P9-CEK-816

A TEXT & TECHNOLOGY SYSTEM FOR WRITING SUCCESS

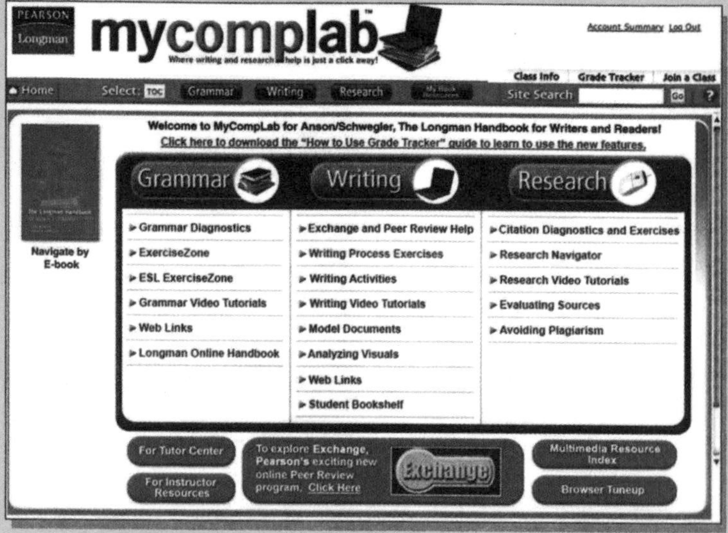

MyCompLab offers dynamic, market-leading tools for improving grammar, writing, and research skills with comprehensive results tracking so students can gauge their progress. Easy to use and engaging, MyCompLab builds confidence as it helps students become better writers and researchers — and helps them to get better grades.

Highlights include: E-book of the text; interactive video tutorials on key grammar, writing, and research topics; ExerciseZone for grammar; Citation Diagnostics and Exercises; Evaluating Sources tutorial; and more!

www.mycomplab.com

*Your text came packaged with MyCompLab access only if your instructor ordered it that way.
To purchase access on your own, go to www.mycomplab.com.

The Longman Handbook for Writers & Readers

Second Custom Edition for University of Illinois at Chicago

Revised Edition

Taken from:

The Longman Handbook for Writers and Readers, Fifth Edition
by Chris M. Anson and Robert A. Schwegler

In Context: Reading and Writing in Cultural Conversations, Second Edition
by Ann Merle Feldman, Ellen McManus and Nancy Downs

Cover photo courtesy of Thomas Moss.

Taken from:

The Longman Handbook for Writers and Readers, Fifth Edition
by Chris M. Anson and Robert A. Schwegler

Published by Longman
New York, New York 10036

In Context, Second Edition
by Ann Merle Feldman, Ellen McManus and Nancy Downs

Published by Longman

Printed in the United States of America

10 9 8 7 6 5 4 3

ISBN 0-536-46279-8

2007240043

KM

Please visit our web site at *www.pearsoncustom.com*

PEARSON CUSTOM PUBLISHING
501 Boylston Street, Suite 900, Boston, MA 02116
A Pearson Education Company

Dear UIC Student:

You hold in your hands *The Longman Handbook for Writers and Readers*. In it, you'll find an incredible amount of information about writing–more than you could possibly absorb in just a few semesters. Running for nearly 1,000 pages, weighing in at 2.4 pounds, and featuring a hefty price tag, you may wonder if this long and heavy book is worth the price–and you should.

In English 160, you will be asked to use *The Longman* as you work on a variety of writing projects, consider various rhetorical situations, and improve your grammar. In English 161, you'll continue to use the book for writing and grammar, and you'll also use it as a research guide. A reference book is necessary for any writer concerned with good writing. *The Longman* is a good writer's reference, and that's why it is required. But there's even more to it than that.

First, this version of *The Longman Handbook* has been customized for UIC students. In the pages that follow, you'll find useful information about resources available to you. Check out the information about the UIC Writing Center and the UIC Library. These are real places here on campus with real people ready (even eager!) to help you with your writing, your research, and your learning. Also included is a genre glossary that you will find useful in your English 160 course and a set of guidelines to give you an idea of how your English 161 instructor will evaluate your research paper.

Yes, there's a lot of information here, but taken a little at a time as needs arise, concepts explained between the covers of this book will make your writing stronger and, better yet, make you a stronger writer. Crack open *The Longman* and take a look. If you're having a problem getting a writing project off the ground, check out Chapter 3 on planning strategies. Perhaps you need guidance navigating Internet resources. If so, check out Chapter 47. Reference guides for the most common citation styles are included, starting on page 638. For advice about putting together an appropriate résumé and job application letter, look at the materials starting on page 855.

Finally, we encourage you to add this reference book to your permanent library. Hold onto it, and don't sell it back at the end of the semester. Why? We believe that success in college and beyond is directly related to your ability to generate ideas and communicate them in writing. We also believe that all efficient writers—no matter how long they've been writing—always have a reference manual within arm's reach. We hope this will be that book for you.

Sincerely,

The Staff of the First–Year Writing Program
comptalk@uic.edu
www.uic.edu/depts/engl/programs/1styearwriting

The Writing Center
100 Douglas Hall
312/413-2206

http://www.uic.edu/depts/engl/writing/
Director: Vainis Aleksa
vainis@uic.edu

What the Writing Center Is:

At the Writing Center, students work with trained undergraduate and graduate student tutors who are prepared to work with writers on a variety of tasks, including the following:

- Business memos or letters
- Resumes
- Lab reports
- Academic essays
- Cover letters
- Personal statements
- Fiction, non-fiction, or poetry
- Proposals
- Research papers
- Annotated bibliographies

We encourage all students, regardless of major, skill level, or experience, to visit the Writing Center. Whether you consider yourself a beginner or an expert writer, there are many ways in which you can make use of the Writing Center's services.

What the Writing Center Can Do for You:

You can work with a tutor on any aspect of your writing, including grammar and style. Tutors and writers often work together on the following:

- Brainstorming
- Structure and organization
- Thesis statements
- Grammar and style
- Proofreading and editing
- Argument/Support
- MLA and APA citations

Please speak with your tutor about what you would like to work on during your session.

Working with a Tutor:

Appointments are required, but we do take drop-ins if someone has been canceled or does not show up for his or her appointment.

To make an appointment to work with a tutor, call the Writing Center at 312/413-2206 or visit us in 100 Douglas Hall, which is located next to Grant and Lincoln Halls. To try to get a drop-in session, simply show up and speak to the person at the front desk.

All appointments begin on the hour (e.g. 9:00 a.m.), and you will work with a tutor for approximately fifty minutes. We recommend that you make your appointment three to five days in advance so that you get the day and time you prefer.

Our hours change depending on the semester, so please call to find out when we are open.

Getting the Most Out *of* Your Time *at the* Writing Center:

We believe that a good, productive session is the result of a conversation between the tutor and the writer, one in which both are talking and asking questions about the writing. To prepare for that conversation, here are a few tips:

- **Make sure you bring whatever documents you need to your session**. This can include a printed copy of your writing, an assignment sheet, and other notes, handouts, instructions, or materials that will help you show your tutor what you've been doing or what you need to do. This will help you get your tutor up to speed.
- **Decide what you want to work on and tell your tutor**. If you can find specific examples of what you want to work on, then this will help the tutor better understand what your immediate concerns are.
- **Be prepared to be flexible. Sometimes tutors notice things about your writing that you have not**. While this may not be what you originally wanted to work on, it may be something that needs addressing.
- **Keep in mind that you may not get everything done in one session**. Tutors do their best, but sometimes you may need two or more sessions. With that in mind, try making your appointments in advance of your due date. While we don't mind working with writers whose papers are due the same day as their tutoring session, it may be less stressful for you and your tutor if there is time to work on the paper after your session has ended.

- **Be prepared to work.** We want your writing to improve, but we also want you to improve as a writer. For this to happen, it is important for you to work with your tutor rather than have the tutor do the work for you. For example, your tutor will be happy to assist you with your proofreading and editing. By doing so, he or she will provide you with knowledge and strategies that will allow you to do these tasks on your own. However, your tutor will not do these tasks for you.

Using Our Other Resources:

In addition to tutoring, we offer other services to writers. These include:

- **Workshops:** During workshops, tutors lead a discussion about a specific writing topic and provide information about that topic. Tutors and fellow students then address the specific concerns of each writer. Past workshops have covered topics such as thesis statements, MLA and APA citations, and incorporating quotes. Call or visit to get more information about upcoming workshops.
- **Online Tutoring:** In addition to face-to-face tutoring, the Writing Center offers a limited amount of online tutoring. Students speak with a tutor in a private, online chatroom for fifty minutes. Sessions are by request only, and requests must be made 36 hours in advance of the desired time. For more information about how you can get an online session or to request a session, email onlinetutor@uic.edu
- **Group Work:** At some point, your teacher may bring your class to the Writing Center for tutor-facilitated group work. In an ideal group work session, you, your classmates, and your tutor participate in a discussion of the assignment and the work you have done.
- **Quick Reference:** We also provide help for those with general questions about writing. If you need an answer, give us a call or stop by. We have a variety of handbooks and other references available for writers to use, and our staff is always happy to assist you.

Getting Involved with the Writing Center:

The Writing Center offers many opportunities for UIC students to get involved in tutoring and writing. These opportunities include:

- **Tutoring:** Tutoring in the Writing Center offers a unique opportunity for students to hone their writing skills, interact with other writers, and gain valuable work experience.

In order to tutor, you must take one of the two classes we offer. Students in every major are welcome to take one of our classes.

- **English 222** is a class offered to sophomores and juniors who are interested in writing and tutoring. The class offers a unique opportunity for students to practice and develop their academic writing skills beyond English 160 and 161. Tutoring other writers adds another dimension to this development.
- **English 482** is intended for undergraduate and graduate students who are interested in teaching writing at the high school or college level or are already teaching. Tutoring is combined with a dynamic discussion of teaching theories and methods, particularly those that emphasize student-centered instruction.

Students who have completed 160 and 161, or who have received equivalent credit, are qualified to take 222 and tutor in the Writing Center. Students majoring in subjects other than English are strongly encouraged to take the class.

If you're interested in becoming a tutor, please stop by and speak with a member of our staff or visit our website at *http://www.uic.edu/depts/engl/writing/*.

- **Staff Tutoring:** Students who take 222 or 482 have the opportunity to apply to become a staff tutor. This experience at the Writing Center has provided many of our tutors with a competitive edge when applying for jobs, graduate school, or other professional programs.
- **Publishing:** The Writing Center also invites you to submit your writing to one of our publications, which include a newsletter, a non-fiction magazine, and a literary magazine. Please call or visit to get more information about submitting your work for publication.

The Writing Center is committed to serving the writing-related needs and interests of UIC students, faculty, and staff. Every effort will be made to accommodate teachers, tutors, and students with disabilities.

We look forward to seeing you at the Writing Center.

Margaret Gonzales
Assistant Director
UIC Writing Center
April 2005

Doing Research at UIC's Richard J. Daley Library

UIC Library homepage: *http://www.uic.edu/depts/lib*

Welcome to the Richard J. Daley Library. Reference librarians at the Daley Library can offer you help with your research inquiry in a variety of ways:

- In person—Come to the Reference Desk on the 2nd floor of the Daley Library
- Via telephone—Call the Reference Desk at 312/996-2726
- Via email—Send us an email question via our "Ask A Librarian" service *(http://www.uic.edu/depts/lib/digital)*
- Via our chat reference service—Get chat assistance via our "Ask A Librarian" service *(http://www.uic.edu/depts/lib/digital)*

How can the Reference Librarians at the Daley Library help you?

- We can help you develop your research question.
- We can help you find books, articles, and other materials related to your research question.
- We can help you evaluate the resources that you find.

The "free Web" vs. Library Resources*

Why use library resources when you can do research on the Web? Although many library resources are Web-based, the information they contain differs significantly from what you would find if you conducted a search on the "free Web" using a search engine such as Google or Yahoo. The UIC Library subscribes to hundreds of databases. You would be unable to find the same books, magazine, and journal articles found in these databases using a free search engine such as Google.

The "free Web" (i.e. Google, Yahoo, Ask Jeeves...)

- **Information on the free Web does not usually go through a review process.** Anyone can publish on the Web without passing the content through an editor. Pages might be written by an expert on the topic, a journalist, a disgruntled consumer or even a child.
- **Information on the free Web is not organized.** Some directory services, like Yahoo, provide links to sites in subject lists. But there are too many Web pages for any single directory service to organize and index.

- **Information on the free Web is not usually comprehensive.** Rarely will you be able to use a search engine on the Web to collect information about your topic from earlier decades and different types of sources.
- **Information on the free Web is not always permanent.** Some well-maintained sites are updated with very current information, but other sites may become quickly dated or disappear altogether without much, if any, notice.
- **Information on the free Web is not always free.** Many Web pages are free to view, but some commercial sites will charge a fee to access their information.

Library Resources *(i.e. subscription databases/ article indexes)*

- **Library resources go through a review process.** Librarians select books, magazines, journals, databases, and Web sites. The library collects sources considered reliable, historically relevant, and valuable.
- **Library resources are free for your use.** Libraries are able to purchase one copy of a book, magazine, or database that can be shared by many people.
- **Library resources are organized.** Items are organized so you can find all the sources on a topic. For example, when you search for a book in the UIC Library catalog you will get a call number. The books shelved near the same call number will cover a similar topic.
- **Library resources are meant to be kept permanently.** A primary function of a library is to be an organized storehouse of information published throughout time. As well as finding very current information, you can also find books that are no longer published and older issues of magazines, newspapers, and journals.

So . . .

Use the Free Web

- To catch up with current news
- To gather opinions and companies
- To learn about organizations
- To find information about the U.S. government
- After you've done your research using library resources

Use Library Resources

- To find books and other materials the library owns
- To find magazine articles
- To find current and historical newspaper articles
- To find scholarly journal articles

*Adapted from *Searchpath* © The Board of Trustees of Western Michigan University

Finding Books, Articles, and Other Materials at the Richard J. Daley Library

The Richard J. Daley Library has books, magazines, journals, videos, and other materials in the humanities, social sciences, business, engineering, and professional studies.

- If you are looking for materials in the sciences, the Science Library is located in Room 3500 SES (Science and Engineering South).
- If you are looking for materials in the health-sciences, the Library of the Health Sciences (LHS Chicago) is located at 1750 W. Polk.

Use UICCAT, the UIC Library's online catalog to find out what resources the library owns. UICCAT is accessible from the UIC Library's homepage: *(http://www.uic.edu/depts/lib).*

How to Search for Books and Articles

In order to find materials on your research topic, you will need to search UICCAT (for books) or an index (for articles).

You can search UICCAT and article indexes in a variety of ways. Most databases allow you to do a Boolean search, which requires you to combine your topic keywords using AND, OR, NOT.

For example, if you are looking for books and articles about the history of public housing in Chicago, a possible Boolean search would be: history and Chicago and "public housing"

Consult the "Help" screens of individual databases for additional searching tips.

Encyclopedias, Dictionaries, and other Reference Materials: Reference books are located on the 2nd floor of the Daley Library. All of the books in the UIC Library are arranged in Library of Congress call number order. To locate reference books on your research topic, search UICCAT or ask a Reference Librarian for recommendations.

Reference books can be a great place to start your research. Use reference books for the following:

- To get an overview of your research topic
- To place your research topic within a historical context
- To find biographical information on a particular person
- To identify keywords and other vocabulary related to your research topic
- To identify experts on a particular topic

Books: Books are located on all four floors of the Richard J. Daley Library. All books in the UIC Library are arranged in Library of Congress call number order. This means you can browse the stacks in a particular call number to find multiple books about the same subject. To locate books on your research topic, search UICCAT.

Use books to:

- focus and look more in-depth at your research topic.
- identify authors/experts in a particular field.
- identify related research (books, articles, etc.) on a specific topic.

Articles: In order to find articles related to your research question, you need to use an article index. The UIC Library subscribes to hundreds of these indexes online, accessible from the UIC Library's homepage.

Use articles for:

- The most current information on your research topic
- A very focused view of your research topic
- To identify authors/experts in a particular field
- To identify related research (books, articles, etc.) on a specific topic

---

Ask a Librarian!

The research process can be daunting due to the sheer volume of resources available in print and online. Reference librarians specialize in helping students refine their research questions, select effective search terms, select appropriate catalogs and indexes, and evaluate materials. Remember, never hesitate to ask for help, either by talking to a librarian at the reference desk on the second floor of the Daley Library, or by using our "Ask A Librarian" service at *http://www.uic.edu/depts/lib/digital.*

Evaluating English 161 Research Papers

Taking a Position: The writer articulates a position that contributes to a significant public conversation. The position relates to key themes discussed in the class materials and work. The writer attends to the consequences of his or her position, its personal relevance, and the potential or real public impact.

5 4 3 2 1

Developing Arguments in Context: The writer understands that arguments emerge from important public conversations in which participants respond to each other as if in dialogue. They question claims, ask questions about evidence, consider the appropriateness of the evidence, qualify their assertions, and respond to counter claims.

5 4 3 2 1

Using Sources Effectively: The writer identifies and reviews appropriate source material relevant to his or her position, characterizes the sources' arguments, discusses disciplinary methods and approaches, provides historical context, critiques the sources, and considers the sources' perspectives.

5 4 3 2 1

Engaging Intellectual Strategies: The writer demonstrates the ability to engage in a dialogue of ideas with the sources used in the paper. The work is enhanced by the ability to summarize, synthesize, and analyze. In addition, writers demonstrate how appropriate paraphrasing and quoting contribute to this dialogue of ideas.

5 4 3 2 1

Using Language Appropriately: The writer makes language and stylistic choices appropriate to the audience and purpose. The writer also cites sources appropriately, integrating the cited material into the writer's work.

5 4 3 2 1

A *Genre* Glossary

The following glossary describes key features of the genres you will find in this book. The concept of *genre* refers to the way a text's content and form are shaped by the situation in which it occurs. When you watch television, you know whether a particular show aims to be comic or dramatic or even a comic takeoff on a dramatic genre. When you read an epic poem, a lease, or anything else, you know—from common sense and experience—what to expect. Genres provide a kind of social agreement between writers and readers.

Each Genre Glossary entry briefly describes the situations, purposes, forms, content, and language and design choices typically associated with that genre. These descriptions can help you in two ways. As you read, they can help you figure out what genre a reading belongs to and how the reading follows or breaks the conventions of that genre. As you write, they can help you think about what genres you might use in a given situation and what readers typically expect from those genres. Then it is up to you to decide which genre to use and to what extent you will meet those expectations.

Academic Article/Research Paper

(Also referred to as academic essay, paper, study, or research report)

Situation/Purpose This entry describes two genres different in many ways but with much in common: articles written by professors and other professionals and published in disciplinary or professional journals or as chapters in books, and research papers written by students as course assignments.

Academic articles are written by professors and other professionals in order to contribute new ideas, arguments, or research findings to their field. Typically they write about a topic that they have specialized in and may have written about before. Some academics and other professionals, especially in the sciences and social sciences, collaborate with others in research or writing or both. But even scholars who work alone are always working within a complex context that includes their own previous work and that of others both past and present. In fact, a hallmark of academic writing is that it is part of an ongoing conversation in which people interested in the same ideas or problems share information and ideas, argue with each other, and try to work together to solve problems and make progress.

Research papers usually have a double purpose: to learn about a topic and to learn about the values and conventions of academic research and writing. Thus, although students are usually writing about a topic that is new to them, teachers often try to create a situation like the ones in which academic articles are written, providing readings and preparatory assignments that give students a context in which to research and make a claim about a topic. Academic articles are usually written to an audience of peers. Students' research paper topics, especially in upper-level courses, may develop into professional interests. Teachers may sometimes encourage students to publish their papers—with the Internet there are many more opportunities—or deliver them at student conferences, in which case they cross a genre boundary and become academic articles. But in most cases teachers and students see research papers as apprentice work in which students learn the subject matter, ideas, and methods of a discipline and have an opportunity to share their ideas at least with their teachers and sometimes with others as well.

Content/Form Despite these differences in situation and purpose, academic articles and research papers have much in common in terms of content and form. Academic articles are often longer, are usually read in their published form, and often begin with an abstract followed by a series of key words to help readers search related topics. Beyond this, there are many similarities.

Both academic articles and research papers conduct an inquiry, and in doing so they make a claim about a problem or issue. This claim is sometimes directly stated in a sentence or two in the introduction, usually after some kind of contextualizing discussion. This direct statement of the claim is often called the thesis statement, especially if the article or paper presents an original argument as opposed to a report of research findings. As part of the introduction or immediately after it, the writer often shows how the claim relates to what others have said; if this is done in an extended or formal way, it is sometimes referred to as a review of the literature. Whether or not the claim is stated directly in the introduction, it is developed and supported in the body of the paper with various kinds of analysis, arguments, and evidence. The analysis and argument are the writer's original interpretations of the evidence or positions on the issue. Evidence might include, depending on the field, research data, descriptions of observations or case studies, quotations from analyzed texts, and references to various authorities in the form of quotations, paraphrases, and summaries. There usually is some kind of conclusion, in which the writer draws together different strands of the discussion to make a synthesizing observation, sums up the main points, reiterates the thesis statement, or makes suggestions about future research. In most of these characteristics, the academic article and research paper overlap with the essay as a genre; see the description of **Essay** in this glossary.

What distinguishes academic articles and research papers from other kinds of essays is the use of formalized documentation conventions to indicate the sources of the evidence presented. The most common conventions for documentation involve the use of parenthetical references and lists of works cited; some fields still use footnotes or endnotes and a bibliography. These conventions are more than just formalities to avoid plagiarism; they are an important way of expressing that academic writing is an ongoing, collaborative effort in which one writer builds on or challenges the work of earlier writers.

The format of articles and papers may differ according to the field. In the sciences, writers may make heavy use of headings to mark sections, which may be organized according to a predetermined structure, and they often include charts and other kinds of graphics. Articles and papers in the humanities may be much more loosely organized and may include no graphics or section markers of any kind, although headings are becoming common even in the humanities. Both professional academics and students sometimes publish their papers on the Internet, and in that case they may use hypertext, allowing readers to follow a particular thread of argument or information through related links.

Language/Design Both academic articles and research papers usually use formal, impersonal language intended to convey unbiased judgment, though in some fields and courses a more informal, personal style is acceptable. Academic articles and research papers may also use specialized language related to the field or issue. This specialized language is an important aspect of academic writing but can cause difficulties.

Academic articles usually use special terminology related to the issue or to disciplinary methods; references to people and ideas familiar to those in the discipline; and quotations, paraphrases, and summaries from sources related to the issue. Some readers see this specialized language as an attempt to make the writers sound important or to confuse outsiders, but writers who use specialized language argue that it captures particular meanings important to the discipline or to the writer's particular argument. Some academic writers, especially if they are writing books aimed at a wider audience, might use a less-specialized language; others, especially if they are publishing in journals likely to be read only by other people in the field, use the highly specialized language that they know their readers expect, understand, and respect.

Research papers, often assigned in college classes, draw ideas and information from academic articles, and students are often encouraged to see themselves as engaging in conversation with the writers of these articles. Students may thus adopt in their research papers the specialized language of these academic articles but may feel awkward putting their own ideas into this language; they may also feel awkward putting new and complex ideas into their own words. Using direct quotations, paraphrases, and summaries from sources is particularly challenging because their use depends on fully understanding the material and being able to integrate the language into the discussion. This struggle, however, is a necessary stage in the process through which a practicing writer develops a language that expresses his or her own thinking but also allows the writer to engage in conversation with experts in the field.

Address/Speech

Situation/Purpose Speeches, also called addresses, are used in a variety of public and private ceremonial occasions including political rallies, dedication and awards ceremonies, religious services, business and educational situations, and weddings, funerals, and graduations. Depending on the situation, the purpose may be to persuade, motivate, celebrate, commemorate, entertain, or instruct.

Content/Form A speech often opens with comments about the specific occasion, remarks to focus the audience's attention and set the tone of the speech, and a statement or foreshadowing of the main idea to be developed. The body of the speech develops this idea with arguments, facts and statistics, and various kinds of examples, including personal anecdotes, depending on the situation and purpose. Speakers must consider how illustrations, pertinent stories, examples, and epigrams can add interest. For example, in commencement addresses, speakers often include personal anecdotes about their education and subsequent use of things they learned in school. Most speeches close with a statement meant to leave the audience reflecting on the topic and the occasion.

Language/Design The tone must of course be appropriate to the occasion. The tone can range, even within a single speech, from casual and humorous to formal and even elevated. Speakers must carefully balance seriousness, demanded by the occasion, with humor, to keep the speech from being dull.

Advice Book/Article

Situation/Purpose Books and articles giving advice are generally written to help people solve problems that are perceived to be widespread. They usually offer solutions that individuals can implement on their own without other outside assistance. More generally, they respond to a desire for self-improvement and for specific and easy-to-follow guidelines on how to achieve it. They cover a wide range of topics including diet, fitness and health, finding a mate, marital success, child rearing, business and financial success, ways to write well, and ways to stop procrastinating. Advice books are often marketed along with, or through, audio- and videotapes, seminars, and even TV specials. Advice articles usually appear in women's magazines, teen magazines, increasingly in men's magazines, and magazines related to health, fitness, and parenting.

Content/Form Writers of advice books and articles often present a philosophy or analysis related to the problem, but the heart of the book is usually the specific advice. The advice is usually broken into short, very readable sections of prose, usually with liberal use of headings, lists, and other formatting devices, and often with pictures or graphs. The writer usually enumerates aspects and consequences of the relevant problem, qualities to be cultivated, goals to be reached, and steps that must be taken. These lists are usually long enough to be useful but short enough to be manageable. Writers often present themselves as mavericks, going against the standard beliefs about the problem and how to solve it. Advice books and articles often include personal anecdotes and testimony from the writer and others who have succeeded by following the advice.

Language/Design The tone of the language is positive and upbeat. The diction and sentence structures are meant to be accessible to most readers. Sometimes the usage is colloquial.

Brochure

Situation/Purpose A brochure's purpose is to promote an idea, distribute information, or market a product. Although we often think of a brochure as a triple-folded sheet of paper. There are as many approaches to designing brochures as you can imagine. For instance, when you purchase a cell phone, the pocket guide describing its use is a brochure. The glossy sales inserts from department stores that accompany your Sunday newspaper are also brochures. A brochure offers an opportunity to illustrate something, explain how a product works, argue that some action be taken, detail a company's accomplishments, or describe an organization and its services. Sometimes it is the only representation of that product and service because readers may not be able to obtain further information. Often, to develop a brochure, a designer is called in to assist. A brochure may dazzle you with its color and design, but these elements must work with the writing to create a document that is meant to persuade or inform an audience.

Content/Form The content and form of a brochure are extremely flexible, but the key is to communicate through a synthesis of visual and textual information. A brochure uses imaginative techniques to express its message, techniques that combine language, color, shape, texture, and form. For example, a corporation might develop an annual report using a form very much like a children's book: bright colors, bold graphic images, a glossy cover, and text arranged like a story, all designed to suggest a particular reality. Or a low-budget brochure for a school might make creative use of a variety of typefaces to illustrate visually a contrast between the chaotic thoughts of students studying a poorly conceptualized curriculum versus the clear, sharp, interwoven thoughts of students attending the school described in the brochure. These brochures are designed to offer a clear and coherent representation of the service or product, usually through a strong visual argument.

Language/Design The rule in designing brochures is "Show, don't tell." Sometimes this is done through examples but can also be achieved through the brochure's physical design, through shapes, size, and use of color, and even through pop-up or pull-tab additions. The particular type or quality of paper also influences decisions about design. Brochures can be designed and produced with a simple word processor, but most often a designer will rely on software such as QuarkXPress, Adobe Photoshop, or Adobe Illustrator.

Business Letter/Memo

Situation/Purpose Although much workplace communication takes place on the phone, through e-mail, or face to face, a great deal of it still takes the form of letters and memos. There are many purposes for business letters and memos, but most fall into one of four categories, according to whether the basic purpose is to inform or to request and according to whether the reader will perceive the message as routine or nonroutine, positive/neutral or negative. Thus the four categories might be labeled routine announcements, routine requests, nonroutine requests (often called persuasive messages), and negative announcements, (often called bad-news messages). But keep in mind that some kinds of messages (for example, thank-you notes or notes of congratulation) do not fit into any of these categories; that most messages have some elements of both informing and requesting; and that the line between routine and nonroutine can be fuzzy. Letters are generally used for external correspondence, though they might also be used for very nonroutine internal correspondence. Memos are generally used for internal correspondence, though they might be used for very routine external correspondence.

Content/Form The kind of information included in a letter or memo obviously depends on the purpose of the message and the specific information depends on the situation. But, in general, use only the most relevant and/or persuasive information. Business correspondence in the United States generally does not include much personal information or many personal remarks, although business correspondence in other cultures often does.

Although letters and memos have different formats (memos do not include internal addresses; letters usually do not include a subject line, though occasionally they do), the overall structure of the message can be the same for letters and memos. In general, the first paragraph should be fairly brief; it either provides a lead-in to the main point or states the main point. The middle paragraphs develop the different points or aspects of the message in some sort of logical order and are generally of medium length. The last paragraph is generally fairly brief, indicates what, if anything, will or should happen next, and includes a polite closing. Although both letters and memos can be of any length, we generally think of memos as shorter and letters as longer. In general, both should be kept to one page if possible.

Language/Design Letters are generally personal (addressed to a single person) but are also usually formal in tone; memos are usually impersonal (addressed to many people) and can be more informal in tone. But the language of both generally follows these principles:

clarity: specific and precise but simple; formal but not pretentious or jargony

conciseness: as brief as possible

coherence: hangs together and flows smoothly

courtesy: reader-focus, positive emphasis, good manners

correctness: no errors in sentence structure, grammar, or punctuation

Business letters and memos should be carefully revised, edited, and proofread, using spelling and grammar checkers.

Codes/Guidelines

Situation/Purpose Codes of conduct, sometimes also called guidelines, are increasingly common in the workplace because they set the standard for employee conduct by establishing guidelines. These codes both protect the employer from unacceptable employee behavior and inform the employee of employer expectations. Some businesses allow employees to contribute to the development of the codes, thus creating a forum for communication between employees and management. These codes are different from procedural manuals such as employee handbooks; they will not tell you how to do a specific job but will help you make general workplace decisions. These codes also serve a public-relations function by announcing the company's principles and standards to its clients and customers. A code of conduct can play a role in inducting new employees into the company's philosophy and can offer guidance to employees when they are confronted with difficult choices while performing their duties. If the code is to play a role in the day-to-day life of the business, it should reflect the particular circumstances and characteristics of the organization and must be adaptable enough to remain relevant as the economic climate changes.

Content/Form Codes are usually divided into numbered sections. They usually begin with a brief description of the company and a statement of its mission and values, setting the context for the guidelines that follow. Middle sections may cover general principles of behavior such as honesty, loyalty, and commitment to excellence, as well as more specific rules relevant to the particular environment of the company. Codes should spell out the kinds of behavior rewarded in the workplace and the kinds of behavior not accepted, and ideally both reasons and consequences should be explained. A good code will strike a balance between spelling out specific rules and advocating employees' use of sound judgment and ethics.

Language/Design The tone of a code of conduct is usually formal, even stern, in order to convey the seriousness of the guidelines. Beyond that, the language follows rules for writing in the workplace with its demands for brevity and standard edited English usage and mechanics.

Comics

Situation/Purpose Comics are a form of visual communication that include everything from the comic strips and books that young people collect to the increasingly popular graphic novels aimed at adult audiences. In addition, as more and more people become accustomed to learning visually, comics have become another way to present complex and technical information such as that found in instruction manuals for loading a digital camera or scanning images into a computer. In this respect, comics can be instructional as well as entertaining. Comics depend on the particular arrangement of the pictures and words to communicate the stories and ideas and are meant to be read in a sequence.

Content/Form Although comics are often thought of as a simple form of communication, they are really quite complex and require a literate audience. The narrative action proceeds in segments called panels or frames that draw on the reading conventions of the Western world and are meant to be read from left to right and top to bottom. Since space is limited, the artist/writer has to make a series of judgments about what to include and depends on the reader to fill in the gaps. For example, the shape of a human head might be used to indicate a human figure, or the profile of a person with her hands on a steering wheel to create the impression of driving a car. The space between the frames also serves a purpose; it requires the reader to supply the transitions between the frames. In this way, comics require a high level of interaction on the part of the reader. Artists introduce comics in a variety of ways; however, one common way is to include a full-page scene—called a splash page—to set the stage. The writer/artist can impact the reading process to some extent by experimenting with framing devices to achieve different effects. Notice the framing devices in the comics in your favorite newspaper or comic book. The size and shape of the frame may convey important information about narrative action or atmosphere. For example, a series of progressively smaller frames conveys a quickening pace of action, while lengthening the shape of a frame can indicate slowly passing time. Sharp lines around the frame can imply a sense of urgency or horror.

Language/Design In comics, the writer and artist are often the same person. Comics are a highly visual medium; the artistry of the images is often the first thing that captures the reader's attention. Many comics rely on images alone. But more often there is a balance between pictures and words. Often the words support the pictures, but at other times the effect is created by the contrast between word and image. Because comics are a static print medium, conveying things such as mood, sound, and motion presents a particular challenge. Visual clues such as speed lines or even footprints create the effect of motion. The characters' facial expressions and exaggerated gestures help create the mood and depict emotions. Sound can be implied through word balloons. The lines around the balloons indicate the words the characters are saying as well as those they are only thinking. Comics appear in both black-and-white and color. Often the colors are the primary colors, which are easily printed in newspapers.

Cover Letter/Reflective Essay

Situation/Purpose A cover letter is any letter that accompanies and explains another document or artifact. The most common use of cover letters is to accompany and introduce a résumé as part of a job application; for a description of this type of cover letter, see **Resume/Cover Letter** in this glossary. But cover letters may accompany a wide range of other kinds of documents. Teachers may ask students to write a cover letter, note, or reflective essay to accompany an assignment or set of assignments, explaining how the assignment(s) was completed, why certain choices were made, and what was learned. For example, an assignment that asks you to reshape material from one genre into another might ask you to include a cover letter in which you discuss what you learned about the nature of and differences between the two genres. The goal is to have you think about how you work as a writer and how the text works as a piece of writing.

Content/Form Cover letters and reflective essays of this type are typically fairly short. The necessary content is usually specified in the assignment and typically includes a discussion of what was written, a description of the writing process, a discussion of the situation that surrounded the writing, and reflection on insights gained from the assignment. They can be formatted as an informal note or a formal letter, with date, greeting ("Dear . . ."), body, closing ("Yours truly," etc.), and signature, and optionally the writer's address and that of the receiver. Typically they are about one or two pages in length, including a paragraph for each topic that the assignment asks you to address, with optional introductory and concluding paragraphs. The teacher will be looking for a frank, thoughtful discussion that refers to specific aspects of the text, its context, or the writing process. Students should use cover letters as an opportunity to gain insight into their own writing and writing in general.

Language/Design The language might be more personal than in the assignment itself since you might be discussing habits, perceptions, and insights related to your own writing. But it should still follow the principles of academic style in terms of diction and the correctness of sentence structure, grammar, and mechanics.

Dialogue/Symposium/Debate

(This description is adapted from William A. Covino's *Forms of Wondering.*)

Situation/Purpose Symposia and debates often occur in public contexts. You may have seen a roundtable discussion on television or heard one on a radio show. Political candidates often defend their platforms through a process of public debates: A symposium offers an opportunity for conversations that explore different perspectives. A debate, on the other hand, highlights the opposing viewpoints of two or more participants who argue through persuasive technique and through the presentation of evidence. The term *dialogue* can mean many different things, but as we use it here, a dialogue is an intellectual exercise in which a writer creates a hypothetical conversation in order to explore different perspectives on an issue; the Platonic dialogues are probably the best-known examples.

In writing classes, teachers often use dialogues to encourage students to explore different points of view, perhaps the points of view of different readings in the course. A related genre is the symposium, which may be either the transcript of a conversation or a set of written exchanges. In both real symposia and imagined dialogues, different points of views are expressed, but in an imagined dialogue the writer has intentionally created these different points of view in order to explore an issue. Ideally, each perspective should be fairly represented.

Content/Form An imagined dialogue resembles a transcript of a real conversation, but it is in fact more carefully constructed. There may be about four or five characters, representing different points of view, usually specific real or imaginary people. Ideally, each character speaks about the same number of times and in mainly paragraph-length comments, though these may be interspersed with shorter comments. Each comment is carefully planned to express the character's views and to respond to the other characters' comments. If the characters are real people, the comments should accurately reflect their actual opinions and attitudes. It is acceptable but not necessary to use exact quotes from writings by these people. When exact words are used, they should be enclosed in quotation marks. When the characters are imaginary, their comments should express consistent opinions and attitudes. Characters should make compelling arguments supported by convincing evidence. They should be consistent but show a willingness to change their views, if that is what the character would do. Comments should demonstrate an understanding of the participants positions. The responses as a whole should make interesting connections among the perspectives.

Language/Design Each response should be written in the persona of the real or imaginary person. They should be written in the first person and should use the words and sentence structures that the character would use.

Essay

Situation/Purpose There are many kinds of essays, from personal narrative or reflective essays that are similar to fiction and even poetry, to impersonal expository essays that are similar to reports and proposals. You may write many kinds of essays in your life, and each might seem very different. But all essays develop a main idea by making connections between related ideas and experiences, whether it is a five-paragraph essay with three examples supporting a stated thesis or a many-page essay interweaving complex ideas and references to develop an implied thesis.

The most common, broadly defined purpose of an essay is for the writer to explore, and allow the reader to explore, ideas and the relationships between ideas. But this broadly defined purpose can be embodied in a variety of situations, each of which will shape the writer's purpose in a particular way. For example, a student might write an essay to analyze the ideas covered in the course or to make connections between the course ideas and the student's personal experience. A public figure might write an essay for a magazine or newspaper in order to persuade an audience about an issue of public concern. In fact, when a persuasive essay is used in this way, we might call it an **Opinion Piece, Column,** or **Commentary**. A novelist or a journalist might write an essay to explore and share with the reader a personal experience and give the reader insight into similar experiences. A professional in any field might write an essay to inform other members of the profession of ideas or discoveries important to the field. In all of these cases, the writing might be called an essay, but in each case the content, form, and language will be different.

Content/Form While literary writing usually involves description and narration, and professional, scientific, or workplace writing usually involves the exposition of facts and ideas, essays tend to include a combination of description, narration, and exposition, with the emphasis depending on the particular purpose and situation. What we often call the personal, informal, or literary essay might be mostly narrative, description, and even dialogue, interspersed or framed with expository comments. Such essays are often written by students or by professional writers in literary magazines. What we often call formal, academic, analytic, argumentative, or persuasive essays give more space to exposition—presentation of information or explanation of ideas—but allow for some narrative or description that illustrates or illuminates the exposition. Such essays might be written about public, professional, or academic issues, by students as well as professionals. At the extremes, an essay might be all narrative/description or all impersonal exposition, but for most essays the essential feature is the combination, which allows the reader and the writer to share an experience and contemplate ideas related to it.

Thus there is no single template for essays, which might have almost any overall shape. But typically the first paragraphs draw the reader into the topic of the essay in a way that is appropriate to the situation and subject. Students often begin an essay as if they are directly addressing the teacher in response to a question. But a convention of essays is that any reader should feel invited into and addressed by the essay, which is why the introduction usually does not begin with a thesis statement but rather with something designed to interest the reader in the topic and lead into a statement of the thesis or otherwise point toward the thesis. The middle paragraphs—which can be of almost any number, from one to dozens, and of varying lengths, averaging about five to ten sentences—develop the topic in a logical or associative way, using transitions to clarify connections; these paragraphs may interweave narration/description and exposition. The final paragraphs reiterate important connections between ideas and point these ideas to the world outside the essay. All essays should have a thesis, which simply means that all essays should have a point that the writer wants to convey to the reader. The thesis, whether simple or complex, may be stated outright in the essay—often toward the end of the introduction or toward the beginning of the conclusion—or implied. But if the thesis is not stated outright, it must be implied strongly and clearly enough that the reader could state it.

Language/Design Depending on the type of essay, the language may be poetic, intimate, concrete, and informal, or highly formal, abstract, objective, or anywhere in between. But wherever the essay is on this spectrum, the language must be clear. It can be informal but should not be imprecise; it can be formal but should not be obscure or full of jargon.

Personal, informal, and literary essays are often written throughout in the first person; the writer's personal and individual voice is absolutely essential to the experience of the essay. Academic, journalistic, and other kinds of persuasive essays may intersperse first-person and third-person discussions; the effect is often to move in and out between close, personal perspectives and wider, more impersonal perspectives. The most formal, objective, and scientific essays typically do not use the first person at all; the writer aims to efface him- or herself and give the impression that the subject matter is simply presenting itself without the medium of a particular writer.

As this description suggests, there are many different kinds of essays, and the boundaries between them are not always clear. For essays specifically characterized by the documented use of sources and usually written in an academic context, see the Academic Article/Research Paper (p. 561). For brief, reflective essays that—typically in school situations—accompany an assignment or set of assignments, see the Cover Letter/Reflective Essay (p. 568). For argumentative or persuasive essays on current issues published in newspapers and magazines, see Opinion Piece/Commentary (p. 578).

In the following section we describe some of the key features of two broadly defined and different kinds of essays, the personal, informal, or literary essay, and the argumentative, analytical, or persuasive essay.

Personal/Informal/Literary Essay

Situation/Purpose The key characteristic of personal, informal, or literary essays is that the focus or emphasis is on the writer's experience or perspective. While analytical, argumentative, or persuasive essays may take their authority from evidence, logic, or methodology, personal essays take their authority from a combination of the significance of the personal experience and the power of the essay's language, and they are usually written to offer a personal perspective or testimony about some phenomenon or situation. Personal essays often appear in the front or back pages of magazines or journals or the "op-ed," page of newspapers, kept separate from more academic, professional, or journalistic writing, but the writers of such essays may include experts writing from a personal rather than an "expert" perspective; professional writers using the power of their language skills to evoke a situation or frame a concept; and ordinary people who want to offer a personal perspective on an issue. These ordinary people may be very skilled writers, but even if they are not, if they have a relevant, interesting experience or perspective to share, their essay may have a strong impact. This may be why teachers often ask students to write personal essays, typically asking them to describe a personal experience and draw some kind of conclusion from it or to comment on a situation or phenomenon, drawing on their personal experience to do so. But although such assignments recognize that anyone has the potential to write a good personal essay, they may not recognize that such essays are more complex and more difficult to write than they may seem at first, for reasons we will see below.

Content/Form Personal essays almost always contain some kind of first-person narrative—a story told from the perspective of the writer and in which the writer usually has a part—and some essays may be almost all narrative and thus may seem to many readers to be almost indistinguishable from short (fictional) stories. But what characterizes most personal essays is an interweaving of narrative and descriptive passages with what we might call expository or discussion passages. An essay might simply begin with a personal anecdote and then go on to make connections between this experience and some larger issues, or it might be a complex interweaving of narrative and commentary in which the narrative gives rise to discussion, the discussion gives rise to further narratives, and so on. But in any case almost all personal essays draw on personal experiences to illuminate, comment on, or testify about larger issues or phenomena, and almost all use some combination of literary techniques and expository strategies to create texts that allow readers to both share an experience and understand its larger significance.

Language/Design The language of personal essays is usually somewhat informal and intimate rather than formal or "professional," and it is often highly descriptive, vivid, and idiosyncratic, often making use of figurative language—images and metaphors, for example—and sometimes using dialogue or otherwise incorporating other voices. But the writer's own individual and recognizable voice is the strongest presence in the essay, determining the overall tone of the essay and synthesizing the other voices that might be incorporated.

Argumentative/Analytical/Persuasive Essay

Situation/Purpose While the emphasis in a personal essay is on the writer's experiences and perspective, the emphasis in an argumentative, analytical, or persuasive essay is on the subject matter and the audience. In a personal essay, the writer reaches inside and draws upon personal experiences in order to share insights with readers; while some personal essays are written in response to ongoing conversations, many personal essays might be said to start new conversations and even to create new audiences. In an argumentative, analytical, or persuasive essay, the writer joins an ongoing conversation in order to state a claim to a targeted audience or persuade that audience to take some action. Such essays are used by academics and other professionals to share ideas and make arguments about issues of professional or disciplinary concern, as well as by public figures or even private citizens to make arguments about issues of public concern. The assumption in a personal or literary essay is often that the writer can speak to anyone, either because the topic is of broad human interest or because the writer's style gives the text an esthetic value apart from its topic and arguments. The premise of an argumentative, analytical, or persuasive essay is that the writer is addressing a particular audience for a particular purpose, and the essay is framed by the expectations of this audience and driven by this purpose.

Content/Form An argumentative, analytical, or persuasive essay usually adheres to generic essay form in a somewhat more disciplined way than the typical personal essay. The introductory section is more likely to state the thesis explicitly, often toward the end of the section. The body paragraphs are more likely to be organized according to some identifiable logic rather than associatively, and the essay is more likely to make use of clear transitional devices. The conclusion is more likely to clearly reiterate the thesis and perhaps to call for further discussion, investigation, or specific action. But perhaps what most distinguishes this type of essay in terms of content and form is the way that it presents its claims or makes its arguments. While a personal essay may make a claim obliquely, indirectly, or by inference, an argumentative, analytical, or persuasive essay usually develops its claims or arguments in very explicit ways, and these all have to do with the important role of the audience in such essays. Because the argument is directed to a specific audience for a specific and fairly immediate purpose, the audience plays an active part in the essay itself. First, as we've already seen, the thesis is usually stated or at least strongly implied in the introduction. Then the body of the essay is developed with the concerns and needs of the audience in mind. The audience might include both those who agree and those who disagree with the claim or argument of the essay, but the disagreers play a more defining role in the essay. Thus, such essays often proceed by first taking into account the arguments or objections to the essay's claims; the paragraphs immediately following the introduction often include a discussion of the issue or question from the perspective of the "other side." Bringing the other side into the essay is a way of both acknowledging the other side and taking control of it by framing and defining it in one's own terms. This is usually followed by, in some cases, an acknowledgment of the legitimacy or force of some aspects of the other side's arguments or view of the situation, then, in most cases, by some kind of rebuttal of the other side's arguments or claims. The rebuttal can take the form of both showing what is wrong or weak in the argument or claim of the other side and presenting arguments and evidence for one's own side. The issue of arguments and evidence is crucial and complex because the arguments and evidence must be defined and presented with a particular audience and situation in mind; what is convincing and even acceptable as an argument and evidence for one audience in one situation may not be acceptable in another. Thus, whereas the content and form of a personal essay may be shaped primarily by the writer's experiences and perceptions, the content and organization of an argumentative, analytical, or persuasive essay are shaped largely by the expectations of a particular audience in a particular situation.

Language/Design At one end of the spectrum, in some literary or personal essays, the writer's individual "voice" is the most forceful source of authority in the essay; and at the other end of the spectrum the writer might try to efface his or her voice so that the argument or evidence seems to present itself directly to the audience without the intervention of a writer. In most argumentative, analytical, or persuasive essays, the voice of the writer is crucial but not in the same ways as in a personal or literary essay. In personal essays, the writer's experience or the esthetic appeal of the writing is crucial; what's crucial in argumentative, analytical, or persuasive essays is the writer's professional, disciplinary, or other kind of expert authority, and of course this must be communicated in a particular situation and to a particular audience. Thus the language of such essays must be not simply generically formal but authoritative to a particular audience. This may involve using a specialized vocabulary, sometimes called *jargon,* though in most situations clarity is valued more than specialized precision.

Feature Story/Profile

Situation/Purpose Feature stories are a regular part of newspapers and magazines, sometimes placed near a related news story or in a special "features" section. Feature stories are a cross between a news story and a work of literature. They usually relate events in the news but do not so much report facts as try to share with the reader an experience related to the news event. Profiles can be either a special kind of feature story or part of a longer feature story. While a feature may present a situation in a broad focus, a profile usually focuses narrowly on a specific person, place, or thing, describing it in evocative detail or telling a compelling story about it. Writers might use a profile of a specific person or group of people in order to characterize a social, economic, or political trend.

Content/Form Feature writers must tell a good story as well as provide an insightful analysis. The organization can be more complex than a news story, for example, which is typically organized as an inverted pyramid. Profiles include information from interviews, personal stories, and quotes from the people interviewed. Writers interweave these elements with narration about and description of the subject. The stories of the people profiled are arranged to support the writer's particular analysis. But, because the main purpose of a profile is to characterize a phenomenon rather than to simply tell a good story, a keen interpretation of the situation is necessary. Charts, tables, and graphs may be included to document the validity of the writer's analysis. Special layouts, often photographs, provide another dimension to the story.

Language/Design Word choice and quotations help evoke an image. Profiles are often characterized by the use of the third person, although the profile is primarily a subjective account of a societal, cultural, or economic phenomenon.

Interview

Situation/Purpose People conduct interviews in order to find out information or different perspectives on a topic and to make the information and perspectives known to others. Common interview subjects are politicians, experts of various kinds, athletes, authors, musicians, artists, and other celebrities. In this textbook you will conduct interviews with others to find out information or learn their perspectives on the issues you're exploring. For example, if you want to learn about marketing strategies in the fashion industry, you might interview someone who works in the industry. If you want to learn different perspectives on the question of whether graffiti is art or vandalism, you might interview a museum curator, a graffiti artist, other kinds of artists, a city official, and someone whose garage door has been tagged.

Content/Form The content of an interview consists of the writer's questions about the topic, the subject's responses, and sometimes other discussion by the writer, for example introductory background or additional information. Interviews usually take the form of questions from the interviewer followed by the subject's response, which may be very brief or quite long. Sometimes interviews take the form of an article in which the subject's responses are woven into the writer's discussion of the topic; sometimes an interview may be only a small part of a longer piece of writing. But keep in mind that the final written version is rarely just a transcript of the interview; rather, the writer has selected and shaped the material to focus on the topic and achieve the desired effect.

The interviewer must carefully plan the questions ahead of time in order to cover all the necessary ground but must also be flexible enough to follow the subject's train of thought and ask good follow-up questions. Interviewers develop strategies for establishing a rapport with their subjects—putting them at ease and getting them to open up—for example by beginning with easy questions or sharing their own views on the topic. Some interviewers like to use tape recorders—with the subject's permission—in order to preserve the subject's exact words; others prefer to take notes. Interviewers typically avoid yes or no questions such as "Do you agree that all graffiti is art?" Rather, they try to draw the subject out by using open-ended questions beginning with phrases like "Tell me about . . . " or "Describe for me. . . . " For example, interviewers will often ask the subject to describe a typical day or specific event.

Language/Design One of the reasons people love to read interviews is that they can hear the subject speak in his or her own voice. Rather than reading someone else's summary or paraphrase, they can read the subject's exact words, which help provide a mental picture of what the subject is like. Thus, in writing up an interview, it is important to use as many of the subject's own words as possible, making sure that the subject is quoted exactly. At the same time, it is important to present the subject's words in such a way that they are not taken out of context and do not misrepresent the subject's intentions.

Letter to the Editor

Situation/Purpose Most newspapers and magazines publish letters from readers, which are usually written in response to an article, column, editorial, or another letter that has appeared in that newspaper or magazine or to issues and events in the news. Letters are usually published on a special page near the beginning of a magazine or on the editorial page of a newspaper. Although they are usually called *letters to the editor,* they are actually aimed more at other readers or the author of an article. Letters to the editor are the most traditional way for ordinary people to communicate their ideas to the public. And although talk radio and the Internet now provide other ways for people to communicate ideas, letters to the editor are still popular. People write letters to the editor when they feel strongly about something or when they feel an issue has not been addressed in the forum they are writing to. The purpose is usually to disagree or agree with a previously published position, to correct a statement of fact, or to add supporting information or ideas to an ongoing discussion.

Content/Form Letters to the editor are subject to screening and editing. This means that a letter is more likely to get published if it meets expectations about form and content. Letters are usually about recently published articles or events and topics currently in the news. They should be as brief as possible while still developing a position convincingly. They usually begin by identifying the topic and/or the article being responded to and briefly stating the writer's position. The position is then developed as concisely but persuasively as possible, making reference to opposing positions when necessary. The ending should be pithy or thought-provoking. Most large newspapers and magazines get more letters than they can publish, so they look for letters that contain very well-argued positions, perspectives that have not been presented before, new information, interesting anecdotes, or humor. Editors usually want to confirm that the letter is authentic and accurate. Most editors will not publish anonymous letters or letters whose authorship has not been confirmed.

Language/Design There is a range of acceptable tones in letters to the editor, from serious, formal, and polite through lightly humorous to angry and sarcastic. But whatever the tone, the language must be clear enough for the average reader of that publication and not offensive or profane, at least not in mainstream publications. The tone and language should follow that used in other letters to that publication but should also express the writer's individuality. Usually letters are edited, but editors might avoid letters that have too many errors; if errors slip by, the writer may feel embarrassed when the letter is published.

Manifesto

Situation/Purpose A manifesto is a public declaration aimed at changing a social situation. Closely tied to a current, often political situation, the manifesto presents an argument that distinguishes itself as a call to action. Writers compose a manifesto to instigate an immediate and often consequential response. A manifesto is intended to change the course of history, shining a light on previously ignored or misunderstood situations. Not only does a manifesto attempt to explain the past or justify future actions, it also attempts to redefine the situation in which these actions occur. The root of the word, *manifest,* suggests that it makes obvious the previously submerged aspects of the situation. Originally, manifestos were proclamations issued, or at least sanctioned, by a head of state, but they have evolved into a genre that anyone can take up. Most often manifestos represent the concerns of a group rather than the thinking of an individual. The best known manifesto, The Communist Manifesto, by Marx and Engels, was written not only to convince workers of the viability of socialism but also to suggest that revolution was a possible consequence of this new understanding. More recently you may have heard of the years-long hunt for the criminal known as the Unabomber, Theodore Kaczynski, whose essay, "Industrial Society and Its Future," was labeled a manifesto by the press. An even more recent and quite different example can be found in a recent book titled *The Cluetrain Manifesto: The End of Business as Usual,* which proclaims that the Internet is turning business upside down and offers a new way to look at business in the information age.

Content/Form The manifesto is an excellent example of how a genre evolves. Having begun as a proclamation by heads of state, it has been adapted for use in a variety of situations, changing its form in each of these new contexts. Overall, though, manifestos typically begin with an introduction offering a general statement about the problem or situation and proceed through a series of short paragraphs or questions and answers that convince readers of the initial proposition's truth. All of the various possibilities for persuasion exist: emotional appeals, a carefully developed series of logical propositions, a series of definitions or even an extended metaphor that tells a story in a new way. Whatever form the manifesto takes, it aims to bring the reader to a new vision and a readiness to act.

Language/Design The language of a manifesto is formal and carefully crafted but incisive, using strong language to startle or shock its readers with a newly unveiled revelation. For example, the Communist Manifesto begins as follows: "A spectre is haunting Europe—the spectre of communism. All the powers of old Europe have entered into a holy alliance to exorcise this spectre" (Marx and Engels, 1848). Marx used an evocative choice of words to set the stage with an "old" Europe that sees communism as a strange and unholy apparition that must be banished. From this beginning he continued to develop his argument for his particular explanation of capitalism and how it should change.

Online Posts

Situation/Purpose Many teachers now use electronic communication in the classroom to allow students to carry on discussions online, just as people outside the classroom use blogs, listservs, bulletin boards, and MOOs or MUDs. Most of the electronic writing assignments in this textbook involve listservs or online threaded discussions. Listservs allow people to send a message simultaneously to all members of a group. Chatrooms, bulletin boards, and threaded discussion forums allow for the development of a conversation online, which all participants can read as it develops. Unlike other electronic discussion groups, online discussions in a classroom are limited to the students in the class, although discussions can be continued outside the class period.

Content/Form Although students are often tempted to use online discussions to chat about personal matters, teachers generally want them to be reserved for discussion of ideas and issues that come up in class, just as in a face-to-face class discussion. It is important to remember that everyone on the listserv, including the teacher, will read the message. The interaction proceeds at a different pace than a face-to-face discussion; there is time for reflection before you respond. Online posts usually conform to the standards of other informal writing activities in this book, for example, a journal entry. If you have kept a journal for a class, you have an idea of the requirements of such informal writing. Generally, the quality of the ideas takes precedence over demands for correctness. Depending on the assignment, you may be asked to reply to a specific question or raise a question relating to the class. You may use your online posts to respond to a specific text or be asked to participate in the discussion of a broader issue.

Language/Design Although online posts are considered an informal type of writing, they should be well crafted and thoughtful. Although the tone can be informal, as in a face-to-face discussion, writers should attempt to use the terminology of the texts being discussed. Online discussions give students a chance to practice using course- or issue-related terminology before they write more formal papers on the topic. Since many people read online posts, the language should not be offensive, personal, or embarrassing. It's a good idea to reread a comment before you post it.

Opinion Piece/Commentary

Situation/Purpose Opinion pieces and commentaries are an important part of a democratic society. They allow ordinary citizens and public figures to exchange ideas about important public issues. Thus most newspapers and other periodicals devote regular space to these commentaries in a section known as the opinion page or op-ed page. Some of these pieces are regular columns written by local or syndicated columnists while others are written by guest contributors; writers may be private individuals but are usually professional journalists or public figures. Local newspapers, campus newspapers, 'zines, and some online publications might publish the opinions of writers with fewer credentials than are customarily required by national publications. This kind of commentary can address a range of topics. Opinion pieces are meant to be persuasive; the writer wants to convince others to adopt a particular position or, at the very least, consider the issue from a new perspective. Opinion pieces allow the writer to develop a position more extensively than does a related form, the **Letter to the Editor,** which is another form for expressing personal views.

Content/Form An opinion piece is essentially a short argumentative essay. (See **Argumentative Essay** for description.) Usually an opinion piece begins by referring to the context of an ongoing debate or some specific recent event, which leads the reader into the argument.

Many systems have been developed for writing arguments. A commonly used one involves making a claim and supporting the claim with evidence. An important step that writers often leave out is establishing the connection between the claim and the evidence; this connection is called the *warrant.* For example, if a writer wants to argue in support of a civic project for youth, the writer's claim is that getting youth interested in a community project like painting a graffiti mural will increase their commitment to the community and reduce the chances that they will vandalize public property. The writer would offer as evidence the fact that similar projects have had these results in other communities. The writer's warrant for using this evidence, which may or may not be stated in the argument, is that using data from similar projects is a reasonable way to make decisions about a present project. But effective arguments do not simply present one side; readers who disagree may simply say, "Well, that sounds good, but the writer hasn't considered this." An argument is more effective when it takes this opposing position into account and responds to it in some way: the *rebuttal.* For example, a writer might acknowledge that the project will cost a lot of money or that such a project will simply encourage more graffiti. After fairly presenting these perspectives, the writer might respond that the money for the project is a fraction of the cost of removing graffiti from city property and that similar projects have in fact resulted in a reduction of graffiti. But developing a logical appeal may not be enough. The writer can also use emotional appeals, for example appealing to the readers' sympathy for the community's youth or invoking the esthetic value of the mural.

An opinion piece may conclude in many different ways—summaries, restatements of the thesis—but however it ends, it should leave the feeling that the writer has considered both sides fairly and chosen the most reasonable position.

Language/Design Opinion columns usually use the first person. The overall tone and specific word choice reflect the writer's own style as well as the nature of the publication. In this textbook you will find examples of opinion pieces that use a wide variety of writing styles.

Proposal

Situation/Purpose In business, the professions, and other areas of public life, people are constantly exchanging goods, services, and money. This exchange is regulated partly by the complex mechanisms of supply and demand. But a special mechanism for the distribution of scarce resources or scarce opportunities is the proposal. When people in the workplace need to persuade an outside agency to give them money or other resources, or if they want to be chosen to provide a product or service, they write a proposal. Sometimes proposals are written in response to Requests for Proposal, or RFPs, which are circulated by agencies with resources to distribute and by companies or agencies who need a product or service. Sometimes proposals are used within a company to persuade someone to do something, usually to make a change or solve a problem of some sort, although in this situation they may be called recommendation reports.

Content/Form Proposals are basically organized as a problem/solution discussion. The problem section usually includes detailed descriptions, sets of facts, and statistics. The solution section includes analyses and recommendations. Since the proposal is used to make important decisions and will become part of a permanent record, the information should be as accurate as possible, based on reliable sources or research methods. When outside sources are used, they should be documented, using a standard documentation system, such as the MLA or APA system. When original research is involved, the research process should be carefully described.

Proposals can vary in length from a single page to hundreds of pages. The form of a typical proposal usually moves from description of a problem to presentation of a solution. A typical proposal will have most of the following elements in roughly this order:

Explain the purpose and scope of the proposal.

Describe and give some background on the situation or problem.

Suggest why the reader needs what you are proposing.

Present and analyze possible alternative solutions.

Explain why your proposal is the best solution.

Describe how your proposal would be implemented, including itemizing the costs.

Ask the reader to take some specific action.

Because proposals are meant to be as reader-friendly as possible, they usually include more elaborate formatting than other kinds of writing: headings, often accompanied by a numbering system; bullets; typographical and spacing variations; graphics are typical.

Language/Design The language is generally formal, impersonal, objective, or even scientific. It may include many technical terms, if necessary, but otherwise should be as clear, concise, and jargon-free as possible. As with other workplace or academic writing, it should avoid errors in sentence structure, grammar, and mechanics.

Report

Situation/Purpose The report is a common, varied, and flexible genre used in all kinds of situations—school, workplace, and other kinds of organizations—in which information must be recorded and communicated. Reports are usually written either to record information for bureaucratic, legal, medical, or scientific reasons or to give decision makers the information they need to make decisions. A student might use a report to record an activity or research findings.

Content/Form Since their purpose is usually to record or present information, reports usually include detailed descriptions, sets of facts, and statistics. They often also include analyses of this information and sometimes recommendations based on the information. Since the report may become part of a permanent record or may influence decisions, the information should be as accurate as possible, based on reliable sources or research methods. When outside sources are used, they should be documented, using a standard documentation system, such as the MLA or APA system. When original research is involved, the research process should be carefully described. Information that is relevant to the report but too extensive to fit smoothly into the body of the report can be included in appendices attached to the end of the report.

Reports vary in form and length. A report usually follows some variation on the following pattern:

Introductory section that might include the purpose of the report, possibly a brief statement of the overall conclusion or recommendation, or background information.

Body section that might include additional background, a detailed description of a situation or problem, a discussion of research parameters and methods, an analysis of alternatives, arguments to support a recommendation, a description of procedures or implementation steps, or a discussion of benefits and drawbacks; it might also include graphics.

Concluding section that might include a summary, a recommendation, or some other kind of concluding statement.

Because reports are meant to be as reader-friendly as possible and because they convey a lot of information, they usually include more elaborate formatting than other kinds of writing: headings, often accompanied by a numbering system; bullets; typographical and spacing variations; graphics are typical.

Language/Design The language is generally formal, impersonal, objective, or even scientific. It may include many technical terms, if necessary, but otherwise should be as clear, concise, and jargon-free as possible. As with other workplace or academic writing, it should avoid errors in sentence structure, grammar, and mechanics.

Resume/Cover Letter

Situation/Purpose At some point in their lives, most people will apply for a job and for most jobs this will include submitting a resume and cover letter. A resume is a document that includes information about a person's education, job history, job-related skills and credentials, and contact information. Usually when people submit a resume as part of a job application, they submit it with a cover letter—a letter focused specifically on one particular job.

Content/Form Resumes usually follow a fairly standard template, with name, address, phone number, and e-mail address at the top, followed by headed sections for Objectives (the kind of job being sought), Education, Job Experience or Employment History, and Skills and/or Credentials. Many also include names and contact information for people that can give references, though some resumes simply say "References available upon request." Some resumes include personal information about age and marital status, though many do not. Most people's resumes are one page, but people with long and complex careers and qualifications may have multiple-page resumes. The section on Job Experience or Employment is usually the longest and includes a list of jobs that the person has had, usually in chronological order beginning with the most recent, and specific details about responsibilities and accomplishments for each job.

Cover letters are also usually a page long and rarely more than two pages, even for people with long and complex careers, and they typically follow some variation on this format: The first paragraph identifies the job being applied for and usually how the applicant knows about the job, for example from a newspaper ad, a school placement office, or a personal contact. This paragraph may end with a brief overall statement about the applicant's interest in and/or suitability for the job. The content and order of the middle two or three paragraphs depends on the type of job and the applicant's background, but typical arrangements include a paragraph on education, training, and credentials; a paragraph on relevant job experiences; and a paragraph on accomplishments, other qualifications, and interests; or one paragraph on education and job experiences and one paragraph on why the applicant is particularly suited for this job or company. The final paragraph usually includes information on how the applicant can be contacted and a strong statement of interest in discussing the job further.

Sample resumes and cover letters can be found in many books or online sites, and word processing programs often include a variety of templates for both resumes and cover letters. These are very useful in helping you understand the reader's expectations, but avoid following these models and templates too closely, especially in terms of specific wording; remember that since many other people applying for the same job may also use these models and templates, employers may see the exact same sentence dozens or hundreds of time. The key to a successful resume and cover letter is to find the delicate balance between meeting the reader's expectations, which may be fairly narrow and even rigid, and creating a picture of yourself as a uniquely qualified individual.

Language/Design The language of a cover letter should have the characteristics of any business letter: sentences should be clear and concise; word choice should be precise and relatively formal; there should be no errors in grammar, punctuation, or mechanics; and connections between sentences and paragraphs should be clear. The layout on the page should be simple and clean, and the formatting should be fairly simple; for example, use the same type face and font size throughout. It's acceptable to put some information—for example, a list of accomplishments or skills—in the form of a bulleted list rather than a traditional paragraph, but don't rely too heavily on bulleted lists in your cover letter; the majority of the letter should be in the form of connected prose.

The formatting for a resume can be more complex and creative, with headings for categories of information like education, employment history, and skills, and bulleted lists for individual items within these categories. But, again, keep the overall layout as simple and clean as possible. Published samples and templates are generally good models for formatting. The language of a resume should also be clear, correct, and relatively formal, though resumes can make more use of phrases in bulleted lists rather than complete sentences in connected prose.

For both resumes and cover letters, use spell check and grammar check, proofread carefully, have someone else proofread carefully, and then proofread again yourself.

Review

Situation/Purpose Reviews are written in response to books, films, plays, restaurants, musical and dance performances, art exhibits, and architecture. Perhaps it is more useful to distinguish reviews by purpose, for example, scholarly reviews written for professional journals, media reviews written by professional writers, and unsolicited reviews written by the general public and published on the Internet. In the first instance, practitioners in specific disciplines assess the contribution of a text or performance to the field as a whole; media reviewers—often writing on short deadlines—give their readers the first public response to new entertainment; and customer reviews give people a forum to share their opinions about a particular book or exhibit. Part of a professional reviewer's responsibility is to discover fresh talent and original work as well as to cover work by prominent artists. It is worth nothing that a review brings a certain amount of notoriety and attention to a subject. Lack of critical attention often prevents less well-established writers or artists from getting the kind of public notice that would give them an audience. A reviewer has a certain amount of power in determining who and what gets the exposure so crucial to finding an audience.

Content/Form Reviews take much of their interest from the works they describe, but reviews are themselves written texts and, as such, should be able to stand on their own as well-organized, interesting pieces of writing. Reviews differ from reports in that they provide a critical analysis. Even an informal review submitted to an Internet bookseller will not be published online if it does not include some discussion of how and why the opinion is formed. Generally, reviews include a description of the text, exhibit, or performance; an analysis of how well it accomplishes its purpose; and an evaluation of the contribution of the work. Within that framework is much room for variation. Reviewers must include enough information for their readers to understand what they are talking about, but the description should be pointed and not include too much information. Reviews customarily include full bibliographic information. The description should provide a context to help readers understand something about the author, artist, and so on; explain why the work was written or produced; and tell something about the particular framework or approach used. The review should address the strengths and weaknesses of the text in terms of its purpose, its comprehensiveness, and its style. Examples or specific quotes help illustrate this information and enhance the reviewer's credibility. Reviewers also evaluate the worth of the work by comparing it to other works of its kind and determining what new ground it has broken or what new perspective it has added to a field.

Language/Design Language may vary depending on who is reviewing, what is being reviewed, and where the review will be published. The overall tone and specific word choice reflect the writer's individual style as well as the nature of the publication. Language may range from casual and hip to formal and academic. Consider whether or not to use the first person. Since the entire review is your opinion, it is not necessary to preface your observations with "I think" or "I believe." Most commonly the first person is reserved to describe the experience of reading or viewing rather than introducing an opinion. For example, "I sat in stunned silence with the rest of the audience after the 20-minute soliloquy." Reviewers usually use the present tense when writing about the text or the author and the past tense when discussing the subject of the book, for example, "This documentary focuses mainly on the alternative rock scene of the 1980s but pays scant attention to rap music, although rap actually contributed more to the reshaping of popular culture while alternative music mainly influenced other musicians."

Web Page

Situation/Purpose Anyone from a kid to a corporation can have a Web page, and it's likely that in the future more people and institutions will use Web pages to communicate in a variety of ways for a variety of purposes. Students at all levels make Web pages as class projects; business people and professionals have work-related Web pages; and ordinary people have Web pages to express opinions, circulate information, and find others who share their interests. Businesses and other institutions of all sizes use Web pages to sell or otherwise promote their products and services. Individuals might have one Web page that they keep updated throughout their life, they might have several for different aspects of their life, or they might create short-term ones for specific purposes. If you are creating a Web page for a class, the purpose may be just to learn how to do it, and in that case your page may simply be an introduction to yourself. Inside or outside of class, Web pages may also have a variety of specific purposes—to make connections around interests, communicate ideas, promote causes, and publicize events. Part of the purpose of a Web page is to attract people to visit and then read the page, but the primary purpose is to inform, persuade, entertain, surprise, and/or challenge those who visit and stay.

Content/Form The content includes background and current information that may be personal, institutional, or issue oriented, depending on the purpose. A Web "page" is usually in fact multiple pages, and hypertext allows readers to move quickly from one page to another in order to follow a thread of information. Hyperlinks allow readers to follow a thread of information to other sites on the Web. Often Web pages include a place for interaction between the owner and the reader or between readers. A great attraction of Web pages is that they combine words, color graphics, and even sound; and the graphics may include designs, drawings, photos, and even animated elements. The choice and arrangement of the elements should be appropriate to the purpose and intended audience. The text and graphics should interact in interesting ways, but the purpose of each element and the relationships between the elements should be clear.

Language/Design Sometimes the language is very plain and straightforward. even formal; often it is playful, casual, and personal; occasionally it is in-your-face, even offensive. As with the elements of content and form, the language should thoughtfully reflect purpose and audience.

Contents

PART FIVE

Researching and Writing 297

PART EIGHT

Sentence Problems 635

PART NINE

Words and Style 721

Preface

All writers, whatever their skills and experience, seek at least occasional advice. We've designed the fifth edition of *The Longman Handbook for Writers and Readers* to provide answers to specific questions as well as extended help with larger concerns.

The handbook provides the following in readily accessible form:

- Advice on composing essays and documents for a wide variety of readers—academic, public, and work—and on understanding the expectations of these readers
- Strategies for research, analysis, and documentation, with special emphasis on the growing number of sophisticated electronic sources for information, ideas, and analysis
- Aid in designing a wide variety of documents, both print and electronic, with special attention to developing new skills for communicating ideas and information
- Answers to questions about grammar, punctuation, and style
- Support for speakers of English as a second language—fully integrated with advice to native speakers, not isolated in a special section of the text
- Help with addressing audiences through the spoken as well as the written word

What makes *The Longman Handbook* unique?

We have written *The Longman Handbook for Writers and Readers* out of a belief that composition instruction will benefit from an innovative approach that responds directly to recent theory and practice while addressing traditional concerns as well. Our aim has been to offer concrete, helpful advice for writers engaging a wide variety of writing tasks and audiences.

- **Writing as social action for communities of diverse audiences.** We emphasize the social nature of writing, especially the ways different groups of readers—in academic, public, and work communities—shape texts and the writing process. We offer specific strategies for responding to these audiences.
- **Critical thinking and reading.** We believe that reading, critical thinking, and awareness of audience expectations are intertwined. For this reason, we emphasize not only the importance of each but also their many interrelationships.

- **A fresh approach to correctness.** We believe that correctness in writing—employing the conventions appropriately and effectively—is largely a matter of social awareness. Errors can undermine the writers' relationship with readers or impede effective, persuasive, and imaginative interaction within a community of writers and readers. Using appropriate conventions of grammar, sentence structure, punctuation, and style is an important part of being able to guide the way readers respond to writing. *The Longman Handbook* treats correctness and understanding written conventions as essential to accomplished writing, helping writers recognize the effect of errors on readers as well as the ways conventions may vary from community to community.
- **Recognize and revise.** We believe that just knowing the definition of an error is seldom sufficient. Writers need *first* to be able to recognize errors. *Then* they need to be able to correct mistakes and internalize the conventions permanently in the process. *The Longman Handbook* helps writers develop the ability to recognize errors in their own writing, an essential step often missing from handbook discussions. Then it provides concrete strategies for revision and correction.

- **Ten serious errors.** We highlight "Ten Serious Errors" in grammar that are most likely to confuse readers and thus should be avoided. These are listed in a table on the inside back cover and highlighted by icons throughout the chapters.
- **Reader's reaction.** Reader's reactions to unedited examples link the writer and reader and show students how their unedited writing could be perceived.
- **Strategies.** Highlighted "Strategy" sections appearing throughout the handbook provide writers with specific steps they can take to accomplish a task; correct an error; or achieve a goal in expression, critical understanding, or style.
- **Online style.** In writing about online communities, we treat online communication not simply as a matter of technological awareness but also as a setting with its own unique rhetorical and stylistic demands and strategies.
- **Research and writing with critical awareness.** We know that information and ideas lie at the heart of good writing, even writing focusing on personal insights and experience. Our discussions of researching and writing pay special attention to critical reading and evaluation of sources. We also give extended emphasis to techniques of summary, paraphrase, synthesis, and critical response. We present techniques for personal inquiry, for drawing on print and electronic resources, and for fieldwork, all designed to add depth and interest to writing, both for the writer and for readers. We pay special attention to new resources for writers, such as the ever-growing number of research databases.
- **Integrating sources and avoiding plagiarism.** From our own teaching, we recognize the importance of both these concerns, and we

provide advice, concrete strategies, and detailed examples to help students create researched writing that gains strength and depth from sources while appropriately acknowledging the origins of ideas and information.

- **Language variation.** Here, we focus on the issue of language variation—home or community language varieties, oral and written dialects, code shifting, the importance of "standard" English in text written for diverse audiences, and the effect that particular choices of personae can have on an audience's reception of a text.
- **Collaboration.** We treat writing, critical thinking, and research as often enriched through collaboration, either with fellow writers and readers or with potential audiences.
- **Speaking.** *The Longman Handbook* offers an entire chapter on speaking, "Speaking Effectively" (Chapter 15).

What's New in the Fifth Edition?

The fifth edition of *The Longman Handbook for Writers and Readers* has been revised, reorganized, and improved in a variety of ways. Note the following changes:

- **How writing differs in academic, public, and workplace communities is highlighted succinctly and graphically in 15 new Communities Boxes.** Boxes are set off from the main chapter text to help students easily reference them throughout the semester and after. Topics include differences among purposes, audiences, thesis statements, style conventions, reading strategies, reasoning and evidence, use of visual elements, library resources, online resources, and fieldwork, among others.

COMMUNITIES BOXES

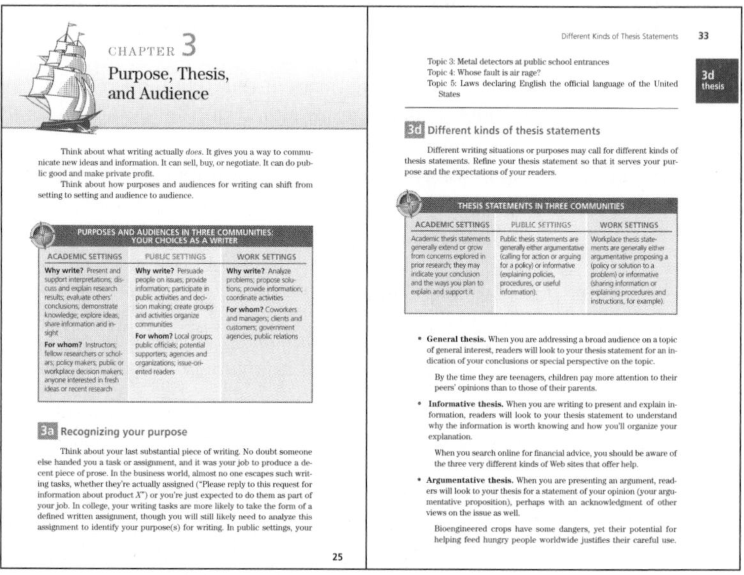

CHAPTER 3
Purpose, Thesis, and Audience

Think about what writing actually *does*. It gives you a way to communicate new ideas and information. It can sell, buy, or negotiate. It can do public good and make private profit.

Think about how purposes and audiences for writing can shift from setting to setting and audience to audience.

PURPOSES AND AUDIENCES IN THREE COMMUNITIES: YOUR CHOICES AS A WRITER

ACADEMIC SETTINGS	PUBLIC SETTINGS	WORK SETTINGS
Why write? Present and support interpretations; discuss and explain research results; evaluate others' conclusions; demonstrate knowledge; explore ideas; share information and insight	**Why write?** Persuade people on issues; provide information; participate in public activities and decision making; create groups and activities organize communities	**Why write?** Analyze problems; propose solutions; provide information; coordinate activities
For whom? Instructors; fellow researchers or scholars; policy makers; public or workplace decision makers; anyone interested in fresh ideas or recent research	**For whom?** Local groups; public officials; potential supporters; agencies and organizations; issue-oriented readers	**For whom?** Coworkers and managers; clients and customers; government agencies; public relations

3a Recognizing your purpose

Think about your last substantial piece of writing. No doubt someone else handed you a task or assignment, and it was your job to produce a decent piece of prose. In the business world, almost no one escapes such writing tasks, whether they're actually assigned ("Please reply to this request for information about product *X*") or you're just expected to do them as part of your job. In college, your writing tasks are more likely to take the form of a defined written assignment, though you will still likely need to analyze this assignment to identify your purpose(s) for writing. In public settings, your

25

Different Kinds of Thesis Statements 33

3d thesis

Topic 3: Metal detectors at public school entrances
Topic 4: Whose fault is air rage?
Topic 5: Laws declaring English the official language of the United States

3d Different kinds of thesis statements

Different writing situations or purposes may call for different kinds of thesis statements. Refine your thesis statement so that it serves your purpose and the expectations of your readers.

THESIS STATEMENTS IN THREE COMMUNITIES

ACADEMIC SETTINGS	PUBLIC SETTINGS	WORK SETTINGS
Academic thesis statements generally extend or grow from concerns explored in prior research; they may indicate your conclusion and the ways you plan to explain and support it.	Public thesis statements are generally either argumentative (calling for action or arguing for a policy) or informative (explaining policies, procedures, or useful information).	Workplace thesis statements are generally either argumentative proposing a (policy or solution to a problem) or informative (sharing information or explaining procedures and instructions, for example).

- **General thesis.** When you are addressing a broad audience on a topic of general interest, readers will look to your thesis statement for an indication of your conclusions or special perspective on the topic.

  By the time they are teenagers, children pay more attention to their peers' opinions than to those of their parents.

- **Informative thesis.** When you are writing to present and explain information, readers will look to your thesis statement to understand why the information is worth knowing and how you'll organize your explanation.

  When you search online for financial advice, you should be aware of the three very different kinds of Web sites that offer help.

- **Argumentative thesis.** When you are presenting an argument, readers will look to your thesis for a statement of your opinion (your argumentative proposition), perhaps with an acknowledgment of other views on the issue as well.

  Bioengineered crops have some dangers, yet their potential for helping feed hungry people worldwide justifies their careful use.

- **Significantly expanded discussions of writing in different communities,** often including examples, have been threaded into most sections of each relevant chapter throughout the book in order to help students connect the topic at hand with real and specific writing situations.
- **Writing Across the Curriculum chapters appear earlier** in the book in the writing process section (Part 4) in order to foreground the importance of applying skills and strategies to different writing environments.
- **New chapter on Writing in the Social and Natural Sciences** (Chapter 18) explains the nature of inquiry and the types of research in different fields. The common genres of different fields are defined and their component parts are explained before a sample is provided of each, offering students guidance for writing throughout their college careers.
- **Thoroughly revised chapter on General Education Academic Writing** (Chapter 16) includes extensive information on analyzing syllabi and assignments, helping students discern the knowledge and skills being assessed, the strategies available to them, and the criteria for assessment.

- **Revised chapter on Writing in Literature and Other Humanities** (Chapter 17) is expanded to include new material on analyzing fine arts such as films, paintings, photographs, and sculpture as well as guidance for writing reviews and critiques, exposing students to different analytical techniques and genres used in the humanities.
- **New chapter on Public Writing** (Chapter 19) helps students to understand the purposes of public writing and anticipate audience needs and expectations. Guidance is offered for two of the most frequent public writing genres: the flyer and the letter to the editor. Students should be able to see how the skills they are learning for rhetorical analysis transfer out of academic and into other writing situations beyond college.
- **Critical thinking and argument is emphasized as integral to the writing process**, with revised critical thinking and argument coverage now appearing in the writing process section (Part 2).
- **Visual argument coverage has been expanded** into a new Chapter 12, and new material helps students better understand when it is appropriate and effective to include graphs, tables, and illustrations in their writing.
- **Research and documentation coverage now appears earlier** in the book, reinforcing for students that asking fruitful questions, researching, drafting, and documenting must precede sentence-level concerns such as grammar, punctuation, and mechanics.
- **Source samples for both MLA and APA styles** demonstrate how to cite those sources students struggle with the most (such as articles taken from online databases) by showing them where in the source material they can find the information their citations require.
- **Avoiding Plagiarism and Integrating Sources have been combined** (new Chapter 26) into one chapter to clarify for students the relationship between working conscientiously with sources and successfully avoiding plagiarism (see p. xviii).
- **Significantly revised online writing chapter** (Chapter 14) now includes extensive information and guidance on blogging, IMing, and text messaging in order to help students understand how these mediums have unique purposes, audiences, and style conventions that differ from more formal academic, public, and workplace writing. Coverage of discussion lists and writing in Web-based forums is also expanded.
- **The chapter on Purpose and Thesis has been combined with the chapter on Audience** to strengthen students' understanding of the connections among these essential elements of writing.
- **The chapter on Revising has been combined with the chapter on Editing and Proofreading** to help students see more clearly important differences among these activities. The discussion of revision continues to emphasize re-seeing of ideas, structure, and strategies while the sections on editing and proofreading focus on smaller, stylistic concerns.

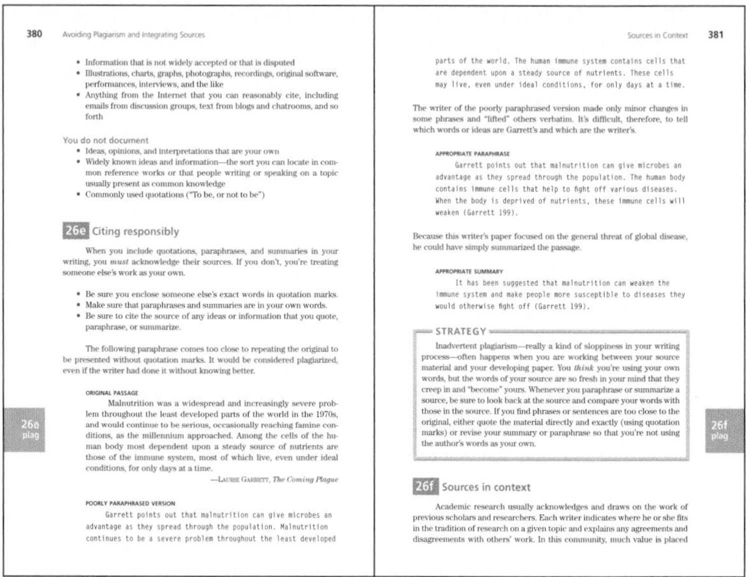

380 Avoiding Plagiarism and Integrating Sources

- Information that is not widely accepted or that is disputed
- Illustrations, charts, graphs, photographs, recordings, original software, performances, interviews, and the like
- Anything from the Internet that you can reasonably cite, including emails from discussion groups, text from blogs and chatrooms, and so forth

You do not document
- Ideas, opinions, and interpretations that are your own
- Widely known ideas and information—the sort you can locate in common reference works or that people writing or speaking on a topic usually present as common knowledge
- Commonly used quotations ("To be, or not to be")

26e Citing responsibly

When you include quotations, paraphrases, and summaries in your writing, you *must* acknowledge their sources. If you don't, you're treating someone else's work as your own.

- Be sure you enclose someone else's exact words in quotation marks.
- Make sure that paraphrases and summaries are in your own words.
- Be sure to cite the source of any ideas or information that you quote, paraphrase, or summarize.

The following paraphrase comes too close to repeating the original to be presented without quotation marks. It would be considered plagiarized, even if the writer had done it without knowing better.

ORIGINAL PASSAGE

Malnutrition was a widespread and increasingly severe problem throughout the least developed parts of the world in the 1970s, and would continue to be serious, occasionally reaching famine conditions, as the millennium approached. Among the cells of the human body most dependent upon a steady source of nutrients are those of the immune system, most of which live, even under ideal conditions, for only days at a time.

—Laurie Garrett, *The Coming Plague*

26e plag

POORLY PARAPHRASED VERSION

Garrett points out that malnutrition can give microbes an advantage as they spread through the population. Malnutrition continues to be a severe problem throughout the least developed parts of the world. The human immune system contains cells that are dependent upon a steady source of nutrients. These cells may live, even under ideal conditions, for only days at a time.

Sources in Context 381

The writer of the poorly paraphrased version made only minor changes in some phrases and "lifted" others verbatim. It's difficult, therefore, to tell which words or ideas are Garrett's and which are the writer's.

APPROPRIATE PARAPHRASE

Garrett points out that malnutrition can give microbes an advantage as they spread through the population. The human body contains immune cells that help to fight off various diseases. When the body is deprived of nutrients, these immune cells will weaken (Garrett 199).

Because this writer's paper focused on the general threat of global disease, he could have simply summarized the passage.

APPROPRIATE SUMMARY

It has been suggested that malnutrition can weaken the immune system and make people more susceptible to diseases they would otherwise fight off (Garrett 199).

STRATEGY

Inadvertent plagiarism—really a kind of sloppiness in your writing process—often happens when you are working between your source material and your developing paper. You *think* you're using your own words, but the words of your source are so fresh in your mind that they creep in and "become" yours. Whenever you paraphrase or summarize a source, be sure to look back at the source and compare your words with those in the source. If you find phrases or sentences are too close to the original, either quote the material directly and exactly (using quotation marks) or revise your summary or paraphrase so that you're not using the author's words as your own.

26f plag

26f Sources in context

Academic research usually acknowledges and draws on the work of previous scholars and researchers. Each writer indicates where he or she fits in the tradition of research on a given topic and explains any agreements and disagreements with others' work. In this community, much value is placed

- **Updated document design chapter** (Chapter 13) includes new tables, graphs, and charts.
- **Comprehensive electronic databases coverage now appears in a new Chapter 23** to offer students easier access to and a clearer focus on these increasingly integral elements of research.
- **Exercises and examples have been revised throughout** with special attention to contemporary issues, themes, and details.

Supplements

The Longman Handbook for Writers and Readers is accompanied by an extensive package of print and media supplements for both students and instructors. Please see your Longman representative for details on these and additional supplements.

For Students

- mycomplab 2.0 MyCompLab (http://www.mycomplab.com) is Longman's umbrella site to support freshman composition and includes extensive resources for grammar, research, and writing. Highlights include: E-book of the text; interactive video tutorials on key grammar, writing, and research topics; ExerciseZone for grammar; Citation Diagnostics and Exercises; Evaluating Sources tutorial; and more. Ask your Longman sales representative for a demonstration or a temporary password.

- vango notes VangoNotes: Study on the go with VangoNotes. Just download chapter reviews from your text and listen to them on any mp3 player. Now wherever you are—whatever you're doing—you can study by listening to the following for each chapter of your textbook:
  - **Big Ideas:** Your "need to know" for each chapter
  - **Practice Test:** A gut check for the Big Ideas—tells you if you need to keep studying
  - **Key Terms:** Audio "flashcards" to help you review key concepts and terms
  - **Rapid Review:** A quick drill session—use it right before your test

  VangoNotes are **flexible;** download all the material directly to your player, or only the chapters you need. And they're **efficient.** Use them in your car, at the gym, walking to class, wherever. So get yours today. And get studying. VangoNotes.com

For Instructors

- The *Instructor's Resource Manual* not only offers instructors support for teaching Parts 1 to 10—with suggested activities, teaching tips, chapter summaries, exercises, and online activities and resources—but also includes opening chapters that discuss other aspects of teaching, such as: the student's approach to using a handbook; advice for adjunct instructors and teaching assistants; online teaching in conjunction with the handbook; and designing a course with the handbook.
- An *Answer Key* is available for the exercises in *The Longman Handbook*.
- The *Diagnostic and Editing Tests and Exercises* aid in analyzing common errors and can supplement the handbook's exercises. (Available in both print and electronic formats.)

Acknowledgments

The fifth edition of *The Longman Handbook for Writers and Readers* reflects important improvements in a book that has experienced more than a decade of development. We are grateful to a number of people for helping to keep moving the book forward.

Many of our colleagues have advised us, reviewed drafts, and provided general responses to our ideas. Our special thanks go to the following people who have reviewed *The Longman Handbook:* James Allen, College of DuPage; David L. Anderson, Butler County Community College (Pennsylvania); Edward Armstrong, University of Arkansas; Lois Ascher, Wentworth Institute of Technology; Valerie Balester, Texas A&M University; James Barcus,

Baylor University; Dennis Baron, University of Illinois at Champaign/Urbana; Sue Beebe, Southwest Texas State University; Rebecca Bell-Metereau, Southwest Texas State University; Steven Bellin, St. Norbert College; Daniel Bender, Pace University; Robin Benny, Chicago State University; Faun Bernbach Evans, Chicago State University; Karen Bilda, Cardinal Stritch University; Wendy Bishop, Florida State University; Peggy Broder, Cleveland State University; Robin Brown, University of Minnesota; Diane Todd Bucci, Robert Morris University; Nancy Buffington, University of Delaware; Jennifer Bullis, Whatcom Community College; Mike Burke, Southern Illinois University–Edwardsville; Norman E. Carlson, Western Michigan University; Tami Carmichael, University of Georgia; Caryn Chaden, De Paul University; Jo Chern, University of Wisconsin at Green Bay; Patricia E. Connors, University of Memphis; Lauren Coulter, Tennessee State; Bonnie Cox, San Jose State University; Carolyn Craft, Longwood College; Katherine Dallen, Whatcom Community College; Susan Dauer, Valencia Community College; Patricia Davis, Pima Community College (Arizona); Susan X. Day, Illinois State University; Marcia Dickson, Ohio State University; Larnell Dunkley, Benedictine University; Janet Eber, County College of Morris (New Jersey); Nancy Enright, Seton Hall University; David C. Estes, Loyola University; Carol Falkenstine de Rosset, Berea College; Jim Farber, Vernon Regional Junior College (Texas); Christine Farris, Indiana University; Barbara Fein, New Hampshire Community Technical College, Stratham; Mary Finley, California State University, Northridge; Michael C. Flanigan, The University of Oklahoma; Cynthia Galivan, Hudson Valley Community College; James Goldstein, Auburn University; Laura Gray, University of Arkansas; Tim Gustafson, University of Minnesota; William Handley, University of California at Los Angeles; Jeannette Harris, University of Southern Mississippi; Vicki Hay, Arizona State University, West; Pam Helberg, Whatcom Community College; Mary Hocks, Georgia State University; Sandra Jamieson, Drew University; Anita Aukee Johnson, Whatcom Community College; Brian Johnson, University of Oklahoma; David Jolliffe, De Paul University; Kathleen Kelly, Northeastern University; Kristen Kennedy, University of Rhode Island; Jeannette Kent, University of Illinois; Millie Kidd, Mount St. Mary's College; Daniel Kies, College of DuPage; Beth Gordon Klingner, Dyson College of Arts and Sciences; Douglas Krienke, Sam Houston State University; David M. Kvernes, Southern Illinois University; Scott Lamascus, University of Oklahoma; Rebecca Lartigue, University of Illinois; Edith Baker Lauerman, Bradley University; Joe Law, Wright State University; Sarah Liggett, Louisiana State University; Mike Little, Texas A&M University; Jane Long, Southwest Oklahoma State University; Diane Lourey, Eden Valley–Watkins High School, Eden Valley, Minnesota; Michael MacDonald, University of Illinois at Chicago; Daiva Markelis, University of Illinois at Chicago; Paul Kei Matsuda, University of New Hampshire; Bruce Maylath, University of Memphis; Kathy McClelland, Auburn University; Rich Meyers, Owens Community College; Terry Miller, Indian River Community College (Florida); Mike Moran, University of Georgia; Kim

Moreland, The George Washington University; Guy Moyer, University of Illinois; B. Keith Murphy, Fort Valley State University; James S. Mullican, Indiana State University; Roark Mulligan, Christopher Newport University; Kaylene D. Nelsen, Lorain County Community College; Justin O'Connell, University of Minnesota; Amy Pawl, Washington University–St. Louis; Carolyn Pearson, Temple University; Tami Penley, Mountain Empire Community College; Teresa Pinney, Whatcom Community College; Mary Ellen Pitts, University of Memphis; Michael Powell, Shawnee State University; Mary Prindiville, University of Wisconsin at Green Bay; Eric Pullin, Cardinal Stritch University; Linda Redelsheimer, Champlin Park High School, Brooklyn Park, Minnesota; Dean Rehberger, Michigan State University; Nedra Reynolds, University of Rhode Island; Elsa Rogers, International College; Robert Ronger, Whatcom Community College; Liv Rosin, Mounds View High School, St. Paul, Minnesota; Donald Ross, University of Minnesota; Carol Rutz, University of Minnesota; Barbara Saez, University of Rhode Island; Lori Salem, Temple University; Mary Sauer, Indiana University–Purdue University at Indianapolis; Sherrie Sawicki, California University, Fullerton; Betty Scott, Whatcom Community College; George W. Semich, Robert Morris University; Linda K. Shamoon, University of Rhode Island; John S. Shea, Loyola University of Chicago; Alice E. Sink, High Point University; Beverly Slaughter, Brevard Community College (Florida); Barbara Sloan, Santa Fe Community College (Florida); Charlotte Smith, Virginia Polytechnic Institute and State University; Susan Smith-Nash, University of Oklahoma; Joyce Smoot, Virginia Polytechnic Institute and State University; Jean Sorensen, Grayson County College; Rita Speltz, Central High School, Red Wing, Minnesota; Roy T. Stamper, North Carolina State University; Jocelyn Steer; Sandra W. Stephen, Youngstown State University; Robert C. Stiepock, University of Rhode Island/Harvard University; Rick Straub, Florida State University; Lida Strot, University of Minnesota; Mark Sutton, Kean University; Anne Tanaka, University of Illinois; Mara Thorson, University of Arizona; Allysen Todd, Community College of Allegheny County (Pennsylvania); John Trimbur, Worcester Polytechnic Institute; Pamela Turley, Community College of Allegheny County (Pennsylvania); Paul Tuttle, University of Louisville; Andrea Van Vorhis, Bowling Green State University; Janice R. Walker, Georgia Southern University; Patricia Webb, University of Illinois; Erin Webster-Garrett, Radford University; Karen Weekes, University of Georgia; Lance E. Wilcox, Elmhurst College; James D. Williams, University of North Carolina at Chapel Hill; Judith Younk, Watertown Mayer High School, Watertown, Minnesota; and Peter T. Zoller, Wichita State University.

Special thanks to Beth Crippen Strauss for her work on the Ebook version. Thank you also to those who worked with us as consultants in the development and revision of selected chapters in previous editions of *The Longman Handbook*—Victor Villanueva, Washington State University; Jim Dubinsky, Virginia Tech; Christina Haas, Kent State University; Elizabeth Ervin, University of North Carolina, Wilmington; Gladys Vega Scott, Arizona State

University; and Mick Doherty and Sandye Thompson. We are grateful for the expertise and creativity of all these writers and teachers.

An extensive team of editors, producers, and managers at Longman were instrumental in the development and publication of the Fifth Edition: A special word of thanks to Lauren Finn, acquisitions editor, for her continued support of the project, and to Anne Brunell Ehrenworth, senior development editor, for her excellent editorial management. Thanks also to Mary Ellen Curley, director of development; Donna Campion, senior supplements manager; Megan Galvin-Fak, executive marketing manager; and Bob Ginsberg, production manager. Susan McIntyre and her team at Nesbitt Graphics did amazing work on a tight schedule to design and typeset the book.

Chris Anson thanks, as always, his wife Gean and sons Ian and Graham for their support and understanding during the revision process, and to the latter for the occasional advice about language, writing, grammar, and contemporary usage that a 12- and 15-year old can provide.

Bob Schwegler would like to acknowledge that he couldn't do any of this work without the advice, insight, and support of Nancy Newman Schwegler, who tolerated with grace and wit the far too many years the project has taken—and the sunny days spent worrying about comma splices. This and many other projects are the happy consequence of her understanding of readers, reading, and the creative ways writers can represent themselves. He would also like to thank Brian and Tara Schwegler for their advice, Christopher for his smiles, Ashley Marie for her inspiration, Lily for hope, and Kira for imagination.

CHRIS M. ANSON
ROBERT A. SCHWEGLER

PART 1

Writing for Readers

CHAPTER 1
Writers, Readers, and Communities

Someone created the Web page you browsed yesterday—wrote the text, designed the layout, and anticipated readers' reactions. Someone else wrote your housing contract, your student loan forms, and the waiver you signed before the technician x-rayed your ankle. Writers worked together to produce the community newsletter you found in your mailbox last Saturday, and one of them gave a presentation on a community issue to the city council.

In each of these examples, people were fulfilling a need to communicate something. Sometimes this "need" can be quite direct: a psychology professor tells you to include summaries of your interviews in your research paper, or a boss expects your sales presentation to explain the contradictory figures from the northwest region.

On other occasions, your need to write (or speak) will come from the goals of a group you belong to, or it will come from within you, as a desire to be heard on an issue. Your writing and speaking give you a voice; they let you do things, express ideas, acquire and share knowledge, and participate in a conversation about issues that matter.

Written and spoken language surrounds us, shaping our lives, choices, responsibilities, and values. This book looks at the roles writers, readers, and speakers play in contemporary culture. It offers concrete strategies for writing, for critical reading and thinking, for oral communication, and for understanding your readers' and listeners' expectations. More broadly, it emphasizes writing and speaking as ways to understand experience and share that understanding.

1a Academic, public, and work communities

Why would an instructor in a physiology course have little patience with a student paper written in the breezy style typical of a health care column from *Cosmopolitan* or *Men's Health*? Why would a corporate executive or a city council member frown on a detailed theoretical presentation of a problem but welcome a much shorter report that gets right to the point and proposes a solution?

These audiences' sharply differing needs and expectations offer typical challenges writers (and speakers) face in knowing what style to use, in deciding what structure a text should have, and in determining what to include (or not) in its contents. How can you recognize and respond to these many differences? First and foremost, you need to envision a *community* of writers, readers, and speakers. A **discourse community** consists of people with shared goals and knowledge, a common setting or context, and similar preferences and uses for verbal and visual texts.

In this book we focus on three broad and important types of communities: academic, public, and work. We suggest ways you can participate in these communities and in other writing and speaking situations you may encounter. We also pay special attention to the way these communities often use electronic communication to carry out their work.

1 Communities in action

What do people in a particular community want? Their preferences and expectations usually reflect shared goals: to exchange information, to debate an issue, to find a solution to a problem. Communities may overlap as well, so you need to be able to participate in more than one community—just as you move from a classroom to a football game or from a book club to a protest rally.

Consider the following example.

> In Greenwood Village, a wealthy suburb of Denver, pets have been disappearing. The culprits are coyotes and other predators, increasingly crowded by new homes and industrial parks. These disappearances are certainly alarming to local residents—will a young child be the next victim? Will the wild animals become even more aggressive?

Much of the real problem solving that takes place in a situation like this starts with the production of written materials and oral presentations. City council members and concerned citizens look for explanations and solutions. They turn to discussions produced within the **academic community:** detailed, complex scientific studies and presentations reporting the effects of development on coyotes and other predators. Wildlife experts, for example, prepare reports that show the effects of development on the habitat and feeding habits of coyotes. A line from one of their documents looks like this.

> This report summarizes and compares the data from two studies of the habits of predators in areas that have experienced significant population growth and urbanization over the past ten years.

Such scientific information is useful, yet its focus is different from the question of concerned parents, pet owners, and others making up the **public community:** How can we protect our children and pets without harming local wildlife? Drawing on scientific detail and knowledge of residents' perspectives, the Colorado Division of Wildlife creates a set of tips, directed at a public rather than an academic audience, which is published in the *Denver Post.*

> *If you see a coyote:*
>
> - Leave it alone; do not approach it.
>
> *If a coyote approaches:*
>
> - Use an animal repellent such as pepper spray to ward off the coyote.
> - Throw rocks or sticks at the coyote to scare it away.
> - Use a loud, authoritative voice to frighten the animal away.
>
> *How to coexist with coyotes:*
>
> - Keep your pet on a leash.
> - Do not let pets out between dusk and dawn, when most predators are active. . . .

A neighborhood action group, which represents a more specific public community, distributes leaflets to residents, urging discussion of the problem, and TV stations turn this material into short oral and visual segments to inform citizens.

> **COYOTE ALERT!**
>
> Are your children safe in their own backyards? Coyotes attacked seven dogs and cats last summer. Find out what we can do. Join the Committee to Safeguard Our Children on Tuesday, October 2, at 7:00 p.m. in the high school gym.

Business leaders, meanwhile, also have views to express. Local officials address the problem with writing directed at several **work communities,** in reports and presentations to the city council, the environmental management department, and municipal development offices. These reports consider options for altering the pace and scope of new developments and for designing educational and management programs to help people, pets, and coyotes live in balance. The Construction Contractors Consortium, for example, sends out a memo to its membership calling attention to the ways that zoning and development restrictions sponsored by environmental groups could hurt their construction businesses.

As you can see from this example, writing and speaking will vary in purpose, organization, and style across these different communities, reflecting different expectations. Ideally, the writers, readers, and speakers within and across these communities will work together to seek a solution that works for everyone.

2 Choices and limits

As you start to write, and then throughout the process, keep in mind the ways the features of the community you are addressing offer you choices and possibilities while also imposing limits. Here are four of the most important features of writing/reading (or speaking) communities (for more details, see the chart below).

- **Roles** that you and your readers (or listeners) occupy
- **Goals** for communication that you and your audience share
- **Forms** that your audience will look for in writing (or speaking) directed toward a particular goal
- **Characteristics** typical of communication that fulfills a particular set of goals and meets an audience's expectations

THREE MAJOR COMMUNITIES OF READERS, WRITERS, AND SPEAKERS

ACADEMIC	PUBLIC	WORK
Roles Students; teachers; researchers; expert committees; specialized readers	**Roles** Neighborhood groups; potential supporters; public officials; government agencies; local political groups; issue-oriented readers	**Roles** Coworkers; supervisors; management; public relations; clients (current or potential); government agencies
Goals Develop new understandings or policies	**Goals** Persuade people on issues; provide information; participate in public decision making	**Goals** Provide information; analyze problems; propose solutions; promote organization
Forms Analytical report; interpretation of text or event; research proposal or report; lab report; scholarly article; annotated bibliography; grant proposal; policy study	**Forms** Guidelines; position paper; informative report; letter or email to agency or group; flyer or brochure; action proposal; grant proposal; charter or mission statement; letter to editor; Web announcement	**Forms** Informative memo; factual or descriptive report; proposal; executive summary; letter or memo; guidelines or instruction; promotional material; minutes and notes; formal reports; internal and public Web sites
Characteristics Clear reasoning; critical analysis; fresh insight; extensive evidence; accurate detail; balanced treatment; acknowledgment of competing viewpoints; thorough exploration of topic	**Characteristics** Focus on shared values; advocacy of cause or policy; fairness and ethical argument; relevant supporting evidence; action- or solution-oriented; accessible presentation	**Characteristics** Focus on tasks and goals; accurate, efficient presentation; promotion of products and services; attention to organizational image and corporate design standards; concise, direct style

Exercise 1

In groups of four or five, draft a "class charter," that is, a formal statement outlining the principles, purposes, or rules that you think should govern your class. Before you start drafting, discuss the roles, goals, forms, and characteristics of this situation. Which members of the class do you need to address? In what ways might their values or interests be similar or different? What do you hope to accomplish with the document you produce? What does a charter look like? How would you present it orally to the class?

1b Identifying electronic communities

On the Web, different communities—academic, public, or work—are often only a click away from each other. You can read an article by an academic researcher, then with a click of the mouse find yourself skimming a site sponsored by a major corporation or filling in an online petition circulated by a political or nonprofit organization.

To recognize the community to which a site belongs or the expectations you need to observe in creating an electronic document, use the TASALS strategy.

Topic: On what subject(s) does the site focus? Do contributors belong to any organization or share any other kind of affiliation?

Attitude: Does the site have a clear point of view or set of values? Do contributors have similar perspectives or values?

Strategies: Does the site use particular writing or visual strategies (see Chapter 13 for examples)? Does the writing have a particular tone or style? Does the design of the site have a particular style or emphasis?

Authority: Does the site try to be authoritative, giving support for claims it makes or information it provides? Do contributors reason carefully and offer evidence, or do they give unsupported opinions and supposed "facts"?

Links: Is the site linked to similar sites? Do postings refer to related online documents, lists, or resources?

Summarize: On the basis of your answers to these questions, summarize the qualities of the electronic community you encountered.

Exercise 2

A. Find the official Web site of your school or city or of an organization to which you belong. Examine the Web site carefully using the

TASALS strategy. How would you characterize the community that sponsors the site? What opportunities, if any, are there to participate in the site—to send comments, to get on a mailing list, or to ask a question of an expert? What kinds of writing or participation would be inappropriate for this site, and why? Write out your observations.

B. Use a Web search engine to locate several Web sites maintained by or catering to professionals in your future field of work. Evaluate the Web site using TASALS. Compare your results with those of your classmates.

1c The composing process: Realities and myths

Effective writers keep in mind the *realities* of the composing process. They know successful writing is almost never a matter of just setting down your thoughts on paper in finished form. Instead, it begins with a *response:* to an idea or experience, to reading or an issue, to a problem or a situation. It calls for planning; for definition of purpose and thesis; for awareness of audience; and for careful attention to drafting, revising, editing, and proofreading (and, for a speech, rehearsing). These various elements of the composing processes are explored in the chapters that follow.

Usually, your composing process won't move in a straight line. When you revise, you may need to go back to more planning or reconsider your first response to the task. Or, in some projects, you might need to work collaboratively with others and interact with potential audiences.

Myths about the composing process can lead to self-defeating habits, however. For example, how many of these statements are true?

- People can easily succeed in the "real world" without needing to write.
- Writing is easy for people who have the knack.
- You can be a good writer without doing much reading.
- It's cheating to ask other people to look over your writing before you turn it in.
- The qualities that constitute good writing remain the same from situation to situation, and audience to audience.

They're all myths. Here's why.

Myth: People can easily succeed in the "real world" without needing to write.

Reality: It's a popular myth that executives don't need to write because their assistants write for them. That's not what the executives themselves say. In Fortune 500 companies, more than half of the employees spend between eight and forty hours writing each week. This statistic shows that the ability to write is crucial for success in the work community. Although the amount of writing on the job varies by type of employment and rank, many workers say that when they were in school, they underestimated the amount of writing they would need to do in their jobs. The same is true in public life and in civic activities.

Myth: Writing is easy for people who have the knack.

Reality: Few of us get to look over the shoulders of good writers. If we did, we would know what researchers know: good writers draft and redraft. They work hard to create effective prose and to consider their work from a reader's perspective. They have become good writers through learning and hard work, not because they were born with a knack for writing.

Myth: You can be a good writer without doing much reading.

Reality: It's not likely. The more you read, the more experience you have with writing. Reading gives you models of writing that work in specific communities; it helps you learn to adjust your writing to the needs of readers; and it increases your options for sentence variety and precise words.

Myth: It's cheating to ask other people to look over your writing before you turn it in.

Reality: It certainly is cheating if you have someone else write a paper or parts of it and then claim the work as your own. But successful writers always depend on readers for feedback. Readers' opinions can tell you how an audience will interpret your writing and can help you anticipate responses and concerns. Especially at work and in the community, important documents are likely to be written in groups for this reason.

Myth: The qualities that constitute good writing remain the same from situation to situation and audience to audience.

Reality: When it comes to good writing, one size doesn't fit all. What works well in one community may not work as well in another; writing that is clear, coherent, and correct for one audience may not seem so for another. The term paper you write for Psychology 265 will have a very different tone, style, and content from the email you write to your cousin or the proposal you write at work.

CHAPTER 2
Discovering and Planning

Imagine assembling tools and building materials without any idea of the structure you want to create: a house, a camp in the mountains, or a simple shed. Think about going into the playoffs without a team strategy just to "see what happens." Success would depend on luck, not design.

The same is true for writing. Whether in college, in a public setting, or on the job, you need to explore your task, consider possible subjects, and identify your purposes for writing before you can really get started. In addition, planning before you begin formal writing—often called **prewriting**—helps you move your project forward more smoothly and confidently. Planning strategies work well at the earliest stages of writing, but they can also help later on as you work out patterns and relationships among ideas or fill in gaps in your knowledge.

2a Getting started

Do you have a reason for writing: a subject, a goal, an assignment, or a task? Or are you getting ready to write without a particular focus for your efforts? Whatever the case, the strategies in the chart on page 10 can be helpful. They can help remind you of what you already know and think about a subject or task. They can suggest a subject worth writing about or help you develop a clear purpose for your writing.

1 Try informal writing

An ideal place to write quickly and informally is in a journal or planning notebook (see 2b). Many accomplished writers use a strategy called **freewriting**—fast, highly informal, unselfconscious writing.

To try freewriting, write quickly for five or ten minutes. Concentrate entirely on *writing without stopping*, even if you think you have nothing to say. Simply writing "I'm stuck, I'm stuck" will at least force you to begin writing. Curiously, such empty or rambling prose will soon begin to bore you, and you'll find yourself almost magically slipping into more interesting ideas, some of which may suggest possible subjects or purposes for writing.

Focused freewriting involves writing quickly about an idea or topic you already have in mind, or one that you began developing through

PLANNING IN THREE COMMUNITIES: IDENTIFYING POSSIBLE TOPICS

ACADEMIC SETTINGS	PUBLIC SETTINGS	WORK SETTINGS
Respond to ideas and questions in textbooks, scholarly articles, or class discussions. **Ask** "Do researchers or experts identify new developments, unresolved questions, or fresh perspectives and techniques?" **Look up** bibliographies or summaries of research as well as newletters and magazines reporting on current research and discoveries. (See 22c–d and 23c–d.)	**Respond** to ideas, problems, and proposals in newspapers, magazines, or Web sites; listen to local and national news programs or talk shows. **Ask** "What local issues or problems engage my interest (and that of others)? What kinds of information do I and others need? What national or global concerns are worth attention?" **Look up** online archives of newspapers and magazines that cover topics of local, national, and global interest or consult publications and announcements from government agencies, public service organizations, or corporations.	**Respond** to challenges and requests posed in memos or organizational newletters or to specific requests for reports and other documents. **Ask** "What significant internal or external challenges does the organization face, and how can I respond to them?" **Look up** articles in business-related journals and magazines for articles, topics, and ideas related to your work; consult professional magazines, Web sites, and newsletters for policy or problem-focused discussions applicable to your work or your organization.

freewriting. For focused freewriting, continue writing as you freely associate ideas, especially if you start with a general topic. Your first sentence might begin, "Antigambling laws—I guess I'm in favor of them generally." As you continue to write, you'll again find yourself exploring what you know or feel about the topic. Consider stating your topic as an assertion so that you can systematically question that assertion, anticipating a spark that ignites your interest.

2 Use listing

Lists can draw out knowledge already in your mind and *create* new ideas through association. Write your topic at the top of a page and then list ten thoughts, facts, or ideas about the subject. Or adapt listing to generate specific ideas. For example, begin with a general impression or idea, and list supporting details and new associations.

As he started working on his proposal requesting permission to allow local bands to perform in the basement of the community center, Morgan Scott listed some of the subjects the report needed to cover.

Space isn't used for anything else during the evenings.
Will give teenagers a safe place to go, especially on weekends.
Need plans for cleaning the space up and maintaining it.
Noise wouldn't bother neighbors.
Plenty of parking for those old enough to drive.
Recreation department and police could easily provide supervision.
Will provide a creative outlet for local residents.
Low cost.
Will have the support of parents.
Add to the city's reputation as a good place to live.

3 Tease out details

Good writing is often detailed. A plea to increase funding in a public school district will be more effective if it includes facts about teachers' low salaries, out-of-date books in the classrooms, and the disrepair of the buildings. Searching for details to particularize general statements can also lead you to new ideas and associations.

To help you increase the level of detail in your writing, make a **detailing list.** For each general idea, opinion, or impression, list specific examples, features, or facts that particularize it. This will give you a rich resource to draw on as you develop your essay.

Heather Strong began writing an account of her trip to the Grand Canyon for her travel club's newsletter.

> When we first looked out over the Grand Canyon, we were just amazed. What a beautiful sight! It was like nothing we had seen before--so impressive and marvelous. It was simply incredible to gaze out over such a spectacle of nature.

This paragraph cries out for specific visual detail. Figure 2.1 on page 12 shows part of a detailing list Heather created to help develop her ideas. These details found their way into her revised draft.

> The view from the North Rim was just as breathtaking. From Tiyo Point we could see Shiva Temple. To its east was the flat-topped formation of Buddha Temple, with its red sandstone lit up like a flaming torch. The effect of these varied red, brown, and gold formations is almost religious. It felt like we were standing in a cathedral of stone, looking down into a million years of spires, statuary, and domes, all bathed in soft, stained-glass hues of light.

2a plan

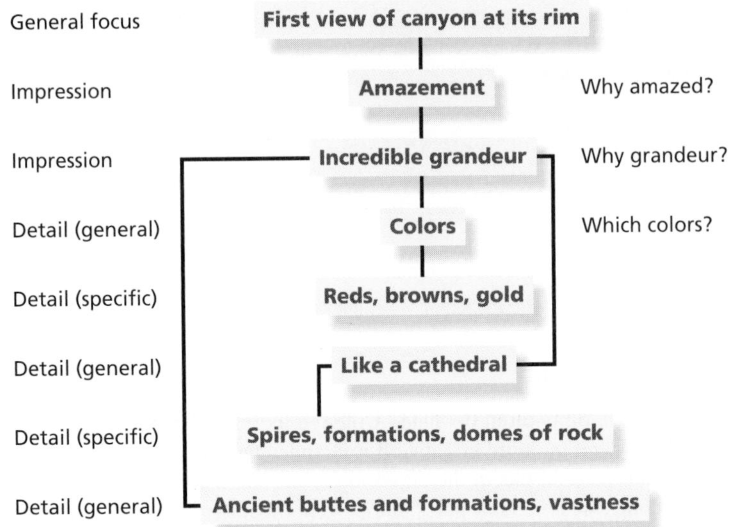

FIGURE 2.1 Detailing list

4 Ask strategic questions

You can generate important information for many writing projects, especially proposals and recommendations, if you try answering the questions *what*, *why*, and *why not* (*where*, *who*, and *how* may also be important questions, depending on your writing project). Brian Corby used this strategy in prewriting for his report arguing that his city's zoning board should not allow a high-rise apartment to be built adjacent to a public park.

What?

- Proposed high-rise apt.
- 18 stories, 102 units plus 3 penthouses
- Overlooking east side of Piedmont Park between Sunrise Ave. and Claremont St.
- Proposal approved by Feb.; Planning by Feb. next yr.; groundbreaking by June
- Finished structure by Aug. of following year

Why?

- Developers profit
- Brings jobs to Lake Walton
- Raises property tax base—supposed to funnel money back into the city and parks

- *Provides medium-cost housing in growing area*
- *Develops ugly vacant property by park*

Why not?

- *"Citifies" one of the few green patches in Lake Walton*
- *Increases traffic, crime rate, park use*
- *Adds to waste; pollution from proposed garbage incinerator in building*
- *Opens the door to other high-rise development because of new zoning ordinance*
- *Blocks sunlight from park*
- *Raises property taxes for longtime and elderly residents*

Exercise 1

Begin with the topic, issue, or problem for a writing project you are working on, or choose a topic that interests you. Then try the listing procedure with your topic. Begin by listing ten things you know about your chosen topic. Then choose one item and generate another sublist beneath it. If you can, keep going to a third or fourth level.

2b Keeping a writing/reading journal

A **journal** is a place to explore ideas, develop insights, experiment with your prose, write rough drafts, and reflect on your reading. Journals are where ideas, observations, and possible topics for writing can take shape or where responses to reading can be developed (see 9b).

A journal is not a diary, however. Diaries record people's daily activities, thoughts, and personal lives. Journals are places where analytical, interpretive, and critical reading take place in the form of written responses and where ideas and observations begin developing into extended writing. Journals are used in academic settings, at work, and in civic contexts, especially to reflect on new ideas or to explore public reaction to initiatives and projects.

Your journal is also where your own writing begins to murmur and find a voice. A journal is a clearinghouse for ideas, speculations, first starts, notes and jottings, drawings and doodles, plans, occasional insights—anything that helps you read and think in depth and begin writing.

1 How to keep a reading and writing journal

Keeping a journal may feel strange or artificial at first. After all, you're writing mainly to and for yourself, with no concern about spelling or grammar. The actual shape and size of your journal is less important to its success than what you do in and with it. It helps to have a journal whose pages can be removed or reorganized. An electronic word-processing document will allow you to do this, as will an inexpensive ring binder.

How much and how often should you write? The more you write, the greater your chances to think about a subject. The length of journal entries will (and should) differ. Working half a day in the library or searching the Internet might yield ten or fifteen pages of notes, speculations, quotations, references, and interpretations, but an idea that comes to you late at night might yield just a few lines of drowsy prose sufficient to jog your memory the next morning. At all costs *write regularly.* Journals abandoned for more than a day or two soon wither and die from lack of nourishment.

Use a personal voice. Use your journal writing to express your beliefs, opinions, and reactions in personal terms. Speculate. Get to know what you—personally—think about an issue or subject. Instead of writing in abstract terms and formal language, go ahead and use phrases like "I wonder if . . . ," "I think it's wonderful that . . . ," or "I can't understand why. . . ." Be conversational. A sentence like "Hmmmmm . . . I guess I never figured zoning board members would get so ticked off about something so silly" would cry out for revision in a formal report. In a journal, you can feel safe using such a casual tone.

Use shortcuts. Try writing quickly. Use abbreviations if you're sure you will remember what they mean. Don't worry at this point about underlining titles, correcting commas in a series, or looking up the spelling of every difficult word.

Experiment with language. Journals encourage the free play of language and thought. Let the poetry emerge, if you wish, from your writing. Be as expressive as you want. Try out ideas that may at first seem outrageous, or write in a style you've never used before. Try imitating or parodying other writers.

2 Thinking, writing, and discovering

Writing in a journal *makes your thoughts visible.* In a journal, you create connections among thinking, writing, and reading.

Translate new knowledge. After reading or hearing about new ideas or information, imagine one or more people who know little about the topic. Explain your new knowledge to them. You'll find, first, that you'll be forced to *speculate* about the meaning of the information and concepts at places you find difficult to understand. Second, you'll often *clarify and resolve* your confusions in the process of writing.

Brainstorm. Instead of staring at a blank piece of paper or screen, waiting for perfect sentences to roll off your pen or keyboard, use your journal for **brainstorming.** When you brainstorm, you think associatively, letting one idea lead to another or exploring the connections among ideas. You create an exploratory, tentative, and often messy set of responses to reading, issues, and experience that can point the way to a focus and plan for a draft of a paper (see Chapter 4).

Extend your thinking. Imagine that you learn this fact from your reading in a sociology article or textbook: Human aggression increases in hot weather. Recording such an observation in your journal may take a few seconds. But imagine *extending* this idea a little, seeing its implications, wondering about possible solutions and applications. Are people more aggressive in hot regions than in cold regions? If discomfort causes aggression, why aren't people just as aggressive in uncomfortably cold weather? Are workers in hot factories more aggressive than workers in chilly factories? Do Northerners become aggressive on vacations to hot places?

Take issue with ideas. Although your journal may feel comfortably informal, it can also be an excellent place to argue with someone else's point of view or criticize a position. Many writers at first react in a combative way to ideas or beliefs that challenge their own. Journals let them "have it out" with an opponent without risking actual confrontation. The result can be a more balanced view of the controversy.

Exercise 2

A. The following journal entry was written by Kelly Odeen, a student in a course on literacy in America. Read Odeen's entry, and then identify specific thinking, writing, reading, or discovering functions for which she is using her journal. What characteristics of her entry suggest these functions?

```
     Reading about the Amish community left me with very mixed
feelings--not sure what to make of them yet. I really admired
the family support of Eli's literacy development. Sounded like
the older family members did just what we've been encouraged to
do as tutors. They gave him positive feedback, etc. Focused on
accomplishments rather than failures. But the setting looked
```

sort of ideal. Everyone in Eli's family reads and writes, even more than in my family. I don't think it's possible to make learning totally individualized in the public school system. Choices have to be made that are better for some children than others. I don't have a solution, but I think the author is being too idealistic to think there can be this match like the Amish have. I'd like to look into this more for my project, maybe. Because I do agree that there are many ways of perceiving literacy, each valid, and we have to be sensitive to where kids are coming from compared with the school system they're going into.

B. Should animals be used in laboratory experiments for the advancement of scientific, medical, and behavioral knowledge? Write a page or two in your journal on this question, considering as many issues and angles on the topic as you can. Then compare your journal writing in a small group. What ideas did the writing yield? How helpful was it? How would you describe the style, organization, and other characteristics of your writing? Which of the purposes described in the preceding section did your writing serve?

2c Structuring ideas and information

Ideas and information alone won't lead to successful writing unless you can find ways to structure them. Some writing tasks, such as business and research reports, need to follow familiar structures. For many other kinds of writing, including essays about personal experience, position papers, critiques, informative pamphlets, and proposals, you'll often need to identify relationships within the information and ideas you've generated.

1 Draw a cluster

A **cluster** is a diagram of interconnected ideas. When you create a cluster, you will find yourself both exploring what you know about a topic and revealing how that knowledge is related.

To create a cluster, begin by writing a concept, idea, or topic in the center of a page, and circle this kernel topic. Then jot down associations linked to this central idea, circling them and connecting them with lines to the kernel topic, like the spokes of a wheel (see Figure 2.2). As you continue to generate ideas around the central focus, think about the ways the subsidiary ideas are connected, and draw lines to show those connections. You can also create clusters in cycles: each subsidiary idea becomes the

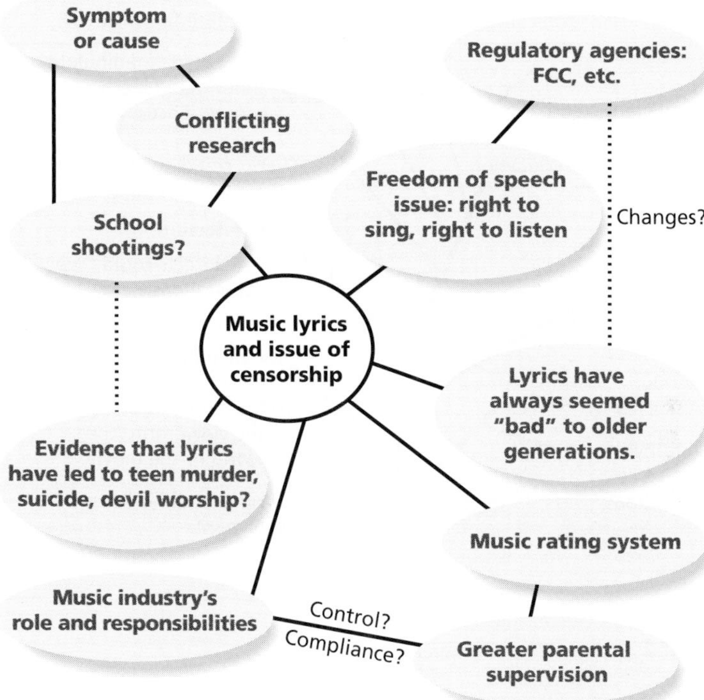

FIGURE 2.2 A simple conceptual cluster

central focus on a new page. The nodes or pieces of the cluster will become a visual representation of how your text might be "chunked" into paragraphs or sections.

2 Create a tree diagram

Tree diagrams resemble clusters, but their branches tend to be more linear and hierarchical, with fewer interconnections (see Figure 2.3 on page 18). Each larger branch can lead to smaller and smaller branches. For this reason, tree diagramming can provide a useful way to visualize the components of your paper.

Start with your main focus or topic as the "trunk" of the tree. As you work upward, create primary branches with centrally connected ideas. You can branch off from these with smaller and smaller branches that each relate in a specific way to the main branch. Consider "revising" your tree diagram into a preliminary outline to use when deciding what to place in each paragraph of your paper.

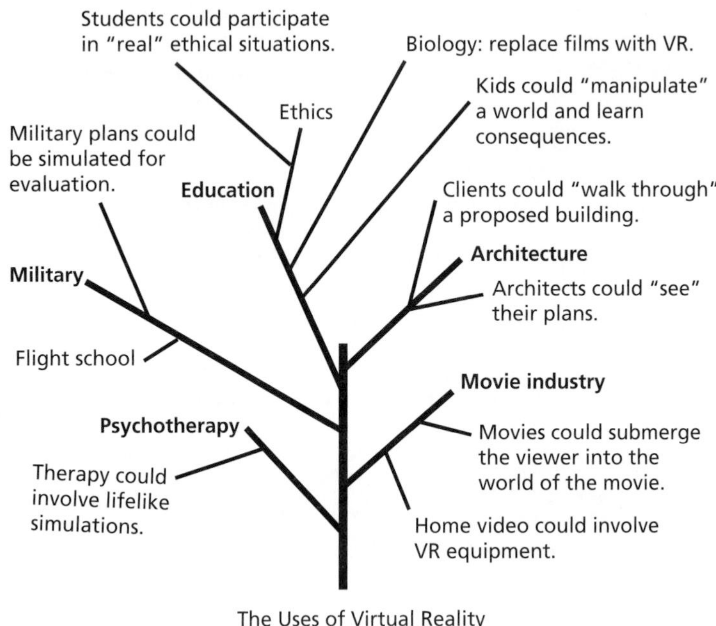

FIGURE 2.3 A simple tree diagram

3 Build a time sequence

If you're writing a paper organized chronologically or involving sequences of time, you may find a **time sequence** useful. To create a time sequence, begin by framing each event along a timeline. Then draw vertical lines of thicker or thinner widths depending on how closely connected one event is to the next.

In planning materials for a self-guided tour of a special museum exhibit on the artist Andy Warhol, James Christenfeld drew a time sequence detailing the history of Warhol's artistic life. With thick connecting lines, he showed how certain pivotal events led to or caused other events or works in Warhol's career. Connections with thin lines were simply chronological.

Exercise 3

A. Choose a simple topic (issue, problem) whose details are familiar to you. Then try creating a cluster or a tree diagram. Does the result suggest a possible structure for a paper or presentation? What problems might arise in "translating" the cluster or diagram into an outline?

B. In a small group, share your cluster or tree diagram and explain its nodes or branches. Then collaboratively try to generate more branches for each writer's diagram.

2d Patterns of generalization and support

For many writing tasks, you will need to arrive at a **generalization** (an interpretation, conclusion, or thesis) about your subject, identify appropriate **support** for your generalization, and arrange these two elements in a pattern that will help convey their relationship to your audience. The following strategies may prove helpful.

1 Highlight generalizations

Any writing task that asks you to draw conclusions about (interpret) the meaning of a situation, text, phenomenon, or experience will require arriving at a generalization about the particulars that make up your subject. First, list as many facts or ideas about your subject as possible, using the listing technique described in 2a. Then ask yourself whether you can draw a generalization (conclusion, interpretation) about these facts or ideas. This strategy is illustrated in Tim Pagenhart's planning for a paper on teenage boys' gang membership. Once his list of facts led him to a generalization, he could look for other facts to support it (see Figure 2.4 on page 20).

2 Create a problem-solution grid

In some writing situations, especially in civics contexts, you may need to focus on a problem and then present an argument for a proposed solution. Proposals, reports, position papers, and other persuasive texts often follow a **problem-solution sequence.** If your writing project calls for this kind of approach, you can use a simple but powerful technique for exploring ideas and information and revealing organizational options for your paper or report: a **problem-solution grid** (see Figure 2.5 on page 20).

Create a problem-solution grid by putting a statement of the main problem at the top of a page. Make a layer of at least two or three possible solutions to the problem. For each, name at least one further problem with that solution. "Solve" each subsidiary problem in turn. You can create as many layers of problems and solutions as you wish, generating many specifics for your paper or presentation.

As Figure 2.5 shows, Paula Masek identified three temporary solutions to the problem of hunger among the homeless. Using a grid to guide her planning and to identify a structure, Masek discussed each boxed item in a separate section of her draft paper.

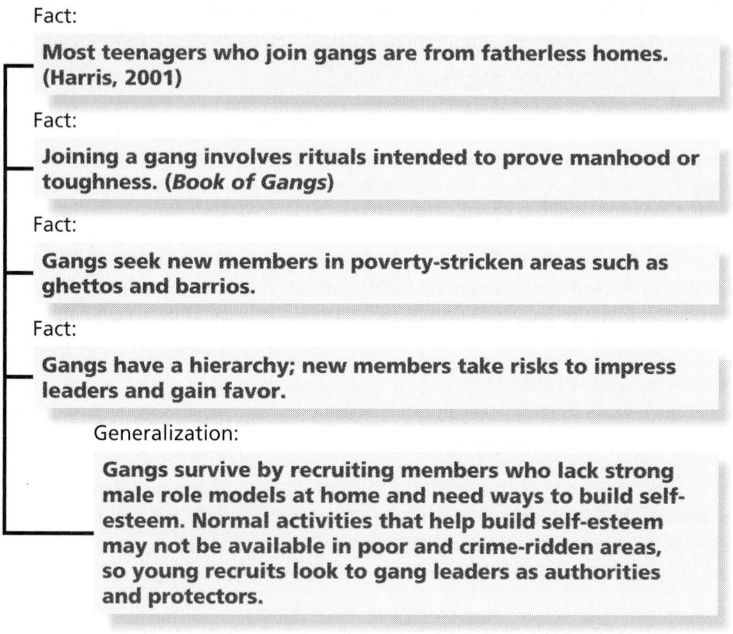

Fact:

Most teenagers who join gangs are from fatherless homes. (Harris, 2001)

Fact:

Joining a gang involves rituals intended to prove manhood or toughness. (*Book of Gangs*)

Fact:

Gangs seek new members in poverty-stricken areas such as ghettos and barrios.

Fact:

Gangs have a hierarchy; new members take risks to impress leaders and gain favor.

Generalization:

Gangs survive by recruiting members who lack strong male role models at home and need ways to build self-esteem. Normal activities that help build self-esteem may not be available in poor and crime-ridden areas, so young recruits look to gang leaders as authorities and protectors.

FIGURE 2.4 Generalizations from particulars

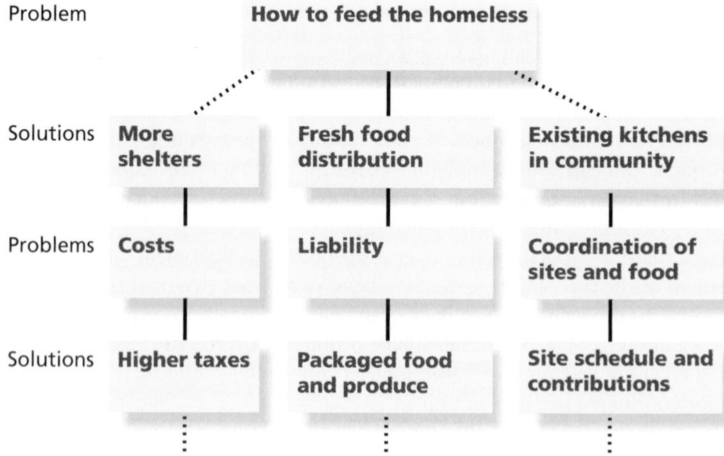

FIGURE 2.5 A problem-solution grid

3 Outline

The best-known traditional prewriting technique is the trusty **outline,** complete with Roman numerals. Unfortunately, the traditional outline doesn't do much to help writers *generate* ideas before they decide how these ideas should be arranged. As a prewriting technique, however, a **working outline** can be useful. The trick is to use the outline to generate new categories of information rather than to label ones you've already discovered.

Try beginning with a simple topic as the main heading of an outline. Commit yourself to three second-level subheadings by writing the letters *A*, *B*, and *C* beneath the main topics. Leave a lot of space between the letters. Then try filling in the blank subheadings. Once you've "discovered" three main subheadings, you can try to create three third-level subheadings by writing *1*, *2*, and *3* beneath *each* of your letters *A*, *B*, and *C*. Then try filling in the new blank subheadings.

Mitch Weber tried this strategy when he began planning the historical section of a report on the nonprofit organization in which he held a summer internship.

III. Creation of the family health center
- A. Founding work of Susan and Roger Ramstadt
  1. The "vision"
  2. Finding the money
  3. The involvement of the Crimp Foundation
- B. The early years (1980–95)
  1. Building momentum
  2. The great financial disaster
  3. Rebirth
- C. Toward maturity
  1. Fund-raising in the 2000s
  2. State recognition and the big award
  3. Health and sustenance
- D. The future
  1. The new board of directors
  2. The new vision

Exercise 4

Create a list of five topics, issues, or problems. Choose the one that most interests you. Then briefly try out three of the planning techniques discussed in 2c–d. After experimenting with them, jot down some notes about which one(s) worked worst and best for you. Why do you think this was the case? What sort of topic did you choose, and how did the technique you used affect its development?

2e Planning in electronic environments

Computer software and the Web offer many kinds of help to writers exploring ideas and information or planning an essay or report. Using a computer's word-processing or note-taking program to help plan your essay can in itself be a useful strategy, because you can easily save your planning materials for later reference when you're drafting, revising, or re-envisioning your writing. Electronic planning can take other forms as well.

1 Use summaries and keywords on search engines

Search engines, such as *Google*, are programs that help you identify Web sites relevant to a topic or issue. Typically, search engines provide the URLs for Web sites, with or without brief summaries of their contents. Some also provide lists of keywords and key phrases.

Select a word or phrase that identifies the topic or purpose of your writing task or that is related to a subject or issue you wish to explore, such as "sports injuries." When the summaries appear on your screen, read them and list any words, phrases, and sentences that suggest ideas or information you might wish to explore in your writing. Here are notes that Heloise Benet took from her preliminary survey of links on the controversy over sleep deprivation among high school students.

Falling Asleep in High School

Most high school students fall asleep because they are sleep-deprived, not bored.

High school day starts early—buses needed later for elementary and middle school routes (schools claim can't afford more buses).

Researchers used to claim high school students were adults and needed same amount of sleep.

Some new research says they may need more than younger students and much more than adults; not all agree.

Do high school students go to sleep late by choice or because their "sleep clocks" are set this way? Lots of controversy over this.

2 Follow links

Web sites contain highlighted words and phrases that provide **links** to sites discussing related issues and ideas. You can use these links to survey subjects, develop ideas, identify possible sources for a report or essay, and explore community-service sites when writing in public settings.

Identify a Web site that discusses ideas and information relevant to your writing task or to a subject you might wish to explore. List any highlighted words or phrases (links) that suggest material worth exploring or possible focuses for your writing. Then click on the links and scan the linked Web sites, writing down words, phrases, and ideas you might develop in your own work. Continue until you have filled a page or two with notes and are ready to look for patterns (see 2c–d) in the material you've gathered.

2f Planning: Paper in progress

Jessica DiGregorio was assigned a paper in a college course focusing on literacy and its consequences for individuals and societies. The task required her to identify a public or official document (such as a charter, certificate, law, set of guidelines, or official publication) and to discuss its consequences for individuals or groups of people. Other people in the class analyzed the effects of documents such as housing contracts, NCAA regulations for college sports, a parent's death certificate, and a "driving while intoxicated" citation. Jessica had always been interested in sports, perhaps because her father was an accomplished basketball player. She decided to do some preliminary listing to see what specific kinds of documents affect participants in sports—amateur, college, and professional (see 2a). Here is a list of questions and ideas she created.

- Injury reports can shape an athlete's participation, the outcome of games, and the emotions of fans and players. Who gives the documents such power?
- Game rules—some rules have serious consequences when broken, but others are less important. Why? Who decides? How do players and fans know?
- Some sports specify the shape, size, weight, etc., of equipment. Does this make a difference? What about the sports that have few regulations on equipment? Do the differences reflect something about the nature of the sports or their roles in society?
- Professional sports contracts seem to be in the news often (Major League Baseball, NBA, NFL). Can they really determine the success or failure of teams? How do they shape the lives of players? My father's contract.
- Following the box scores. What happens when people regard games as box scores?
- Drug regulations. Laws or informal rules. What's the difference?

After deciding on the consequences of professional contracts on players' lives as a focus for her work, Jessica made the following list.

- Contracts in the news—what kinds of things they cover.
- Odd things that some sports stars request.
- My father's NBA contract. What's in it?

- What he had to do as a result of the contract. What the team had to do.
- What it meant for his life. My family. Me?
- Similar to other contracts at the time?
- What if you break a contract?
- What is a contract? Legally. What exactly can contracts do and not do?

Exercise 5

Study Jessica DiGregorio's two planning lists. What other topics on the first list do you think would have been worth developing in ways that addressed her assigned task? What questions would you ask her about the topics on the second list? What advice would you give her for either elaborating her second list or choosing specific items on it to include in (or exclude from) her paper? Generate a list of additional particulars that DiGregorio could use to develop her topic.

CHAPTER 3
Purpose, Thesis, and Audience

Think about what writing actually *does*. It gives you a way to communicate new ideas and information. It can sell, buy, or negotiate. It can do public good and make private profit.

Think about how purposes and audiences for writing can shift from setting to setting and audience to audience.

PURPOSES AND AUDIENCES IN THREE COMMUNITIES: YOUR CHOICES AS A WRITER

ACADEMIC SETTINGS	PUBLIC SETTINGS	WORK SETTINGS
Why write? Present and support interpretations; discuss and explain research results; evaluate others' conclusions; demonstrate knowledge; explore ideas; share information and insight	**Why write?** Persuade people on issues; provide information; participate in public activities and decision making; create groups and organize communities	**Why write?** Analyze problems; propose solutions; provide information; coordinate activities
For whom? Instructors; fellow researchers or scholars; policy makers; public or workplace decision makers; anyone interested in fresh ideas or recent research	**For whom?** Local groups; public officials; potential supporters; agencies and organizations; issue-oriented readers	**For whom?** Coworkers and managers; clients and customers; government agencies; public relations

3a Recognizing your purpose

Think about your last substantial piece of writing. No doubt someone else handed you a task or assignment, and it was your job to produce a decent piece of prose. In the business world, almost no one escapes such writing tasks, whether they're actually assigned ("Please reply to this request for information about product *X*") or you're just expected to do them as part of your job. In college, your writing tasks are more likely to take the form of a defined written assignment, though you will still likely need to analyze this assignment to identify your purpose(s) for writing. In public settings, your "assignment" will often come to you in the form of a need or problem you can best address through writing (or formal speaking).

One of your early steps in planning for any piece of writing, therefore, should be to analyze the task and setting, taking time to identify what you're being asked (or what you're motivated) to do.

1 Identify the focus

In many writing tasks, your focus or topic may be defined for you in advance. In a memo to the YMCA volunteer tutoring staff, for example, your topic might be an upcoming training session. On other occasions, you may need to identify the topic in a task that's given to you, or even come up with a topic on your own. In all these cases, it helps to articulate for yourself just what it is you're writing about.

Look for key noun phrases. Your written assignment or task description will inevitably contain nouns that signal the main topics you need to address. Look for key nouns or noun phrases in the assignment and underline them. In your planning notes, write these nouns and then, by freewriting or writing conceptual maps (see 2a–d), begin inventing possibilities for your paper's contents.

In analyzing a writing assignment in his child development course, for example, Dennis Buehler underlined three key noun phrases.

> The purpose of this assignment is to integrate what you have learned in the area of cognitive development. Focusing on the second year of life, what are the most important skills that emerge in different domains (attention, language, and perception)? Give specific examples from the studies we have read so far.

The underlined topics can be stated more simply as *cognitive-developmental skills in the second year of life.*

Create a focus statement. When your writing task isn't an assignment given to you by someone else, write your own focus statement. Include key nouns or noun phrases (as in the preceding example). This can help you to keep your writing from straying from the point. Karla Spellman was asked to write a page for the Web site of a city project called "Green Chair," explaining how volunteers made green Adirondack chairs that were sold to raise money for creating play spaces in inner-city parks. She wrote the following focus statement and underlined the key noun phrase in it.

> In a page for the City Projects Web site, write a description of the Green Chair project, including its goals, how people can volunteer to build the chairs, and where they can buy one.

2 Define the purpose

Identifying nouns—topics or focuses—gives you a clear sense of what your writing is *about*. But nouns don't act: they're just things that sit, inert, on the page. Your writing doesn't just need to say something; it also needs to *do* something. This "doing" is the rhetorical action—the purpose—of your writing, and it usually appears in a verb or verb phrase.

Look for key verb phrases. In an assignment someone else gives to you, the central purpose for your response will appear in key verbs and verb phrases—statements of action and agency. Underline all key verbs or verb phrases that appear in the assignment or task description. Then circle those that appear to be the most important or central—the ones that tell you what to *do* with your writing. Use one or more of the planning techniques (see 2a–d) to generate material for your writing.

In analyzing the second writing assignment in her composition course, Corinth Malletas underlined two key verb phrases.

> *Assignment 2:* Find an advertisement that catches your attention in a popular magazine. Then analyze the ad for its hidden cultural assumptions, being sure to describe exactly what is happening in the ad. Include techniques of camera angle, coloration, and focus.

Create a purpose statement. For self-motivated writing, create your own purpose statement and underline the key verb or verb phrases. In planning an announcement recruiting acoustic bands for a new coffeehouse, Ty Brown wrote the following purpose statement and underlined two key verb phrases.

> Create a flier directed at band members and leaders to encourage their application to audition for the X-Tra Coffee House and explain the process to them as well as details about the coffeehouse.

Notice that these verb phrases contain important assembly instructions for Ty's flier. "Encourage" implies "getting attention," "being positive," and "advertising." "Explain" implies "giving information," "being clear," and "avoiding deception." Here are some of the more common verbs used in writing situations, especially in college writing assignments, along with brief definitions and examples.

VERBS USED IN WRITING ASSIGNMENTS OR SITUATIONS

Describe. Show how something might be experienced in sight, touch, sound, smell, or taste. *Example:* "Describe the obstacles experienced by wheelchair-bound or vision-impaired visitors to historic homes in the area."

(*continued*)

VERBS USED IN WRITING ASSIGNMENTS OR SITUATIONS *(continued)*

Analyze. Divide or break something into its constituent parts so you can analyze their relationships. Begin with careful description and observation. *Example:* "Analyze the causes of increased wildlife roadkill in a suburb."

Synthesize. Combine separate elements into a synthesis, producing a single or unified entity. *Example:* "Synthesize this list of disparate facts about energy consumption."

Evaluate. Reach conclusions about something's value or worth. Substantiate all evaluations with evidence based on careful observation and analysis. *Example:* "Evaluate the proposals submitted by three different groups who each want to organize this year's charity auction."

Argue. Argue to prove a point or persuade a reader to accept or entertain a particular position (see Chapters 10–11). *Example:* "Write a letter to the college senate arguing your position on the campus-wide ban on indoor smoking."

Inform. Present facts, views, phenomena, or events to inform your reader. *Example:* "Inform homeowners about the hazards of lead paint."

Extend. Apply an idea or concept more fully. *Example:* "Extend the production figures to take into account the mechanics' work slowdown."

Trace. Map out a history or chronology, or explain the origins of something. *Example:* "Trace the development of Stalinism."

Discuss. Provide an intelligent, focused commentary on a topic. *Example:* "Discuss citizens' primary objections to the proposed tax hike."

Show. Demonstrate or provide evidence to explain something. *Example:* "Show how specimen transport problems contribute to operating room delays."

Exercise 1

Below are two writing tasks, one in the form of a college writing assignment, the other in the form of a work assignment to a writer working in an internship at a local nonprofit agency. Locate the noun(s) that indicate the *focus* of each task, and find the verb(s) that indicate its *purpose*. Restate the focus and purpose in your own words if necessary.

Sample Assignment: At some point, most people recognize in themselves a prejudice against another person or group. These prejudices often come from stereotypes—inaccurate generalizations made on the basis of limited experience, rumor, or what others tell us. Choose some past action in your life that came out of a prejudice. What was the cause of the action? If the same circumstances arose today, would you behave differently?

Sample Task: Draft a proposal to the State Board on Aging for our planned ElderHelp Transport System. Refer to the current guidelines for contents of the proposal, length, and format. It would be useful to include some information on actual beneficiaries of our plan, so you will want to conduct a few informal interviews with some seniors—possibly ones who use our center. Rose has written successful proposals to the state board in the past, so get her input early. Of course, you should also run your draft past Jim.

3b Using purpose to guide your writing

Now that you've analyzed the general purpose of a writing task, you can begin to consider more specific effects you want your writing to achieve. These effects are your **rhetorical purposes** for writing: what you want your writing to *do* at each stage. Do you want your first paragraph to grab your reader's attention with something really alarming, or is it more important to begin on a cool note of academic objectivity? Should you use a personal anecdote in the middle of your document to show how you understand a problem, or would it be better to launch into a description of research studies? Do you want to leave your reader hanging at the end by suggesting unexplored questions, or will you wrap everything up with a really strong, opinionated conclusion?

1 Rough out a purpose structure

As you think about how you want to affect your reader, it helps to plan a general **purpose structure** for your paper's contents. Begin with a few simple categories, such as "beginning, middle, end," or "introduction, body, conclusion." Your categories should correspond to the main parts of your paper or document. Then explain what each of your categories will *accomplish*. Use verbs: "show," "explain," "make the claim that," "create interest," "build up to," "disprove."

In planning to write about housing options for a section of her school's student guide, Carol Stotsky defined her general purpose as explaining the benefits and drawbacks of various housing options. But then she needed to get more specific. She decided to *draw her readers in* by *showing them* that it's important to think carefully about housing options.

> **Beginning: Why consider housing options?**
> (*Draw* readers in; *show* that the topic is important to them)

Carol decided that she would then discuss each housing option in detail, analyzing the advantages and disadvantages of each.

Middle: *Explore* housing options in detail.

She then decided to move her final section toward a *recommendation* by presenting a scheme in which students start college by living in a dorm or at home and then move toward greater independence in their third or fourth years by considering off-campus housing.

Ending: *Recommend* that students start secure, then move toward independence.

This formal purpose structure gave Stotsky a tentative order and direction for her contribution to the student brochure.

Exercise 2

Roz Dane is a nurse practitioner in a family clinic. Clinic physicians have been seeing many patients who have suffered complications from more unusual body piercings, such as tongue studs. In some cases the patients were not aware of the potential complications or dangers. After some discussion, the physicians who own the clinic have asked Roz to produce a short, informative, and unbiased pamphlet on body piercing, which they can make available to patients before they consider various piercings.

Write a purpose statement for Roz's task, and plan a multipart structure for her pamphlet based on that purpose.

3c Defining a thesis or main idea

Most writing has a point, but if that point isn't clear within the first page or so of a text, readers may become frustrated and give up reading. In a public context, for instance, a pamphlet will need to grab readers' attention immediately. Or in the work community, an executive summary might appear first, before a full report, to clarify the main points right away and give readers a sense of what's to follow. In contrast, academic readers may be expected to have more patience as the writer gives background information that leads up to a main point.

One way you can be clear about your purposes and avoid bland, generalized prose is to develop a specific **thesis** for your writing, which you then explore, support, or illustrate using specific examples or arguments. Although you'll hear the term *thesis* almost exclusively in college (with terms like *main idea*, *message*, *story*, or *point* being used more often in business and community writing), the principle of the thesis remains the same across contexts: a thesis is the controlling idea of a piece of writing. Many college papers contain a thesis statement, usually a single sentence, that appears somewhere early in the text, most often at the end of the first paragraph. In other writing, the thesis may be more subtle, but it still has the effect of telling the reader what the writing will say and do.

Depending on your writing situation, you can begin a paper with a clear thesis in mind or discover your thesis later and revise accordingly. You can also begin with a clear thesis and then modify it as you look for evidence or **supporting ideas** to back up your assertions.

1 Turn topics into theses

When you begin a piece of writing, do you think about large areas of knowledge or experience that often appear as nouns or noun phrases? These usually take the form of *topics:* "conservation versus jobs in the timber industry," "the use of laser surgery in female infertility treatment," "death penalty by lethal injection in the state of Texas." Developing a thesis means *narrowing* one of these topics into something more specific and verbal, some statement of principle, action, or belief.

To develop a thesis from a topic, first try **narrowing** the topic to a specific angle or perspective. Then begin turning the topic from a noun (a "thing") into a statement that contains a verb. Lynn Scattarelli narrowed her topic in an informational pamphlet she designed for a community parenting group.

VAGUE TOPIC	Ritalin
STILL A TOPIC	The use of Ritalin for kids with attention-deficit disorder
STILL A TOPIC	The problem of Ritalin for kids with attention-deficit disorder
ROUGH THESIS	Parents should be careful about medicines such as Ritalin for kids with attention-deficit disorder.

2 Complicate or extend your rough thesis

Early thesis statements often beg for clarification or elaboration. In Lynn Scattarelli's rough thesis, it's not clear what she's suggesting to parents about Ritalin: that it shouldn't be used? that it should be used judiciously? that it's inappropriate for kids with ADD? Answering these questions led her to a more complex and interesting thesis.

FINAL THESIS	Although Ritalin is widely used as a drug treatment for children with attention-deficit disorder, parents should be careful not to overrely on such drugs until they have a complete picture of their child's problem and have explored all the options for treatment.

Lynn complicated her final thesis by accepting Ritalin as a legitimate treatment for ADD. The main point—a caution about overreliance and the exploration of other options—*qualified* or *extended* her rough thesis.

3 Expand your thesis with specifics

Think about how a thesis or main idea helps your reader. Knowing something about what you're going to say, your reader can organize the information that follows in chunks, fitting the ideas communicated by paragraphs and sections into the larger statement of purpose. But you need to decide on these ideas in the first place. Consider using the planning processes described in Chapter 2 to create a series of points or ideas that extend, support, or illustrate your thesis. Start with a simple list—three items, for example—and then work from there. Each item can form a kind of "minithesis" for its paragraph or section, guiding the ideas and focus of that paragraph.

4 Modify your thesis

Don't force yourself to stick too closely to your original thesis. As you plan, you may find yourself entertaining other ideas, especially those that seem to contradict your main idea or thesis. In such cases, your writing may be more interesting if you can qualify your earlier position or perspective, revising your thesis and its supporting ideas.

Exercise 3

Turn each of the following topics into two different thesis statements or main ideas. Be as inventive as you like.

EXAMPLE

TOPIC Saw-blade sabotage in the timber industry

THESIS Spiking trees to sabotage the saw blades of timber workers is both illegal and extremely dangerous, but it should be understood as a subversive act intended to stop further depletion of virgin forests.

THESIS Protests that include the illegal spiking of trees to sabotage the saw blades of timber workers actually help the timber industry by suggesting to the public that conservationists are less concerned about human safety and human life than about trees.

Topic 1: Grandparents' visitation rights, which allow them to see grandchildren against the parents' will

Topic 2: Gay rights in the Boy Scouts

Topic 3: Metal detectors at public school entrances
Topic 4: Whose fault is air rage?
Topic 5: Laws declaring English the official language of the United States

3d Different kinds of thesis statements

Different writing situations or purposes may call for different kinds of thesis statements. Refine your thesis statement so that it serves your purpose and the expectations of your readers.

THESIS STATEMENTS IN THREE COMMUNITIES

ACADEMIC SETTINGS	PUBLIC SETTINGS	WORK SETTINGS
Academic thesis statements generally extend or grow from concerns explored in prior research; they may indicate your conclusion and the ways you plan to explain and support it.	Public thesis statements are generally either argumentative (calling for action or arguing for a policy) or informative (explaining policies, procedures, or useful information).	Workplace thesis statements are generally either argumentative (proposing a policy or solution to a problem) or informative (sharing information or explaining procedures and instructions, for example).

- **General thesis.** When you are addressing a broad audience on a topic of general interest, readers will look to your thesis statement for an indication of your conclusions or special perspective on the topic.

  By the time they are teenagers, children pay more attention to their peers' opinions than to those of their parents.

- **Informative thesis.** When you are writing to present and explain information, readers will look to your thesis statement to understand why the information is worth knowing and how you'll organize your explanation.

  When you search online for financial advice, you should be aware of the three very different kinds of Web sites that offer help.

- **Argumentative thesis.** When you are presenting an argument, readers will look to your thesis for a statement of your opinion (your argumentative proposition), perhaps with an acknowledgment of other views on the issue as well.

  Bioengineered crops have some dangers, yet their potential for helping feed hungry people worldwide justifies their careful use.

- **Academic thesis.** When you are addressing an academic audience, readers will look to your thesis statement for your specific conclusion and a plan to support it in terms appropriate to the academic discipline.

  My survey of wedding announcements in local newspapers from 1970 to 2004 demonstrates the extent to which religious background and ethnicity have decreased in importance as factors in mate selection.

3e Recognizing your audience

Many writing experts use the term **audience** to refer to actual or implied readers or listeners. An audience may be one person (such as the city official you address in a letter complaining about the poor condition of the neighborhood sidewalks), or it may be dozens, hundreds, or thousands of people (such as the readers of the newspaper that publishes your letter about the same problem).

Your first question in any analysis of audience will be, "Who am I addressing?" Is it a flesh-and-blood person you know intimately? Or is it a shadowy, unknown reader, with only a faint silhouette to guide your thinking? Is your reader a single person or a large group?

To begin answering these questions, study Figure 3.1 below. This illustration shows an audience continuum, beginning with the most intimate reader on one end (yourself), addressed in journals, diaries, or plans for a per-

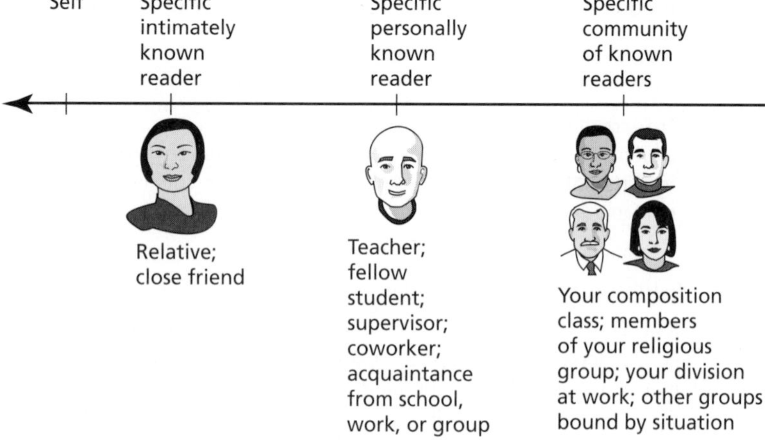

FIGURE 3.1 The audience continuum

sonal project, and ending with the remote and amorphous "general community of unknown readers" on the other.

Audiences themselves can also be multiple. A memo requesting personal leave will be read not only by your direct supervisor but by her supervisor as well. Members of your working group will probably receive a copy of the memo, even though they can't make a decision about your request. If your request is approved, the payroll and personnel departments may also see the memo.

Exercise 4

Imagine that you're living on Shell Island, located in a small estuary along the coast of Florida. A favorite winter vacation spot, the area boasts some excellent shelling beaches. But now, after years of ravenous beachcombing, fewer shells appear at low tide, and the area is attracting a more limited variety of birds and other wildlife. The local city council has proposed a general ban on beachcombing and plans to pass an ordinance that would require visitors to obtain a beach permit, at a cost of $30, to use the public beaches. The money would be channeled back into the study and preservation of the local environment.

You're planning to write a position statement on the proposed ordinance. Choose one of the three contexts listed on page 36. Then, referring to the audience continuum, analyze the audience for your position statement. Take a position on the issue, and consider which readers will disagree with your position and why.

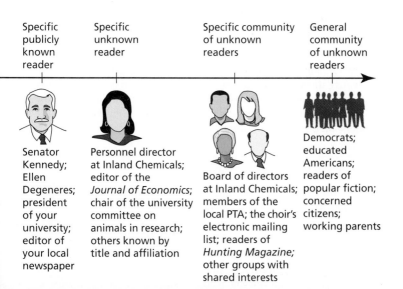

Specific publicly known reader

Senator Kennedy; Ellen Degeneres; president of your university; editor of your local newspaper

Specific unknown reader

Personnel director at Inland Chemicals; editor of the *Journal of Economics*; chair of the university committee on animals in research; others known by title and affiliation

Specific community of unknown readers

Board of directors at Inland Chemicals; members of the local PTA; the choir's electronic mailing list; readers of *Hunting Magazine;* other groups with shared interests

General community of unknown readers

Democrats; educated Americans; readers of popular fiction; concerned citizens; working parents

Context 1: Surfriders is a small organization for active surfers who visit Shell Island almost daily and are interested in keeping the area clean and safe. Write a letter to Todd Gray, president.

Context 2: Winter Birds is a newsletter sent to retired people who live in Northern states but have properties on the island and migrate there for two or three months during the winter. It is published and mailed by a local association for retired people. Write a letter to the editor.

Context 3: Nan Brown is the director of the Shell Island Chamber of Commerce. Business owners, rental agents, and tour operators rely heavily on the Chamber of Commerce for support. Write to Brown.

3f Specific readers and communities of readers

Although you might identify actual people as readers (your mother, your rabbi, the First Lady, the owner of the gas station down the street), at some level your writing is shaped by how *you* think of your audience and how you understand the communities of interest and purpose to which they belong (academic, public, and work). Constructing audiences also draws on your social and cultural knowledge. If you know very little about feminism, for example, and you write to an audience of feminists in a public setting, you may address them inappropriately. Knowing that there are many varieties of feminism complicates your audience, but the result is a richer and more accurate picture that leads to a better-informed and more incisive piece of writing.

When developing a profile of your audience, be aware that you're dealing with *tendencies.* Not all members of a group or community can be expected to agree with each other, so ask yourself whether you are unfairly stereotyping your reader(s). *Feminism* may suggest one set of policies to some members of an audience (family-friendly workplaces) and a different set to other members (elimination of sexist images in advertising). Or both.

Often, the more specific kinds of knowledge you have (or can gather) about potential readers, the more you can anticipate about their likely responses. Employing sets of questions like those below can help you develop an understanding of your readers.

ANALYZING YOUR AUDIENCE

Use the following questions to think critically about the nature of your readers as you plan and revise your writing.

1. **Size and relationship.** How large is your audience, and how generalized? How intimately do you know your audience? What sort of relationship do you have to your audience?
2. **Prior knowledge.** How much does your audience know about the subject of your writing? Are your readers complete novices or just short of

being experts? Do they share your prior knowledge of the subject? Are they young or old? Are they wise or inexperienced and naive?

3. **Physical context.** Where are your readers situated geographically? Is it possible to pinpoint their location? If not, can you generalize about it (e.g., Florida State University, San Francisco, Capitol Hill)?
4. **Social context.** What characterizes your audience socially and culturally? Are your readers educated? poor? middle class? Do they spend their time watching TV or reading books? Do they listen to Brahms? Do they go to tractor pulls? Do they spend time at singles bars or PTA meetings?
5. **Intellectual disposition.** How would you characterize your readers' way of thinking? Are they highly conservative? radical? apathetic? Where would they stand on certain major issues? Are they more likely to read and enjoy the *National Enquirer* or the *National Review*? *Science* or the *Christian Science Monitor*?
6. **Conditions of reading.** Under what conditions will your audience be reading your writing? Will readers be at home? at school? at the office? at the breakfast table? Will they be studying your writing closely at a desk or reclining in an easy chair after a good meal? Will they be busy or distracted? Will time be on their side, or will they be wishing they could buy a few extra hours?
7. **Power.** What is your status relative to your reader? Are you expecting the reader to accomplish something? Is your writing accomplishing something for someone else, such as a supervisor? Is that person also going to read your writing?

Exercise 5

Imagine that your longtime next-door neighbors rent their house and take a temporary position in another country. Soon after the renters move in, they begin piling up the yard and driveway with junk cars, old refrigerators, tires, and other debris. The situation becomes so intolerable that you decide to write to the renters, calling attention to the problem. You also decide to write to the local city inspections office, which is responsible for enforcing various codes on yard debris.

Write the two short letters, addressing the first to John and Susan Valentine and the second to Betsy Lewis, City Inspections Office. Then analyze the style, tone, and content of your letters. In each case, you were writing to a specific audience. How did their positions on the continuum influence your decisions? What general principles can you infer about the relationship of audience analysis to certain choices you made in your writing style?

3g Adapting to readers and communities of readers

Imagining audiences means more than gathering isolated facts about them (average age, occupation, and so on). In analyzing your audience, stopping at facts is like lining up the cumin, coriander, oregano, and basil without knowing how much of which spices you should add to the stew. Analyzing an audience can influence many decisions you make as you plan and revise your writing.

1 Genre, content, structure, and style

In particular, consider how audience influences your *genre*, *content*, *structure*, and *style*.

- **Genre.** What sort of text you choose for your writing—its **genre**—will depend in part on your audience. People who want to fix a slow drain themselves by consulting a public handyman site on the Web will not expect a poem or a long philosophical treatise but a clear, concise, and helpful set of tips. Choices of genre are especially important because they often give you guideposts for other decisions regarding length, style, structure, and purpose.
- **Content.** What specific information you put into your writing also depends on your audience.
- **Structure.** How you arrange and organize your ideas will likewise depend on your audience.
- **Style.** How you think about your audience will influence the style of your writing. How informal or formal should your writing be? how clinical or emotional? how friendly or hostile? how embracing or adversarial?

2 Your relationship to a community of readers

While it may seem as though you've almost always written for a teacher, you actually participate in conversations in many communities through your reading, writing, and speaking. Your college, public, and work communities give you a rich assortment of audiences to address. A campus alone consists of a loose confederation of scholars and teachers, students, administrators, members of teams and clubs, and people serving in many public and private capacities. In some circumstances, you may need to address or think of more than one of these types of readers, which complicates your task. Strategies for addressing different communities of readers depend partly on your relationship to your reader(s).

Writing for authorities. Writing for people in positions of authority can be especially challenging; after all, your performance and reputation may be on the line, and the stakes (such as a grade or the renewal of a contract) can be high. In academic settings, for example, a common first-day activity is figuring out the teacher. Is she tough or easy, rigorous or undemanding? Does she expect flawless, highly polished papers, or is she more concerned with the messy, exploratory side of writing? Does she seem to welcome diverse views, even if they don't match her own? In business settings, knowing what a supervisor expects can be just as daunting—and important.

STRATEGY

Always attend to the specific guidelines for completing a writing task (see 3a). If these are provided orally, write them down carefully. Reread all directions several times. Above all, *ask questions*. Most teachers, supervisors, or superiors are willing to elaborate on their expectations. Their answers often tell you how they will evaluate your writing in light of its purposes.

Writing for communities of peers. Many public and civic contexts in which you might write or speak are organized democratically. You don't have a supervisor as much as a series of self-appointed roles (such as membership on a committee), so you are on more-or-less equal footing with others in your group. (In other public settings, of course, power takes more complicated forms: a city council member has a certain kind of authority in her work above that of an ordinary citizen, but citizens themselves hold the power to vote such a person out of office.)

STRATEGY

During the planning stages of your writing, be sure to discuss your ideas and intentions with members of a peer group. Their initial responses (as "themselves") will give you valuable insights from the perspective of a general academic audience. If you have a specific audience you are addressing, ask your peers to role-play that audience for you so you can test how well you've achieved your purposes. (For more on peer groups during revision, see 5c.)

Writing for broad public communities. A murky and ill-defined audience, but one often alluded to in directions for or evaluations of writing assignments, is the "general reader." Although no one yet has defined this audience very clearly, it usually refers to reasonably educated people—for example, most people in your college or university. Many teachers favor the undefined "general academic audience" for classroom writing for the very reason that opinions among this group will vary widely and require of the writer more thought—hence, deeper learning.

Readers in broad public communities are themselves very diverse. Some are well educated, well informed, and interested in the pursuit of knowledge (often for its own sake). Others read very little—just a weekly newspaper, for example—in order to keep up on current events. Some readers have incisive, critical minds and like to be entertained with new and stimulating ideas; others read only when they have to and prefer not to spend much time talking about ideas.

In reading your writing, teachers often allude to various public communities with statements like "How would the audience for this piece react to so radical a statement?" or "Are you sure you've considered the opposing views your audience might raise here?" or "How would people opposed to gun control respond to this?" Such statements assume different audiences with different dispositions. Interestingly, academic readers will take you seriously if you can show, through your prose, that you've considered a range of public responses to an issue or idea. That sort of awareness of audiences can also make your writing in work and nonacademic communities stronger and more convincing.

STRATEGY

In your planning notes, circle any assertions or points that readers in various public communities could challenge. Then brainstorm to develop several responses to the challenges. Are the challenges well reasoned? If so, consider acknowledging or incorporating them in your paper.

3 Writing for yourself and forgetting about audience

Writing for yourself can help you to formulate or explore new knowledge. If you're responding to a task or an assignment given by a teacher or supervisor, ask yourself what the writing process can do for *you*. What sort of learning is implied by the design of the project? How can you maximize your own interest in the subject? What will *you* get from your efforts?

Writing to or for yourself can also help you in the early stages of your writing, when "audience paralysis" can set in. Tough-minded audiences can make you so self-conscious that you can hardly produce a word that will survive your scrutiny. The result is frustration, procrastination, and anxiety.

Exercise 6

A. Pick a specialized magazine with which you are very familiar (such as *Road & Track*, *Cooking Light*, or *Wired*). Get a recent copy of the magazine and glance through it, noting the topics, lengths, and formats of its articles; its advertisements; its layout; and its writing style. Then, using the advice outlined in this chapter, select one method for analyzing the magazine's audience. If you can't answer a question definitively, make as educated a guess as possible, and state what further information you'd like to have.

B. Join a group of three or four other students. Briefly describe and compare your magazines, and then discuss your audience analyses. What issues surface about the relationship between the writing and the audience? What problems or questions about audience would you like to discuss?

CHAPTER 4
Drafting

Drafting means stringing words together into sentences and paragraphs that will begin to make some sense to a reader. All your planning, purpose, setting, and audience analysis will prepare you to write. But don't expect to sit down and immediately write a smooth, coherent paper simply because you've accumulated a lot of material. A **rough draft** is necessary to begin to create something that resembles a fully elaborated text. This process of pulling your information together and *writing* will always be intellectually challenging: drafting is hard work.

4a From planning to drafting

Your use of various planning strategies should produce more than enough material to begin drafting. The problem you face at this stage is knowing how and where to begin writing your draft. You need to assess what you have and start turning your material into sentences that move your ideas forward.

1 Draft in manageable parts

Conceptual outlines do more than simply help you generate ideas. A good cluster, for example, will also show you relationships among connected ideas and ways you might think about organizing your paper.

The items in your planning materials will usually suggest chunks of text that you can draft in one sitting. Look for specific ideas that suggest paragraphs or sections of your paper. Then choose one idea and write about it, either in draft form or in the form of lists, notes, or sentences. If your fifteen-page paper on the relationship between asthma and ozone levels seems like a daunting task, begin by writing a fairly easy section—for example, two pages summarizing recent research studies.

2 Develop a general structure

The kind of material you're writing may determine the way you organize it. A narrative, for example, will probably be arranged *chronologically* (each event following the previous event in time); an argument may be organized *logically,* by paragraphs supporting some assertion. Much of the writing done in the workplace or the public arena is highly structured. Whatever you're writing, you need to think about what should come first, second, and third in your paper.

Most academic writing will contain at least three parts: an **introduction,** a **body,** and a **conclusion.** This simple structure can help you to make some preliminary decisions about how to group your ideas.

By thinking about this three-part organizing scheme, Amy Burns was able to generate ideas for a paper on superstition and develop a preliminary structure.

INTRODUCTION	Fear; people who believe in superstitions; origins
BODY	Examples of superstitions (black cat, #13, crossing fingers, walking under a ladder, rabbit's foot)
CONCLUSION	Truth and falsity of superstitions; mystery surrounding them; concepts of reality

When she began drafting her paper, Burns used the ideas from this preliminary plan to write an introduction about how superstitions originate in a fear of the unknown.

> Many people are superstitious or at least practice some of the bizarre rituals of superstition, but very few know why or have thought about the reason. A lot of people practice superstitions without realizing that what they are doing is superstitious. The biggest percentage of people practice superstition because of a fear of the unknown. You might have heard some superstitions from parents or grandparents, been influenced by school or religion, or perhaps even read about them in books. However or wherever you heard of them, you practice superstitions because you are afraid of what will happen if you do not.

Although the introduction-body-conclusion structure can be helpful, much of the material you will write outside the academic community may require another approach (see the chart on page 44). Petitions, newsletters, sales letters, problem descriptions, status reports, and some Web sites, for example, don't follow a rigid structure with set headings; but readers do have expectations about how such pieces should be organized.

3 Assess your purpose and redraft

Even before you've written a full draft, you may want to stop to think about whether the material is achieving your general purposes for writing (persuading someone of a position, telling a story, explaining how to do something) or your more specific purposes for different parts of your paper

DRAFTING SUGGESTIONS FOR THREE DIFFERENT COMMUNITIES

ACADEMIC SETTINGS	PUBLIC SETTINGS	WORK SETTINGS
Consider drafting quickly to set down the links in a chain of reasoning, leaving space to develop detailed discussions, support, and summaries of other interpretations later in the drafting process. Use lists of main points and evidence or informal outlines to maintain the direction of your reasoning as you draft.	Consider creating a list of main ideas and points of information to keep focus on your readers' needs and interests as you draft. Enlist others from your organization or potential audience as respondents during drafting to keep your focus on the ideas and arguments you need to include.	Consider dividing the task according to the conventional sections of a report or other document (see Chapter 20), completing first those sections for which you have the clearest or most complete understanding of information and ideas. When working with a group, consider dividing the work of drafting according to parts of the document or assigning various drafts (first, second, etc.) to individuals according to their knowledge and abilities.

(providing information, livening up a paragraph with an anecdote, illustrating a point with an extended example). (See Chapters 3 and 6.) Read your early material and extend, cut, or redraft it to more adequately reflect your intended purposes.

In her paper on superstition, Amy Burns's broad purpose was to inform her readers about the nature of superstition and to encourage some enjoyable reflection. Her first *specific* purpose statement was "I want to grab my readers' attention and get them thinking about the nature of superstition." From this statement, she realized that her introduction was informative but too dull. She drafted new sentences and then followed them with her earlier material.

> Do you knock on wood after making a prediction? Shiver when a black cat crosses your path? Consider the number 13 unlucky? If so, then you have already been swept into the fantasy world of superstitions. Many people are superstitious or at least practice some of the bizarre rituals of superstition, but very few know why or have thought about the reason.

4b Drafting strategies

What makes drafting so challenging? Partly, it's the need to get a complicated job done, finding the right words while you're still figuring out where to begin. It's also dealing with apprehensions, such as feeling the focus slipping away, or thinking your writing isn't working, or revising every sentence instead of moving quickly ahead. You can meet these challenges successfully if you practice some useful techniques for getting words down on the page.

1 Write about your writing

Worrying about your writing probably won't ever go away—even the pros do it. Worrying yourself into avoidance or confusion, however, won't help you write your draft.

A very common fear is the deadline. Strangely, many writers react to deadlines by putting off the writing until the specter of doom is practically breathing down their necks (often in the wee hours before the writing is due). For these procrastinators, just about any other task, even the most unpleasant, will be worth doing just to avoid sitting down and starting to write.

Begin drafting not by writing your paper but by writing *about it.* What's foremost in your mind about your paper? What do you hope to do with it? What possible ways might you start it? As you make these notes, you'll soon find yourself a little less anxious about starting—after all, you *have* started. As your anxiety lessens, you'll find yourself more willing to take risks and try out a few lines.

2 Draft quickly

Another source of frustration comes from the struggle to find the right words. Sometimes every sentence seems to tangle you in a mess of contradictions, until you're no longer sure what you want to say. In this situation, you want to gain momentum, to feel that your ideas are smoothly giving way to words.

The solution is to draft quickly. As you begin, don't worry about writing perfect sentences and paragraphs. Just aim to get as much material on paper as you can, right from the start. Writers often find that when they write quickly, they feel a momentum developing, a kind of "flow." If you can type faster than you can handwrite, using a computer may encourage this momentum.

ESL ADVICE: DRAFTING

Paying more attention to grammar, vocabulary choice, and style than to ideas and information while you draft can make your writing harder to do and less effective. As you draft, pay attention first to *what* you are saying and then to *how* you are saying it. You will have time later to revise and correct your grammar and the specific words you have chosen. Worrying about these matters too much as you draft may slow your writing down so much that you lose track of the ideas you wish to develop.

3 Semidraft

Writing a first full draft in one sitting, especially of a major document, may be too ambitious a goal; you'll need to divide the task into several drafting episodes. Some writers, however, can't seem to continue drafting anything for more than a few minutes before they stall out. They can't come up with the words to describe a particular idea, often because they're tired or haven't thoroughly considered their ideas.

Semidrafting is the process of writing full sentences until you feel you're about to stall out. At that point, you simply write the word *etc.* and then continue on to your next point. Or you insert a brief direction to yourself in brackets to remind you what to do when you return to the draft to push that section a little further along.

4 Talk it out or take a break

Sometimes nothing works. You simply can't, at that moment, put coherent sentences together on the page, and your frustration can cause you to lose interest in the project.

Writing isn't like breathing, something you do as a matter of course. It's more like eating, which depends on your appetite. If you simply can't write, no matter how many techniques you try, then don't. Put off your writing until a little later. Just set a time to return to the task—preferably on the same day, but no later than the same time the next day. In the meantime, try the following Strategy to keep going.

STRATEGY

Send an email about your writing project to someone you know well, or talk with this person. Explain what you're trying to do. Expressing your concerns may help you alleviate tension and may even show you some solutions. Your listener may also have suggestions to help you get started.

Exercise 1

Try out one of the Strategies for drafting described in this chapter. Jot down some notes about how well it worked to get you started drafting and keep you moving forward. Then compare the results of your experiment in a small group, identifying strategies that seemed to work well.

4c Collaborative drafting

Different groups work together in different ways depending on the composition and purpose of the group. A committee formed to revise production standards at a manufacturing plant might consist of department managers who each have an area of expertise, whereas a Sunday school parents' committee might include people who have no experience in running a school but share the goal of increasing enrollment. Each group will distribute writing tasks in the way that seems most efficient for its resources and purposes. If your group is uncertain about how to proceed, consider one of the following suggestions.

1 Do parallel drafting

In **parallel drafting,** your group divides the proposed document so that each member is responsible for drafting a particular section. Members can exchange drafts as they revise and edit. This strategy allows writers with different specializations to work comfortably together yet draw on individual expertise, but it may require one person to act as editor, integrating the drafts.

2 Do team drafting

In **team drafting,** the group agrees on first and second authors for each section. The first author begins drafting and continues until he or she gets stuck. Then the draft passes to the second author, who begins where the first writer stopped. This method works well when various writers share similar ideas and approaches. The drafts are recirculated when the group is ready to revise and edit.

3 Do intensive drafting

Intensive drafting is most successful when you are working with a close friend or colleague. You need to find a location where you can assemble your materials and work undisturbed. Decide where each person will start, begin drafting together, and exchange sections at a certain time or as each of you finishes a segment. You continue your intensive, undisturbed work—exchanging drafts and reworking the document—until you are both satisfied with the result.

STRATEGY

Make use of the "track changes" feature in most popular word-processing software to draft collaboratively in an electronic document file. This function allows changes to the original draft to appear in a different color on screen. Drafts can be circulated by disk or email, edited by group members using the tracking feature, and returned to the author. Every member's changes will appear (color-coded by editor in some software) in the draft for review.

Exercise 2

Imagine you are part of a student organization that is raising funds for a community project in which volunteers read to children in school libraries. Your organization intends to submit a grant proposal to a local foundation or philanthropic group. Plan how the members might use the following equipment to draft the proposal collaboratively: telephones, email, computers, fax machines. What steps would be involved in your plan?

4d Drafting: Paper in progress

Recall that Jessica DiGregorio had developed a generalized topic: the consequences of professional contracts on the lives of sports players (see 2f). After listing some possible examples to support this topic, she tried freewriting for a few minutes on selected items in her list. Here is her freewriting passage on the item "What he [her father] had to do as a result of the contract."

- Keep himself fit for five years (meaning?)
- Not indulge in bad habits
- Not stop playing basketball
- Stay clear of ice-skating, skiing, other strenuous activities to avoid injury

Exercise 3

A. Examine DiGregorio's freewriting. At this point she wanted to use some ideas in her freewriting to begin drafting. What advice would you give her about the ideas she has begun to explore? What other details on the subject of the contract requirements could she include in her rough draft? Is there anything in the freewriting that suggests a good place for this passage in her paper (beginning, middle, or end)?

B. In a small group, compare your responses to Exercise 3A. What elements did the members of your group agree could be profitably expanded from the freewriting as DiGregorio drafts her paper? Was there any consensus in your group about where to place this section of the paper?

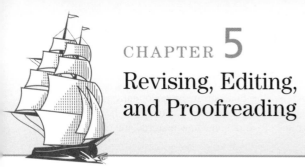

CHAPTER 5
Revising, Editing, and Proofreading

Because so much of what we read is in a final, published form, we often forget how much work goes into a good piece of writing. Invisible to us are the hours the author spent in the process of **revision**—considering and reconsidering content and structure, tearing out whole sections and redrafting them, honing and refining paragraphs, polishing the style, and finding just the right words to express a thought.

Revision is not simply **editing,** a fine tuning for style, grammar, and problems with sentences and wording. Nor is it **proofreading,** a final-stage cleaning up of typographical errors or a search for missing commas and apostrophes. These important activities generally come after revising, but are different in important ways.

When accomplished writers say the word *revision,* they mean mentally "stepping outside" a draft, assessing its strengths and weaknesses as if reading it for the first time; deciding what parts need to be expanded, clarified, elaborated, illustrated, reworded, restructured, modified, or cut; and then actually making the changes.

REVISION HIGHLIGHTS FOR THREE COMMUNITIES OF READERS

ACADEMIC SETTINGS	PUBLIC SETTINGS	WORK SETTINGS
Pay special attention to these:	**Pay special attention to these:**	**Pay special attention to these:**
Clarity of conclusions and thesis statement	Clear statement of policy, cause, or position	Clear statement of problems, solutions, tasks, and goals
Topic sentences and section headings	Relevant and accurate supporting evidence	Explanations and proposals presented concisely and directly
Integration of quotations and supporting information	Direct and clear presentation of ideas and explanations	Factual accuracy
Acknowledgment of competing viewpoints	Fairness of reasoning and in treatment of opposing points of view	Section headings and conventional elements of document
Critical analysis and fresh insight	Focus on actions or solutions	

5a Major revisions

When you begin revising, concentrate on major concerns. A **major revision** is a large-scale change in your draft. For example, if you've left out a major point, you may need to draft some new material and change your conclusion.

1 Redraft unworkable material

Read through your draft as if you were seeing it for the first time. It helps if you have left your draft alone for a short while so that you can see it afresh. As you read, place a question mark next to sections that seem confusing or garbled. You may need to **redraft** these parts entirely. Go back to the parts you've marked and bracket the specific places where your writing seems to lose its vitality, meaning, or style. Ask yourself what you're trying to accomplish in a particular passage. Then, without even looking at the draft, try again on a new sheet of paper to write what you mean.

Jessica DiGregorio shared with her classmates a draft of her essay reflecting on her father's professional sports contract. They felt the first paragraph didn't capture much tension or create interest, and they placed brackets around sentences that seemed particularly weak. After changing a few words, DiGregorio realized she really needed to redraft the entire paragraph.

ORIGINAL DRAFT WITH BRACKETS FROM PEER GROUP

[A few days ago I decided to go through the musty old cedar chest in my living room and dug up some of the old documents that I had read years earlier.] I came across the Contract marked NBA (National Basketball Association) [that I had looked at before, but remembered that it was very confusing.] It contained words such as: hereunder, however, notwithstanding, and hereof, but when I read this over for the second time it made me realize that my father, [for a total of five years was bound to this document,] and chose to live his life according to what it said.

REVISED DRAFT

I had looked at the contract in the musty cedar chest when I was in high school, but words like *hereunder*, *however*, *notwithstanding*, and *hereof* left me confused. This time, when I saw the papers with *NBA* written on top and glanced through the provisions, I realized that when my father signed this, he gave the National Basketball Association control over his life and his family.

2 Reorganize poorly arranged paragraphs or sections

Structural problems are common in early drafts. Often you find that you've written your way "into" your main point, discovering later what you

STRATEGY

Number each paragraph in your draft. Then, on a clean piece of paper, explain in a phrase or a single sentence what each numbered paragraph says (its main point). When you've finished, look back at your list of statements.

- Could any paragraphs be consolidated?
- Are any paragraphs ineffectively ordered?
- Could you arrange the paragraphs or parts of the paper to yield a clearer, smoother flow of ideas?

want to say earlier in the draft. Or you may recognize that two different paragraphs are making the same point and should be consolidated.

Keyshawn Williams drafted a section of his paper on the problems of electronic archives. Reading over his draft, he noticed that the parts seemed out of order and that two short paragraphs said similar things. He began revising by identifying the main points of the paragraphs, and he could then arrange the paragraphs in a more logical order. Having done this, he realized that his new paragraphs needed considerable elaboration. He also added a sentence that helped to focus his next two paragraphs.

ORIGINAL

Although most people think that electronic archives can store written documents permanently, they would be surprised to learn that medieval parchment makes a far more lasting medium than computers. In fact, electronic media will begin decaying rapidly.

To create a digital archive that will last without being recopied, you would have to preserve the original system software, hardware, operating manuals, recording devices, and all the other apparatus that did the original archive.

decay

The decay is so rapid that the federal government requires its records to be recopied every ten years and "exercised" once a year. A congressional report notes that there are now only two machines in the world that can read the electronically stored information from the 1960 U.S. Census. Another problem concerns the fact that some records are written in programs that are obsolete, making it impossible to read the data even if the disk is in good shape.

obsolescence

REVISION

Although most people think that electronic archives can store written documents permanently, they would be surprised to learn that medieval parchment makes a far more

> lasting medium than computers. **There are two main reasons why electronic document storage is highly questionable even as our society plunges into the electronic age.**
>
> **First,** electronic media will begin decaying rapidly. [Explain why the magnetic medium decays.] The decay is so rapid that the federal government requires its records to be recopied every ten years and "exercised" once a year.
>
> Another problem concerns the fact that some records are written in programs that are obsolete, making it impossible to read the data even if the disk is in good shape. A congressional report notes that there are now only two machines in the world that can read the electronically stored information from the 1960 U.S. Census. To create a digital archive that will last without being recopied, you would have to preserve the original system software, hardware, operating manuals, recording devices, and all the other apparatus that created the original archive.

3 Add new material

Because you may write your first draft quickly, just to get it down on the page, you may find places where something is missing. Added material can enliven a dull description, clarify or extend a point, or provide essential information for your readers.

As you reread your paper, mark any cases in which a paragraph or sentence doesn't connect clearly enough to the one before it. Also note any gaps in information or detail. Try making a detailing list if you need to add information to your draft (see 2a-3).

Looking over her draft Web page telling employees how to transfer to a new email system, Gina White noticed some gaps and filled them in.

> Your new email address is listed below. It should be easy to remember **because it consists of the first four letters of your name and the last four numbers of your Social Security number.** Our company's address is the same: @Wishfactory.com. You may send your new address to people or discussion groups that send you frequent email, but you don't need to. **Our server will automatically forward any mail directed to your old address.**

4 Delete unnecessary or redundant material

Reread your draft as if an editor has accepted it for publication in a magazine with the stipulation that you trim at least ten percent. Too much prose can be just as distracting or frustrating to a reader as too little. What can you cut? Could some paragraphs be eliminated altogether, perhaps by merging just the essential material from them into another paragraph? (See also 6e.)

Exercise 1

Compare the following first-draft and revised versions of Maureen Lagasse's paper on racism. Describe the nature of Lagasse's changes—did she redraft, reorganize, add, or cut? What do you think motivated her revisions?

FIRST DRAFT

In setting out to write this paper my concept to explain was racism, and in doing some reading and thinking, I realized that racism can't be defined or explained in one simple definition. In the dictionary the definition of racism is "the practice of racial discrimination or segregation, etc." Although this is what racism is, this definition doesn't fully explain racism. What exactly are races, and how do people actually develop these discriminations against people of different races?

REVISED DRAFT

Have you ever wondered why people view interracial relationships as unacceptable? Have you wondered whether there really is a difference between you and someone of another race? In the dictionary the definition of racism is "the practice of racial discrimination or segregation." Although this is a legitimate definition, it doesn't fully explain racism.

5b Minor revisions

Minor revisions are fairly small changes, mostly in the individual sentences of your prose, with the goal of refining and polishing. Most minor revisions are made for three reasons: *sense* (how clear and understandable is your prose?), *style* (how elegant and smooth is your prose?), and *economy* (how much can you say in the least space?).

1 Revise for sense

Read each sentence of your paper individually and test its clarity: does the statement *make sense* in the context of the paper? Don't let your mind float back into your own construction of ideas; instead, imagine yourself as your intended reader. If you have peer readers, ask them to place question marks next to any statement or group of statements they find confusing or garbled.

2 Revise for style

When you revise for style, you're concerned with the way your prose "sounds"—that is, with its rhythm, complexity, and diction or word choice (see 46b–d). When you read a rough draft, some parts will usually sound better to you than others. Use your intuition as a reader.

In his report on the environmentally threatened wild mustangs of Nevada, Paul Tichey placed an asterisk next to a paragraph he had already revised for sense. Paul liked the clarity of his revision, but the end of his new sentence seemed awkward because so many words began with a *d* ("dehydration and death during the duration of the drought"). He also thought that "during the duration" seemed redundant. Here's his further revision.

> The Air Force, which was partly responsible for the demise of the wild mustangs on the Tonopah missile range, has now joined forces with the Bureau of Land Management and a group of wild-horse preservationists to help save the mustangs from **fatal** dehydration ~~and death during the duration of the drought.~~ **while the drought persists.**

STRATEGY

Place an asterisk in the margin next to any paragraph that seems to need polishing. Then go back to the first paragraph you marked and code each sentence according to what you feel about it: + (positive), ✓ (neutral), – (negative), ? (unsure). Now concentrate on revising the sentences you do not like in that paragraph. Move on to revising the questionable sentences. Reread the entire paragraph. When you are satisfied, go to the next paragraph you marked with an asterisk. If you're still uncertain about any sentence, ask peer readers for their impressions. *When in doubt, try an alternative.*

3 Revise for economy

To revise for economy, read your writing and think about what you can cut from it *without causing it to lose sense or coherence.* In the middle of Paul Tichey's paper, one paragraph included too much material. He decided that half of it could be cut.

SECOND DRAFT

> A serious problem confronting groups who want to manage wild mustangs on military sites in Nevada is the relative inaccessibility of the sites, since many require security passes or are fenced off, and environmentalists can't come and go as they please, as they can on public or even some private land. It's simply harder to study or help horses on restricted military installations. Open rangeland has easier access, and inspectors can simply move in and out at will.

THIRD DRAFT

Restricted access to Nevada military sites presents a serious obstacle to successful horse management. In contrast to open rangeland, where inspectors can come and go as they please, military sites are often fenced off and require security clearance.

In the revised paragraph, Tichey said essentially the same thing in thirty-eight words that he had said before in seventy-eight—a cut of over 50 percent!

Exercise 2

Examine the following paragraphs from Anita Jackson's paper on Buddhism. Then characterize the sorts of minor revisions Jackson made. Did she revise for sense, style, or economy? What sorts of changes did she make? How successful were the changes?

EARLY DRAFT

The man who became the first Buddha was named Siddhartha. Siddhartha was a prince in northern India who lived in a large palace. His father didn't allow him outside the palace because he wanted to spare Siddhartha from the miseries of the world.

Siddhartha became curious and one day he went riding outside the palace. What he saw would forever change his life and influence the lives of many thereafter. That which Siddhartha saw has since been named the Four Sights.

REVISED DRAFT

The man who became the first Buddha was Siddhartha, a pampered prince of northern India who lived in a lavish palace. Yet for all his riches his father would not allow him to venture beyond the castle walls because he wanted to spare Siddhartha the miseries of life. Siddhartha grew extremely curious about the outside world and one day went riding beyond the limits of the palace. What he saw that day would forever change his life and influence the lives of many thereafter.

What Siddhartha saw has since been named the Four Sights.

5c Collaborative revising

Professional writers rarely produce a good piece of writing without getting responses from many readers along the way. Follow their lead: *make sure to ask at least one person you respect to read your papers and give you some honest feedback, and promise you'll do the same in return.* Here are some tips for getting and giving helpful feedback in **collaborative revision.**

1 Respond helpfully

When you're reading someone else's writing in order to offer constructive criticism, remember that your most helpful role is not as proofreader or editor but as real, warm-blooded *reader*.

- Find out the writer's purpose for the paper. What is the writer trying to accomplish? What sort of paper is this?
- Who is the writer's intended reader?
- What are the writer's main concerns at this point? What would the writer most like to learn from you?

Once you have answers, read the paper through, jotting comments in the margins and keeping track of your thoughts and impressions.

When you convey your responses, remember you'll need to balance praise with helpful criticism. Don't just say, "I liked it. It was really good," or give directions like "You should move this paragraph up to page 3." Instead, offer diplomatic advice; ask, "What would happen if you moved this paragraph?" or suggest, "I wonder whether that paragraph would fit better on page 3."

2 Make the most of responses

Remember, you're not out to collect pats on the back; you want the most useful, constructive commentary you can get from astute, honest readers. This means accepting even hard-hitting reactions and suggestions with grace and diplomacy. If you react defensively to a peer reader's criticism, that person is not likely to keep giving you much feedback. If a reader questions something you especially like in your draft, *remember that no one can force you to make a change*. You have the final say.

- Give your readers a list of specific concerns you have about your draft. Do you want them to comment on tone? style? structure? logic?
- Keep your apologies to a minimum. You may feel anxious about sharing a first draft with your classmates, but as writers you're all facing the same situation.
- If all of your group members are working on papers at the same time, forming a writer's group and spending time on each of your drafts can be an especially valuable experience.
- Using your readers' responses, *spend some time planning your changes*. A few minutes planning your revisions may save you time experimenting.

3 Workplace collaboration

Collaborative revision is often the norm outside the school setting. However, workplace collaboration may be somewhat different from sharing your draft with classmates.

- In the workplace, many people will have a stake in your text. They are more likely than fellow students to be willing—even eager—to review it for you.
- Supervisors, in particular, may be direct and insistent about making certain changes.
- It helps to solicit responses from individuals with a range of perspectives and with different kinds of knowledge about your topic or problem.

ESL ADVICE: REVISING WITH A PEER READER

If you are worried about your grammar or spelling, you might want to review these items quickly before sharing your rough draft. Look for a peer reader who is willing to ignore these details. Ask this reader to focus on specific issues (such as the order or development of your ideas) or on problems you often have in your papers (such as weak first paragraphs). Consider sharing your draft with several readers, including native speakers of English, to get a range of responses.

Exercise 3

A. If you haven't done so, form a small revision group and circulate rough drafts of your papers in progress. Using the tips in this section as well as the techniques for major and minor revision described in 5a and 5b, comment on your partners' drafts. Then meet in a revision group to discuss your drafts. Keep track of the group's comments on your own paper.

B. Analyze your group experience. What was helpful? What comments will lead (or have led) to specific revisions? What comments did you choose not to act on? Why?

5d Revising: Paper in progress

After semidrafting several paragraphs about items on her list of particulars, Jessica DiGregorio was prepared to write the following full rough draft of her paper about her father's sports contract.

First Draft of Sports Contract Paper

Jessica DiGregorio

A few days ago I decided to go through the musty old cedar chest in my living room and dug up some of the old documents that I had read years earlier. I came across the Contract marked NBA (National Basketball Association) that I had looked at before, but remembered that it was very confusing. It contained words such as: hereunder, however, notwithstanding, and hereof, but when I read this over for the second time it made me realize that my father, for a total of five years was bound to this document, and chose to live his life according to what it had said. This twelve-page "AGREEMENT" caught my attention from the time I was young, but it did not make sense to me until now.

When I was younger I never took interest in my father's past mainly because I was tired of hearing people telling me "Did you know your father was the best basketball player?!" and "If you could have seen him play!" I used to just smile and not say anything because I never thought my father could be an athlete as good as Michael Jordan or Larry Bird. My perspective on his basketball career changed as I got older, I became interested in watching videos of him and asked him questions on what it was like to be a basketball legend.

"CLUB DOES HEREBY EMPLOY PLAYER AS
A SKILLED BASKETBALL PLAYER"

This statement which was said on the first page of his contract set the setting for all of the other statements that followed. Since the NBA decided that my father was good enough to play the sport, a contract was made to fit the needs of both the Club (the Buffalo Braves) and the Player (my father). After my father read the first line he was honored and knew that all of his hard work and determination had paid off. The Club which drafted him in 1973 knew that he was a person of great charisma and talent including basketball legend Red Auerbach. This contract was the beginning of a five-year long agreement which was taken very seriously.

"HE WILL TO THE BEST OF HIS ABILITY MAINTAIN HIMSELF IN
PHYSICAL CONDITION SUFFICIENT TO PLAY SKILLED BASKETBALL"

This rule stated in the contract meant that my father had to keep himself fit for the next five years, and not allow himself to overindulge in bad habits. The Club made up this rule to insure themselves that they were signing someone who was serious about the game. This meant that my father had to stay physically fit and never stop playing basketball. He was advised to stay clear of skiing, ice-skating, or any other strenuous activity not related to basketball so that he would not get injured. If my father, or any other player disobeyed this part of the contract it stated that, "the club shall have the right to suspend the player for a period of one week . . . and will be examined by a physician."

"IN THE EVENT OF THE DEATH OF THE PLAYER PRIOR
TO THE TERMINATION OF ANY SEASON . . .
THE CLUB SHALL PAY TO THE PLAYER'S HEIRS . . ."

This particular part of the contract interested me the most. It stated that if my father had died, all of the money which was already promised to my father within the contract went to my mother. This was very important to my father since my mother was a housewife and stayed home with my older sisters. The Club added this statement to the contract to give the player's family the proper amount of financial help after the loss of their loved one. Basically after the death of a player the money which was promised throughout the five year term is terminated and the family only received what the player lived for. If there was to be a breach in the contract then lawyers would have had to be appointed to the family of the deceased, and determining where money goes can be a sticky situation if it is not written down and documented properly.

"THE CLUB SHALL HAVE THE OPTION IN ITS SOLE DISCRETION
TO TERMINATE THIS AGREEMENT AND RENDER IT NULL AND VOID"

This final part in this contract stated that the Club had the final say in any of the decisions that would have come along. This meant my father had to follow all of the requirements made within the document which he had signed. If he or anyone else did not follow any of the regulations, then they would have no say if their contract was to be null and void. This left the final power up to the Club and gave them the upper hand in everything that dealt with the players. This was an important part of his contract because it allowed the Club to demonstrate how powerful it really was in the make or break of a person's professional basketball career.

Contracts and legal documents shape our everyday life. Some people underestimate the power of legal documents which bind and connect us to different things. A single piece of paper can determine where we live or how we live our lives. The contract which bound my father to the NBA shaped his life in a major way. For five years he lived by rules and regulations created by the Club to which he belonged. He became a basketball legend and lives in the memories of some people, but to me he is just my dad.

Exercise 4

A. Study Jessica DiGregorio's first draft. Assuming that she has drafted with a loose structure in mind, how would you describe that structure? What is your impression of the draft as a whole, and what suggestions would you make for its organization and its supporting points relative to the main goal of examining her father's NBA contract?

B. In a small group, compare your analyses of DiGregorio's first draft, and try to reach some consensus about what she should focus on in her revision.

5e Editing your own writing

After making major and minor revisions in your writing (see 5a–b), you should turn your attention to editing. **Editing** means fine-tuning your work for a reader—adjusting sentences and words for clarity, for precise meaning and effect, and for correctness. It means identifying problems in grammar and sentence structure as well as glaring omissions or repetitions. And it means looking for consistency in style, punctuation, word usage, and tone.

Recognizing and revising such problems is not the same as proofreading, however. When you proofread a paper, you hunt for distracting or careless typographical errors such as misspelled words, transposed letters, and incorrect hyphenation or word division. Proofreading is your last chance to make sure that errors in presentation don't distract and annoy your reader.

Successful editing also means recognizing and using the conventions of specific communities. Some conventions don't vary much across communities: a spelling mistake stands out in your document regardless of its intended readers or context. Other conventions, however, may not be so rigid. For example, newspaper or magazine readers wouldn't be surprised to find only one comma in this sentence: *The suspect jumped from the car, evaded the officers and ran into the motel.* In an academic context, though, many readers would argue that a second comma ought to follow *officers*, and for evidence they might cite the well-known guides of the Modern Language Association or the American Psychological Association (see Chapters 28 and 29). Likewise, a scientist would use numerals (such as *12* or *84*) for the numbers in a lab report, while an art historian might spell out *twelve* or *eighty-four* in an interpretive paper. Many workplace communities use particular "local" conventions that you'll need to learn as you adapt your writing to those contexts.

To edit successfully, you need to read your writing with an editor's eyes, focusing hard on a text and reading carefully and slowly. You can't edit well if you're skimming a paper twenty minutes before class.

Editing for style and correctness calls for a special kind of reading, one that shifts away from content (what's being said) and toward form (how it's being said). Focus on each sentence, and scrutinize it for smaller stylistic concerns, grammar, and punctuation. Problems, inconsistencies, and errors will emerge, and you *must* fix them before your paper can be considered finished.

Often, editing requires you to keep in mind a certain concern (commas, for example, or sexist language) while you scour your entire text for specific cases. It's hard to look for too many kinds of problems at once. Sometimes you may need to read your text four, five, six, or more times, keeping in mind a different cluster of concerns for each reading.

1 Final editing for economy and style

Even after major and minor revisions have tightened the focus and eliminated inessential or repetitive sections, most papers can still profit from some final cosmetic surgery. If any part of a sentence adds little or nothing to style or meaning, eliminate it during a final check for redundancy or wordiness.

NEAR-FINAL DRAFT In actual fact, the aligned pulleys are lined up so that they are located up above the center core of the machine.

READER'S REACTION: **This seems repetitive and confusing.**

EDITED The aligned pulleys are **positioned** above the **machine's core.**

STRATEGY

Use the following questions to help you edit your draft for final trimming and styling.

- **Are my sentences reasonably easy to read?** Try reading your sentences (especially out loud) from the perspective of a reader unfamiliar with their content and purpose. Whenever you stumble over a phrase or a whole sentence, try rearranging the structure for easier reading.
- **Do any words stand out as odd or inappropriate for my purpose?** Try to choose a more appropriate word. Consider turning to a dictionary or thesaurus for help (see 46e).
- **Have I used some sentence structures too often?** Try varying sentence structures. For example, do almost all sentences begin with nouns or with a pronoun like *I*? Then try starting some sentences with prepositional phrases or subordinate clauses.
- **If I had to cut ten words from each page, which ones could I eliminate?** Cut the excess if you can do so without creating new problems in style (for example, short, choppy sentences) or meaning.

Exercise 5

In a brochure-writing assignment, Kim Francis wrote the following draft paragraph for a pamphlet describing tourist attractions and accommodations near her Wisconsin home. Read the paragraph once for meaning and then a second time for editing. During the second reading, ask some of the questions listed in the Strategy above. Then edit the paragraph to make it more effective.

After spending a day exploring the countryside, rest and relax at a quaint country inn, relaxing by the fire and sipping on some mulled wine. After spending a quiet night in a room decorated with beautiful old antiques, wake up to a country breakfast. Then after your pleasant stay at the inn, explore

```
the quaint towns and roads that have made Door County,
Wisconsin, such an attractive vacation destination for people
who like to escape and get away from it all.
```

2 Editing for grammatical problems

When you edit your writing for grammatical problems, first you need to *identify* or *recognize* a problem, and then you must *edit* your prose to fix the problem. Many writers spend too little time identifying problems and simply correct those few they spot while skimming their drafts. Don't leave it to your reader to find errors you missed.

Identifying known errors. All writers make easily identifiable mistakes while immersed in thought during the writing process. These are the easiest problems to spot because you already know what's wrong.

Read your paper slowly from start to finish but don't become immersed in the ideas. Instead, look carefully and deliberately at each paragraph, circling or marking any errors in grammar, punctuation, and sentence logic. If you can quickly correct an error along the way, do so. If you're not certain how to correct the error, wait until you've finished identifying problems; then refer to the appropriate sections in this handbook or other reference tools for advice.

"Before" and "after" passages from Jim Tollefson's newsletter article on the Endangered Species Act for his local conservancy group show his circled errors (labeled in the margins) and his edited version.

DRAFT WITH ERRORS IDENTIFIED

caps/fragment/ apostrophe Who?/comma splice

Critics of the endangered species act think it is too broad. Because some specie's may be less vital to environmental balance than others. They want to protect species selectively, however, scientists still do not know which species are more important.

EDITED

Critics of the Endangered Species Act think it is too broad because some species may be less vital to environmental balance than others. These critics want to protect species selectively. However, scientists still do not know which species are more important.

Serious errors. Here is a list of the ten errors many instructors are likely to consider quite serious because they confuse or irritate readers. Refer to the section of the text listed in parentheses for more information on identifying or correcting the error.

Fragment (37a)
Fused Sentence (38b)
Unclear Pronoun Reference (39a–b)
Double Negative (36d)
Dangling Modifier (40b)
Missing Possessive Apostrophe (50a)
Missing Punctuation Marks (48a, 48c, 48e, 48h, 48i, 49a-4, 51a)
Lack of Subject-Verb Agreement (35a–b)
Shifts in Person or Tense (41a)
Unnecessary Commas (48j)

Other areas of special concern include the following:

Comma Usage (Chapter 48)
Lack of Parallelism (Chapter 43)
Misplaced, Dangling, and Disruptive Modifiers (Chapter 40)
Mixed Sentence Structures (Chapter 42)
Problems with Verb Form and Tense (Chapter 33)
Spelling (Chapter 59)

Identifying suspected errors. Other kinds of problems that require editing may be somewhat less obvious. You may suspect that you've made an error but aren't sure. *Don't take a risk.* Check the rule or convention, and edit accordingly.

STRATEGY

- **Circle or mark all suspected problems or errors in your paper.** Then check appropriate sections in this handbook or another reference work, and edit those that are, in fact, errors. If any suspected errors are still unresolved after a thorough check, ask a teacher, editor, or knowledgeable peer or friend to help you.
- **Create an editing checklist of problems or errors that you often encounter in your writing.** Apply the checklist to each paper you write. Begin by analyzing your own papers and by giving some samples of your writing to a teacher or expert writer. Ask that person to identify *patterns* of errors in your writing, and also look for them on your own. Using this handbook, study the errors and try to identify their causes. Then create your own strategies for recognizing the errors, and turn these into a personalized editing checklist for your papers and other writing.

After editing her paper on the effects of loud music, Carrie Brehe put three more items on her editing checklist.

1. A lot—sounds like one word but is actually two. Think of an entire "lot" full of whatever. Think of the opposite of a little. From the noise paper: "Alot of teenagers have no information about how their hearing works." Search for all cases of alot.
2. Their vs. there. Sound the same. I usually write "there" for "their" when I make this mistake, but not the reverse. "Their" is possessive only, and "there" is location. From the noise paper: "Most people are not even aware that there hearing can be damaged by lawn mowers, chain saws, and even jets taking off." Search for all cases of there/their.
3. If they would have known. I say this a lot (ha!). I'm still not sure what the subjunctive means, but this problem shows up when I write "if." Correct to "if they had" or "if they were." Search for all cases of "if + would." From the noise paper: "If they would have known what the concerts were doing to their eardrums, they might have stopped going."

Identifying unknown errors. A final category of mistakes consists of those you have no idea you're making. Writing courses and tutoring services are designed to help you identify and edit such errors. Studying handbooks and reading as much professional prose as you can may help, but by far the best strategy is to work with your own writing.

Read your writing, preferably aloud. Sometimes this will help you to locate problems intuitively. Or you may recognize them because you encounter difficulty reading a passage. Circle everything you question; then use the Strategy on page 64 to check suspected errors. Add *all* previously unknown errors to your editing checklist (see above).

Ask someone to read your paper and to mark or circle any problems he or she encounters. Your reader doesn't need to be a grammarian to call attention to problems with sentences, usage, and the like. Because they're not as close to the text as you are, these readers may find problems you overlooked. (See 5f for more on collaborative editing.)

5f Collaborative editing

When you edit collaboratively, you identify and talk about specific problems in a paper with one or more "consulting readers," usually friends or peers. Your goal is not just to rid your paper of errors but to learn to identify and correct errors on your own. Whether you are the consulting reader in a group *or* the writer, use these suggestions for providing and receiving good advice.

- When someone asks you to read his or her paper for editorial feedback, be sure the paper is finished enough for this kind of work, so you don't waste time.

- Use familiar language and symbols for your comments so the writer will readily understand them. The terminology used in this handbook is generally accepted in education and business. You may need to explain your suggestions in more detail when working in public communities.
- If you're uncertain about a feature, just note your uncertainty. Let the writer use a reference source (a dictionary, a style guide, or this handbook) to identify and correct the problem.
- Avoid "taking over" the writer's draft. Identify outright errors, but don't rewrite whole sentences and paragraphs.
- If you think that a writer has been unnecessarily sloppy, hoping that you'll clean up the mess, don't spend much time working on the paper.
- Comments about style are always more helpful when they're specific. Marginal comments like "awkward," "good," or "I like this" won't always help the writer know specifically what works or doesn't work.
- If something is good or bad, explain why. But don't spend time on long explanations.
- Try to identify patterns of error in the writer's prose. If the writer repeats the same mistakes, point the repetition out.

Exercise 6

On the day your teacher returns drafts or finished papers with comments, look for any errors he or she has noted or identified. Working in groups of three or four, read each other's papers, looking for patterns of error. Compare these patterns and, as a group, try to write "rules" explaining how to fix them. In creating the rules, feel free to use your own terms and ways of explaining. Add any new items to your editing checklist.

5g Editing on the computer

Editing has its share of "quick fix" remedies. Among the most attractive are computer programs that "read" a piece of prose and then tell you how to correct or improve it. Before using or buying such a program, learn something about what it can and can't do.

1 What computer editors can do

When examining an editing program, see whether it will meet your specific needs. Use the following questions as a guide.

- Does the program identify errors in spelling, punctuation, capitalization, and usage? Does it identify incorrect sentence structure? How reliable are the identifications?
- Will the program alert you to unclear sentences, problems with subject-verb agreement or modifiers, sexist or discriminatory language, and vague expressions?
- Is it linked to a spell checker, thesaurus, dictionary, synonym finder, or other utility? Will it identify clichéd or vague expressions and commonly misused words?
- Does it allow you to design and add your own rules, tailoring the program to your editorial needs and to meet the conventions of use within your writing community? Does it reflect the expectations of a particular community, such as business readers and writers?

2 What computer editors can't do

Although they may claim to answer most of your writing problems, computerized editing programs are no match for human readers and editors. Most programs will alert you to a potential problem but leave you to identify and repair it yourself. Grammar and style checkers also take a lot of time for what they deliver, and they can check only material that has been typed into the computer. The programs provide few options for different kinds of writing or for audiences that differ in sophistication and background knowledge. Beware, therefore, of blanket pronouncements from the program. They may be inappropriate for your writing situation.

5h Proofreading

After you've made as many conscious decisions about your writing as possible and you are ready to submit it, it's time for **proofreading,** looking for errors you may have missed during the editing process. No writer produces an absolutely flawless document every single time, and one or two insignificant mistakes may have little impact, especially if the work is otherwise powerful. But as the slips accumulate, the author's credibility diminishes, and this can ruin the effectiveness of your ideas and lead to a poor assessment of your work.

Proofreading is the simplest of all the processes a paper must go through before it's finished. You submit a piece of writing to a meticulous reading. Focus consciously on every word of your document. Don't let your eyes blur; move from word to word, fixing your eyes on each word to be sure it doesn't contain transposed letters, typographical errors, and the like. Use a spell checker. Or try reading your writing out loud. Every error you identify is a prize catch that increases your credibility.

When working in public settings, it also helps to have several people proofread separately to catch as many errors as possible.

Exercise 7

Two versions of a paragraph follow—one in an unedited form, the other partly edited. Without looking at the edited version, read the unedited draft as an editor. Scrutinize the passage ruthlessly, making any corrections you wish and explaining them in a notebook. Then compare your editing with the changes made in the second paragraph. What differences do you find between your editing and the writer's editing?

UNEDITED DRAFT

At the start of her career, historian Barbara Smithey, felt forced to choose between a life of: public service vs. research. As curator of the Westville Museum of New England culture in Westville, Ct, she was passionatly devoted to preserving or restoreing old houses in disrepair and seeing to it that they were entered if they qualified into the National Register of Historical Places. At the same time, she had a kean interest in research on the town of Westville which had been settled in the early 17th-Century. She manfully seized control of all public documents on the area, that were not already protected and got them housed in the local historical archives. These included, some early notes about the Indian savages that the White men encountered when they settled the land. Also some personal diaries lady settlers kept.

EDITED DRAFT

At the start of her career, the historian Barbara Smithey~~,~~ felt forced to choose between a life of~~:~~ public service ~~vs.~~ and research. As curator of the Westville Museum of New England Culture in Westville, ~~Ct,~~ Connecticut, she was passionately devoted to preserving or restor~~e~~ing old houses in disrepair and seeing to it that they were entered (if they qualified) into the National Register of Historic~~al~~ Places. At the same time, she had a ke~~a~~en interest in research on the town of Westville, which had been settled in the early ~~17th-Century.~~ seventeenth century. She ~~manfully~~ seized control of all public documents on the area~~,~~ that were not already protected and ~~got~~ had them ~~housed~~ placed in the local historical archives. These included~~,~~ some settlers' local Native Americans, as well as

early notes about ~~the Indian savages that the White men encountered~~

of women settlers.

~~when they settled the land. Also~~ some personal diaries ~~lady settlers~~

~~kept.~~

CHAPTER 6
Paragraphs

Every time you begin a new **paragraph,** you send a signal to readers: you tell them to watch for a shift in topic, a different perspective, or a special emphasis. You make promises, too: you say that you will develop ideas and details in ways appropriate to your writing task, and that you'll link sentences and ideas in ways that make their relationships clear.

Whether you're writing a short documented essay for a history class, a business letter at work, or a grant proposal for the soccer team you coach, you need to create paragraphs with a clear *focus* (*unity*), *coherence* among sentences, and adequate *development* of ideas and content. If you fail to do these things for your readers, they may have trouble deciding what a paragraph is about, and following your reasoning from sentence to sentence, as in this example.

> The caffeine in popular beverages comes from natural sources: coffee beans (coffee), tea leaves (tea), evergreen leaves (maté), and kola nuts (colas). Tea comes from the leaves of bushes native to Asia. Maté comes from a South American shrub similar to holly. More caffeine is found in coffee or tea than in maté. Tea and maté are made in similar ways except that the water for maté is heated in a gourd. People often drink the beverage through a straw stuck into the gourd. In Paraguay, Argentina, Chile, and the southern regions of Brazil, many people find refreshment in a maté-filled gourd.
>
> READER'S REACTION: **What is the topic of this paragraph: tea and coffee? caffeine? caffeinated beverages? maté? Every time one sentence focuses on a topic, the next sentence suddenly changes direction.**

By making the relationship among and within paragraphs clear, you can help readers keep track of a line of argument or the logic of an explanation.

6a Focused paragraphs

By making a paragraph's topic, main idea, or perspective clear to your reader, and by maintaining this focus throughout, you can create a paragraph that is focused or unified. A **focused paragraph** is effective because it doesn't confuse or mislead readers by straying into unrelated or loosely related details and statements. In a **unified paragraph,** all the sentences are clearly and directly related to the main idea, as in the following selection.

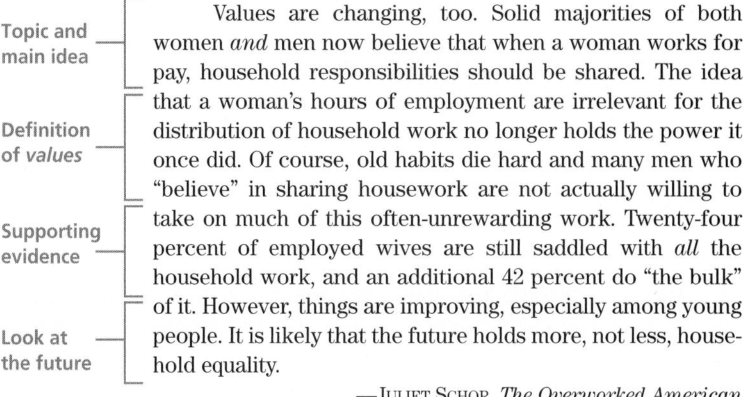

Values are changing, too. Solid majorities of both women *and* men now believe that when a woman works for pay, household responsibilities should be shared. The idea that a woman's hours of employment are irrelevant for the distribution of household work no longer holds the power it once did. Of course, old habits die hard and many men who "believe" in sharing housework are not actually willing to take on much of this often-unrewarding work. Twenty-four percent of employed wives are still saddled with *all* the household work, and an additional 42 percent do "the bulk" of it. However, things are improving, especially among young people. It is likely that the future holds more, not less, household equality.

—JULIET SCHOR, *The Overworked American*

Schor unifies this paragraph by making sure all its parts develop and support the main idea: people are beginning to view housework as a responsibility shared by women and men.

STRATEGY

Use the following questions to identify and revise any unfocused paragraphs in your draft. Ask a peer reader to apply them to your draft, or use them as a framework for self-assessment and revision.

- **What is my main point (or topic) in this paragraph?** For a paragraph lacking a central theme, decide on a focus.
- **How many different topics does this paragraph cover?** For a paragraph with many possible centers of interest, decide which one you will emphasize.
- **Have I announced my focus to readers? Where? How?** Look for sentences or phrases announcing the focus or clearly implying it. Add such statements if necessary.
- **Do statements in the paragraph elaborate on the main idea? Do details fit within the topic?** Look for material not directly related to a paragraph's focus and decide whether it undermines the unity or adds interesting variety.

6b Creating paragraph focus

To bring focus to a paragraph, you need to decide what you want the paragraph to do for readers. Do you want it to announce and explain your conclusion or recommendation? Do you want it to explain a concept or process? Do you want it to support your arguments on an issue?

One way to keep a paragraph focused as you write, and to help readers recognize that focus, is to state your topic and your main idea or perspective in a single sentence, a **topic sentence.** As you write, you can use a topic sentence as the focal point for the other sentences in a paragraph. When you revise, you can often easily improve an unfocused paragraph by adding a topic sentence, placing it in an effective position in the paragraph.

PARAGRAPHING STRATEGIES FOR THREE COMMUNITIES

ACADEMIC SETTINGS	PUBLIC SETTINGS	WORK SETTINGS
Use introductory paragraphs to announce a thesis, to indicate the method of discussing and supporting the thesis, and to summarize prior research. Use paragraphing to indicate stages in the chain of reasoning and different kinds of supporting evidence, and use clear topic sentences and transitional expressions to announce steps in reasoning and highlight evidence. Develop relatively long paragraphs presenting and discussing detailed evidence and integrating supporting or competing points of view through quotation, paraphrase, or summary.	Use introductory paragraphs to highlight a situation requiring action or to introduce a need for information or changes in policy. Use concluding paragraphs to summarize recommendations or to call for action. Develop paragraphs with examples, narratives, and causes or effects that appeal to values and emotions while providing clear support for a thesis or necessary information.	Use introductory paragraphs to outline a problem or to describe a situation requiring response from members of an organization. Use concluding paragraphs to restate the importance and implications of the proposed actions or policies. Develop problem-solution or question-and-answer paragraphs to focus readers' attention on tasks and goals.

1 Topic sentence at the beginning

When you want readers to grasp the point of a paragraph right away, state it in a topic sentence at the beginning. In the following paragraph, the author uses the topic-sentence-first strategy to comment on the art of comedy.

Topic sentence — Supporting example

When writing jokes, it's a good idea to avoid vague generalizations. Don't just talk about "fruit" when you can talk about "an apple." Strong writing creates a single image for everyone in the crowd, each person imagining the same thing. But when you say "fruit," people are either imagining several different kinds of fruit or they aren't really thinking of anything in particular, and both things can significantly reduce their emotional investment in the joke. But when you say "an apple," everyone has a clear picture, and thus a feeling.

—JAY SANKEY, "Zen and the Art of Stand-up Comedy"

2 Topic sentence plus a limiting or clarifying sentence

If you're covering a broad topic or offering much detailed information, you can give a paragraph a sharper focus by creating a **limiting** or **clarifying sentence** (or two) following the topic sentence. The added sentence tells readers which specific aspects of the topic you will discuss or clarifies your point of view.

Topic sentence
Clarifying sentence

In the Marine Corps appearance counts mightily, today as always. The corps insists that "no eccentricities of dress will be permitted" even in civilian clothes, and of course "the wearing of earrings by male Marines, under any circumstances, is prohibited." Likewise, when in uniform or out of it, Marines must obey certain specific rules about personal grooming. "No eccentricities in the manner of wearing head, facial, or body hair will be permitted." And there's official advice presumably aimed at female Marines, but nice to contemplate if aimed at all: "If worn, wigs will comply with grooming regulations."

—PAUL FUSSELL, *Uniforms*

3 Topic sentence at the end

A topic sentence at the end of a paragraph can summarize or draw conclusions from the information that comes before. This strategy can show how your perspective grows logically from the evidence, and it can tie together details with a forceful generalization.

Album after album was littered with rap songs referring to Black women as bitches, gold diggers, hos, hoodrats, chickenheads, pigeons, and so on. Music videos with rump shaking, scantily clad young Black women as stage props for rap artists soon became synonymous with rap music. Though dominated by what feminist critic bell hooks called "sexist, misogynist, patriarchal ways of thinking and believing" (*Z Magazine*, February 1994), rap lyrics simultaneously addressed every gender issue imaginable from dating, gender equality, and domestic violence to rape and sexual harrassment. Due to its role in shaping a whole generation's worldview, including our ideas about sex, love, friendship, dating, and marriage, rap music is critical to any understanding of

Topic sentence

the hip-hop generation's gender crisis. More importantly, rap music is one of the few existing arenas where the full range of gender issues facing young Black men is documented in the voices of Black youth themselves.

—BAKARI KITWANA, *The Hip-Hop Generation*

ESL ADVICE: ADJUSTING TO PARAGRAPH CONVENTIONS

In English, readers expect paragraphs to have a specific focus and often look to a topic sentence for guidance. In other languages, however, paragraph conventions can take quite different forms. For example, Hindi paragraphs need not focus on a sharply defined topic, do not require a clear topic sentence, and often contain discussion of loosely related ideas or information. Paragraphs in other languages, such as Thai, also differ from English paragraphs. Consequently, become familiar with paragraph conventions as you learn to write in a second language.

—ROBERT BICKNER and PATCHARIN PEYASANTIWONG, "Cultural Variation in Reflective Writing," and YAMUNA KACHRU, "Writers in Hindi and English," *Writing Across Languages and Cultures*, ed. Alan C. Purves (Newbury Park: Sage, 1988) 160–74, 109–37.

4 Topic sentence implied rather than stated

At times, the main point is so clear that you can rely on readers to recognize it without a topic statement. Omitting a topic statement is useful when you don't want to state a very obvious point or when an explicit statement might distract from examples and details. This strategy is also helpful when a topic clearly continues for more than one paragraph.

Whenever we went to my grandfather's house, he would lead the three of us to the closet stocked with toys, saying "I bought these especially for you" as his crystal blue eyes twinkled. I can remember playing with the toys outside on the lawn and running through the sprinkler he set up for me and my brothers on sunny days. Just when we started getting tired and hot, he would call us in for a lunch of hot dogs or tuna sandwiches with plenty of potato chips and soda pop. And there were always popsicles for dessert.

—CAREY BRAUN, College Student

READER'S REACTION: **Your grandfather seems like a person who understands children and knows how to make them feel cared for and loved.**

Exercise 1

Identify any topic sentence and clarifying or limiting sentence in the following paragraph. Analyze how the paragraph makes use of these sentences to create focus and emphasis.

Kids are in the mall not only in the passive role of shoppers—they also work there, especially as fast-food outlets infiltrate the mall's enclosure. There they learn how to hold a job and take responsibility, but still within the same value context. When *CBS Reports* went to Oak Park Mall in suburban Kansas City, Kansas, to tape part of the hour-long consideration of the mall, "After the Dream Comes True," they interviewed a teenaged girl who worked in a fast-food outlet there. In a sequence that didn't make the final program, she described the major goal of her present life, which was to perfect the curl on top of the ice-cream cones that were her store's specialty. If she could do that, she would be moved from the lowly soft-drink dispenser to the more prestigious ice-cream division, the curl on top of the status ladder at her restaurant. These are the achievements that are important at the mall.

—William Severini Kowinski, "Kids in the Mall: Growing Up Controlled"

6c Paragraph coherence

When your readers can move from sentence to sentence within a paragraph without any trouble following your train of thought or explanation, the paragraph displays **coherence.** Lack of coherence comes from abrupt changes in your topic from sentence to sentence, or from a lack of transitions or other devices to guide readers from statement to statement. A paragraph like the following one is hard for readers to understand because it offers them little guidance.

LACKS COHERENCE

Captain James Cook discovered the island of Hawaii in 1779. Mauna Kea, on Hawaii, is the tallest mountain in the Pacific. Cook might have noticed the many mountains on the island as he sailed into Kealakekua Bay. The island also has five major volcanoes. Mauna Loa, another mountain on the island, is a dormant volcano that last erupted in 1984. Kilauea is the most active volcano on earth. It continues to enlarge the land that makes up this largest island in the Hawaiian chain. The volcano sends forth lava continuously.

READER'S REACTION: This paragraph jumps from sentence to sentence without saying much about the way the ideas and details fit together. It's just hard to read and remember.

STRATEGY

Use the following questions to test your paragraphs for coherence.

- Does the paragraph highlight and repeat words naming the topic and main points?
- Do transition words alert readers to relationships between sentences?
- Do parallel words and structures highlight similar or related ideas?
- Do sentence beginnings identify a topic and stick to it?

6d Creating paragraph coherence

1 Repeating words and phrases

By repeating words and phrases that refer to your topic and main point, you keep readers aware of a paragraph's focus and link one sentence to another. Synonyms and related words can also be part of a pattern of effective repetition, as in the following paragraph.

> **"Childhood is the kingdom where nobody dies"** is a line, from the poem by Edna St. Vincent Millay, that has stuck in my mind ever since I first read it, when I was in fact **a child** and **nobody died.** Of course **people did die,** but **they** were either very old or **died** unusual **deaths, died** while rafting on the Stanislaus or loading a shotgun or doing 95 drunk: **death** was construed as either a "blessing" or an exceptional case, the dramatic instance on which **someone else's** (never **our own**) story turned. Illness, in that **kingdom** where I and **most people** I knew lingered long past **childhood,** proved self-limiting. Fever of unknown etiology signaled only the indulgence of a week in bed. Chest pains, investigated, revealed hypochondria.
>
> —JOAN DIDION, "After Henry"

2 Supplying transitions

You can use **transitional expressions,** statements, and paragraphs to alert readers to relationships among sentences and paragraphs and to highlight a paragraph's design and purpose.

Think about the possible connections among the ideas and information you are discussing; then decide which connections you wish to highlight. Draw on the following techniques to link paragraphs in ways that emphasize connections and that call attention to your line of reasoning.

- Use transitional words and phrases (see the chart on pp. 77–78)
- Announce your purpose
- Provide boundary statements
- Create transition paragraphs

Note how the use of transitions makes the following paragraph easy to read.

> Many people still consider the choice of college the most important career decision you can make. **These days, however,** graduate school is the most important choice **because** the competition for all kinds of jobs has gotten fiercer. **For example,** business positions at the entry level often go to people with MBAs and law degrees. **In addition,** many good jobs require advanced training and skills. **More-**

over, employers pay attention **not only** to the presence of an advanced degree on your résumé **but also** to the program of study **and** the quality of the school. **Therefore,** think about going to graduate school, **and** choose your school carefully.

You can use a direct or an indirect statement to announce your purpose and organization near the beginning of a new section, and to help readers anticipate the line of reasoning you will use to develop and support ideas.

DIRECT STATEMENT — The next section looks at the new generation of situation comedies that has taken over the top of the ratings chart in the last two years.

INDIRECT STATEMENT — Advertisers have developed sophisticated ways to identify the tastes, purchasing power, and needs of consumers. Each of these tactics needs to be examined in detail.

To help present detailed reasoning or information, consider opening paragraphs with a **boundary statement**—a sentence at the start of a paragraph that acts as a bridge from the paragraph before. A boundary statement begins with a reminder of material covered in the preceding paragraph (or paragraphs). It then presents the topic sentence of the paragraph to come. For example, in the following sentence the writer briefly mentions the subject he has just finished discussing and then highlights the main point of the paragraph itself.

The rise of the Sunbelt in recent years has been accompanied by **the decline of rural America.**

—BRAD EDMONDSON, "Making Yourself at Home"

In short essays, simple transitions or boundary statements generally provide adequate guidance for readers. In longer essays or complicated discussions, you may need to give readers extra guidance with one- or two-sentence transition paragraphs. Brief transition paragraphs perform the same functions as transitional expressions and statements.

TRANSITIONAL EXPRESSIONS

TIME AND SEQUENCE	next, later, after, while, meanwhile, immediately, somewhat earlier, first, second, third (firstly, secondly, thirdly), shortly, thereafter, in the future, over the next two days, concurrently, subsequently, as long as, soon, since, finally, last, at that time, as soon as
COMPARISON	likewise, similarly, also, again, in the same manner, in comparison

(continued)

TRANSITIONAL EXPRESSIONS *(continued)*

CONTRAST	in contrast, on one hand . . . on the other hand, however, although, even though, still, yet, but, nevertheless, conversely, at the same time, regardless, despite
EXAMPLES	for example, for instance, such as, specifically, thus, to illustrate, namely
CAUSE AND EFFECT	as a result, consequently, since, accordingly, if . . . then, is due to this, for this reason, as a consequence of
PLACE	next to, above, behind, beyond, near, across from, to the right, here, there, in the foreground, in the background, in between, opposite
ADDITION	and, too, moreover, in addition, besides, furthermore, next, also, finally
CONCESSION	of course, naturally, it may be the case that, granted, it is true that, certainly
CONCLUSION	in conclusion, in short, as a result, as I have demonstrated, as the data show
REPETITION	to repeat, in other words, once again, as I said earlier
SUMMARY	on the whole, to sum up, in short, to summarize, therefore

3 Using parallel structure

You can link elements within a paragraph by using **parallelism**—repeating the same grammatical structures to highlight similar or related ideas (see also 42c). Note how the parallel words and phrases in the following paragraph create coherence.

> I have a place on the West Coast **where** my relatives still farm, **where I heard** the stories of feuds and backbiting, and **where I saw** that people **survived and flourished** because fundamentally they **trusted and relied** upon one another. **A death in the family** is not just **a death in a family;** it is a **death in the community. I saw people** help each other with money, materials, labor, attention, and time. **I saw men** gather once a year, without fail, to clean the grounds of a ninety-year-old woman who had helped the community **before, during,** and **after** the war. **I saw her** remembering them with birthday cards sent to each of their children.
>
> —KESAYA E. NODA, "Growing Up Asian in America"

Exercise 2

A. In the following paragraph, increase coherence and readability by repeating words, adding transitions, using parallel structures, and making any other changes necessary.

Heart attacks have many causes. Some heart attacks occur because a blood clot closes a coronary artery. Sometimes a mass of fatty substances (plaque) has the same effect. Heart attacks with these causes are the most frequent. A spasm in an artery may also close it and prevent blood from reaching the heart. Smoking, hypertension, and diabetes can create conditions that keep blood from reaching the heart. The blood-starved tissue may die. This will cause permanent damage to the heart's ability to pump blood. A dead portion of the heart is called a myocardial infarction.

B. Copy a paragraph from one of your own essays, scrambling the order of the sentences, and then exchange scrambled paragraphs with a fellow student. Rewrite and strengthen your partner's paragraph by putting the sentences in the most effective order and revising to increase coherence among sentences.

6e Developed paragraphs

Suppose you encountered the following paragraph at a public Web site on choosing a pet. How would you react?

> Dogs and cats make wonderful pets, but certainly not trendy ones. Exotic animals of all kinds, including Vietnamese pot-bellied pigs and llamas, have begun appearing in living rooms and backyards.

You would probably respond that the paragraph has a clear main point and a potentially interesting example but seems skimpy and uninteresting. Without supporting details, the paragraph is neither informative nor convincing. **Paragraph development** provides the examples, facts, concrete details, explanatory statements, or supporting arguments that make a paragraph informative and supportive of your ideas and opinions, as in this fully developed version of the paragraph.

Topic sentence

Brief examples

> Dogs and cats make wonderful pets, but certainly not trendy ones. Exotic animals of all kinds, including Vietnamese pot-bellied pigs and llamas, have begun appearing in living rooms and backyards. About the size of beagles, the pigs are affectionate and easy to care for. Llamas require more room and care, but these gentle animals are now in demand as well—at least among people who can afford the one or two thousand dollars needed to buy one. Ferrets, Amazon parrots, pygmy goats, and dwarf rabbits have been finding places in fashionable homes as well. People who want to keep well ahead of the crowd might consider Old World chameleons or dart-poison frogs (the source of poison for blowdarts used by jungle hunters).

1 Developing paragraphs with details

The details of how you dangled from the sheer rock face when your climbing equipment failed may thrill the readers of your essay in an outdoor magazine. They'll look for long paragraphs filled with specifics. The equipment recall announcement you write for the Consumer Product Safety Commission will probably offer more compact paragraphs with relevant statistics, specific warnings, and product-identifying information. Your memo for the equipment company would probably contain several concise paragraphs, each with the precise information needed to answer key questions: How did the equipment fail? Why did it fail? How can we correct the problem?

CHECKLIST FOR DEVELOPING PARAGRAPH CONTENT

- **Examples.** Use brief, specific examples or an extended, detailed example.
- **Concrete details.** Recreate sights, sounds, tastes, smells, movements, and sensations of touch.
- **Facts and statistics.** Offer precise data from your own field research or from authoritative sources, perhaps in numerical form. Summarize the results or quote your sources. Facts and statistics are the kinds of evidence many readers consider convincing proof of generalizations and opinions. They also help readers understand complicated social and natural phenomena.
- **Summaries.** Summarize other people's opinions, conclusions, or explanations (21g). Tell how they agree with and support your conclusions. Or point out their omissions and weaknesses as a way of arguing for your own conclusions or insights.
- **Quotations.** Use statements you have gathered from field, electronic, or library research (26g) as ways of supporting your conclusions or as ways of making your discussion more dramatic and memorable.

Fully developed paragraphs give readers an in-depth picture of a subject when this is necessary for the purpose and context of the writing. Your readers will usually expect two kinds of statements in a paragraph: those presenting ideas (including your own conclusions) and those presenting information. Beyond this, however, you have many choices, depending on what you want a paragraph to do.

Rely on examples. Whether brief or extended, examples are effective strategies for paragraph development because they help you clarify difficult concepts, provide good reasons for readers to agree with your opinion, or show how widespread a phenomenon is. Extended examples can draw readers into an event and connect with their emotions. Brief examples can play important roles, especially in work and public settings where readers have little patience for long explanations but still expect you to justify your opinions and recommendations. Brief examples can be particularly effective when blended with facts and statistics, as in this excerpt from a newsletter published by the Consumer Product Safety Commission.

> All kinds of products have been included in the fast-track recalls. For example, a major manufacturer recently recalled tens of thousands of humidifiers that could potentially overheat or catch fire. A leading manufacturer of children's products recalled tens of thousands of baby monitors that could smoke and flame. A prominent clothing retailer recalled more than 100,000 children's jackets with zipper pulls containing unacceptable levels of lead. A well-known company recalled tens of thousands of gas grills because a defective hose could leak gas or cause fires.
>
> —"Fast-Track Recalls," *Consumer Product Safety Review*

Interpret for your readers. When you use examples, details, facts, and statistics to develop a paragraph, you can make them more persuasive and easier to understand by providing interpretive statements of your own to link them to the paragraph's main point.

Interpretive statement

> Breakfast cereals can differ radically in serving size even though most cereal boxes define a single serving in the same way, as a one-ounce portion. A one-ounce serving of Cheerios is $1^1/_4$ cup, for example, while a one-ounce serving of Quaker 100% Natural Cereal is $^1/_4$ cup. Weight measurements can disguise the differences between products; measurement by volume reveals the contrasts. For dieters, volume can be as important a measure as the number of calories per serving because the volume indicates how much cereal you will have to appease your appetite: two bites or a bowlful.
>
> —Sara Brilliant, College Student

Exercise 3

First, examine the paragraph in Exercise 2A and identify the various strategies of development used by the writer. Which seem particularly effective, and why? Which, if any, seem ineffective?

Next, for each of the following topic sentences, explain which kind or kinds of supporting information (examples, concrete details, facts and statistics, or supporting statements) you believe would create the most effective paragraph.

1. The fall promotional campaign increased sales of our October and November issues.

2. Upgrading our computer software would result in more efficient handling of our customer accounts.
3. Increased funding would enable us to extend our after-school basketball program for preteen boys and girls.
4. Should our budget surplus be used to fund additional hours at the senior center or to assist meal-delivery programs for the homebound?

---

2 Creating paragraph structures

How will you arrange the content of your paragraphs? **General patterns of development** such as narration, comparison, and cause and effect offer you ways to develop a paragraph's content as well as its arrangement. **Specific patterns of development** reflect the outlook of readers and writers in specific settings (academic, public, or work) on useful ways to develop paragraphs.

General patterns of development. Each of the general patterns enables you to accomplish a different writing task, as the following chart indicates.

PATTERNS FOR PARAGRAPH DEVELOPMENT

TASK	DEVELOPMENT STRATEGY
Tell a story; recreate events; present an anecdote	Narrating
Provide detail of a scene or object; portray someone's character; evoke a feeling	Describing
Explore similarities or differences; evaluate alternatives	Comparing and contrasting
Provide directions; explain the operation of a mechanism, procedure, or natural process	Explaining a process
Separate a subject into parts; explore the relationships among parts	Dividing
Sort things or people into groups; explain the relationships among the groups	Classifying
Explain the meaning of a term or concept; explore and illustrate the meaning of a complicated concept or phenomenon	Defining
Consider why something happened or might happen; explore possible causes and consequences	Analyzing causes and effects

Narration presents events in the past, the present, or even the imagined future. In academic writing, for example, narratives can provide historical background, and in public settings narratives can help readers understand how an issue or disagreement came about. In work settings, narratives can provide information necessary for understanding a problem or challenge, but their focus generally must be limited to details relevant to the current situation.

Description helps you create images of a place or object (often using a spatial organization), sketch a person's character, or evoke feelings. In a technical or business report, however, description can convey important details of a product or physical setting.

You can use paragraphs built around **comparing** and **contrasting** to evaluate alternative policies or products. In arranging comparison paragraphs, you can employ a **point-by-point organization,** examining each comparable feature for first one subject and then the next.

Topic sentence — But biology has a funny way of confounding expectations. Rather than disappear, the evidence for innate sexual Feature 1 — differences only began to mount. In medicine, researchers Feature 2 — documented that heart disease strikes men at a younger age than it does women and that women have a more moderate Feature 3 — physiological response to stress. Researchers found Feature 4 — subtle neurological differences between the sexes both in the brain's structure and in its functioning. In addition, another generation of parents discovered that, despite their best efforts to give baseballs to their daughters and sewing kits to their sons, Feature 5 — girls still flocked to dollhouses while boys clambered into tree forts. Perhaps nature is more important than nurture after all.

—CHRISTINE GORMAN, "Sizing Up the Sexes"

Or you can use a **subject-by-subject organization,** considering each subject in its entirety, as in the next example.

For everyone, home is a place to be offstage. But Topic sentence — the comfort of home can have opposite and incompatible meanings for women and men. Subject 1 — For many men, the comfort of home means freedom from having to prove themselves and impress through verbal display. At last, they are in a situation where talk is not required. They are free to remain silent. But Subject 2 — for women, home is a place where they are free to talk, and where they feel the greatest need for talk, with those they are closest to. For them, the comfort of home means the freedom to talk without worrying about how their talk will be judged.

—DEBORAH TANNEN, "Put Down That Paper and Talk to Me!"

To explain a **process**, you may need to provide readers with a paragraph of **directions** or an **explanation** of how a mechanism or procedure works. You can also divide or classify. When you divide a subject, you split it into parts. A **division** paragraph offers you a chance to explain a subject in detail and to highlight the relationship of its parts. When you classify, you sort several subjects into groups based on their similarities. A **classification** paragraph is an opportunity for you to identify the groups and explore similarities within them or the differences and relationships among them.

When you need to introduce a term or concept to your readers, you may need to write just a phrase or sentence to define it, or you may need to create a **definition** paragraph if the term is complicated.

> When you hear the word crystal, many people think of a mineral dug from the ground. But the lead crystal used to make beautiful plates, glasses, and vases does not come from this source. The crystal in these objects—artworks, actually—is glass with a high lead content. The glass is made from a mixture of sand and other ingredients like potash (potassium) or soda that help the mixture melt. The various minerals also affect the color and clarity of the glass. Lead crystal must contain at least 30 percent to 35 percent lead oxide (by weight) in its ingredients. The resulting material is easier for artists to work with as they grind intricate facets into the surface to create designs that sparkle and intrigue like a finely cut diamond.
>
> —Andrea Herrmann, College Student

When you wish to explain why something has occurred, you might focus a paragraph on causes; to explore consequences, you might focus on effects. Or you might combine them, to create a **cause-effect** paragraph.

Problem-solution pattern. In longer business reports, writers often devote separate paragraphs to problems and recommendations. In shorter documents such as letters and memos, however, writers often turn to **problem-solution** paragraphs like the following, from a memo.

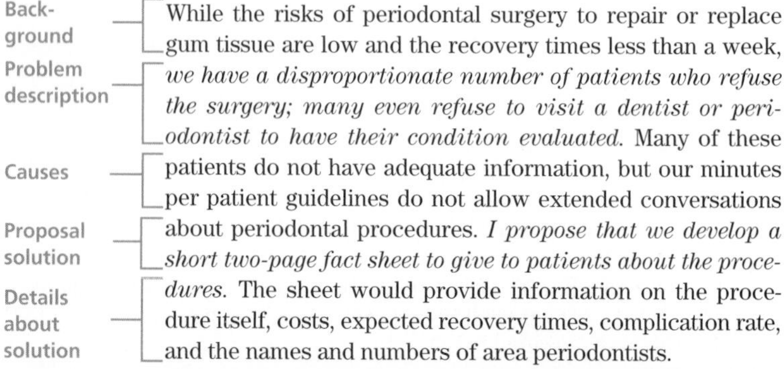

While the risks of periodontal surgery to repair or replace gum tissue are low and the recovery times less than a week, *we have a disproportionate number of patients who refuse the surgery; many even refuse to visit a dentist or periodontist to have their condition evaluated.* Many of these patients do not have adequate information, but our minutes per patient guidelines do not allow extended conversations about periodontal procedures. *I propose that we develop a short two-page fact sheet to give to patients about the procedures.* The sheet would provide information on the procedure itself, costs, expected recovery times, complication rate, and the names and numbers of area periodontists.

Question-and-answer pattern. Another paragraph structure that addresses problems and recommendatons is the **question-and-answer** pattern. This pattern is particularly useful in public settings because the question segment allows writers to raise concerns they share with readers while the answer segment allows writers to explore possible policies or recommendations for dealing with the concerns. The following paragraph from a Web site on athletic nutrition <www.athleticnutrition.com/Stjohns.html> uses the question-and-answer pattern to share research relating the use of St. John's Wort, an herbal antidepressant, to athletic workouts.

> What research has been done on St. John's Wort?
>
> The active derivative in St. John's Wort is called hypericin. This active ingredient . . . has been shown to increase the half-life of certain neurotransmitters and thus, by extending the time that these neurotransmitters are in the brain, extend and enhance their positive effects. Most studies done on St. John's Wort have explored its possible antidepressant activity. These double-blind studies indicate that indeed, St. John's Wort does possess these antidepressant capabilities and can stave off mild depression. Finally, some studies have shown that St. John's Wort may inhibit cortisol secretion, as well as possibly block the release of other catabolic hormones. This is of particular significance to weight-training athletes as this can lead to better gains and increased strength and size.

Summary-and-statement pattern. Paragraphs in public discourse often begin by stating or summarizing facts or information (such as statistics, quotations, events, or studies) and then moving into interpretation, critique, or application of information; a statement of need; or a plan or request. This is especially true of the first paragraph of a public document, such as this grant application.

> Recent research in gerontology suggests that nursing home residents benefit from regular contact with animals. Such benefits include enhanced motor skills, increased interest in physical activities such as walking or dancing, decreased loneliness and stress, and increased appetite. Despite these benefits, no nursing homes in the tri-county area have made "therapeutic animal" programs available to their residents. In the hope of putting our facility at the forefront of senior care in this area, I am requesting $300 to purchase a therapy dog from the local organization Paws with a Cause.

Exercise 4

A. Choose one of the following pairs of topics. Drawing on your own knowledge, develop each topic into a paragraph, using the pattern of development indicated in brackets.

1. A paragraph about finding a part-time or summer job [process] and a paragraph on an unusual or memorable person [description or narration]
2. A paragraph exploring different outlooks on the relationships of parents and children [comparison-contrast] and a paragraph providing advice about dealing with a difficulty in parent-child relationships [question and answer]
3. A paragraph identifying the differences between educational requirements, expected income, and working conditions for two jobs (such as restaurant manager and doctor, or teacher and chemical engineer) [comparison-contrast] and a paragraph exploring a common work or college problem and offering possible solutions [problem-solution]
4. A paragraph identifying the reasons some students do well (or poorly) on tests [cause-effect] and a paragraph describing a good way to study for tests [process]
5. A paragraph exploring different views people hold about taking buses and driving cars [subject-by-subject comparison] and a paragraph identifying differences between educational requirements, expected income, and working conditions for two jobs [point-by-point comparison]

B. Working in a group, identify the patterns of development in the following paragraph. There may be a single dominant pattern or more than one. Explain how each pattern or combination is used.

None of the foreign geologists had ever encountered anything quite like the disaster at Lake Nyos. Our earliest hypotheses seemed to be almost as numerous as the scientific teams present. Some workers, impressed by the accounts of survivors who reported smelling rotten eggs or gunpowder and hearing explosions, were convinced that a volcanic eruption beneath the lake had released sulfurous gases. Others, including me, suspected that the gas had come from within the sediments on the lake bed. Eventually, though, geological and chemical investigations made it obvious that the lake had released carbon dioxide from within its own waters—independent apparently of any other process. Like an enormous bottle of soda water, it belched and fizzed gas from its depths.

—Samuel J. Preeth, "Incident at Lake Nyos"

6f Introductory and concluding paragraphs

The paragraphing strategies you use to divide the body of an essay or report into parts don't work for beginnings or conclusions. For these you need some special-purpose paragraphs.

1 Creating introductory paragraphs

In the opening paragraphs of an essay, report, or public document, you create a relationship with your readers, inviting them to learn about a subject, explore ideas, address a problem, or examine a line of argument. Examples of different types of introductory paragraphs follow the chart.

TWELVE WAYS TO DEVELOP AN EFFECTIVE INTRODUCTORY PARAGRAPH

PROVIDE BACKGROUND

Provide background information on a topic or problem; present an issue in context; give the history of the subject.

TELL A STORY

Open with a brief anecdote or story.

OUTLINE A PROBLEM

Outline a problem, danger, or challenge.

EXPLAIN AN ISSUE

Present the different sides of an issue, along with any particularly well-known or controversial events relevant to the topic.

PRESENT A SITUATION

Describe a situation, a set of relationships, or recent events that require some response from readers or an organization to which they belong.

OFFER A DEFINITION

Define an important concept or term that will recur throughout the piece.

ASK A QUESTION

Present provocative questions or opinions that require further discussion.

USE AN EXTENDED EXAMPLE

Start with an extended example related to the topic and main idea.

PRESENT A QUOTATION

Quote from an authority or from someone whose opinion leads into the topic or highlights key ideas.

MAKE A COMPARISON

Highlight the importance of a topic or issue by comparing it to another situation, historical period, subject, or issue; offer an intriguing analogy.

PROVIDE STATISTICS

Supply facts and statistics that introduce the topic or that help define an important issue or problem.

DESCRIBE A MYSTERY

Present a mysterious or interesting phenomenon worth exploring or explaining.

ANECDOTE

It was advertised as the biggest non-nuclear explosion in Nevada history. On October 27, 1993, Steve Wynn, the State's official "god of hospitality," flashed his trademark smile and pushed the detonator button. As 200,000 Las Vegans cheered, the 18-story Dunes sign, once the tallest neon structure in the world, crumbled to the desert floor.

—MIKE DAVIS, "House of Cards"

Davis introduces the environmental threat posed by Las Vegas culture.

DEFINITION

It used to be that a diner was a lowly place to eat. It was known as a greasy spoon, a hash house, or—in trucker lingo—a choke and puke. Diners were where the city's fallen angels went for a cup of mud (coffee) and a sinker (a doughnut) beneath fluorescent lights; where night hawks and wandering hoboes whiled away the wee hours. As for the food at diners, it was strictly for the crude of palate—heavy on the starch, grease, and gristle.

—JANE STERN and MICHAEL STERN, *Roadfood*

The Sterns are about to review a different kind of diner: clean, with good food and more fashionable customers.

PROBLEM

A candle-lit Christmas tree at Grandmother's house may be a thing of the past, but fire hazards still loom in American homes, ready to turn this season's joy into holiday tragedy.

—"Fire Safety Tips for a Safe Holiday Season,"
<www.sema.state.mo.us/firexmas.htm>

2 Creating concluding paragraphs

Paragraphs that conclude essays should generally remind readers of key ideas and encourage them to think about information or proposals you have presented. The following paragraph illustrates one strategy used in concluding paragraphs.

SUMMARY OF MAIN POINTS

So if it's any consolation to those of us who just don't manage to fit enough sleep into our packed days, being chronically tired probably won't do us any permanent harm. And if things get desperate enough, we just might have to schedule a nap somewhere on our busy calendars.

—DANIEL GOLEMAN, "Too Little, Too Late"

EIGHT WAYS TO DEVELOP AN EFFECTIVE CONCLUDING PARAGRAPH

SUMMARIZE MAIN POINTS

Review the main points briefly; a detailed summary will seem repetitive.

RESTATE THE THESIS

Put the thesis in different words to drive home the essay's main point.

RECOMMEND ACTIONS OR SOLUTIONS

Repeat, for emphasis, the specific solutions, policies, recommendations, or actions proposed in the text, perhaps summarizing them in a list.

PREDICT FUTURE EVENTS OR SPECULATE

Look at relatively clear consequences, not those requiring explanation; keep speculations interesting but not so provocative that they require extensive discussion.

USE A QUOTATION

Provide a quotation that makes key ideas memorable or supports your conclusions.

OFFER A STRIKING EXAMPLE, ANECDOTE, OR IMAGE

Supply a mental picture or brief narrative to reinforce an essay's message.

ECHO THE INTRODUCTION

Use this echo to create a sense of completion.

RESTATE IMPLICATIONS

Review the implications of actions or policies discussed in the text.

Exercise 5

A. Revise the following concluding paragraph to make it more effective.

I probably have left out some of the arguments for and against gun control, though I think I have covered the main ones. The point I really want to stress most is that gun control is a difficult question. Simple proposals such as banning all handguns or getting rid of all regulations won't work. We need new ideas that balance the rights of gun owners with the right to be free from violence and crime. Though I have not explained it in detail, we probably need a program like the national registration and education system that has been recently proposed. And we certainly need to do something about the many handguns readily available to teenagers.

B. Have each of the members of a writing group bring in a popular magazine containing relatively long articles. As a group, examine the articles and choose three openings and three conclusions that you consider successful. Identify the strategies used in each.

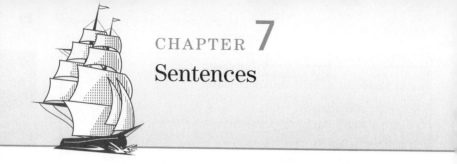

CHAPTER 7
Sentences

Most people would find the following sentences hard to read and understand.

> Our ski club president did not, because he was embarrassed by his lack of advanced skiing experience, sign us up for the University Ski Clubs Association trip to Utah.
>
> It is suggested that employee work cooperation encouragement be used for product quality improvement.

You can make sentences like these clearer and easier to read with some simple revision strategies.

SIMPLE AND DIRECT: Because he was embarrassed by his lack of advanced skiing experience, our ski club president did not sign us up for the University Ski Clubs Association trip to Utah.

CLEAR: We will try to improve the quality of our products by encouraging employees to work cooperatively.

But don't just create sentences that are clear and direct. You can also use a number of strategies to create appropriate emphasis and pleasing variety, and to meet the demands of different writing situations: academic, public, and work, as shown in the chart on page 91.

7a Clear sentences

Generally, the clearest sentences answer the question "Who does what (to whom)?"

CLEAR: The research team [subject; Who?] investigated [verb; does what?] seizure disorders [object; to whom?] in infants.

CLEAR: The seizures [subject; Who?] often become [verb; does what?] harmful.

SENTENCE STRATEGIES FOR THREE COMMUNITIES OF READERS

ACADEMIC SETTINGS	PUBLIC SETTINGS	WORK SETTINGS
Use direct, clear sentences for statement of thesis or conclusions and for summaries of others' research. Use emphatic sentence patterns to highlight relationships among ideas and supporting information. Consider using *I* or *we*. Avoid excessive nominalization and use of passive voice. Use summative and resumptive modifiers.	Use direct, clear sentences to present key ideas, recommendations, information, or proposed actions. Use clear and specific verbs. Prefer active to passive voice. Limit use of nominalizations. Use sentence variety and emphasis to keep an audience attentive and involved.	Use direct sentences with significant subjects and specific verbs, especially when discussing problems, solutions, or key ideas. Consider using *I*, *we*, and *you* frequently to establish direct contact with readers. Prefer active to passive voice. Limit use of nominalizations, noun strings, and expletive structures.

Many sentences in good writing are more complicated than those that move directly from subject to verb (to object), yet you can still make them clear by helping readers to answer the question "Who does what (to whom)?"

1 Use significant subjects

Sentences with subjects that name important ideas, people, topics, things, or events are generally easy for readers to understand. You can create sentences with significant subjects by asking, as you write, "What (or whom) am I talking about in this sentence?" and "Is this the subject I want to emphasize?" You can also use these questions to identify and revise sentences whose subjects are not significant. Consider this sentence from an essay titled "Should You Try to Get a Tan?"

UNFOCUSED — The greatest risk comes from exposure to a tanning machine as well as the sun because both of them can damage the skin.

READER'S REACTION: I thought this essay was about the dangers posed by sunbathing and tanning salons. Why are these subjects buried in the middle of the sentence?

POSSIBLE REVISION — Either **the sun or a tanning machine** can damage the skin, and the greatest risk comes from exposure to **both** of them.

2 Avoid unnecessary nominalizations

When you create a noun from another kind of word, the result is a **nominalization.** A verb like *complete* can become a noun like *completion;*

an adjective like *happy* turns into a noun like *happiness*. Some nominalizations play important roles in effective sentences, often naming ideas and issues essential to a discussion; others act as stumbling blocks for readers. Used inappropriately, nominalizations may obscure important information or lead you to omit it entirely.

USEFUL NOMINALIZATION **Distractions** like television, the VCR, and electric lights (for reading or conversing) keep us up at night, robbing us of the hours of sleep previous generations enjoyed.

Distractions, a nominalization, comes from *distract,* a verb.

VAGUE Dissatisfaction among employees often leads to shoddiness in products.

Nominalizations created from adjectives may lead to vague statements, as is the case with *dissatisfaction* and *shoddiness* in this sentence.

REVISED Dissatisfied employees often make shoddy products.

The new verb, *make,* specifies the action more clearly.

STRATEGY

As you write or as you review a draft, pay special attention to nominalizations that

- Draw readers' attention away from a sentence's proper focus
- Lead to vague sentence subjects or objects
- Cause you to leave important information out of a sentence

Revise sentences with these nominalization problems by making sure every sentence indicates clearly who did what (to whom). To do this, replace an inappropriate nominalization with a word indicating a clear and significant subject (or object), and name the sentence's action (did what?) in the verb.

COMMON NOMINALIZATIONS

Spotting nominalizations can be difficult at first, but you can quickly turn this search into a useful habit. Words ending in *-tion, -ence, -ance, -ing,* and *-ness* are often nominalizations. Here is a list of some common nominalizations to watch for.

NOUN	VERB	ADJECTIVE
analysis	analyze	
appropriateness		appropriate
beginning	begin	

NOUN	VERB	ADJECTIVE
calculation	calculate	
comparison	compare	
convenience		convenient
delivery	deliver	
denial	deny	
guidance	guide	
investigation	investigate	
opening	open	
openness		open
preference	prefer	
solution	solve	
suggestion	suggest	

3 Use *I, we,* and *you* as subjects

Although *I*, we, and *you* are often inappropriate in academic and professional writing, there are many settings in which these pronouns can act as clear subjects in effective sentences. Workplace documents such as reports, proposals, and memos; writings in the public sphere, such as election campaign materials, posters, reports, petitions, and magazine articles; and even an occasional academic text—all of these can benefit from careful use of *I*, *we*, and *you*.

Using *I*. When you are the subject of an essay, when you are speaking directly to readers, or when you are reporting on your own investigations or conclusions, *I* is an appropriate subject.

> In designing the survey, **I** avoided questions likely to embarrass respondents.

On the other hand, adding statements like *I think* and *I feel* when you are already clearly stating your point of view makes your writing more wordy but not more effective.

Using *we*. *We* is appropriate when you use it to report the actions of a group or to discuss experiences you as a writer share with most readers.

> **We** [North Americans] consume a large portion of the world's resources.

Using *you*. *You* is appropriate when used to mean "you, the reader." Consider using *people*, *individuals*, or a similar word if your reader will incorrectly assume you are referring to him or her and not to people in general.

APPROPRIATE Before asking a large number of people to complete the survey, **you** should test it on a few individuals to identify any major flaws in the design.

INAPPROPRIATE According to an article in *Rolling Stone*, **you** were less drawn to the 1960s British rock invasion if **you** lived in the Midwest than if **you** lived on the East or West Coast.

READER'S REACTION: I was born in 1990. Is the author writing to my parents?

REVISED According to an article in *Rolling Stone*, **people** were less drawn to the 1960s British rock invasion if **they** lived in the Midwest than if **they** lived on the East or West Coast.

4 Be careful with strings of nouns

In a **noun string,** one noun modifies another.

NOUN	NOUN	NOUN
hip	joint	replacement
computer	network	server

Or nouns plus adjectives modify other nouns.

ADJECTIVE	NOUN	NOUN	NOUN
triple	bypass	heart	surgery
preliminary	digital	array	radar

Familiar noun strings can help you create concise yet clear sentences. Unfamiliar noun strings, however, can make sentences hard to understand. Readers may have trouble deciding which noun represents the focal point.

CONFUSING The team did a ceramic valve lining design flaw analysis.

READER'S REACTION: Did the team analyze flaws or use a special procedure called flaw analysis? Did they study ceramic valves or valve linings made of ceramic material?

One solution is to turn the key word in a string (usually the last noun) into a verb. Then form the other nouns into prepositional phrases.

REVISED The team **analyzed** flaws **in** the lining design **for** ceramic valves.

Another strategy involves turning one noun into the subject.

REVISED **Flaws** in the lining design for ceramic valves were analyzed by the team.

This version highlights the subject being analyzed.

Exercise 1

Revise the following sentences to create clear subjects and make the sentences easier to understand.

EXAMPLE

We expect ~~Our expectation is that~~ athletic shoes to ~~will~~ look good as well as feel comfortable.

1. Our expectation is that our elected officials will look like the populations of people they represent.
2. Fifty years ago, election of only one gender of people, male, and of only one race, white, was possible.
3. Today, politicians boast of every level of our government's racial and gender diversity.
4. Choice between candidates is on the basis of their stand on the issues, their media savvy, and their ability to communicate.
5. Choice of candidate is not always on the basis of race, in other words.

5 Use clear and specific verbs

Clear, specific verbs can make sentences forceful and easy to understand. Overuse of the verb *be* (*is*, *are*, *was*, *were*, *will be*) can lead to weak sentences. Always consider replacing forms of *be* with more forceful verbs.

WEAK Our agency is responsible for all aspects of disaster relief.

STRONGER Our agency **plans, funds, delivers,** and **monitors** disaster relief.

Look for predicate nouns (nominalizations) you can turn into clear, specific verbs (see 7a-2). Eliminate general verbs (*do*, *give*, *have*, *get*, *provide*, *shape*, *make*) linked to nouns by turning the nouns into verbs.

WEAK Our company **has done a study** of the new design project and **will provide funding** for it.

STRONGER Our company **has studied** the new design project and **will fund** it.

6 Keep subjects and verbs clearly related

Clear subjects and verbs play key roles in effective sentences. When subject and verb are separated by long phrases, readers may have trouble identifying these elements and may find the sentence difficult to understand.

> The veterinary association **in response to concern about the costly facilities required by new guidelines for animal care and disposal of medical waste** has created a low-cost loan program for its members.

Separating the parts of a verb phrase (see 32a-3) with a long phrase or other group of words can also make sentences difficult to read.

> Manufacturing companies **can** if they wish to improve product quality, cost, and reliability, **contact** the university's Design for Assembly program.

7b Direct sentences

A direct sentence structure moves from subject to verb (to object). An indirect sentence structure uses an **expletive construction** (*there is*, *there are*, or *it is*) to control the arrangement of the words. Much of the time, expletive constructions make your sentences wordy and hard to understand.

EXPLETIVE It is important for us to increase community awareness of our services in order to reach target audiences.

REVISED We should increase community awareness of our services to reach target audiences.

An expletive construction may also enable you to withhold information about the "doer," the person or thing responsible for an action. You need to decide whether this is appropriate, given your context and purpose, or whether you are omitting details important to your readers.

DOER NOT NAMED There was considerable debate over whether to build a new library or renovate the old one.

DOER NAMED Members of the fund-raising committee debated whether to build a new library or renovate the old one.

MORE SPECIFIC Veit, Gould, and Clifford, the three members in charge of studying the issue, debated whether to build a new library or renovate the old one.

You can sometimes use expletive constructions to good effect. By waiting until late in a sentence to name the subject, you can create suspense and surprise. And you can use expletives to introduce topics that will be taken up in following sentences. (See 7d-3.) A sentence with an expletive construction may also be the clearest and most precise way to make a statement.

> Historians used to believe that a sudden invasion by shepherding tribes caused major changes in the region's culture. Now, however, **there is** new archaeological evidence that the "invasion" was actually a gradual resettling that took about a century.

ESL ADVICE: *THERE IS* AND *THERE ARE*

Academic writing in English often contains sentences beginning *there is* or *there are*. Sometimes the strategy is appropriate; often, however, the sentences are hard to write and read. Whenever you can, avoid opening sentences with these words so that your sentences are easier to write and read.

Exercise 2

A. Rewrite the following sentences, using clear verbs to make them easy to understand.

EXAMPLE

induces stress
Negotiating ~~is a stress-inducing experience~~ for many people in business.

1. Negotiating, regarded by many experts as an important element in successful business careers, especially on the executive level, is not offered as a course at many colleges.
2. Included among the programs offered by our consulting company is a course in professional negotiation. It is considered to be very useful.
3. We also give demonstrations of how to prepare effective proposals, counter-offers, and other negotiation-related documents.
4. Our consultants can, if a company wishes, provide training for both small and large groups.
5. It is generally agreed that the training program is a confidence builder for many people.

B. Work with several other writers to turn the sentences in Exercise 2A into a clear, forceful paragraph that a consulting company might include in a pamphlet advertising its services. Add material if necessary to produce an effective paragraph, and combine or rearrange sentences as appropriate.

7c Emphatic sentences

You want your readers to notice the most important ideas and information in a sentence. In drafting and revising, you can highlight this material by placing it at the beginning or end of a sentence, by presenting it in a special sentence pattern, or by using the passive voice in a careful manner.

1 Use sentence beginnings and endings

A reader's attention gravitates toward sentence beginnings and endings. Shift material you wish to emphasize to a sentence's opening or closing.

UNEMPHATIC Gases produced during the cheese-making process by the "eye former," a bacterium, create the holes in Swiss cheese.

REVISED **The "eyes,"** or the holes in Swiss cheese, are created during the cheese-making process by gases produced by a bacterium, **the "eye former."**

Words at the beginning and end emphasize the unusual names. The verb shifts from active to passive voice (see 7c-3).

REVISED **Called "eyes" and produced by gases from a bacterium called the "eye former,"** the holes in Swiss cheese are created during the cheese-making process.

Phrases at the beginning emphasize the names.

2 Create emphatic sentence patterns

Inverted sentence order, climactic order, periodic sentences, and cumulative sentences—which you've seen many times in your reading—all offer ways to create emphasis.

Inversion. By inverting the normal subject-verb-object/complement word order, you can shift the focus of a sentence. **Inverted sentence order** often calls attention to the element you have moved to the initial position.

INVERTED **From the darkness near the rear of the auditorium thundered the director's voice** with criticisms of our acting.

NORMAL **The director's voice thundered** from the darkness near the rear of the auditorium with criticisms of our acting.

Because inversion creates emphasis in part by disrupting a reader's expectations for sentence order, overuse of it or other exotic sentence arrangements will confuse or irritate readers.

Climactic order. Using **climactic sentence order**—in which elements build to a climax—can create powerful emphasis, especially on the last item in a series.

What every truly modern home has, she said, is a dishwasher, a gas grill, a Jacuzzi, **and a divorce.**

Periodic sentences. A **periodic sentence** piles up phrases, clauses, and words at the beginning, delaying the main clause of the sentence. The suspense casts a spotlight on the main clause.

Because she knows that inspired designs often spring from hard work, because she loves perfection yet fears failure, and because she believes that risk-taking does not eliminate attention to detail, Jennifer is working eighteen hours a day on her fall clothing collection.

The risk, of course, lies in delaying so long that the reader loses track of the meaning, as in the following example.

CONFUSING
Having begun the business as much to escape from boredom as to make a profit, and also suffering from a lack of skill in accounting and an unwillingness to listen to the good advice of the professionals they hired to review the management and recordkeeping procedures that were causing dissension among employees, Sheila and Stefan decided to declare bankruptcy.

Cumulative sentences. To build a **cumulative sentence,** you start with the main clause, then add details and statements in the form of modifying phrases, clauses, and words. The main clause provides a firm base to which you can add details and ideas, bit by bit.

A cumulative sentence allows you first to emphasize the main clause, then the successive words, phrases, and clauses that work cumulatively to build a detailed picture, an intricate explanation, or a cluster of ideas and information.

Main clause	Varna stumbled down the stairs,
Details	the flowerpot falling from her grip,
Details	spilling dirt into the air,
Details	shattering on the linoleum floor just seconds before she landed among the shards of pottery and fragments of geranium,
Details	the loud thud bringing everyone in the house to attention.

3 Use the passive voice with care

When a sentence's verb is in the active voice (see 33e), the doer (or agent) is also the subject of the sentence.

doer action goal
The outfielder caught the towering fly ball.
subject verb object

When you choose the **passive voice** for the verb form, you turn the sentence's goal into the subject and make naming the doer optional.

goal action [doer]
The towering fly ball was caught [by the outfielder].
subject verb [prepositional phrase]

Using the passive voice, you de-emphasize the doer by placing it in a prepositional phrase or by dropping it altogether (see 33e). In addition, you create sentences that are generally wordier than corresponding versions in the active voice. Note how emphasis and length differ in active and passive versions of the following sentence.

doer (subject)
ACTIVE VOICE **The Centers for Disease Control** interviewed three thousand people affected by the toxin.

subject
PASSIVE VOICE **Three thousand people** affected by the toxin were interviewed by **the Centers for Disease Control.**
doer

If you wish to emphasize the *doer*, use the active voice. If you wish to draw readers' attention to the goal or outcome of an action rather than its doer, consider using the passive voice.

ACTIVE **Poorly trained contract workers** caused the explosion and fire at the refinery.
Subject emphasizes cause.

PASSIVE **The explosion and fire** at the refinery were caused by poorly trained contract workers.
Subject emphasizes result.

You can also use the passive voice to highlight significant elements in a discussion.

Refineries are potentially dangerous workplaces. **Most accidents** can be prevented, however, by careful training of workers.
Passive voice in the second sentence keeps attention on the dangers.

You can choose whether or not to name the doer in a sentence written in the passive voice.

Requirements for the term paper were distributed in all sections of the psychology course [by the individual instructors].

When the doer is unknown, unimportant, or obvious, you can appropriately omit it.

> Federal income tax forms will be mailed on January 1.
> By the IRS, of course.

But when leaving out the doer would omit important information or mislead readers, include it.

> Consumers were not informed of their right to sue for damages.
> The sentence doesn't say who withheld the information.

Exercise 3

A. Revise the following sentences to eliminate passive voice.

EXAMPLE

Grocery stores sell many
~~Many~~ different kinds of ice cream ~~are sold by grocery stores~~.

1. The superpremium ice cream brands are chosen by many people.
2. More butterfat and less air is contained in superpremium ice cream than in regular ice cream.
3. The high fat content ought to be considered before the ice cream is purchased.
4. The rich, tasty ice creams are being challenged by the new frozen dessert products.
5. Frozen yogurts with candy and nuts mixed in have been heavily promoted.

B. Examine the following passage carefully and identify the strategies the author uses to create emphasis. Then share your responses.

There was a time when people who wanted to keep the peace and keep the crockery intact held to a strict dinner-table rule: Never argue about politics or religion. I don't know how well it worked in American dining rooms, but it worked pretty well in our schools. We dealt with religion by not arguing about it.

Children who came out of diverse homes might carve up the turf of their neighborhood and turn the playgrounds into a religious battlefield, but the public classroom was common ground. Intolerance wasn't tolerated.

In place of teaching one religion or another, the schools held to a common denominator of values. It was, in part, the notion of Horace Mann, the nineteenth-century father of the public-school system. He believed that the way to avoid religious conflicts was to extract what all religions agree upon and allow this "non-religious" belief system into schools.

I wonder what Mann would think of that experiment now. Was it naive or sophisticated? Was it a successful or a failed attempt to avoid conflict in a pluralistic society?

—ELLEN GOODMAN, "Religion in the Textbooks"

Working with a group of fellow writers, try to agree on answers to these questions about the Goodman passage: Which sentence strategies add to the effectiveness of the passage, and why? Which, if any, detract from its effectiveness?

7d Revising for variety

Too many sentences of similar length, type, and structure can create unemphatic writing that bores readers. Variety helps. Many of the strategies that create emphasis (see 7c) can also create variety, and the two qualities often go together. This is especially important in public contexts, where you need to sustain your readers' interest.

1 Vary sentence length

Revision is a good opportunity to pay attention to varying the length of sentences. Use short sentences for dramatic contrast and for emphasis. Create longer sentences to explore relationships among ideas and to add rhythmic effects to your prose. Use middle-length sentences as workhorses, carrying the burden of explanation and description.

Note how variety in sentence length helps make this explanation easy to read and interesting.

> The real country ham may or may not be smoked after curing. Smithfield, Virginia, hams are smoked over hardwood or hardwood sawdust. Unscrupulous producers use smoke flavoring. But Mac Pierce, who runs the country's largest retail pork market, Nahunta Pork Center in Pikeville, North Carolina, says less than 1 percent of his hams are smoked, and most of those are bought by northerners. "Smoke masks a good ham's flavor," says Mac.
>
> —BILL NEAL, "How to Cure a Pig"

The sentences contain twenty-two, five, thirty-six, and fifteen words, respectively.

2 Vary sentence types

It's easy to get into the habit of using only **declarative sentences,** sentences that make statements (see 32d for sentence types). An occasional exclamation (**exclamatory sentence**), a mild order (**imperative sentence**), or a question (**interrogative sentence**) can vary the pace of your prose effectively, making it more lively and memorable.

VARIED

Some of the less familiar sports offer good opportunities for entertainment and exercise. Are you looking for fast-paced, thrilling events? Go see a soccer game, a lacrosse match, or a bicycle race. Do you want strenuous exercise and vigorous competition? Sign up for a rugby team, a badminton class, or a squash league. To benefit from these activities you need only take a simple step: Get involved!

A **rhetorical question** is one that requires no answer or that you plan to answer yourself in the course of an essay.

These are all ways you can get more time for sleep, even in the midst of a busy schedule. **But is it really important for most of us to get more sleep?** It is, and staying healthy and staying alert aren't the only good reasons for doing so.

ESL ADVICE: SENTENCE VARIETY

You may be tempted to use and re-use sentence patterns with which you are particularly comfortable. Readers are likely to consider overuse of a limited number of patterns monotonous, however. As you write, and especially as you revise, analyze the sentence patterns you use regularly. Then consider introducing more variety to add emphasis and interest to your writing.

3 Vary sentence structures and patterns

You can create variety by blending sentence structures in your writing (use simple, compound, and complex sentences; see 32d) and by varying the kinds of coordination and subordination you employ (see Chapter 44). You can also create variety by using periodic and cumulative sentence patterns and inversion (see 7c-2). By trying different sentence openings (see 7c-1), you can make sure your sentences vary in arrangement.

EXPLETIVE Then there was the time we painted our house.

PHRASE **To our neighbor's eyes,** the house seemed to belong to somewhere else.

PHRASE	**Looking for a bargain,** we bought paint at a discount store.
PHRASE	**The paint having been cheaply made,** the house began peeling within a year and a half.
DEPENDENT CLAUSE	**If you want to be happy with a paint job,** spend the money for quality materials.
TRANSITIONAL EXPRESSION	**In addition,** choose the color carefully.

Exercise 4

Rewrite the following passage to add variety. You may wish to rearrange the order of statements, to cut or add words, or to combine some sentences and divide others.

Psychologists have been studying what events people remember. People from middle age on remember events from their early years more clearly than they remember more recent events. People in their seventies have clear memories of their thirties but less clear memories of their fifties. Most of us remember very little about childhood. Almost no one remembers events from before four years old. Researchers think that we tend to remember events that are new or exciting to us and to forget routine events. Memorable events are most likely to occur early in life. Infants probably have not developed the mental abilities necessary to create memories, however.

---

4 Create surprise

Good writing often employs strategies that intrigue readers. **Summative modifiers, resumptive modifiers,** and **antithesis,** which change—or seem to change—the direction of a sentence, are particularly effective at creating surprise and interest.

A **summative modifier** summarizes the preceding part of a sentence and then sends it off in a new direction.

> To protect your vegetables against harmful insects, you can use soap sprays, scatter insect-repelling plants among the beds, or introduce "friendly" insects like ladybugs and praying mantises—**three techniques** that will not leave a harmful chemical residue on the food you grow.

A **resumptive modifier** extends a sentence that appears to have ended, adding new information or twists of thought.

People who are careful about what they eat may lead healthier lives—**healthier,** though not necessarily longer.

The advertising campaign is a surprising failure, **surprising** because it worked so well with test audiences.

Antithesis—the use of parallelism to emphasize contrast—can be witty, dramatic, cynical, ironic, or memorable.

To err is human, to forgive divine.

—Alexander Pope

Can an honest politician be smart, or a smart politician honest?

Exercise 5

A. Browse through some current magazines, looking for one that contains relatively long essays with varied and often surprising writing style. You might look at *Vogue, The New Yorker, Rolling Stone, Business Week, GQ, Vanity Fair, Advertising Age, Utne Reader, Commentary, Tikkun, Scientific American*, or *Details*. Choose two paragraphs whose style you admire, and identify any of the sentence strategies discussed in this chapter. Be ready to discuss why the sentences can be considered effective in communicating the author's ideas.

B. Although correct and carefully crafted sentences are important for writing in most communities, sometimes complex sentences are unnecessary or even distracting. Make a list of types of writing that don't require complete sentences (for example, classified ads). Then speculate about when sophisticated or complex sentences are necessary and appropriate and when they are not.

PART 2

Critical Thinking and Argument

CHAPTER 8 Thinking Critically

What convinces people to accept your conclusions about a subject? to share your opinion on an issue? to follow your recommendations? or to trust the explanations you offer? Many things do, of course. Perhaps the most important of them is the quality of your reasoning: the kind of careful, logical, insightful thinking your writing embodies. Thinking that displays these qualities is called **critical thinking** (sometimes called **critical reasoning**).

Whatever its focus, critical thinking in general calls for attention to logic, evidence, and accuracy, as well as awareness of alternative perspectives and opinions. What's more, the quality and design of your thinking contribute significantly to the representation of yourself that you create for an audience. Do you present yourself as thoughtful, informed, and fair-minded—hence persuasive? Or do you undermine your effectiveness by coming across as illogical, careless about ideas and information, and uninterested in other points of view? What constitutes critical thinking may also differ markedly depending on the community you are addressing: academic, public, or work (see 8d). In public contexts, for example, you can stand out from biased or one-sided views by representing yourself as sensible and balanced.

8a What is critical thinking?

Critical thinking is any process of reasoning, inquiring, or explaining that displays the following qualities.

- Attention to the logic or reasonableness of conclusions, and to the evidence supporting them.
- Willingness to question one's own assumptions and consider differing outlooks.
- Concern for precise information and clearly defined ideas.
- Desire to go beyond superficial explanations and opinions to reach fresh insights.

Consider the contrasts between the following two examples of reasoning offered in a public context; both are letters to the editor about a controversial proposal to build a greenway between two parks, one of which is in

Coolidge (an economically depressed neighborhood) and the other in Lake Stearns (a wealthy, stable neighborhood of fine older homes).

LETTER 1 (LACKS CRITICAL THINKING)

Doesn't consider other points of view
Little evidence
Vague details and ideas
Logical?
Reasonable?

City planners must be out of their minds to cook up this crazy idea. Drug pushers and thieves will have a field day preying on the people who use Lake Stearns Park, and soon the whole neighborhood will be destroyed by crime. We must stop these public officials before they totally destroy our lives with their senseless fantasies.

READER'S RESPONSE: This is just a collection of assertions with little evidence. The writer doesn't try to explain why the assertions are reasonable but feels free to dismiss other perspectives as unreasonable and illogical—without presenting any evidence.

LETTER 2 (DISPLAYS CRITICAL THINKING)

Goes beyond the obvious
Acknowledges other perspectives
Carefully presented evidence and clearly defined ideas
Logical reasoning
Reasonable conclusion

The proposal to create a greenway between Coolidge and Lake Stearns Parks appears to bridge the gap between these two different communities. But the greenway will not solve the existing problems in Coolidge Park. Residents near Lake Stearns are unlikely to ride their bikes or jog into Coolidge, and the presence of Coolidge residents in Stearns will only create a feeling, unjustified though it may be, of defensiveness. City funds could better be used to improve Coolidge Park by adding lighting, a basketball court, and an updated community center.

READER'S RESPONSE: The problem isn't simple, and the writer gives it a careful, balanced treatment. The reasons both for objecting to the proposal and for an alternative solution are supported by specific details.

The lack of critical thinking displayed in Letter 1 undermines its persuasiveness, except perhaps for those few readers who already agree with its conclusions. In Letter 2, the depth of critical thinking invites readers to take the writer's reasoning seriously, forming their own opinions and agreeing or disagreeing in response.

8b Building a chain of reasoning

Critical thinking works toward creating a **chain of reasoning,** the path you take in linking ideas, conclusions, evidence, and alternative perspectives to convince your audience. Some links in a chain may consist of *information:* examples, facts, evidence, details, and scientific or scholarly data. Other links may offer *ideas:* reasons, analysis, logical argument, citations from authorities, or differing points of view. It is crucial to be able to turn your thinking into a chain of critical reasoning that gives shape to your writing.

CRITICAL THINKING STRATEGIES FOR THREE COMMUNITIES OF READERS		
ACADEMIC SETTINGS	**PUBLIC SETTINGS**	**WORK SETTINGS**
Make the steps in the chain of reasoning particularly clear, stating them specifically and addressing possible objections. Provide extensive evidence and a balanced treatment of competing viewpoints. Emphasize fresh insight and accurate detail. Highlight conclusions.	Focus on clear statement of conclusions, recommendations, or solutions. Provide relevant, varied supporting evidence that meets the concerns of the variety of outlooks likely to be present in the audience being addressed. Pay special attention to fairness and ethical concerns in drawing conclusions or in presenting recommendations and information. Make the reasoning and evidence clear and accessible. Acknowledge opposing points of view and incorporate competing viewpoints whenever possible into recommendations.	Focus on values and goals of the organization when making recommendations or promoting policies, but acknowledge broader ethical concerns as well when the reasoning and proposed actions raise possible ethical issues. Provide clear statement of conclusions and easily summarized reasoning and evidence consistent with the organization's standards for decision making and the problem or policy being addressed. When working with a group, consider dividing the work of drafting according to parts of the document or assigning various drafts (first, second, etc.) to individuals according to their knowledge and abilities.

1 Focus on conclusions

The links in your chain of reasoning may include supporting conclusions and related (though nonessential) observations, interpretations, or recommendations. The end point of the chain—the **main conclusion**—is the most important. In some cases, you may offer more than one conclusion; for example, both using electronic tags *and* upgrading software to keep better track of inventory.

List your conclusions to strengthen your chain of reasoning.

- **List** all your conclusions (interpretations, opinions, and so on), both major and minor. Decide which make up your main area of focus, and which offer support as part of the chain of reasoning. Create two more lists, one for main and another for secondary conclusions.
- **Review** your two lists of conclusions. Do any more come to mind? Are any important assertions missing? If so, do you need to develop them?
- **Consider** the lists as readers might. Will they see any assertions as interpretations or judgments? Will they expect your conclusions?

2 Include information and inferences

A chain of reasoning needs both information and inferences. **Information** includes facts of all kinds—examples, data, details, quotations—that you present as reliable, confirmable, or generally undisputed. **Inferences** or **generalizations** are conclusions you reach based on and supported by information. Information turns into **evidence** when it's used to persuade a reader that an idea or proposition is reasonable.

Distinguish between information and inference.

- **List the key facts** relating to your subject. Which facts will readers regard as undisputed? Which can you confirm with observations, details, or a reliable source? If facts are in dispute, what are the reasons for accepting them as you present them?
- **List your inferences.** What do the facts imply? Which inferences reflect your understanding of the subject? What *might* happen or be true as a result of the facts?

3 Assess evidence and reasoning

Readers expect you to select evidence carefully, and to link it reasonably with assertions—that is, to proceed logically.

Use these questions to evaluate evidence as you read and write.

- How *abundant* is the evidence? Is it *sufficient* to support your claim?
- Does it *directly* support the claim?
- How *relevant, accurate,* and *well documented* is the evidence?

Proceeding logically is complicated when evidence that would persuade one group of readers would not convince another group. Consider, for example, how two citizens' groups might respond to the proposal to build a greenway between two parks, one in Coolidge (an economically depressed neighborhood) and the other in Lake Stearns (a wealthy, stable neighborhood of fine older homes). Starting from the assumption that the generally law-abiding residents of Coolidge are deprived of shopping and services that have left the area because of a high crime rate, the Coolidge Citizens' Consortium logically supports the greenway because it will give residents access to recreation and shopping in Lake Stearns. In contrast, starting from the assumption that the balance of a peaceful, low-crime neighborhood can easily be upset, another group, Preserve Lake Stearns, argues logically that though most Coolidge residents are law-abiding, the greenway will draw some habitual criminals who will undermine the quality of life in both neighborhoods. Each side reasons logically, but each starts with different assumptions and arrives at different conclusions. (See also Chapters 10–11.)

STRATEGY

Ask questions to evaluate your assumptions.

- How do I view the groups of people on each side of this issue?
- What will my readers want in a plan that addresses this problem?
- What do specialists in this field see as questions worth investigating?

4 Consider your readers' assumptions

Some assumptions and values are easy to identify, but others are unspoken. After hearing a lot of talk at work about efficiency, you might think that your coworkers and readers want only to cut costs. But preserving jobs and offering a quality product are also shared goals. The success of your reasoning may depend on how closely your assumptions correspond to those of your audience.

STRATEGY

Focus on assertions to anticipate how readers may respond to your reasoning.

- List your assertions that identify cause-effect links, classify or compare, connect generalizations and examples, or define. Delete or rethink any that are weak or possibly illogical (see 11a–b).
- To spot weak reasoning, imagine a skeptical reader's reaction to each assertion.

WEAK Violence in schools is rising because of increased violence in movies and on TV.

READER'S REACTION: **Is this true? My kids watch a lot of TV, but they aren't more violent than I was as a kid, when TV was far less violent.**

Exercise 1

Locate a document whose success or failure depends on the quality of its reasoning: a proposal, a position paper, an editorial, an academic article, or a memo on an important issue. Read it carefully, and identify its conclusions and the main kinds of evidence it presents. Next, try to identify any assumptions the writer makes that differ considerably from yours or those of another possible audience. Finally, use the questions posed in 8b-3 to assess the quality of the evidence.

8c Persuasive reasoning

The way you represent your reasoning in writing or speaking is crucial to the acceptance of your information and ideas. Will your audience know that you have analyzed information and ideas critically? Will they recognize that you are presenting your ideas and those of others in balanced, thoughtful ways?

Look again at the ways the writers of two letters to the editor represent themselves in arguing about the Coolidge/Lake Stearns greenway project.

WRITER 1

City planners must be out of their minds to cook up this crazy idea. Drug pushers and thieves will have a field day preying on the people who use Lake Stearns Park, and soon the whole neighborhood will be destroyed by crime. We must stop these insane public officials before they totally destroy our lives with their senseless fantasies.

WRITER 2

The proposal to create a greenway between Coolidge and Lake Stearns Parks appears to bridge the gap between these two different communities. But the greenway will not solve the existing problems in Coolidge Park. Residents near Lake Stearns are unlikely to ride their bikes or jog into Coolidge, and the presence of Coolidge residents in Stearns will only create a feeling, unjustified though it may be, of defensiveness. City funds could better be used to improve Coolidge Park by adding lighting, a basketball court, and an updated community center.

Both letters argue the same point: the greenway proposal is shortsighted. But think about the way these two writers present themselves.

WRITER 1	WRITER 2
Attacks proposers and Coolidge residents	Focuses on the proposal
Uses emotionally charged words (*insane, crazy*)	Uses balanced language
Comes up with vague ideas (stopping officials)	Offers specific alternatives
Stereotypes Coolidge residents	Suggests enhancing quality of life in Coolidge
Seems impulsive, shallow, uninformed	Seems balanced and thoughtful

Clearly, the representation created by the first writer is unlikely to lend credibility to what the writer has to say, and it may discourage readers from agreeing with the writer's point of view. What can you do to avoid representing yourself in such a negative manner? What can you do to create a representation that encourages an audience to respect and trust what you have to say? The following suggestions may help.

1 Be well informed

Whether you're writing an academic paper or making a public statement, you need to be well informed and to help your audience benefit from your knowledge, through both the quality of your insights and the depth and relevance of the information you present. Information, issues, and ideas are rarely isolated; they're embedded in the social, occupational, historical, or disciplinary contexts that surround a topic.

Explore what you know, and draw on the insights and perspectives of others. List what you know about your topic and what surrounds it. Identify the most important areas, given your purpose, and try to define what's still unclear and where you might find material to fill the gaps.

- Use face-to-face or electronic discussions (see Chapter 14) to identify issues, conclusions, evidence, and possible objections to your reasoning.
- Put your thoughts on paper tentatively, and then identify gaps in your evidence or logic by reading what others say about the topic or issue.
- Ask others to read your drafts critically and to identify reasonable objections that you can address as you revise.
- Put your work aside for a while; then read it as your readers might, noting any gaps that undermine clarity, persuasiveness, or credibility.

2 Acknowledge other perspectives and anticipate readers' reactions

If you fail to acknowledge other views, contrary arguments, conflicting evidence, or alternative solutions to a hotly contested issue, your readers may find your presentation one-sided and question your credibility. By anticipating such reactions, you can complete your chain of reasoning, building readers' confidence in you and your conclusions.

3 Be balanced and reasonable

Emotional language may be appropriate when you're urging a public audience to act on the basis of shared belief. The same language would probably irritate, even offend, coworkers or academic readers, who generally expect critical analysis of information. As you select the words and tone to represent your thinking, you create an image of yourself whose qualities may shape readers' responses. Your image can make your reader trust and respect you, distrust and dislike you, or find you imbalanced and your conclusions ridiculous or unconsidered.

UNCONSIDERED The greenway will just transport the Coolidge low-lifes into Lake Stearns Park and destroy its peace and quiet.

READER 1: What's a "low-life"? Is this term based on race? or class? Is everyone in Coolidge a "low-life"?

READER 2: Why—and how—would people from Coolidge destroy the "peace and quiet" of Lake Stearns?

4 Assess the appropriateness of strong bias to the occasion

To write effectively, you must know when to be cool and logical and when to show emotional commitment. At work, bias is expected when you represent an organization, but you'll need to write objective internal memos and reports. In public, your devotion to a cause generally will be accepted as such. Your academic writing, however, should lean toward unimpassioned, reasoned assessments.

STRATEGY

Adjust your bias to the occasion. Try to judge whether strong opinion is appropriate for your writing situation. Imagine a scale running from biased, opinionated writing to objective, neutral writing. Put an *X* somewhere on the scale to indicate your best assessment of your readers' expectations. Now put an *O* on the scale to indicate your best assessment of where your draft fits. If you find any distance between the *X* and the *O*, rework your word choice, your sentence structures, and the claims you're making until your draft better suits your situation.

BIASED, OPINIONATED ⟷ OBJECTIVE, NEUTRAL

Exercise 2

Locate an essay, article, or report on a controversial topic or issue, and analyze the ways in which the writer succeeds or fails to convincingly represent his or her thinking. Begin by deciding what community or communities of readers the author is addressing. Base your judgments on the presentation's appropriateness for particular readers, and on its purpose. Use the following questions to guide your analysis:

1. Does the writer appear well informed?
2. Does the writer acknowledge other perspectives?
3. Does the writer seem to respect his or her audience?
4. Is the presentation balanced and reasonable?
5. Does the writer anticipate readers' reactions?
6. Is the writer's bias appropriate for the occasion?

8d Critical thinking: Academic, public, and work

Researchers looking for ways to develop alternative-fuel vehicles will take different paths with their critical thinking than public officials trying to create (or repeal) regulations, or business executives developing new products. In this case as in many others, though the subject remains the same, the goals and procedures of critical thinking are likely to differ from setting to setting, according to audience and occasion.

1 Academic contexts

Working in academic communities, researchers and students alike analyze and interpret their subjects (social or natural phenomena, texts, artworks, and so forth). Their critical reasoning aims to offer interpretations, explanations, and insights. The reasoning process (both as an act of discovery and in the final written product or oral report) has the following characteristics.

- Detailed reasoning and critical analysis, often explained at length, with careful attention to the logic leading up to conclusions
- Special attention to insights and conclusions that go beyond the obvious and beyond common knowledge
- Care in gathering and presenting extensive evidence and accurate detail to support conclusions
- Balanced treatment acknowledging and explaining other viewpoints

Balanced treatment

Goes beyond obvious

Detailed reasoning and analysis

Regardless of whether there has been a shift in attitudes among employers, race is obviously a factor in many of their current decisions; however, the issues are complex and cannot be reduced to the simple notion of employer racism. Let me pursue this point by first focusing on the way in which employers themselves perceive the issues of prejudice and discrimination and, second, examining black employers' perceptions of inner-city workers.

Care in presenting accurate evidence

If discrimination is a significant factor in the employment woes of inner-city blacks, it is not recognized as such by a substantial majority of the employers in this survey. When asked the reason for the high levels of unemployment in Chicago's inner-city neighborhoods, only 4 percent of the 179 employers mentioned discrimination.

—William Julius Wilson,
"The Meaning and Significance of Race"

ESL ADVICE: CRITICAL THINKING IN ACADEMIC CONTEXTS

Academic writing in English generally follows a pattern of generalization and support in both reasoning and expression. Readers will generally expect you to state a conclusion first, then offer evidence and reasons to support it. Academic traditions in some cultures follow a different approach: data and evidence first, then conclusions that emerge logically. Follow the conventions your particular audience expects, even if doing so, for example, putting your conclusions first, seems unnatural or uncomfortable.

2 Public contexts

In public settings, reasoning often focuses on issues or policies as part of democratic decision making, with the goal of persuading or providing issue-oriented information. As a result, the process of reasoning and its expression in writing or speaking emphasizes the following elements of critical thinking.

- Concentration on author's point of view and provision of plausible, logical reasons for agreeing with this perspective
- Special attention to shared values and goals that support advocacy of a cause or policy, and to the need for specific kinds of information
- Awareness of the importance of relevant evidence in supporting positions or claims
- Fair recognition of others' interests, goals, and points of view

Shared values; concentrates on own point of view

How is health care like going to the grocer? The more you put in the cart, the higher the bill. But unlike your grocery expedition, where all you pay for are the items in your own cart, with health care the other customer's cart is on your tab, too.

Fair recognition of others' outlook

Nor will the tab get any better with the patient protection legislation being considered in Washington. Sure, Americans will get guaranteed access to emergency rooms, medical clinical trials and specialists. Senate legislation even provides the right to sue your insurer and be awarded up to $5 million in punitive damages. . . .

Relevant supporting evidence

According to the Employee Policy Foundation, the right to sue in the Senate's so-called Patients' Bill of Rights will add up to $16.3 billion per year to health care costs. The litigation costs, and the efforts by some employers to avoid liability, could lead to an additional 9 million uninsured Americans by 2010.

—"Restrict Right to Sue or We'll Pay in the End,"
Atlanta Journal-Constitution, July 19, 2001

3 Work contexts

Analysis of problems, proposal of solutions, and provision of information are often the focus of critical thinking, writing, and speaking in work settings. These tasks call for focus on the following elements of critical thinking.

- Accurate analysis of problem or need for information; clear explanation of solution, with special attention to its reasonableness and logic
- Sharp focus on task, problem, or goal
- Attention to evidence that indicates the importance of the problem or task and the appropriateness of the solution
- Awareness of alternative explanations or solutions; concern with the likely consequences of actions

Exercise 3

A. Locate a site where two or more people discuss the same topic in writing or speaking, preferably directly addressing each others' reasoning: an online discussion, a newspaper opinion page with contrasting editorials, a magazine article or interview, or records of a debate. Briefly summarize the position of each participant, and then discuss how each addresses or criticizes flaws or gaps in the reasoning of the other, either directly or by implication.

B. Working with a group in class or online, begin discussion by briefly stating your conclusions on an issue and giving the most important evidence for them. Pass this statement on, asking the next person to add other conclusions, evidence, objections, and counterarguments. Have the last person summarize conclusions, evidence, and objections and circulate the original document and the summary to the rest of the group. Discuss how your group's reasoning was changed by the serial dialogue.

CHAPTER 9
Reading Critically

Critical reading is the kind of reading that leads to writing. It begins with your understanding what you have read; moves to response, evaluation, and even argument; and ends with the development of your own ideas and insights.

Critical reading helps you to evaluate the ideas and information you encounter and to develop alternative points of view and interpretations (see also Chapter 8). Reading critically, which puts your mind to work on a text, gives you new ideas by helping you link what you read to your own experience, to other texts of all kinds, to issues and information, or to a problem or responsibility. Your writing then *adds* to the discussion of a topic by incorporating insights you've gained from your critical reading.

If you place critical response before your understanding a text, however, you may miss important ideas and information in what you have read. As a consequence, your responses may lack depth and relevance and your writing will fail to engage readers in an ongoing conversation about the subject.

All the elements of the critical reading process are important if you wish your writing to build on what you have read. This principle applies equally to reading in academic, public, and work settings.

9a Read to understand

If you are like most people, you begin reading on the first page of an essay, report, book, or foldout pamphlet. You go on, reading from sentence to sentence, paragraph by paragraph, paying attention to interesting information and ideas but often getting so involved in the details that you miss the ways in which the writer ties them together. As a result, you may struggle with the answers to questions like "What is the essay about?" "What is the point of this brochure?" "What problem is being described?" "How valid is the solution?" "What other issues need to be considered?" and "What further conclusions does this suggest?" Yet these are the kinds of questions you need to be able to answer in order to read critically and turn your reading into writing.

Simply put, by "starting cold," you are trying to do too many things at once. Instead, you need to "warm up" by previewing the text and any specific situation, issue, or audience it addresses. As you read, you need to take time to develop an overall understanding and to identify key ideas. And you need to read responsively, raising questions that help you understand the text and develop your ideas and insights.

1 Prereading strategies

What "big" features of reading that shape a text's meaning, ideas, or relationship to readers are you likely to miss if you jump right into reading? You may fail to recognize the text's overall design, the specific situation (academic, public, or work) that it addresses, or the writer's particular purposes. Fortunately, you can use prereading strategies to develop an understanding of these features before you begin your careful reading.

Preview the organization. For books and long articles or reports, preread by skimming the table of contents to see how a work is organized. What appears first, second, third? In magazine articles, essays, scholarly papers, or reports without tables of contents, look first for any headings or subheadings; these road maps tell you where the reading will take you and help you to plan your time.

Develop a reading plan: If you have only half an hour to read before you must do something else, knowing that the first section of a scholarly article ends on page nine may help you plan your time accordingly.

Examine the context. Begin by skimming the table of contents and headings in a text or paging quickly through it to get some idea of its subject and focus. Then consider the social setting in which the text was produced and the audience or community it seems to address. Use the following questions about context to guide your prereading when you approach a text for the first time.

- Does the text reflect the concerns of a specific academic, public, or work community, or does it appear to address a more general community of readers? (See 8d.)
- Which of the typical forms and characteristics of that community appear in this text? Which do not? (See the chart on p. 5.)
- Does the text appear in a publication (journal, periodical, or Web site) with a particular point of view (conservative or feminist or pro-choice, for example)? Is it associated with a particular industry or political organization? Does it cite or link to other texts endorsing particular perspectives or with common interests?

Develop a reading plan: What goals, generalizations, or funds of information will you and other readers need to pay attention to in writing produced for this context? (For some ideas, see the chart "Three Major Communities of Readers, Writers, and Speakers," p. 5.)

Sample the content. Good writing presents new ideas and information; you can make sense of these elements if you prepare yourself to read more effectively by sampling the content and by bringing to mind what you already know about the topic, the writer's outlook, or the issues being addressed. Use the following questions about a text's content and author to focus your scanning as you preread.

- Is the text by a single author or by a group of people representing an organization?
- When was the text published, and how current are the information and ideas?
- Who are the intended readers? Are they identified in the text, and is the purpose clearly stated in the title, headings, or highlighted portions of the text?
- Do visuals, graphics, or text layout provide obvious clues to the writing's purpose(s), focus, and intended audience? (See Chapter 12 for advice on understanding the visual elements of a text.)
- If the text is in electronic form, do any other texts within the site or linked to it provide any hints about its focus, purpose, and audience?
- Is there any evidence of how popular or well received the text is? Has it appeared in numerous editions? Are there testimonials from authorities on the subject? If the text is on a Web site, does a "hit counter" indicate the number of people who have visited the site?
- What does the back or front of a book tell you? What information can you gather from any abstracts or summaries at the beginning of a report or scholarly article?

Develop a reading plan: What kinds of information and ideas in the text are unfamiliar to you? What generalizations or conclusions does the author offer that help explain the unfamiliar material? Make these two steps part of your reading plan: (1) Look for generalizations and conclusions that aid your understanding of unfamiliar content. (2) Set aside extra time for sections of the text devoted to new information and insights.

Sample key words and specialized terms. If you notice unfamiliar terms, look for patterns of related terms, or consult a dictionary or online glossary. Consider the following excerpt from an internal memo on market competitiveness for an air carrier.

> As per Strategic Plan: Two goals will require further delineation from your group. These are the goals pertaining to fleet types and to industry performance on DOT metrics. The original proposal for fleet type reduction was to reduce from 16 to 6; new proposals, based on year-end figures, suggest that this may need to be revised to 4 fleet types. The key DOT metrics to address include on-time performance and mishandles.

CRITICAL READING STRATEGIES FOR THREE COMMUNITIES OF READERS

ACADEMIC SETTINGS	PUBLIC SETTINGS	WORK SETTINGS
Critical reading in academic settings calls for attention to reasoning and evidence as well as the claims (thesis) a writer advances. Check that interpretations and conclusions are each supported by evidence that is accurate, specific, and convincing. See that alternate scholarly perspectives have been taken into account. Verify that the theory or method used to analyze and interpret the subject is applied correctly and consistently.	Critical reading in public settings calls for special attention to the clarity of the writer's recommendations or judgments as well as evaluation of supporting evidence. Note how effectively the writer deals with alternative policies or value judgments. Evaluate the writer's position according to what you know about the context and about alternative points of view. Take note of any objections or reservations that come to mind as you read.	Critical reading in work settings focuses on how accurately the writer analyzes problems or challenges. It pays particular attention to proposed solutions, policies, or other actions, especially to their practicality, efficiency, and likelihood of success. It also evaluates the ethical dimensions of any proposed action or policy.

Note how the example uses a number of terms its writers assumed readers would understand: *fleet types, DOT metrics, mishandles.* By glancing through the text first and noting such terms, you'll gain a sense of what the document is about. (Note that for the intended readers of this memo, "insider" terms like these would be common knowledge.)

Develop a reading plan: If you read complex, challenging texts often—as you do in college—create a regular reading place with resources such as dictionaries close at hand. (When you read in a college library, such resources are always nearby.)

Make predictions. Sample some paragraphs, sentences, or visuals, and try to predict what the text is about and where it will take you. Do your samples imply a particular direction, focus, or purpose? Jot your predictions down and note which ones are later confirmed as you read.

Develop a reading plan: Use these questions to help make predictions.

- What is this text about?
- What is the writer's point of view on the topic?
- How does the writer want me to feel or think about the topic?
- What parts of the selection are likely to be most demanding for readers?
- Which parts are likely to be most informative or enjoyable?
- Where in the selection is the writer most likely to announce conclusions or generalizations?

Exercise 1

Locate a short article, a short electronic document, or a portion of a longer text that has no overt structure—no headings, section divisions, or other organizational signals. Then skim (preread) the material and create headings or divisions for the main parts of the reading.

2 Reading strategies during and after

You've probably had the experience of reaching the end of a passage in an essay, report, Web site, or book (or the end of the work itself), only to realize that you don't have even the vaguest sense of what you've been reading. To avoid this problem, try the following strategies.

Pause and assess. When you reach a place at which you can stop reading without interrupting a line of reasoning or a crucial narrative, put the reading aside for a moment. Where are you? What have you learned so far? What do you think? What still confuses you? Jot down answers to these questions in your journal or on a piece of paper. Then go back and skim what you've read. If you're uncertain about something, reviewing the text can sometimes clarify it.

Highlight important information. If you're an avid highlighter *while* you read, try to change your style. Don't spend a lot of time attending to tiny details the first time through your reading. Instead, read to capture the essential points of the piece. This will let you see a "bigger picture," a set of organizational or argumentative structures, without getting lost in the details.

STRATEGY

Do most of your highlighting *after* your first reading. Go back and write notes in the margins of your reading to identify important points and details, or use your highlighter to identify what's *really* important.

Highlighting an electronic document is more of a challenge. Sometimes it helps to print a copy and highlight this paper record of what you've read. You might also find it easier to read analytically when the text is on paper rather than on a screen. If your computer software allows, you may be able to print out selected portions of a document. This can be a form of highlighting, though it detaches the highlighted text from the original, making it more difficult for you to consult the entire document at a later date. You can also try to save electronic documents on a word processor and then add boldfacing, underlining, or font highlighting to especially important sections or passages.

Identify generalizations. General statements of all sorts help organize information and ideas and help readers understand the insights and line of reasoning a writer is offering. Identifying them helps you understand and remember an essay or article's main points, line of reasoning, and overall organization. Look for generalizations near the beginning of a selection (including a thesis statement), at the beginning of each section of the text (including any headings and subheads), at the beginning or end of paragraphs, or in special paragraphs that summarize main ideas and the organizational plan (see 3c–d, 6b and f).

Annotate. At one time, students were punished for writing in books (even their own copies). For some people, this history has turned to habit. If you own the book or document you're reading, go ahead and annotate it using whatever white space is on the page. If you don't own it, consider making a photocopy of relevant material, perhaps reducing it to give you more marginal space for your notes. If you're reading a Web page or other electronic document, consider downloading and printing it so you can make annotations—unless your software allows you to open a note-taking document that you can link to the text you're reading.

Read with your audience and purpose in mind. Often we read in order to write: to gather information and ideas or to develop insights and solutions that we plan to share with readers. If this is your goal, highlight or make notes on those sections of a text that are relevant to the community of readers you plan to address, or to your specific purposes for reading.

Reread and review. If you're learning sophisticated concepts, studying complicated issues and problems, or working through difficult arguments, you may need to read material more than once. Every time you read something again, you'll find more information or new ideas.

Exercise 2

Find a relatively challenging article, electronic document, or book chapter, or choose one that you've begun to read for a specific purpose, perhaps as a course assignment or in preparation for a report or other writing task. Then try several of the reading strategies outlined in this section, taking note of which best aided your understanding and which seemed most likely to be useful to you as a writer.

9b Read to respond and evaluate

What is the central idea a writer is trying to convey? Have you got a better or different idea of your own? What new insights does a piece of writing offer you? What insights of your own came to mind as you read? Can you describe the writer's opinions, generalizations, or attitudes toward the subject matter? Do you agree with them? Has the writer missed important points? What are your opinions? How might you state your perspective for readers?

When you read for response and evaluation, these are some of the questions you try to answer. They link an understanding of the text to an evaluation of its content and then to the development of your own perspective. Clearly, this kind of reading is *active* and *engaged*. This form of reading is also *responsive*—you respond to the content and strategies of a text by evaluating them according to your purposes for reading and the situation to which the text is addressed (academic, public, or work). You respond by developing your own ideas and interests and by beginning to think about the kinds of writing you might produce as a consequence of your reading.

1 Make responsive annotations

As you read or reread, it's important for you to keep track of your questions, thoughts, reactions, agreements, and disagreements. Putting them in writing helps you focus on them and to begin developing them into a text of your own. You can do this in the margins of a book or article; on a separate sheet of paper; or on your desktop, laptop, or handheld computer.

Use the following kinds of annotations and leading questions to develop responses and evaluations.

- **Interpretations.** What does the writer mean in the text as a whole or in each part? How might I revise or add to the insights or conclusions? Where and how does my outlook differ from the writer's?
- **Confusions.** At what points in the text are readers likely to become puzzled, and why? How would I revise the text to eliminate the confusion? Are the potential points of confusion significant enough to deserve a text of their own, and could I address them in a paper?
- **Questions.** What more will readers need to know about the subject, issue, or problem? If I were the writer, what would I want them to know?
- **Disagreements.** What disagreements does the text (writer) seem to anticipate? What does the writer fail to anticipate? Where and why do I disagree? Are my disagreements worth writing about?
- **Evaluative responses.** What do I like or dislike about the text as a whole or about specific parts? Do I like it enough to extend the writer's approach in a text of my own? Do I dislike it enough to be willing to answer it or argue with it in my own writing?
- **Restatements.** How might I restate the text's key ideas in my own words? Does my restatement reveal any ideas that deserve further exploration or development—perhaps in my own writing?

- **Communities.** What will different communities of readers perceive as the most important ideas and information in the text? Why might people in two different settings, who may be affected by or interested in the subject, respond in different ways?
- **Memories.** What experiences, memories, or related issues or problems come to mind as I read? Is it likely that the writer anticipated such reactions?
- **Retentions.** Which details, insights, or opinions from the text are most likely to stick in readers' minds after they have finished, and why?

Clint Graff made some responsive annotations to a passage from a document about the information provided to consumers on food labels.

A recent review on communication of food, nutrition, and health messages did not include dietary supplement labeling specifically but did address consumer understanding of nutrient content and health claims on food labels (80). In an appendix to this report, Levy (83) indicates that consumers in focus groups were interested in having information about the relationship between diet and disease. Some commissioners interpret this study as suggesting that consumer research has not yet established a "mandate" for having health information on food labels as opposed to obtaining such information from health care providers, books, or the print and telecommunications media. Moreover, considering that food labels are viewed by consumers as reflective of the manufacturer's interest in selling the product, consumers are skeptical about the veracity of health messages on food labels.

What were they asked? And do people really read the info?

How does this study lead to this conclusion?

Points to tension between consumer desire for info & fear that it's just hype. I'm skeptical too. But aren't there ways to get trustworthy information to consumers? Write about this?

Note repetition and emphasis. Words, phrases, ideas, and details that appear repeatedly in a text may shape its meaning and its effect, even if the writer didn't fully intend to provide such emphasis. Devices for creating emphasis—headings, thesis statements, topic sentences, vivid detail, sentence structure, and parallelism or other stylistic strategies—also highlight and create meaning and focus a text's purpose.

Summarize in chunks. Most texts have natural "resting points," often marked with road signs like headings and subheadings, or shifts in focus.

These are good places to take stock of what you've learned or how you are reacting to the reading. This can help you to monitor your comprehension and begin interpreting the piece.

Share interpretations and insights. Go public with the "conversation" you're having internally with a piece of writing. If other people have read the same piece, their responses can help you to formulate and test your own interpretation.

Respond in writing. A journal or reading log provides an especially effective method for reading critically (see 2b). If you're keeping a journal, jot down your conclusions about the writer's purpose(s) and key ideas. Be ready to reread the text to check your perceptions and understandings. By struggling to put the text's ideas into your own language, you are already developing your interpretation—and working toward ideas you might develop later in your own writing.

Exercise 3

A. Obtain a copy of the minutes from a recent city council or other public meeting (these may be available online). Read the minutes carefully, making responsive annotations as you read; then, summarize the document for a partner. Once you have done this, speculate about the ways different communities might read this document. Is there any specialized terminology that might be confusing to some audiences? Did any one issue seem like an ongoing problem or controversy? If so, were solutions proposed? Can you tell, from the minutes, who the most influential or powerful participants were?

B. Compare the interpretive reading of an academic text to that of a workplace document. Select a challenging excerpt from some of your course reading, and locate a text from a workplace context. (You might use a document from a current or former job, ask individuals you know in the working world to share a text with you, or locate a relevant document from a work- or profession-related Web site.) Use interpretive reading strategies (making responsive annotations, noting repetition and emphasis, summarizing in chunks, sharing interpretations, and responding in writing) as you actively read the two pieces. Then reflect, in writing, on the differences between your interpretive readings of the two texts: Does one lend itself to this kind of reading more easily? Which strategies were most useful with each text? Which text elicited the strongest response?

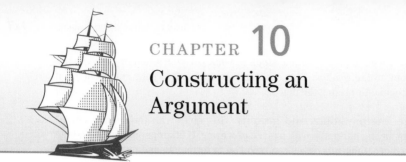

CHAPTER 10 Constructing an Argument

Why argue? If you could prove absolutely, to everyone's satisfaction, that your approach to limiting undergraduate alcohol use (or to funding a new community park) is the best one, you wouldn't need to argue for your position. You could simply present your conclusion and explain the strong logic and evidence supporting it.

But matters like use of alcohol, and taxpayers' money, and business strategy seldom lend themselves to such certainty. Readers (and listeners) will be aware of competing opinions and policies as well as contradictory evidence. They will know that despite their importance, many issues do not allow for absolute answers. This is especially true for value judgments, policy questions, and proposed courses of action. On such questions, members of your audience will probably begin by regarding your opinion as one possibility of many; they will expect you to argue for it with good reasons, logic, evidence, and attention to alternative opinions before they decide to agree with you.

Argumentative writing has specific qualities that set it apart from other kinds of writing, which aim to explain, inform, or interpret.

- **Argument deals with issues and opinions, not certainties.** It addresses situations in which more than one opinion, interpretation, or course of action is possible.
- **Argument is evaluative.** It takes a stand, presenting and endorsing an outlook, judgment, or opinion.
- **Argument aims at persuasion.** It focuses on reasons, evidence, and values most likely to encourage readers (or listeners) to share an opinion or undertake a proposed action.
- **Argument interacts.** It engages an audience's attitudes and values as well as alternative points of view (pro or con).

10a Occasions for argument

If you think for a moment of the kinds of writing you may have occasion to do in academic, public, or work settings, you will recognize that much of it is **argumentative,** designed to persuade readers to share your opinion or perspective rather than a differing point of view.

At the heart of most occasions calling for **argument** is an issue, a topic about which people may hold sharply differing points of view. How you

ARGUMENTS IN THREE DIFFERENT COMMUNITIES

ACADEMIC SETTINGS	PUBLIC SETTINGS	WORK SETTINGS
Anyone advancing a new interpretation, perspective, or conclusion may need to argue why it is superior to other points of view. Prior research often provides unresolved issues and problems as a focus for arguments.	Proposals for new policies, projects, or procedures often take argumentative form in order to gather public support or to demonstrate why they are preferable to the alternatives. Even suggestions for adopting noncontroversial practices or presentations of useful information may need to take argumentative form. Controversial practices and information generally require argumentative presentation.	Discussions of problems and solutions generally take argumentative form to create agreement in understanding a problem and to encourage group action in solving it. Arguments also build support for policies or programs and create agreement on goals and values.

go about building an argument to address an issue may vary from context to context, however.

1 Existing issues

Many arguments you construct will address existing issues. Some, such as gun control or responses to global warming, will have broad relevance; others will be of concern to a specific audience, for example, proposals for a new campus drinking policy or limitations on business or residential development. An existing issue is a matter of ongoing disagreement or of a continuing struggle to find a satisfactory solution. Issues of this sort come to you partially formed: other people have already identified the dimensions of disagreement, gathered supporting ideas and information, and taken stances, pro and con.

The presence of so much activity surrounding an issue is generally a sign that it is truly a matter for argument—not a question that can be easily or quickly resolved. The activity also bears witness to the ongoing importance or significance of the questions involved—as long as it is recent activity. Twenty years ago, for example, the policy of requiring deposits on soft drink and beer bottles was widely debated; while the issue is certainly not "resolved" on a national basis, it is no longer a matter of widespread concern or discussion.

List current issues. Keeping in mind the signs of an existing, viable issue—continued disagreement as well as new arguments and counterarguments—you can probably make a list of current issues in varied communities.

	ACADEMIC	PUBLIC	WORK
GENERAL	Standardized testing Affirmative action in college admissions	Genetically altered foods Violence and sex on television	Child care at work Ethnically targeted marketing
LOCAL	Housing regulations at Nontanko River State University	A local crusade against a television series	Discipline policies at Abtech's Child-Care Center

Listing is a good discovery strategy if you are responding to an assignment to prepare a written (or oral) argument about an issue, but it has other uses as well. Listing can help you spot the disagreements or problems that define (or divide) communities; it can help you begin to develop your own responses to the issues.

Get involved in issues. Involve yourself in the flow of opinions and ideas surrounding issues.

- **"Talk" to yourself.** In a journal, on a piece of paper, or on a screen, "talk" to yourself about problems, controversies, trends, or ideas that concern you or influence the ways we live. Try making a list, adding to each item a short (one- or two-sentence) summary of at least two different opinions on the subject. To identify and explore different opinions, try adopting different voices in your writing by imagining yourself as a person who has a very different outlook from your usual one.
- **Interview friends, family, or coworkers.** Ask them about questions and problems that concern them and inspire strong opinions. Keep a record of their responses, and add your own ideas. Identify subjects about which there are at least two reasonable and differing opinions. (Issues of limited or local concern—such as oil- versus gas-fired electric generation or possible dredging of a polluted river—may provide a clearer focus and draw more interest than overly broad issues, even ones of global concern.)
- **Read and listen.** Leaf through news and opinion magazines such as *The Nation* and *National Review* or listen to issue-oriented discussion shows on television and radio. Look at editorials in local and national newspapers (available in your library and online). Consult online discussion groups or issue-oriented electronic publications such as *Salon*. List issues interesting to you, and write down any opposing opinions and important information or ideas.

Exercise 1

A. Using the strategies (described above) for involving yourself in the flow of opinions and ideas, prepare a list of issues or controversies that interest you. Choose one, summarize the issue or controversy in a sentence or two, and then summarize the main conflicting opinions (pro and con), each in a sentence.

B. Working in a group, share your lists of issues. Choose an issue on someone else's list (other than the issue they have expanded) and expand it in the same manner that you did in Exercise 1A by summarizing the issue and the main conflicting opinions.

2 Potential issues

When you focus on a problem others have not identified, offer an opinion or evaluation likely to be controversial, or propose a change in a long-agreed-upon policy, you address a potential issue. Though a potential issue is not yet a focus of argument, you can probably anticipate some members of your audience responding with opposing opinions and contrary proposals that will turn the potential issue into an actual issue.

STRATEGIES FOR RECOGNIZING POTENTIAL ISSUES

Use these strategies to help recognize potential issues and to deepen your and your audience's understanding of a subject or situation.

- **Review the consequences.** A policy, program, or organization often starts out with specific goals. Question and evaluate the consequences of policies or actions as a way of uncovering issues worth discussing.

  Have there been unintended consequences? good or bad?

  Has the situation changed? the facts of the matter? Are new responses or conclusions called for?

  What problems have appeared? Are there different ways to solve them?

  What do participants say about disagreements or problems that emerged? What do outsiders say?

  Has the policy or program been successful enough to act as a model for dealing with similar solutions?
- **Question the "taken-for-granted."** The opinions or activity that many people take for granted may mask important disagreements and issues.
- **Question assumptions.** Make a list of some things you think most people take for granted, for example, economic prosperity is good; diesel engines are dirty and polluting. Or make a list of things you think a particular group of people assumes, for example, environmentalists: prosperity increases pollution; regulations lead to cleaner air and water. Then look for contradictions within and among your lists: economic

(*continued*)

STRATEGIES FOR RECOGNIZING POTENTIAL ISSUES (*continued*)

prosperity is good vs. prosperity increases pollution. Or raise questions about an assumption: Do diesels always pollute? When have regulations made water dirtier?

- **Question definitions and categories.** Use questions to probe taken-for-granted definitions and classifications. People frequently talk and write about "chick flicks," that is, films that appeal to women (*not* men) by focusing on relationships and emotions rather than action. Do men really dislike such films? Do women actually prefer such films to action films or comedies? Are there enough films of other types incorporating the characteristics of "chick flicks" to call into question the existence of the category on its own?
- **Question evaluations.** An evaluation or judgment is an opinion—subject to challenge, of course—and therefore always a potential issue. Raising questions about an evaluation or judgment can help you probe the reasoning behind conclusions and decisions and turn potential issues into real ones:

  Opinion: Early decision programs benefit college applicants.

  Response: That's what a lot of people say, but really? What about people who need to choose among financial packages? Aren't regular applicants disadvantaged when a large percentage of the spaces in an incoming class are already filled by the time they apply?
- **Question silence by developing contrasts.** An absence of open disagreement does not mean an absence of potential issues. Quite often, people address an issue like the clash between wildlife and housing developments or discriminatory practices within an institution only when a crisis arises. Try focusing on an organization, community, or policy. Identify a loosely similar one (two communities with youth sports programs, for example). Use contrasts to identify potential issues. A seemingly issue-free college athletic administration can appear as a source of potential controversy when viewed in contrast with a differently structured, perhaps more successful, program.
- **Offer an evaluation.** When you state a judgment about the quality of a film, a book, a performance, a policy, a program, or anything else that can be legitimately evaluated, you create an issue, at least to the extent that you intend for others to share your opinion and are not simply expressing your personal taste—which is, of course, a personal statement rather than a subject for debate.

Exercise 2

A. Use two of the strategies (described above) for identifying potential issues. Identify at least five potential issues, making sure you employ both techniques at least twice. Then summarize each issue in a sentence or two, and summarize any potentially conflicting opinions about it in a sentence each.

B. Choose one of the potential issues from your list in Exercise 2A. Explain briefly why you think an audience should be concerned about it.

---

3 Identify arguable issues

Your feelings about some things may be so strong that you want to argue with anyone who disagrees with your position. But what if no one really disagrees? What if no one thinks the subject is worth arguing about?

To have an argument in a formal sense, you must begin with an arguable **issue,** a subject about which your audience can recognize two (or more) clearly differing, worthwhile opinions. No one, for example, is willing to say that driving while intoxicated is a good thing; anyone who tried to advance this opinion would be considered foolish, at best. Drunk driving is not an issue. However, reasonable people disagree about which policies are most likely to discourage people from driving while intoxicated—strict laws, harsh punishments, roadblocks, advertising campaigns, door-to-door public information programs, programs for high school students, and so on. For most people, this question is certainly an arguable issue, and they would probably be glad to listen to differing opinions in hopes of discovering the best way to deal with the problem.

Use the following questions to help determine whether you have chosen an issue worth arguing about.

1. *Is the issue clearly debatable?* A fact is something about which there can be no debate ("Mice are rodents," "President John F. Kennedy was assassinated on November 22, 1963"). The only facts that can be debated are those that might be reasonably challenged *as* facts. For example, it was widely held as "fact" that peptic ulcers were caused by excess acidity in the diet, and for years treatment involved changes in eating habits, antacids, or acid-inhibiting drugs. New evidence, however, now supports a theory that ulcers are caused by a bacterium able to be treated with antibiotics. The question "Are peptic ulcers caused by diet?" is, in light of this information, a much more debatable issue than the question "Does the earth have a moon?"
2. *Can you explore the issue with something more than pure speculation?* Claims that can't be verified often make for interesting philosophical discussion, but they don't lend themselves fully to argument. The question "Where do we go when we die?" is impossible to answer conclusively and therefore hard to develop into an arguable issue. Statements for which there is only tentative supporting evidence ("There may be life on other planets") also make difficult choices for argument.

3. *Is the issue more than a matter of pure taste or preference?* An author's own values and beliefs need to be supported in argument with sound reasoning or evidence. Statements such as "I hate anything with tomatoes in it" can't be supported with anything more than circular reasoning ("because I hate tomatoes"). However, evaluative statements based on comparisons or analyses, such as those found in reviews, can become reasonable supporting evidence for a broader assertion ("The food at Alfredo's Restaurant is highly overrated").

4. *Does the issue avoid assumptions that are so deeply or universally held that they cannot be argued?* Although some of the most important social and political issues of our time seem like good topics for argumentative writing, they may seriously frustrate your composing process. Arguments about topics such as the right to die and capital punishment may invoke systems of belief, including religious belief, that can't be logically debated. Debates between nonreligious students and their fundamentalist peers rarely end in resolution or change—interesting or confrontational though the discussions may be. When you choose a topic, ask yourself whether and how it can be explored through the use of sound reasoning and evidence.

DEVELOPING A DOCUMENTED ARGUMENT: IDENTIFYING AN ISSUE

When he heard of people who were suing fast-food restaurants for causing obesity, Paul Pusateri thought they had no case. But the question intrigued him: Does fast food cause obesity? He did a bit of research, and, to his surprise, he discovered a debatable issue. Are fast-food restaurants at least partly responsible for growing rates of obesity? Some people argue that consumers have a choice and are responsible for choosing fattening foods. Others argue that the policies and practices of fast-food chains encourage overeating and unhealthy diets. At this point, Pusateri decided that he had identified an issue worth arguing about—one that affects the lives of millions of people.

Exercise 3

A. Examine the following five issue statements. Decide which of the issues could be developed into argumentative papers and which would not lend themselves to such development. Explain why.

1. Banning campus visits by environmentally insensitive firms
2. The taste of fresh orange juice
3. The sale of pharmaceuticals (aspirin, sunscreen, condoms, tampons) in campus vending machines
4. Belief in the sacredness of cows

5. The reinstitution of chain gangs (prisoners shackled together at the legs) to do highway work

B. In a small group, compare your analysis of the items in Exercise 3A. Collectively choose two issue statements that would make good argumentative papers.

10b Developing your stance

You construct an argument to help persuade people to accept your opinion. To argue effectively, therefore, you first need a clear idea of your own opinion and of the reasons why you hold it. Even at this early stage, however, thinking about how readers (or listeners) will respond to your reasoning is important. For instance, if you want to present your views about a plan to allow large billboards in your community, it doesn't help if you haven't thought through all the issues. Argument is interactive: to persuade others to accept your perspective, you need to engage their opinions, values, and likely objections.

It is often easy to voice opinions in a lively discussion among friends—if another person disagrees, you can immediately defend or clarify what you have said or you can challenge the person with another point. In written argument, however, you don't have this luxury. Because readers aren't responding to you "live," you need to anticipate their reactions and counterarguments.

To develop your argumentative stance, you need to do two things.

1. *Articulate* your opinion along with supporting reasons and information to yourself.
2. *Clarify* your ideas and supporting evidence through interchange with competing perspectives.

It is crucial that you do these things through *writing*, because the act of writing pushes your thinking and reasoning.

1 Articulate your stance

Begin by exploring your stance on paper as a way of focusing your ideas, values, and feelings.

- **Write informally** (perhaps in your journal) about your intuitive reactions to your chosen issue. Does the issue make you feel scornful, pitying, fearful, or outraged? If the issue angers you, exactly what about it makes you angry?
- **List the specific elements of the issue** to which you have responded emotionally, and briefly summarize your responses. Add to this list other points that you may not react to emotionally but that, on an intellectual level, support your first reaction.

- **Identify facts, examples, and ideas** that support your opinions. Also begin thinking about objections to your point of view. If you need to go outside your experience to provide support or to deal with opposing opinions, make a preliminary research plan identifying the kinds of information and ideas you may need to gather.

2 Clarify your ideas

Clarify your ideas through interaction with competing perspectives.

- **Read** about the subject, focusing on ways others have defined the issue, on their opinions, on the kinds of support they cite, and on potentially useful information they present.
- **Talk** with people about the issue, gathering their opinions and feelings into an understanding of how perspectives on the subject differ.
- **Listen** to debates in person, on television, or on the radio, and record the differing opinions, supporting ideas or evidence, and counterarguments.
- **Visit** an online discussion group to observe and take note of the varying points of view on an issue as well as the ways participants respond to and counter each others' arguments.

10c Developing a thesis

As you begin identifying your point of view, try to limit the scope of your argument. If your issue is too broad, you will have a hard time covering it in reasonable space and time and an equally difficult time persuading audiences to agree with you. Most of all, however, work toward developing a clear statement of your own opinion—the point of view with which you wish to persuade readers to agree. Your opinion (**thesis** or **argumentative claim**) will eventually become a major focus as you develop your argument in writing. You will need to make sure the ideas, supporting information, and organization you choose all help further your thesis or claim. (In a letter to the editor, for example, you may need only one or two paragraphs to make your point.)

1 Focus on an argumentative claim

One good way to focus your effort is to ask yourself what kind of **argumentative claim** you plan to make (a **claim** is the opinion you plan to argue for).

- *Do you want to argue that an activity, belief, arrangement, or performance is good or bad (effective or ineffective, healthful or harmful, desirable or undesirable)?* If so, you are asking readers (or listeners) to agree with a **value judgment.**

- *Do you want to persuade your audience that a particular course of action ought to be undertaken or avoided?* If so, you are asking for agreement on a particular **policy.**
- *Do you want people to agree that a particular explanation is correct or incorrect?* If so, you are asking them to endorse or reject an **interpretation.**

Put your claim in writing so you can share it with others and analyze it carefully yourself. Your claim needs to be relatively specific; after all, when you ask people to agree with you, they will be unlikely to do so unless you can indicate your opinion and purpose clearly and specifically.

STRATEGY

Make sure you agree with yourself on the purpose and goals of your argument. Write a memo to yourself explaining your goals. Use the memo as an opportunity to think out loud and clarify your purpose as you write.

To: Self
From: Me
I find using roadblocks as a way of catching drunk drivers really disturbing. I know it is important to keep drunk drivers off the road, of course. I think this remedy is extreme. I guess what I really want to do is to get my audience to agree that the roadblocks are a violation of civil liberties and should be banned.

A memo to yourself taking into account fresh evidence, new ideas, or counterarguments you have encountered can be a good place to revise and redirect your opinion and the direction of your argument.

DEVELOPING A DOCUMENTED ARGUMENT: FOCUSING ON A CLAIM

As he worked on his paper about fast food and obesity, Paul Pusateri concluded that the fast-food chains are responsible in significant ways for encouraging people to develop unhealthy eating habits. To begin turning this stance into writing, he prepared a memo to himself:

To: Paul P.
From: Paul P.
I started out thinking that fast-food chains weren't to blame, and I still think customers are responsible too—partly. But in my judgment, the heaviest blame goes to the companies. I want readers to agree with me that the companies have been wrong in many of their policies and actions.

Be ready to revise your claim. As you construct your argument, bringing together your ideas and evidence to support them, you may decide to modify your argumentative **claim,** that is, the opinion, judgment, or course of action you wish your audience to adopt.

> To: Self
> From: Me
> Subject: Roadblocks are effective
> Roadblocks violate civil liberties, but the three studies I found online through NorthernLight.com say that the roadblocks take a lot of drunk drivers off the road and may reduce accidents. Self, you've got to deal with this evidence and the arguments for roadblocks it suggests. Perhaps you can propose an effective alternative that does not violate civil liberties.

2 Create a thesis statement

An explicit **thesis statement** makes your argumentative claim (opinion or proposal) clear and helps your audience follow your reasoning and evidence.

Develop a tentative thesis statement as you plan and draft your argument, and revise it as you refine your ideas and evidence. Make sure your thesis statement is not just a general statement of your point of view but an **argumentative thesis** specifying your opinion on an issue. An effective thesis does these things.

1. Identifies a specific issue and your opinion
2. Provides a clear and logical statement of your argumentative claim
3. Suggests a general direction for your argument
4. Indicates related claims or opinions

DEVELOPING A DOCUMENTED ARGUMENT: CREATING A THESIS STATEMENT

Here is the initial thesis statement Paul Pusateri developed.

> Although customers make the food choices, the unhealthy choices they make at fast-food restaurants are often the result of advertising strategies, lack of clear information, and other practices of the fast-food chains.

In the course of developing his argumentative essay, Paul revised this statement several times, yet his initial thesis statement gave him a good place to start.

Arguments are often complex and involve several closely related claims. Pay special attention to making such relationships clear. For example, imagine that you are working on a thesis statement for your essay arguing that stopping all cars on a highway to search for drunk drivers is a violation of civil liberties, so roadblocks should be replaced with another technique for keeping intoxicated people from driving. You need to recognize that this claim commits you to arguing both a value judgment (roadblocks violate civil liberties) and a policy (another technique for enforcing laws against drunk driving); if you do, you can make sure your thesis (and your essay as a whole) does not blur these points and the evidence you use to support them.

3 Revise your thesis statement

In a sentence (or at most two sentences) state your thesis (your opinion or proposal) and indicate the general kind of reasoning you will offer to support it.

Suggestion: Try using sentence patterns like "*X* should be altered/banned/etc. because . . ."; "I propose the following plan/policy/actions/etc. because . . ."; or "*Y* is inappropriate/ineffective/harmful/etc. because. . . ."

Next, check specifically whether your tentative thesis blurs your specific purposes for arguing or is illogical.

BLURRED AND ILLOGICAL Police should stop conducting unconstitutional roadblocks and substitute more frequent visual checks of erratic driving to identify people who are driving while intoxicated.

The value judgment and policy proposal are blurred in this thesis statement. In addition, the thesis is potentially illogical because the writer seems to assume that the roadblocks are unconstitutional and does not acknowledge that this value judgment needs to be argued (see "Begging the Question," p. 166).

Make sure that your thesis either focuses on a single claim or identifies two related claims you will argue in an appropriate order.

SINGLE PROPOSITIONS Roadblocks used to identify drunk drivers are unconstitutional.

Police should make more frequent visual checks of erratic driving to identify people who are driving while intoxicated.

RELATED PROPOSITIONS The current practice of using roadblocks to identify drunk drivers is unconstitutional; therefore, police should use an alternative procedure such as instituting more frequent visual checks of erratic driving behavior.

Exercise 4

Examine the following propositions as possible thesis statements for argumentative essays. Decide whether each example provides an adequate thesis, and explain your judgments.

1. The United States should deregulate all mail service in order to increase competition and improve the quality of service.
2. Rap music, which is violent, vulgar, and sexist, should be banned from public consumption, and fines should be imposed on anyone listening to it in public places.
3. The demands for "computer literacy" (knowledge of how to use computers on the job, at home, and in all aspects of public life) will keep increasing with each generation; therefore, public schools should be required to have courses in computer literacy for all students.
4. All Americans select and wear their attire on the basis of a discriminatory class system which, in the schools, distracts students from their education; therefore, we should pass a federal law requiring all students in public schools to wear identical uniforms.
5. Arson is not a crime; it is a mental disease and should be treated as such.
6. If children read when they are growing up, they will become literate.
7. Orange juice tastes better than cranberry juice.
8. Recirculating the hot air from your clothes dryer into your basement during the cold winter months can significantly reduce your heating costs.
9. Humanity's woes began when Eve tasted the forbidden fruit in the Garden of Eden.
10. The telephone resulted in a society less prone to writing, but email will likely lead us right back into the written word as a primary form of communication.

CHAPTER 11 Developing, Supporting, and Documenting an Argument

To encourage readers to agree with your argumentative claim—your opinion, interpretation, or proposal—you need to give them good reasons in the form of ideas and evidence that support your proposition.

11a Developing reasons that support your claim

If you consider your argument from your audience's point of view, the reasoning you use to support your claim is as important as the claim itself. Viewed from this perspective, an argument is a series of reasons that help audience members convince themselves to agree with your point of view and prefer it to competing ones.

Envision your argument as a claim linked to a series of reasons. One good way to create a link between your claim (opinion) and the reasons supporting it is to envision a working thesis statement centered on the word *because* (or *since*, *therefore*, *consequently*, and the like) followed by the supporting reasons.

CLAIM (IN THE FORM OF A WORKING OR PRELIMINARY THESIS STATEMENT)

Coursework for teacher certification should continue after people have started working as classroom teachers *because* this approach will be more effective and efficient, *because* it will help increase the number of new teachers, and *because* it will help others decide more quickly if teaching is the right career for them.

REASON 1

We learn about a professional skill or activity best while we are also doing it.

[Evidence: compare to examples of medical internships and residencies; examples and charts drawn from research on innovative teacher training programs]

REASON 2

Practicing teachers are often more motivated learners than are pre-service teachers.

[Evidence: information from scholarly article comparing responses of participants in pre-service and in-service courses]

REASON 3

College instructors can design more efficient post- or in-service courses by eliminating the background information pre-service teachers require, leaving time to focus on important issues and the latest research and curriculum resources.

[Evidence: quotations from editorial in magazine dedicated to issues in teaching]

REASON 4

Reducing the amount of time people have to spend before they begin teaching will help increase the number of new teachers available in a time of teacher shortages.

[Evidence: interviews with fellow students; statistics and examples from news reports and online discussion groups]

REASON 5

People who decide after teaching for a short time that they have made the wrong career choice will not have spent as much time in coursework and will be able to redirect their education more easily.

[Evidence: statistics and quotations from online version of report of a state commission on teacher preparation]

REASON 6 (COUNTERARGUMENT)

New teachers will still be capable of doing good work in their first teaching jobs, especially if they are adequately supervised and supported by the schools that hire them.

[Evidence: newspaper reports, interviews with two school superintendents]

Think of your argument as reasons *plus* evidence

Reasons alone are seldom enough to convince an audience. They need to be developed with evidence (see the example above) that does a number of things.

- Provides logical justification for the writer's (speaker's) opinions and reasoning
- Encourages audience members to trust the writer's conclusions and proposals
- Enables an audience to understand the reasoning in depth and perhaps draw links between it and their own experiences
- Points out similarities among the values and attitudes underlying the writer's claims or proposals and the values and beliefs of the audience
- Helps readers (listeners) envision a proposed course of action or new policy and regard it as plausible or desirable

11b Using varied kinds of evidence

As you explore an issue, examining what others have said about it, pay attention to the ideas and information they use to support their arguments. Think of ways you might acknowledge and incorporate their ideas and details in your own work. Then as you work on your own reasoning, consider the possible sources of support discussed below. Choose those that are most relevant to the reasons supporting your claim and that address most directly your audience's concerns as well as any opposing arguments.

Pay attention to variety and balance in evidence, too. If, for example, all your evidence comes from your own experience, some in your audience might argue that because other people don't share those experiences, your argument is not entirely valid. Try to achieve a balance of facts and statistics, quotations from experts, examples, and personal knowledge.

1 Use examples

Examples drawn from your own or others' experiences can be among the most persuasive kinds of evidence. Events, people, ideas, objects, feelings, stories, images, and texts—all these and similar "instances" can be turned into examples to support a claim and encourage readers to share your point of view.

Relying on examples is something we and our readers do every day. When we are trying to make a decision or form an opinion, we often call to mind our own experiences or those we have read or heard about. Almost without thinking, we then try to decide whether the experiences are representative or unique and whether they apply to the issue or situation we are considering.

In choosing to provide examples in support of an argument, therefore, you need to keep in mind both the readiness of readers to be persuaded by examples and the likelihood that they will approach examples critically. Remember, too, that the power of examples to persuade often rests in the concrete detail a writer provides. Detail serves to illustrate and explain the point being made as well as to support the writer's conclusions.

A fully developed example uses explanation to provide readers with the information they need if they are to come to agree with an opinion or judgment. It uses specific details to help persuade readers of the ethical or emotional importance of a proposition and of its relevance to the reader and to other people. The following extended example does these things by drawing on the writer's experiences.

> I am afraid to grow old—we're all afraid. In fact, the fear of growing old is so great that every aged person is an insult and a threat to the society. They remind us of our own death, that our body won't always remain smooth and responsive, but will someday betray us by aging,

wrinkling, faltering, failing. The ideal way to age would be to grow slowly invisible, gradually disappearing, without causing worry or discomfort to the young. In some ways that does happen. Sitting in a small park across from a nursing home one day, I noticed that the young mothers and their children gathered on one side, and the old people from the home on the other. Whenever a youngster would run over to the "wrong" side, chasing a ball or just trying to cover all the available space, the old people would lean forward and smile. But before any communication could be established, the mother would take her child back to the "young" side.

—SHARON CURTIN, *Nobody Ever Died of Old Age*

Brief examples often serve more to explain than support, but by providing several related examples, you can often create a cluster of instances with considerable persuasive force, as in the following passage.

The era of the modern family system had come to an end, and few could feel sanguine about the postmodern family condition that had succeeded it. Unaccustomed to a state of normative instability and definitional crisis, the populace split its behavior from its beliefs. Many who contributed actively to such postmodern family statistics as divorce, remarriage, blended families, single parenthood, joint custody, abortion, domestic partnership, two-career households, and the like still yearned nostalgically for the *Father Knows Best* world they had lost.

—JUDITH STACEY, "The Family Values Fable"

2 Use quotations and ideas from authorities

By turning to the words or ideas of a recognized authority on a subject or issue, you can add to the reasons for readers to agree with your point of view. After all, we identify people as experts or authorities because we believe that they know more about a subject than we do, and the idea of expertise includes a general willingness to agree with the expert's opinion.

Most readers are nonetheless likely to maintain an intelligently critical attitude toward your use of ideas and quotations from experts. They will expect you to cite generally recognized authorities or to indicate why the person you are citing should be viewed as an authority. They may also reject the perspective of someone whose biases suggest a lack of fairness or balance, particularly if these biases differ from their own. As a result, you may need to present the words or ideas you are citing in ways that make clear that your source is both fair and authoritative, just as the writer of the following passage does.

Another role of the [African American] family is to pass along different kinds of successful coping strategies against racism. One

> strategy, the heightened sensitivity to the potential for exploitation by white persons, has been referred to by Grier and Cobbs in *Black Rage* as cultural paranoia. While this heightened sensitivity often has been pathologized by the dominant culture, it is a realistic and adaptive way of approaching situations that have frequently been antagonistic. Hopson and Hopson in *Different and Wonderful* suggest that another important coping strategy and a major source of psychological resilience is reflected in the sharing of African cultural derivatives with children while encouraging them to take pride in their ancestry. In *Long Memory*, Mary Berry and John Blassingame note that each generation of African Americans prepares the next for survival in a society that devalues them by passing along "searing vignettes" about what has preceded them. They view this process as a long collective memory that is in and of itself an instrument of survival.
>
> —BEVERLY GREENE, "African American Families"

Do not expect an authority to do all the work for you. After all, you cite an authority simply to add weight to your own thesis and perspective. You encourage readers to agree with you by pointing out that someone whose opinion carries considerable weight already agrees with you. For this process to be effective, you need to make sure that your words appear along with those of your source. This is important even when you include a quotation because you feel that your source makes a particular point more effectively and persuasively than you can. In the following paragraph, for example, the writer uses the final sentence to make sure readers see how the information he is citing fits his argument.

> Accompanying this modern view of the nuclear family were the sentiments that enlivened it. The first of these was the sentiment, as described by Edward Shorter in *The Making of the Modern Family*, of *romantic love*. Beginning with nineteenth-century individualism, the belief arose that for each of us there is one other individual who was created as our perfect mate. Once we encountered that person, we would know it instantly and proceed to spend the rest of our lives forever "happily-ever-aftering." An essential condition of this romantic ideal was that a young woman would "save" herself for her fated partner. In this romantic context, [her] virginity was a valuable commodity that could be exchanged for a lifelong commitment to the relationship. Romantic love worked to keep couples together even when they were unhappy. **While this ideal was unfortunate for parents in unrewarding relationships, it often benefited children because parents stayed together and usually did not blame the children for the failure of the marriage.**
>
> —DAVID ELKIND, "The Family in the Postmodern World"

As you search for examples to support your points, remember the importance of your own writing. No matter how well written your source, readers will ultimately be persuaded by what your own words say rather than by selected statements from someone else.

3 Use detailed information

The range of detailed information available to you on most issues is wide, including statistics, technical information, the results of surveys and interviews, background information, and historical detail. Which of these sources you choose and the role each plays in your writing will depend on the particular issue you are addressing, your point of view, and the views or knowledge of your intended readers. Be alert to these kinds of information as you think about an issue and undertake research, and consider the many different ways you can use the information to support your argument. Here are examples of different kinds of detailed information used to support an author's thesis.

> Meanwhile, young people find it harder and harder to form or sustain families. According to an Associated Press report of April 25, 1995, the median income of men aged twenty-five to thirty-four fell by 26 percent between 1972 and 1994, while the proportion of such men with earnings below the poverty level for a family of four more than doubled to 32 percent. The figures are even worse for African American and Latino men. Poor individuals are twice as likely to divorce as more affluent ones, three to four times less likely to marry in the first place, and five to seven times more likely to have a child out of wedlock.
>
> —Stephanie Coontz, "The Way We Weren't"

4 Use comparisons

One important way to arrive at a judgment is to compare a particular issue, problem, policy, or situation about which you are uncertain to one about which you are more certain. In trying to decide whether to expand a local recycling program, for example, you might reasonably look at the success of current efforts. In arguing for restrictions on television programs or for wider access to technical information gathered by governments or corporations, you might look at the success or failure of such practices in other countries.

Comparisons can be particularly useful when you are arguing for a particular policy. Your readers will be concerned about the consequences of a policy and its likelihood for success or failure. No one can predict the future, of course, but comparisons can help you persuade because they point to the probability of certain outcomes.

At the same time, you should expect readers to approach comparisons critically, being skeptical of those that are far-fetched or unreasonable and judging whether the comparison speaks directly to the issue at hand. Instead of asking a comparison to stand on its own, therefore, spend some time pointing out its applicability and answering possible objections to it. The author of the following passage, for example, uses comparison to argue for two-parent, child-centered families even though he acknowledges that one-parent families can raise children successfully.

> Infants and children need, at minimum, one adult to care for them. Yet, given the complexities of the task, childrearing in all societies until recent years has been shared by many adults. The institutional bond of marriage between biological parents, with the essential function of tying the father to the mother and child, is found in virtually every society. Marriage is the most universal social institution known; in no society has nonmarital childbirth, or the single parent, been the cultural norm. In all societies the biological father is identified where possible, and in almost all societies he plays an important role in his children's upbringing, even though his primary task is often that of protector and breadwinner.
>
> —DAVID POPENOE, "The American Family Crisis"

STRATEGY

Develop a list of questions that can guide your search for facts, ideas, and experiences that support your proposition. Here are possible questions.

- What are some good or bad consequences of this policy?
- What do experts say about solutions to the problem?
- What religious or moral values support my position on this issue?
- Are there any comparisons that might help readers understand my perspective?

Trying to answer these questions can help you decide whether you can use your own knowledge to support an assertion or whether you need additional facts, opinions, and information.

11c Incorporating counterarguments

Traditional argumentation is like debate: you imagine an adversary, someone who doesn't go along with your ideas, and try to undermine that adversary's points or **counterarguments.** Most contemporary approaches to argument aren't quite as battle-like. Your point should be not so much to "win" as to acknowledge other people's perspectives yet still try to convince them of the validity of your views. With either kind of argument, however, you need to anticipate your readers' reactions.

STRATEGY

Use lists and columns to help develop counterarguments. Divide a sheet of paper into three columns. On the left, list the main points supporting your opinion. Write opposing points in the middle column. Put yourself wholly into the other position's point of view when you are listing opposing points. Pretend you are a person diametrically opposed to your original stance. Try to find weaknesses in the points in the left-hand column. Be as critical as possible. In the rightmost column, list the possible defenses to the counterarguments you listed in the middle column. List any known or potential outside sources that would support your argument.

Sometimes it may be difficult to imagine any point of view other than your own. The process of inventing counterarguments may need to move beyond your own frame of reference and beliefs. This is where taking your thesis or position into a more public forum can help. Use various audiences as a "test" for your assertions. Put the idea forward tentatively, so that you will be seen as searching openly for differences of opinion. You might, for example, ask some friends or acquaintances, "What do you think about this issue?" or "Do you think that we ought to do *X* to solve *Y*?" Then listen carefully, and take note of the responses. You might gently extend your friends' reasoning by raising a subsidiary issue or counterargument: "But what about the fact that . . . ?" Again, listen.

Exercise 1

A. Using the strategy described in 10c, develop a workable thesis statement. List at least three pieces of supporting evidence or arguments for your assertion.

B. In a small group, use the Strategy in 11c to create a list of counterarguments against each member's main supporting arguments. In a discussion of each thesis statement, try collectively to respond to those counterarguments in ways that weaken the objections to the original arguments.

11d Building an argument: Paper in progress

Knowing that he had to begin writing a short argumentative paper, Zachary Carter began jotting ideas in his journal. As he walked through the student union on his way to a class, he noticed a group of students crowding around a table where several members of the Coalition on Animal Rights sat. Large posters on the wall showed cruelties allegedly inflicted on monkeys, dogs, and other animals as a result of medical experiments. The students and the Coalition members were carrying on a lively debate about the animal experiments. As Zachary listened, he knew that he had stumbled on an idea for his paper. He grabbed some leaflets and hurried to class.

1 Identify an issue

At lunch, Zachary Carter glanced through the leaflets he had taken. He couldn't help feeling that they turned an enormous, undefined topic ("animal rights") into something very specific by focusing on only one issue (the morality of performing medical experiments on animals). He started writing about his own feelings on this subject in his journal.

> One day when I was little, I came across some neighborhood kids taunting a frog they'd found. They were kicking it, tossing it to each other, rolling it down the sidewalk. I was horrified, but the kids were a lot bigger than I was, so I just stood a few yards away, ready to run to my house if they turned on me. I found the frog's bashed-up body in the grass the next day.
>
> Animal rights. Maybe this violation was outrageous because there was no purpose but a sick pleasure for the kids. Experiments inflict pain, too, but we're supposed to think it's all for the good of human beings. I don't know. A frog, some experiments. These seem so small. The problem is so much bigger than this. It's humans as a species, multiplying, taking over the planet and pushing out other creatures.

On his way to class, Carter continued to puzzle over the question of animal rights. The experimentation problem seemed like a complex argument, since people can claim that animal experiments have led to cures for dozens of diseases and thus made our lives better. At the same time, it seemed manageably narrow, since experiments can be studied, monitored, and controlled. But what about other aspects of animal rights? What about the destruction of rain forests, the wiping out of entire species by human development, or pollution killing off organisms by the thousands?

2 Investigate an issue

The day after his encounter with the animal rights group, Zachary Carter was checking his email messages on his computer when he decided to try out his thoughts on an electronic mailing list for students in his writing class.

> Hi, people. I've been thinking about animal rights. (I'm sure you saw the table in the student union.) I guess I'm more worried now than before about what happens to animals in experiments. But I keep thinking that the lab issue is missing the point. It seems so small compared to the huge injustices we keep doing to animals on the whole planet. If we stopped all the experiments in the world, animals still would have no rights because of what we are doing to their environment. What do you think?

Within a day, about a dozen students had posted responses. Several students offered sensible replies and even suggested where Carter could get more information.

> In response to Zachary Carter's message: Take a situation like human hunger. Big problem, right? So some people create a food-shelf program in one city, and it helps a few dozen families. It doesn't get rid of the problem, but it's a start. Same with taking care of our environment.
>
> Zach Carter: Check out Richard Wagner's book Environment and Man, and while you're at it, Al Gore's Earth in the Balance.

3 Articulate a stance

After thinking about the mailing list responses, Zachary Carter knew that he had to work to articulate his stance. Was he concerned primarily about animal experiments? Or was his point more solution based—that we should do something more fundamental about animal rights? But what was that something? Returning to his journal, he wrote a page exploring his ideas.

A day later, Carter had narrowed his opinion into something approaching a claim or thesis. In his brainstorming, he realized that he wanted to take a broader view of animal rights, and he settled on a tentative proposition for his paper.

> *In considering the rights of animals, we must begin shifting our focus from small controversies such as animal experiments or the survival of a single species to the true injustice, the large-scale destruction of animals' habitat by humans.*

Carter felt generally satisfied with his focus but also knew that he really didn't have an argument, just a way of thinking about a problem. What exactly was he proposing—just that we should think more broadly, or that we should take some sort of action?

4 Find supporting evidence

Taking the advice of one of the mailing list respondents, Carter went to the library in search of the books by Wagner and Gore. He found that they dealt broadly with the issue of the environment. As he read, he was drawn again and again to passages dealing with the issue of human overpopulation. Was there a way to link animal rights to human overpopulation? Searching the electronic databases in his library, he located a series of books by Edward Abbey dealing with the environment. The anthology in his composition course also included a useful article titled "The End of Nature." There was plenty here, he thought, to help him support his ideas. He started jotting down useful quotations.

> "Global warming, ozone depletion, the loss of living species, deforestation—they all have a common cause: the relationship between human civilization and the earth's natural balance." (Gore 31)

Especially powerful for his paper were various proposals for reducing the human population, or at least keeping it from growing out of control. This one main argument, Carter thought, could lay the foundation for an approach to animal rights in which the earth would be balanced between humans and animals in a harmonious ecosystem.

5 Recognize counterarguments

Because Carter had already received some email objections to his original thoughts about animal rights, he decided to do most of his work on counterarguments by himself, trying to put himself in the shoes of people (including some of his friends) who would object to the idea. Using a listing strategy (see 11c), he divided a piece of paper into three columns, wrote down key supporting points, then imagined what people would say against his supporting points. After trying to come up with valid counterarguments, he looked for ways to defend his original supporting points. The result was a chart of ideas that he could develop in his paper.

> Tentative thesis: In considering the rights of animals, we must begin shifting our focus from small controversies such as animal experiments or the survival of a single species to the true injustice, the large-scale destruction of animals' habitat by the overpopulation of humans.

Supporting Points	Opposing Points	Defenses
Humans are pushing the balance of nature askew with their ever-increasing population.	We haven't yet mined the earth for all its resources, so we could support many more people in the future.	Mining all the earth's resources will inevitably destroy the existing ecosystem.
Large-scale tips in the balance of nature will cause a domino effect as inter-dependent species die off.	Entire species have gone extinct without major effects on ecology.	In the past, extinction has happened slowly and naturally because of changing conditions.
More humans need more water, leading to more dams, in turn leading to the destruction of submerged habitat.	Dams create lakes, which create new opportunities for plant and animal life.	Dams like the Glen Canyon Dam upset fragile ecosystems miles downstream.
Male sterilization can effectively curb over-population, as shown in Barbados, etc.	Sterilized men may change their minds about fathering children and then be unable to do so.	Semen can be collected prior to sterilization for later use in artificial insemination.

After creating this list, Carter felt he was ready to begin more formal work on the structure of his paper in preparation for a preliminary draft. Note how he develops a complex argument that includes a definition of his key terms, adequate quotations from his sources to support his points, and a clear, crisp, readable style to engage his readers.

Animal Rights: The Big Picture

by Zachary Carter

1 The issue of animal rights is a multifaceted one, and, upon examination, it tends to make one follow a circle of logic which leads from one conclusion to the next, without the benefit of a final outcome or decision. But there is a way out of this circle, and that is to shift the focus of the issue away from small controversies such as animal experiments or the survival of a single species of tiny fish

to the true injustice, the large-scale destruction of animals' habitat by the overpopulation of humans. Upon exploration, this particular avenue yields astonishing and interesting--even horrifying--results. Clearly an intense effort must be made to preserve the rights of animals (as defined later in this essay) for the benefit of every species involved, including the human race.

2 In order to examine this issue thoroughly, we must find a definition of both "animal" and "rights" and stick to them. So, for the purpose of this essay, "animal" will be defined as any creature that belongs to the kingdom Animalia, which includes reptiles, birds, insects, amphibians, and mammals (even humans). As for a concept of "rights," one must first look at what is most important for the whole of nature. The earth is a vast, spinning ecosystem, teeming with countless forms of life, all in diverse conflict and chaos. Yet amid all the confusion there is an order, a balance, an underlying simplicity. The food chain, photosynthesis, the Krebs cycle, the water cycle, migratory patterns--all these things indicate the presence of an underlying balance, a large-scale cooperation of organisms, the purpose of which is to promote life.

3 Al Gore tells of this in his book <u>Earth in the Balance</u>: "All its parts exist in a delicate balance of interdependency" (50). This balance is important to the continuation of life as we know it on earth because "any interruption of this natural process can have a magnified impact" (51). A large-scale tip in this balance can result in devastating effects on the lives of all creatures, <u>Homo sapiens</u> and other species alike. It is apparent that the preservation of this balance must be the paramount concern of any society because all members in any society are integral parts of nature. If the situation is viewed in this light, then it becomes not only humanity's right and every other species' right, but our duty as well, for the very preservation of life and nature as we know it, to live peacefully

within the balance of nature. Consequently, we arrive at the most fundamental definition of "rights": the right to exist within the balance of nature.

4 And now we come to the problem. Humans, driven by natural instinct, are slowly pushing the balance askew and, in the process, trampling on the rights of other species to exist inside the balance. Because of the population boom, humans have spread across every continent, developing, settling, industrializing, mining, setting up agriculture, and so forth. Gore speaks of human intrusion into the balance: "Global warming, ozone depletion, the loss of living species, deforestation--they all have a common cause: the new relationship between human civilization and the earth's natural balance" (31).

5 The human race has destroyed vast areas of native habitat and cut down billions of trees which--at that volume--are virtually irreplaceable. As Gore notes, "when we scrape the forests away, we destroy these crucial habitats along with the living species that depend on them" (116). Predatory species such as the wolf, coyote, and mountain lion, which are an important part of the ecosystem (because they dwell at the apex of the food chain), have been virtually wiped out in many areas. Deer and elk feel this loss through their subsequent boom in population, which in turn causes a demand for food which cannot be met. As a result, there are millions of starving deer and elk, all because of the destruction of a few predators.

6 These examples of habitat destruction and the killing of species are clearly a violation of animals' rights to exist within the balance. Another type of disruption is the damming of rivers, which not only submerges vast areas of habitat, but also upsets the fragile river ecology for hundreds of miles downstream. A prime example of this is the former Glen Canyon in Utah, now under Lake Powell, a result of the construction of the Glen Canyon Dam. In South America, huge amounts of the Amazon rain forest are being burned, leaving

billions, perhaps trillions, of animals homeless if not killed. Extinctions are on the rise: "Living species of animals and plants are now vanishing in the world at a rate one thousand times faster than at any time in the past 65 million years" (Gore 25). The destruction of an entire species is an example of another clear violation of the rights of animals to exist within the balance. And there are more subtle and terrifying problems than these: global warming, the greenhouse effect, the rising of the oceans. These, in the words of Bill McKibben, can lead us "if not straight to hell, then straight to a place with a comparable 'temperature'" (274). But the underlying cause of all this injustice, the mother of all problems, is overpopulation.

7 We face a future in which there is no longer physical space on the earth for the human race, much less the billions of other species that inhabit the planet. In the words of Edward Abbey:

> The sea will be farmed, all deserts irrigated, whole mountains pulverized, the last forests turned to pulpwood plantations, in order to satisfy the ever-growing needs (no doubt as desperate as in the past) of a human population much larger than at present. (Down the River 117)

Richard Wagner, author of Environment and Man, states that "adding four billion more [people] staggers the imagination, for the earth is barely able to support its present population" (553). He also says that "overpopulation is one problem the entire world must share" (538). Clearly the population explosion must be stopped. This is the only way to make room for all species to have their rightful place within the balance, for the benefit of human beings and the whole of the natural world.

8 First, a move must be made to prevent future development of similar problems, and the only way to do this is to curb the population explosion. Several things can be used to this end.

Abortion, while morally objectionable to many people, is a natural form of population reduction. Rabbits in the wild, for example, will abort their unborn fetuses if the local environment is insufficient for survival. If moral imperatives preclude the use of this method, then there are other equally effective chemical and mechanical methods, "but the most reliable method is sterilization" (Wagner 547). A simple operation performed on a man renders him unable to conceive offspring, and this does not affect sexual impulses. The irreversibility of this method can be combated by taking samples of semen before the operation. Then, at any time, the partner can be artificially inseminated (Wagner 547). A reduction in population <u>can</u> be achieved. This is demonstrated by the efforts of "Barbados, Taiwan, Mauritius, Hong Kong, Tunisia, Singapore, Costa Rica, Egypt, Chile, and South Korea," which have achieved a reduction (Wagner 554). This proposed reduction in population will help to prevent further encroachment upon the natural habitat of animal species by human expansion and exploitation.

9 As for the present, efforts should be made to develop new and streamline old technology in order to make more efficient use of resources. Gore says, "It is now an axiom in many fields of science that more new and important discoveries have taken place in the last ten years than in the entire previous history of science" (31). This trend is expected to continue, and, if so, efficiency of production and use of natural resources should be steered in that direction. Subsequently, waste disposal, energy production, and manufacturing should be improved significantly. Gore also says that "the transformation of the way we relate to the earth will of course involve new technologies, but the key changes will involve new ways of thinking about the relationship [between people and nature] itself" (35).

10 The first and most important imperative is that all individuals make a conscious effort to improve this relationship to the balance of nature, for the sake of animal rights, themselves, and their children. Without this effort to preserve the balance, all members of the human race are on a collision course with destruction, taking millions of innocent species along with them:

> [D]evelopers were bulldozing the last hundred acres of untouched forest in the entire area. As the woods fell away to make way for more concrete, more buildings, parking lots, and streets, the wild things that lived there were forced to flee. Most of the deer were hit by cars; other creatures--like the pheasant that darted into my neighbor's backyard--made it a little further. (Gore 25)

11 An effort to curb these injustices is in order immediately, for the sake of the balance. For "the earth, like the sun, like the air, belongs to everyone--and to no one" (Abbey, Journey 88). And if no effort is made . . . very well then . . . let the world rot.

Works Cited

Abbey, Edward. "The Damnation of a Canyon." Beyond the Wall. New York: Holt, 1984.

---. Down the River. New York: Plume, 1991.

---. The Journey Home. New York: Plume, 1991.

Gore, Albert. Earth in the Balance: Ecology and the Human Spirit. New York: Houghton, 1992.

McKibben, Bill. "The End of Nature." The Informed Argument. Ed. Robert K. Miller. New York: Harcourt, 1992. 264-74.

Wagner, Richard H. Environment and Man. New York: Norton, 1978.

11e Logical strategies

When you employ **logical strategies** for argument, you arrange your ideas and evidence in ways that correspond with patterns of thought that most people accept as reasonable and convincing. You do not have to provide absolute proof for your opinion; if you could, there would be no real need to argue. After all, arguments help to resolve disagreements precisely because an absolutely correct position cannot always be identified. In such a case, an argument helps readers choose among opinions that are reasonable alternatives.

Here are four of the most commonly used logical strategies.

- **Reasoning from consequences.** You argue for or against an action, outlook, or interpretation, basing your argument on real or likely consequences (good or bad).
- **Reasoning from comparisons.** You argue for or against a policy or point of view, basing your argument on similar situations, problems, or actions.
- **Reasoning from authority and testimony.** You draw ideas and evidence to support your outlook from recognized experts or from people whose experience makes them trustworthy witnesses.
- **Reasoning from examples and statistics.** You draw on events, situations, and problems presented as illustrations (examples) or in summarized, numerical form (statistics) to support your point of view.

Induction and deduction are other commonly used logical strategies. A **deductive argument** begins with an explicitly stated **premise** (or assertion or claim) and then goes on to support that premise. It uses **syllogistic reasoning** as the basic logical format. A **syllogism** includes a **major premise,** a **minor premise,** and a **conclusion.** Here is a simple truthful syllogism.

MAJOR PREMISE All landowners in Clarksville must pay taxes.

MINOR PREMISE Fred Hammil owns land in Clarksville.

CONCLUSION Therefore, Fred Hammil must pay taxes.

Faulty syllogistic reasoning is easily illustrated in a flawed syllogism.

MAJOR PREMISE All Ferraris are fast.

MINOR PREMISE That car is fast.

CONCLUSION Therefore, that car is a Ferrari.

In a complex argument, of course, these kinds of reasoning are much more elaborate. You might begin an argumentative paper, for example, by saying something that your readers would generally hold to be true, go on to show that specific examples of that assertion must also be true, and end with your argumentative assertion. This basic sequence can be used to shape each paragraph as well as to frame the paper as a whole.

In contrast, an **inductive argument** does not explicitly state the premise; rather, it leads readers through an accumulation of evidence until they conclude what the writer wants them to. Such arguments usually begin with a **hypothesis,** which differs from an assertion in being tentative, an idea that the writer wants to consider but as yet has not reached any hard-and-fast conclusion about. Of course, in a finished written argument, this hypothesis is somewhat disingenuous since the writer *does* have a conclusion but withholds it until the readers are convinced by reading through all the supporting points.

This form of argument is effective when you are taking a controversial stand on an issue. If you asserted your stand explicitly at the beginning of the paper, you might put many of your readers on the defensive, ready to criticize your argument right from the start. However, if you hold off your assertion, your readers may also hold off their judgment.

Exercise 2

Compose a simple proposition or thesis, and then try to support it with each of the four logical strategies described in 11e (reasoning from consequences, reasoning from comparisons, reasoning from authority or testimony, and reasoning from examples and statistics). Invent authoritative statements or statistics if you wish.

EXAMPLE

Simple proposition: The student senate's proposal to allow alcoholic beverages to be served in the student union should not be passed.

Reasoning from consequences: The consumption of alcohol will increase crime on campus, especially personal assaults, drunk driving, and rape.

Reasoning from comparisons: Easy availability of alcohol deters students from their academic work; when a bar opened briefly three years ago near fraternity row, every fraternity experienced a drop in average grades.

Reasoning from authority and testimony: Having alcohol so easily available on campus may subvert our college's mission by contributing not to students' growth but to their deterioration. According to research conducted by Legman and Witherall, a large percentage of alcoholics over the age of thirty reported that their college binge drinking set a strong pattern for their later addiction.

Reasoning from examples and statistics: Bars on campus draw students away from more beneficial activities. Two years after Carmon College opened a wine and beer hall on campus, participation in lectures and special events had dropped by 26 percent; attendance at the film series declined by 18 percent; and weekend library usage between 5 P.M. and midnight dropped by 43 percent.

11f Emotional strategies

In drawing on **emotional strategies,** you focus on the values, attitudes, belief systems, and emotions that guide people's lives and that are central to any decision-making process.

Values and beliefs. You may present examples, ideas, or statements that confirm or contradict your readers' probable values.

Emotions and values. You may present examples or use language that draws emotional responses (positive or negative) from your readers ("The consequence of this policy will be an increase in the already horrifying flood of bruised, battered, undernourished two- and three-year-olds brought into emergency rooms by parents who deny even the most obvious evidence of abuse").

Be aware that readers often see emotional strategies as weaker support for a point than reason or logic. In an argument against the use of animals for research, for example, an emotional appeal about cruelty to animals could be countered by an emotional appeal about the need for research to cure terrible diseases. A general emotional appeal about animal suffering is not as strong as specific, verifiable accounts of animals being subjected to unbearable pain in the name of research. Often the most powerful emotional appeals will be those directly linked to other forms of logical support.

11g Data-warrant-claim (Toulmin) reasoning

In *The Uses of Argument* (1964), Stephen Toulmin proposes **data-warrant-claim reasoning,** which draws on several kinds of statements reasonable people usually make when they argue (statements of data, claims, and warrants), highlighting a way of relating these statements in order to convince readers.

Data corresponds to your evidence and *claim* to your conclusion. *Warrant*, however, is a more complex term; it refers to the mental process by which a reader connects the data to the claim. It answers the question "How?" Another way to understand this is to think of data as the indisputable facts and the warrant as the probable facts and assertions. As in an inductive argument, you present the data that lead to your claim, but you also present the warrants, the probable facts and assertions that will encourage readers to accept the validity of your claim.

For instance, as data you might have the results of a detailed study establishing the likelihood of injury in each of the many different models of cars currently on the market. You could make a number of interpretive statements about the data (warrants) and point out patterns you see (probable facts—warrants) in order to provide reasoning that links the data to your claim: for the average consumer, buying a large car is a good way to reduce the likelihood of being injured in an accident.

To argue effectively, you need to show your readers *how* the data and the claim are connected. To warrant such a claim, you could say that there are small, medium, and large cars in the ratings and extend this warrant by pointing out that the large cars have a higher safety rating. To back up this warrant, you point out that although some of the smaller cars on each list are quite safe, in general, the large cars are the safest. You could extend the argument by citing further statistics (data) about safety along with arguments and reasoning from other sources (warrants).

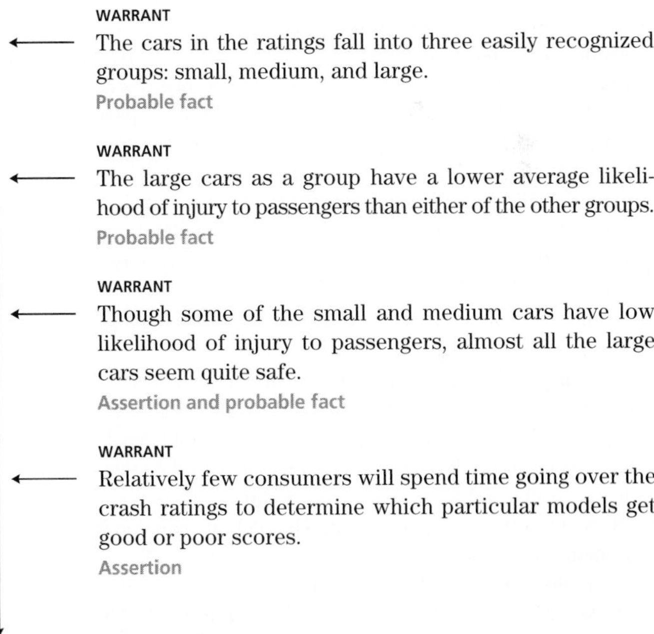

DATA
Ratings of each car model according to likelihood of injury to driver and passenger (scale: 1 = low to 10 = high)
WARRANT
The cars in the ratings fall into three easily recognized groups: small, medium, and large.
Probable fact
WARRANT
The large cars as a group have a lower average likelihood of injury to passengers than either of the other groups.
Probable fact
WARRANT
Though some of the small and medium cars have low likelihood of injury to passengers, almost all the large cars seem quite safe.
Assertion and probable fact
WARRANT
Relatively few consumers will spend time going over the crash ratings to determine which particular models get good or poor scores.
Assertion
CLAIM
For the average consumer, buying a large car is a good way to reduce the likelihood of being injured in an accident.

The data-warrant-claim approach to constructing an argument does not assume that an argument can provide absolute proof of a proposition. It aims instead at showing readers that an opinion or proposed action is plausible, grounded on good evidence and reasons, and worth their endorsement. Arguments that employ this kind of reasoning may sometimes seem more like purposeful dialogues than debates. If you employ this approach, you should take the attitude that your argument is open to other viewpoints, to compromise, and to negotiation.

11h Audience and purpose

Remember that you won't write an effective argument if all you do is stridently voice your opinion on an issue. An argument is effective only if it's part of a relationship between you and your audience. Defining who your audience members are, how you want them to perceive you, and what you want to convince them of is the essential first step to constructing an argument (see Chapter 3).

Your audience is partly determined by your topic and by your own stance. If you are writing about the abortion issue, for example, you need to be clear in your own mind whom you are addressing. Argument papers on this topic are often not well written because the audience is usually a vague "the other side." Remember, it is a fallacy to divide an issue into only two sides (see the discussion of the either/or fallacy in 11i). Likewise, it is ineffective to think of your readers as belonging to one of only two camps.

Rogerian argument, based on the theories of psychologist and group therapist Carl Rogers, provides a useful perspective for considering the responses of your audience. Rogers argued that people's minds can more easily be changed when their opponent seems like an ally instead of an enemy. A highly combative or adversarial approach immediately puts a reader on the defensive, thus setting up a barrier to your ideas. The reader's psychological reaction is "Oh yeah? Well, let me tell you something, Buster!" rather than "Hmmm, that's an interesting point worth considering."

Identifying alternative views. To practice Rogerian strategies, imagine for a moment that you share the views of someone who is opposed to your actual position or solution. What is your opponent's frame of reference? What assumptions might have led him or her to these views? Giving, for the moment, a charitable response that acknowledges someone else's right to hold an opinion you disagree with, what validity can you see in anything your opponent might say?

Rogers also found that a good way to understand someone's view is to try restating it rather than immediately countering it. When participants in a discussion negotiate their positions, sentences often begin not with statements of judgment or reaction ("Well, I think . . ." or "That point doesn't hold water"), but with statements of reflection and repetition: "What I hear you saying is . . ." or "It sounds to me like you're trying to. . . ." This allows not only for mutual understanding of each person's points but for mutual respect for differences of opinion once those points are clearly articulated.

Making a concession. When you understand your opponent's ideas, you may be prepared to work a **concession** into your argument. You make a concession when you acknowledge or consider a view opposed to one you are arguing. A concession does not have to be so strong that it undermines your entire argument. But placed strategically, it can help your reader to see that you have, in fact, tried to be fair-minded. A reader who recognizes that attitude will be more likely to trust your judgment and listen to you.

Concessions may appear briefly, embedded in the structure of a sentence, or they may be elaborate, sometimes taking one or more paragraphs to describe. Concessions embedded in single sentences often involve words like *although*, *while*, *while it may be true that*, *of course*, or *but*.

In a letter to the editor bemoaning the extinction of local, family-run hardware stores in the shadow of huge, warehouse-sized lumber centers, Angie Krastaat made an extended concession that consumers may be attracted by the lower prices and large selection at the lumber centers, but then countered it with an anecdote that led to a generalization.

> Of course, the lumber centers do have their draws: paint in every color, discounted power tools, and items too large to fit into most small stores. But what they gain in selection and pricing they sorely lack in their robot-like relationship with their customers. Where else can you get a single nut, bolt or nail—just one—than a local hardware store? What large lumber center will replace that torn screen or broken window while you wait? Where can you find someone at Mega-Hardware who will work with you in the store to repair something, using ingenuity and bins full of single items?

STRATEGY

To make your argument on "hot" issues more effective, try limiting your audience. Focus on a particular group of people concerned about the issue—on abortion, for example, focus on reaching sexually active teens, unmarried mothers, or the people who protest at abortion clinics. Also consider your image as an arguer. How do you want your readers to perceive you? Do you want to be perceived as erudite, rational, and coolly objective; as passionate and moving; as outraged; as reflective and forgiving?

11i Misleading and illogical reasoning

A **fallacy** is a flaw in the reasoning of any persuasive work, whether it's an argumentative essay, an interpretation of a literary work, a report of the results of a study, or a review. Fallacies often show up in advertisements, stated directly in the copy and implied in the visual images. An ad for beer that shows attractive, bikini-clad women and muscular, handsome men romping on a California beach implies (illogically) that drinking the beer will get you that lifestyle. This example of faulty cause-effect reasoning implies that *because* you drink the beer, you'll be like the people in the ad. The same fallacy can be a problem in academic and professional writing as well but may not be as blatant. For instance, if you read an article that says legalizing marijuana will result in a dangerous increase in cocaine use, you ought to question how the writer demonstrates that cause-effect relationship and supplies evidence linking marijuana use to cocaine use.

Faulty cause-effect relationship. This problem is also called *post hoc, ergo propter hoc* (Latin for "after this, therefore because of this") or just a **post hoc fallacy.** This flawed reasoning attempts to persuade you that just because one event happens after the other, the first event causes the second.

FAULTY CAUSE-EFFECT The increase in explicit violence on television is making the crime rate soar.

READER'S REACTION: This *may* be true, but no evidence is presented here linking the two situations.

False analogy. **Analogies** are comparisons between two things, often on the basis of shared characteristics. In a false analogy, the things may at first glance seem to be comparable but really are not. (See the discussion of the red herring and *ad populum* fallacies in this section.)

FALSE ANALOGY Raising the national speed limit is like offering free cocktails at a meeting of recovering alcoholics.

READER'S REACTION: I don't see the connection. Most drivers aren't recovering from an addiction to high-speed driving, and a legal limit is not the same thing as self-restraint.

Misleading language/misleading evidence. This fallacy is also called **equivocation** and **slanted statistics**. A writer can use misleading language by beginning with one definition of a term (usually one everyone agrees with), then shifting to another sense of the word, one that supports the writer's argument but that not all readers may agree with.

MISLEADING LANGUAGE — Everyone has the right of free speech, so censoring films by rating them Triple X is against one's constitutional rights.

READER'S REACTION: This tries to pass off the *rating* of films as censorship (which it is not) and assumes that *free speech* and *censorship* are directly opposite terms (which they are not necessarily).

Misleading evidence includes statistics, survey results, and expert opinions stacked in favor of one side of the argument. For instance, someone who used an opinion poll to argue for the preservation of the spotted owl but polled only people at an environmental rally would have overwhelmingly favorable but misleading evidence.

Red herring. Similar to misleading evidence is the red herring fallacy. A *red herring* is something that distracts readers from the real argument.

RED HERRING — Gun control laws need to be passed as soon as possible to decrease the rate of domestic violence and home firearms accidents. The people who think guns should not be controlled are probably criminals themselves.

READER'S REACTION: The second sentence doesn't logically follow from the first; it just attacks the people who would oppose the writer's argument instead of supporting the initial assertion.

Ad populum. *Ad populum* means "to the people" and refers to an argument that appeals to the audience's biases instead of using rational support.

AD POPULUM — All doctors should be tested for AIDS and should not be allowed to practice if they test HIV-positive, so they don't spread the disease to their patients. Do you want to be one of those patients?

READER'S REACTION: This writer is obviously trying to invoke my fear of getting AIDS. The claim that HIV-positive doctors will pass on the disease to patients is not founded on valid research.

Ad hominem. Another faulty argument based on audience biases is the *ad hominem fallacy*, which means "to the man." This is a personal attack on the opponent rather than a debate on the issue.

AD HOMINEM — Of course Walt Smith would support a bill to provide financial assistance to farmers—he owns several large farms in the Midwest. Besides, how can he be a good senator after cheating on his wife?

READER'S REACTION: I'd like to hear reactions to Walt Smith's ideas, please. I don't really care whether he had an affair fifteen years ago.

Bandwagon. This fallacy is also called *consensus gentium*, "consensus of the people." A **bandwagon argument** is one that tries to convince you that everyone else agrees with the idea already, so you ought to join in.

BANDWAGON Each year an increasing number of people are quitting smoking, so you ought to quit, too.

READER'S REACTION: **This writer is trying to convince me to quit by saying that other people are doing it. Even though the assertion may be valid, the support is not.**

Begging the question. This fallacy also is called **overgeneralization** or **hasty generalization.** An argument is begging the question when it presents assumptions as if they were facts, sometimes using words and phrases like *obviously*, *certainly*, *clearly*, *people always/never*, and even the seemingly innocuous *some people say*.

BEGGING THE QUESTION Most people these days are trying to be more physically fit; obviously, they are afraid of getting old.

READER'S REACTION: **No evidence is presented for either the claim that most people are trying to be more fit or the claim that they are afraid of getting old. On what basis are these stated as facts?**

Either/or. An **either/or strategy** oversimplifies an issue, making it seem as if it has only two sides.

EITHER/OR On the matter of abortion, there are two positions: either we support a human's right to life, or we allow women to have complete control over their bodies.

READER'S REACTION: **Why can't someone endorse protecting life while also supporting the right to choose what happens to one's body?**

Circular reasoning. *Circular reasoning*, also called **tautology**, is an attempt to support an assertion with the assertion itself.

CIRCULAR REASONING The university should increase funding of intramural sports because it has a responsibility to back its sports programs financially.

READER'S REACTION: **All this really says is that the university should fund sports because it should fund sports.**

Exercise 3

A. Choose a controversial topic you know something about—gun control, abortion, the death penalty, the right to die. Now choose any three of the fallacies described in 11i and write one example of each fallacy to make claims about your topic. (Don't identify the names of the fallacies in your response.)

B. In a small group, exchange copies of the fallacious arguments you wrote for Exercise 3A. Discuss each set of fallacies, trying to identify the logical problems and to suggest revisions or identify specific kinds of support needed.

11j Documented argument or position paper

A **position** paper or **documented argument** is a sharply focused form of argumentative writing that draws heavily on research to take a stand on a question of action or policy, generally an issue of considerable concern in academic, public, or work communities. A position paper defines its issue, considers its audience, and draws on evidence and logical strategies to make its point.

1 Sample position paper

In the following paper, note how the writer frames his argument with an opening reference to fast-food chains and the growing problem of obesity in America. As you read, consider who the writer's audience is, what the main argument is, and how he constructs the support for the argument. What are the counterarguments, and how does he address them? What kind of support, if any, is missing? What fallacies, if any, do you detect?

Pusateri 1

Paul Pusateri

Dr. Drept

WRT 101

15 October 2006

Running Uphill

1 Who is at fault? Is it the fast-food chains for putting such fattening items in front of consumers with endless promotions and marketing schemes? Or is it the consumer's fault for eating the unhealthy meals knowing full well the negative consequences? Suing a fast-food chain for causing your own obesity, as some people have done (Cohen), may be extreme. As one report puts it, "Fast-food litigation has been greeted coolly so far

Defines the issue

Mentions authorities

11j arg

Pusateri 2

because it appears to run up against a core American value: personal responsibility" (Cohen A24). At the same time, this does not mean that the fast-food chains are free from significant blame for the rise of obesity and similar health problems that affect many people today (Surgeon General). The truth is that most people know fast food may not be good for them; they simply don't realize just how unhealthy it is. For example, how many of us know that a "quick lunch" at McDonald's, including a Big Mac, fries, and a Coke, has 62 grams of fat and 1,500 calories (Barrett 74)? Even though the chains are starting to make their menus healthier, they are still to blame. Their pricing policies, overall menus, and marketing techniques lead people to eat fast food no matter how much fat it contains or how many calories it provides.

Argumentative proposition

2 How are we to know what is good for us and not so good in the food we eat? What standard can we use to judge the meals offered by fast-food restaurants? To maintain a desirable, healthy weight, men need about 2,700 calories per day, and women need about 2,000. The American Heart Association recommends less than three hundred milligrams of cholesterol and fifty to eighty grams of fat per day, while the National Academy of Sciences recommends 1,100 to 3,300 milligrams of salt per day (Minnesota Attorney General). In each case, the national average intake is higher (Minnesota Attorney

Standards for evaluating audience

Pusateri 3

General), driven in part, perhaps, by the amount of fast food we eat.

3 Not all fast food contains excessive salt, cholesterol, and calories, of course, but the items that dominate the menus at a Wendy's, Burger King, McDonald's, and other fast-food restaurants and that appear frequently in advertising generally do. For example, a report by the Minnesota Attorney General gives these nutrition facts for two staples of fast-food menus, a cheeseburger dinner and a pizza dinner.

Supporting evidence

1. Quarter-Pound Cheeseburger, large fries, 16 oz. soda (McDonald's)

This meal:	Recommended daily intake:
1,166 calories	2,000-2,700 calories
51 g fat	No more than 50-80 g
95 mg cholesterol	No more than 300 mg
1,450 mg sodium	No more than 1,100-3,300 mg

2. Four slices sausage and mushroom pizza, 16 oz. soda (Domino's)

This meal:	Recommended daily intake:
1,000 calories	2,000-2,700 calories
28 g fat	No more than 50-80 g
62 mg cholesterol	No more than 300 mg
2,302 mg sodium	No more than 1,100-3,300 mg

4 The information in these charts is probably astonishing to most of us. Even though restaurants make nutrition facts available to customers and publish them

Brief concession followed by supporting arguments

online--for example, at a McDonald's Web site (McDonald's USA)--the "need for speed" and convenience that makes us turn to fast-food restaurants in the first place means that most of us do not consult the lists of nutritional facts. Instead, we order foods prominently displayed on menus or we order by price, from a value menu or a promotional special, both of which in my experience feature familiar and relatively unhealthful choices. In so doing, we often pass by the better choices, the small fries rather than the large, for example. At McDonald's, instead of a quarter-pound cheeseburger and large fries, we might choose a hamburger and small fries with 481 calories and 19 grams of fat, a healthier solution (Minnesota Attorney General).

Concession

5 Admittedly, fast-food chains have been adding healthier options to their menus. Arby's Light Roast Chicken has 276 calories and only seven grams of fat; Wendy's has a healthy chili with 210 calories and seven grams of fat. Burger King and McDonald's offer a vanilla shake with five grams of fat and a chicken salad with only four grams of fat, respectively (Minnesota Attorney General).

Menu placement

6 These items often do not receive adequate emphasis in advertising or menu placement, however. In addition, the lack of adequate emphasis frequently means that customers end up thinking that some kinds of food are healthy when they are not. As Kelly Frey points out in "Salad Not Always Healthiest Fast-Food Choice," a Crispy Chicken Salad with

ranch dressing at McDonald's has eight more calories and nineteen more grams of fat than a Big Mac. Salads from Wendy's and Burger King may also have more fat and calories than the burgers. Even a Cobb Salad with low-fat dressing at McDonald's would take a 150-pound person sixty minutes to walk off all 320 calories it contains (Barrett 74).

Advertising and marketing

7 Even television ads that pass certain tests for truthfulness can be misleading. The ads for Subway, for example, leave the impression that the chain's sandwiches are healthful. Some are, yet many are not. Subway's advertising is factually true. The specific sandwiches advertised as healthful actually are; it is the others that are not, but they tend to fall within the general impression of healthfulness created by the advertising. At Subway, a six-inch BMT Italian sandwich has thirty-nine grams of fat, the same as a Big Mac from McDonald's and a Bacon Double Cheeseburger from Burger King (Diet Riot). A Quarter Pounder or a Whopper Jr. would be a better choice for me than the Cold Cut Trio I commonly eat at Subway.

Modifies argumentative proposition

Proposes course of action

8 The blame may lie with the fast-food chains, but the responsibility for making healthier choices is ours as well. There are ways we can do this, but even the available healthy choices are outside the range of those usually marketed by the chains. Nonetheless, an article like Jo Lichten's "Healthiest Fast Food for Busy Travelers" can be a guide. From it I learned that Burger King's Mustard Whopper Jr., which replaces mayonnaise

with mustard, decreases calories by eighty. I thought that Mexican fast food could not taste good and be healthy; I found that a Bean Burrito from Taco Bell can be a complete meal with only 370 calories and twelve grams of fat (Lichten). It's like running uphill, but it is possible to begin reversing the unhealthy practices for which fast-food chains are still to blame.

Works Cited

Barrett, Jennifer. "Fast Food Need Not Be Fat Food." Newsweek 13 Oct. 2003: 73-74. Academic First Search. EBSCO. U of Rhode Island Lib. 21 Oct. 2006 <http://search.epnet.come/direct.asp?an=10997141&db=aph>.

Cohen, Adam. "The McNugget of Truth in the Fast-Food Lawsuits." New York Times 3 Feb. 2003, A24.

"Diet Riot." DietRiot.com 14 Oct. 2003. 19 Oct. 2006 <http://www.dietriot.com/fff/rest.html>.

Frey, Kelly. "Salad Not Always Healthiest Fast-Food Choice." The Pittsburgh Channel.com 15 May 2003. 19 Oct. 2006. 19 Oct. 2003 <http://www.thepittsburghchannel.com/health/2206321/detail.html>.

Pusateri 8

Lichten, Jo. “Healthiest Fast Food for Busy Travelers.” American Woman Road And Travel. 2003. 5 Oct. 2006 <http://www.roadandtravel.com/health/healthiestfastfood.htm>.

McDonald’s USA. “McDonald’s USA Nutrition Information.” 21 Oct. 2003. 31 Oct. 2006 <http://www.mcdonalds.com/countries/usa/food/nutrition/categories/nutrition/>.

Minnesota Attorney General. Fast Food Facts. 19 Oct. 2006 <http://www.olen.com/food/book.html>.

Surgeon General of the United States. The Surgeon General’s Call to Action: Prevent and Decrease Overweight and Obesity. Washington: GPO, 2003.

2 Comment on Paul Pusateri’s Paper

Pusateri’s argumentative thesis is clear, if a bit complicated. He does a good job of supporting it with a variety of evidence. Some readers are likely to agree with his outlook, at least in part. As he admits, however, many are likely to prefer to put the responsibility elsewhere: on the people who choose the food they eat, not on the restaurants that serve it. Whether or not they are persuaded, however, most readers are likely to agree that he has made a sound case for his point of view.

CHAPTER 12
Creating a Visual Argument

Suppose you want to convince readers that your ideas for an ecologically sound yet also student-friendly dorm were worth serious consideration even though your proposals were created by a group of students. You could argue for your plan with words alone, but pictures and drawings would be both more informative and more persuasive. Figures 12.1 and 12.2 show two visuals a student created as part of *EcoDorm: An Independent Student Project at the University of Idaho.*

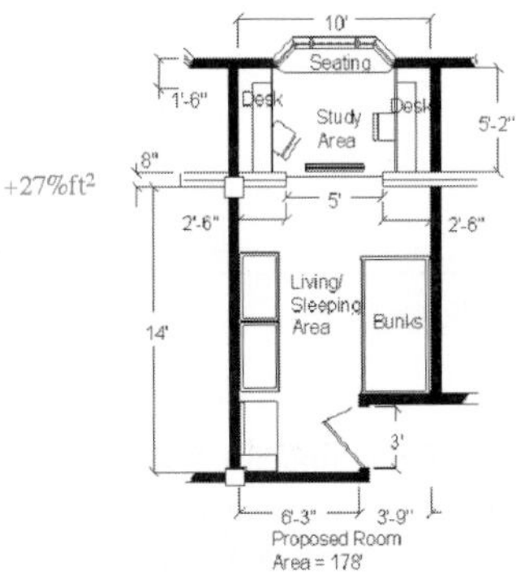

FIGURE 12.1 Drawing of proposed dormitory room. Source: <http://www.uidaho.edu/ecodorm>.

FIGURE 12.2 Computer-generated picture of proposed dormitory room. Source: <http://www.uidaho.edu/ecodorm>.

Visuals can be an important and even critical component of argument. They can help explain an issue or problem. They can clarify supporting evidence. They can draw on emotions and values to make your argument especially persuasive. However, visuals can't do all the work of argument and shouldn't be expected to substitute for careful reasoning and detailed supporting evidence.

12a Presenting an issue

An issue you address in an argument can be complex and detailed, yet you generally need to introduce it clearly and concisely so you can move on to your primary tasks—introducing your perspective (argumentative proposition, 10c) and providing support for it. Visuals can emphasize the importance of the issue while providing details at a glance.

1 Graphs, tables, and charts

When an issue or problem needs to be understood in terms of numbers, statistics, or relationships among facts, a table (p. 177), graph (p. 178), or chart (below) can substitute for sentences filled with potentially confusing detail.

COMPLICATED A recent survey showed considerable support for noise reduction efforts in the town. Of the respondents, 45 percent strongly supported the efforts; 20 percent gave moderate support; 15 percent gave mild support; and 20 percent offered no support.

CLEAR AT A GLANCE

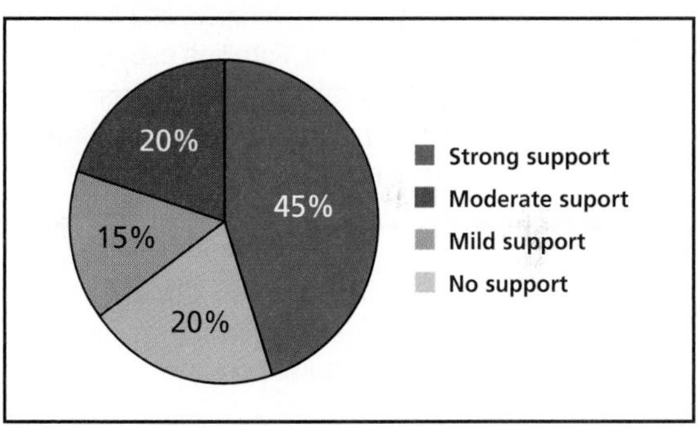

FIGURE 12.3 Survey results: Support for noise-reduction laws

2 Pictures and drawings

Pictures can help readers understand complicated physical settings or problems such as dorms that pose a fire hazard or neighborhoods that need to be revitalized. They can present social relationships or issues, including those that involve values or emotions. The organization Save the Children, for example, uses photographs integrated with text to emphasize the poverty and need of the children it serves as well as the urgency of the problem (See

Omar is 13 years old and has experienced the violent uprooting of his family and extreme personal loss. He has missed out on most of his education and his sense of security and stability has been shattered. Save the Children opened a children's center at the camp where Omar and his siblings live and now he spends every day there.

"I come to the centre because I like to learn new things"
Omar's Story >

Fifty-five thousand children have already attended these centers, which have been established in eleven different locations around West Darfur. The child-friendly spaces provide a secure location for children like Omar who have become, through conflict, part of a new and transient community facing special risks. Some are neglected, most miss out on adult attention and guidance, and they are at risk of abuse if left unsupervised. Families can make use of the centers for temporary child care as an alternative to leaving their children alone. At the same time they can learn basic literacy, numeracy, hygiene practices and social skills.

FIGURE 12.4 Omar's story: Save the Children.
Source: <http://www..savethechildren.org/campaigns/rewrite-the-future/omars-story.html>.

Figure 12.4). The photos also support the agency's attempts to persuade readers to contribute to the organization.

12b Providing evidence

Visuals can add depth and detail to reasoning and evidence you present in words, or they can stand more or less on their own, relying on verbal commentary in the visuals themselves. Visual evidence is of two kinds: (1) details, facts, and statistics presented in the form of graphs, tables, or other figures, and (2) photographs or drawings that are evidence in themselves. Facts and statistics presented as columns of figures (tables) or in graphs and charts can simplify the presentation of complex evidence. They can also highlight key points. They make evidence easier to understand and more persuasive. For example, comparative data about the relative pace of life in different countries is efficiently summarized in the following table.

THE PACE OF LIFE IN 31 COUNTRIES

Country	Overall Pace of Life	Walking Speeds	Postal Times	Clock Accuracy
Switzerland	1	3	2	1
Ireland	2	1	3	11
Germany	3	5	1	8
Japan	4	7	4	6
Italy	5	10	12	2
England	6	4	9	13
Sweden	7	13	5	7
Austria	8	23	8	3
Netherlands	9	2	14	25
Hong Kong	10	14	6	14
France	11	8	18	10
Poland	12	12	15	8
Costa Rica	13	16	10	15
Taiwan	14	18	7	21
Singapore	15	25	11	4
USA	16	6	23	20
Canada	17	11	21	22
S. Korea	18	20	20	16
Hungary	19	19	19	18
Czech Republic	20	21	17	23
Greece	21	14	13	29
Kenya	22	9	30	24
China	23	24	25	12
Bulgaria	24	27	22	17
Romania	25	30	29	5
Jordan	26	28	27	19
Syria	27	29	28	27
El Salvador	28	22	16	31
Brazil	29	31	24	28
Indonesia	30	26	26	30
Mexico	31	17	31	26

FIGURE 12.5 The pace of life in 31 countries.
Source: Levine, Robert. "The Pace of Life in 31 Countries." *American Demographics,* 19 (1997): 20–29.

Visual presentations can also appeal to values and emotions, as does the following map, in which the color red indicates states with what the author considers fewer or inadequate gun control laws.

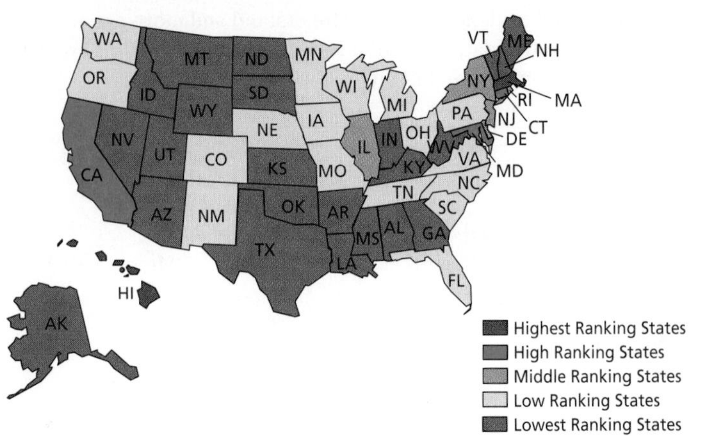

FIGURE 12.6 A comparative survey of state firearm laws.
Source: <http://www.soros.org/initiaves/justice/articles_publications/publications/gun_report_2000401/GunReport_Chart1.pdf>.

(Note: Using such strategies to add emphasis to weak or questionable evidence is, of course, unethical.)

Photographs and artwork (including line drawings) can highlight evidence's appeal to values and emotions and create vivid representatives of a larger group of examples.

Visuals can also help explain complicated reasoning, as in the following graph highlighting the consequences of failing to decrease birth rates in lesser developed countries.

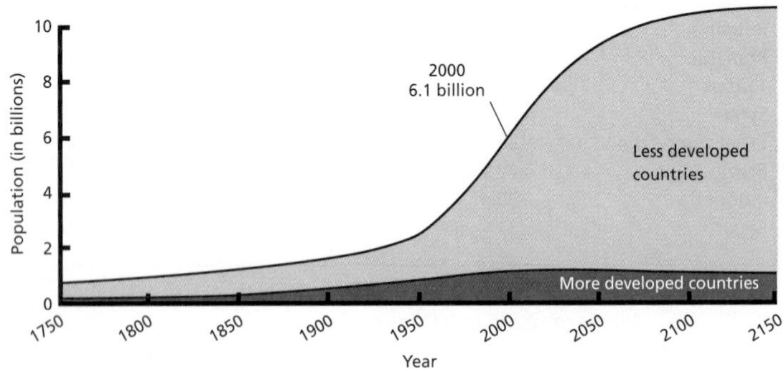

FIGURE 12.7 World population growth, 1750–2150.
Source: <http://www.prb.org/PrintTemplate.cfm?Section=Population_Growth&template=/ContentManagement/HTMLDisplay.cfm&ContentID=5602>.

Presenting Your Work

CHAPTER 13
Designing Documents

With all of the electronic resources available today—pictures, graphs, color, type fonts, even streaming video—it's obvious that writing is far more than words alone. Writing now means producing an entire document, not just the words, and the final product can take many forms: paper, electronic, and multimedia. You can combine these elements in many ways, making choices appropriate for the community of readers you are addressing, the information you are presenting, the ideas you are exploring, and your purposes for writing.

SELECTED ROLES FOR VISUAL RESOURCES IN THREE COMMUNITIES

ACADEMIC	PUBLIC	WORK
Summarize and clarify complex relationships. Present complicated data. Highlight conclusions.	Emphasize appeals to emotions and values. Highlight elements of a policy or proposed action. Summarize key information.	Outline features of a problem. Summarize goals. Highlight recommendations or solutions. Enumerate procedures or elements of an agreement.

Academic. In an academic report on sleep deprivation, for example, you might use such visual strategies as graphs and tables to supplement and extend your written discussion (see Figure 13.1 and the table on page 181). (In MLA style, the word *Figure* is abbreviated *Fig.)* Visual resources can summarize and clarify complex relationships.

Public. In a campus newspaper article on student sleeplessness, however, you might use a photograph of students sleeping in the library just before exams, placing it near the beginning of your text. A carefully chosen photograph would do more than grab the attention of your readers; it would help prepare them for the article by bringing to mind their memories of similar experiences relevant to the subject you are presenting.

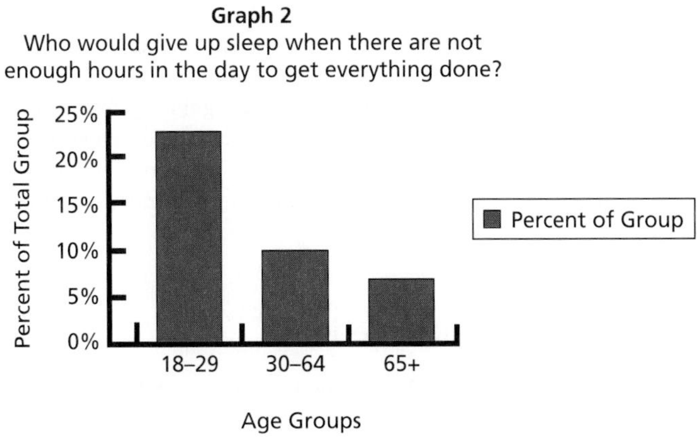

Graph 2
Who would give up sleep when there are not enough hours in the day to get everything done?

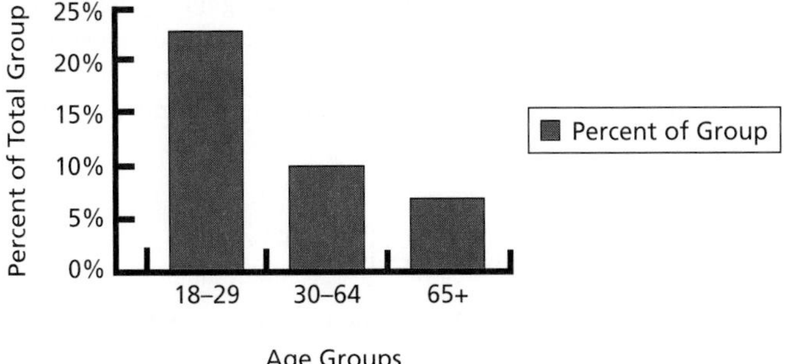

FIGURE 13.1 Graph used in academic report on sleep deprivation.
Source: "Sleep Is One Thing Missing in Busy Teenage Lives," *New York Times,* 5 Nov. 2002.

Table 2 Proportion of High School Students Who Experience Various Problems—By Sleep and Grades

		GET ENOUGH SLEEP		GRADES IN SCHOOL		
	All %	Yes %	No %	A's %	B's & C's %	D's & F's %
Often have difficulty waking up in the morning	58	37	70	56	60	67
Often fall asleep during class	12	7	15	10	13	27
Feel tired during class	53	34	64	54	48	65
Daydream during class	42	31	48	39	43	60
Have difficulty paying attention in class	27	16	34	23	28	58
Often feel bored	55	43	61	53	54	76
Often feel lonely	28	18	34	28	25	42
Have thought of dropping out of school	20	15	23	12	26	57

Note: Base: High school students (grades 7–12)

FIGURE 13.2 High school students who experience problems—sleep and grades.
Source: <http://www.harrisinteractive.com/harris_poll/Index.asp?PID=372>.

Work. In creating a Web site on the causes and dangers of sleep deprivation for a mattress company, for example, you'll want to pay attention to the *layout*, the arrangement of the page. You might choose, for instance, to include a column on one side of the page that highlights key features of your site and enables readers to move directly to the discussion most interesting or relevant to them: discussions of the causes, effects, or dangers of sleep deprivation or advice about sleep basics, including information about your company's practices.

13a Goals of document design

The choices you must make in designing a document fall into five categories: *goals*, *format*, *content and style*, *layout*, and *medium*. The goals you set for document design ought to shape all your other choices.

A well-designed document can achieve many goals.

- **Alert readers to your purpose(s).** Headings, illustrations, charts, and special typefaces will all help readers understand and remember your specific aims.
- **Emphasize key points or ideas.** Boldface or colored type will make your key recommendations stand out. Material set off from the text in a box gets special attention. A split screen on a Web site can list key points alongside the text that discusses them.
- **Help readers locate information.** Headings can identify the parts of a report containing specific information. A line drawing can highlight parts of a mechanism. Links in an electronic document can take readers directly to summaries of different kinds of information.
- **Explain relationships or support arguments.** Tables or graphs of data can help readers visualize complex relationships. Adding color to a chart, using graphics to highlight parts of a picture or drawing, and adding marginal commentary to a text drawn from one of your sources are all effective ways to emphasize your interpretation or link evidence to your thesis.
- **Help readers visualize information and heighten the effect of your words.** A chart can help readers understand the relationship between education and income level in a dramatic fashion. A photograph can bring home the terrible effects of tornadoes or encourage readers to take steps to confront a problem. Video clips and sound in an electronic document can add a sense of immediacy and vividness to the information you present while reinforcing your descriptions, discussions, and interpretations.
- **Make your writing more persuasive.** By using images and design strategically, you introduce varied perspectives on your subject while

highlighting your own point of view. Blended with effective reasoning and clear expression, your visual design for a document can encourage readers to pay special attention to your conclusions.

13b Format choice

Imagine trying to draw a reader's attention to an upcoming event with a bulletin-board flyer using a 10-point font and no other visual effects. Designing effective documents requires more planning. There is no substitute for taking the time to consider your writing task and audience before you determine what format, layout, and visual aids (if any) you will use to support and enhance your presentation.

1 Consider your rhetorical situation and readers' needs

Your document design choices are affected by the same concerns that define your writing task: audience, purpose, and context. Readers need different things from different documents. The same reader approaches an essay about air pollution quite differently from a set of instructions for the operation of a chain saw. Equally true is the fact that two people might approach the same document in different ways. An engineer for a chemical plant that seeks to comply with EPA guidelines will read the essay about pollution with concerns very different from those of a homeowner who lives downwind from the plant.

As you participate in various communities, pay special attention to the way information is presented and received. For example, while your academic readers will expect to read a document from beginning to end, readers in a work community, eager to get to the point, are likely to limit their reading to the introduction and the conclusion.

2 Determine the form and shape of your document

As you begin considering document design, start with the "big picture"—the entire document and its overall shape—and then move to the important details of how you will integrate the various design elements.

- What format or document type will you use? How will you lay out the pages?
- What highlighting devices will you use to make your organization readily visible?
- What kind of font, typeface, and type size will you use?
- Will you use visual aids? If so, which ones?
- If you use certain aids, such as photographs or drawings, are there copyright issues or legal concerns you must address first?

After you answer these questions, you should create a mock-up version of your document—a sketch that will help with planning. Such quickly sketched versions of a document enable you to visualize how the various design elements addressed in Sections 13c–e will work together.

13c Layout

Layout is the arrangement of elements such as words, paragraphs, lists, tables, graphs, and pictures on a page or computer screen. Laying out your document effectively involves presenting information in a way that is easy to read, access, understand, and use.

1 Use visual cues

To increase the readability of your document, use visual cues such as boldface text and color. These devices will simplify your readers' task and influence their attitudes. Be careful to avoid overwhelming your text with visuals. Simplicity—a few well-chosen visual cues—often works best.

Use highlighting to direct the reader's eye and create emphasis. Typographic devices (see 13d) such as **boldface,** *italics*, shading, underlining, and boxes signal distinctions among items in a text, create impact by emphasizing a specific section, and help the reader locate main sections.

STRATEGY

- Use italics for emphasis or when irony or humor is intended. (See Chapter 55 for more on using italics.)

  His rent was late for the *third* straight month.

- When you want to emphasize something, consider using **boldface type.**
- Use capital letters for emphasis only, and use them infrequently. Use of all capital letters in a text's body becomes monotonous and hard to read. (See Chapter 54 for more on using capital letters.)
- Don't overuse exclamation marks and underlining. Be **angry,** or perhaps *angry,* but not angry!!! Underlining on Web pages can cause confusion because hypertext links are almost always underlined. (For more on exclamation points and underlining, see 52c and 55b.)

Use color to create order. Using color effectively can help readers identify recurring themes (titles and subtitles), can reveal patterns and relationships (charts and graphs), and can speed searches. It can aid in decision making. Be aware, however, that colors have different connotations among professional audiences (as shown below) and that color is not appropriate or necessary in all contexts.

COLOR	ENGINEERING	MEDICINE	FINANCE
blue	cold/water	death	reliable/corporate
red	danger	healthy/oxygenated	loss
green	safe/environmental	infection	profit

STRATEGY

As you draft and revise your documents, consider color carefully. Follow basic principles for the use of color in effective document design.

- Use color to accomplish specific goals (to warn or caution, for instance), not just to decorate.
- Use color to prioritize information. Readers will go to bright colors first.
- Use color to symbolize. Draw on your knowledge of your readers.
- Use color to identify a theme that recurs or to sequence information.
- Use color to code different symbols or sections and make searching for information easier.

2 Arrange information effectively

Effective document design enables users to locate important information quickly.

Use white space. White space can organize information into chunks and guide the reader's eye. *White space* is the term for open space not filled by design elements. It can be the spaces between letters, words, lines within a paragraph, or paragraphs. It also includes the margins (top, bottom, and sides) of a page, usually one or one and a half inches wide, and the space surrounding graphics. Used effectively, white space can guide the reader's eye from one point to another. Crowded pages are never crowd pleasers; always be sure there is adequate white space on every page of your document.

Use informative headings. Headings are concise phrases that forecast or announce content in upcoming sections. Because they are usually larger and darker than the basic text of a document, headings work to catch the reader's eye—as they do in this handbook. Headings also move readers along, helping them to see the organization of a document (the big picture) and to find the specific information they seek.

STRATEGY

Considering the organization of your information and how efficiently readers will be able to make sense of it, create appropriate headings for your document. Adhere to the following principles as you create your headings.

- Use consistent type font and style for headings.
- Use different size type to indicate different levels of headings.
- Make your headings stand out—use boldface type and/or white space between headings and text.
- Position your headings consistently (for example, if you center first-level headings, as in the example that follows, do so throughout your document).
- Make headings content-specific and task- or reader-oriented (*"Deducting Student Loan Interest"* rather than *"Student Loan Interest"*).
- Make headings parallel in structure (see Chapter 43).
- Use only those headings you need; avoid clutter.

Notice how this handbook makes use of headings. You are reading at this point in the chapter:

Use lists. Lists are an effective way to present information, making it easy for readers to grasp your major points. They break up dense text and make your document look more pleasing. Lists also help you complete tasks (a "to do" list, for example), and they are useful whenever you need to group related items (a list of healthy food groups versus not-so-healthy food groups). Consider highlighting list items with visual cues such as bullets or numbers.

Rely on visual conventions. Just as our language has grammatical conventions, there are conventions for document design. Depending on the community you're in and the document you're writing, readers will expect to find certain features. Humanities papers written in MLA style will follow MLA formatting conventions (see Chapter 28); APA papers will follow APA guidelines (see Chapter 29). Letters, memos, reports, and brochures all require their own formatting conventions. Your history teacher will expect to see a report that follows certain conventions while your prospective employer will look for others in your résumé.

13d Typeface choices

In preparing your document, you can take advantage of the large variety of fonts, typefaces, and type sizes available with today's computers and software. But do so judiciously, always being sensitive to your audience and purpose. Most readers would rather see no more than two or three different fonts in a single document. In addition, always select a typeface or font that speaks to the audience in a tone that best reflects the subject matter without sacrificing readability.

- **Use a proper type size and weight to influence readers and help them read the text quickly and easily.** Type size affects legibility. Standard type size is 10 or 12 point because both are easy to read (see the sample font sizes below). Type size also affects how the reader will perceive the information: the larger the type, the more important the information will appear. Twelve-point type is the standard in academic texts appearing in word-processing programs.

12 point	10 point
A New Deal.	A New Deal.

  Type weight (letter width and stroke thickness) is also important in reinforcing your message levels. Because some fonts have thicker or wider letters, you can use them to highlight messages without relying on the use of boldface, italics, or shading.
- **Make reading easier by using serif and sans serif typefaces appropriately.** Serif typefaces have the "feet" or small strokes at the end of each letterform. Sans serif fonts lack them.

Serif	Sans serif
N	**N**

  Readers tend to find serif typefaces easier on their eyes in long documents. Sans serif fonts are harder to read in long documents but work well in titles, headings, and labels. They also work well for material that will be presented on a computer screen. (Notice how serif and sans serif fonts are used in this handbook, for example.) There are many variations of serif typefaces. Examples include Times New Roman, Courier, Garamond, and Century Schoolbook. Sans serif faces include Arial, **Impact,** and Tahoma.

- **Add interesting flourishes with display or decorative fonts** such as Mistral, Sand, **Cooper Black,** or Harrington. Some documents, such as brochures, invitations, and posters, require special touches to catch readers' attention or sway their emotions. Decorative fonts have personality and do this well. However, because these fonts are intended to be more ornamental than informative, they should be used with discretion.
- **Add emphasis or direct attention with symbol fonts.** Used carefully, symbol fonts (such as those you find in Zapf Dingbats, Monotype Sorts, and Wingdings) can direct a reader's attention, emphasize a point, and add simple graphic flourishes to your documents. There are many of these special characters, and you'll often find them listed under "symbols" in a pull-down menu in a word-processing program or in a list of fonts. You may find ornamental symbols and icons like these in your font menu.

ϑ □ Ξ [! / 3̄ ♥

13e Visuals

Albert Einstein once said, "I rarely think in words at all." He thought in symbols and pictures; he envisioned concepts and information. This is essential for writers to understand. Sometimes words aren't sufficient or aren't as efficient as tables, graphs, charts, photographs, maps, and drawings are in making a point. These visual aids, or graphics, are effective in bringing information to life.

- Graphics communicate what words cannot.
- Visuals are understood more quickly than words.
- Tables, charts, and other visuals help readers learn and retain information.
- Graphics entice readers, especially in public settings, where attention-getting is at a premium.

1 Tables organize information

Tables are useful when you present information—usually text or numbers in columns and rows—in a relatively small space. They also help in displaying complex information. Tables (see Figure 13.3) are labeled as such and are numbered and titled, as in the example that follows; all other graphics are **figures**.

2 Graphs and charts represent relationships among data

If you want to emphasize trends, add credibility, interest the reader in data, or forecast future values, then graphs or charts will be very useful. Graphs, like Figure 13.4, rely on two labeled axes (vertical and horizontal) to

Table 1 Web Site Services, 2005 (percentages, by sector)

	PUBLIC UNIVERSITY	PRIVATE UNIVERSITY	PUBLIC 4-YR. COLLEGE	PRIVATE 4-YR. COLLEGE	COMMUNITY COLLEGE
Undergraduate application	99	90	95	96	96
ePortfolio	32	27	37	28	10
Journals & reference	92	96	92	94	84
Course reserves	78	81	66	67	35
Course registration	97	94	97	80	97
Online course	95	67	88	54	94
E-Commerce capacity	92	81	87	57	85

Source: "The Campus Computing Project," www.campuscomputing.net

FIGURE 13.3 Usage rates of Web site services among colleges

show relationships between two variables. Charts display relationships in other ways. Some, such as pie charts (Figure 13.5 on p. 190), show percentages of a whole; others, such as bar charts (Figure 13.1 on p. 181), compare items or show correlations. Graphs and charts need to be labeled with a figure number and a brief caption.

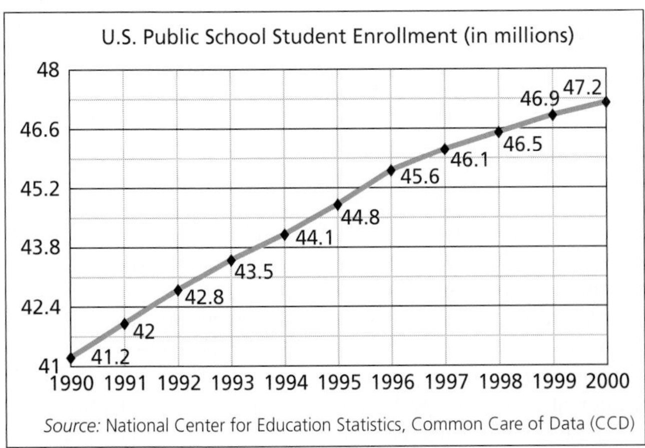

FIGURE 13.4 Number of students enrolled in public schools. Source: <http://nces.ed.gov>.

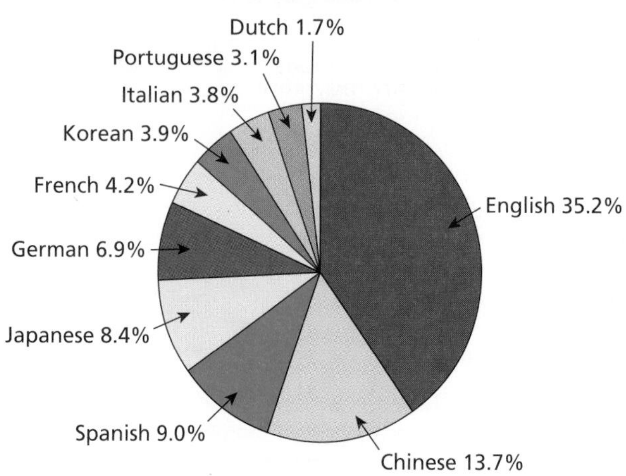

FIGURE 13.5 Online population by language group. Source: GlobalReach, <http://global-reach.biz/globstats/index.php3>.

3 Other visual devices serve varied purposes

Use drawings and diagrams to present physical appearances, to show connections among parts, and to illustrate spatial relationships. Think of the diagrams you've seen in manuals for using a new car or assembling a model or the diagrams you've used to set up a priority schedule for schoolwork. All such diagrams and drawings aid readers by helping them actually *see* what to do.

You can also use photographs and illustrations to record reality, to define and provide examples, just as newspapers and magazines do. Photographs and illustrations are useful when you don't have the time or expertise to create a drawing or when the external appearance (rather than the components) is the focus. But keep in mind the need to credit sources and the appropriateness of such visual devices in various contexts—and avoid overusing them.

Some word-processing programs include a selection of "clip art"—simple drawings that you can easily paste into your document to enhance a point or draw a reader's attention. You can also purchase CD-ROMs of clip art and photographs (try an art supply store) that you can use to enhance your documents, and many Web sites offer clip art and stock photography. In all cases, however, you must be sure that your use of images complies with copyright rules. Most disks, publications, and Web sites of clip art and photographs include information on copyright; if you aren't certain, and no contact information is given, you should look for an alternative image.

STRATEGY

- Choose the appropriate visual aid.
- Use the visual to illustrate one point, and make sure it supports that point. Don't use graphics as decoration or filler.
- Keep graphics as simple as possible to achieve your end.
- Set graphics off with white space. Don't crowd them.
- Use textual cues to guide the reader: label the graphics consistently, number them, and provide accurate, concise captions that explain the relationship of the graphic to the text.
- Help readers make sense of your graphics by positioning them as close to their text references as possible.
- Be sure to credit sources for borrowed graphics.

13f Web pages

Whether you have had experience creating simple (or complex) Web pages or you're just a frequent Web surfer, you know that well-designed Web pages are easy to navigate, are attractive, and represent their company, organization, or creator well, while those that are poorly designed are hard to use and leave a poor impression.

There are various types of Web pages. The most common is the **personal home page,** an individual author's effort to create a place for herself online. Additionally, you will see commercial sites (including corporate pages, sites sponsored by nonprofit organizations, and online shopping opportunities), educational sites (including school and university pages, scholarly journals, and free informational presentations), and news/entertainment sites (including newspapers, magazines, and other media).

1 Establishing a purpose and a persona for your Web page

If you're building a personal home page on the Web, consider what you want the general format to be. Are you fulfilling an assignment for a biology class project on coral reef preservation? You might include maps and photographs of reefs to illustrate your research, along with links to sites sponsored by environmental organizations. Are you setting up an "online business card"? Limit the material to very general information and contact listings. Will your site function like a résumé? Provide detailed information about your professional interests and abilities, perhaps with links to volunteer organizations you have worked with and classroom projects you are proud of. Are you designing a resource for people with interests similar to yours? Add links and commentary on sources you find useful. Or are you producing a kind of autobiography, so your friends and family can see what you're up to?

You need to determine your audience and what aspects of yourself you want to present to the online community. If your site is designed for your instructor and your fellow students, will you be surprised or annoyed if someone you do not want to hear from or have never met sends you email commenting on your site? If your autobiographical page shows off your keen sarcastic wit and your political views, are you comfortable knowing that a potential employer may find that site by using a simple search engine?

STRATEGY

Before building any Web site, spend time studying sites with similar purposes. Make lists of what you do and do not like about these sites. Consider contacting the authors and designers of those pages to ask for advice before you start, or for feedback after you have begun. And, just as you would ask for peer feedback on a paper in progress, ask fellow students, colleagues, or friends for comments and suggestions.

Be careful about naming your site. Search engines will index it based on the words that appear in the title and in the text of the site. Select your words carefully, and when you're ready to publish, visit the major search engine sites to learn the process of registering and indexing your site and its title. When writing for the Web, effective search engine registration is almost as important as making sure the actual information in your site is accurate.

2 Considering your audience

Getting feedback from your intended Web audience is the best way to "user-test" your site and find out how others feel about its layout. Keep a few simple rules in mind when constructing and maintaining a site.

- **Content is key.** Most Web users are looking for information, not "cool" design and graphics. Make sure any graphics reinforce your topic rather than just take up space.
- **Allow ample "white space."**
- **Test your Web pages on various platforms and browsers.**
- **Always include contact information,** preferably in the form of an automatic email link. However, *never* put your full name, address, and phone number (or other vital information) in this space.

13g Model documents

The following model documents show how the principles of document design outlined in this chapter work in action.

1 Daisy Garcia
Professor L. Miles
HPR 101
17 December 2003

Rebuilding

September 11, 2001, marks a day when your feelings of shock and loss of direction matched with others across the country no matter where you were or what you were doing when the twin towers of the World Trade Center collapsed. Deciding what, if anything, to build on the site has been a process of differing emotions, perceptions, and plans. The various proposals have been ambitious, breathtaking, moving, and, above all, quite different in perspective and style.

. . .

Freedom Tower is designed to stand as the tallest building in the world in its completion at a symbolic height as a 1,776-foot spire. The antenna structure will be the home of various channels in the NY area and have a representational design relating
2 to the Statue of Liberty. David M. Childs is collaborating with Libeskind as the design architect. It will contain a vertical garden known as "Gardens of the World," observation decks, and programs for recreational commercial use. The commercial buildings are going to be designed by the other three architects chosen by Silverstein.

There are about 10 million square feet of office space in five towers and 880,000 square feet of retail space. The Wedge of Light is an area designed and aligned with the heavens so that on September 11th of each year, it is lit.

Sample page from student paper on the World Trade Center memorial.

1 MLA opener
2 Integration of photograph

Thursday
July 8th, 2003

Volume XX
Issue 2

The Daily Moose

North America's Only Newspaper Devoted to Moose Lovers Everywhere. Twenty-Two Years and Growing.

1

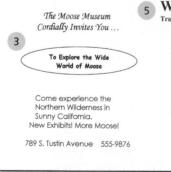

Big Moose Comes From Small Dreams

Staff Reporter: Andrea White

Growing up, your favorite animal may have been a cat, dog, or turtle. Even as exotic as parrots, giraffes and elephants. But in areas north of Chicago and Boston, children wish for pets like deer, caribou and even moose. Moose usually occupy areas in the northern United States and Canada, finding them in southern California is quite unusual. However, traveling to Orange County, California you might see dozens, even hundreds of these winter-weather giants. Mainly Seconds, a craft/antique store in Orange County, has a display of numerous moose paraphernalia all collected by the "Moose" himself, Mike Bonk.

2

The Moose Museum Located at Mainly Seconds,

In 1982, Mike's first store opened and received a gift from his wife and former employees. It was a corduroy moose head with a plaque inscribed, "The Moose is Loose". This present hangs on the wall near the entrance next to painted words, *The Moose Museum.* The museum started when Mike put his personal items on display around the store. It seemed that as the store increased and prospered, his collection did also. Soon there was so much moose collectibles; it formed itself into a museum.

This museum is not like any other. Set in the back section of the store, it consists of about fifty cases and 10 aisles of various products either resembling or being moose associated. "If it's moose, it's in here" Mike said during a recent interview. And it's true (Cont. on page 2).

The Moose Museum
Cordially Invites You . . .

3

To Explore the Wide World of Moose

Come experience the
Northern Wilderness in
Sunny California.
New Exhibits! More Moose!

789 S. Tustin Avenue 555-9876

Warning: Moose X-ing

Travel columnist: Caroline Cesserta

My family and I always agonize about where to travel for our yearly summer vacation. This year, my daughter and I agreed on a nice mountain lodge in Colorado while my husband and other daughter sided on a tropical getaway to Mexico. To compromise, we decided to tour California starting from the Mexican border up to Oregon. One of my personal favorite spots is very unusual store I discovered when we were stopped at a rest stop and someone noticed my moose decal on the back window. (Cont. Pg. 2)

Student newspaper devoted to moose lovers.

1. Uses varied typefaces and sizes for a system of headings
2. Integrates photograph and text
3. Encloses highlighted text in oval-shaped "box"
4. Single-column format for lead story
5. Double-column format for additional text

13g models

4

1 Phillips Park

ZOOLENNIUM Fall Festival

2 **Sunday, September 28th from 11 a.m. to 3 p.m.**

The Friends of Phillips Park and the City of Aurora invite you to take in the park's beautiful array of fall colors while you enjoy a day filled with activities, attractions and fun for the whole family.

FREE
Pony Rides
Pumpkin Painting 3
Petting Zoo
Hay Rides
Super Slide
Jumping Castle
Face Painting
Scratch Art & Sand Art

LIVE ENTERTAINMENT......

11 am Buttons The Clown
12pm The Aurora Suzuki Violins
1pm Dave Rudolf
2pm The Truly Remarkable Loon

VISIT THE PUMPKIN PATCH

Stop and shop for your Halloween Pumpkins and fall decorations from A-1 Farms large on-site selection.

5 **Be among the first 1,200 youngsters to visit the Pumpkin Painting Tent and you'll receive a free pumpkin to paint and take home with you. In the display area you'll find fire trucks, emergency vehicles, D.A.R.E.-Mobiles and K-9 Units, along with special appearances by "McGruff" the crime fighting police dog, "Ozzie" the Kane County Cougar's mascot and "Ollie" the Phillips Park Zoo mascot. If you relish food with an Oktoberfest flair, bratwurst, sauerkraut, hot dogs and pork chop sandwiches - will be served up hot off the grill, along with hot apple cider, fresh donuts and hot pretzels.**

Be sure to visit the Phillips Park Zoo, where you'll find bald eagles, wolves, foxes, otters, elk, goats, pot-bellied pigs, llamas, swans, reptiles and peacocks. Located on more than 325 acres, attractions at Phillips Park include the Visitors Center & Mastodon Gallery, the Sunken Garden, the Phillips Park Golf Course, the Aquatic Center, Mastodon Lake-a twenty-eight acre fishing lake with a 1-mile jogging/bike path and island exhibits, the waterfall, World War I cannons, and several veteran related monuments. Among the amenities you'll find a large state-of-the-art playground, softball fields, picnic pavilions, sand volleyball courts, tennis courts, horseshoe courts and more.

Parking lots are located along Moses and Wyeth Drives and at the Aquatic Center. Additional parking is available along Smith Boulevard. For more information visit the City of Aurora web site at *www.aurora-il.org* and go to Parks & Recreation, or call (630) 898-7228.

Details are subject to change.

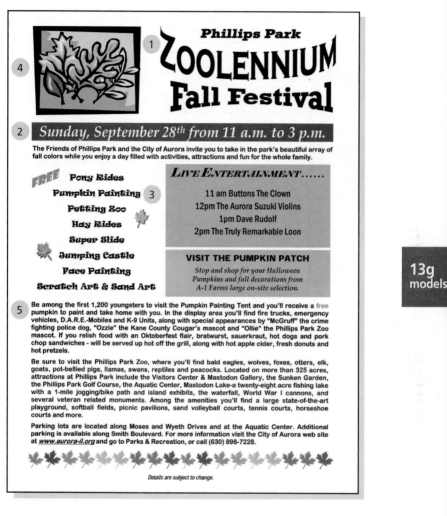

Flyer from a community-based organization.

Source: <http://www.aurora-il.org/Parks%20Operation/zooleniumfallfest2003.html>.

1. Unique font draws attention to headline
2. Date and time of the event prominently placed
3. Activities separated into scheduled (right side) and constant (left side)
4. Color and artwork add visual interest
5. Details provided in carefully organized paragraphs and legible font

13g models

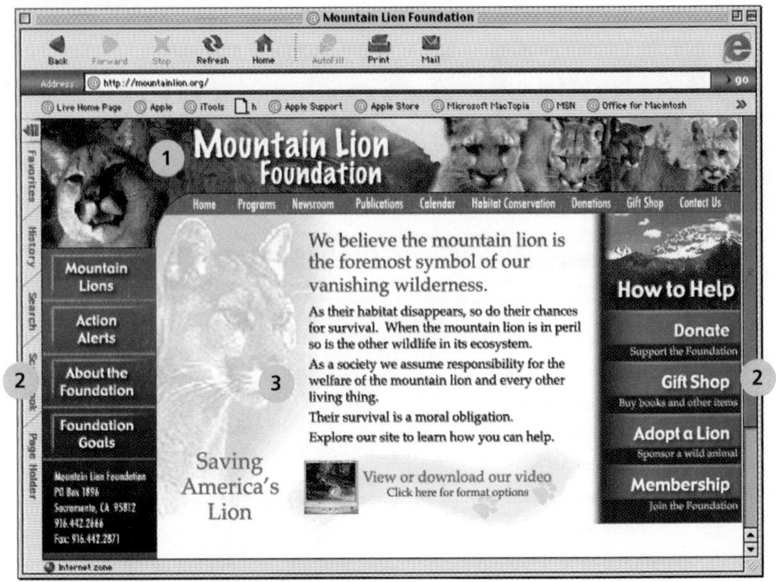

This first page of a newsletter from an organization dedicated to informing the public about mountain lions entices the reader with both photos and buttons leading to additional pages of information and a video.

1. Picture highlights beauty of animal and calls attention to the site
2. Buttons provide map of information in site and access to each category of information
3. White background makes text easy to read. Ghosted profile of mountain lion emphasizes elusive nature of the animal

CHAPTER 14 Writing Online

Thanks to digital technology, vast amounts of information are now just a few keystrokes or mouse clicks away. Easy access to this information has improved the lives of students, researchers, and the general public; helped civic groups to publicize their efforts; made government information more accessible to citizens; and provided an entirely new domain for the work of business and industry.

Some online environments are like libraries: you go there and retrieve information, opening Web sites and downloading documents. But many other online environments involve more than the passive receipt of information: they involve different kinds of interactive *exchange.* Whenever you participate in an online course, chat with friends through an instant messenger (IM) service, email a question or comment to a nonprofit organization, read and write on a Web-based forum, or post a response to a blog, you are participating in an **online community.** Each of these communities has certain expectations and follows certain standards for people's membership in the group.

14a Writing online

Whether you are writing an email message to classmates about a collaborative project, building a personal Web site to supplement your résumé, or participating in an online discussion about a local environmental issue, you're writing in a *context:* you need to consider the specific needs of your online audience, your purpose for writing, how you want to represent yourself to others, and what "rules" govern the way you can participate.

1 Understanding your online audience and your purpose

Online writers must tailor their messages to specific audiences to communicate effectively. People often join online communities because they're interested in a particular topic. Fans of the Dallas Cowboys can chat daily about the latest trade rumor or game story. Students in a course on African American literature and culture might design a Web-based forum to share interviews with local African American artists and activists. Opponents of a bill in Congress can use email to gather "electronic signatures" on petitions to their legislative representatives.

If you're not sure about the audience expectations for a particular online exchange, Web forum, or other online community, try a brief period of "lurking" (reading without participating). Lurking can help you to see who else participates, learn the rules of participation, and pick up terms or ideas commonly used by the participants. You will find IMs have a more restricted set of participants, the sender and receiver, so the expectations grow out of the relationship between the two, as in a personal conversation (see 14d-3).

Because it's so easy to send information and messages online, you may be tempted to participate spontaneously in online communities. Be aware, however, that your audience may be irritated if your message doesn't really contribute anything new or have a clear purpose. If you send an email response to a discussion you've just joined, without taking the time to see what messages have already been sent, you may seem to be "out of the loop" and lose credibility. Even in IMs and brief text messages (see 14d-3), the recipient has more time to study your message than during oral interchanges. Briefly considering your message and planning its wording can help avoid embarrassment or misunderstanding by making your meaning clear.

STRATEGY

Before you commit to sending something electronically to an online community, consider carefully your readers and, above all, what you want to tell them.

- What's the context of your message? How does your information extend, amplify, or clarify prior information?
- Why will readers find your information helpful or interesting?
- What do you want readers to *do* with the information or ideas: respond? take action? think more deeply about the issue?

2 Creating an online persona

When you participate in an online community, your **persona,** or how you define yourself to others, can be developed in depth because you can make repeated contributions in response to what others say. Still, this aspect of online communication differs from face-to-face communication in important ways.

- You can often remain anonymous.
- You can identify or conceal your gender or ethnicity.
- You can choose to be a "silent" type and contribute rarely, or you can contribute often.
- You can represent yourself in different styles or voices.
- You can use your real name or choose a made-up name or even an online personality (an "avatar").

Many blog writers create strong, easily identifiable, though partly fictional personas: the sarcastic observer of contemporary politics, the "wild child" turning up his or her nose at conventional morality, the traditionalist criticizing current social trends. This may at times be an important element of blogging, but it can be problematic if some readers, potential employers, for example, assume that the persona is an accurate representation of your traits or a literal record of your behavior.

Your choices, when made honestly and ethically, can be useful as you join new online communities or participate in them regularly. Tailor your persona to suit your purpose. If you're contributing your knowledge and expertise, for example, present yourself as helpful and concerned, not as a know-it-all. If you're contributing to an online peer review of a classmate's paper or presentation, you'll want to be supportive and friendly—neither too casual nor too harshly critical. If you are blogging, consider the possible effects of the online record you are leaving behind.

3 Netiquette

Online communities vary widely in the kinds of language and behavior they tolerate and expect from members. It's your responsibility to familiarize yourself with commonsense guidelines (known as **netiquette**) that apply across nearly all Internet communities and to learn the standards of the specific group you want to address.

- **Think before you click.** You can't take back a sent email. Avoid putting anything in an email message you wouldn't want your mother or a future employer to read.
- **Learn before you send.** Lurk and learn the norms of the community. If a discussion group has a searchable archive, see if a previous discussion already provided information that can help you to answer a question.
- **Consider off-list responses.** If you post a question that you think most of a discussion list's members will not be interested in, ask respondents to write to you "off list" (using your email address, not the list address).
- **Act, don't react.** Avoid posting "flames" (personal attacks) to contributors you disagree with.
- **Don't use ALL CAPS.** Like shouting, this practice is considered rude.
- **Attend to grammar.** Even if online messages seem informal, bad grammar, spelling mistakes, and poor word usage still convey a feeling of sloppiness or a lack of concern for readers. (When sending IMs or texting, however, use abbreviation conventions to save space—but don't carry them over to email or printed documents, where they will seem out of place and careless.)
- **Cut the fat.** Include only *relevant* information from previous messages to which you are replying.

- **The Golden Rule of netiquette.** Don't forget that there are real people behind every computer that receives your email or downloads your Web site.

14b Avoiding plagiarism and acting ethically online

Online environments now offer you access to almost limitless texts, images, and other media, including music and streaming video. Because digital technology allows you to download this material to your own computer—and then to CDs or disks—it's tempting to see all of it as yours, free for the taking. But it's not. Worse, it's not always obvious whether something on the Internet is copyrighted, which makes it unclear whether you're doing anything wrong when you copy or distribute something. Downloading a song from your favorite band or printing and circulating a story or cartoon may violate federal copyright laws, resulting in fines (or worse) if you're caught. When working online, avoid practices that are illegal or unethical, and avoid those that can create suspicion or investigation. When in doubt, err on the side of caution.

1 Always document or credit information borrowed from others

It's so easy to forward electronic mail, download software programs and images, create Web pages, and copy material published online that governments worldwide are being forced to reconsider the concept of "intellectual property." Who owns the rights to words, images, or ideas? How can those rights be protected without prohibiting the free flow of information that the Internet makes possible? The issues make it important for you to document every online source you use in developing your writing.

Remember too that your credibility depends on the credibility of the community resource you choose to rely on. If you're writing a paper about diabetes, citing sources from a collection of official American Diabetes Association Web pages and a moderated discussion group for endocrinologists is far more effective than citing email from a local bulletin board about a new home remedy. For all information from online sources you wish to cite, ask yourself "Where did it come from?" If you are not confident about your answer, your instructor might be able to help you evaluate the credibility of a source. You should also be prepared to find an alternative site. (Remember to acknowledge and document your sources; see Chapters 28–31.)

Cutting and pasting information from Web sites and other Internet resources into a single document for later use is a good way to consolidate your research. This new form of note taking, however, can lead to accidental plagiarism. It is easy to forget where something originally came from and mistakenly convince yourself the writing is your own!

STRATEGY

- Always write down the address of any Web site you are using, and clearly label text you copy from that site. Print the first page of each Web site you're using for easy reference in case your later drafts require further documentation. The printout should include the site's URL so you can return to it for future reference and also for citation purposes.
- Always note the date you found the information. Web sites can be updated every day, and your cited information may disappear. In addition, you will need to provide the access date in your citation if you use the information in your final document. (For more on citation issues, see Chapters 28–31.)
- If you're citing an email, listserv, or Web forum message that has not been posted to a publicly accessible location, ask the author's permission before quoting. It's a good idea to do this even if the posting is public.
- Corroborate your sources. Follow the journalist's rule: If you can't find information in at least two credible places on the Internet, don't use the material.

2 Do your own work

Never buy or download papers and claim they represent your own work. No doubt you're already aware of paper mills—sites where you can get or buy prefabricated college papers on different topics. Additionally, many writing classes now post their work to the Web for peer review, and you may find these papers and projects when you use a search engine. But consider the moral implications and the consequences of borrowing Internet resources and claiming them as your own. Remember that your instructor has access to those same sources; a common practice among teachers who suspect plagiarism is to input random phrases from student papers into a search engine to see whether those phrases appear anywhere on the Web. Plagiarism detection services do much the same thing. (See Chapter 26.)

3 Know the rules

When you're using an email account provided by a college or university or by a business or public organization—even when you access it away from the institution—you are responsible for adhering to the institution's policies and regulations. If you access the Internet through a service provider, you're obligated to abide by the client rights and responsibilities outlined in your contract. Policies on computer use can be extensive, and you should thoroughly review them.

14c Email choices

Email is a popular means of communication primarily because it's *fast.* But its speed shouldn't be an excuse to avoid writing carefully and thoughtfully before your message speeds through cyberspace to its destination(s).

1 Email for different communities

There are two main types of electronic mail: individual mail and list-based mail. When you write individual mail, you decide exactly who will receive your message. When you write list-based mail, you address a predetermined audience of subscribers to a list (an online community, see 1b), all of whom will receive what you write.

Don't assume, though, that individual mail is more "personal" while list mail is more "professional." Many lists are chatty with informal conversation between friends, and individual mail might be written as an introduction to a potential employer or to complain about a rent increase. As in any other type of writing, you have to adopt the appropriate tone for your audience. If you don't adjust your persona to suit your purpose for writing, your message will likely not be communicated to your audience in the way you intended.

2 Elements of email

Every email message has elements that convey a specific kind of information and help you effectively communicate your purpose. While you are probably familiar with the basic components of email, it helps to consider how certain choices create an online persona.

From. While some email programs show a sender's address in the "from" section, others display a chosen **screen name,** a self-identifier the user chooses for herself. A screen name like *BradFan* might entertain your friends, but it won't make a positive impression on a potential employer.

Sent. This line displays the date and time your mail is sent. Because recipients may need this information, make sure your computer's time and date settings are correct.

To. It's good practice to check the "to" line every time before sending your email—just to be sure it's going to the right place. Two other lines—"cc:" (carbon copy) and "bcc:" (blind carbon copy)—enable you to send mail to people who are not part of the primary audience but who might be interested in the subject matter. With a blind carbon copy, you can send copies without the main recipient's knowing because the addresses for the copies will not appear in the text sent to the main recipient.

Subject. Use this line to draw readers into reading the actual message. Short and clear subject lines are best.

Message body. Long messages are more likely to be deleted, left unread, or only partially read. If you're replying to someone, make clear what it is that you are replying to, but don't include long strings of previous messages.

Signature or sig file. Sign your email. If you have a mail program that allows you to attach a signature file automatically, write out your full name and some contact information. Many people include clever quotations, song lyrics, and jokes in their signature files; be aware of how such additions affect your online persona.

3 Email appearance

Most email systems produce "primitive" text, without the formatting options that you have in word-processing programs. For the purposes of a vast number of daily email messages, it doesn't much matter what your text looks like. Yet a few considerations can make your communications more efficient and show your sensitivity to the needs of your audience.

- Don't let email do the work of full-length documents. If you need to send a paper, report, or other substantive text to someone, send it as an attached document.
- Break your messages into paragraphs. People become tired and frustrated when they must read long blocks of email text.
- Use emoticons and acronyms appropriately, based on your audience. **Emoticons** *(emotion + icon)* are a kind of shorthand code that allows writers to add a jolt of feeling to their text. Emoticons (such as smiling or frowning faces) can be drawn with keyboard characters; increasingly, many mail programs now convert typed emoticons into graphic representations. Internet **acronyms** (FYI, BTW) are abbreviations of common phrases, used to speed up communication.

Emoticons and acronyms are generally considered to be appropriate for casual communication but not for professional or academic writing.

4 Using the functions of email

Just as each email message has certain elements (see 14c-2), every email program has buttons or commands that allow you to manage your correspondence in a variety of ways. When you're working quickly, it's sometimes easy to forget the consequences of choosing certain options.

Reply and **Reply-all.** Remember that when you use the *Reply-all* function, your message will go to any other people who received the original communication. Be careful that you don't accidentally post a personal note to a public space.

Forward. Before forwarding other people's messages, consider whether the original author would want his or her message forwarded to someone else. When in doubt, urge the original author to send the message to the person(s) you have in mind.

Attach. Not all mail programs support attachments (such as word-processed files, spreadsheets, and pictures), so you can't assume your recipients will always be able to read your document. Give the recipient time to open the attachment or write back to you if there's a problem, and be ready with alternative formats or ways to send the information.

14d Participating in online communities

The three most common formats for online communities are discussion lists; Web forums (blogs); and "real-time" writing, including IMing and texting. Each format plays host to communities engaged in writing on a variety of topics.

1 Discussion lists

Most discussion lists come to you; however, you go to a particular kind of discussion list known as a newsgroup. The writing format and style concerns of each are similar.

To join or subscribe to a **discussion list,** you send an email message to the service that hosts the list. You then automatically receive all the messages from the list at your email address. When you post a message, usually it's first reviewed by the list moderator (some lists are not moderated). If it passes the moderator's standards, he or she sends it to the personal addresses of all the people subscribed. It's important, then, to adapt to the community's standards, or your messages will never be made available to your peers. Sometimes someone else (such as a teacher or the leader of a group) may subscribe you to a list. In such cases, you'll probably receive an automated notification that you have been added to the list, along with instructions for managing your subscription or leaving the list.

You can access **newsgroups** without having email messages sent to your personal address. You can scan the topics and threads for a subject that interests you and choose the individual posts you wish to read. The message you send to a newsgroup is immediately posted and available for reading by anyone. Newsgroups are usually not moderated.

In all unmoderated situations, it's easy to become careless, especially because they often have an informal tone. But messages sent to listservs and newsgroups can be read by anyone; if your messages are archived, they can be accessed and read for years to come.

2 Web-based forums: Blogs

Web-based forums allow users to easily access sites where they can participate in conversations with others who share interests. More than a quarter of a million Web forums are already in existence, covering topics that range from current events to entertainment. Some Web-based forums are moderated. Many, such as the popular CollegeEdge forums, ask you to set up a user name with a password; a few charge a fee for participation.

Writing in Web-based forums makes frequent use of informal language, emoticons, and abbreviations, and the citing of previously written material to provide context.

Blogs, for "Web logs," are interactive Web sites where the blog owner posts information, reflections, news stories, and the like; those who visit the blog can then post responses. The blog can have more than one response location—for example, one that allows anyone access and another that allows access only to specific persons.

Many people use blogs to present their own personal reflections, sometimes attaching graphics, background music, and pictures or video clips. Or they present political or social commentary, either the views of a single person or a group. A few bloggers have achieved such prominence that they are cited frequently by other writers or television commentators; some have books collecting and reprinting their daily musings.

3 Real-time writing

The Internet now supports a variety of ways for people to participate in "real-time" electronic discussions and communities. **Real time** means that the discussion takes place without delay: your words appear on the screen of every user involved in the discussion as soon as they are typed. Such conversations can take place between participants who are in the same classroom or scattered around the world.

The most popular real-time communities in current use are **chat rooms** hosted by private Internet services or available via the Internet relay chat (IRC) network. Chat rooms are usually quite informal and have become a popular way for celebrities to "meet" their fans online. Chats open to the public, such as interviews with politicians and "town hall" meetings, are almost always moderated, so your writing will be controlled by an "editor" who decides whether you may post your questions or comments.

An **IM** (Instant Messaging) service allows you to chat in real time with a limited number of people (often one to one). IMing allows for the spontaneity and directness of conversation, but because most people type more slowly than they talk, IMing makes frequent use of radical abbreviations (RU OK?) and short statements in order to keep the exchange going at a comfortable pace. This style of communication is highly informal and depends on the participants' mutual understanding of the abbreviations and of each other's habits of expression. This makes it clearly inappropriate for most other means of formal communication.

Texting is a type of short message service (SMS) that is available on most cell phones, pagers, and hand-held devices. Texting is similar to IMing, in which compressed, IM-like messages are sent to a mobile device.

14e Participating in virtual classrooms

Many teachers across the college curriculum are now using digital technologies to enhance or supplement their classroom instruction. Typically, students meet in a traditional classroom two or three times a week, then continue to discuss the course material online, sending and receiving messages or documents, visiting links, and submitting and getting back homework. On many campuses, students are also taking entire courses online, meeting, if at all, only occasionally with the instructor. In all such cases, your virtual persona will be crucial to your success, just as it would be in the classroom. Opting out of participation, being disruptive, dominating the conversation, using inappropriate diction—these and other unacceptable aspects of face-to-face communication also count against you in the online environment.

1 Using electronic courseware

Most courseware that supplements classroom instruction can be easily navigated, with plenty of help screens in case you're not familiar with some elements. It helps to explore such systems before your course and assignments officially begin, so that you will be familiar at the outset with how they work.

WebCT™ and *Blackboard* are popular commercial courseware systems that help teachers create information-rich, interactive Web sites to enhance learning and productivity in their courses. Courseware commonly includes a home page where you can get assignments and schedules, information about your grades or progress, and links to other Internet sources on the subject of your course. In addition, *WebCT*- or *Blackboard*-enhanced courses often provide a course chatroom, a discussion board, and an "internal" email system. Chatroom discussions are scheduled in advance; some may involve several different rooms, and the electronic conversations may be recorded so your instructor can assess your contributions. Bulletin boards, where you post information asynchronously, are usually organized by topic; be sure you choose the correct topic when you post a message.

When using courseware, it's important that you read the rules and operating procedures carefully. Explore the site fully, taking note of how it works and what you're required to do. Many teachers also post ground rules for participation, and these rules may stipulate the kinds and amount of your interaction.

2 Taking courses online

Many universities now offer courses that you can take entirely online. If such a course is offered at your own institution, you may be registered with students who live on, or within a few miles of, your campus, and others who may live at a much greater distance. In such courses, you'll continue to do much of your work independently, but almost all the interaction will take place online instead of in a classroom.

Although each online course will be uniquely organized, with its own particular requirements, schedules, and procedures, some general strategies are helpful for working in such an environment.

STRATEGY

- Read everything. You may be so used to "surfing" and "skimming" the Internet that online courses trigger a similar process when you first enter or log on to a course site. Slow down. Read the screens carefully, particularly the introductory information on the course. Take notes or print out the most important information.
- Know the rules. Internet courses are often carefully controlled to avoid electronic chaos. Just as in regular courses, Internet courses will have tardy or absence policies, ground rules for participation, and due dates.
- Think "community." Although sitting at a computer may make you feel like there is no social accountability in your course, just the reverse is true. To work well, Internet courses require full participation from all members. Learn the names or avatars of the other students, try referring to their ideas, and generally make yourself a member of the virtual community.

Exercise 1

Reflect in writing on your experiences with electronically enhanced learning. How did it work? What was your role? Can you think of any instructive stories or anecdotes?

DOMAIN NAMES AND TYPES

A **domain name** locates an organization or other entity on the Internet. A number of suffixes used by American Web sites can tell you a great deal about what you are reading.

.com	commercial site
.edu	educational site
.gov	government site
.net	network site
.org	nonprofit organization

CHAPTER 15
Speaking Effectively

Surveys show that people are more afraid of public speaking than almost anything else they can imagine, including being fired from a job—but why? Like driving a car or playing tennis, public speaking can be learned effectively and performed well. Good presenters will tell you that, instead of dreading the moment when they must stand in front of a group of people, they look forward to the challenge. Anxiety about public speaking never goes away; good speakers turn that anxiety into a kind of energy that helps them to present their ideas clearly and enthusiastically.

But effective oral communication is not just standing up and delivering a carefully scripted address. At meetings of city councils or education boards, citizens often express opinions from a place in the audience. In college, you may be asked to explain your response to another student's paper in a small group. In business settings, you may need to give an impromptu report to a dozen people. These and many other forms of oral communication follow certain conventions of length, style, delivery, and persuasive strategy. Knowing some of these conventions can help you to be effective as a speaker in a range of settings. You can greatly improve your performance if you break the presentation down into four stages: *planning*, *practice*, *delivery*, and *reflection*.

15a Effective oral presentations

It's Shaun's turn. He makes his way awkwardly to the front of the room, saying, "OK, I'm gonna talk about, um, my project is, let's see, what I want to tell you about is what I, what my project, what I researched for this unit, the real story of the *Exxon Valdez* oil spill ten, fifteen, after, um, you know, like what biologists found and stuff when they, like what the data says about it all." Twenty-three faces are staring at him. He fumbles for some notes he had jotted down the night before, spilling the pages from the folder onto the floor. The seconds tick by, an eternity of silence. "Um, let's see," he continues, still sorting the pages. "Um, like I said, this, my project, what I want to say, to tell you about. . . ." He avoids eye contact with his audience, desperately trying to collect his thoughts.

Startled awake by his alarm, Shaun is relieved to find that the presentation was just a bad dream. Luckily, he has several more days to prepare for the real thing. Careful planning and rehearsal will eliminate all but the most unforeseen problem.

1 Planning your presentation

Before beginning to draft and practice your presentation, you'll need a plan.

Analyze your situation. To plan effectively, begin by writing down everything you know about your speaking situation.

- What's the occasion?
- How many people will be there?
- How long is the entire gathering, and how long will you speak?
- What sort of place or space will you speak in? Where will you speak from?
- How will you know when to speak?

A clear understanding of your speaking situation can help you to plan the content and delivery of your remarks. For example, knowing how much time you have to speak will help you determine how much detail to provide, points to cover, and materials to prepare. It's always helpful to go to the place where you'll be speaking when it's empty and "scope out" the room, noting its size, lighting, and seating arrangement.

Shaun's planning notes help him begin visualizing his presentation.

> Oral presentation on project: 25% of grade. Purpose is to report main findings of research on topic (Exxon Valdez oil spill a decade and a half later); audience is class (23 students); front of room; teacher announces; total time no more than 15 minutes.

Focus on your purpose and your audience. Knowing something about the people you will address helps you make important decisions about your presentation. You wouldn't say the same things about your science project to a group of middle-school kids as you would to a group of judges at a college science fair. What do you know about your audience? What might they already know about your subject? What do they expect to find out from your remarks? (See also Chapter 3.)

You'll also want to ask yourself what *you* hope your presentation will accomplish. Are you trying to persuade people to take action or vote a certain way on an issue? Are you giving them information they can use in their own work or activities? Do you want them to learn something new and come away from your remarks feeling enlightened and interested in a subject? (See also Chapter 3.)

Research your topic. Unless you're an expert on the topic of your presentation, you'll need to consult external sources to plan your remarks, just as you would in a documented paper. (See Chapters 21–27.) Remember, live audiences have even less tolerance than readers for abstract information presented in dull, lifeless language. Choose information that makes your presentation come alive without leaving out essential facts or details.

Organize your content. Instead of trying to write your talk like a paper, begin by creating an outline. Usually your talk will consist of three parts.

- **Introductory remarks,** in which you introduce yourself and give your audience a preview of what you'll say (or prove, show, cover, and so on).
- **Content or substance of the presentation,** which consists of your main ideas, illustrations, and material.
- **Conclusion,** which sums up and restates your purpose, reminding the audience of what you have shown or offered.

Create talking points. Talking points are key phrases, words, visual cues, or other reminders that guide you through your speech. They include not only your main points, but signals to help you coordinate your talk: "check time," "change overhead," "circulate handout." Most of the time, talking points will be words or short phrases, but you should write out all of your introductory remarks and your conclusion. Doing so will help lead you into your presentation smoothly and allow you to wrap it up cleanly and dramatically. Use typical transitional phrases, such as "next," "now let's consider," "in conclusion," "finally," or "to sum up" (see the chart on p. 77). Remember that paragraphs or sections of a "paper" are invisible to your audience; you need to signal your intentions and structure verbally or by other means, such as overhead visuals.

Your talking points should include transitions that link one part to the next. These transitions, which you should write out as phrases or full sentences, are important guideposts for your audience. In one of Shaun's transitions, he moved from the immediate impact of the oil spill to the main part of his presentation: "As we've seen, the *Valdez* oil spill had a devastating short-term effect on the Alaskan shoreline and its ecosystem. I want to turn now to some of the research that has been conducted to assess the long-term environmental impact of the spill."

Plan your timing. If your presentation can be no longer than, say, fifteen minutes, begin by estimating the time for each of the components, and then divide the middle part into more specific chunks of time.

As Shaun planned his presentation, he created the following outline.

Introduction (2 minutes): "Have any of you been to Alaska or seen it in films?" (wait . . .) "Someone describe the land for me." (Get 2–3 brief responses.) Unfortunately, all that beauty you describe is seriously threatened by pollution, oil exploration, and development. A case in point is the infamous Exxon Valdez oil spill of 1989. In March of that year, [explain]. My purpose is to give a status report, based on secondary research, of the environmental impact of the Exxon Valdez oil spill fifteen years later, and to reach a conclusion about the total impact of the spill and whether Exxon met its obligations to restore the environment.

Substance:

Background (3 minutes): (Put up Overhead #1.) Remind audience of the original situation and promised restitution. (Pause for effect and check time.)

—What I did (2 minutes): (Put up Overhead #2.) Explain how I gathered information and from which sources. Special focus on Valdez Oil Spill Trustee Council. (Check time.)

—Major findings (6 minutes): (Put up Overhead #3.) Summary of the most important findings, divided into three categories of assessment (soil/beach, wildlife, long-term ecology). (Be sure to cover statistics.)

Conclusion (2 minutes): "In summary. . . ." Explain results of the study and answer question it asked. "As illustrated by this presentation and the evidence I have provided, we must use whatever means—through new legislation, public protest, and private foundations—to safeguard our pristine Alaskan wilderness and shoreline so that we never experience another Exxon Valdez. All of us, no matter what our political leanings, have a fundamental responsibility to protect our environment."

Use note cards. After sketching out your talking points, creating an outline, and working out a time plan, transfer your material to note cards. Use the main categories in your outline to organize your cards. In some cases you may need more than one card for a single section of the presentation. Your cards will include major categories of content as well as presentational cues (reminders, transition notes, and so on). Finally, number the cards so you'll always know where you are in your presentation.

Exercise 1

Choose a subject that you know something about and that would make a good informative presentation. First describe a purpose for conveying this information and an audience that might find it useful. Create an outline for a ten-minute oral presentation on this subject to this audience; then sketch out a series of talking points, following the advice in 15a-1, including transitions between points and an estimate of the time for each part of the presentation.

---

2 Rehearsing your presentation

As you plan your presentation, don't assume you have to "get it right" before you can begin rehearsing. Hearing yourself talking out what you've written down will give you new ideas that, in turn, will alter your plans.

Stand and deliver. If you recline in a comfortable chair to rehearse your presentation, you won't be building the confidence you need to speak to your audience. Standing up will match the physical and spatial conditions of your talk. Your body, your breathing, the placement of your feet, your eye movements will all be affected by where you're positioned during your rehearsals.

Rehearse alone, then with an audience. If possible, the first few times you rehearse your presentation, do it alone. You won't be embarrassed about stopping and restarting or talking to yourself. As you build confidence and iron out the wrinkles in your talk, it helps to give a "dry run" of your talk to one or more trusted listeners. Work through the entire presentation at once, then ask them for their suggestions.

Try videotaping or recording your presentation. If you have access to a camcorder or other video equipment, tape your presentation and then watch it several times to see if you can discern problems, distracting habits, inappropriate pace, poor transitions, or unclear statements. At first you may be embarrassed or self-conscious to see yourself on tape, but remember that everything you learn about yourself will help you become a more effective presenter.

Rehearse with your visual aids. Visual aids help your audience but they also add a layer of complexity to your presentation. Be sure to include any visual aids in your rehearsal, so you can practice your timing and transitions. If possible, set up the visual-aid equipment that you will use. This step will allow you to find out where to stand so you don't block the screen, how to coordinate your visual aids with your remarks, and how to operate the equipment effectively.

Practice. Keep rehearsing until you know every part of your presentation—its transitions, dramatic pauses, reminders to look at your audience, and so on. The longer your presentation, the more complex your remarks, and the more formal the occasion, the more you should practice.

3 Giving your presentation

Think of an especially effective presentation you attended recently. The speaker probably connected with you in some way, interested you in the subject, and presented his or her information in a lively, engaging manner. He or she probably looked at the audience in strategic ways, modulated his or her voice, and was careful about gesticulation or body movement. The following suggestions can help you develop these skills.

Avoid reading verbatim. Good public speaking involves more than reading a printed paper aloud. Reading aloud is common in some fields, yet most audiences prefer speakers to *present* their ideas instead of *reading* them. This kind of speaking is called **extemporaneous speaking** or **conversational speaking,** a mode of delivery that emphasizes greater interaction among speaker, audience, and ideas. In this kind of speaking, you prepare a set of ideas, not a verbatim text, and you speak from and about those ideas. This is not to say that you don't craft the words for your presentation in advance; you just recall what you want to say from memory and from your note cards rather than reading long, boring sentences out loud.

Speak loudly and clearly. Project your voice over the entire audience. It's important for you to be heard, and speaking up will also affect your confidence. Articulate your words clearly, and monitor your speech rate, being careful not to race through your talk. Vary the pitch and cadence of your voice to accentuate certain points you're making, but don't exaggerate your emotions.

Use purposeful, natural gestures. Standing stock-still may not give your presentation variety, but be careful not to get carried away with wild gestures or movements. Move around if you wish but don't pace or make repeated motions. Avoid distracting movements (drumming the lectern, jingling change in your pocket, twisting your hair, or shifting your weight). Instead, subtly accentuate your remarks with gestures and facial expressions.

Maintain eye contact. As you begin your remarks, look at your audience. Look directly at individuals in the audience, but don't do so for more than two or three seconds unless you are in a question/answer mode, and don't keep returning to the same person. Vary your eye movement so that you don't "favor" one part of the room or one group of people. If it helps, work in a pattern, such as front-left, front-right, center-left, center-right, rear-left, rear-right. If you're using visual aids, glance at them from time to time but keep your focus mainly on your audience.

Use visuals effectively. If you use a chalkboard or flip chart to call attention to certain ideas, prepare everything ahead of time. Audiences become impatient if they must wait for you to write something down during your presentation. A more effective way to present information visually is to use a prepared overhead transparency and project it on a screen. If you use transparencies, make sure that anything you project is readable from anywhere in the audience.

Certain software programs, such as *PowerPoint*, allow you to create stunning slides that include words, pictures, and other media. If you use such programs, be sure to follow the suggestions that accompany them; learn and practice with the technology before using it. Always bring backup overhead transparencies with you whenever you use computer projection devices, in case of equipment failure. Be careful not to make your visual presentation so gimmicky with motion and sound that your ideas are lost in the glitz.

Avoid reading every word on your slides: the audience is capable of doing that themselves. Instead, paraphrase or call attention to the material on the slides, or let bullet points summarize points you are making in more detail.

Don't panic. If something goes wrong during your presentation—the projector won't turn on, a microphone isn't working, or you lose your place in your talking notes—remain calm. It's better to focus on the source of the problem for a few seconds, even if this is a distraction, than to allow yourself to lose your thoughts or become confused about what to do next. Audiences are more forgiving than you think. If the problem can't be fixed, such as a broken bulb in a projector, move on without it.

4 Assessing the results

Although most presenters can tell the difference between a stunning job and a mediocre one by the enthusiasm of the audience, you need a better source of feedback to know what you did well and what you can improve. Don't be satisfied to step down and put your presentation behind you; actively seek further information so you can develop your abilities.

Ask a confidante to be in the audience. If possible, ask someone you trust and respect to attend your presentation, and ask that person to look for specific areas you're concerned about, such as your body movements or the rate of your speech.

Carefully study any scoring guides or remarks you may receive from a teacher. Teachers often use sets of criteria to judge the quality of a presentation. If they aren't accompanied by explanations, ask your teacher for more specific feedback. If you're doing more than one presentation, work on the weakest categories in the assessment of the first one.

Do a self-assessment. Although you can't see or know everything about your presentation, you'll probably have some immediate impressions. Write them down as soon as possible. After identifying justifiable areas of concern, spend some time thinking of strategies to overcome the problems.

Exercise 2

Write down what you consider your two primary delivery difficulties (nervous gestures, filler words, or voice projection). For each, describe (1) when the difficulty usually happens (for example, during transitions or when you look at notes) and (2) something you can do to resolve this difficulty (such as pausing instead of using filler words or placing your hands on the table instead of in your pocket).

15b Managing speech anxiety

Speech anxiety affects people differently. No one is entirely immune to the apprehension of public speaking, yet some people handle the pressure reasonably well, whereas others have intense emotional responses. Much anxiety comes from lack of experience. Giving oral presentations in college provides you with experience and confidence. To help overcome your anxiety, try these strategies.

1 Analyze the causes of your anxiety

Write down what makes you most anxious about public speaking. Does it have to do with the audience? the subject? your preparation? what you will look like? what people will think? Compartmentalize your fears, then work through each one, finding productive, personal strategies for overcoming them.

2 Be prepared physically

Humans are biological organisms with automatic physical responses to certain situations (the "fight/flight" reaction, for example). Speech anxiety is part of a cycle: the more afraid we are, the more unpredictable and vulnerable we feel . . . which only generates more fear. We are far more prone to this cycle when we're exhausted or physically deprived (of nutrition, oxygen, or fluids).

Before any presentation—and *especially* before one in which the stakes are high—be sure to rest and eat well, even though you may be anxious. Put your presentation aside for at least an hour before bed, and do something else to take your mind off it.

3 Control your breathing and calm your body

Public speaking affects every speaker's heart rate, respiration, and other physical properties. The fact that your palms sweat before you speak, or your neck flushes, or your stomach gets butterflies doesn't predict anything about the quality of your presentation; all it means is that you're like most other people, even highly effective speakers. If you let these physical responses control your presentation, they will. You need to control them instead.

Start with your breathing. Discreetly taking long, deep breaths before you talk will help to slow your heart rate, calm your nerves, and provide oxygen to your brain. Think about your entire body from top to bottom, and find the places where you're most tense. Then deliberately relax those tense spots, continuing to breathe slowly and deeply. Keep your focus on your ideas, not on yourself, how you look, or what your audience will think about you.

4 Move confidently and purposefully

When it's your turn to speak, focus first on getting to your speaking position. Move deliberately and carefully; you don't need to rush. Don't begin to speak until you're facing your audience; you can even take a second or two to organize yourself if you have notes or if you need to adjust a microphone. Focus entirely on your opening statement. If you've rehearsed well, your first few remarks shouldn't be difficult, and once you've made it through thirty seconds of your presentation, you'll begin to feel less tense.

5 Practice, practice, practice

Nothing reduces the fear of public speaking more than the confidence that comes from rehearsal. The more you practice, the less deeply anxious you'll feel. You may still feel a kind of superficial tension, but if you keep reminding yourself that you're thoroughly prepared, that tension will turn into energy and excitement.

6 Remember that you're not on trial

Anxiety often comes from fearing that we'll be "found out," that we're not really experts but frauds. Our audiences seem like examiners or tribunals, ready to pounce on every flaw in our reasoning or to demand complicated explanations that we can't provide. Remember that your audience probably knows very little if anything about your topic. You're not the world's expert, but the audience isn't expecting you to be, either. Admit your limitations, stick to what you know, and try to present your ideas in ways that will stimulate and interest your audience.

STRATEGY

Expect questions from your audience, and use the following guidelines for responding effectively.

- Anticipate the kinds of questions you may be asked; where necessary, prepare brief answers ahead of time that you can recall during your presentation.
- Ask for clarification if you don't understand a question.
- Respond directly, not evasively. If you don't know the answer, admit it, and don't make one up. Instead, perhaps say that the question suggests a fruitful area for further study or investigation.
- Don't indulge "hostile" questioners. Answer them briefly and diplomatically, with a yes or no, or "I'm not sure," and move to the next questioner.

Exercise 3

List and describe your greatest fears about public speaking. Are you afraid you will lose your place? forget your material? say something wrong? Are you fearful that your voice will shake or your hands tremble? For each fear, consider what you can do ahead of time to reduce your anxiety.

15c Group presentations and other public forums

Public speaking includes occasions when one person or a small team addresses people in a public or group setting. The need to be articulate and focused is just as great in these settings as it is in a traditional "speech." If you're being interviewed by the local news media about an event you witnessed, you'll want to be clear and accurate; if you're speaking at a public meeting in order to express your opposition to a proposal, you'll want to persuade with sound reasoning and a balanced perspective. A few strategies can help you present yourself effectively.

1 Effective group presentations

Split up the responsibility for researching your presentation, then come back together to create joint talking points. It's essential that all members of your team participate; don't allow one member to sketch out his or her remarks briefly and tell you it will all work out. Everyone should have a copy of all the talking points for the group.

Behave as a team. During your presentation, an initial lead presenter should introduce the other speaker(s) on the team. Each presenter should create a transition to the next presenter, but these transitions should, whenever possible, be oriented toward your content, not the fact that you're changing speakers. Instead of saying, "Now Ephraim will talk," try something like "The underlying social causes of this phenomenon, to which Ephraim will now turn, help to explain why it became popular in the 1960s."

Speak to a common theme. Even if members of your team have come up with different information and ideas, don't place yourselves in opposition to each other. Instead, create a single presentation that allows you to reveal differences in your subject matter: "Ephraim has described one way of interpreting this social phenomenon; now I'd like to explain it from another perspective."

Divide your time and stick to the plan. Audiences are aware of imbalances in the time each presenter takes. Don't have someone speak for one minute simply to give her a voice; divide your time evenly among your team. Monitor your own time carefully so that you don't take away from the time of presenters who follow you.

2 Effective speaking in public forums

Every day in your community, people gather to share ideas and opinions about local concerns. You can speak effectively in these settings by using some simple but powerful strategies.

Become informed before voicing an opinion. Don't rush to a meeting of your city council armed with opposition to a proposal until you're well informed. Better still, if you don't know enough about an issue to speak to it, attend the meeting in order to learn.

Bring information. If you feel confident enough about an issue to voice an opinion, bring information and evidence that support your points (see Chapter 11 on supporting evidence). Opinion alone will help decision makers to know how a community feels, but it may not persuade them as powerfully as facts and details will.

Plan your remarks. In many public forums, you'll have much less time to speak than you would in a traditional presentation—perhaps only a minute or two. Just as you would for a longer speech, plan and rehearse your remarks. Don't alienate those who might disagree with you; instead, try to strike a balanced, reasonable posture while making your own position clear.

Assess the progress of the meeting. A badly timed comment won't do much to contribute to a forum or discussion. Wait until the focus of the discussion aligns with what you want to say, then try to make your comments when they will have the most impact. If possible, tie your remarks to the discussion by referring to something someone else has said.

Make your comments clear and persuasive. Although emotional appeals (especially empathy) sometimes help support a cause, emotion is usually less effective in persuading a diverse audience than careful, balanced reasoning. Fear and nervousness also tend to affect people's demeanor in public settings, causing them to speak angrily, make accusations, or even cry. If you prepare for a tense public meeting by thinking through your ideas carefully and framing a clear, logical argument for your position, you won't fall prey to your emotions, and your audience will be more likely to think about your ideas and modify their positions on an issue.

3 Effective comments on boards and committees

When you play an active role in a business, in school, or in your community, you'll find yourself participating on various boards and committees. These settings have their own "rules" or conventions of successful communication, which, if violated, can lower a member's standing and weaken his or her participation. Because the rules vary from group to group, it's important for you to listen and observe carefully during the first meeting or two, until you have a clear understanding of how people interact. As you participate in such groups, a few general strategies may be helpful.

Prepare for the meeting. Boards and committees usually announce an agenda before each meeting. Study the agenda carefully, reading any documents that will be discussed or collecting enough background information to be informed. If you are formally placed on the agenda (to give an update on a project, for example), prepare and rehearse your contribution in the same way that you would an address to a larger audience (see 15a).

Choose when and how to participate. During an open discussion on a board or committee, ask yourself whether the comment you want to make will advance the discussion or offer new ideas. Listen carefully to what others say, so that your own contributions aren't thought to be irrelevant. Keep your comments focused and, when appropriate, brief; don't belabor points or ramble. When possible, directly link your ideas and remarks to what others have said.

Find an appropriate style for your comments. If you have carefully gauged the level of formality and rules of participation that characterize your board or committee, you'll find you can more easily adjust your language to fit your situation. Of course, you don't want to speak in a way that's unnatural to you. But if your committee deals with difficult issues and has taken on a somewhat formal nature, don't use casual, slang-ridden language. The kind of discourse may also change *during* a meeting—with more casual, social discussion before and after the "business" part of the meeting.

Use language sensitively. Consider the makeup of your board or committee. As you frame your remarks, think about how various members may react to any assumptions implied by your words. Keeping your emotions under control will help you to avoid unconsidered, rash, or potentially offensive remarks or terms (see also Chapter 47).

Exercise 4

Watch a brief oral presentation. If you can't find a nonprofessional example and decide to use television, don't choose a news broadcast or other journalistic presentation, but look for a presentation that is given to a live audience, such as a speech in Congress. Local and cable-access stations may broadcast town council meetings, school board meetings, and the like. Choose one that lasts at least five minutes. As you watch, jot down notes about topics discussed in this chapter: the method of delivery, eye contact, the use of notes, body and facial movements, pauses, distracting features, and so on. Write a brief analysis and evaluation of what you saw.

PART 4

Writing for Specific Communities

CHAPTER 16
Academic Writing: General Education

The kinds of **general academic writing** you do in many college courses require similar ways of thinking and working with information and texts. General academic writing is common in introductory courses that are not designed for majors or specialists (often referred to as general education courses). In introductory psychology, for example, you might be asked to write summaries, term papers, or short documented papers—tasks similar to those in an introductory anthropology course or in a history of Western civilization course. These kinds of writing often call for reasoning that weighs two sides of an issue, analyzes why something happens, or summarizes the main ideas in an article. What differs is the content and subject matter you're writing about.

In more advanced courses and in your academic major, you do more **discipline-based writing.** This kind of writing draws on forms, styles, structures, and other characteristics shaped by the community of people who work within a field, such as sociologists, anthropologists, biologists, economists, architects, music historians, or engineers. It is still academic writing—writing in courses, labs, and seminars—but it shares some features with the writing of professionals in the field. (See Chapters 17–18 for the characteristics and appropriate strategies for discipline-based writing.)

Being able to recognize the kind of general academic writing a course calls for and having the skills that will enable you to respond appropriately are important to your success as a college student.

16a Analyzing assignments

College writing begins with an assignment, and assignments are usually announced in a course syllabus, at least in general form. (More specific information may come from the instructor later, when you begin working on the task.)

1 Syllabus assignments

Begin by looking through a course syllabus for general statements about the nature and purpose of writing in that course. Then take the following steps.

- Note titles and due dates of writing assignments.
- Make a separate list of all the writing assignments. Next to each assignment, jot down any information that explains its nature, purpose, or complexity.
- Note whether the assignments appear to be *sequenced* in some way. Do they build on previous assignments? Does the *type* of writing change in any way? Note patterns in the assignments, such as three "short analyses" (one due every five weeks) and a large term paper at the end.
- Look for relationships between and among the assignments and the overall coverage of course material.

In the syllabus for her history of science course, Amanda Loh noted the following general statement:

> You will write often, both to reflect on the material and to show your understanding of it. There will be informal response papers of about one page. There are three formal essay assignments of 800–1,500 words each, to be explained in class and in handouts: a *document comparison*, a *change essay*, and a *comparative analysis*.

Loh noticed that the assignments were spread over the course duration and that each was accompanied by a short description.

> **Document comparison:** Write a thesis-based paper describing two historical documents and analyzing the differences between their authors' perspectives and biases.
>
> **Change essay:** Explain how a scientific concept or process changed over time, with reference to an original conception and a later conception (this requires a bit of research).
>
> **Comparative analysis:** Compare and analyze how two cultures viewed or developed a particular scientific or technological perspective, approach, or method.

Loh could see that the assignments became more complex, starting with a comparison of two documents and ending with a synthesis of multiple sources of information. The names of the essays were rather unfamiliar but made sense. Still, she knew she would need a lot more information and guidance.

2 Detailed assignments

Instructors' assignment methods vary greatly. Some like to hand out brief descriptions, perhaps a single paragraph or half a page in length. Others like to describe the assignment in class, clarifying it based on students' questions.

Still others create Web pages with lengthy explanations and links to evaluation criteria, suggestions, and resources.

Whatever the method, you need to spend time analyzing an assignment carefully, noting specific or unusual expectations. Pay special attention to four key elements of any writing assignment.

1. **Level of formality.** Usually, the longer an assignment, the more formal it is. Your instructor assumes that you won't spend a lot of time on an overnight response paper of one page, but a fifteen-page term paper assigned at the start of a course and collected at the end will assume multiple drafts, careful revision and editing, and flawless grammar and documentation.

2. **Freedom versus constraint.** Some assignments will be "open" in terms of what you can say or what information you can use. Others will limit you to specific readings or information or ask specific questions you need to answer in your paper.

3. **Purpose(s).** An assignment may be designed to give you practice or to help you learn something specific. It may have a rhetorical purpose, requiring you to convince someone about a point or perspective; to share new information with an interested audience; or to reveal a new understanding about a text, phenomenon, object, or process. Purposes are usually revealed by specific nouns and verbs in an assignment (see 3a).

4. **Audience(s).** The "default" audience for most college writing assignments is the instructor, but instructors often push aside their own tastes and opinions to play the role of a wider, "educated" college audience when they read your work. Sometimes instructors will ask you to address a specific audience, such as the people opposed to your solution to a problem or members of a professional group. In addition, you may be asked to share your writing with your peer audience in the classroom (see 5c).

STRATEGY

- Examine the description of the assignment carefully.
- Take notes: What is the task called? Is its name unfamiliar? If so, does it seem to be a name that's shared within the field of study, or is it a name that the instructor has created for classroom purposes?
- Describe its level of formality, its freedom versus constraint in subject matter, its purpose(s), and its audience(s).
- If any assignments include longer descriptions, "assignment guides," suggestions for completion, or grading scales, circle key words and identify verbs that signal what you need to do. Look for clues about the structure, style or voice, and content of the task.
- Figure out whether you are supposed to report information "neutrally" or to take a position and argue a point (see 10a).

3 Assignment goals

Assignments have specific *learning goals:* they're designed to help you gain knowledge in an area or practice a skill (such as researching a topic or summarizing information). Writing assignments also have *rhetorical goals*, such as presenting information or arguing a point. Finally, assignments have *assessment goals;* they give your instructor a piece of evidence about how well you've accomplished the learning and/or rhetorical goals of the assignment.

A good way to understand a writing assignment is to identify these kinds of goals. Sometimes the goals are clear and specific, as in the following excerpt from an assignment in an introductory psychology course, asking students to summarize, analyze, and critique a journal article.

> There are two main goals for this assignment: first, to give you practice summarizing the main points of articles that report original psychological research; second, to help you to critique research by asking questions about its design and conclusions.

In other cases, the learning goals won't be so clear. You may need to look at an assignment's **assessment criteria** to figure out how you will be graded and what the instructor is emphasizing in the task. (If the assignment criteria are unclear, ask the instructor to explain the assignment's goals to you.)

General academic assignments can also be divided into those that ask you to report information objectively (**information-driven;** see 16b) and those in which you make a case for your own interpretation or evaluation (argumentative, or **point-driven;** see 16h). For information-driven writing, you are like a reporter: your job is to gather information carefully and thoroughly, and then present it, often in distilled form, as clearly and objectively as you can. Informational papers include summaries and syntheses, reports, and objective documented papers or research papers. On the Web, information-driven writing will include material found at many government and public sites, and at information clearinghouses such as Wikipedia.

Here is a typical information-driven writing assignment from an introductory course in anthropology.

> **Overview:** For this assignment you will write a descriptive report of a cultural observation. You will need to find a social context, preferably one you are not accustomed to (and not one you yourself are usually in, such as a family meal), and spend one hour taking notes on what you see in as much detail as possible. You will then turn your notes into a description of the cultural and social behaviors of the people and events you observed.

16b Common types of information-driven assignments

Some college writing assignments ask you to gather information and present it objectively to others. Such information-driven writing doesn't aim to support your opinion or your critical insights. Instead, it asks you to adopt the stance of a careful reporter or an informed synthesizer.

Good information-driven writing relies on thorough gathering of information, careful analysis and synthesis, and a presentation shaped by both the subject matter and readers' needs. Instead of thinking of your readers as people who need to be sold something, imagine that they are already your clients, and that they want you to supply information thoroughly, objectively, and clearly.

Remember to offer your readers accurate information that is new, interesting, or useful to them. Your own values, attitudes, and opinions are less important than the information, its clarity, and the fairness of your presentation.

16c Summaries

A **summary** is a general term for any piece of writing in which you present concisely the key elements and details (content) of a longer text (or of an event), without extraneous detail or embellishment. In an **objective summary,** your job is to present in compressed form the substance of a text, using your own words, without evaluation or commentary (see 21g-1). (In an **evaluative summary,** you add an evaluation of the coverage, accuracy, or value of your source; see 21g-1.)

Most often, instructors assign summaries of chapters in textbooks or other readings, partly to help you identify the most important (main) ideas and information without getting caught up in less important details. A summary is much shorter than the original; a good summary might provide in less than a page the essential content of a fifteen-page article.

Before you can write a summary, you need to be very familiar with the work you are summarizing. Reread the text, underlining key passages and taking notes. If the "work" is not a text but an event, such as a lecture, presentation, or class discussion, take good notes during the event. Identify the main points in the text or the most important elements you included in your notes about an event, and state them in a sentence or two. Then create an outline of subpoints, either chronologically as presented in the text, or hierarchically, from most to least important. You can begin your summary with the main point (usually an extensive introduction is not necessary) and then explain the subpoints in order.

Here are the opening sentences to a summary Jen Halliday wrote for her introductory sociology course, summarizing an article reporting changes in white students' racial attitudes when they had increased contact with African American students. Notice how she provides the central point of the reading first, then begins moving into the substance.

> In this article, the authors report on a study of change in the racial attitudes of a sample of White college students when they had increased contact with African American students and were exposed to increased information about racial issues. To conduct their research, the authors first randomly selected a group of ten White college students between the ages of 18 and 23 at a midsized Midwestern university. To gauge these subjects' existing attitudes and feelings toward African Americans, they used a combination of surveys and interviews. . . .

Because it is easy to include more information than necessary when summarizing, ask yourself whether you are providing more detail than is needed to understand the author's key points and the way he or she arrived at them.

In a philosophy course focusing on contemporary ethical issues, Pete Sodeberg and his classmates were required to write brief summaries of the discussion in each class session so they would pay attention and think about the material more fully. Here is the start of one of Sodeberg's summaries.

> Today we extended our discussion of ethical issues in medicine following several pro/con readings about harvesting cells from frozen embryos for purposes of research. First, Dr. Schmidt asked us to review the main arguments (ethical and otherwise) for and against the question, which he listed on the board. We then considered the lists from the perspective of their ethical arguments. On the support side, we noted that the ethical issues are driven by the principle of the most good for the least sacrifice, while on. . . .

Notice that Sodeberg begins with a global statement about the focus of the class, then summarizes the process that led to the main part of the discussion, but without providing the actual list of pros and cons. In this case, the discussion of the list, which he then describes for two paragraphs, is more important than the list items themselves.

Checklist for an effective summary

- Begins with a concise (one- to two-sentence) overview of the work or event
- Provides enough detail to give readers a sense of the event's contents at a level of generality high enough to help avoid excessive detail

- Presented in an objective style, without personal commentary or evaluation (unless commentary and evaluation are parts of the assignment)

An **abstract** is a special form of summary, often accompanying a lab report, detailed study, or research paper. An abstract provides a summary of the content of a paper or article. Instructors may ask you to submit an abstract with a paper; you may also encounter abstracts in research databases and on Internet sites (see Chapters 23–24).

Abstracts are entirely objective, restating the content of a paper without extraneous commentary. For scientific papers, an abstract typically includes information about various sections of a paper: hypothesis, method, results, and discussion (see 18i). By reading an abstract, someone not familiar with a paper should be able to understand its general contents, methods, stance (theory or opinion), and conclusions.

16d Literature reviews

A **literature review,** sometimes called a *survey paper* or *review of the literature*, is often part of a longer paper, yet instructors sometimes assign it as a paper on its own. A psychology paper reporting the results of an experiment, for example, generally provides a literature review right after the introduction.

A literature review synthesizes the existing research on a topic—describing the content, similarities, and disagreements among previous research efforts. A literature review thus provides a backdrop for the study or analysis that follows. As a writer (and researcher), you would not repeat in your work what others have already done but you might want to build on earlier work: testing or retesting conclusions, analyzing aspects overlooked by previous researchers, or drawing on conclusions and methods and applying them to a different subject. Or you might use prior work as a springboard for your move into a fresh (though related) topic. A literature review establishes a context for your work and helps readers understand it, or (as a freestanding document) helps readers understand what we know (or do not know) about a topic or question.

Most literature reviews present the findings of others in a fair and balanced manner. Two or more studies may reveal major disagreements in a field, but the job of a literature review is to document those disagreements without judging the studies themselves, at least initially. Some kinds of literature reviews do judge the works being analyzed; for example, an author of a medical research article may present the findings of previous studies while criticizing their methods. Such a review tends to be more point-driven because the writer is laying the groundwork for a claim that his or her own methods are superior. In most college courses requiring a literature review, however, you will be asked to summarize the literature, not criticize it. Your reviews will be informative, aiming at summary (21g-1) and synthesis (21g-3) of knowledge.

(The research papers in Chapters 17 and 18 of this text provide examples of literature reviews used to open longer papers. Note how the writers use the reviews to explain and justify the goals of their studies and to provide necessary background for readers.)

Checklist for an effective literature review

- Summarizes the results of prior research accurately and concisely
- Synthesizes the conclusions and information from prior research, noting overlaps but giving credit to individual researchers
- Notes major disagreements among the studies being reviewed
- Establishes a justification and framework for the current study or research paper

16e Annotated bibliographies

An **annotated bibliography** is similar to a regular bibliography (see Chapters 28–31) except that each entry also includes an annotation describing the aim, purpose, or content of the work cited. Annotated bibliographies help readers survey what has been written on a topic and suggest specific works they may wish to consult for their own research. College instructors commonly assign annotated bibliographies to help students survey and report on a body of scholarship or to help them prepare for an extended research paper.

Annotated bibliographies usually begin with a brief introduction to the topic, perhaps highlighting the kinds of works covered in the bibliography. Next, they present citations for each work followed by annotations, usually no longer than a paragraph or two in length. Annotations often employ abbreviated sentence structures, omitting the subject on the grounds that it is understood to be the work given in the citation: "Summarizes research on the development of the Cherokee syllabary."

The annotation below comes from student Ian Preston's annotated bibliography, which consisted of an introduction to the topic followed by sixteen entries. He prepared his bibliography for a project focusing on bilingualism in the United States.

Glazer, Nathan. "Where Is Multiculturalism Leading Us?" Phi Delta Kappan 75 (1993): 319-24. This article describes the Center for the Study of Books in Spanish for Children and Adolescents, an organization that promotes the positive aspects of bilingualism.

```
Unlike other organizations that portray their ethnic
groups as victims, the Center, Glazer argues, ought
to be followed as a model of a bilingual program.
```

Notice how Preston writes objectively (neutrally) even as he *represents* the argument of the author.

Checklist for an effective annotated bibliography

- Introduction orients readers to the topic being covered
- References employ a consistent documentation style (Chapters 28–31)
- Annotations provide a brief summary of the work, accurately representing its contents and perspective but without unnecessary detail
- Works are presented in alphabetical order by authors' last names. Long or complex bibliographies may be separated into sections, sometimes chronologically ("Nineteenth-Century Studies," "Twentieth-Century Studies"), sometimes by general topic or focus ("Critical Studies: General Satire," "Critical Studies: Individual Satirists")

16f Essay exams (informative)

In many classes, instructors use **essay exams** to evaluate your skills as a synthesizer of information and as a critical thinker, skills that cannot be demonstrated in true/false or multiple-choice tests. Exams in which you provide clear and objective information in essay form, that is, **informative exam essays,** can be short—a paragraph or two describing a phenomenon, for example—or long, calling for elaborate descriptions and data. (For essays in which you defend and explore a claim or point, see 16k.)

To create carefully organized, clearly written, and detailed essay exams, spend a few minutes at the start developing a simple outline. Separating your answer into three to five sections (or paragraphs)—more, if appropriate—can help you organize information into clear and easy-to-understand chunks you can use to direct your reader from point to point logically so your instructor can see quickly that your essay embodies adequate knowledge of the subject.

To begin the exam, *read the question(s) carefully.* You need to write quickly and concisely in a limited time yet you also need to answer the question(s) specifically and with as much support as possible. Understanding what kind of answer the instructor expects is crucial; your planning before you write, though brief, needs to address the question directly. Writing as much as you can without a specific focus, hoping to "hit" the right points, will not impress your instructors.

On an exam in a general biology course, Nicholas Branahan responded to this question: "Define the concept of natural selection, being sure to explain its main features and how it affects behavior." Here is the opening of his response.

> Natural selection is a process in which the characteristics of an organism that best promote its ability to reproduce are selected and the characteristics that hinder it are weeded out. As random gene mutations form new characteristics, natural selection will select those that enhance the organism's ability to reproduce. Ability to reproduce depends on adaptability to the weather, ability to find food, avoidance of predators, and other aspects necessary for survival.

Notice how Branahan first defines the concept briefly (as requested) and then begins to explain its main features. In two subsequent paragraphs, he explains how natural selection affects behavior and what happens to the organism when the environment changes.

Checklist for a successful informative essay exam answer

- Addresses the exam question directly, without providing loosely related information
- Is organized clearly and logically, with each paragraph focusing on a different section of the topic
- Includes, as much as possible, brief examples, cases, and references

16g Short documented paper

In many courses, you may be asked to write a relatively brief informative paper, drawing on a limited number of library, database, or Internet sources, although not as many as in a typical research paper/project and with a less-extensive focus. Informative documented papers do not argue a point but present information objectively with a narrow or specific focus.

The techniques useful for an extended research project (see Parts 5 and 6) apply to shorter documented papers (including use of a specific documentation style) but in shorter and more focused form. Typically, a short informative paper does not provide a detailed examination of a topic or answer a complicated research question, but instead offers an overview of an issue, phenomenon, or event by drawing on three to five sources. Such papers are designed to *inform* readers but not to analyze a topic or issue exhaustively.

David Aharonian wrote his paper, "Desperate Times for Teachers," for an education course in which the instructor asked students to explore issues relating to the teaching conditions in the United States. Note that even though it is informative, citing facts and statistics from four articles, the paper still has a thesis. Unlike an argumentative thesis (see 3d), however,

Aharonian's thesis presents a conclusion based on his synthesis of research studies. Note, too, that he does not recommend a course of action, which would require taking a position. Instead, the paper stops short of argument, allowing the reader to take the next step based on a considered response to the information presented. Here are some selections from the paper.

> There is a major controversy regarding teacher salaries in this country. Many people feel that teachers are overpaid because they have summers off from work. They feel that teachers do not truly work year-round and therefore are either getting a fair rate of pay or getting too much. Many teachers, however, disagree with this assessment. They feel that they are underpaid for the work that they do. Most teachers find it very difficult just to make ends meet on a teacher's salary, and often they resort to moonlighting.
>
> Moonlighting means that a person holds another job in addition to his or her career. . . .
>
> **[The next four paragraphs supply information and statistics on moonlighting teachers, drawn from two sources.]**
>
> But there really are no easy solutions to the problem. One obvious answer would be to increase teacher salaries (Alley 21). This would lead to less moonlighting and allow teachers to concentrate more on their primary occupation. But there are still many people who oppose raising teacher salaries. Because public school teachers rely on taxes and bond referendums for increased salaries, they often go two or three years without any raise in their pay. When pay does increase, it may go up only 2-3 percent. This lowers teacher morale and can lead to frustration or burnout (Henderson 12). As one teacher in Oklahoma put it, "It's hard to look across the hall and see a teacher who's taught fourteen years, making only $4,000 more than you are" (Wisniewski and Kleine 1).
>
> **[The paper ends with a list of works cited.]**

Checklist for a successful short documented paper

- Summarizes or synthesizes the views, research results, or positions of other writers concisely and accurately
- Offers conclusions based on a reasoned consideration of works examined in the text but generally allows readers to decide on the significance of the conclusions for policies, beliefs, and possible action
- Employs a clear, easy-to-follow organization

STRATEGY

Informative writing relies on a careful internal logic that helps readers to process and understand information. To find an internal logic to your information, try some informal grouping and outlining techniques (see also Chapter 2).

- **Chunks.** List the main areas your paper will cover. All the information you have gathered should fit into these "chunks." If something doesn't fit, reconsider your list. Perhaps you can create additional categories.
- **Patterns.** Look for patterns in your information. For example, if you are **comparing** or **contrasting** two objects or phenomena, then your work will involve dividing your paper into two large sections or into a number of subtopics, each of which covers part of the two main topics. If you use **classification,** you will organize information in terms of groups, categories, or parts, each presented in its own section. (See also 6e on patterns in paragraphs.)
- **Sequence.** Consider presenting information in **sequential order,** perhaps in a *spatial sequence* (describing physical features in relationship with each other), a *chronological sequence* (describing events in a series to explain a history or the stages in a process), or *hierarchical sequence* (describing relationships and the relative importance of a subject's features or parts).

16h Common types of point-driven assignments

When you write point-driven papers, you comment on material you read or information and ideas you gather through research. Your writing conveys and supports your point: the commentary, opinion, analysis, or arguments you present to readers.

Such writing usually requires you to *begin* in the role of a reporter, collecting information, opinions, or data (see 10b). When you begin drawing on this material for a paper, your role will change into something like that of an arbitrator, jurist, or judge, weighing various issues, evidence, or opinions. This kind of writing requires *critical analysis* and care in representing yourself and your reasoning (see 8b).

16i Critiques

A formal **critique** summarizes a text and offers a critical reaction to it. The summary should objectively condense the work, including all of its main ideas. The critical response is a subjective reaction to the work, but not necessarily negative or based purely on opinion without supporting evidence. A good critique tries to explain *how* and *why* a work is written as well as *how well.* In a critique, you make a point about a body of knowledge and opinion, helping readers interpret it and look at it from fresh perspectives.

College student Reid Nelson's critique begins with an objective summary.

> In the speech "Some Concerns Central to the Writing of Indian History," Alfonso Ortiz addresses the inadequacies created when non-Native American historians write Native American histories. Ortiz feels there is a need for historians to develop "greater sensitivity toward, and respect for, tribal traditions, and . . . learning Indian languages" (20).

The summary continues for five more paragraphs. Nelson then shifts to critique.

> Ortiz's simple and straightforward argument uses neither complex theorizing nor bewildering terminology. He clearly spells out the negative consequences that occur when academics are not confronted with responses from the groups they are writing about. In this case, the consequences are the continued misunderstanding of Native Americans and poor relations between the two groups. The point is strengthened through Ortiz's use of repetition. Of course, the reception of his ideas will depend on whether historians agree that there is a problem in the way they write history, and whether they agree that Ortiz's proposals will benefit non-Native Americans' understanding of Indian history.

Notice how Nelson moves from description to evaluation in the sample paragraph, interpreting what Ortiz has done (and how successfully he has done it) and analyzing how historians might accept his ideas. The paper continues in this direction and ends with full references to the printed source for the speech.

Checklist for a successful critique

- Does not confuse objective summary with subjective opinion
- Summarizes all the text's main ideas and important questions
- Expresses a critical opinion of the text fairly, stressing how and why it works and balancing positive and negative points
- Gives the reader a clear picture of the text's content, its writer's stance, and the strengths and weaknesses of its argument

16j Reviews

A **review** is a critical appraisal of an event, object, or phenomenon, such as an art show, concert, book, or restaurant. Reviews help people make decisions or test their own judgments against those of another person. In a review, you describe, analyze, and evaluate your subject from an informed but opinionated perspective, ranging from fairly objective and descriptive to strongly judgmental. In general academic courses, reviews will most often focus on works or events tied to the discipline you are studying.

Some reviews use a simple two-part structure: a description followed by an evaluation. Others begin with an evaluative point in a kind of thesis statement: *Subject X is a success (or failure), good in some areas but poor in others*. Whatever the format, good reviews don't just state an opinion but support it with specific information and details. In addition, good reviews are informed by knowledge of the subject and form. In writing your own reviews, therefore, it helps to read professional reviews of the same work or event to note important features of style, structure, and choice of language.

Note how Amy Singh, a student in an introductory linguistics course, introduces the subject of the book she is reviewing before she moves on to the review itself.

> The preservation of a language, though the community that uses it may be small, is crucial. Language is not just a communicative amenity--it is a reflection of (and an influence on) a specific culture. Not only does a language allow a culture to flourish, but it allows the people within that culture to flourish. In some cases, a language is particularly well suited to a specific culture because it is all that allows its users to function in society. To allow or force a language so tailored to die is to leave the culture with no effective means of communication, only whatever its people have managed to acquire, usually by bare necessity, of the surrounding, dominant language.
>
> Cathryn Carroll's book, *Laurent Clerc: The Story of His Early Years* (Washington, D.C.: Kendall Green Publications, 1991) gives the reader a broader platform on which to base these convictions. Set in the early nineteenth century, *Clerc* examines the beliefs, stereotypes, and attitudes surrounding the deaf and their language. . . .

Singh's paper continues for another five paragraphs, detailing the contents of the book and commenting on the importance of its points. Although she doesn't spend much time evaluating the book, the way she describes its content implies that she thinks the book is successful and worth reading. She makes this clear in her conclusion.

> Carroll's fascinating book illustrates the folly of expecting one mode of communication--one language--to suffice for every member of society. Her book portrays the struggle of the deaf to gain equal standing in a greater society that had so much trouble accepting them. . . .

Checklist for a successful review

- Describes the subject of the review at the start, providing all the information a reader needs to understand it
- Offers a reasoned, supported evaluation of the subject's main elements
- Demonstrates the writer's knowledge of the subject so that readers are more likely to respect any conclusions presented (and supported) in the review
- Offers reasonable support for conclusions so that readers are likely to respect them even if they do not agree with the evaluations

16k Essay exams (point-driven)

A **point-driven essay** responds to an exam question asking you to present a position or argue for your own interpretation of a work, phenomenon, or event. In such an essay, listing bits of information without discussing their significance or making connections is not acceptable. You will need to offer a conclusion or interpretation—a thesis (Chapter 3)—for which you provide supporting evidence and reasoning.

First, *read the exam question(s) carefully.* You need to write quickly and concisely, answering the question with as much support as possible. It's crucial to understand what kind of answer the instructor expects and to plan the essay, even briefly, before actually writing. Decide what position you want to take or what point you will make. This will become your working thesis or proposition—a perspective or interpretation that you will support with evidence. Try creating a brief outline for your answer, even just a few lines or items listed on the facing page of the test booklet or an extra sheet of paper. Working from an outline will help make your paper more focused, point-driven, and clearly organized. Avoid going off on tangents, and keep from making especially complicated arguments (unless you have time to revise).

The following sample opens an essay in which student Ted Wolfe answered a question asking him to identify and discuss a major theme from a survey course in American literature, drawing examples from two stories. (Students were allowed to use their books to find quotations.) Note how

Wolfe focuses on one theme (the conflict between good and evil) and draws on elements of a story to illustrate this theme.

> Hawthorne's "Young Goodman Brown" explores the conflict between good and evil. Young Goodman Brown has his religious faith tested during a journey into the woods. In what may or may not have been a dream, the devil shows him that everyone he believed to be good is evil. . . . When the devil is about to baptize him, Brown calls out for Faith, his wife, telling her to resist temptation. He is really calling out for faith, as in faith in God. When he does this, the hellish vision passes, and he is alone in the woods. From this, we can conclude that Hawthorne believes people should try to resist temptation and lead moral lives.
>
> Goodman Brown is never the same after the experience, be it a dream or reality. He becomes "a stern, a sad, a darkly meditative, if not a desperate man."

As Wolfe continues his answer, he argues that Hawthorne is not just offering a pious message but suggesting that "one should not get so caught up in trying to be morally perfect that it ruins one's life. People must learn to 'find the perfect future in the present.'" Wolfe explores the theme effectively, with evidence and quotations from the text.

Checklist for a successful point-driven essay exam

- Addresses the exam question directly, taking into account all parts of the question
- Uses references—quotations, facts, and other information—to support the writer's conclusion, but does not overload the essay with detail
- Synthesizes material, makes connections among references, interprets the evidence, and discusses the significance of the material; does not merely list information

16l Position papers

Many instructors assign **position papers.** This type of paper presents a position on an issue or controversy and then supports that position, sometimes with material from the course, sometimes with outside reading and research. Position papers must focus on an actual controversy, meaning others need to have expressed different opinions on the issue. Some topics that are not "arguable" are your own likes and dislikes, matters of indisputable fact, and beliefs that are based on conviction and not empirical evidence (including most religious beliefs).

Once you have determined that your topic is not in one of these categories, make sure you can identify two (or more) distinct positions on the topic. In a position paper you will advocate a specific perspective, interpretation, or solution; therefore, your paper will follow conventions of argumentative writing (see Chapters 10–11). Your position paper may be documented, using outside sources to support your points, or it may be argued using internal logic, personal experience, or anecdote, as appropriate. For example, if you argue that recent global warming has (or has not) been caused by human activity rather than natural climatic variations, your position will likely find better support in the scientific literature than in a description of your trip to Alaska, where you saw hunks of ice "calving" from glaciers. However, if you are arguing that millions of gallons of gasoline could be saved by gas-saving driving habits, such as accelerating less quickly, solid reasoning and an appeal to readers' experience may be enough to support your point.

For an example of a position paper, see 11j.

Checklist for a successful position paper

- States a clear position on an arguable issue
- Uses factual knowledge, statistics, logical reasoning, or carefully selected, relevant anecdotes to support the writer's opinion or interpretation
- Includes discussion of alternate points of view to indicate that the reasoning is careful and thorough (see 11c)
- Contains an introduction that explains the issue, a thesis or position statement, and paragraphs arguing for the position with appropriate supporting evidence

CHAPTER 17
Writing in Literature and Other Humanities

What are the humanities? Literature, philosophy, history, art history, music, languages, classics, performing arts, cultural studies, and related fields of study. What kinds of thinking and writing do people explore in the humanities? They interpret texts, performances, and artworks, looking for meaning, the relationship of various elements, and techniques. They develop theories to help us understand our lives and our cultures. They look for patterns of meaning in past events and suggest ways to deal with the future. And they evaluate (or review) texts, performances, ideas, and interpretations.

As you move from general education courses into upper-level courses in the humanities, the writing tasks you encounter will begin to differ in complexity and in subject matter. Some kinds of writing may be similar to those you encountered earlier, yet they will require greater awareness of techniques of understanding and interpretation.

The range of fields making up the humanities is so wide and their subject matters so different that discussing the kinds of writing each requires is particularly challenging. Fortunately, a discussion of each field of study is not necessary. Writing in many humanities courses takes forms similar to those explained in Chapter 16, "Academic Writing: General Education." In addition, humanities courses often require interpretive, critical writing similar to the kinds of writing assigned in literature and film courses. We discuss these kinds of writing in sections 17a–e. You can transfer the advice in these sections to related fields of study such as art history, languages, cultural studies, classics, and performing arts. Finally, humanities courses often call for reviews and critical analyses of books, performances, or works of art. We discuss these in section 17f.

17a Research in literary study and related fields

Research in literary study, film study, cultural studies, languages, music, and similar fields focuses on verbal, aural, or visual texts. It pays attention to the actions of people being represented in the text, to the ideas being conveyed, to the visual images and patterns, and to the techniques being employed. Researchers try to interpret the relationships of these elements and what the elements of the text and its content convey (intentionally or unintentionally) about ideas, culture, society, or history.

Writing in literary study, therefore, often takes the form of **analysis** (understanding the elements of a work) and **interpretation** (understanding the relationship of the elements and the overall meaning, either of the work itself or of the culture/society it embodies).

In works regarded as imaginative literature (fiction, poetry, drama, and often film), the author generally calls special attention to the techniques of presentation, such as characterization, plot, symbolism, and figurative uses of language. In addition, imaginative literature often conveys its meanings through a fictional representation of some setting or human activity: the events of a story, a confrontation between characters, a monologue revealing thoughts and emotions, or a scene in which events take place. To understand the meaning of such texts, you need to read them with a different kind of attention than you give to other kinds of writing. Likewise, to present in writing your interpretation of and responses to literary texts, you need to employ special strategies of explanation and support.

17b Reading literary texts

When you read a novel, short story, or poem or view a drama or a film, you need to pay attention to both meaning and artistic technique. In doing this, however, you should be aware that there are many different strategies for reading and interpreting such works. Your choice of a reading strategy can determine the way you interpret a work's meaning and the way you respond to the writer's forms of expression. Your goal as a reader and writer is to develop and present interpretations that your readers will consider insightful and convincing.

1 Reading for meaning

For many critics and students of literature, to read for meaning is to read for theme. You can view **theme** as an idea, perspective, insight, or cluster of feelings that a work conveys or that permeates a work, organizing the relationships among its parts. Or you can view theme as the responses and insights readers are likely to derive from their experience of reading a work. In reading for meaning, therefore, you need to pay attention to theme, both as it is developed in a work and as it develops in your responses to the work.

STRATEGY

As you read, write down any ideas, perspectives, insights, or clusters of feelings the work seems to focus on. Pay attention to the various techniques writers generally employ for conveying meaning (see 17b-2): characterization and dialogue, events and conflicts, descriptions or scenes, and discussions of ideas and emotions (either by characters, the speaker, or the writer addressing readers directly). Write down potentially important ideas or themes in the margins (if you own the book), on a sheet of paper, or in a journal you keep while you read. You need not explore potential themes in depth; for a first reading, at least, an informal list can be very valuable.

Look especially for repetition and contrast as a key to importance. Repeated words and ideas, contrasting characters or events, and patterns of images can signal themes worth noticing.

In the following marginal notes on Anson Gonzalez's short poem "Little Rosebud Girl," for example, Sevon Randolf, a college student, indicates some repetitions and contrasts that reveal an important cluster of feelings and ideas (a theme) that she thinks the poem conveys.

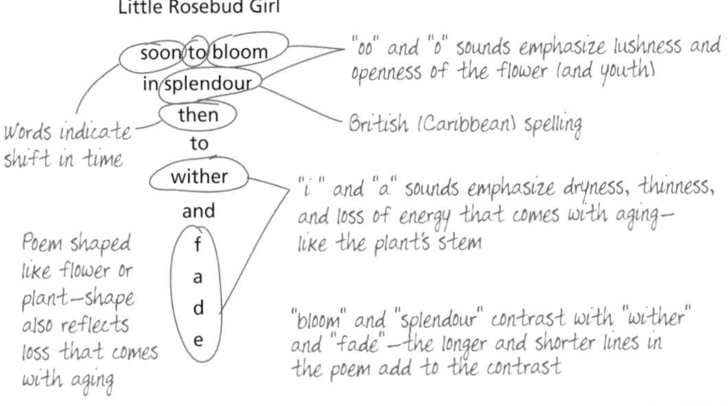

Little Rosebud Girl
soon to bloom
in splendour
then
to
wither
and
f
a
d
e
"oo" and "o" sounds emphasize lushness and openness of the flower (and youth)
British (Caribbean) spelling
Words indicate shift in time
"i" and "a" sounds emphasize dryness, thinness, and loss of energy that comes with aging—like the plant's stem
Poem shaped like flower or plant—shape also reflects loss that comes with aging
"bloom" and "splendour" contrast with "wither" and "fade"—the longer and shorter lines in the poem add to the contrast

—ANSON GONZALEZ, "Little Rosebud Girl" (1968)

The perspective you take as you read may suggest meanings and interpretations. If you know something about psychology, for instance, you might notice that the characters in a novel embody different psychological types or that the main character's actions can be explained as an attempt to overcome feelings of abandonment as a child. If you know something about history or political theory, you might be able to explain the events in a play as a reflection of an attempt to resolve contradictions affecting a particular society or culture. For example, you might be able to show that Shakespeare's plays *Macbeth* and *Henry IV* deal with questions of power and the proper form of government, major concerns in Elizabethan England. Finally, if you are familiar with contemporary feminist thought, you might note that the psychological and social portraits in a work seem to follow recognizable patterns of dominance and oppression and that the work seems to be designed as a commentary on the ways society has often distorted the lives of women. (Jennifer O'Berry's paper on "The Yellow Wallpaper" in 17d-2 draws on several such approaches.)

2 Reading for technique

When you read for meaning, you inevitably read for technique. A writer cannot create events, portray characters, represent scenes, or elicit a reader's reactions without using techniques of characterization, plot, setting, or imaginative language. Nonetheless, because these techniques are such an important feature of every literary text, you may wish to focus on them as you read, either to understand a writer's artistry or to cite the writer's use of the techniques as evidence for your discussion of a work's meaning.

As you read, pay particular attention to the following elements of a novel, short story, poem, or drama and to the techniques the writer uses in creating these elements.

Character. Identify the major and minor characters and their personality traits. Are they represented in depth with a variety of traits, even contradictions, or are they one-dimensional? Observe how the characters change and develop—or fail to change—in response to events. Note how self-aware the characters are. Which ones are presented positively, which negatively? Consider which characters, if any, represent values that the work seems to endorse.

Plot. Identify the order of events. Is it chronological, or have events been rearranged in some way? Decide what role conflicts play in developing the plot. Ask whether the events spring from the characters' personalities or serve primarily to reveal character traits. Is there a main conflict, a chain of conflicts, or a climax to which the work builds? Weigh the possibility that not all events are to be taken at face value. Watch for subplots alongside the main plot. Is the meaning of events clear to characters (and readers) from the start or only later? Pay attention to techniques of foreshadowing and suspense.

Setting. Note the time and place in which the events occur, along with any extended descriptions or background information relating to the place and time. Does the setting help explain the character's actions or reactions? Does it convey a mood that shapes the readers' reactions or the work's meaning? If the work is from an earlier period, check for elements in the setting that require historical explanation.

Point of view. For novels and stories, decide who is telling the story. Stories can be narrated in the first person (*I*) either by a character in the narrative or by a narrative voice (sometimes representing the author). They can also be told in the third person by a narrator who speaks of the characters as *he* and *she* but does not identify himself or herself as *I*. Narrators may be limited in what they know, be omniscient (knowing and seeing things the characters cannot), or combine both. Narrators may be reliable and truthful, unreliable and deceptive, or mix these and other traits. The speaker in a poem may be a character or may be a persona, a voice that speaks for the poet.

Language. Look for special uses of language: similes, metaphors, understatement, paradoxes, ironic comments, and the like. Pay attention to vivid language that creates scenes and images (sight, sound, and the like). Look for unusual word choice and striking or emphatic arrangements of words. Be alert for rhythms in the wording and for patterns of sound and rhyme.

Genre. Pay attention to **genre**—the specific form or kind of work: novel, short story, poem, drama, or film. Be especially alert to the techniques and conventions characteristic of each form, and note how writers use these conventions to convey meanings and shape readers' reactions. Note instances in which the writer varies or alters conventions, perhaps by undermining them or developing them in unusual directions.

STRATEGY

As you read a literary text, make notes on the large-scale techniques the writer uses to shape the work (genre, plot, and point of view, for example) and also on the smaller-scale techniques that appear to be important in a particular passage (language and character, for example). If you make your notes in the margins of your book, you can highlight passages you may wish to cite later in a paper. If you make notes in your journal, however, you will have more room to explore your responses and the ideas you may wish to develop in a paper. (Your journal entries also should note important passages for later use.)

Whenever possible, relate your observations on technique to your perceptions of a work's meaning. This will help you understand the purposes behind the techniques. It will also help you identify evidence for your interpretations of a work.

Note how T. J. Corini's marginal notes on the opening paragraph of John Edgar Wideman's novel *Philadelphia Fire* identify techniques and link them to meaning in a way that points toward a paper he might write.

What's going on?

On a day like this the big toe of Zivanias had failed him. Zivanias named for the moonshine his grandfather cooked, best white lightning on the island. Cudjoe had listened to the story of the name many times. Was slightly envious. He would like to be named for something his father or grandfather had done well. A name celebrating a deed. A name to stamp him, guide him. They'd shared a meal once. Zivanias crunching fried fish like Rice Krispies. Laughing at Cudjoe. Pointing to Cudjoe's heap of cast-off crust and bones, his own clean platter. Zivanias had lived up to his name. Deserted a flock of goats, a wife and three sons up in the hills, scavenged work on the waterfront till he talked himself onto one of the launches jitneying tourists around the island. A captain soon. Then captain of captains. Best pilot, lover, drinker, dancer, storyteller of them all. He said so. No one said different. On a day like this when nobody else dared leave port, he drove a boatload of bootleg whiskey to the bottom of the ocean. Never a trace. Not a bottle or bone.

Whole ¶ presents contrasts of character, attitude, perspective, and detail

first character—a hero? an outlaw?

The bones symbolize the contrast

His actions make him seem verbal, self-assured

Repetition and parallelism help emphasize his growing legend

2nd character Cudjoe uncertain of his manliness? Admires Z?

Z. self-sufficient? Sure of himself? Characterization —Z.'s actions and attitudes contrast w/C.'s contrast

Contrast

17c lit

Exercise 1

A. Choose a short text or part of a text you are planning to write about. Read it, making notes on the meaning and technique in the margins or in a journal.

B. Ask a classmate to read the same text and make the same kind of notes that you made in Exercise 1A. (Return the favor by reading and annotating a text for your classmate.) Compare your notes, looking for points of agreement. Discuss any annotations or interpretations that need explanation or support.

17c Writing about literary texts

When you write about a literary text, you interpret and analyze an author's words and techniques. To do so, you must arrive at conclusions—judgments and observations—with which another reader may agree or disagree. Consequently, you need to convince readers that your conclusions are both reasonable and well founded. You can generally do this by offering evidence from the text or from secondary sources.

1 Writing about meaning

In writing about the meaning of a literary work, you may explain and support your conclusions about its theme. Or you may focus on insights you develop by applying a particular perspective to the work (a historical perspective or a feminist perspective, for example).

Developing a thesis. If you are writing about a work's theme, make sure readers can easily identify your statement of the theme. Presenting your conclusion about the theme early in your paper in a thesis statement is an effective strategy. In addition, if you develop a working thesis early in your drafting, you can revise it and use it to help focus your supporting paragraphs.

Selecting evidence. Suppose you developed the following working thesis.

> In "Young Goodman Brown," Hawthorne focuses on dangers to human relationships and community posed by excessive concern with the self.

For supporting evidence, you can turn to passages in the text itself, either those that seem to state this theme or those you can analyze and explain in ways that support your conclusion. Simply quoting passages from the work is not enough. You need to discuss and analyze them in detail in order to show readers why the passages support your interpretation. You can also cite or summarize other elements of a work, such as events, characters, and symbols, analyzing them in detail to show that the text and the techniques it employs are consistent with your interpretation. Finally, you can turn to the writing of critics and scholars to support your thesis.

Organizing. Because a paper about meaning focuses on your view of a text's theme or on your interpretation of the work, you need to organize the paper to explain and defend your perspective. There are two general ways to do this (with many variations, of course). One way is to separate your thesis into parts and take up each in a different section of your paper. In writing about Hawthorne's "Young Goodman Brown," for instance, you might first demonstrate that the story deals with a character obsessed with the self, then look at what the story says about the consequences of this behavior. The other way to organize your paper is to divide it into parts corresponding to different segments of the work (beginning, middle, end) or different elements (characters, language, symbols), showing in sections of your paper how the particular part or element supports your thesis.

STRATEGY

Follow these conventions for writing about literature.

- Use the present tense when summarizing literary texts ("In the next section of the play, Falstaff *acts* in a manner that calls into question the kind of morality he represents").
- Use the present tense for discussing what a writer does in a particular work or group of works ("Dickens *uses* descriptive passages in *Bleak House* to develop symbols that comment on the action and the characters").
- Use the past tense for discussing a work in historical context ("During the Vietnam War, Levertov's poetry *took* on a distinctly political tone").

2 Writing about technique

In writing about technique, you explain the choices the author has made from the resources available for creating fiction, poetry, or drama. You also try to highlight the author's variations on the techniques, if any. Finally, you draw conclusions about the roles the techniques play in shaping the work's meaning and the likely responses of readers.

Developing a thesis. Since your purpose in this kind of paper is to describe and analyze one or several techniques and then relate technique to meaning, your thesis statement should reflect this dual emphasis. In writing about the story "Young Goodman Brown," for example, you might say, "Hawthorne uses ambiguity in setting, symbolism, and characterization to suggest how excessive concern with the self can alter one's perception of everyday events."

Selecting evidence. The primary evidence in a paper about technique is the text itself, presented either through quotations or through paraphrase and summary. But details from a text are not enough on their own to support your conclusions. You need to discuss the evidence, explaining the particular ways a technique is used and pointing out how this use supports your conclusions about the text's meaning. (The work of critics and scholars can also provide supporting evidence.)

Organizing. If you are examining a single technique, consider dividing your essay into parts corresponding to different sections of the work, demonstrating how the technique is employed in each section and for what purpose. (For a short work such as a poem, you might examine the work line by line or sentence by sentence, creating an **explication.**) If you examine more than one technique, you can divide your paper into parts, each concerned with a different technique. Or you can take up each section of a work in turn, looking at the various techniques used there.

Exercise 2

A. Choose a work you plan to write about. Read it, and write out a tentative thesis statement presenting your conclusions about the work's meaning and technique. Then prepare a list of particular passages or sections of the work you plan to use as evidence in your paper. Finally, create a rough outline or some other kind of plan for this paper.

B. Present your tentative thesis, list of evidence, and plan to a group of writers working on the same project. Discuss each writer's material, offering criticisms and suggestions to help each other prepare a draft. Draft your paper, and then share it with the same group for advice about revision. Take the group's advice into account as you revise and prepare the final draft.

17d The text analysis

A **text analysis** is a frequent assignment in many courses across the college curriculum. The first of the three examples here focuses on literary techniques in a poem. The second focuses on meaning in a short story.

1 Sample text analysis: Focus on technique

As you read the following paper, note how the writer goes through the poem line by line, accounting for nearly every image and phrase. This form of analysis is often called explication.

"Under Stars": A Portrait

by Chantele Giles

Under Stars

Tess Gallagher

The sleep of this night deepens
because I have walked coatless from the house
carrying the white envelope.
All night it will say one name
in its little tin house by the roadside.

I have raised the metal flag
so its shadow under the roadlamp
leaves an imprint on the rain-heavy bushes.
Now I will walk back
thinking of the few lights still on
in the town a mile away.

In the yellowed light of a kitchen
the millworker has finished his coffee,
his wife has laid out the white slices of bread
on the counter. Now while the bed they have left
is still warm, I will think of you, you
who are so far away
you have caused me to look up at stars.

Tonight they have not moved
from childhood, those games played after dark.
Again I walk into the wet grass
toward the starry voices. Again, I
am the found one, intimate, returned
by all I touch on the way.

1978

1 With the use of visual imagery in the poem "Under Stars," Tess Gallagher paints a romantic, yet lonely portrait of the relationship between the speaker of the poem and her long-distance lover. Although the speaker's emotional state is plagued with images of loneliness, she projects the long-distance romance as a positive relationship that is warm and caring.

2 As Gallagher brushes "The sleep of this night deepens" of the first stanza onto her canvas, her poetry begins to take shape. The word "sleep" implies that the relationship with her lover is

peaceful. Since the "night" personifies the relationship, the phrase implies further that the relationship is past the early stages and is deepening with the "sleep" of the night. In the next lines the speaker is walking "coatless from the house / carrying the white envelope." She walks "coatless" because she does not need to cloak the relationship; she is neither afraid nor ashamed. Since the "white envelope" connotes purity, goodness, and truth, it symbolizes the relationship as being true. The word "coatless" implies not only that the speaker has nothing to hide, but that the affiliation is warm and caring. If it were cold and dysfunctional, the speaker would not be without a coat.

3 In the last two lines, Gallagher applies the final strokes to the first stanza. The first of the two lines implies that the speaker is consumed with thoughts of her lover. With the image of the "little tin house by the roadside," Gallagher suggests that the speaker's lover is some distance away, which implies that the speaker is trying to bridge the distance between the two of them. She accomplishes this by composing a letter and placing it in the "little tin house."

4 Since the second stanza exposes the inadequacies of the relationship, Gallagher applies a darker paint to her canvas. The "metal flag" suggests the cold reality of a long-distance relationship, since metal is cold to the touch; the flag's "shadow" implies that the relationship cannot be touched by the speaker. The association with her lover leaves only a lonely "imprint" on the speaker's heart, which is symbolized by the "rain-heavy bushes." The final three lines are painted a lighter color. With these lines, the speaker implies that the "shadow" of loneliness is not permanent. Since the "town a mile away" symbolizes the future, the speaker implies that the future is close at hand. The "few lights" of the town suggest that there is hope in the near future.

5 Gallagher allows the readers into the realm of the speaker's fantasy, as she begins the third stanza. The "millworker" and "his wife" represent her fantasy relationship. The warm atmosphere created by the "yellowed light" implies that the speaker's fantasy is cheerful and bright. In this relationship, the couple reside and share their meals together. The "white slices of bread" connote food, nourishment, and sustenance. Since the "wife has laid out the white slices of bread" for the "millworker," the speaker implies that not only does she want to be her lover's sustenance, but she also wants to be consumed by him (the way the "millworker" will consume the "bread").

6 The last lines of the third stanza illustrate the speaker's need for closeness. Since the lover is "so far away" and the speaker looks "up at the stars," the speaker feels closer to her lover because of the possibility that the lover may be looking "up at the stars" also. This possibility creates a connection between the speaker and her lover. In the fourth stanza, Gallagher strokes onto her portrait "Tonight they have not moved / from childhood, those games played after dark." These lines suggest that the distance between the speaker and her lover has done little to change the affection she feels for her lover. "Those games played after dark" may refer to romantic liaisons; since these liaisons involve intense feelings, the speaker implies that the intensity of her feelings "[has] not moved from [the] childhood" of the relationship. Therefore, the speaker's connection to her lover is permanent.

7 With "Again I walk into the wet grass," Gallagher demonstrates that the speaker looks "up at the stars" on a regular basis, thus reinforcing the various images of the poem such as walking coatless and the "rain-heavy bushes." The "starry voices" recall the images set forth in the third stanza and the first part of the fourth stanza.

This line reinforces the images of the speaker's heavenly fantasy, as well as the feelings of permanence.

8 In the last lines, Gallagher displays the speaker's final analysis of the relationship. It is long-lasting and can survive the long-distance barrier. Since she considers herself to be "the found one," she implies that her lover is her one and only true love. She says further that her love is "returned by all" she touches, implying that their love is a powerful, all-encompassing natural force.

9 Tess Gallagher creates a gentle but stirring portrait of true love. Although the images suggest that the speaker endures the heartache of the separation, she does not succumb to the depression usually associated with it. Instead, she embraces the negative aspects of the situation and disempowers them through her fantasies and stargazing.

2 Sample text analysis: Focus on meaning

As you read, note how the writer backs up her interpretation with quotations from the story but does not let the quotations dominate the paper. If you have read this short story, consider other ways it could be interpreted; if you have not read the story, consider other ways the quotations used in this sample could be interpreted.

Images of Self in "The Yellow Wallpaper"

by Jennifer O'Berry

1 During the 1800s the idea of the "new woman" was appearing. Women began to realize that they were seen only as their husbands' and society's "property." They began to pursue their independence and create their own identities. In Charlotte Perkins Gilman's short story "The Yellow Wallpaper," a nameless woman is searching for her personal identity and freedom from the oppressive childlike treatment inflicted on her by her doctor/husband. Gilman presents an elaborate metaphor about the images seen by the woman within the wallpaper

found in her nursery/bedroom. This metaphor and the images the woman finds in the wallpaper play a significant role in the woman's achievement of finding her true self. Her state of insanity at the end of the story serves as a safe mask for her newly found freedom from alienation and oppression.

2 Gilman presents the woman in her story as a somewhat unstable character who believes that she is sick, although John, her doctor/husband, believes that she is only suffering from a "slight hysterical tendency" (416). This characterization seems intentional on the part of Gilman because it makes the reader see clearly that the woman's ideas are oppressed, even from the beginning, by her husband. John thinks that all his wife needs is a strict rest schedule in which she is "absolutely forbidden to 'work'" (416) until she is "well" again. Gilman seems to suggest, by putting work in quotes, that the duties of the woman, and all women at that time, were not truly considered work. She was forbidden to write and to have visitors. Early in the story, when the "rules" for her recovery are stated, the woman begins to comment on her disagreement with her husband, but she stops abruptly, as if she does not dare to have such thoughts. She believes that she would more quickly recover if, instead of being quarantined and forbidden from such pleasures as her writing, she "had less opposition and more society and stimulus" (416).

3 The woman tells the reader that "Mary is so good with the baby" (417), implying that she herself does not want to spend time with the baby. The child is also never mentioned by the woman as being with her or spending time with her. This seems to suggest that she may actually be experiencing a type of postpartum depression, causing her to want to abandon her child. The thoughts that lead her to feel that she may be ill may actually be due to her desire to abandon her role of wife and mother which was so rigidly demanded by society at that

time. She gets "unreasonably angry" (416) about the condition of things sometimes, but she blames this anger on her "nervous condition" (416). She tries to dismiss these thoughts because she feels that they are not proper. Therefore, she feels that she must be ill.

4 Gilman uses many images to enlighten the reader about the childlike treatment of the woman by her husband. The woman is directed by her husband to rest in a bedroom that used to serve as a nursery. Gilman chooses this room to show how John thinks of his wife. When referring to his wife, John commonly chooses names such as "blessed little goose" (418), "blessed child" (420), and "little girl" (421). This shows that he does not see his wife as an equal but rather as a helpless child who is solely dependent on him. As the woman begins to realize that she has been a subject of this type of oppression, she begins to be "a little afraid of John" (422) and to "wish he would take another room" (424), which exhibits her awareness of this treatment and the desire to be free from it, and from him.

5 Because of her rigid rest schedule, the woman is forced to spend most of her time in her nursery/bedroom, where she begins to explore the "worst [wall]paper" (417) she has ever seen in her life. Since she is not allowed to do much else, she commits herself to "follow that pointless pattern to some sort of conclusion" (419). She finds many images in the pattern, all of which aid in her "improvement" (423) "because of the wallpaper" (423) out of her mother/wife roles. She describes the pattern as images that will "plunge off at outrageous angles, [and] destroy themselves in unheard-of contradiction" (417). These "contradictions" seem to be referring to the contradictory treatment of her by her husband and society's contradictory expectations of her to be the perfect wife and mother. She becomes entranced by the wallpaper and "follows the pattern about by the hour" (419). With each second, the images become more numerous

and complex. She begins to see "a broken neck and two bulbous eyes" (418), a woman behind the pattern in the wallpaper. This woman "is all the time trying to climb through . . . but nobody could climb through . . . it strangles so" (424). She begins to identify with the woman and decides that she will stop at nothing until the woman is released from her entrapment.

6 At the end of the story, the woman is simultaneously on the brink of self-identity and insanity. On the last night she is to stay in the house, she is left alone in the room where she finally frees the woman in the wallpaper. When the woman in the wallpaper begins to "crawl and shake the pattern" (425), the main character "[runs] to help her" (425). Through the night, the two women pull and shake the bars and are able to "peel off yards of that paper" (425). She breaks down some of these cultural bars with the help from the woman in the wallpaper. When morning arrives, there is only one woman--the two have merged, and the woman's true identity has been found. In the remaining wallpaper are "many of those creeping women" (426). This symbolically represents the great number of women who also desire to be freed from the bars put up by society. She wonders if those women will ever "come out of the wallpaper as [she] did" (426). This shows her symbolic escape and her desire for other women to experience this personal freedom.

7 John returns at the end of the story to discover his wife in a state of insanity. When he sees her as the woman in the wallpaper, creeping around the room, he faints. She "had to creep over him" (426) because he was blocking her path. This strongly symbolizes the conquering of her husband because of her dominant position over him. She tells him that he cannot "put [her] back" (426) because she is finally free. Her creeping, which is like that of an infant, seems to represent a birth of her new self. At the same time, she has become completely insane. It is rather ironic that she must move into this state in order to be free from oppression. This seems to represent

society's view of a liberated and self-identified woman. John believes that his wife is not ill before she begins her pursuit of self-discovery. When this discovery is complete, he sees her as insane. The opposite is true for the woman herself. She sees herself as ill before her process of identification and fully healthy afterward.

8 The woman in Gilman's short story uses the yellow wallpaper as a tool to find her true self. The color of the wallpaper itself seems to represent the brightness and hope of a new horizon, yet at the same time, it is a reminder of the "old, foul, bad yellow things" (423), like a fungus that grows and decays. This is representative of the woman's life. She can never truly be free, because society's views and ideas will never acknowledge that a liberated woman can achieve her own identity.

Checklist for a successful text analysis

- Presents a unified interpretation that attempts to convince its readers of one specific way of reading the text
- Accounts for every idea, argument, image, or allusion; does not overlook elements that don't fit into the interpretation
- Does not try to hide behind a facade of objectivity, presenting opinions as absolute truths, but neither does it resort to the relativist plea that "one person's opinion is just as valid as another's"
- Attempts to add a new way of reading the text to the existing ways; does not merely repeat what has already been written about the text
- Assumes a dialogue with the reader

3 Commentary on students' papers

Chantele Giles (17d-1) was faced with the problem typical of writing explications of poetry, that of making the explication as lively and as engaging as the poem itself. Knowing that she must account for every line and image of the poem, she starts at the beginning and moves line by line to the end. To add interest, she frames the explication with an analogy of the poet to a painter, but her prose still sounds too dry. She could enliven her paper by varying the organization, perhaps by using the analogy as a frame to begin and end the paper rather than to begin each paragraph. She could also alternate the line-by-line approach with an occasional comment on the overall meaning of the poem. And she could move beyond discussing the meaning of the poem to other ways of looking at it, such as analyzing its effect on her or other readers or comparing it to other poems.

Jennifer O'Berry (17d-2) uses quotations from the text well; she seems to have an intuitive sense of what is significant about them and how they relate to each other. She could improve the paper by discussing these quotations in more depth, explaining why they are significant in understanding how this story illustrates the ways women were oppressed. As the paper is now, the significance of the quotations is a bit unclear, mainly because Jennifer does not define the terms that she uses to explain their significance (terms such as *self-identity, true self, insanity*, and *oppression*). Defining these terms would help strengthen the connection between the quotations and the discussion.

17e Analyzing and interpreting visual texts

Visual texts such as films, paintings, videos, photographs, architecture, and sculpture call for a different approach than novels, poetry, or drama. In part, the difference is one of technique: films and videos draw on the technical resources of photography and animation, for instance. The difference is also a matter of space and time: photographs, paintings, sculpture, and architecture occupy space but don't unfold in time as novels or films do, for example.

How scholars and researchers analyze visual texts and their meaning or significance differs from their approach to written texts. An analysis of visual texts pays particular attention to features and qualities like the following.

- **Arrangement.** How are the visual elements placed with regard to each other? Where are the figures in a picture, the objects in a photograph, or the parts of a building situated with regard to the elements?
- **Color.** What color scheme dominates the visual (pastels, sepia, shades of gray), and which patterns in the use of color are apparent?
- **White space.** How much of the work is filled with visual content and how much is left empty or "white"? For example, is a central figure surrounded by white or neutral space or is the entire frame of the painting, photograph, or film scene filled with people, objects, and background material?
- **Cinematography/photographic style.** What film or video techniques does the work employ (fading, quick cuts, slow motion)? What uses of lenses or recording material (film, tape, digital) characterize the work (long distance, graininess, sharp or blurred focus)?
- **Realism/abstraction.** Are the representations of people, objects, or scene presented in realistic detail, or are they abstracted to a greater or lesser extent (a realistic still life of fruit, an abstract representation of a human figure, nonrepresentational masses of color and form)?
- **Sound.** Does the work include oral speech and sound (as in most movies and videos), or does it consist simply of form, shape, and volume (as in a building) occupying space (paintings, sculptures, architecture, photographs)?

- **Eye movement.** Do the eyes of viewers move around a visual based on the ways people (or animals) in the film, cartoon, or picture look at or relate to each other (**gaze movement**)? Or do their eyes move around the visual according to geometrical, structural, or similar relationships among the objects and colors (**structural movement**)?

Understanding how these elements are related to each other and to the work as a whole is the key part of analyzing visual texts. This task is also an essential part of interpreting the ideas a visual text conveys or the psychological, cultural, social, or philosophical insights and meanings it embodies.

The elements of Figure 17.1—a Web page—are organized to interest viewers to enter the site. Bright, colorful images, coupled with sleek design and use of vibrant hues, encourage viewers to take a closer look at the products offered and potentially make a purchase.

FIGURE 17.1 Main menu for Inanimate.

Source: <http://www.Inanimate.com>.

17f Reviews and critical analyses (critiques) in the humanities

In many humanities courses, instructors will ask you to analyze, evaluate, and respond to what someone else has to say about a text, a performance (literary, visual, or aural), or about events and social patterns (present and past). Writing in fields like history, art history, and music history focuses on events and social or artistic developments. Writing in fields like literary study, cultural studies, music, languages, performing arts, and classics usually focuses on texts and performances.

A **review** is a critical appraisal of a text, performance, artwork, or event. Reviews evaluate using specific standards (or criteria) drawn from a field of study (for example, criteria for a successful novel, biography, nonfiction work, historical work, film, painting, or song). Academic reviews aim at conveying a judgment about achievements and weaknesses based on the standards of a field and comparisons with similar works. They may also incorporate your more personal judgments. The goal of an academic review is to convey an opinion about the work's overall value to other people working and researching in the field. (For a detailed discussion of reviews, see 17f-2.)

A **critical analysis** or **critique** is similar to a review, yet it has a stronger emphasis on analysis of particular parts of the work and on their implications for further research and theory or for the field as a whole. While it is possible to critique performances, artworks, or musical pieces, critiques are more likely to focus on written texts, either on literary or visual texts or on scholarly and theoretical texts. For example, in a history course, an instructor might ask you to critique a recent work of historical analysis focusing on an earlier period or to critique a representative text from the same period. In a music course, an instructor might ask you to critique an account of the origins and social roles of hip hop or an account of Mozart's role in musical and social history. (Such critiques are sometimes referred to informally as "book reports.")

Critiques typically begin with background information on the work being examined along with an overview of the standards (or criteria) the writer plans to use to evaluate the work. Following this, critiques usually offer a brief summary of the work being analyzed and an analysis of its major elements, ideas, key information, and presentation techniques. *Analysis* in this context means identification of the most important information, ideas, and strategies in the work and judgment about their success or failure relative to either the standards of the field, to general standards for scholarly or informative writing, or to the achievements of similar works. The last section of a critique typically offers the writer's judgment of the overall value of the work, its ideas, the policies it proposes, and the interpretations it offers.

This judgment relates the work to knowledge and research within the field, to current social and political developments, or to the writer's own perspective.

Here are the opening paragraphs of a critique Samantha Ann Rode prepared for a history course.

Parallel Universes

Fools Crow, a novel by James Welch, vividly describes the life of Blackfeet Indians and their conflict with the expanding American nation. For many people, the term "Native American" calls up a romanticized version of events involving feathered headdresses and loincloths. In his novel, however, Welch portrays the complex history and heritage involved in Indian ritual and belief once deemed "savagery." Welch's detailed accounts of Blackfeet heritage and religious beliefs give the culture the credibility it deserves.

A common understanding of American history, often expressed in textbooks, makes the westward expansion of the country during the nineteenth century seem a necessary evil and portrays Plains Indians as the beneficiaries of encroaching civilization. As Welch's work indicates, however, the Blackfeet had their own civilization, complete with a version of creation, centering on the sun and moon, not unlike the Christian story of Genesis. In addition, the Blackfeet considered their tribal lands sacred, full of heritage and history. Forced movement to a new territory completely uprooted the foundation upon which Blackfoot society was based. The Blackfeet had a deep respect for the land and all its elements. The way the new settlers treated the land and the animals violated these beliefs. In portraying these contrasts in the novel, Welch makes the reader aware of the natives as human beings, not just obstacles in the way of expansion. Welch's novel adds to historical understanding by helping explain the roots of misunderstandings and conflicts between Native Americans and settlers.

Differences in language contributed to barriers between the two groups, of course, but the novel helps us understand why the attitudes of the settlers were probably even more important sources of conflict. The belief systems of the Native Americans and the settlers were not completely incompatible; the settlers just never took the time to understand or to work toward compatibility. In the novel, for example, when Fools Crow and Red Paint were married, they took a very similar course to that taken in European-American society. Fools Crow asked Red Paint's parents for permission; gifts were exchanged; and the marriage ceremony followed. The Blackfeet also had tribal councils for discussion of problems and possible courses of action, just as in the social and political structures of American society. Native Americans and European Americans did not need to be in conflict, but the desire on the part of the newer Americans to dominate and suppress what they considered an inferior culture made hostility inevitable. By providing an understanding of Native American culture, Welch explores the roots of the conflict that ended with many Native Americans being moved to reservations and their lands being occupied by settlers, and he helps readers understand continuing conflicts.

1 Sample text analysis: Focus on technique (film)

As you read, notice how the student writer organizes his paper and uses details from the film to illustrate and support his points.

Realism and Visual Effect in Educating Rita

by Jason Fester

1 Educating Rita is a realistic film. It depicts an older woman hairdresser who returns to college to become educated. As a realistic film it presents itself very conventionally with authentic sets, vernacular dialogue, and routine eye-level shots with conversations consisting of medium two-shots and close-ups. Since the film

concentrates on language and the interaction of characters, the other elements of cinematic technique seem secondary, and as a realistic film, this seems appropriate. "Realists . . . try to preserve the illusion that their film world is unmanipulated; an objective mirror of the actual world" (Giannetti 3). But the director inconspicuously uses color to parallel character development and contribute to the theme of his movie.

2 When Rita is first seen, she is light-skinned and has bleached blond hair. She wears red lipstick, a thin white shirt, high heels, and a tight hot-pink skirt. The next time she is seen, she wears a white shirt, a bright red skirt, high heels, dangling silver earrings, and this time pink highlights adorning her hair. Rita is a vivacious, vivid woman, and the colors of her wardrobe reflect this. Her appearance presents her as sexual and corporeal.

3 The university, however, is a dull, colorless place. The building's walls are dirty white and gray stone. Frank's office is a dungeon of brown curtains, olive walls, and a drab red carpet, all bordered by a montage of tan, matte yellow, earth brown, and olive drab books. Everything associated with the university is plain, colorless, and somber. Frank's house continues the decorum of his office with brown curtains, muted yellow, and olive drab wallpaper. Frank wears suits exclusively in varying tones of tan; his friend exists in the same gray suit throughout the movie, and even Julia limits her wardrobe to red-browns. There is no vividness to any of these places or people. Everything, except Frank, is sober.

4 This is the world to which Rita commits herself, regardless of Frank's warning that she will have to "suppress, perhaps even abandon altogether, [her] uniqueness." Thus it is appropriate that at the stage of her development when she has chosen to commit to her education, saying "I want to change," she is wearing a tan jacket with a brown skirt.

5 With the advent of spring comes the next phase of Rita's transformation: summer school. Here her apparel consists of the light blues and greens of the fertile season, suggesting that Rita herself is flourishing and growing. Upon her return to Cambridge, she responds to a compliment on her appearance with "I got a whole new wardrobe." Her appearance is now quite different from when she was first introduced. Her hair is now her natural brown; she is unadorned with jewelry or makeup; and she is clothed in a blue blazer, loose-fitting white pants, and a long white scarf. These neutral, asexual colors and styles continue throughout this period of her activities: light blues, greens, and soft grays cause her to blend with the garments of her student peers and the lusterlessness of the college.

6 Exceptions to this pattern are the retrogressive Roaring Twenties outfits Rita wears for the bistro. They consist of hot pinks, turquoise, pink and blue leopard skins, and lime greens arrayed in clashing ensembles. But these serve to mock her original style, for when she jokingly displays one outfit to Frank, he humourlessly replies, "Why can't you just be yourself?"

7 The end of the movie presents a Rita vastly different from the one introduced at the beginning. Rita is now merely Susan, a confused, unfulfilled woman. She is dressed in blue jeans, common and ordinary. She wears no makeup. Her long brown hair hangs limply on her shoulders. As she walks along, her blue clothes merge with the dreary blues and grays of the wet rained-on streets. She doesn't know where she's going; she doesn't know what she wants to do.

8 The director uses the colors of Rita's clothes contrasted against the colors of her environment to further express the character changes she undergoes. Even though this is a realistic film, the director surreptitiously manipulates one technique, color, in a way that affects the emotions and responses of the viewer.

Work Cited

Giannetti, Louis D. Understanding Movies. 10th ed. Englewood Cliffs: Prentice, 2004.

Checklist for a successful critical analysis (critique)

- Provides a concise summary of the work being analyzed
- Makes a clear statement of standards (criteria) being used to evaluate a work's success and indicates the relevance of these standards to the goals of the particular field of study to which the work belongs
- Provides specific examples and details from the work (or from similar works) to support the analysis and evaluation of its success or limitations
- States clearly an estimate of the work's overall value and significance and provides concrete examples or careful reasoning to support this estimate

2 Commentary on student review

Jason Fester assumes that readers will be familiar with the film he is discussing, and as a result, he does not adequately identify some of the characters, scenes, and relationships he discusses. At the same time, however, his discussion of Rita's appearance and its relationship to her character is especially clear. He organizes his discussion so that it follows the chronological order of the film. This is particularly appropriate not only because the organization aids him in demonstrating the pattern in Rita's changing dress but also because it allows him to draw parallels with Rita's changes in character and the themes developed through these changes. He also presents detailed evidence about the film's techniques so that he is able to show convincingly how the evidence supports his interpretations of the director's work.

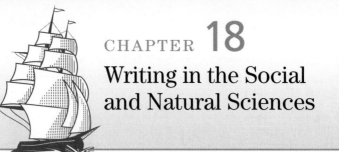

CHAPTER 18 Writing in the Social and Natural Sciences

As you move from general education courses to more advanced courses or begin studying for a major or minor, your writing tasks will change, along with the depth and complexity of the subject matter you write about. Instead of reading summaries of research in a textbook, you will begin reading research articles and looking at the results of scientific studies, and you will prepare reports and reviews of the scholarly literature with the goal of presenting the information and insights you gain through your reading. You will create lab reports to describe your work in a chemistry, biology, or pharmacy course, or a similar field. You will do fieldwork of your own (observations, surveys, and interviews; see Chapter 25) and report the results in your sociology, anthropology, folklore, or linguistics course.

The kinds of written documents you create will be similar to the kinds professionals create, but (in most cases) without the level of complexity and detail typical of advanced research and scholarship. Some of the writing tasks you encounter, such as lab reports or reviews of the scholarly literature, will be parts of coursework in a variety of fields. Others will be unique to a specific field of study or practice, as in the case of nursing care plans, a form of writing characteristic of nursing and allied health sciences.

In this chapter, we look at kinds of **writing in the disciplines** useful in a range of fields, both in the social sciences and in the natural sciences.

18a Research in the social sciences

The **social sciences** study human behavior and relationships, including both individual behavior and group characteristics and actions. Some fields, such as psychology and sociology, fall neatly into the social sciences. Others are less easy to categorize. Historians, for example, often argue whether their field should be part of the humanities (see Chapter 17) or belong with the social sciences.

Social Science Fields

anthropology (cultural, social, linguistic)
archaeology
business
communications
economics
education
folklore
gender studies
geography
history
linguistics

peace and conflict studies
political science
psychology
social policy
social work
sociology
urban studies

Typically, social scientists study data gathered from observing human behavior or by obtaining information from individuals or groups. Studies may report on selected aspects of individual or small-group behavior over an extended period (**case studies**), or they may provide information about varieties of behaviors characteristic of a particular location (rural town, city neighborhood, manufacturing plan) or group of people such as elementary school students, restaurant workers, professional athletes (**ethnographies**). Methods of study can include gathering opinions and responses from a substantial number of people (**surveys**); focusing on the behaviors, attitudes, and ideas of individuals or small groups (**interviews, observations**); or conducting **experiments,** comparing behaviors of groups acting in normal situations (**control groups**) with those acting in altered situations (**experimental groups**).

In published form, social science research has titles like "Mass Media Advertising and the Reinforcement of Gender Roles," "Success Rates for Current Approaches to Trauma Therapy," and *Unraveling Somalia: Race, Violence, and the Legacy of Slavery.* In many cases, the title indicates both the subject and the method used to investigate it: "Economic Decision Making: Findings from Simulated Market Experiments," "Organizational Behavior in Crisis Settings: Observations from a Case Study," "Effects of Negative Political Advertising as Measured by Telephone Surveys."

18b Common types of writing assignments in social science courses

Writing assignments in social science courses often ask for reviews of current research or opinion (see 18c), informative or interpretive reports on current issues or problems (see 18d), reports of original research (surveys, interviews, case studies; see 18e), policy proposals (a form of argumentative writing, see Chapters 10–11), and critiques or reports on articles and books (see 16i, 16j).

18c Reviews of research

An effective review of research reports the conclusions, methods, strengths, and weaknesses of current research on a topic of significant interest in a field of study. The writer selects the ideas and information for the review based on both the content of the research (conveying it accurately and concisely) and the purpose(s) of the review.

Some reviews focus on a problem or challenge, using current research to define and explain it. Some reviews examine current research to identify unanswered questions or possibilities for further research, often using the review to introduce and justify the writers' own research or to lead up to research questions they plan to explore (for a discussion of research questions, see 21e). In either case, writers need to be both accurate and selective, presenting the key ideas and details of a source while putting greater focus on those that help define a problem or question.

In a political science course focusing on current issues, student Andrew Quadros looked at arguments for and against the use of harsh interrogation methods or torture in wartime and in other crisis settings. His aim was to develop a research question that might be answered through a survey: How do contemporary college students view the use of harsh interrogation methods or torture in combating terrorism? Here are the opening paragraphs.

Is Torture Ever Justified?

Andrew Quadros

Are harsh interrogation methods, even torture, ever justified? Before the events of 9/11 and the ongoing war on terrorism, most Americans would have answered "No!" They would probably have regarded such tactics as violations of the Geneva Conventions and therefore unacceptable. Maria Trombley, of the Society of Professional Journalists, summarizes the ban this way: "Torture is forbidden by the Geneva Conventions, both in cases of internal conflicts (Convention I, Art. Section 1A), wounded combatants (Convention I, Art. 12), civilians in occupied territories (Convention IV, Art. 32), civilians in international conflicts (Protocol I, Art. 75, Sec. 2Ai), and civilians in internal conflicts (Protocol II, Art. 4, Sec. 2A)" (2003).

Recently, other voices have attempted to re-open the argument. The most notable is that of Charles Krauthammer in an article titled, "The Truth About Torture" (2005). Krauthammer argues for the necessity of torture in "ticking time bomb" situations where torture of a terrorist is necessary to get information to avoid the death of many people and should therefore be considered ethical. Moreover, writing in the *Deakin Law Review*, John Kleinig (2005) outlines situations in which, he believes, most people would agree that torture is necessary because it is an effective means of extracting vital information from dangerous people in order to save many lives.

In response to Krauthammer's article, Michael Kinsley (2005) points out that creating broad policies on the basis of unlikely situations is a bad idea and that in the present case, doing so is likely to lead to an expansion of torture in cases where it is not justified on the grounds of its absolute necessity.

[The paper goes on to explore other recent positions on the issue, explaining the current state of the discussion and noting how many of the writers develop their outlooks in direct response to each other.]

References

Kinsley, M. (2005, December 13). Torture for dummies: Exploding the "ticking bomb" argument. *Slate*. Retrieved October 23, 2005, from http://www.slate.com/id/2132195

Kleinig, J. (2005). Ticking bombs and torture warrants. *Deakin Law Review, 10*, 617-627.

Krauthammer, C. (2005, December 5). The truth about torture. *The Weekly Standard*. Retrieved October 22, 2006, from http://www.weeklystandard.com/Content/Public/Articles/000/000/006/400rhqav.asp

Trombley, M. (2003). Reference guide to the Geneva conventions. *Society of Professional Journalists*. Retrieved April 24, 2006, from http://www.genevaconventions.org

Checklist for a successful review of research

- Begins by identifying the specific topic, issue, or problem that is the focus of research
- Identifies clearly each piece of research; summarizes concisely what it says about the topic
- Highlights the most important, most controversial, and most influential contributions of the researchers
- Identifies the current state of knowledge or opinion and suggests future directions for research and discussion
- Points out what each piece of research has contributed to the development of current knowledge

18d Informative reports

An informative report in the social sciences brings readers knowledge drawn from research. It addresses a need for practical knowledge, a desire for greater understanding, or even simple curiosity. An informative report makes clear to readers the sources of information: articles, books, newsletters, or research databases. In most cases, however, an informative report is not arranged as a survey of the sources and the conclusions they offer, in the manner of a review of research (see 18c). Instead, effective informative reports focus on the information readers need; the reports are arranged to cover different aspects of the topic and to highlight key points for readers.

Checklist for a successful informative report

- Draws on recent, reliable research and other sources for information
- Identifies a need for information and responds to it
- Provides clear explanations, including visuals, and presents the information in ways that are accessible to readers
- Follows an organization that highlights important facets of the subject and information most likely to be of use or interest to readers

18e Research reports

A research report in the social sciences often follows the arrangement of a typical scientific paper: introduction and research question(s), materials and methods, results, and discussion. (For further discussion of scientific papers, see 18f.) This kind of paper reports on a tightly focused, controlled study that aims to answer a particular research question or questions, for example, "What elements of student loan procedures do college students find most confusing?"; "Are there psychological consequences for professional athletes using steroids?"; or "Do high school students retain language abilities gained in elementary school foreign language classes?"

Typically, successful research reports focus on questions developed from reading current research and understanding the ongoing research "conversation." They identify a particular population to be studied, and they report the results of a particular method of inquiry (interview, observation, survey, or experiment). Not all social research takes this "scientific" form, however. Often, researchers conducting extended and detailed observations and interviews with an individual (case studies in psychology or education, for example) or long-term observations of activities in a particular setting (ethnographies of a social or cultural group in anthropology, for instance) report their data and conclusions through extended narration and description accompanied by discussion and conclusions.

Nonetheless, understanding and using the elements of a research report can help you focus your research and share the results clearly and effectively.

- **Introduction.** Survey of prior research and statement of research question(s).
- **Methods.** Identification of people (population) studied and description of research method. (May include copy of a survey or interview questions.)
- **Results.** Detailed presentation of results or data from the study.
- **Discussion.** Presentation of conclusions about the results including key observations and discussion of extent to which the data provide an answer to the research question(s).

In a course on American folklore and folklife, student Justine Buhl read about beliefs and superstitions that persisted from generation to generation of college students through word-of-mouth transmission. She decided that conducting a survey might help her identify and study the phenomenon on her own campus, and she presented the results of her (admittedly limited) survey in a research report, portions of which appear below.

Food Folklore: Still Alive on Campus

Justine Buhl

[Introduction]

On any given day, in one of the many colleges around the country, students are, as they say, “grossed out” by the food served in their college dining halls. If you listen carefully, you will most likely hear students asking, “What is that? It looks disgusting!” or “Is this even real chicken?” Many of the things students say are similar to, or even the same as, things students have been saying for many years. There are stories and beliefs, passed down by word of mouth from generation to generation that are a kind of college folklore of dining hall food.

[Provides a brief review of relevant research on college folklore.]

I have encounted beliefs and stories about dining hall food enough times to be curious about them and about their similarities to the food folklore on campuses other than my own. I therefore decided to interview students at my own university and to do some research on college folklore, in order to answer two questions: (1) What are stories and beliefs about dining hall food that circulate among students at the University [a state university in the Northeast]?

and (2) How similar are these stories and beliefs to those that circulate on other campuses?

Method

To answer these questions, I interviewed twenty students from the University and asked each six questions:

1. What are some of the stories you have heard about the food in our dining halls?
2. What similar stories (if any) have you heard from students at other colleges?
3. What special names have you heard to describe dining hall food on this campus?
4. What similar names (if any) have you heard from students at other colleges?
5. What are some of the common myths you have heard about dining hall food on this campus?
6. What similar myths (if any) have you heard from students at other colleges?

[The discussion goes on to describe the interviewing procedure and some minor difficulties the writer encountered during the process.]

Results

In response to question one (stories about food), eight people said they thought laxatives were put in the food. One each responded that “they put poison in the food” and “they spit in the food,” and

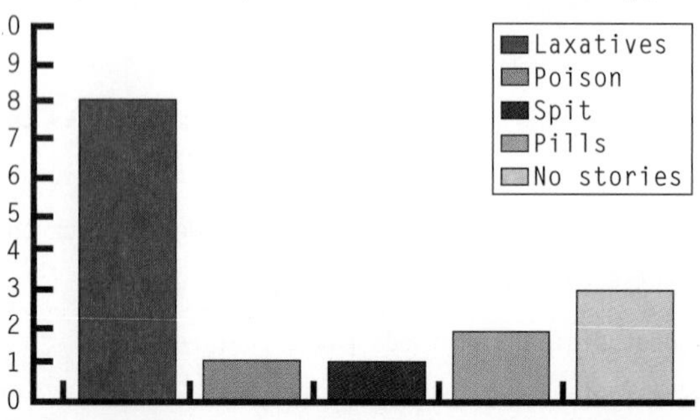

Figure 1. Kinds of stories.

two people said that "they put pills in the food." The results are presented in Figure 1.

[The discussion goes on to summarize the results for each of the other questions.]

Discussion and Conclusion

Students at the university have clearly encountered stories about dining hall food ("laxatives") and names for the food ("Mystery Meat"). They have also heard some gruesome urban myths about the food. They have heard these from their friends at other colleges as well. What is particularly interesting, however, is that all three forms of folklore have been in circulation for generations at American colleges.

[The discussion goes on to draw on scholarship on campus folkore, pointing out how stable it has been for more than one hundred years, including the examples obtained through the interviews. It suggests that the stability may reflect enduring concerns and fears of college students.]

Checklist for a successful research report

- Provides a brief review of prior research and explains reasons for conducting the study
- Identifies a clear research question or set of questions
- Identifies the group of people (population) studied
- Specifies the method of investigation and provides detailed information about interview questions, surveys, or other instruments
- Provides an account of the process of investigation, indicating any problems or noteworthy events
- Specifies the data gathered through the investigation, providing examples or tables and charts to supplement written presentation when appropriate
- Discusses the extent to which the data provide answers to the research question(s) and the extent to which the study is consistent with prior research or identifies new directions for investigation

18f Research in the natural sciences

The subjects of research in the natural and medical sciences are familiar to most of us: the natural world (including rocks, weather, oceans, stars, planets, chemicals, and atoms); organisms of all kinds; plants and animals (including humans). We are all familiar with the methods of inquiry, both from studying them in natural science courses and from portraits of scientific research in films, novels, and television: detailed observations in the field, microscopic examination in a laboratory, and experiments in laboratories, hospitals, or special facilities like wind tunnels or cyclotrons.

Natural Science Fields

anatomy	genetics	paleontology
astronomy	geology	pharmacy
biology	kinesiology	physical anthropology
chemistry	medicine	physics
environmental science	meteorology	
	oceanography	

Typically, natural scientists gather data by careful observation and collection techniques, often employing sophisticated equipment to measure phenomena not apparent to the human senses, such as electrical waves or atomic and subatomic particles. They also use recording techniques to observe and collect data that change slowly over time (such as the growth of an organism) or that are dangerous to sample (such as fumes from a volcano). Measurement of changes or of the physical dimensions and components of a subject are key techniques for natural scientists. Looking for relationships among events, materials, or matter and energy are key focal points for scientific research, especially the search for mathematical correlations or likely cause-effect relationships. The sheer volume of inquiry in the natural sciences means that a researcher needs to be aware of the likelihood that any topic will be the subject of numerous research articles and reports. In addition, the complexity of the phenomena studied by natural scientists means that individual research projects tend to focus only on a small part of a phenomenon.

Complexity and narrow focus mean that many natural science research publications have titles indicating that they are intended for a limited number of specialist readers: "A Gas-Phase Chemiluminescence-Based Analyzer for Waterborne Arsenic" (from the scholarly journal *Analytical Chemistry*) or "Reversal of Myotonia in Myotonic Dystrophy" (*New England Journal of Medicine*). Fortunately, many informative research reports in the natural sciences are directed at more general audiences, and these reports can provide a bridge to understanding more technical discussions. General reports may take the form of magazine or newspaper articles, or reports: "Rising, Not Shining" (article summarizing current sleep research, from the *New York Times*) or "DNA Is Not Destiny" (*Discover*). Even scholarly journals may contain more accessible articles: "Survival in Stage I Lung Cancer Detected on CT Screening" (*New England Journal of Medicine*).

18g nat sci

18g Common types of writing assignments in natural science courses

Writing assignments in natural science courses often ask for reports of students' laboratory work (lab reports; see 18h), informative or interpretive reports on current issues or problems (see 18j), abstracts (see 18i), reviews of current research (18c), or reports of original research (observations, experiments, reports of innovative practices; see 18k).

18h Lab reports

Instructors assign lab reports in order to read, quickly, what you did in an experiment, so you will need to make your report as concise and clear as possible. The format of a lab report can help you organize information clearly, yet you will still need to avoid ambiguous language and unclear references.

A **lab report** represents a kind of informative writing in its sharp focus on the objective description of causes and effects. If certain aspects of an experiment or procedure are irrelevant to the cause-effect relationship, you need not include them. However, it is important to describe very clearly just what was done in the experiment and what happened as a result.

Lab reports follow different formats depending on the field of study and even the requirements of individual instructors. Some instructors value conciseness and require all reports to be no longer than two double-spaced pages. Others expect more details and may stretch the length to five or ten pages. Check with your instructor about format, style, and other requirements, such as specific section numbers and headings. A typical structure begins with an overview (or *abstract*) of the experiment, including its focus or goal (why it was done). Following this comes an *introduction* to the problem or principles involved (what it shows), a description of the *methods* used (how it was done), an explanation of the *results* (what happened), a *discussion* of the outcomes (what the results mean), and a *conclusion* (what the experiment shows).

Here are the two opening paragraphs from a lab report Michael Perry prepared in his introductory physics class.

Speed of Sound in Water

Michael Perry

I. Abstract

This experiment was designed to measure the speed of sound in water and determine how changes in the properties of the water affect the speed of sound. First, the speed of sound in water at room temperature was measured using a "time of flight" method. Then the speed of sound was measured at different temperatures to determine the change in the speed with varying temperature. The speed of sound from part 1 of the experiment was 1479.7 m/s. In part 2 the speed of sound was found to vary from 1419.7 m/s at 10.8°C to 1581.03 m/s at 33.10°C.

II. Introduction

A wave traveling through a material causes quick compressions and expansions of the material. The pressure and density oscillate where these compressions and expansions take place. The speed of the wave is determined by how much the density changes with a given pressure change. Water is a liquid and is therefore less compressible than a gas (for example, air). So it takes a greater pressure in water to change density a given amount. We can therefore expect the speed of sound in water to be greater than that in air.

[The paper continues with the following sections: III. Experiment, IV. Results, V. Discussion, and VI. Conclusion.]

Checklist for a successful lab report

- Strictly follows the lab report format required by the instructor
- Does not digress into unnecessary commentary on the experiment
- Uses specific terminology and unambiguous language
- Presents data and results accurately, without distortion

18i Abstracts

Lab reports, informative reports, and reports of original research in the natural sciences often begin with an **abstract,** and many instructors require abstracts along with the papers they assign. An abstract is a concise summary of a paper. It is entirely objective, restating the content of the paper without extraneous commentary. An abstract for a scientific study must include, at a minimum, a summary of the hypothesis, the method, the results, and the discussion sections of the paper. An abstract of the review of literature might be needed as well. The reader of an abstract, with no familiarity with a paper, should be able to understand not only the gist of the paper but also the method, stance (theory or opinion), and conclusions. (See the abstracts in 18h and 18j, introducing the reports.)

Checklist for a successful abstract

- Summarizes all the important sections of a paper
- Defines key terms used in unique or unusual ways
- Presents information concisely, eliminating all unnecessary words and phrases

18j Informative reports

Knowledge produced in the natural sciences is important and interesting, yet complex. Consequently, informative reports presenting and interpreting scientific knowledge play important roles. They can identify problems, provide practical solutions, or suggest policies. In the course of exploring recent developments or outlining problems and policies, reports often provide reviews of current research (for reviews of research in the social sciences, see 18c).

For courses in the natural sciences, students are often asked to write informative reports as a way of developing an understanding of topics or problems that call for further scientific research. For a course in the health sciences, student James Newlands wrote a paper on ADD/ADHD misdiagnosis, explaining the problem and emphasizing its seriousness. Here are the opening paragraphs of his paper.

ADD/ADHD Misdiagnosis

James Newlands

Abstract

Research was done on the misdiagnosis of ADD/ADHD. Most misdiagnoses result from similarities with other disorders. The disorder most often confused with ADD/ADHD is Childhood Bipolar disorder. Misdiagnosis is due to both similarities between the diseases and lack of widespread knowledge of Childhood Bipolar disorder. In addition, females are often misdiagnosed with depression because they frequently display inattentiveness rather than the hyperactivity generally associated with ADD/ADHD.

In the last ten years there has been a considerable increase in the number of ADD/ADHD cases diagnosed, along with a marked increase in medication. In 2000, more than 19 million prescriptions for ADHD drugs were filled, a 72 percent increase since 1995 (Lebelle, 2000). The increase is due both to increased awareness of the disease and to misdiagnosis. Increased awareness among teachers means that it is usually the school that approaches parents to have an assessment for

ADD/ADHD and parents often feel pressured to use drug treatment to "correct" their children's behavior (Lebelle, 2000).

There is no independent valid test for ADD/ADHD. Instead, health professionals rely on a list of behaviors (inattention, hyperactivity, impulsivity, academic underachievement, or behavior problems); diagnostic interviews; and anecdotal information from family and school staff (Lebelle, 2000; ADHD M.S.). The lack of an objective test leaves diagnosis open to interpretation by the doctor. Combined with pressure from schools to "correct their child's behavior," diagnosis by a doctor causes many parents to allow their children to go on medications such as Ritalin. What consequences do these medications have for children? How and how often are children being misdiagnosed? In this paper I discuss the main causes of misdiagnosis and the consequences of medication for children.

Checklist for a successful informative report

- Provides accurate summaries of research
- Clearly identifies problems, solutions, or policies
- Provides details, ideas, and research conclusions relevant to a problem, solution, or policy and identifies sources of the information and ideas
- Provides visuals to explain complicated information, including pictures, tables, and graphs

18k Original research reports

Even in undergraduate courses students may conduct original research, working on their own or with an instructor. Their papers report on observations or on experiments that test hypotheses. The elements of a research report in the natural sciences are as follows.

- **Introduction** providing a review of research and a statement of questions guiding observations or of a hypothesis being tested through experiment.
- **Materials and methods** discussion outlining materials used in an experiment; describing measuring tools for observation; explaining methods of observation; or presenting the design of an experiment.

- **Results** presenting data observed or gathered in detail, often in tables or graphs as well as written discussion.
- **Discussion** of the extent to which the data answer research questions or support a hypothesis as well as exploration of relationships among the data.
- **Conclusion** highlighting results of the study and providing suggestions for further research.

Each of these elements appears in the research report written by Anne Bloomfield for a study she conducted in her wildlife management course. The report is printed in Chapter 31. The report itself is somewhat technical, yet its design and content are clear and understandable.

Checklist for a successful original research report

- Contains all the expected elements of a scientific report
- Provides a careful summary of relevant prior research
- States a hypothesis or research question(s)
- Provides clearly organized data in concise sentences, providing tables or graphs when these strategies help clarify the presentation
- Discusses the extent to which the data support or do not support the hypothesis or the extent to which they answer the research question(s)

CHAPTER 19
Public Writing

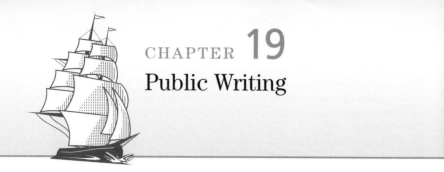

In every public and civic context, people write to convey information, express their views, organize collective efforts, and challenge injustice. Such writing not only improves your skills and flexibility but also helps you to become a better-informed citizen.

19a Goals of public writing

When you address a public audience, you're likely to think of yourself as a volunteer, an activist, or a committee member, not as a writer. Your first concern will be to organize a beach cleanup or elect a mayor. You'll write to achieve your civic goals: to motivate others to support your cause, to influence policy decisions, and to promote democratic processes.

19b Analyzing public audiences

When you prepare a meeting reminder for your book club or a newsletter for your neighbors, you will know your readers personally. They expect clear information and may appreciate motivation, but they often already agree about issues or activities. But when you begin to draft publicity for the tennis club's pasta dinner—its big fund-raiser—you'll need to address a wider circle, readers you don't know personally and who won't support the dinner unless you can persuade them that your cause is worthwhile.

Connect readers and goals. Use questions like the following to frame your writing in a strong relationship to your audiences' values and expectations.

- Why are you writing? What do you hope to accomplish?
- Who are your readers? What do they value? How much do they know or care about your project or issue?
- Do you primarily want to inform or to motivate them? Do you want readers to agree with you or to take action—go to a meeting, contribute time or money, vote "yes" or "no," call an official, or join your group?
- To persuade your readers to do what you want, what might appeal to their anger, passion, or fear—your sincerity, testimonials from others, information, or connections to their own interests or community values?

- How might you approach these readers? Will they respond best to impassioned appeals, logical analyses, or combined strategies? Will they expect a neighborly letter, a flyer, or a polished brochure?
- How can you contact prospective readers—through flyers at a meeting, appeals by mail or email, or letters in the newspaper?

STRATEGY

Work with others to answer these questions and make appropriate decisions in focusing your public writing.

- What is your task? Who will do what as you work on it?
- What's your deadline? How soon will recipients need information? How much time should you allow for printing, mailing, or other steps?
- What type of material should you prepare? What is the usual format? Do you have models or samples of past materials?
- Does your material require approval from anyone?
- Do you need to reserve a meeting room, coordinate with another group, or make other arrangements before you can finish your text?
- How will you distribute your material? Do you need to arrange duplication, mailing, or volunteers to deliver or post materials?

19c Types of public writing

Many types of public writing—letters, flyers, pamphlets, newsletters—are flexible documents. They can be directed to different readers, such as group members, newspaper readers, officials, or local residents. They can address different—or multiple—goals by providing information, building support, motivating to action, or supporting participatory democracy.

19d Flyers

A common form of public writing is the flyer informing people about a meeting, activity, or event. Flyers also supply directions, advice, and information to residents, citizens, and other groups. Sometimes they are prepared as companions to posters—which may supply similar information as they promote events.

ELEMENTS OF A PUBLIC FLYER

- It may open with its topic ("Hostetler Annual Reunion"), a general appeal ("Light a candle for peace!"), or a greeting ("Dear Choir Members").
- It clearly presents the essentials needed to attend or participate: date, time, place, directions, plans, equipment or supplies, contact and emergency telephone numbers, rain date, and so forth.

TYPES OF PUBLIC WRITING

TYPE	CHARACTERISTIC ACTIVITIES	COMMON FORMS
PROVIDING INFORMATION	Gathering information, exploring issues, examining other views and alternative solutions, comparing, summarizing, synthesizing, and presenting material	Flyer, newsletter, fact sheet, informative report or article, letter (to group supporters, interested parties, officials, residents, or community in general), pamphlet, poster
BUILDING SUPPORT	Reaching consensus within a group, articulating a stance, defining a problem, proposing a solution, appealing to others with similar or different values, presenting evidence, finding shared values, advocating, persuading	Position paper, letter (to prospective supporters, officials, newspaper, or others concerned or involved), policy guidelines, statement of principles
MOTIVATING TO ACTION	Defining action, orchestrating participation, supplying information about involvement, motivating participants	Action proposal, grant proposal, flyer, letter, call to action in newsletter or other publication
PARTICIPATING IN DEMOCRATIC PROCESSES	Attending public meetings, meeting with officials, understanding legislative processes and timing, advocating civic involvement, distributing information on public or civic actions	Meeting minutes, committee report, legislative update, letter to officials, letter to group members, call to participate in newsletters or other publications, summary or analysis of public actions, petitions

- It sticks to essentials and omits long explanations or background.
- It uses visual features, headings, graphics, and white space to highlight the most crucial information. (See 13c–e.)
- It may be informal or formal, depending on the group and the topic.

The following flyer announces a group's special event—a meeting to collect signed petitions for presentation to the school board.

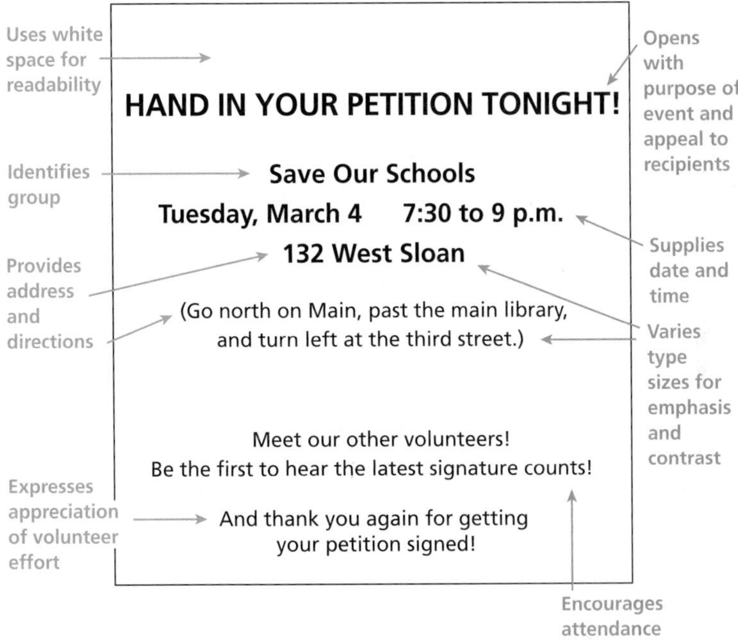

Uses white space for readability
HAND IN YOUR PETITION TONIGHT!
Opens with purpose of event and appeal to recipients
Identifies group
Save Our Schools
Tuesday, March 4 7:30 to 9 p.m.
Supplies date and time
132 West Sloan
Provides address and directions
(Go north on Main, past the main library, and turn left at the third street.)
Varies type sizes for emphasis and contrast
Meet our other volunteers!
Be the first to hear the latest signature counts!
Expresses appreciation of volunteer effort
And thank you again for getting your petition signed!
Encourages attendance

19e Letters to the editor

Both partisans and interested citizens submit letters to the editor in order to comment on current issues or engage in topical debate. Check the opinion section of your local or campus paper, either in print or online, to read the current letters selected for publication and to locate directions for submitting your own letter.

ELEMENTS OF A LETTER TO THE EDITOR

- It respects the length limit established by the newspaper or publication.
- It clearly identifies its topic and its point of view or proposal.
- It briefly supplies reasons and evidence that may persuade readers to consider or agree with its point of view. (See Chapter 11.)
- It treats other views and writers respectfully, even if it disagrees with their opinions.

Following are two letters to the editor (see pp. 284 and 285), the first primarily informative, the second defending a group criticized by the writer of an earlier letter.

Letter to the Editor
April 16, 2007
Greeks Wrong in Punishing Critics

I am writing in response to the recent letter from Jillian Soares (April 14, 2007). As president of the Pan-Hellenic Council, she claims that the Council has the right to fine a fraternity or sorority if any of its members "speak publicly in ways that undermine the integrity or reputation of the Greek societies at Central Range State University." She uses this passage from the Pan-Hellenic Council's bylaws to justify fining Nina Campbell's sorority for statements she made in a recent Snowcap Advocate column. In it, Campbell criticized lack of fraternity and sorority support for the University's "All Campus Diversity Initiative."

As a sorority member myself, I think Campbell's criticisms were inaccurate and overstated. Certainly the Greeks can do a better job of promoting diversity—but then everybody can. After all, would a "Diversity Initiative" be necessary if everyone were doing a good job? But I think the Greeks have done more than most others on campus and that Campbell simply ignores all sorts of positive evidence. Campbell's opinions aren't the real problem, however. The proposed punishment is, along with the policy that makes it possible.

In her letter, Soares claims that the issue isn't a question of free speech because no one is trying to prevent Campbell from stating her opinion. She says that Campbell can avoid the fine for her sorority by resigning from the organization. She also states that the Council is not trying to prevent any Pan-Hellenic members from criticizing fraternity or sorority activities—the policy is only for statements that "distort the facts" or that are "needlessly insulting." But who is to determine the "facts"? When people don't like what they are hearing, they often claim that critics have "got the facts wrong."

The biggest problem with the policy is that it might discourage people from speaking out about actions that are truly discriminatory, unjust, or illegal. Soares says that anyone who wishes to speak out without violating the policy can resign from the fraternity or sorority. The policy might not prevent people from making reasonable criticisms, but it would certainly discourage them. Even when a person knows she is right to criticize, she might not want to cause trouble or expense for her "sisters."

Do we really want to force people to resign when they are speaking from the heart about things they believe are wrong—even if we disagree with them or even if they see the "facts" differently? Isn't this discriminatory?

Rebecca Fala

Sorority Circle

19f Speaking in public settings

People gather daily to exchange opinions about local concerns. Citizens lobby officials for actions. Campus forums draw students, faculty, and administrators to discuss policies. Interest groups engage members and visitors. Use the strategies on page 285 when preparing to speak in a public setting.

Letter to the Editor
February 18, 2007
"Balanced Education" Limits Diversity in Ideas

Last week at the South Valley School Board meeting, Concerned Citizens for a Balanced Education made a proposal that ought to be voted down at the next meeting. Concerned Citizens is critical of student government at South Valley High for sponsoring a talk by Malcom Zindt, who disapproves of the current president and many of his policies. They want to ban any speakers who "do not offer students a balanced perspective on issues or current events" in order to guarantee that "a South Valley education is a balanced education."

I believe that there are three important reasons for voting against this proposal.

(1) The proposal requires that any speakers present a "balanced" view. Speakers worth listening to generally present their own views, however. We want to listen to them because they offer special insights or because they are strong representatives of a point of view. Speakers who offer balanced perspectives are often less interesting—even boring. As a result, fewer students will attend their presentations and fewer will have a chance to encounter challenging ideas.

(2) By requiring that each speaker provide a balance of ideas, the proposal will eliminate the possibility of a set of lectures that create balance by presenting speakers with very different points of view. The student government has already set up a talk by Rose Azavone, a well-known critic of Zindt's and a supporter of current government policies. Concerned Citizens opposes this proposal because it would "require spending extra money for a job that one speaker could do." I believe Concerned Citizens is less interested in balance than in making sure students do not get to hear ideas the Citizens don't like!

(3) Concerned Citizens makes it clear that its idea of "balance" is pro versus con, left versus right. They seem to think that each issue has only two sides. This view is too simple. As a college student, I have come to realize that there are usually more than two ways of looking at an issue.

I hope the Concerned Citizens proposal will be defeated. I would like students at my former high school to get a chance to hear many voices and then make their own conclusions.

Ken Park, S.V.H.S., Class of 2004

STRATEGY

- Attend meetings, listen, and read to get informed about issues.
- Plan and rehearse (see 15c), even to speak for a minute or two.
- Be reasonable; don't alienate those who are undecided or disagree.
- Use facts, details, and other evidence—not emotion—for support.
- Stay calm at a tense meeting so that fear and nervousness don't lead you to speak angrily, make accusations, or even cry.

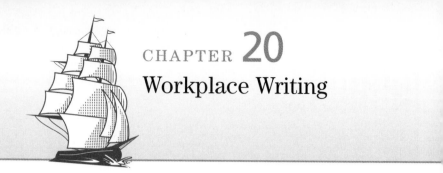

CHAPTER 20 Workplace Writing

Enhanced by new technologies, communication between individuals and groups is a critical factor in virtually all workplace tasks. A complete discussion of workplace communication would take a book in itself. This chapter has more modest goals: to introduce you to some proven strategies that will help you achieve success in workplace writing, and to acquaint you with some standard styles and practices.

20a Goals of workplace writing

Business writing is reader centered: you're writing to persuade, inform, or meet the needs and expectations of your audience. Your audience's expectations are less likely to reflect individual outlooks than general goals and conventions for workplace writing, however. In many settings, moreover, conventions may be relatively specific and even rigid, while in others they may be more open to negotiation and innovation.

1 Plan according to your readers' needs

Your main focus while planning workplace writing will be the relationship between your information and your audience. Sometimes your audience will be made up of people working in different positions (for example, someone in the marketing department and someone else who handles shipments in the warehouse). Be sensitive to the needs and perspectives of your various intended readers.

Because your readers are likely to be busy and impatient—whether they are other people at work or members of the general public to whom you are writing in your professional capacity—you need to be especially careful in organizing your information.

Workplace documents should have a "friendly" design and layout, inviting the reader to read and to continue to read. Is there enough white space in your document to make it look uncluttered? Are your margins sufficient? What does the spacing of your document look like—are sections squeezed together, or have you left enough space to show blocks of information? Remember that a readable document is attractive and inviting, not tight and cluttered.

STRATEGY

Using the audience continuum in 3e, spend a few minutes writing about your intended readers. What do they know about the topic? How will they use the document? What do you know about their technical background, their level of education, their interest in the topic, and their need for what you have to offer?

2 Draft as clearly as possible

As you draft, remember to emphasize clarity. Effective workplace writing is easy to read—unambiguous, uncluttered, and direct.

STRATEGY

Instead of drafting with an eye to style, try to write the essential information as clearly and directly as you can. As you write, concentrate on exactly what you need to say. You can revise for a smoother and more appealing style after you've presented the main information directly.

3 Revise and edit

In some workplace settings you may be under pressure to write a document quickly—even more quickly than a paper due in two days for your composition class. Under these circumstances it's easy to skip the editing and revising process. Be especially careful not to fall into this trap. Reread *all* your documents. Plan your schedule so you have at least some time for revising and editing. Even a single badly chosen word, one garbled sentence, or a lone case of misinformation can be embarrassing.

In addition, set specific goals for your revising. Plan, for example, to eliminate wordy passages, extraneous information, and irrelevant facts. Or aim to avoid clichés, exaggeration, passive voice, and overly technical language. Try to choose vocabulary appropriate to your audience's level of expertise, and revise accordingly.

Workplace writing often makes use of graphics to present information clearly and concisely. When you use graphics, label them carefully, and mention them in the text of your document before they actually appear in the text. (See Chapter 13.)

20b Workplace writing process

As a new employee, one of your best resources is the fresh set of eyes you bring to the workplace. While observing the writing process in your organization, look for answers to the following questions, which will accelerate your understanding of the ways in which the writing process is organized locally.

1 How are writing projects assigned?

Are assignments made by email, by memo, or by word of mouth? If your supervisor assigns projects orally, then be sure to take careful notes. However the assignment is made, be sure to check and double check that you have followed instructions exactly. If you have questions about the assignment, be sure to ask the supervisor, but don't pepper the boss with questions unless you have learned that she or he welcomes frequent discussions about work-in-progress.

2 Is most writing done individually, or in work groups?

If writing is done collaboratively, how is it done? Are individuals assigned to write sections of the project which are then assembled into a document, or do writers brainstorm and draft the document as a team, working around a conference table? Does collaboration occur electronically? If so, then it is important that you learn the conventions for electronic collaboration (see the section on email later in this chapter). Some companies use software packages, such as *Lotus Notes*, which provide an electronic environment for collaborative writing. Other companies simply use email but have conventions for file sharing and revision. Your coworkers are a good source of information regarding the ways in which your company approaches the invention and drafting process.

3 Does the company have a formal editing process?

Time is money is a mantra many businesses follow, and good editing takes time. Some companies have established formal levels of editing that will be assigned based on the type of document being produced. For example, an internal company memo might require only light editing for usage and clarity; a letter sent to an external supplier might require medium editing, which includes the elements of a light edit plus checking for passive construction, standard company formatting, and other stylistic issues; a proposal to win a competitive contract probably requires a heavy edit, which includes the elements of a medium edit, plus checking for organizational soundness, tone, coherence, and other more global issues. Regardless of the kind of editing process used by your company, it is important that you learn the expectations of your supervisor. Some supervisors want to see a draft quickly and care little about usage, mechanics, and style. Other supervisors want to see complete, well-edited drafts, regardless of the time constraints. Until you learn the needs and desires of your supervisor, careful self-editing is a must. Part 9 of this handbook will be an invaluable aid to you in this process.

As you get feedback from your supervisor about your writing, start using that feedback to create a personal editing and revision checklist to ensure that you don't repeatedly make the same mistakes. This checklist can also help you better adapt to the stylistic preferences of your supervisor.

4 Does the company have a formalized set of writing genres?

Many companies have a set of document templates they expect writers to use. Other companies just direct their writers to a model document to follow. Many scientific and professional organizations publish style guides that resemble the MLA and APA styles you are familiar with. For example, a chemical company might expect its writers to conform to the style guide of the American Chemical Society. Some very large businesses and governmental organizations have created their own style guides. Again, your fellow writers can be a helpful source for this kind of information.

5 How are revisions to documents such as work procedures and technical specifications controlled?

Documents that are used to create a product, or that define the materials that go into the product, require careful control. It is important that companies have procedures to ensure that products are built to the plans and processes expected by their customers. Many manufacturing firms have a technical library or a document control office that controls the revision of such critical documents. Usually these offices are located within the engineering departments of manufacturing firms. If you are assigned to write this type of document for the first time, be sure to talk to the personnel who administer these systems to ensure that you meet the stylistic and administrative expectations of the manufacturing community.

Exercise 1

A. Interview a supervisor or a writer at a local company. Ask the person to describe how the editing and revision process is controlled in the company. Also ask which type of errors are most troubling. Prepare a short presentation to share what you learned about this local business community with the class or your collaborative group.

B. In a small group, compare your findings from the interview you conducted for Exercise 1A. Find common processes and themes, and note those processes and themes where interviewees differed. Prepare a short presentation to share what you learned with the class.

20c Business letters

Good business letters follow standard practices and established formats. Most business letters are written using **block format** on company letterhead, or a letterhead template where the company's name, postal address, phone and facsimile numbers, and Web address are centered at the top or bottom of the letter. All other paragraphs (including the inside address, greeting, closing, and signature) are flush with the left margin. Some longer business

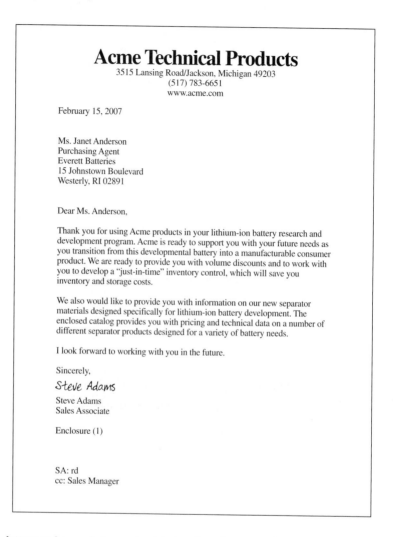

Acme Technical Products
3515 Lansing Road/Jackson, Michigan 49203
(517) 783-6651
www.acme.com

February 15, 2007

Ms. Janet Anderson
Purchasing Agent
Everett Batteries
15 Johnstown Boulevard
Westerly, RI 02891

Dear Ms. Anderson,

Thank you for using Acme products in your lithium-ion battery research and development program. Acme is ready to support you with your future needs as you transition from this developmental battery into a manufacturable consumer product. We are ready to provide you with volume discounts and to work with you to develop a "just-in-time" inventory control, which will save you inventory and storage costs.

We also would like to provide you with information on our new separator materials designed specifically for lithium-ion battery development. The enclosed catalog provides you with pricing and technical data on a number of different separator products designed for a variety of battery needs.

I look forward to working with you in the future.

Sincerely,

Steve Adams

Steve Adams
Sales Associate

Enclosure (1)

SA: rd
cc: Sales Manager

letters and many letters not printed on letterhead use a **modified block format** in which the return address, greeting, closing, and signature are centered on the page. In both styles, notations following the signature are flush left along with the body of the letter, including initials for the writer and typist (RL: gw), *Enc.* or *Enclosure*, or *cc: Nancy Harris* (the name of a person sent a copy). Follow these additional guidelines for business correspondence.

- **Stationery.** The best is 25 percent or 50 percent white cotton bond paper at standard business weight (20 pound). Résumés and letters of application are often printed on a more durable weight paper (24 pound). Avoid colors and fancy paper styles.

- **Print quality and style.** Check that your printer, word processor, or typewriter is in good repair. While both laser and ink-jet printers will deliver high print quality, the laser printer has the advantage of delivering waterproof text. Avoid nonstandard or stylized fonts—they can be difficult to read and are often associated by readers with personal or nonprofessional correspondence.
- **Salutations.** Use the first name of your recipient only if you are already on a first name basis. Use the full name if you don't know the person's gender. Avoid gender-specific salutations such as "Dear Sir" or "Gentlemen"; they are not appropriate. If you do not know the name of the person to whom you are writing, use general salutations and titles such as "Dear Accounts Department" or "Dear Credit Manager."
- **Longer letters.** Use plain paper of the same weight and color as the first page. Use letterhead stationery only for the first page.
- **Envelope.** Envelope paper should be the same color and weight as the letter, and the font should match that of the letter.

20d Memos

Although some companies still use preprinted forms for memos on which a person can hand write or print a message, most companies use a corporate memo template or one of the standard templates for a memo found in word-processing programs. The organization's name and logo, or letterhead, may appear at the top of the memo, but no address information is needed since memos are internal company documents.

The words *To*, *From*, *Subject*, and *Date* appear on all memos, often in the order shown on the memo on page 292. Spacing, notations for enclosures, additional pages, and copies all follow the same pattern as in letters.

20e Email

The email message is replacing the memo as the preferred genre for internal communications within many organizations, and the phone call for communication outside the organization. Because the use of email is becoming such a commonplace part of business and personal communication, people have developed the habit of writing email without using the same composing processes they previously used for writing memos and letters. Yet a poorly composed email can damage a writer's credibility with readers in the same way a poorly composed letter or memo does. Developing the following habits when using electronic communication will help you avoid this pitfall.

Everett Batteries: Internal Memo

TO: Bob Rogers, Director of Battery Research and Development

FROM: Janet Anderson, Purchasing Agent

DATE: October 11, 2007

SUBJECT: Evaluation of Future Separator Needs

I recently received correspondence from Acme Technical Products with pricing information on their battery separator, as well as a catalog of new separator products. I am in the process of developing a purchasing plan detailing our separator needs for the next twelve months. Could you please provide me with a forecast of your department's projected use of Acme separator material on a month-by-month basis? I need this information by November 12 in order to meet MRP system deadlines.

I have enclosed a copy of the new catalog which contains technical specifications and pricing information for your use.

jck
Attachment

- **Choose your addressees carefully.** Organizational lore is full of stories of persons who inadvertently sent a personal response to a message sent by an electronic mailing list or to a group of recipients. Such a response is thought of as *spam* (junk mail) within electronic communities and in some cases might inadvertently insult a reader *lurking* (silently reading messages) within the electronic community.
- **Proofread your message.** Use the same standards for grammar and punctuation you would use in a memo. Don't use abbreviations, acronyms, or jargon unless you are certain all recipients will understand

them. Don't use all capital letters within an electronic message unless you intend to strongly emphasize that point. Typing a message in all-capital letters is considered "shouting" by electronic communities.

- **Use a subject line.** Many recipients are overwhelmed with the volume of email they receive. Most email programs index incoming messages by date, time, sender, and subject. A clear subject line will help the recipients to screen and identify those messages they need or wish to read immediately, and to delete unimportant messages.

20f Résumés and application letters

Résumés and the accompanying cover letters are among the most important sales documents you will write; the "product" is, after all, yourself and everything you have accomplished. There are countless "right" ways to prepare these documents. This section offers guidelines for the content, design, and construction of a résumé and letter of application.

Your letter of application should be closely related to your résumé. The documents should work as a unit to convey the necessary information and to make you appear professional and organized. Letters of application offer you the chance to discuss or highlight skills or experiences mentioned in your résumé or to add information not in your résumé. These letters function best when the writer tailors the cover letter to connect skills and educational requirements found in the job advertisement or the description of the position to the résumé.

The purpose of the résumé package (résumé and application letter) is to get an interview, not a job. Few employers hire using only the information contained in a résumé package. Many employers receive hundreds of résumé packages for every job position posted, so when constructing a résumé concentrate on trying to create a professional identity for yourself. Highlight your skills and achievements objectively and clearly, and be sure to proofread. Some employers look for grammar or punctuation errors in their résumé screening process.

Employers favor job candidates who are motivated, mature, and responsible. You can't simply state these things; your résumé package must exemplify these traits. For instance, employers like applicants who know how to start and finish a project independently and who are self-motivated, capable, and willing to face challenges confidently. Describe your experiences not only in terms of what you have actually done, but in terms of what you have learned from the experiences and how they will help you in the future.

1 Begin with a résumé preparation checklist

Before you start to prepare your résumé, you need to reflect on both your career goals and your own qualifications and background.

STRATEGY

Write informally in response to the following questions. Jot down your ideas and as many examples from your background as you can remember. Later you can select the best ideas and examples for your purposes.

1. What kind of work do you want to do? What kind of job do you want?
2. What are your career goals?
3. What jobs have you held?
4. What volunteer positions have you held?
5. What are your skills, abilities, or interests? (Include items even if you have not been formally educated in these things.)
6. What are the main features of your educational background? Consider the following points.
   a. College major, minor, and concentrations
   b. Special projects or research
   c. Honors and awards
   d. Memberships and offices in organizations
   e. Volunteer positions
   f. Special skills
   g. Grade-point average (overall, and within major field)
7. What other awards or special honors, if any, have you received (from work, volunteer efforts, or community organizations)?
8. Who might make a good reference for you? Try to identify at least one former or current professor, one former job supervisor or employer, and one personal reference.
9. What makes you different from other applicants? Why should a prospective employer interview you rather than someone else?

2 Use categories to construct your résumé

After you've collected the information for your résumé, your task is one of construction—placing the information into appropriate categories, phrasing it concisely, and arranging it in a visually appealing way that stresses your strongest traits first.

Career objective. When you write your career objective, be specific! Avoid empty phrases like *position of responsibility in a fast-growing firm.* Consider tailoring your objective to each type of position for which you apply.

Job experience. When you get ready to describe your job experience, list all the duties you had, and then choose the ones that are most similar to those of the job you want. If you have held many jobs, don't list them all in your résumé. List those jobs which you held the longest, the ones that are

Carol E. Westermeyer

College Address:
Apt. 22 College Park
Greenville, Virginia 20205
(804) 555-3345
cwesr@school.edu

Home Address:
7562 Galsworth Road
Squires, Texas 30303
(512) 555-7912

Objective Entry-level position as an electrical engineer

Education

- **B.S. Electrical Engineering, May 2007**
  Virginia Polytechnic Institute, Blacksburg, Virginia 24060
  G.P.A. 3.18/4.0 Minor: Economics

Experience

- **Technician/Assembler, May 2003–September 2003**
  Communication Technology, Inc., Fairview, Virginia 24059
  -Developed cost analysis and designed prototype wireless communication products for Masters Mountain Laboratories.
  -Built and tested various AF and RF products: transmitters, receivers, headsets, amplifiers, and antenna networks.
  -Served as company representative to demonstrate a new generation of wireless radios at Atlanta National Radio Conference.

- **Interoffice Administrator (part time), 2003–present**
  Bergland Technology Associates, Lakeview, Virginia 24051
  -Updated and reorganized shop inventory control using Microsoft Office software.

Project

- **Member, Design Team for Electric Vehicle**
  Department of Electrical Engineering, Virginia Polytechnic Institute, Blacksburg, Virginia 24060
  -Controller group duties included design and programming of a constant velocity transmission (CVT) controller.

Skills Experienced with a variety of computer software programs, including Microsoft Office, Autocad, and Statistica.

Activities Vice President, Student Senate, Virginia Polytechnic Institute

most similar to the job for which you are applying, or the ones that demonstrate your most employable characteristics. If you think that you have little specific experience that relates to the job you seek, highlight other job skills, such as the ability to work as part of a team, to handle responsibility, to supervise others, or to work with little or no supervision. When possible, don't simply state these skills; provide examples from your experience.

Volunteer experience. If you've held volunteer or unpaid internship positions that may be attractive to an employer, list them. They are often considered important experience. Note that the position was voluntary, but handle the rest of the information just as you would for any other job experience. Don't use an apologetic tone here; the fact that you were not paid for the job doesn't mean it was not serious work in which you developed valuable skills.

Sequence of experience. Typically, jobs are listed in reverse chronological order (with your most recent job first). If your most important job experience is not your most recent, however, list that one first, and then list the remaining jobs in reverse chronological order.

References. Unless the employer has specifically asked for references, use the general statement *References available upon request.* Few employers will want to look at your references unless they wish to interview you. You should bring a separate page listing the names, addresses, and phone numbers or email addresses of three or four references with you to the interview. (Always ask permission *before* you use someone as a reference.) Most colleges have placement services that will send out dossiers that include confidential reference lists or letters of reference.

A number of programs provide templates for creating a résumé on a computer. Most of these programs provide several different formats for a standard résumé. These programs allow you to spend your time focusing on the text of your résumé rather than spacing and layout.

Some companies may prefer that you submit your résumé electronically. If so, be sure to follow any instructions they may provide for formatting the electronic file. Frequently the résumé file will be attached to an email that will function as your letter of application. Another way of getting your résumé to a number of potential employers is to submit your electronic résumé to an Internet job service.

Many people are now creating résumés on the Web. Some advantages of Web-based résumés include the ability to "nest" information on subsequent pages without cluttering the main résumé page. For example, you might include links from the positions you have held to pages that describe these positions and your accomplishments in them. If you choose to develop a Web-based résumé, however, be sure to pay special attention to issues of layout and design, and make navigation through the site easy and "user-friendly" for your readers. Like paper résumés, Web-based résumés need to present you and your work elegantly and without error.

PART 5

Researching and Writing

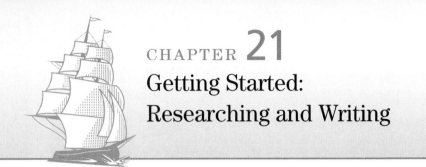

CHAPTER 21
Getting Started: Researching and Writing

Research is systematic inquiry into a subject through written sources (print or electronic), fieldwork (interviews, surveys, ethnographic observation), or even a systematic examination of your own experience. You can use the depth of information, ideas, and insights you develop through research for many purposes. You might create an **informative** essay, report, or brochure.

"Everybody's Wheezin': My Generation's Collective Journey with Asthma"
Informative essay on the rising incidence of the affliction

"'Buy U.S. Bonds': How Posters Helped Shape Public Opinion During World War II"
Informative report on the ways the government employed posters

"What Linux Can (and Can't) Do for Your Computers"
Brochure or pamphlet

"Unions versus Tobacco Growers in Mid-Twentieth Century America"
Academic paper

You might create an **argumentative** paper that takes a stand on an issue or a **proposal** that supports a particular course of action.

"Bring the Gray Wolf Back to the Adirondacks"
Argumentative essay or editorial

"Dealing with Objections to Gray Wolf Reintroduction in the Adirondack Region of New York"
Position paper

"A Three-Step Process for Reintroducing Gray Wolves to Adirondack State Park"
Proposal

Or you might explain and support an **interpretation** or **analysis.**

"Dream Interpretation: Three Current Approaches"
Academic report including one of the writer's dreams interpreted according to each of the three approaches

"Diversity on Campus: What Do Western College Students *Really* Think?"
Analytical paper

"Rebuilding America: Images of National Identity in Contemporary Popular Song"
Interpretation of contemporary song lyrics and music videos

21a Identifying a subject or project

Research is a careful, sustained inquiry. It is guided by research questions that set goals for gathering and examining information. The process usually begins simply enough, either with your own experience and reading or with an assignment in class or at work.

1 Experience

Research can begin with your personal or professional interest. For example, you've probably walked past the perfume counters of department stores many times. What would happen if, on every such occasion, you found yourself overcome with a fit of sneezing? You might share that experience with others to get their reactions, and you might try an informal experiment, seeing how close to the perfume area you could get without sneezing. Eventually, your curiosity would get the best of you, and you would begin searching for an explanation: what's the relationship between perfume and sneezing? You would be asking a **research question** (see 21e).

If your personal interest continues, it might well lead to a full-scale research paper for a course, perhaps starting with a Web search for a site that reports the results of studies on the relationship between perfume and allergies (such as the Health and Environment Resource Center, <http://www.herc.org>).

2 Reading

Written conversations among people inquiring about a topic offer many places for research to begin. A word or phrase you encounter in reading (or hear spoken) can spark an interest worth pursuing through research. Here is how one student, Jenny Latimer, describes the start of her research.

> After my coworker Kate turned down my offer of a red licorice stick, having first briefly viewed the ingredients on the wrapper, I asked her to explain why. She told me they contain hydrogenated oils, which are, according to research articles she had read, "silent killers." She went on to describe in brief what she considered the horrors they do to your body

```
and the many varieties of foods that contain them as well as
the extent to which she goes to avoid hydrogenated oils. I was
shocked by this news. I was also somewhat intrigued.
```

3 Assignment

If a research project comes to you in a written assignment, read it carefully. Look for key words and phrases that specify a topic or question. If the assignment begins with an occasion or with a problem your instructor identifies, write down whatever words you and your readers are likely to associate with it.

Use the words and phrases you have identified to help develop a topic for your research and writing (see 21c-1). Take them into account also when you develop a purpose and focus for your project. Summer Arrigo-Nelson and Jennifer Figliozzi did so in an intermediate composition course. The assignment asked them to "investigate the psychological or social dimensions of a local or campus problem" by drawing on print or electronic sources and field research of their own, and to present their conclusions in the form of an academic research report. They underlined the words *psychological or social dimensions* and *campus problem* in the assignment and used these terms later to develop a topic and specific focus for their work (see 21c-1).

4 Audience

Your purpose for researching and writing, the kinds of questions you ask, and the sources you consult will depend to a considerable extent on your audience.

Exercise 1

Start your research project in one of four ways.

1. Create a journal entry in which you explore your experience, looking for incidents, interests, or questions that suggest a subject for research and writing.
2. Look through magazines, newspapers, or Web sites for discussions and topics that interest you as a subject for research; take notes on the areas of interest you encounter.
3. Underline key words in your assignment, then create a paragraph explaining your understanding of the assignment and naming one or more subjects you consider appropriate to it.
4. Identify an audience for your research paper or report and then write out an explanation of what your potential readers might look for in a choice of subject and goals for the writing. (Draw on the chart on p. 301.)

AUDIENCE EXPECTATIONS FOR RESEARCH WRITING

	ACADEMIC	PUBLIC	WORK
GOALS	Explain or prove, offer well-supported interpretations or conclusions, analyze or synthesize information for use in other settings	Support arguments for policy or course of action; inform or advise for the public good	Document problems, propose a project or course of action, compare information, improve performance
TYPICAL QUESTIONS	What does it mean? What happened? How does it occur? How might it be modified?	How can this policy be made better? What do people need or want to know?	What is the problem? How can we solve it? What course of action will help us achieve our goals?
TYPICAL FORMS	Interpretive (thesis) paper, informative paper, research report, grant report	Position paper, editorial, proposal, informative article, pamphlet, guidelines	Proposal, report, feasibility study, memorandum
AUDIENCE EXPECTATIONS	Detailed evidence from varied sources including quotations, paraphrases, and summaries; documented sources that acknowledge scholarship	Accessible, fair, and persuasive information with evidence; informal documentation	Clear, direct, and precise information; appropriate detail; less formal documentation

21b Kinds of research writing

No matter what subject you set out to investigate, your research will be heavily influenced by your answer to this question: Will I use my research to *inform* or to *persuade*? The answer you give early in a research project is important because it helps shape your decisions, yet it is not final. Be ready to modify your purpose (or change it altogether) as you research and write.

1 Informative research project

Informative research writing focuses on the *subject* you are planning to explore and explain. You therefore focus your research and writing on discovering information and ideas about your subject and sharing them with readers: your efforts will be *subject-driven.*

Taking this approach does not mean your writing will be an unoriginal reciting of facts and statements from sources. On the contrary, successful informative research writing is guided by the writer's understanding of a subject, insights, and conclusions. The writer draws ideas and information from sources, then organizes them to aid readers' understanding or to answer potential questions, and finally offers (and supports) insights or conclusions about the topic.

An informative research paper often takes shape from the writer's initial questions about a subject or from the questions it aims to answer for readers. If questions about the nature and consequences of a subject seem most important in your thinking, then the reasonable goal for your project may be to explore and inform. You may even be able to develop such questions into a more formal research question to guide your research (for a discussion of research questions, see 21e).

In an early entry in her research file (see the chart on p. 303 for guidelines), Jenny Latimer recorded a recent experience and the questions it brought to mind. In doing so, she came to recognize her informative purpose.

> After I had stuffed a couple of red licorice sticks into my mouth in front of my coworker Julie, she picked up the wrapper and said, "I didn't realize they had hydrogenated oils in them. I'll never eat them again!" I started wondering about a number of things. What are hydrogenated oils, and why do they seem to be in everything we eat? When did this start? Is there a proposal to get them out of foods? What do they do to you? Do we really need to worry?

2 Persuasive research project

Persuasive research writing focuses on your **thesis** or **conclusion.** Your research and writing will concentrate on evidence and explanatory details, chosen for their logical support of your point of view, their persuasiveness for readers, and their usefulness in explaining issues or problems. (See Chapters 8–12 for a discussion of argumentative writing.)

Your research should focus on more than just the evidence and ideas that support your conclusions, however. An argument will not be likely to persuade readers to agree with your thesis unless it offers detailed information about the issues or problem you are addressing.

Your research will help you explain a particular issue or problem on which you wish to take a stand or a subject you wish to analyze and interpret. It will also help you develop, refine, and support your thesis, your proposal, or your interpretation.

Exercise 2

Choose a format for a research file: folder, electronic file, notebook, word-processing document, or whatever form you find comfortable and useful. Make sure it can be divided into parts for your various research and writing activities. Create some initial entries, perhaps the activities described in Exercises 1 and 3, to see if the format you have chosen is accessible and useful. Then, take the file with you wherever you plan to do research—at the library, online, or in field research such as an interview—and add information to the entries you have already created. If the format you have chosen seems cumbersome, revise it before you move further into the research process.

CREATING A RESEARCH FILE

Keeping track of the information and ideas you gather through research is important because you will draw on them frequently as you draft and revise your document. One good way to accomplish this task is to create a research file. A **research file** is a place where you record and store systematically your activities throughout the research and writing process—ready to be recalled for later use. These activities include:

- Identifying a *specific topic* (21c) and developing a *research question* (21e) or *tentative thesis* (21f)
- Creating a *search strategy* (21j), listing *resources* (21j-1), and assembling a list of sources or a *working bibliography* (21j-4)
- *Note taking*—making a record of relevant ideas and information from sources, including summaries, paraphrases, and quotations; copying (or recording) passages (or images) for possible inclusion in your writing
- *Documenting sources* (Chapters 28–31)
- *Drafting* and *revising* (Chapter 27), including integrating your insights with ideas and information from your sources (Chapter 26)

You can keep a research file in a notebook, in a folder, on note cards, or in a computer file. Your file should contain sections corresponding to each of the main stages of your research and writing, along with a timeline for completing your work.

A research file is an excellent place to probe ideas through freewriting or other discovery techniques (3a). It is a good place to record evolving versions of a thesis statement or of a plan for a paper, and it is a good place to record brief observations you may expand on later.

21c Choosing a topic

Your research can grow from a personal interest, an assignment, a strong feeling or point of view, a pressing issue or problem, a desire for understanding, or the interests and needs of potential readers. Remember, however, that your choice of focus for your research needs to be guided by the space, time, and resources available to you.

1 Respond to your assignment

Read your assignment carefully, underlining key terms (see 21a-3). Then respond to the assignment in the following ways.

- If a word or phrase immediately suggests a topic, write it down, and add a list of synonyms or alternate terms.
- If you can't identify a topic at first, take key words and phrases, write them down, and brainstorm related words and phrases along with the topics they suggest.
- Consider asking whoever made the assignment for thoughts on a potential topic—and for further topic suggestions. Consider asking potential readers for their reactions.

After they had underlined the words *psychological or social dimensions* and *campus problem* in their assignment, Summer Arrigo-Nelson and Jennifer Figliozzi made a list of campus problems.

low class attendance	new majors	date rape
inadequate library	role of sports	student alcohol use
living conditions	cancelled classes	student fees
parking	drugs	crime

They chose "student alcohol use" as a focus; the topic interested them. They also thought that they could easily find research sources and that doing field research of their own wouldn't be too difficult. Some initial reading and brainstorming led them to wonder about the role of parents in determining the drinking habits of college students, and they decided to address this question in their research.

2 Recognize your interests

Perhaps you have an interest, a passion, a job you like (or hate), a sport or recreation, a curiosity, or some other involvement that is part of your life and might be intriguing to readers—if you can bring together what you already know with what you discover through research.

You don't need a precise opinion, a specific proposal, or even a well-formed conclusion in order to identify a topic for a thesis-centered or persuasive research paper. A strong feeling, general awareness of a problem, or curiosity will do. It will help you identify specific issues or subjects worth further study. Here is how several students turned their feelings, interests, general awareness of issues, and curiosity into research projects.

INTEREST	TITLE OF FINAL PAPER
Curiosity: Why do so many workers in fast-food restaurants seem to be recent immigrants?	Easy to Hire, Easy to Fire: Recent Immigrants and the Fast-Food Industry
Job: I have been working as an EMT, but I'll bet most people don't know anything about the job.	You Won't Meet Us Until You Need Us: What EMTs Do
Strong Feeling: I like my SUV, and I'm sick of hearing people criticize SUVs and their owners.	What's *Good* About SUVs
General Awareness: I've seen a lot more deer grazing beside highways lately, and I've been hearing about many deer-related car accidents.	Keeping Deer and Cars Apart: A Proposal

3 Browse for an issue or problem

You can recognize "big" issues easily enough: "Global Warming: Real or Not?" "Does Television Violence Lead to Violent Behavior?" So much has been written about "big" topics that they easily exceed the scope of even the most ambitious research paper. However, a bit of browsing can lead you to more focused issues, problems, and topics. Glance through one or two issues of a magazine or newspaper; scan the entries in a database; consult informational Web sites. Look for words, phrases, and titles that suggest topics, especially questions that remain unanswered and issues that (for most people) have not been resolved.

- **Print and online magazines and newspapers** (local, campus, and national)—"Antibacterial Products: Harmful or Helpful?" (article title from online *New York Times*)
- **Online discussions of issues**—post to a discussion group talking about a work-related injury (carpal tunnel syndrome) affecting fitness workouts and inquiring about nonsurgical cures (Newsgroup: misc.fitness.weights)
- **Databases**—"Strategies of Professional Assistance After Traumatic Deaths: Empowerment or Disempowerment?" (article from *Scandinavian Journal of Psychology*, April, 2004, *Academic Search Premier*)
- **Informational Web sites**—"Swimming Pools Linked to Hay Fever." (online article from ABCNews.com)

Exercise 3

While browsing a print or online source for possible topics, write down those you discover in your research file. As you make notes, try turning the topics into paper titles; in this way, you begin to envision the kinds of research you will need to do and the kind of paper you will write.

4 Identify keywords

As you have no doubt discovered when searching the Web for information, writers of electronic documents use **keywords**—words or phrases identifying important ideas and clusters of information—to link discussions of a subject and identify them through electronic search engines (24b). As you browse print or electronic sources for subject ideas, make a list of what you or the writers identify as keywords.

When you have assembled a substantial list, bring together those words and phrases that most interest you as subjects for research. See if you can identify a potential focus for your research from your choices, or use the keywords to identify sources for further browsing.

Exercise 4

Choose one of the following general subject areas as if you were going to write a research paper on it. Using the strategies in 21c, explore the subject and list two or three keywords or phrases that help sum up areas of interest you find within the subject.

"No Child Left Behind"
Road rage
Cures for Lyme disease
Depression among college students
"Slow growth" methods for containing suburban sprawl
Recent trends in body piercing and tattoos
Threat of terrorism
Hormone replacement therapy and breast cancer
Lifelong sports and physical health

21d Narrowing a topic

Perhaps you have already identified a subject, issue, or problem. Maybe you have made an entry in your research file clarifying your interests and purpose(s) for writing. You aren't quite ready to begin, however. First you need to focus or narrow your topic so you can do the necessary research in a reasonable amount of time and cover the important elements in specific detail in a paper that isn't overly long.

1 Broad subject to limited topic

Think of a subject as a broad field filled with clusters of information, ideas, and written interchanges—clusters that are often only loosely related to each other even though they fall within the same subject field. A **topic** is a single cluster of ideas and information within a broader subject, usually the *topic* of an ongoing *conversation* involving writers and readers.

By limiting your attention to a particular topic or conversation (or to some element within the conversation—a *subtopic*), you take an important step toward making your research project manageable. But how can you identify the various conversations in a subject field in ways that help you narrow the topic for your own research and writing? You can survey briefly some of the same kinds of resources you will revisit later as you plan and execute your *search strategy* (21j): databases, indexes of articles, electronic search engines, magazines and journals, library catalogs, and printed books. At this stage, however, limit yourself to a sampling of potential resources.

Here are notes student Tou Yang made in his research file (p. 301) from his survey of the database *Academic Search Premier* on the subject *athletic dietary supplements*, along with his comments on two potential topics the notes helped him identify.

> "Eat Powder? Build Muscle! Burn Calories!"—creatine monohydrate, lots of athletes swear by it, claim it has only good effects
> "Effect of Creatine Supplementation on Aerobic Performance and Anaerobic Capacity in Elite Rowers in the Course of Endurance Training"—it seems to work, a little bit at least
> "Creatine Monohydrate Supplementation Enhances High-Intensity Exercise Performance in Males and Females"—controversy over whether creatine works or not; they claim it does
> "From Ephedra to Creatine: Using Theory to Respond to Dietary Supplement Use in Young Athletes"—understanding why athletes use dietary supplements even though they are probably not effective
> Some disagreement over whether creatine works or at least over how well it works—take a position on this? Or explain how it works and what it seems to add to sports performance?

2 Surveying potential topics

For your preliminary survey of potential topics, turn to the same categories of resources you will examine in depth later, but sample and browse instead of reading critically and taking detailed notes.

Use a library's online catalog. Using the built-in search engine in a library's online catalog, search the *subject* category and, if possible, the category *words and phrases* in titles and a book's description. Browse the list of works you locate, writing down (preferably in your research file) words and phrases that suggest specific, limited topics. Pay special attention to books containing collections of articles on a topic; the terms that appear in the titles of individual selections often identify specific topics and subtopics. Also pay attention to the names of authors, recording for later use the names of any who have written extensively on a topic.

Browse magazines and journals. At a newsstand or in the periodical room of a college or university library, browse the titles and contents of magazines and scholarly journals. Note important words and phrases in the article titles and in the selections you skim. Scholarly articles often begin with abstracts highlighting important ideas, information, and conclusions; read the abstracts, turning to the texts of the articles only when you know they are relevant to your search.

Use databases and indexes. College and university libraries subscribe to many specialized databases and indexes like *InfoTrac* and *First Search*, which list articles of general interest and also scholarly articles (searchable by title, author, and keywords). The databases generally provide abstracts (summaries) and oftentimes full texts of the articles.

Use search engines for electronic resources. Web search engines enable you to use words and phrases to search Web sites and online discussion groups and newsgroups. Use the titles and descriptions or scan a sampling of sites to identify topic clusters and ongoing conversations about the topics. Highlighted links within the sites also help identify topics and are evidence of conversations among electronic texts and their writers or creators. The statements and responses posted to online discussion groups and newsgroups can provide direct evidence of the questions and concerns that readers are likely to bring to your discussion of a topic.

Interview an authority. Researchers, college teachers, professionals, public officials, and people engaged in an activity can often provide you with an overview of recent developments, questions worth addressing, and significant controversies. Most people will be gratified by your interest in their work and glad to help.

Exercise 5

Create an entry for your research file in which you record the steps you have taken to narrow your topic. List the different options you have for narrowing your topic and the advantages or disadvantages of each one. Then create a statement identifying the focused topic you have chosen and your reasons for choosing it.

21e Research questions

Research writing, especially informative writing, aims to answer questions, both those raised in the conversation among members of a research community addressing a subject and those likely to be raised by readers. By developing a **research question**—formulating a few simple questions about your subject early in the research process—you can set limits on the scope of your topic and focus on the most important ideas and information you gather through research.

STRATEGY

Work toward forming two or three questions early in your research process. Relate your questions to your general and specific goals for writing. Design questions to enlighten both yourself and your readers.

Summer Arrigo-Nelson and Jennifer Figliozzi developed the following questions for their academic research project on the relationship of parental behaviors to college student drinking.

> Will students with permission to drink at home show different drinking behaviors at college than those without permission to drink at home?
>
> Do the students feel that a correlation exists between drinking behaviors at home and at college?

Research questions can take several forms, depending on your own preferences and your purposes for writing. Some writers prefer questions that focus on factual or informational matters: *who*, *what*, *where*, *when*, *why*, and *how*. Other writers prefer questions that suggest both a purpose and an eventual organizational pattern for writing. Jennifer Latimer arrived at her research questions in this way:

> I looked at the licorice package, the sour candy package, the snack crackers box, even the pudding pack—all contained hydrogenated oils. I did some preliminary research and developed two questions for my research and my readers:
>
> What effects do hydrogenated oils have on us?
>
> Should I (and we) ever again eat delicious treats containing them?

Still others prefer questions that arise from their research: questions asked by other writers, questions they raise in marginal notes on a book or article, questions they develop through freewriting or brainstorming in a research file.

By limiting the number of research questions for your project and keeping them simple, you can narrow your topic and focus your efforts on providing satisfactory answers for your readers.

STRATEGY

Devote one section of your research file to developing one or a limited number of research questions that you can modify later to reflect your increasing knowledge and insights about your topic. The following question patterns may be helpful to you in developing your research question.

How did *X* come about? What are its consequences?
What are some new developments? What benefits or dangers do they involve?
What is *X* and into what categories does it fall?
Why is *X* a problem? What can we do in response to it?
What unusual (intriguing, surprising) features does *X* have? Why are they important to us?
What choices does *X* pose?
Is *X* as important (dangerous, valuable, unusual) as many people claim?
Who is affected by *X*? What should they know about it or do about it?

21f Preliminary thesis

Almost all research essays, reports, documents—even Web sites—use a **thesis statement** (3c–d) to guide readers' attention and state the writer's key idea or theme. The form and scope of a thesis statement will vary according to your purpose for writing. In persuasive writing, a thesis statement plays a special role by presenting the argumentative proposition (10c), proposal, or interpretation your writing supports.

By creating a thesis statement early in the research and writing process, you can narrow your topic and shape your search strategy (21j) accordingly. Later you will modify your thesis in response to what you have learned, but formulating a thesis at the beginning of the process can help you plan your research effectively. Thesis statements that guide research often follow one of four patterns.

- **Issue.** What is the issue, and what is my stand on it?
- **Problem.** What is the problem, and what solution am I offering?
- **Public question.** What is the situation we are facing, and how should we respond?
- **Academic question.** What is the phenomenon, and what is my analysis and interpretation?

Revise your thesis statement regularly, perhaps devoting a section of your research file to this effort. Use the opportunity to consider changes in direction or emphasis triggered by what you learned through research and to begin envisioning the strategies you will use in writing your paper.

Exercise 6

Create a preliminary thesis statement to narrow your focus to a specific issue or problem. You might use several sentences at this point in the process, one stating the issue, problem, question, or phenomenon you are addressing, the other offering your (tentative) opinion or conclusion.

21g Summarizing, paraphrasing, and synthesizing

You can't identify and use research sources without reading them. But if you read your sources in superficial ways, your research project and your writing will suffer. A research project calls for two types of reading: reading for understanding and critical reading.

Both kinds of reading contribute in significant ways to the outcome of a research project. Reading for understanding leads to the summaries, paraphrases, syntheses, quotations, and details you will draw on as you write. Critical reading leads to many of the insights you will offer to readers.

In a **summary,** you present the essential information in a text without interpreting it. A summary is shorter than the original, *compressing* the information and presenting only the key ideas and support. In a **paraphrase,** you restate an author's ideas in your own words, retaining the content and sense of the original but providing your own expression. A **synthesis** brings together summaries of several sources and points out the relationships among the ideas and information.

1 Summarizing

You create summaries as a concise way of presenting ideas and information from a source in your own writing. In an **objective summary,** you focus on presenting the content of the source in compressed form and avoid speculating on the source's line of reasoning. In an **evaluative summary,** you add your opinions, evaluating or commenting on the original passage.

PREPARING A SUMMARY

To prepare a summary of information relating to your topic, follow this process.

- **Read** the selection, looking for the most important ideas, evidence, and information. Underline, highlight, or make note of key points and information that you think should be mentioned in your summary.

(*continued*)

PREPARING A SUMMARY (*continued*)

- **Scan** (reread quickly) the selection to decide which of the ideas and bits of information you noted during your first reading are the *most* important. Try also to decide on the writer's main purpose in the selection and to identify the major sections of the discussion.
- **Summarize** *each section* of the source (each step in the argument, each stage in the explanation) in a *single sentence* that mentions the key ideas and information.
- **Encapsulate** the *entire passage* in a *single sentence* that captures its main point or conclusion.
- **Combine** your section summaries with your encapsulation (above) to produce a draft summary of the main point, other important points, and the most important information.
- **Revise** to make sure your summary is logical and easy to read. Check against the source for accuracy.
- **Document** clearly the source of your summary using a standard style of documentation (see Chapters 28–31).

In a summary, you can present the key ideas from a source without including unnecessary detail that might distract readers. Arrigo-Nelson and Figliozzi used two one-sentence summaries of research to help introduce one of the questions for their academic research paper.

> First, research has shown that adolescents who have open and close relationships with their parents use alcohol less often than do those with conflictual relationships (Sieving 1996). For example, a survey given to students in seventh through twelfth grades reported that approximately 35 percent of adolescent drinkers were under parental supervision while drinking (Dept. of Education 1993). Based on this research, we are interested in determining if students who were given permission to drink while living with their parents would possess different drinking patterns, upon reaching college, than those who did not previously have permission to drink.

2 Paraphrasing

A good paraphrase doesn't add to or detract from the original but often helps you understand a difficult work. When you want to incorporate the detailed ideas and information from a passage into your own writing but don't want to quote your source because the wording is too dense or confusing, then a **paraphrase** can be the answer.

As part of her research for an editorial supporting a new alcohol abuse program on her campus, Figliozzi encountered the following passage in a report on current programs at various schools.

> The university also now notifies parents when their sons or daughters violate the alcohol policy or any other aspect of the student code of conduct. "We were hoping that the support of parents would help change students' behavior, and we believe it has," says Timothy F. Brooks, an assistant vice-president and the dean of students at the University of Delaware.

Because she wanted to avoid long quotations and instead integrate the information smoothly into her discussion, she paraphrased part of the passage.

> Officials at the University of Delaware thought that letting parents know when students violate regulations on alcohol use would change students' drinking habits, and one administrator now says, "We believe it has" (Reisberg 42).

PREPARING A PARAPHRASE

To paraphrase part of a source, put the information in your own words, retaining the content and ideas of the original as well as the sequence of presentation. (Many paraphrases contain sentences that correspond with the original except for changes in wording and sentence structure.)

- **Read** the selection carefully so that you understand the wording as well as the content.
- **Write** a draft of your paraphrase, using your own words and phrases in place of the original. Rely on synonyms and equivalent expressions. You can retain names, proper nouns, and the like from the original, of course.
- **Revise** for smooth reading and clarity. Change sentence structures and phrasing to make sure your version is easier to understand than your source.
- **Document** clearly the source of your paraphrase using a standard style of documentation (see Chapters 28–31).

Exercise 7

Choose an article that interests you in a magazine such as *Natural History* or *Scientific American*. Paraphrase the first paragraph or two or any passage of a few lines or more. Do as Figliozzi has done above, and try to integrate the passage into an imaginary research report, putting much or most of the passage into your own words.

3 Synthesizing

By bringing together summaries of several sources and pointing out their relationships in a **synthesis,** you can use your sources in special ways:

to provide background information, to explore causes and effects, to look at contrasting explanations or arguments, and to bring together ideas and information in support of a thesis.

PREPARING A SYNTHESIS

To create a synthesis of your source materials, use the following strategy.

- **Identify** the role a synthesis would play in your explanation or argument as well as the kind of information and ideas you wish to share with readers.
- **Gather** the sources you plan to synthesize.
- **Read** your sources, and prepare to summarize them.
- **Focus** on the purpose of your synthesis, and draft a sentence summing up your conclusion about the relationships of the sources.
- **Arrange** the order in which you will present your sources in the synthesis.
- **Write** a draft of your synthesis, presenting summaries of your sources and offering your conclusion about the relationship(s).
- **Revise** so that your synthesis is easy to read. Make sure readers can easily identify the sources of the ideas and information.
- **Document** clearly the sources for your synthesis using a standard style of documentation.

Many academic papers begin with a summary of prior research designed to identify a need for further research and to provide justification for the research questions. The opening section of Summer Arrigo-Nelson and Jennifer Figliozzi's academic research paper uses synthesis for this purpose.

> Research dealing with student alcohol use most often focuses on children's perceptions of their parents' actions and on the relationship between child and parent. Studies conducted with high school students have supported the hypothesis that positive family relationships are more likely to be associated with less frequent alcohol use among adolescents than are negative relationships. Adolescents model the limited substance use of their parents where there is a good or moderate parent/adolescent relationship (Andrews, Hops, and Dunkin 1997). Other factors the studies found to be associated with positive family relationships, along with substance use, were academic achievement, family structure, place of residence, self-esteem, and emotional tone (Weschler, Dowdall, Davenport, and Castillo 1995; Martch and Miller 1997).

Public and work writing often use synthesis in a similar fashion to identify a problem that needs to be addressed or a policy that needs to be examined or reconsidered.

STRATEGY

You can "quote" pictures and graphic representations by reproducing them within your own text (with appropriate documentation). Paraphrasing and summarizing are more difficult, though not impossible. To paraphrase pictures, drawings, or graphic presentations, you need to "extract" information and concepts from them and "translate" the material into your own words. Instead of paraphrasing a paragraph reporting the results of a study on car theft in major U.S. cities, for example, you would describe the bar graph that reports the statistics.

21h Reading sources critically

To read critically, you must be able to do four things: (1) *identify* in your sources any unanswered questions (academic), unresolved issues (public), or unsolved problems (work) that you can make the focus of your research and writing; (2) *synthesize* different perspectives among sources; (3) *interpret* your sources; (4) *evaluate* your sources.

1 Identifying questions

A final research report or essay often begins by identifying an unanswered question, an unsolved problem, or an unresolved issue in a way that highlights its importance for readers, going on to address this concern in detail. As you read and reflect on your topic, record and explore unanswered questions, unsolved problems, and unresolved issues. Try stating them as concisely as you can in a *question paragraph* (or a *problem* or *issue paragraph*). Such a paragraph can suggest ways for you to develop your paper or report, and you may even include all or part of it in the finished product. Here are critical notes student Lily Germaine made for a paper about bodybuilding.

21h resrch

Tucker, Larry A. "Effect of Weight Training on Self-Concept: A Profile of Those Influenced Most." Research Quarterly for Exercise and Sport, Introduction, pp. 389–91.

Tucker uses the word "although" at least four times when summarizing other studies, and he tends to use phrases such as "only a few studies have shown. . . ." He's being nice on the surface but is setting his readers up to find fault with the other studies. That basic fault is their lack of objective methodology, which he seems to plan on rectifying by using mathematical measurements and rigid definitions of terms. A glance through the rest of the article reveals lots of equations and two tables of statistics. He seems to think he can be completely objective in determining such a slippery thing as "self-concept." I really have to question this assumption.

Germaine's question paragraph begins with insights and wording from her notes.

Does bodybuilding affect self-concept? Before we can answer this question, we need to ask if we can accurately measure such a slippery thing as "self-concept." Some researchers, like Tucker, believe that self-concept can be accurately gauged using mathematical measurements and rigid definitions of terms. For several reasons, however, this assumption is questionable. . . .

2 Synthesizing perspectives

To offer your readers an in-depth understanding of a subject, use a **critical synthesis** to bring together perspectives, opinions, interpretations, and evidence from a variety of sources and explore their potential connections. Critical synthesis provides readers with a unified discussion reflecting your understanding of the various perspectives, but it also pays special attention to highlighting and summarizing differences and to presenting your conclusions about the sources.

Be alert to agreements and disagreements as you read and take notes on your sources, identifying and exploring the various perspectives. When you are drafting your paper, consider preparing a critical synthesis that may become an important element of the finished project, such as a review of prior research (academic), an overview of differing stands on an issue (public) or a consideration of alternative responses to a problem (work).

Look over your sources and notes, then synthesize (sum up) the main ideas, positions, or facts of your sources, building on the techniques you use to prepare a synthesis (21g-3). To do this, imagine that you're an expert on the topic and that you're trying to give someone a quick state-of-the-art overview based on your sources. Here are guidelines.

1. Be true to the ideas and information in your sources.
2. Suggest relationships (among conclusions, opinions, ideas, and facts) that go beyond those relationships discussed in your sources.
3. In a thesis statement (3c) or a statement of the central idea of the synthesis, summarize the relationships you observe.
4. Be selective. Focus on material that relates directly to your central idea.

5. Be balanced. Acknowledge facts, opinions, and alternative perspectives that contradict the central idea of your synthesis.
6. Base your synthesis on your own thinking as well as material from your sources.

Here is a critical synthesis Kimlee Cunningham used to introduce the thesis of her academic paper on three Disney animated feature films.

> It is probably an exaggeration to say that a character like Belle in Beauty and the Beast is a lot like a contemporary feminist. As one critic suggests, "She wants adventure and he wants commitment; he holds a mirror and she hugs a book" (Showalter). However, we should not simply ignore an interpretation like this by claiming "that it takes a classic fairy tale, and turns it around and analyzes it from a modern feminist view" (Hoffman). Even if many people view a film like Beauty and the Beast (or Aladdin) as "just a love story" (Hoffman), the films nonetheless grow out of the complicated values and roles that shape relationships today. Disney's contemporary portrayal of women characters shows a willingness to change with the times but also a reluctance to abandon traditional values and stereotypes.

3 Interpreting sources

Most research papers or reports should present a point of view about their topic: a conclusion about its meaning or causes, a commitment to a particular course of action, or a stand on an issue. At the same time, you need to share with your readers the differing outlooks embodied in your sources, and to indicate why readers should accept your interpretation. Here are basic questions concerning the outlook (or bias) of your sources.

1. Does the source display a balanced perspective in offering its conclusions?
2. Does the source advocate strongly, though fairly, for a particular point of view?
3. Does the source display one-sided bias, including misrepresentation of facts and distortions of others' positions?

In an **interpretation,** you build on synthesis (see 21h-2) by explicitly including your opinions and giving priority to your own ideas and points of view. Interpreting involves **generalizing** (coming to broad conclusions about what your research has to say about your topic) and **extending** (going beyond this to connect your source's ideas to your own).

PREPARING AN INTERPRETATION

Begin an interpretation by stating the point of view of your source(s) as accurately as possible. Add your own ideas and conclusions. Take into account any strong advocacy (or questionable bias) in the source(s).

1. Present material from your sources accurately. Select material most relevant to the point you want to make, but do not suppress contradictory, biased, or partisan material.
2. Present your point of view and provide supporting evidence, perhaps comparing the perspective of one source to that of another and to your own.
3. Add interpretations and conclusions of your own not present in the sources, or present in a different form.

21i Audience inventory

As you identify the "conversations" that writers are having about your topic and as you begin your own research, remember that various communities of readers may expect different things from a report or paper. Academic readers look for detailed evidence from a variety of sources and expect carefully documented sources and quotations. Readers in a work setting expect a clear and direct presentation, accurate information, and detail appropriate to the subject and the audience's expertise, along with less formal documentation. And readers in public communities expect information and supporting evidence that is accurate, clear, accessible, and persuasive, without quite as much attention to documentation.

STRATEGY

Create an **audience inventory**—a checklist or set of questions adapted to a specific audience that helps tailor your research and writing to the specific concerns of that audience. Answer the following questions in constructing your inventory.

What problems or issues has the audience been facing?

What new discoveries or information might interest the audience or be useful to it?

What policies or programs are causing your readers difficulty or might be helpful to them?

Arrigo-Nelson and Figliozzi prepared an audience inventory to help plan their paper on the effects of alcohol consumption among college students. Below is a sample of their inventory, which focused on the audience of their own campus community.

AUDIENCE INVENTORY QUESTION	What new discoveries or information about student alcohol use might benefit the campus community?
WRITER'S RESPONSE	Our conclusion about the relationship between student drinking behavior in college and parental permissiveness for drinking in the home could be important for a campus program aiming to reduce student alcohol use.

Exercise 8

Develop a set of potential questions to help understand your audience's interests, needs, and expectations. Then use these questions to develop an audience inventory.

21j Developing a search strategy

A good **search strategy** is a plan for locating the resources you need to answer your research question and support your thesis. It will help you to consult a variety of sources providing different kinds of information and points of view. A search strategy has five elements: resources; search tools; keywording; working bibliography; and timeline.

1 Resources

Your search strategy should begin with a list of the kinds of resources you plan to use—printed books, scholarly journals, newspapers, databases, Web sites, interviews, and surveys, for example. Draw on your preliminary research (21d) to create your initial resource list, and update it as you discover further potential resources. If you have specific titles, Web sites, or people in mind as sources, list them.

STRATEGY

It is easy to focus your research on familiar resources—printed books, Web sites, scholarly journals, magazine articles—while ignoring less familiar but often highly valuable resources such as bibliographies, abstracts, and government documents. To make use of less familiar resources, include *What about . . . ?* sections in your research file. Under the heading "What about . . . ?" list resources you might not normally consult, and investigate them the next time you visit the library or go online for research (see 22a, "Organization of library resources"; 24b, "Search engines"; and 25b, "Meaningful field research").

2 Search tools

Obvious search tools come readily to mind when you begin researching: your library's online catalog and Web search engines like *Google*. They are adequate starting points but not always the best or most precise means of locating resources, particularly when your research moves beyond information and ideas that are generally known.

Here are four kinds of specialized research tools.

- Indexes of magazine and periodical articles: *Readers' Guide to Periodical Literature*, *InfoTrac*, *New York Times Index*, *Wall Street Journal Index*
- Indexes of articles in scholarly journals and professional publications: *Social Sciences Index*, *Applied Science and Technology Index*, *MLA International Bibliography*, *Humanities Index*, *Education Index*
- Academic and professional databases with built-in search engines: *EBSCOhost*, *LexisNexis*, *OCLC First*
- Specialized Web search engines and indexed databases: *Cata List*, *Metacrawler*, *Dogpile*, *PAIS*

STRATEGY

Begin by listing the most familiar search tools you plan to employ, then add "What about . . . ?" entries for less familiar or more specialized tools, perhaps drawing them from those listed in 22c, d, and e. In the course of your research, update your "What about . . . ?" entries to reflect whatever new tools you discover.

3 Keywording

Many people begin searching for sources by using general terms to identify a topic, only to discover that these are not the terms used in an index or search engine. Indexes, databases, library catalogs (22c–e), and many other reference sources are arranged (or searched) by **keywords.** If you identify the keywords or phrases for printed or electronic indexes, you can usually locate all the resources you need. If you don't, you may waste time following the wrong paths and locating useless sources.

Of course, you may not know which are the preferred terms and phrases until you begin your search, and there may be some necessary trial and error in your work. Sometimes it helps to have in mind two or three alternative keywords or phrases. If a particular database or other resource yields little under one keyword, you can try others before moving to another resource.

Exercise 9

As part of your developing search strategy, make a list of possible sources you have discovered and a list of keywords and phrases that may help guide your research.

4 Working bibliography

Your search strategy should make provision for recording information that will help you or your readers locate a source. A list of sources you have examined and may decide to draw on as you write is called a **working bibliography.** In a working bibliography, you should record the types of information you will need to provide in your final paper in a list of works cited, a references list, a list of works consulted, or footnotes (see Chapters 28–31).

INFORMATION FOR A WORKING BIBLIOGRAPHY

When you examine a source, record the following kinds of information in your working bibliography, ready to use in compiling the list of sources for your final paper.

PRINTED BOOKS

- Author(s) or editor(s)
- Title
- Publication information: place of publication, name of publisher, date of publication
- Volume or edition numbers, if any
- Call number (to locate the book in library stacks)

PRINTED ARTICLES

- Author(s) or editor(s)
- Title
- Name of journal, magazine, newspaper, or collection of articles
- Publication information
  - Article in a periodical: volume number, issue number, month or day of publication, page numbers of article (inclusive)
  - Article in a collection: title of collection and editor's name, place of publication, name of publisher, date of publication, page numbers of article (inclusive)

ELECTRONIC OR ONLINE WORK

- Author(s), editor(s), or group(s) responsible for the document
- Title or name of Web site
- Information about any corresponding print publication (as above)

(*continued*)

INFORMATION FOR A WORKING BIBLIOGRAPHY (*continued*)

- Electronic publication information: date of electronic publication or latest update, date you accessed document, and complete URL; (for an online journal) volume and issue number, publication date; (for a database or CD-ROM) document access number or version number; (for email or post to a discussion list) name of sender, subject line, date of posting, name of list, date of access.

When you are doing research, keep a copy of your working bibliography close at hand so you can make notes about entries to add or delete.

Organizing your working bibliography. You can organize the entries in a working bibliography in several ways.

- **Alphabetically,** as they will eventually appear in a list of works cited or a references page. This strategy can save time and effort when you prepare your final text.
- In **categories** reflecting the parts of your subject or the kinds of evidence they provide for your argument. This strategy can help you identify at a glance areas for your work and those needing further investigation.
- **According to the plan** for your paper. This strategy can help you gather your resources efficiently as you write.

Annotating. Some writers add comments, evaluations, or brief summaries to the references in their working bibliographies (for a discussion of annotated bibliographies, see 16e). The annotated bibliographies they create in this manner can be papers in their own right or part of a longer research project.

Exercise 10

Assemble the notes you have taken for your working bibliography. Use them to create a working bibliography as part of your research file. Organize the entries in a manner appropriate to your purposes for researching and writing. If possible, link the entries electronically to notes you have taken on the sources.

21k Timeline

Planning involves dividing up your work and sticking to a schedule. By being methodical in the process of your research, you'll make the most efficient use of your time.

Answer the following questions to help create a timeline for your work.

1. **How much time do I have?** When should my report or document be in final form? Do I have to produce intermediate assignments, such as a progress report, drafts, or notes?
2. **What kind of report or document will I be creating, and for whom?** What form will my work take? What resources will I have to gather or develop in order to produce such work? What audience or community of readers will I be addressing? What will I need to learn about them and their expectations? Will I need to share or discuss the project with them while I'm researching and writing?
3. **What kind of research must I do?** Will I be doing research in printed sources (articles, books), electronic sources (databases, Web sites), or field sources (interviews, surveys, observations)?

WHAT TO INCLUDE IN A TIMELINE OR CALENDAR

When you create a calendar for your research, include the following tasks, allowing four days to a week for each.

1. Choose a subject. Do the preliminary research necessary to identify a specific topic.
2. Narrow your topic so that it is realistic in the time you have available for research and writing. Begin identifying possible resources.
3. Develop a research question or tentative thesis. Create an audience inventory. Develop a search strategy. Begin a working bibliography.
4. Begin research. Identify possible resources, read and evaluate them, and take notes. Record bibliographical information for sources.
5. Review your research notes. Begin looking for patterns in the information and ideas you consider appropriate for your project. Begin summarizing key ideas or information; begin drafting those sections of your project you see as important parts of the final document. Identify areas needing further investigation and continue your research. Revise your research question or tentative thesis in a form close to the version that will appear in the final paper.
6. Start writing your first draft. Develop a plan for your paper and begin drafting. Include preliminary in-text references or endnotes. Maintain a working list of sources cited as you draft. Check for missing bibliographical information.
7. Finish drafting. Review your draft for areas needing further research; share it with others who can give you honest, practical responses and advice. Revise your paper and prepare documentation in final form.
8. Polish and proofread the final draft; share it with someone who can help spot problems, omissions, or errors you did not notice. Submit your work.

Put your plans into calendar form so you can envision the process as a whole and evaluate your plan. Be ready to revise your calendar to accommodate the realities of research and writing and to reflect changes in the direction of your work.

You can maintain your calendar in handwritten form on a paper calendar or in a dated list of activities.

> Do preliminary research to analyze task and audience and to arrive at a focused topic—October 15–18
> Draft a research question—October 19

Or you can use the calendar and planning programs in your desktop, laptop, or hand-held computer to create a timeline and revise it as needed. In choosing a format for your calendar, make sure you can include it in your research file. This is an especially important consideration for electronic calendars. If you use a project planning program to create a calendar, check that the document you create can be integrated with the documents that make up your research file.

STRATEGY

Work Backward. Create a research and writing plan by working backward from the due date for a project. Even if you don't follow the plan precisely, a calendar, list of dates, electronic project planning graph, or chart of activities can help you get started on a project and give you a sense of direction.

Exercise 11

Develop a timeline for your research and writing project. Put it in the form of a calendar, a project graph, or a chart of activities. Work backward from your due date and estimate the amount of time you will need to allot to each activity.

CHAPTER 22
Library Resources

Libraries give you access to books, periodicals, recordings, government documents, microforms, historical archives, collections, and, through computer terminals, CD-ROMs, and online resources (see Chapter 23). Libraries are important places to visit for research; nonetheless, some of their resources are available elsewhere, in electronic databases (see Chapter 23), for example, or on the Internet (see Chapter 24). Libraries have some distinct advantages (and disadvantages) as research locations, however.

Advantages

- Scholarly publications, technical and specialized reports, and government publications are more likely to be available at libraries than on the Internet.
- Books, microforms, and other publications like pamphlets may not be available online.
- Reference librarians can provide considerable help and advice—and are eager to do so.
- Libraries often provide Internet access, so you can follow a strand of research at *one* location, whether it takes you to printed sources, databases, or the Web.

Disadvantages

- Library research may require a considerable block of time, and library schedules may not correspond with your schedule.
- Library resources may be difficult to navigate, especially when you are not familiar with the organization of research libraries.

22a Organization of library resources

Your library research strategy should take into account both the kinds and the arrangement of resources in research libraries.

1 Kinds of library resources

In general, library resources fall into two categories, each with its own system for locating specific sources.

LIBRARY RESOURCES FOR THREE COMMUNITIES

ACADEMIC SETTINGS	PUBLIC SETTINGS	WORK SETTINGS
Research libraries offer resources often unavailable in public libraries or through the Internet. Scholarly journals, specialized books, government documents, and limited circulation magazines offer access to current research and information about work in technical fields. Microforms and recordings provide records of unpublished papers, conference presentations, and artistic performances. Online catalogs often include the holdings of more than one library and enable access through interlibrary loans.	Research libraries generally subscribe to a wide range of national and international magazines, enabling researchers to identify public concerns and needs for information. Local, national, and international newspapers provide opportunities to note current issues and problems that concern either specific or general public audiences. Government documents provide access to important information for the public and to the services and actions of public agencies.	Research libraries subscribe to magazines, newsletters, and newspapers, often directed at business or professional audiences, enabling researchers to identify current challenges or recent developments of importance to their organizations. Government documents provide information about regulations, policies, and programs of interest to readers in the workplace. Research librarians can help locate information about companies, financial organizations, or international trade and governmental relations.

- Books, pamphlets, and miscellaneous resources including photographs, films, and recordings: Use **online catalogs.**
- Articles in magazines, scholarly journals, and other periodicals: Use **electronic and print indexes,** some of which may be accessed through a library's Web site.

2 From general to specific resources

Your research will usually move from general, less detailed sources to more specific, more detailed ones as you narrow your topic and begin adding depth of detail and evidence to your writing. The distinction between general and specific treatment of a topic holds true for online and field resources also, but it is especially sharp for library resources. Often some sections of a library are dedicated to general reference works, other sections to field- or discipline-specific texts.

22b General resources

You can use general resources to gain a broad overview of a topic, including background information, and a sense of relationships to other subjects. General references can also provide names, keywords, and phrases useful for tracing a topic, as well as bibliographies of potential resources. (Commercial Internet services like America Online also offer access to online reference works, databases, reference services, and collections of resources.)

General encyclopedias, ready references, maps, and dictionaries. These works provide very basic information on a wide range of topics. They are good places to find an overview of your topic, but they don't usually provide in-depth information. Resources of this sort are generally available in both print and electronics formats.

> *New Encyclopaedia Britannica, Columbia Encyclopedia, Microsoft Encarta, World Almanac and Book of Facts, Canadian Almanac and Directory, Statistical Abstract of the United States, National Geographic Atlas of the World, The American Heritage Dictionary of the English Language, Oxford English Dictionary*

Specialized encyclopedias and dictionaries. These volumes provide greater depth of coverage of a specific topic or area. Such works can be easily located in a library's catalog or by searching online. The range of resources is wide, and these texts are usually available in print and electronic formats.

> *Dictionary of the Social Sciences, Dictionary of American Biography, Current Biography, Who's Who in America, McGraw-Hill Encyclopedia of Science and Technology, Encyclopedia of World Art, International Encyclopedia of Business and Management, Encyclopedia of Advertising, International Encyclopedia of Film, International Television Almanac, Encyclopedia of Computer Science, Encyclopedia of Educational Research, Dictionary of Anthropology, Encyclopedia of Psychology, Encyclopedia of the Environment, New Grove Dictionary of Music and Musicians, Encyclopedia of Nursing Research, Encyclopedia of Religion, Encyclopedia of Sociology, Women's Studies Encyclopedia*

Bibliographies. These works provide organized lists of books and articles on specific topics within a field of study or interest. Most are available in regularly updated electronic form as well as in print.

> *Bibliographic Index: A Cumulative Bibliography of Bibliographies, MLA Bibliography of Books and Articles on the Modern Languages and Literatures, International Bibliography of the Social Sciences, Foreign Affairs Bibliography, Film Research: A Critical Bibliography with Annotations and Essays*

22c Online catalogs

Library catalogs give you access to books and to many other resources, including periodicals, recordings, government documents, films, historical archives, and collections of photographs. Your library's catalog is most likely an **online catalog,** though **card catalogs** are still in use in some small libraries. You can search under the *author's name*, the *title of a work*, the *subject area*, the title of a *series or periodical containing the work*, and, in some libraries, *words in the title or in a work's description.* Some catalogs list not only works in their home library but also works in other libraries within a region or in a consortium, such as a group of college libraries.

Rachel Torres discovered that her library belonged to just such a group when she began her search for resources, especially printed books, on her topic: Afro-Cuban music. She began by typing her topic into the search screen, and the catalog returned a number of possible sources (see Figure 22.1).

She chose item 4 from the list, and the next catalog screen provided detailed information about the book along with the location of an available copy at a cooperating library (see Figure 22.2 on p. 330).

The copy in her university library was checked out, but Torres was able to get a copy from another library a short drive away. If none of the libraries had had the book in its collection, she would have been able to get a copy through a lending service called **interlibrary loan.** To use such a service, ask a reference or circulation librarian. Some libraries will also give you the option of electronically requesting interlibrary loan materials. Many online catalogs even allow you to search the catalogs of other libraries, nationwide and worldwide.

22d Periodicals, print and electronic indexes, and government documents

Periodicals are publications containing articles by different authors. **General-interest magazines** appear once a month or weekly, with each issue paginated separately. **Scholarly journals** generally appear less frequently than magazines, perhaps four times a year, with page numbers running continuously through the separate issues that make up an annual volume. **Newspapers** generally appear daily or weekly and frequently consist of separately numbered sections.

Most scholarly journals are still available primarily in printed form, though many colleges and universities now subscribe to journals in electronic form, with current and back issues available online, either through terminals in the library or through the library's Web site. Many general-interest magazines and newspapers are now available in electronic as well as printed form.

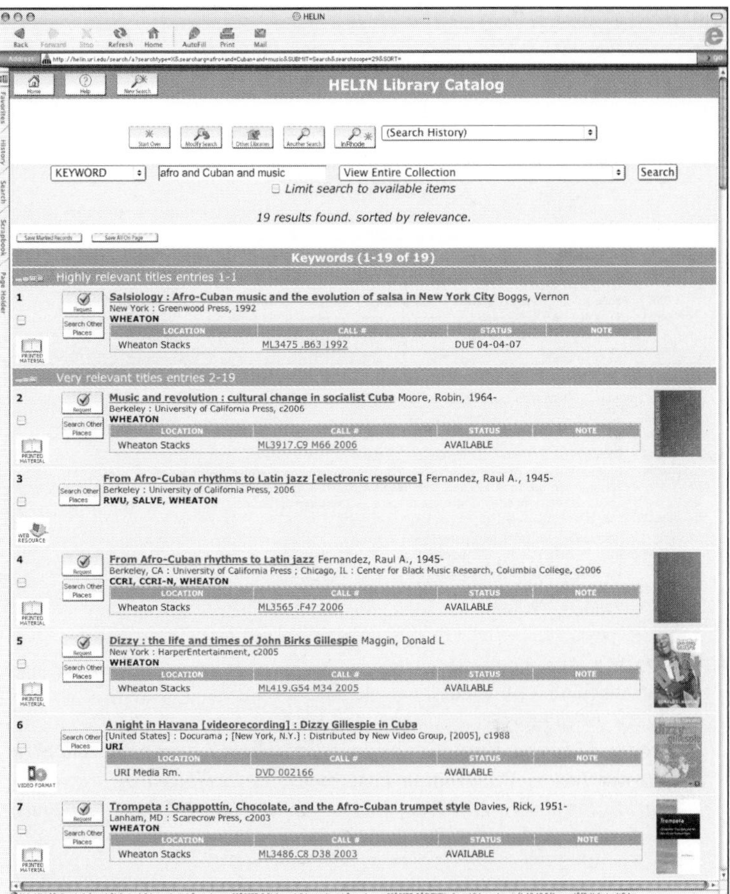

FIGURE 22.1 Search results for the keywords *Afro-Cuban music*

22d source

You can locate articles in print (and in electronic form) by consulting the many print and online **indexes.** Most indexes are currently available in both print and electronic forms. Many of these aids are quite specialized in coverage, providing lists or electronic links to related resources. They may also offer brief summaries (or **abstracts**) of the contents of articles and books.

General and newspaper indexes. These indexes give you a way to search for topics in newspapers, magazines, and other periodicals intended for the general public as well as some intended for more specialized audiences.

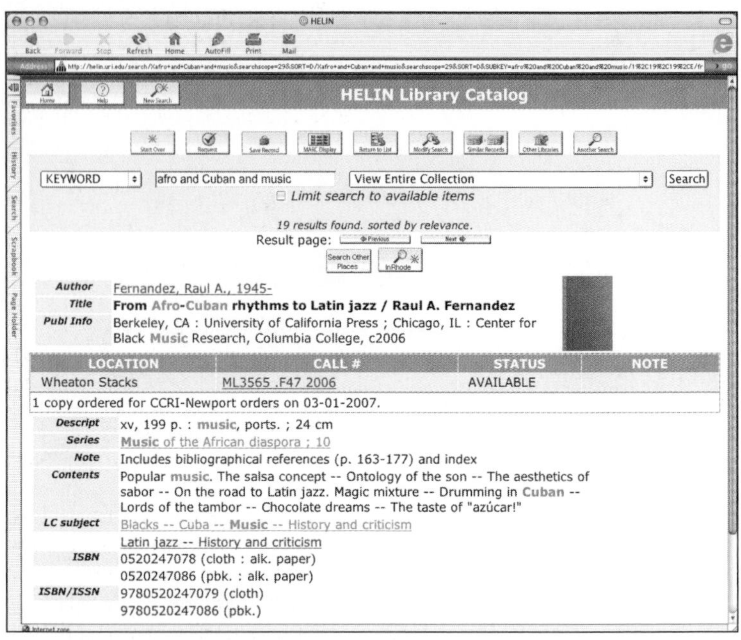

FIGURE 22.2 Detailed information for one entry under *Afro-Cuban music*

Academic Index, Readers' Guide to Periodical Literature, Wall Street Journal Index, Washington Post Index, PAIS (Public Affairs Information Services), InfoTrac, Editorials on File, Hispanic American Periodicals Index, OCLC/ World Catalog

Specialized indexes. Specialized indexes provide ways to search through publications that contain professional, technical, and academic resources.

Anthropological Literature, Art Index, Humanities Index, Music Index, BIZZ (Business Index), EconLit, Education Index, ERIC Current Index to Journals in Education, Index to Legal Periodicals, Social Sciences Index, Applied Science and Technology Index, General Science Index, Geobase, Index Medicus, Medline

Abstracts. Collections of abstracts bring together brief summaries of articles in specialized fields.

Abstracts of English Studies, Biological Abstracts, Chemical Abstracts, Dissertation Abstracts International, Historical Abstracts,

Language and Language Behavior Abstracts, Newspaper Abstracts, Psychological Abstracts, Sociological Abstracts

Government documents are reports of information and research, records of hearings, pamphlets, public information publications, and regulations issued by Congress, federal agencies, and state and local governments. These documents, rich sources of information both general and technical, are sometimes housed in separate collections in a library.

To access government documents published after 1976, search the *Catalog of U.S. Government Publications*. Its Web site is <http://www.access.gpo.gov/su_docs/locators/cgp/index.html>. Follow the directions on screen to locate the records for publications you want to consult. Copy information about the documents, including the SuDocs number, which many libraries use to identify documents on their shelves. (Note: Many government documents are available electronically.) For government documents published before 1976, consult the printed *Monthly Catalog of United States Government Publications*. Use its index to find information about the publications you need, including the SuDocs number.

In reading several magazine and newspaper articles about tornadoes, Michael Micchie noticed that some writers cited government documents and government-sponsored research as the source of their information. He decided to see what government publications he could find that addressed tornadoes and especially the problem of detecting them before they do harm. His search using the keyword *tornadoes* returned nineteen citations, each with a link to a full description of the document and a link to a list of libraries likely to have a copy of it. Figure 22.3 on page 332 shows part of the response he received.

Exercise 1

Make a list of the resources named in 22b–d that you are not familiar with but that might be appropriate for your research. Choose two and examine them briefly. List the potential sources about which they provide information.

22e Evaluating library resources

Library sources—books from reputable publishers, articles from scholarly or well-known periodicals, government documents—often have been reviewed by experts and produced with editorial checks. Even so, once you locate these sources, you'll need to decide whether they are appropriate for your research community and your questions and whether they support or deepen your thesis.

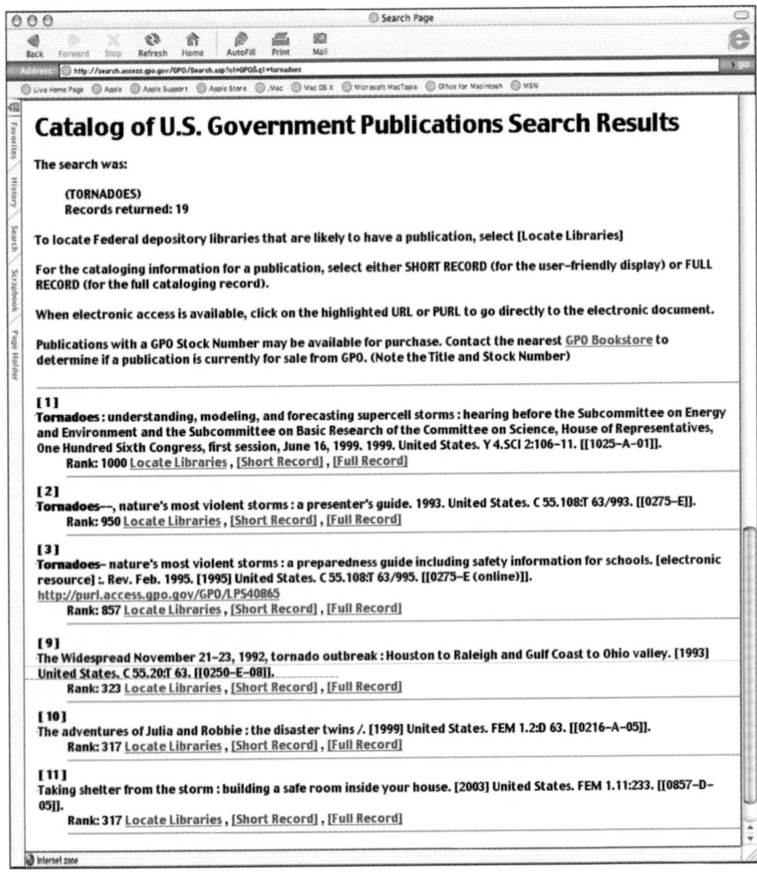

Search Page

http://search.access.gpo.gov/GPO/Search.asp?ct=GPO&q1=tornadoes

Catalog of U.S. Government Publications Search Results

The search was:

(TORNADOES)
Records returned: 19

To locate Federal depository libraries that are likely to have a publication, select [Locate Libraries]

For the cataloging information for a publication, select either SHORT RECORD (for the user-friendly display) or FULL RECORD (for the full cataloging record).

When electronic access is available, click on the highlighted URL or PURL to go directly to the electronic document.

Publications with a GPO Stock Number may be available for purchase. Contact the nearest GPO Bookstore to determine if a publication is currently for sale from GPO. (Note the Title and Stock Number)

[1]
Tornadoes : understanding, modeling, and forecasting supercell storms : hearing before the Subcommittee on Energy and Environment and the Subcommittee on Basic Research of the Committee on Science, House of Representatives, One Hundred Sixth Congress, first session, June 16, 1999. 1999. United States. Y 4.SCI 2:106-11. [[1025-A-01]].
Rank: 1000 Locate Libraries , [Short Record] , [Full Record]

[2]
Tornadoes--, nature's most violent storms : a presenter's guide. 1993. United States. C 55.108:T 63/993. [[0275-E]].
Rank: 950 Locate Libraries , [Short Record] , [Full Record]

[3]
Tornadoes- nature's most violent storms : a preparedness guide including safety information for schools. [electronic resource] :. Rev. Feb. 1995. [1995] United States. C 55.108:T 63/995. [[0275-E (online)]].
http://purl.access.gpo.gov/GPO/LPS40865
Rank: 857 Locate Libraries , [Short Record] , [Full Record]

[9]
The Widespread November 21-23, 1992, tornado outbreak : Houston to Raleigh and Gulf Coast to Ohio valley. [1993] United States. C 55.20:T 63. [[0250-E-08]].
Rank: 323 Locate Libraries , [Short Record] , [Full Record]

[10]
The adventures of Julia and Robbie : the disaster twins /. [1999] United States. FEM 1.2:D 63. [[0216-A-05]].
Rank: 317 Locate Libraries , [Short Record] , [Full Record]

[11]
Taking shelter from the storm : building a safe room inside your house. [2003] United States. FEM 1.11:233. [[0857-D-05]].
Rank: 317 Locate Libraries , [Short Record] , [Full Record]

FIGURE 22.3 Search results for the keyword *tornadoes* in U.S. government publications

22e source

Questions for evaluating library sources

- Does the publisher, journal, or sponsoring organization have a reputation for balance and accuracy? Is it an advocate whose views require caution?
- Is the author's reputation clear? What do other sources think of the author's fairness, reliability, and importance?
- How accurate is your source, especially if it presents facts as truth? Can you spot obvious errors? Which points are well documented?
- How does the author support generalizations? Do they go beyond the facts? Are they consistent with your knowledge?

- Are the ideas generally consistent with those in your other sources? If not, do they seem insightful or misleading and eccentric?
- Does the source meet the expectations of your research community?
- Does the source appropriately document information, quotations, and ideas or clearly attribute them to other authors?
- Has the source appeared without an editorial or review process? Does it apply only to a specific setting? Is its information outdated? Does it cite experts who have political or financial interests? Does it try to obscure its own bias? If so, consider it questionable; use it with caution.

CHAPTER 23 Databases

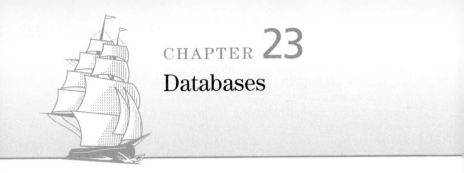

In recent years, texts in electronic form have begun replacing printed articles, documents, and even books, especially texts of scholarly and technical articles and general-interest periodical articles. College, university, and public libraries have greatly increased the number of online collections (or databases) of electronic documents they make available, and they will probably continue to do so. These electronic databases have some clear advantages as well as some disadvantages.

Advantages

- Because printed collections of scholarly publications are expensive to maintain and take up considerable space, the number of journal articles and technical publications to which a library provides access is generally greatly increased by the number of texts electronic databases make available.
- The texts available through databases are often identical in content and presentation to the printed versions.
- Many databases provide both abstracts (summaries of content) and full texts of documents.
- Databases often provide search engines useful for locating a document as well as related publications.
- Databases are often available both through library terminals and on the Web, through a library's Web sites.

Disadvantages

- The most recent issues of scholarly journals and technical publications are sometimes not available in database form.
- The range and number of texts available through databases are growing rapidly, yet not all publications are available through electronic databases.
- Some articles are available only in abstract form, not full-text form through databases.
- Most databases and search engines do not enable you to look at entire issues of a scholarly journal or periodical, only at individual articles you locate using keywords, titles, author's names, or electronic links. As a result, you may not be aware of groupings of texts created by the editors of a journal or periodical.

RESEARCH DATABASE RESOURCES FOR THREE COMMUNITIES

ACADEMIC SETTINGS	PUBLIC SETTINGS	WORK SETTINGS
Research libraries offer database resources and generally pay the subscription fees for users. (Large public libraries may also offer access to research databases.) The high cost of print subscriptions to scholarly publications means that libraries are often able to offer access to a wider range of online scholarly journals, specialized books, government documents, and limited circulation magazines than to their print equivalents. Specialized searching tools in databases help researchers identify technical and scholarly sources not accessible through Internet searches. Databases provide full texts of hard-to-locate sources.	Research and public libraries subscribe to databases providing access to articles in popular and specialized magazines, local and national newspapers, and professional or technical newsletters addressing topics of public interest. Databases contain current publications, and their search engines may allow users to highlight a specific set of dates, a locale, an issue, or a topic. Databases may provide collections of materials on a particular topic or issue.	Research and public libraries subscribe to databases providing information on profit making and nonprofit organizations, including their operations, policies, management strategies, and financial condition. This information is sometimes not available in print form or it is available only after it is no longer current. Information on the latest regulations or developments often appears in online publications indexed and made accessible through databases.

23a Reference databases

Reference databases are simply files of information available through the Internet or the Web or, occasionally, on CD-ROMs. Most databases focus on specialized or technical fields. As a result, they are likely to be consulted primarily by researchers with a special interest in a field. The limited number of users of online databases stands in contrast to the large numbers of people who access general-interest sites and search engines on the Web. At the same time, specialized databases are expensive to construct and maintain; they index hundreds of thousands of documents and must be updated continually to serve the needs of researchers who require access to the latest information, ideas, and results of experiment and inquiry. Consequently, most databases restrict access to paying customers, but access is allowed to students and faculty at most universities, their fees paid by the library making the database available.

How specialized are most databases? Quite specialized, but also quite useful to people interested in the topic areas they cover. Here, for example, is a description of one such reference database, *Family Index*, which covers a range of topics most people would consider well worth learning about.

> *Family Index*
> Lists recent articles on the family from a wide range of journals. Subjects include family history and trends; education; economics, public policy and the law; health care; gerontology; religion; diverse families; marriage; parenthood and child development; sexuality; abuse and neglect; and other problems. Updated frequently.

This description of a typical reference database highlights characteristics common to others as well. The database has a specific focus yet provides a wealth of material within that focus. It provides information about articles from a large number of journals, more than would be indexed by a Web search engine (24b). It is updated on a regular basis so that its contents are current. Its focus is up to date and contemporary, with references to recent documents only. If you need to access earlier publications, this resource will not be helpful, but if you want to know about the latest work in the field, this may be your best choice.

Databases are of several kinds, varying according to the kinds of information they provide: *full-text databases, databases containing abstracts*, and *indexing* or *bibliographic databases.* Other kinds of databases include those providing research aids and those housing various kinds of information such as pictures or statistics. Databases also differ according to field of study or interest and in the number and range of resources they contain.

Databases are generally searchable by author, title, and keyword or by special categories that reflect the scope and emphasis of the particular materials included in a collection.

23b Full-text databases

Full-text databases list articles and other documents and provide brief summaries of the content of each item. In addition, they provide the entire texts of all or most of the items indexed. As a result, they can save you time and effort in locating texts of potential sources. In their coverage, full-text databases range from extensive collections of scholarly or general interest articles like *Academic Search Premier* and *Academic Universe* to highly focused collections like *Health Reference Center Academic.*

Some of the most useful full-text databases are listed below.

- **General full-text databases**

  Academic Search Premier (EBSCOhost)
  Full texts of thousands of scholarly publications in such fields as social sciences, humanities, education, computer science, engineering,

language and linguistics, arts and literature, medical sciences, and ethnic studies. Most entries are from early 1990s to the present.

Academic Universe (LexisNexis)
News, law, and business information. Includes news from national and international newspapers and wire services; articles from hundreds of periodicals; and other reference sources.

ArticleFirst (FirstSearch)
Articles from approximately 13,000 journals.

National Newspapers
Indexing, abstracts, and full text of the *New York Times*, *The Wall Street Journal*, the *Washington Post*, and the *Christian Science Monitor*, beginning in the 1980s.

InfoTrac OneFile (InfoTrac)
News and periodical articles on topics such as business, computers, current events, economics, education, environmental issues, health care, hobbies, humanities, law, literature and art, politics, science, social science, sports, and technology.

- **Specialized full-text databases**

CQ Researcher
Weekly reports on topics such as social issues, environment, health, education, science, and technology. Each report focuses on one issue and includes pros and cons, charts and graphs, lengthy bibliographies, and discussions by a variety of researchers or experts.

Biography Resource Center
This database provides biographies and periodical articles. Searches can be made using a variety of facts: year of birth or death, occupation, gender, ethnic background, or nationality. Information is drawn from a wide range of sources.

National Environmental Publications Internet Site
More than 6,000 full-text EPA documents published since 1977.

Health Reference Center—Academic (InfoTrac)
Provides articles from the last twenty-five years on subjects such as fitness, pregnancy, medicine, nutrition, diseases, public health, occupational health and safety, alcohol and drug abuse, HMOs, and prescription drugs.

Jenny Latimer (see Chapter 21) was looking for detailed information to use in her paper about the presence of hydrogenated oils in snack foods, especially candy. She knew her research would involve technical information, but she didn't know which field of study would be most likely to provide the information she needed: food science and nutrition? health sciences? chemistry? biology? She also thought that such fields as psychology, sociology, and anthropology might help her explain why we prefer certain kinds of foods over others. In addition, she was worried about finding herself limited to sources that were too technical for her to understand or explain to readers. As a result, she decided to consult a database that covered general-interest as well as academic publications and to use one that provided both abstracts and full texts. She hoped that by sampling the available sources online, she would be able to decide whether they were appropriate for her project or too technical to be useful.

Here are some of the steps she followed. First she entered her search terms into the query screen of the database, using the terms *hydrogenated oils* and *candy*. When the search engine was unable to identify any sources using these terms, she broadened the search by using the terms *hydrogenated oils* and *food* (using the Boolean operator AND; see p. 349). This search identified sixteen sources, some of which seemed promising (see Figure 23.1).

Latimer looked at the first four articles, both the abstract and the full text, and took notes on several. One of them provided specific examples she felt might be important for her paper (see Figure 23.2).

After reading and taking notes, Latimer decided that the areas of study most likely to provide her with the kinds of information and insights she needed for her paper were nutrition studies and health sciences.

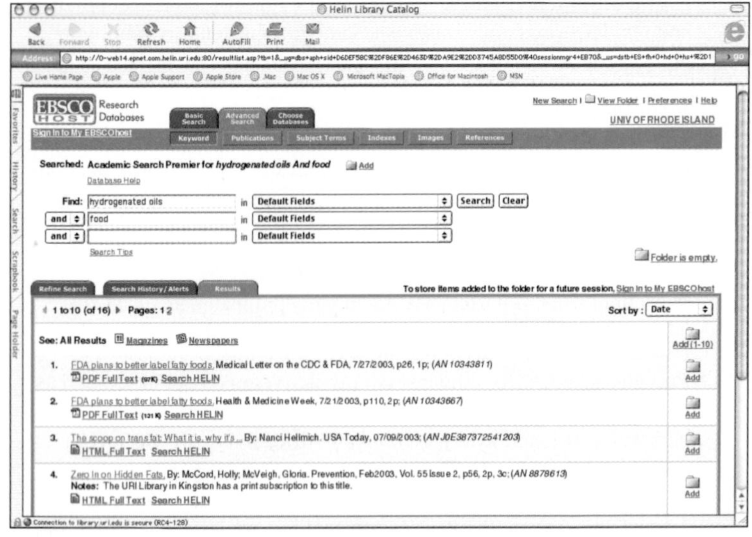

FIGURE 23.1 Database search results for the terms *hydrogenated oils* and *food*, using a Boolean operator

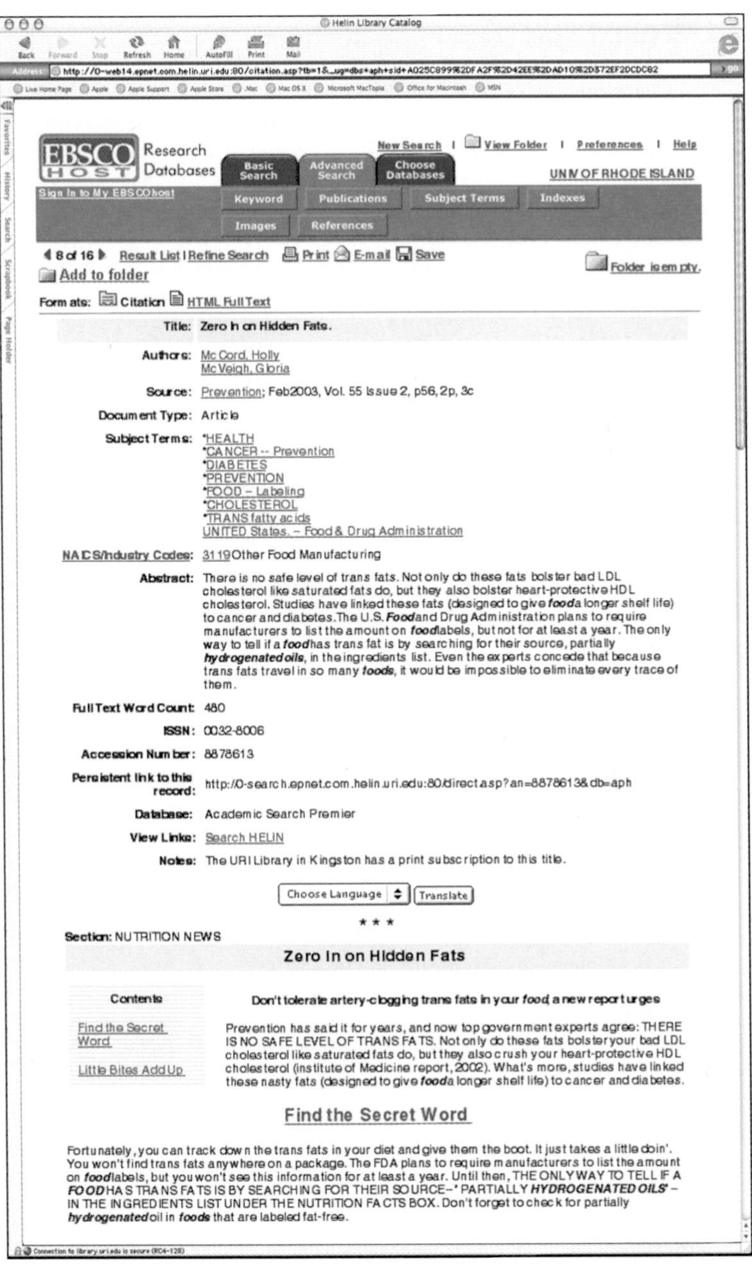
Helin Library Catalog
Back Forward Stop Refresh Home AutoFill Print Mail
Address: http://0-web14.epnet.com.helin.uri.edu:80/citation.asp?tb=1&_ug=dbs+aph+sid+A025C899%2DFA2F%2D42EE%2DAD10%2D372EF2DCDC82
EBSCO HOST Research Databases
New Search | View Folder | Preferences | Help
Basic Search
Advanced Search
Choose Databases
UNIV OF RHODE ISLAND
Sign In to My EBSCOhost
Keyword
Publications
Subject Terms
Indexes
Images
References
8 of 16 Result List | Refine Search Print E-mail Save
Add to folder
Folder is empty.
Formats: Citation HTML Full Text
Title: Zero In on Hidden Fats.
Authors: McCord, Holly; McVeigh, Gloria
Source: Prevention; Feb2003, Vol. 55 Issue 2, p56, 2p, 3c
Document Type: Article
Subject Terms: *HEALTH *CANCER -- Prevention *DIABETES *PREVENTION *FOOD -- Labeling *CHOLESTEROL *TRANS fatty acids UNITED States. -- Food & Drug Administration
NAICS/Industry Codes: 3119 Other Food Manufacturing
Abstract: There is no safe level of trans fats. Not only do these fats bolster bad LDL cholesterol like saturated fats do, but they also bolster heart-protective HDL cholesterol. Studies have linked these fats (designed to give food a longer shelf life) to cancer and diabetes. The U.S. Food and Drug Administration plans to require manufacturers to list the amount on food labels, but not for at least a year. The only way to tell if a food has trans fat is by searching for their source, partially hydrogenated oils, in the ingredients list. Even the experts concede that because trans fats travel in so many foods, it would be impossible to eliminate every trace of them.
Full Text Word Count: 480
ISSN: 0032-8006
Accession Number: 8878613
Persistent link to this record: http://0-search.epnet.com.helin.uri.edu:80/direct.asp?an=8878613&db=aph
Database: Academic Search Premier
View Links: Search HELIN
Notes: The URI Library in Kingston has a print subscription to this title.
Choose Language Translate
Section: NUTRITION NEWS
Zero In on Hidden Fats
Contents
Find the Secret Word
Little Bites Add Up
Don't tolerate artery-clogging trans fats in your food, a new report urges
Prevention has said it for years, and now top government experts agree: THERE IS NO SAFE LEVEL OF TRANS FATS. Not only do these fats bolster your bad LDL cholesterol like saturated fats do, but they also crush your heart-protective HDL cholesterol (Institute of Medicine report, 2002). What's more, studies have linked these nasty fats (designed to give food a longer shelf life) to cancer and diabetes.
Find the Secret Word
Fortunately, you can track down the trans fats in your diet and give them the boot. It just takes a little doin'. You won't find trans fats anywhere on a package. The FDA plans to require manufacturers to list the amount on food labels, but you won't see this information for at least a year. Until then, THE ONLY WAY TO TELL IF A FOOD HAS TRANS FATS IS BY SEARCHING FOR THEIR SOURCE—"PARTIALLY HYDROGENATED OILS"—IN THE INGREDIENTS LIST UNDER THE NUTRITION FACTS BOX. Don't forget to check for partially hydrogenated oil in foods that are labeled fat-free.

FIGURE 23.2 Detailed information for one entry under *hydrogenated oils* and *food*

23c Databases containing abstracts

A large number of databases, especially those focusing on academic or technical fields, provide abstracts (brief summaries of a document's content) and sometimes full texts of selected items. A new feature of some of these databases is a link to a library's online subscription to academic and technical journals. It allows readers to obtain the full text of an article in a journal for which the library has an online subscription. (This feature is likely to become more widespread as libraries shift to taking online rather than print subscriptions to scholarly journals.)

PsycINFO
Indexes and provides abstracts of journal articles and books in psychology from 1872 to the present.

CINAHL (OVID)
Indexes and provides abstracts of articles on nursing and other health-related subjects.

Sociological Abstracts (CSA)
Contains abstracts and indexes of articles, books, dissertations, and conference papers in sociology and behavioral sciences. Entries begin in 1963.

Biological Abstracts
Indexes and provides abstracts of articles in journals in the life sciences, beginning in 1990.

America: History and Life (ABC-CLIO)
Abstracts and indexes of journal articles and other materials covering the history of the United States and Canada. Begins in 1964.

MLA Bibliography (FirstSearch)
Provides indexes and abstracts of journals, books, and other materials in language and literature. Begins in 1963.

ComAbstracts
Abstracts of articles in the field of communications, usually covering the latest ten years.

MEDLINE (FirstSearch)
Indexes and provides abstracts of journals in medicine, beginning in 1985.

Historical Abstracts (ABC-CLIO)
Indexes and provides abstracts of articles and other materials on the history of countries other than the United States and Canada, from 1450 to the present.

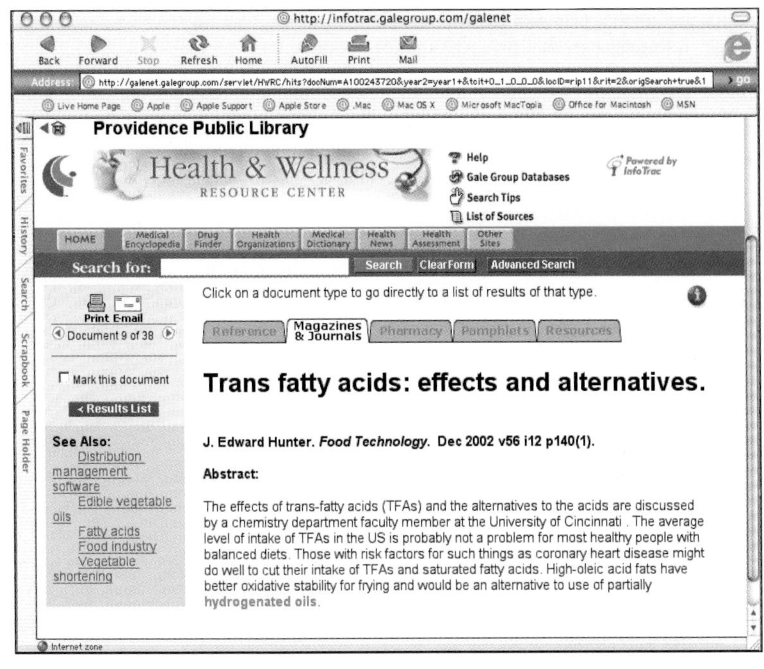

FIGURE 23.3 An abstract from the database *Health Reference Center—Academic*

ERIC (FirstSearch)
Indexes and provides abstracts of journals and other materials in education beginning in 1966.

Jenny Latimer's search for information on the presence and effects of hydrogenated oils in foods, especially snack foods and candy, led her to research in nutrition and health sciences and to the database *Health Reference Center—Academic*, which provides abstracts of scholarly articles and conference presentations. In this database she found an abstract that enabled her to argue in her final paper that the dangers of hydrogenated oils are not as clear as many people claim (see Figure 23.3 above).

23d Indexing or bibliographic databases

Many databases provide titles and publication (or access) information for articles and documents in a specialized field. They can be quite useful for identifying and locating potential sources. But you will generally need to locate the texts of these sources by other means, though some databases do provide a link to a library's online subscription to a scholarly journal.

Art Index (FirstSearch)
Indexes over 400 publications in the arts.

GEOBASE (FirstSearch)
Indexes over 2,000 journals on topics in geology, geography, and ecology.

23e Resource databases

Resource databases provide access to information, images, and documents arranged in the form of an electronic reference work, or they offer tools for researchers. Three databases you might find helpful in conducting research and writing a research paper are listed below.

Web of Science (ISI)
Provides Web access to ISI citation databases (*Science Citation Index*, *Social Sciences Citation Index*, and *Arts & Humanities Citation Index*). Citation indexes allow you to identify the sources used by researchers in their work and to track the strands of a research "conversation." In doing so, you can trace influences on a researcher's or writer's work and identify issues and controversies.

RefWorks (CSA)
Web-based service that helps you to create reference lists or lists of works cited by drawing bibliographical information from online sources. Creates bibliographical entries in more than 100 documentation styles.

WorldCat (FirstSearch)
Catalog of library holdings and Internet resources worldwide.

STRATEGY

These suggestions will help you make effective use of reference databases.

1. Use the databases described in this section only as a starting point. Watch for databases that are even better suited to your needs.
2. Most libraries prepare handouts describing the online databases to which they subscribe and providing detailed, practical advice. The number of available databases and their sophistication are increasing rapidly. These handouts will provide you with up-to-date information on the availability and features of the library's databases and tell you about the latest additions to the collection.
3. Unless your research is in a relatively advanced state, requiring that you focus on specific issues or kinds of information, you should be moving from general databases to more specialized ones.

4. Keep detailed records of the databases you have consulted, the possible sources you have identified, and any abstracts or full texts you have located. Download or print out copies and include them in your research file if you can.
5. Pay attention to links and alternative search paths suggested by a database; they may lead you to unexpected and worthwhile resources. They may also lead you astray, so keep a record of the screens you have viewed in case you need to retrace your path.
6. When the full text of an article is not available online, check your library's catalog to see if it is available. (Many libraries provide links to their catalogs as part of their database programs.)
7. If a database provides only an abstract or a bibliographical reference to an article, check if the database will email you the full text of articles you believe will be useful. Some databases charge for this service; others will provide texts for free.

Exercise 1

Spend some time searching electronic databases (general and specialized) for possible sources, and take notes on one or more full-text documents appropriate for your project. Then list briefly what you consider the advantages and disadvantages of databases as a resource.

23f Evaluating database resources

Database texts are often electronic versions of printed texts—books from reputable publishers, articles from scholarly or well-known periodicals, government documents—which have been reviewed by experts and produced with editorial checks. Even so, once you locate these sources, you'll need to decide whether they are appropriate for your research community and your questions and whether they support or deepen your thesis.

Other database texts appear only in electronic form, created by organizations, individual authors, or even database providers themselves. To evaluate both kinds of texts, the questions on pages 332–333 for evaluating library sources will be helpful. Some additional questions for database sources follow.

Questions for evaluating database sources

- Does the database provider, the journal or periodical, or the sponsoring organization have a reputation for balance and accuracy? Is it an advocate whose views require caution?

- Is any abstract or summary consistent with the title of the source (if the full text is not provided) or with other texts by the same author or from the same organization?
- Is the electronic document complete, or has it been excerpted or otherwise altered from the print original? Are changes from the original indicated clearly? Are the changes consistent with the purpose and perspective of the original text?
- Are the sources of documents clearly indicated in the electronic text?
- Do the electronic documents cite sources in conventional ways?
- Are the goals and coverage of a database indicated clearly?

CHAPTER 24
Internet Resources

Many writers begin their research on the World Wide Web. They do so because of its accessibility, the vast number and wide range of resources available, and the currentness of much of the information and opinions that Web sites offer. But Web research has important limitations, too. The texts are often shorter, less detailed, and less fully developed in explanation or argument than print texts. The reviewing and editorial processes to which print texts are often submitted are frequently missing from Web sites. And the absence of cataloging and indexing systems like the Library of Congress classifications for printed books makes the use of search tools and a well-thought-out search strategy a necessity.

Critical evaluation, an important part of your research in printed sources, is even more important when you review Web sites (see 24d). As a consequence, you should generally make these sources only a part—not the whole—of the resources on which you draw.

24a Internet search strategy

Your search strategy for Internet resources should be part of your general search strategy, which also covers library and field resources. In creating your Internet search strategy, emphasize diversity. Go beyond Web sites to electronic versions of printed texts (books, magazines, scholarly and professional journals, newspapers); electronic databases and collections of documents (including government publications, discussed in 22d); Internet discussion groups and newsgroups; visual and audio resources on the Web; synchronous devices including Webcams; and the links embedded in Webbed texts.

The sheer volume of available resources and the lack of a standard catalog or classification system for Web and Internet documents mean you should know the available search tools, their strengths and their weaknesses, and you should include these tools in your search strategy.

> **STRATEGY**
>
> Turn your plan for Internet research into a checklist. The checklist can help you to avoid following distracting paths and options and to focus on the worthwhile leads you discover during the research process.

Electronic Resources: A Planning List

Use the following list as a reminder to include a wide range of electronic resources in your research.

- Web sites
- Online versions of printed texts
- Online databases (see Chapter 23)
- Online collections of documents
- Discussion groups and newsgroups
- Visual and audio documents
- Synchronous devices
- Links

24b Search engines

The Web consists of documents ("pages" and "sites," which are collections of pages) that you can access using an address called a URL (Uniform Resource Locator) or by a link embedded in a Web document (usually a logo or a highlighted portion of text). To contact a Web site, you need a browser such as *Internet Explorer* or *Mozilla Firefox*. (The electronic addresses for Internet sites, such as discussion groups, work in similar ways except that the sites do not employ links.)

INTERNET RESOURCES FOR THREE COMMUNITIES

ACADEMIC SETTINGS	PUBLIC SETTINGS	WORK SETTINGS
Some scholarly and technical resources are available online. Researchers need to evaluate the information and conclusions carefully, paying particular attention to the people or organizations responsible for a document and to the accuracy and level of bias in a text. Some Web search engines, such as <*Google.scholar*>, specialize in locating scholarly and technical Web resources. More general search engines may not identify such resources.	Web sites provide insights into public concerns and issues, along with detailed information. Discussion sites may provide an in-depth view of differing opinions, arguments, and counterarguments. Accuracy and bias is always a concern with Web and Internet documents, so researchers need to evaluate carefully the sources of documents and the information they contain as well as the purposes and biases of the people responsible for them.	The Web provides many up-to-date documents for organizations responding to internal or external challenges. Information on the Web may be copyrighted or proprietary, however, so borrowing or implementing material may require formal permission from those responsible for a Web site. Web sites may also provide the most current information on new developments or policies—information whose accuracy generally needs to be carefully evaluated.

To locate sites relevant to your research, use a **search engine,** an electronic search tool that identifies and gathers data about Web sites and organizes information about those sites for your use. (Many search engines will also identify Internet sites such as discussion groups.) The kinds of sites a search engine identifies, the kinds of information it gathers, and the ways it selects and organizes information depend on two things: (1) the principles on which the search engine operates and (2) the questions you ask of it.

1 General search engines

General search engines typically search for resources according to keywords or phrases you type into a field. Different search engines are likely to produce different lists of sources. Search engines do not index the entire Web; each one examines only a part of the potential sites on the Web, some more, some less. When their coverage overlaps, you will get similar results; when it does not, each search engine will provide useful references not reported by the others. It is worth your while, therefore, to use several search engines.

GENERAL SEARCH ENGINES

Google	<http://www.google.com>
AltaVista	<http://altavista.com>
Yahoo!	<http://www.yahoo.com>
AllTheWeb	<http://alltheweb.com/>
Wisenut	<http://wisenut.com>
Lycos	<http://www.lycos.com>
Teoma	<http://www.teoma.com>
HotBot	<http://hotbot.com/>

In addition, the Web site descriptions that different search engines provide can vary considerably. Since these descriptions often shape your decision to consult or ignore a site, you need to read them carefully.

Rashelle Jackson was working on a project guided by this research question: "What techniques used in hip-hop performance make it different from other kinds of music?" She typed the words *hip hop techniques* into several search engines, and each responded with lists of resources that included a site with the title "The Phonograph Turntable and Performance Practice in Hip Hop Music." She realized right away that the title of the site indicated it was appropriate for her topic. However, the first three descriptions she read were uninformative, incomplete, even misleading. Only the fourth gave her a good idea of the site's contents and its relevance to her search (see Figure 24.1 on p. 348).

The Phonograph Turntable and Performance Practice in **Hip Hop** ...
... This transformation has been concurrent with the invention by the **Hip Hop** DJ of a ... sliding lever which allows the performer to effect certain **techniques** on a ...

The **Phonograph Turntable** and Performance Practice in **Hip Hop** Music
The **Phonograph Turntable** and Performance Practice in **Hip Hop** Music Miles White ... globalization of **Hip Hop** music and culture ... invention by the **Hip Hop** DJ of a new technical ... capabilities of...

The **Phonograph Turntable** and Performance Practice in **Hip Hop** Music
White. Introduction...

The **Phonograph Turntable** and Performance Practice in **Hip Hop** Music
The **Phonograph Turntable** and Performance Practice in **Hip Hop** Music Miles White ... globalization of **Hip Hop** music and culture ... invention by the **Hip Hop** DJ of a new technical ... capabilities of the **phonograph**, a process which ... Description: The popularization and globalization of **Hip Hop** music and culture over the past twenty or so years has provided new and refreshing areas of inquiry and research across a number of academic disciplines and critical approaches. The scholarly work...

FIGURE 24.1 Search engine results for the keywords *hip hop techniques*

For every potentially relevant or useful Web site your search engine returns, you will likely have to peruse many, many descriptions of sites that are clearly irrelevant, oversimplified, dated, or untrustworthy. Others may seem loosely related or possibly relevant, however, and worth a look. They could provide fresh perspectives and useful examples or information.

2 Disappointing searches

Standard searches sometimes return disappointing or confusing results. The keywords or phrases you enter may not be the ones used by some sites, and the search engine passes them by. When that happens, try synonyms or related words and phrases. In searching for information on techniques employed in hip hop performances, Rashelle Jackson employed a variety of terms: *hip hop techniques*, *DJ techniques*, *scratching*, *cueing*, *beatboxing*, *crossfader technique*, *beat matching*, and other terms she drew from her own knowledge and the sources she consulted. Each term produced a slightly different list of sources, with some overlap.

Your query may be appropriate but the results disappointing because of a quirk in the search engine. For instance, in researching a paper on the singer Amy Grant, you might type in her name and get a few useful references and others that appear simply because they contain the two words of her name—in unconnected form: "List of recent graduates: . . . **Amy** Hollings, Rebecca Olivera, **Grant** Snyder. . . ."

3 Advanced searches

Some search engines allow you to avoid disappointing results by conducting more focused searches using **Boolean** terms (or **operators**) to construct your queries. To expand or limit your electronic search, use Boolean logic to link terms with the operators OR, AND, and NOT. Consult the instructions on the main page of the search engine to see if this strategy will help; *Google*, for example, does not require Boolean operators because they are built into the system.

OR (expands): *X* OR *Y*	Search for either term (documents referring to either *X* or *Y*)
AND (restricts): *X* AND *Y*	Search for both terms (documents referring to both *X* and *Y*, but not to either alone)
NOT (excludes): *X* NOT *Y*	Search for *X* unless *X* includes the term *Y* (documents referring to *X*, except those that also refer to *Y*)

Other search engines offer advanced options (or screens) that enable you to specify and focus the conditions of a search (see Figure 24.2 on p. 350).

Some general search engines return references to Internet resources other than Web sites, including discussion lists, newsgroups, and chat rooms. Be alert for these resources; they can expand the range of your research.

DISCOVERING A SEARCH ENGINE'S CAPABILITIES

At the main page of your search engine, find the link to the page that explains the system ("search tips," "about this site," etc.). Find answers to as many of the following questions as possible.

- How is the system organized?
- What are the basic search procedures?
- Does the engine recognize Boolean operators? Which ones?
- Does the engine exclude "stop words" such as *where* and *how,* which slow down a search? If so, what command executes that exclusion?

(continued)

DISCOVERING A SEARCH ENGINE'S CAPABILITIES (*continued*)

- What are the advanced search features? What procedures can you use to conduct a search *within* preliminary results?
- Can you personalize the engine to save yourself time whenever you use it?
- How are results displayed? Can you vary the parameters of that display, such as increasing the number on each page while decreasing the length of the annotations, or vice versa?

4 Metasearch sites

A **metasearch** site enables you to conduct your search using several search engines simultaneously—and then to compare the results. Conducted early in your research, a metasearch can help you identify which search engines are most likely to be useful for your task. Metasearches can also suggest interesting new directions for your inquiry. Here are three useful sites.

Dogpile	<http://dogpile.com>
Momma	<http://www.momma.com>
Metacrawler	<http://metacrawler.com>

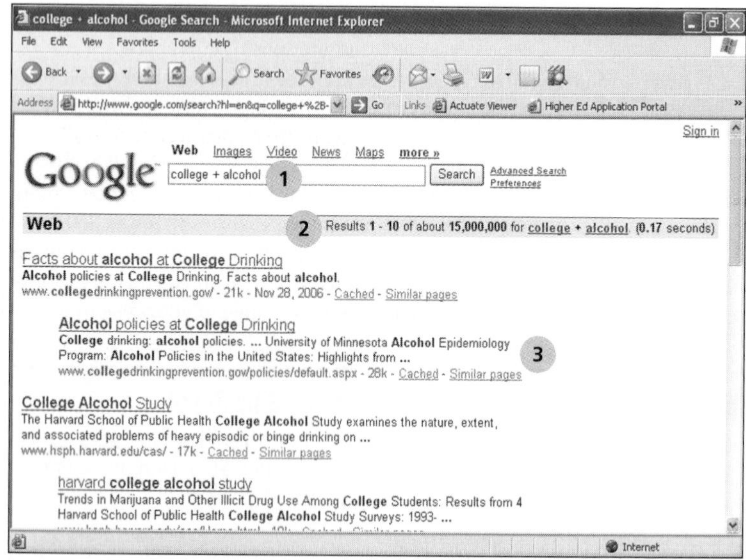

1 Keywords used in search
2 Results of search
3 One source with annotation

FIGURE 24.2 Results of a *Google* search using the keywords *college* and *alcohol*

5 Focused search sites and question-oriented sites

Some search sites focus on specific disciplines, fields of inquiry, or content areas. As you narrow your search or look for more complex information or the results of academic studies, these focused search sites become more useful. Academic research papers (in sociology, art history, and literature, for example) can benefit especially from specialized sites such as *Google Scholar* at <http://scholar.google.com>.

Other search tools allow you to ask questions rather than use keywords: for example, *Ask* at <http://ask.com>. Or they may link keyword queries to what (sometimes) are related, relevant resources as does *WebReference* at <http://webreference.com>.

24c Kinds of Web sites

To identify and use appropriate resources on the World Wide Web and the Internet, you should recognize some important kinds of Web sites and Internet sites, their content and purposes, and their uses.

1 Individual Web sites

Individual Web sites are not necessarily *about* individuals, though they may be, as is the case with *home pages* created by individuals to share events in their lives, to broadcast their opinions or share their collections—of memorabilia, texts, and the like. Although many Web sites are so idiosyncratic or personal as to be of little use for research (unless you are researching the home page phenomenon itself), others may prove to be good resources. Some home pages share accounts of experiences you can cite as examples: white-water rafting, service on a United Nations peacekeeping force, work on an oil rig in Northern Alaska.

Many people maintain Web sites about topics that fascinate them or about issues on which they have strong opinions (see 24c-2). Though some such sources are sloppy, out of date, inaccurate, or misleading, others are rich sources of information and ideas and may offer links to more valuable resources. Approach these resources critically, but with an awareness of their potential usefulness. At the very least, they may help you understand the attitudes at least some of your readers will have about your topic.

STRATEGY

Home pages maintained by researchers often contain links to their research articles, both those that have appeared in print and those in progress. If you encounter the work of active researchers in the course of your inquiries, consider looking up their home pages to see if they provide easy access to the researcher's ongoing work or to related work by other researchers.

2 Blogs

Blogs are Web sites offering daily or weekly accounts of one person's activities and thoughts. From people in war zones, in dangerous parts of the world, or in important jobs, they can be fascinating sources of information. Others can be just plain boring. Nonetheless, important public figures, corporate executives, and scientists and researchers in many fields maintain blogs, as do ordinary people caught up in extraordinary circumstances, such as a natural disaster or individuals and groups providing political commentary.

The material available on blogs can be fascinating and useful, especially when they are maintained by people of power and influence, by authorities in a field, or by writers of special skill. Yet such blogs can be untrustworthy, especially those maintained by people about whom we readers know little or nothing. Before drawing on blogs or home pages for your research, find out as much as you can about the person(s) responsible for them, and evaluate their contents critically (see 24d).

3 Sponsored Web sites

Organizations of all kinds sponsor Web sites: public, private, corporate, academic, governmental, religious, and social. The suffixes on the electronic addresses often indicate what kind of organization the sponsor is.

edu	educational institution
gov	government agency
org	nonprofit or service organization
com	business organization (commercial)
net	network organization

A sponsored Web site may be little more than a billboard or a marketing device, yet sponsored Web sites can also be sources of up-to-date information and articulate, fair advocates for a cause. The usefulness and the integrity of a site generally depend on the character of the sponsoring organization and the resources devoted to creating and maintaining it. When examining sponsored Web sites, use the evaluation questions for online resources (24d) and draw information and ideas from the site with an awareness of its purpose and the bias of the sponsoring organization.

4 Advocacy Web sites

Advocacy Web sites explain or defend an organization's actions and beliefs and argue for specific policies (see Figure 24.3). Although they are biased in favor of the organization's position—after all, they *advocate* for their own point of view—many are of high quality, explaining positions, answering critics, and providing *detailed* supporting evidence and documentation along with lists of readings on a topic or issue. Some even provide links to Web sites with opposing points of view as a way of stimulating open discussion.

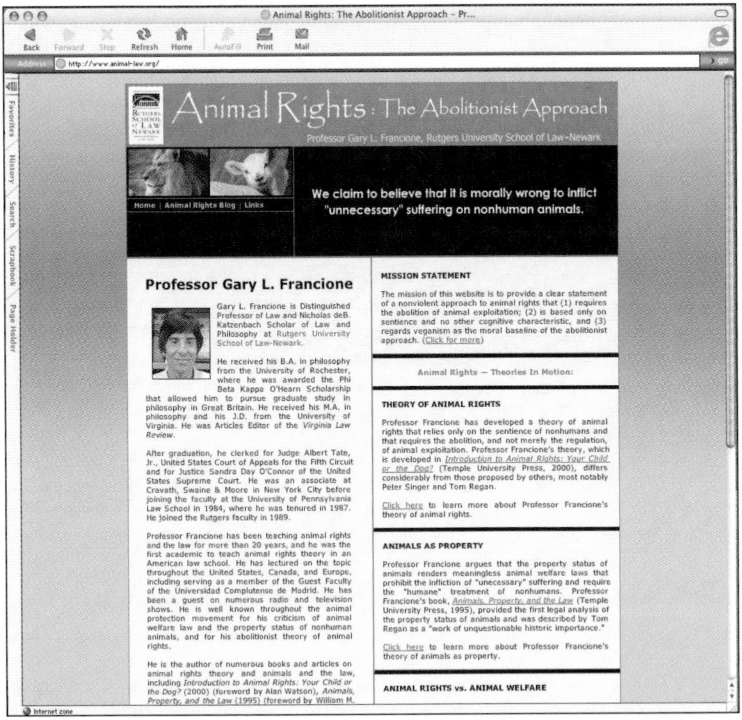

FIGURE 24.3 Home page of an advocacy Web site

Advocacy Web sites include public service Web sites that encourage responsible behavior or action for public health and safety. Unfortunately, good intentions do not guarantee the accuracy or currency of information, and you need to approach these sites critically as you would any other.

5 Informational Web sites

Informational Web sites may focus on a particular subject such as sleep research, horror movies, or poetry from the Beat Generation of the 1950s, or an activity such as an environmental project or steps to developing a healthy lifestyle. Or they may focus on the sponsoring institution itself, providing information about its activities, ongoing research projects, and research results. Carefully organized informational Web sites provide tables of data, historical background, reports of research, answers to frequently asked questions (FAQs), links, and lists of references. Large Web sites may also provide site maps and allow keyword searches.

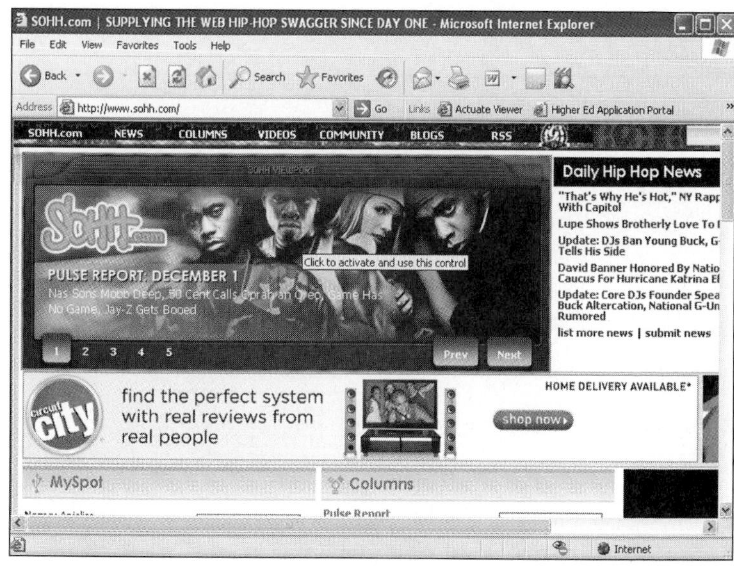

FIGURE 24.4 Commercially sponsored Web site SOHH.com devoted to hip hop

While looking for information for a paper on the techniques used in hip hop performances, Rashelle Jackson encountered the Web site shown in Figure 24.4. She identified it as a commercially sponsored Web site featuring hip hop related products, but it also offered the kinds of information she wanted and links to a host of other potentially useful sites.

Be aware, however, that many informational Web sites are poorly organized, unevenly developed, and even untrustworthy. Look on the Web site for information about the sponsoring organization, how information for the Web site is gathered and maintained, and the date of the last update. To investigate the usefulness and trustworthiness of a particular informational Web site, draw on the advice for evaluating online sources presented in 24d.

6 Research-oriented Web sites

Research-oriented Web sites are in a broad sense informational, but they are more narrowly focused than most informational Web sites, and they are arranged in different ways. Research-oriented Web sites typically contain one or more of the following.

1. Full texts of research reports (sometimes twenty-five or more pages long)
2. Summaries of completed or ongoing research projects

FIGURE 24.5 Home page for the American Psychological Association Web site

3. Electronic texts of research articles that appeared in print journals or book-length collections
4. Extensive data frequently presented in the form of downloadable tables, graphs, and charts or available as texts of field notes and discussions of statistics
5. Reviews of current research
6. Texts of unpublished conference papers and other presentations
7. Announcements of grants, conferences, and forthcoming publications
8. Addresses or phone numbers for researchers
9. Bibliographies of books and articles; links to related Web sites

Universities, research institutes, and professional organizations often maintain research-oriented Web sites, as is the case with the Web site maintained by the American Psychological Association (see Figure 24.5).

7 Archival Web sites

Web sites can act as repositories, or **archives,** for collections of documents, images, data, and sound recordings. Web site creators have assembled archives on a wide range of subjects. Most useful are historical records, records of recent events, and records of artistic performances and creations.

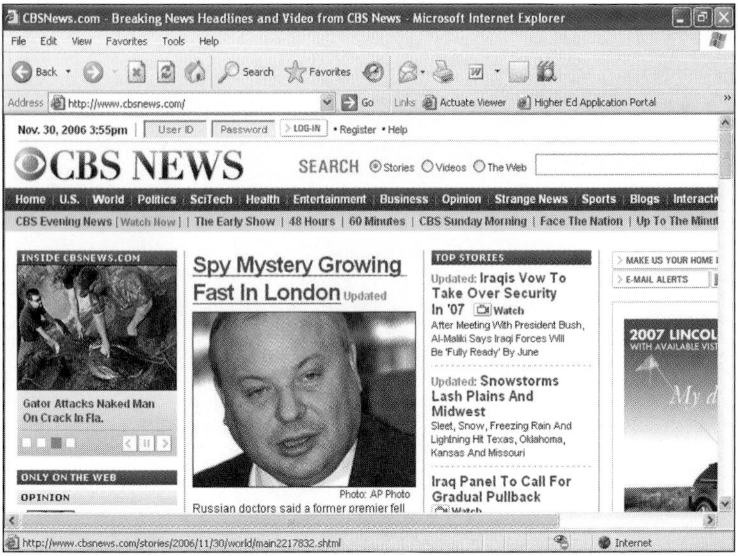

FIGURE 24.6 Current events Web site with photos; such sites may also include audiovisuals

1. **Historical records.** Important events (Easter Uprising in Dublin, Ireland, 1916; Gulf War; Presidential Election of 1948); technological developments (history of flight, early microcomputers); historical periods (T'ang Dynasty, Mannerist Period in Italian Art); and similar historical subjects all have online collections of materials.
2. **Records of recent events.** Collections recording recent occurrences, gatherings, and political events appear on the Web as soon as a day or two after the event, with updates and expansions occurring frequently (see Figure 24.6). Sites devoted to important events often provide images, texts, streaming video, and audio while the events are occurring.
3. **Records of artistic performances and creations.** Background information, production details, reviews and interpretive studies, and interviews with artists and participants are available on Web sites devoted to specific creations and performances (films, concert tours, shows in galleries). See Figure 24.7.

8 Online periodicals and books; electronic versions of print publications

Online magazines, newspapers, and scholarly journals are similar to print publications in many ways. Indeed, many appear in both online and print versions.

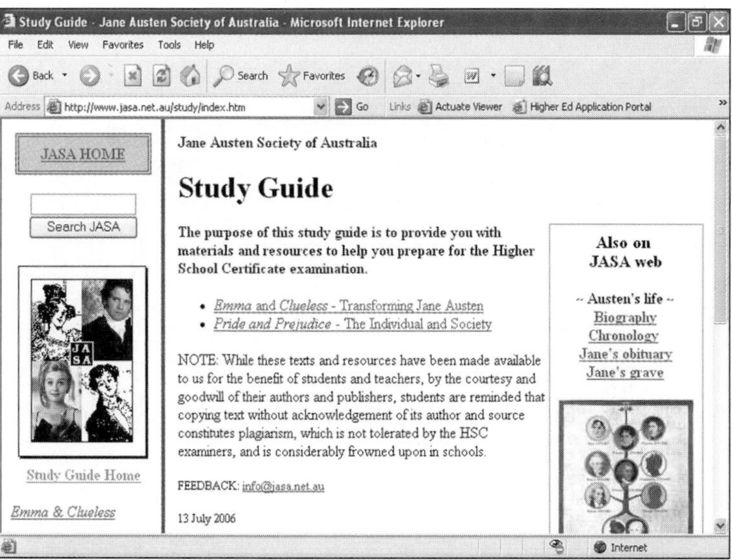

FIGURE 24.7 Web site devoted to Jane Austen weaves literary history with information on film performances

Newsweek <http://www.newsweek.com>
Business Week <http://www.businessweek.com>
Weekly Standard <http://www.weeklystandard.com>
The Nation <http://www.thenation.com>
Dallas Star-Telegram <http://www.dfw.com>

Many online sites go one step further and make back issues or selected articles available, as is the case with the following publications.

Scientific American (general interest magazine of science and technology) <http://www.sciam.com>
Social Text (academic journal of social and political issues) <http://www.nyu.edu/pubs/socialtext>
Salon (general interest magazine of social and cultural commentary) <http://www.salon.com>

24c source

Online publications like these often make use of the Web's ability to incorporate audio clips and streaming video or to display simultaneously different sections of text in contrasting formats or *frames* (see Figure 24.8 on p. 358).

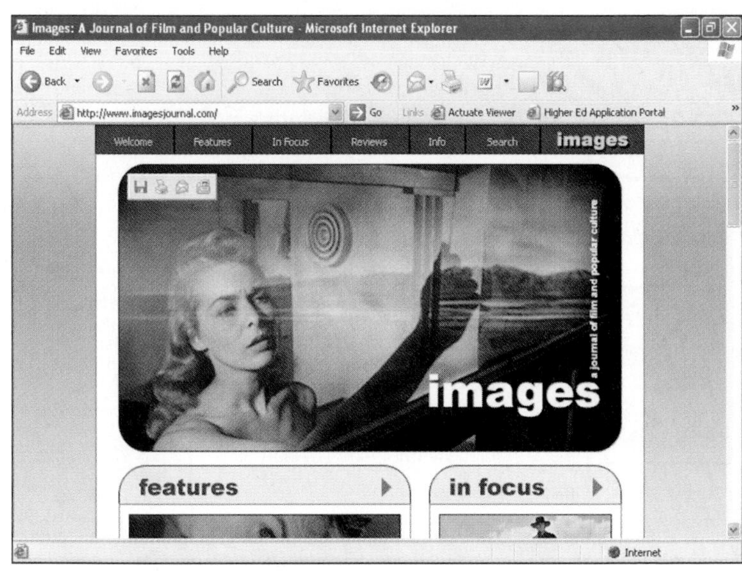

FIGURE 24.8 A Web site that incorporates audio clips and streaming video

Classic works of literature, major historical texts, biographies, and similar works that appeared first in print are now available in online libraries like *Berkeley Digital Library SunSite* at <http://sunsite.Berkeley.edu> and *Gutenberg Project* at <http://promo.net/pg/>. Some books now appear only online, though that trend is developing slowly.

9 Government publications sites

Government publications on an astonishing range of topics are available in print form in most college and university libraries (22d). In addition, many government agencies have spent considerable effort developing Web sites for access to their reports and documents. Use the following sites to identify government publications relevant to your research.

FirstGov	<http://www.firstgov.gov>
Catalog of U.S. Government Publications	<http://www.access.gpo.gov/su_docs/locators/cgp>
FedStats	<http://www.fedstats.gov/search.html>
FedWord	<http://www.fedword.gov>

10 Discussion groups and newsgroups

The Internet and the Web play host to many discussion groups, some focusing on highly specialized topics like beekeeping, small countries in Eastern Europe or Africa, and poetry slams. The postings to such lists vary in quality, from inquiries by novices to discussions and responses from nationally recognized experts. It can be difficult to judge the quality of contributions because the writers may identify themselves only by screen names. (See 24d for a discussion of ways to evaluate materials from such sources.)

A **discussion group** posts messages from members of a mailing list to all other members and gives them a chance to respond. **Newsgroups** or **bulletin boards** are open sites where you can post messages or questions of your own and read postings from other people. Many search engines will help you locate postings. Those in Figures 24.9 and 24.10 on pages 360 and 361 are from *Google*.

24d Evaluating online resources

Online sources pose special problems for evaluation. Many Web sites are produced without the editorial checks and balances that make books from reputable publishers or articles in scholarly journals and well-known magazines relatively trustworthy sources. You can begin evaluating Internet and Web sources using questions developed by Paula Mathieu, formerly at the University of Illinois, Chicago, as part of the Critical Resources in Teaching with Technology (CRITT) project.

Evaluation questions

1. **Who benefits? What difference does that make?** The Web pages accessible at <http://www.got-milk.com/mmmilk/index.html>, for example, seem dedicated entirely to the reader's health, as illustrated in Figure 24.11 on page 362. Perhaps the three cups will indeed benefit most readers. With a little bit of critical thinking, however, these readers can easily recognize that milk producers and distributors will also benefit from sales of those three cups a day.
2. **Who's talking? What difference does that make?** The "speaker" responsible for all the positive facts about milk is not clearly identified in the pages. The speaker is, in fact, the Southeast United Dairy Industry Association (SUDIA), an organization of 5,000 dairy farmers. Can readers trust the "facts" presented by this group that goes unnamed in the pages? Perhaps. But it seems unlikely that all the "facts" will appear on the pages, especially those that might call into question an unqualified endorsement of milk's goodness.

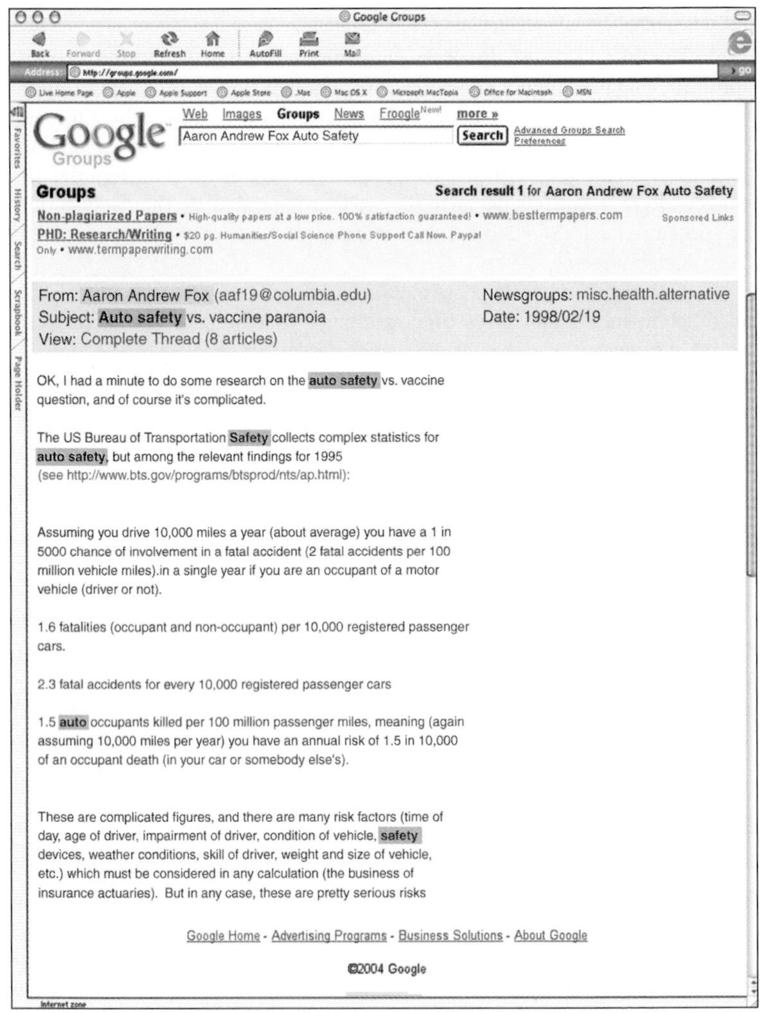

FIGURE 24.9 Discussion group message from *Google* with data on driving fatalities

In contrast, consider the Web page at <http://www.notmilk.com/drlarsen.html> (see Figure 24.12 on p. 363). This site provides a contrary voice, linking milk drinking to disease. The article first appeared in *International Health News*, which is published by the author of the article. The Web site for *International Health News* contains the disclaimer: "International Health News does not provide medical advice."

Jongwon Park Beekeeping – Google Groups

Back Forward Stop Refresh Home AutoFill Print Mail

Address: http://groups.google.com/groups/search?q=Jongwon+Park+Beekeeping&qt_s=Search+Groups

Live Home Page Apple Apple Support Apple Store .Mac Mac OS X Microsoft MacTopia Office for Macintosh MSN

Favorites History Search Scrapbook Page Holder

Google Groups

Web Images **Groups** News Froogle[New!] **more »**

Jongwon Park Beekeeping **Search** Advanced Groups Search Preferences

Groups **Search result 1** for **Jongwon Park Beekeeping**

From: **Jongwon Park** (jongwonp@vt.edu) Search Result 1
Subject: Help for Research: The Technology Transfer in **Beekeeping** Through Internet.
Newsgroups: sci.agriculture.**beekeeping** This is the only article in this thread
Date: 1995/12/20 View: Original Format

Please, allow me to introduce myself. I am a graduate student of Science and Technology Studies Program in Virginia Polytechnic Institute and State University. For my graduate seminar class -- "Technology Transfer", I am writing the term paper about the use of Internet in **beekeeping** community for the technology transfer.

Traditionally, technology transfer was viewed as; First, the technology is developed in the place of research (usually in the laboratory) and applied in the place of production. Second, the artifacts or the piece of machinary travels from one place to the other place. In these view, the transfer is one-directional and simple displacement of the machine (usually from the so called first worlds to the third worlds).

In my study, I am trying to understand the interactions between different communities and show that the transfer occurs in both directions between research and practical application. I also would like to argue that the travels of the technological artefacts involves cultural changes. In **beekeeping** community, I think that academic researchers, commercial beekeepers and hobbyists forms a distinguishable sub-communities. I also think that these three groups have different interests and cultures. Sometimes these groups do not agree with each other about some technical knowledge such as **beekeeping** management techniques. (i.e. How to find the queen?) Moreover, the researchers and beekeepers learn from each other rather than the researchers teach the beekeepers what to do. Since **beekeeping** involves many factors which are very difficult to control, it seems to me that **beekeeping** practice provides a great example of technology transfer.

I am interested in the discussion occured in this newsgroup in which the researchers and practical beekeepers disagree with each other. In other words, I am interested in the contraversial stories about **beekeeping**. Or, the cases in which researchers learned from beekeepers. In addition, I am also interested in what can be called, "Falklore Wisdom" in **beekeeping**. If anybody can remember the beekeepers' maxims or saved the threads of contraversial discussion, please send it to me to the address; JONGWONP@VT.EDU
I also welcome any suggestions for my research.

I have followed discussions in this newsgroup for three months now. I also reviewed the logs of bee-list. However, I was not able to find enough cases I am interested in. I was advised by Adam Finkelstein (the discussion with Adam inspired my research) to post my request in this newsgroup. After I finish my termpaper, I will post it to this newsgroup.

Please forgive me if I interupted the discussion of this newsgroup.
Jongwon Park

Google Home - Advertising Programs - Business Solutions - About Google

Internet zone

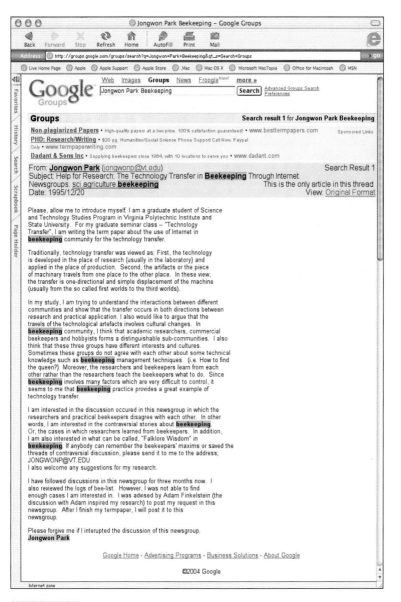

FIGURE 24.10 Discussion group message from *Google* requesting help with personal research

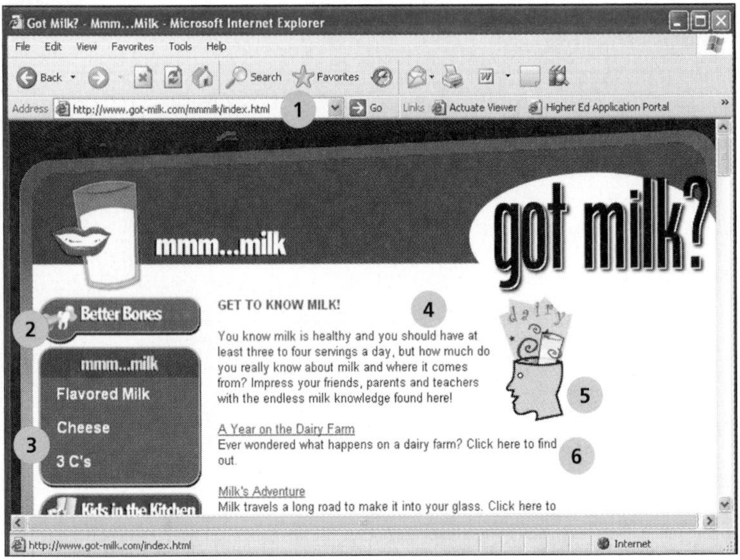

1. Commercial site
2. Includes features designed to appeal to readers
3. Offers personal analysis of diet and exercise
4. Advocates drinking milk
5. Uses graphics to convey information
6. Offers more information

FIGURE 24.11 Web page sponsored by the Southeast United Dairy Industry Association (SUDIA)

The *International Health News* Web site also announces its focus on alternative forms of medicine. The author, Hans R. Larsen, says little about his training or scientific experience except to indicate that he has a Master of Science degree in chemical engineering. For the most part, therefore, the author leaves readers to judge what he says based on the quality of his evidence and reasoning. He does provide scientific support, but some readers may find the reasoning strained and the tone a bit extreme.

A third Web site, <http://digestive.niddk.nih.gov/ddiseases/pubs/lactoseintolerance.htm>, offers an additional perspective on milk and dairy products, pointing out that between 30 and 50 million Americans are lactose intolerant, including 75% of African Americans and Native Americans and 90% of Asian Americans (see Figure 24.13 on p. 364). This site, sponsored by the National Digestive Diseases Information

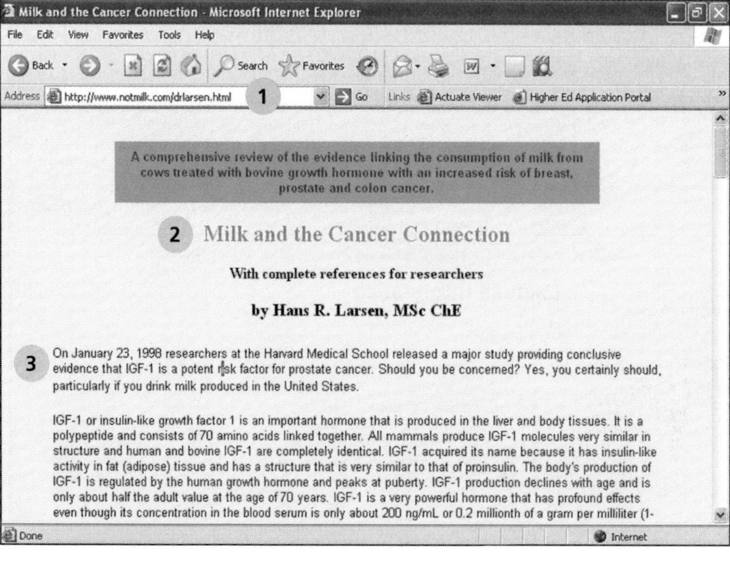

1 Organizational site
2 Uses title to introduce position
3 Cites authority

FIGURE 24.12 Web page sponsored by <notmilk.com>

Clearinghouse (an organization that is part of the federal government's National Institutes of Health), certainly can be trusted for its authority and integrity. Notice that the authors, who "are" the NDDIC, make no judgments about the value of dairy products; their role is to present information impartially and truthfully.

To critically analyze and interpret these sites, the motivations of each "author" clearly must be taken into account. One has a commercial interest: sell as much milk, and as many dairy products, as possible, regardless of the consequences. Another has a political and social interest: stop the consumption of dairy products with an unnatural additive. A third has an informational interest: give the public up-to-date, factual information and recommendations from the most authoritative research and sources possible, regardless of what consequences that information may have for different organizations and businesses.

3. **What's missing? What difference does that make?** Why does the first Web site ignore all kinds of milk other than cow's milk: soy milk, rice milk, goat's milk, sheep's milk, coconut milk? The selective nature of the presentation, its commercial purpose, and its strategies become

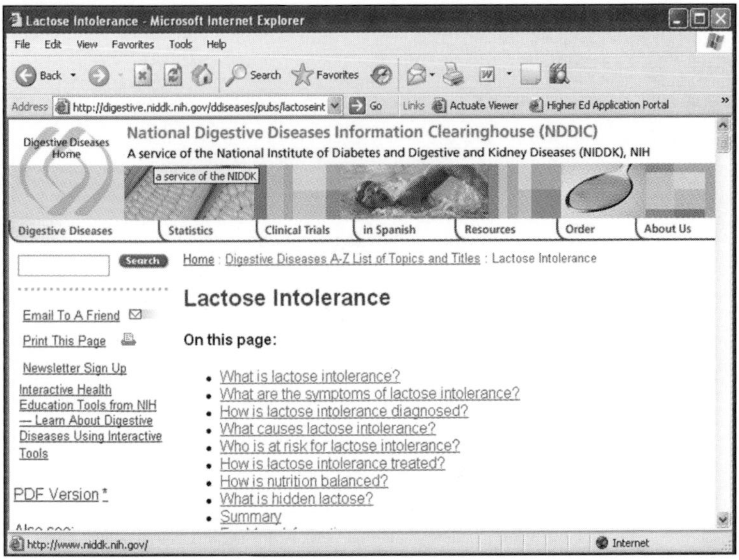

FIGURE 24.13 Web page sponsored by the National Digestive Diseases Information Clearinghouse

even clearer when a reader asks what is left out and why. On the second site, the writer dismisses research in favor of the use of IGF-1 by saying that the data come from the drug's manufacturers and that questions have been raised about its use—without pointing out specifically what is wrong with the data or indicating what the questions are.

STRATEGY

Some Web pages may provide you with no information about the source or author. How, then, can you begin to figure out where it came from? Start by looking carefully at the URL. Web searches often take you to a page deep in the hierarchy of a Web site. You may need to "back up" to a higher level. Remember that main Web sites end in several major suffixes (*org*, *edu*, *gov*, and *com*, meaning "organization," "educational institution," "government site," and "commercial site"). To get back up to higher pages, erase a section of the subsidiary suffix and enter that address into your browser. To get to the main or "home" page, erase everything after the *org*, *edu*, *gov*, or *com*.

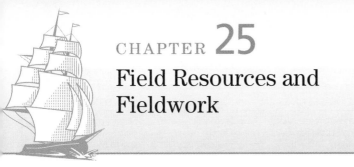

CHAPTER 25 Field Resources and Fieldwork

Much of the research you've done in school has probably focused on published sources (books, articles, Web texts). Many researchers, however, also gather information firsthand, "in the field." When you conduct **field research,** you collect information directly from the observation of events, places, and phenomena, or from **informants,** people you interview or survey.

25a Field research

You may wonder what you can learn from people and events "out there," beyond a library or research lab. But if you drove a car today, you probably passed a traffic light that was timed as a result of field research on traffic patterns in the area. If you picked up something to eat at the drive-through of a fast-food restaurant, the service and food you received were probably influenced by surveys other patrons had filled out for market-research companies. If you drank from a water fountain on your way to class, the source of that water is likely to be tested constantly, through field research, to assess its contents and safety.

Researchers have many reasons for wanting to collect and analyze information through field research. Consider the range and variety of field research being conducted in various settings.

- **Academic settings.** Field researchers in disciplines like sociology, psychology, business, education, and urban planning often want to study people's behaviors or outlooks in order to identify patterns or causes and effects. Anthropologists, for example, study human and social behavior by immersing themselves as much as possible in a culture: they make observations, participate in events or rituals, take copious notes, and try to make sense of their experiences and records. When field research takes the form of scientific inquiry in disciplines like chemistry, engineering, and pharmacy, it investigates how substances, organisms, objects, and machines work or can be constructed.
- **Public settings.** Field researchers in public settings often collect and interpret people's opinions, attitudes, and values, especially in relation to policies, public programs, and institutions as well as to issues affecting all or part of a society. Government-sponsored research in the

FIELD RESEARCH IN THREE COMMUNITIES		
ACADEMIC SETTINGS	**PUBLIC SETTINGS**	**WORK SETTINGS**
Interviews with researchers and specialists can provide useful information on the current state of knowledge and on current topics of interest. Surveys, observations, and interviews can be used to gather data to address research questions that build on prior research or to address fresh topics.	Surveys can identify public opinion, needs, and concerns. Interviews may provide in-depth understanding of policies and problems. Observations and ethnographic studies may help identify the success or failure of policies and procedures.	Surveys can identify procedures, attitudes, and shared concerns or problems. Interviews and questionnaires can provide information on possible solutions to problems or on new products and services. Ethnographic research can uncover difficulties in operations or with an organization's structure and policies. Surveys and ethnographic research can also help gauge the likely success of a new procedure or product.

public interest provides important information that can have profound effects on laws and regulations. Researchers working for the Environmental Protection Agency, for example, collect samples of soil, water, and air from across the country in order to measure the levels of pollutants or contaminants.

- **Work settings.** Field researchers in businesses and other organizations often look at how customers (or staff) act and interact, focusing on problems, programs, or future actions and choices. Industrial researchers study a particular manufacturing plant to see if they can find inefficiencies in production; market researchers conduct extensive polls and surveys to gauge the public's interest in a certain product, and they may recruit people to take taste tests or engage in "focus groups" to provide information for the purposes of improving a product or refining a marketing strategy.

In these and thousands of other cases, research involves the firsthand collection and analysis of data.

Yet fieldwork doesn't exclude information from published resources. In most cases, field researchers supplement their work with data gathered by other researchers and writers, or they refer to prior research in order to extend or refine it. Still, your own fieldwork will yield original results—that is, the material in your research paper or report will come from your work, not from somebody else's research, and the information and ideas you present are more likely to be fresh and original.

25b Meaningful field research

Because field research usually involves gathering and analyzing "raw" data, the results of research can be surprising. For example, you might believe that most students on your campus have similar opinions about campus food. But after conducting a survey or questionnaire, you could find that opinions are more varied or complicated than you thought, depending on whether respondents live in the dorms and eat the same food for dinner ("too much of the same") or live off campus and find that the food isn't too bad compared to what they usually prepare for themselves. So it's important that you begin your field research with a completely open mind or a "neutral" perspective on what you're investigating.

If you launch your original field research too quickly, you might overlook important perspectives or miss the chance to think more carefully about your data-gathering process. Instead, do some background research before beginning a field research project. What have other people said or found out about your topic? What problems or unanswered questions arise from their work? Be sure to plan your fieldwork carefully (see pp. 369–370, 371, and 374) so that you won't feel you've missed something important.

Good field research also involves interpretation. Be prepared to give the data you collect the same kind of critical "reading" and analysis you give to print and electronic resources (see 22e, 23f, and 24d). Those same sources can help you to make sense of your data or reach conclusions from it. Of course, the goals of your fieldwork and the method you employ should depend on both your writing tasks and the research community you're addressing.

25c Surveys, polls, and questionnaires

A common type of field research for college papers involves collecting attitudinal or factual data from students, faculty, or people in the vicinity of the campus. Research in public and work settings often relies on these techniques, and they're common in academic research as well.

Surveys, polls, and questionnaires can be administered orally (a researcher asks questions in a mall or on the phone), on paper (an informant fills out a satisfaction survey in a restaurant), and increasingly on computers. Regardless of the format you choose, you'll need to think through your questions carefully and test your instrument before you administer it for real.

1 Surveys and polls

Surveys and **polls** collect short answers, often in *yes/no* form. They provide statistics you can present in charts and tables, measure against research findings, and use to support your opinions. In a project for the student activities board on his campus, Eric Poritsky designed a poll to find out how much time students spent using computer terminals on campus (away from their dorm rooms). The board used the results in a proposal to the Coffee Bean, a national chain coffeehouse with a franchise in the union, that it install a dozen computer terminals in its facility so that students and faculty could access the Internet while having coffee. Poritsky's poll asked respondents a few simple *yes/no* questions about their computer use. His "key" questions were the following:

- Is the prospect of having access to a computer inside the Coffee Bean attractive to you?

  ☐ Yes ☐ No ☐ Maybe

- If there were free computer terminals in the Coffee Bean, would you use them?

  ☐ Yes ☐ No ☐ Maybe

Remember that simple polls and surveys provide only basic information (which can be useful in the first phase of a research project). What they gain in simplicity and speed, however, they lack in depth and complexity.

2 Questionnaires

Questionnaires allow you to gather more in-depth information, sometimes from a large number of people. Because they're usually mailed or offered on the Internet, most questionnaires don't require the "live" contact time of interviews, but they need to be prepared carefully so they don't confuse respondents and ruin a project.

Questionnaires contain sections that focus on specific aspects of people's experiences or opinions. This format helps organize respondents' thoughts, so they don't feel they're jumping from topic to topic. More complex questionnaires have sections that respondents answer (or skip), depending on how they answered one or more questions in a previous section. Some questionnaires use both simple, multiple choice or *yes/no* questions and more open-ended questions respondents can answer in narrative form.

The University of Florida's Office of Financial Aid, for example, uses an opinion survey to gauge satisfaction with its services. After some factual, poll-like questions (status of the respondent, number of times he or she used the service), the questionnaire uses a combination of multiple-choice questions and open-ended questions (where respondents can type their thoughts inside boxes). Figure 25.1 shows each type of question. Notice especially the range of possible responses and the relationship between the multiple-choice question (which provides the surveyor with numerical data) and the open-ended question (which allows the respondent to explain his or her choices).

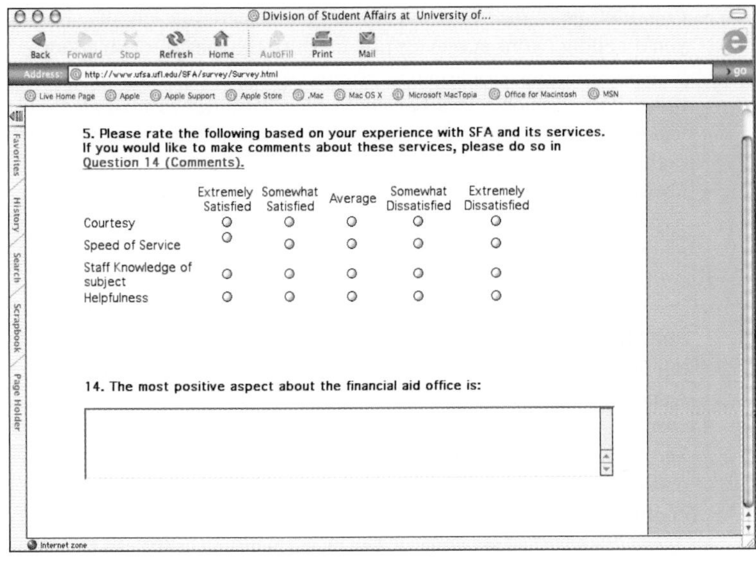

Division of Student Affairs at University of...

http://www.ufsa.ufl.edu/SFA/survey/Survey.html

5. Please rate the following based on your experience with SFA and its services. If you would like to make comments about these services, please do so in Question 14 (Comments).

	Extremely Satisfied	Somewhat Satisfied	Average	Somewhat Dissatisfied	Extremely Dissatisfied
Courtesy	○	○	○	○	○
Speed of Service	○	○	○	○	○
Staff Knowledge of subject	○	○	○	○	○
Helpfulness	○	○	○	○	○

14. The most positive aspect about the financial aid office is:

FIGURE 25.1 Sample multiple-choice and open-ended questions from an opinion survey at <http://www.ufsa.ufl.edu/SFA/survey/Survey.html>

STRATEGY

- *Consider your purpose.* Begin your survey, poll, or questionnaire with a clear sense of what you want to find out and why. Creating and refining a research question (see 21e) will help you to focus on relevant questions or data.
- *Consider your subjects*, the people you will question. Do you want to select them on the basis of gender, age, or occupation? If you are comparing the opinions of college students and parents about alcohol use, you will need a large enough sample from each group to enable you to generalize about the differences you find.
- *Consider what you're expecting.* If your questionnaire is long or complicated, will your respondents tire and toss it away? Consider providing a reward of some sort for answering lengthy surveys and questionnaires. If you're creating a Web-based questionnaire, give respondents a sense of its length before they begin, especially if they can't see all the screens at the start.
- *Consider what you're asking.* Will your respondents be uncomfortable? Will they be able to provide the information without becoming frustrated or finding that "it all depends"? Are your questions too subjective?

- *Consider your location or context.* Think carefully about where you'll conduct your survey or poll because the location you choose may determine what particular groups of people answer your questions. Polling people in a bar about their attitudes toward alcohol use will yield quite different results from conducting the same poll in the parking lot of a health food co-op.
- *Consider the form of your instrument.* Will you ask respondents to write out explanations, check boxes, or circle choices? Will you use a multiple-choice format or a rating scale?
- *Anticipate responses* and design questions accordingly. If you ask a *yes/no* question, will a *yes* or *no* answer give you enough information? If you ask an open-ended question (requiring a freeform written or oral response), how will you organize and make sense of the responses?
- *Draft a list of questions* that will yield the information you want. Scrutinize your wording carefully, and test your draft on at least two or three people. Ask them to describe points at which they were confused or needed more information.
- *Above all, test the instrument.* Ask class members or friends to take your survey, poll, or questionnaire, and to tell you when they were confused or frustrated, or felt something was "oversimplified" or too subjective. Take note of their problems.
- *Revise the instrument and prepare it for distribution.* You may need to test and revise your instrument several times to get it right. Remember that it's very difficult to readminister a survey or questionnaire if you find serious problems with it after gathering your data (which may be unusable). In your final version, fit your questions on one page (front and back) if possible, but leave room for longhand comments if you have time to analyze them.

Here are a few of the questions student Shane Hand asked people about recycling. As they answered, he marked a tally sheet.

DO YOU . . .

use coffee mugs instead of polystyrene cups?	(Yes)	No
reuse plastic wrap, foil, and plastic bags?	Yes	(No)
recycle newspapers and/or magazines?	(Yes)	No

ARE YOU WILLING TO . . .

take your own bags to the store?		No
shop at a store that's harder to get to but carries biodegradable products?	Yes	

25d Interviews

Field researchers use interviews to gather in-depth information from informants or subjects about their opinions or experiences. You can use interviews to supplement your research in print and electronic resources either by talking with experts or by contacting people whose experiences may help you test the validity of conclusions offered in other sources. You can also decide to make interviews your main method of research.

Interviews can be highly planned or open-ended. As you plan your interview questions, think carefully about your goals and shape the interview protocol accordingly.

STRATEGY

1. *List possible interviewees.* Begin by formulating questions you'd like to have answered; then list the people who might be able to answer them. Consider whether you'll need to do a thorough, lengthy interview or just collect short answers to a few questions.
2. *Write out questions you want to ask your interviewees.* Arrange your questions logically; avoid those that can be answered *yes* or *no* unless you plan follow-ups. If possible, rehearse questions with friends to discover those that are ineffective.
3. *Be courteous when you contact your interviewees.* Explain your project and ask permission to do the interview. (See 25e.)
4. *Use your list of questions, but don't be shackled by it.* Follow the train of new information and ideas as long as it serves your purpose.
5. *Consider recording your interview instead of writing everything down.* Using a tape recorder or other recording equipment will let you focus on the content of the interview. Always ask permission to record your interview, and bring along extra tapes.
6. *After the interview, send a thank-you note to each interviewee.* Not only is this polite procedure, but you may also need a follow-up interview.

Exercise 1

A. Imagine you're writing an interview paper describing someone's unusual occupation. Choose an occupation and draft a list of questions you might ask a person with that occupation during an interview.

B. In a small group, compare and discuss your list of questions. Concentrate on the form of the questions and the sorts of information they might elicit. Consider role-playing parts of your interviews to tease out potential problems in the phrasing of the questions and in the ways an interviewer might follow up on them during the interview.

25e Obtaining human subjects' consent and approval

Whenever you conduct research on human subjects, even in administering a questionnaire, you need to abide by certain ethical and legal principles to avoid injuring your subjects. "Injury" doesn't just mean harming someone physically, such as having people test a product known to cause cancer. It can also refer to psychological injury, such as interviewing children about traumatic events in their lives. Furthermore, subjects are protected by privacy laws; although most people know when they become uncomfortable answering questions, they may not always be aware of how the law protects them. Consulting with a teacher or a human subjects board member on your campus will help ensure that your research meets the proper standards.

Most campuses have a committee, board, or administrative unit that provides information and advice on the involvement of human subjects in research. The group may have an acronym such as HSCC (Human Subjects Consent Committee), IRB (Institutional Review Board), IEC (Independent Ethics Committee), or OHRP (Office for Human Research Protection). Such boards or committees are responsible for approving plans for research after considering the legal and ethical implications of those plans. If an expert in child language development wanted to see whether humans develop the capacity to speak "innately" by isolating an infant from all forms of human communication for the first five years of its life, any human subjects review board would disallow the study because it would harm the child. Such boards also consider the kinds of information a researcher proposes to gather from subjects, and these boards can approve or disapprove the proposal or send it back for revision. If a researcher wants to collect sensitive information from subjects, such as in-depth interview data about their sexuality, the human subjects committee may approve or reject the plan after considering the entire project, its goals, its subjects, and so on.

Approval to conduct human subject research is usually required on most campuses—and it has the benefit of protecting the researcher as well as the subjects. Whether you need approval for field research involving human subjects will depend on various factors. In some cases, an entire class can receive general approval to conduct surveys, polls, or questionnaires; in other cases, no approval may be necessary. Be sure that you and your instructor know the practices on your campus, and follow the requirements accordingly.

STRATEGY

In addition to meeting guidelines and regulations, ethical field research involves some commonsense principles. As you design your research plan, consider the following.

- Explain your research to your subjects. In some cases, you may need to keep the explanation general so that you don't influence their responses, but you should not conceal the purpose and nature of your study.
- Make clear to your subjects what will happen with the data you gather. Who will see the data? How long will it be kept? (IRB committees have requirements for the collection, use, storage, and disposal of data, and you should follow those requirements.)
- Explain that your subjects' anonymity will be preserved or that they will have the option of anonymity. If you need to use names, will you use pseudonyms?
- Give your subjects the option of seeing the results of your research.

25f Ethnographies

You can use **ethnographic research** to interpret the practices, behaviors, language, and attitudes of particular groups that may be tied together by their interests or ways of understanding and acting in the world. Such cultural analyses are at the heart of much important research on human belief and ritual. *Ethnography* means, literally, the writing ("graphy") of culture ("ethno"). A written report of ethnographic research (an **ethnography**) aims to provide an in-depth understanding of its subject. For this reason, you may need to use several methods to gather pertinent information about your subject: the **observation** of people, events, and settings; **interviews** with **informants** (people who provide you with information about the group to which they belong); and the collection of **artifacts** (material objects characteristic of a group or culture). Most full-scale ethnographies require months or even years of participation in a community, but you can use the principles of ethnographic research for more modest "quasi-ethnographies" or "qualitative" sorts of investigations.

In its fullest manifestation, ethnography is not a practical research method for a single college course. Some master's and doctoral students design ethnographies for their theses and dissertations because they have enough time to immerse themselves in a social or cultural context to meet the general standards of this kind of research. (Some ethnographers distrust any study calling itself an ethnography unless the researcher has spent at least a year on site.)

A popular kind of paper in college courses draws on the general principles and methods of ethnography without meeting its requirements for sustained immersion in a context. Such studies are sometimes called "microethnographies," "mini-ethnographies," or "cultural analyses." Their aim is to introduce you to the methods of careful sociocultural analysis without demanding a huge investment of time. Such investigations may require you to choose a group or subculture with which you're unfamiliar, and then spend considerable time "on site," learning about its customs, beliefs, practices, behaviors, and norms. For example, you might spend several weekends at the airfield and hangars of a skydiving club, or a series of evenings at the local meeting place of an Alcoholics Anonymous group, or regular hours at the meetings and the convention of a Japanese anime club.

To understand your subject in depth, you'll have to focus your fieldwork on a specific setting, activity, person, or group of people to which you can devote enough time and energy to arrive at worthwhile conclusions. You'll conduct **structured observations** in which you carefully and objectively look at a situation, behavior, or relationship in order to understand its elements and processes. (For instance, in researching the ways preschoolers use language during play, you might arrange and plan in detail a series of structured observations at a day-care center.) You'll interview participants, trying not to make your interviews too "formal" or to put your subjects on guard. You'll talk to them about their activities and be as spontaneous as possible, writing down as much detail as you can about the physical location and the participants' actions and behaviors.

STRATEGY

1. Choose the site and, if necessary, get permission to conduct your observation or participate in the group.
2. Decide how to situate yourself. Will you move around or remain inconspicuous? How will you explain your presence to the people you are observing?
3. Decide what information you want to gather and why. Consider how you will use it in your report.
4. Consider your means for recording information: tape recorder, camera, notepad, video camera. (The more intrusive your methods, the less likely you may be to get spontaneous data.)
5. Make a list of problems that might arise and develop strategies for dealing with them.
6. Between visits to your site, be sure to reread your notes and reflect on them, generating questions and hypotheses for your next visit.
7. Above all, don't think one visit to your site will suffice. Make multiple visits—the more, the better. People, rituals, agendas, activities can all change between visits, and you'll want as full a picture of your culture or community as you can create.

CHAPTER 26
Avoiding Plagiarism and Integrating Sources

Kim Kim has put off working on her major research paper for so long that she can't imagine getting it done on time and still earning a passing grade. A friend thinks her topic—allowing incarcerated mothers time to parent their children while they are in jail—is broad enough that Kim could probably buy a research paper on the topic at one of the many Internet paper mills. Kim spends an hour searching sites and finds a paper that should work. She pays the service $50 with her credit card, downloads the paper, and prints it out. She puts her name and the date at the top of the paper and turns it in to her instructor.

Paul After getting a *B* in a human biology course during the fall semester, Paul is now enrolled during the spring semester in a course in introductory biochemistry. He has to write a term paper on a topic of his choice. He realizes that the topic he wrote about for his fall semester term paper—which focused on the human body's reaction to living at high altitudes—is relevant to his spring semester biochemistry course. He makes a few minor changes in the original paper and adds a page on chemical processes. After printing out the new version, he turns it in to his biochemistry professor without mentioning that he originally wrote it for another course.

Tisha Tisha is working on a short documented research paper for her composition class. She has found an excellent source. She incorporates a paragraph from the source directly into her paper and dutifully cites it in her references. A paragraph later, she adds some more from the same source but neglects to put quotation marks around the text. Although it's clear that the words are not hers, she has not indicated this in her writing.

Which of these is a case of plagiarism? Which might be called academic dishonesty? Are they of equal severity? If Tisha makes an "honest" mistake while writing a paper, should she be guilty of plagiarism and suffer the full consequences?

26a What is plagiarism?

Plagiarism, which comes from a Latin word for "kidnapping," refers to the theft of another person's ideas or words. However, plagiarism is fundamentally a cultural concept, part of a system of beliefs and regulations that

AVOIDING PLAGIARISM AND INTEGRATING SOURCES IN THREE COMMUNITIES

ACADEMIC SETTINGS	PUBLIC SETTINGS	WORK SETTINGS
College professors, researchers, and other professionals view documents and research results as intellectual property of considerable importance. They have high standards for the acknowledgment and documentation of material drawn from print, electronic, or field sources. They also expect conclusions to be supported by extensive use of quotations, ideas, conclusions, and data drawn from a variety of authoritative sources.	Failure to acknowledge sources of information or texts being summarized and paraphrased can undermine confidence in public documents and in the writers responsible for the documents. Careful acknowledgment (and documentation) of sources, especially for paraphrases and summaries, not just for quotations, is necessary for public writing. Quotations and data from sources are important in informative writing and in argumentative writing, though their use may sometimes be less extensive than in academic documents.	Many organizations are dedicated to producing business surveys, collections of information, and compilations of opinions. Using their work without acknowledgment (and, sometimes, without paying for permission to use it) is wrong. Quotations, graphs, tables, and summaries of information drawn from sources are persuasive and useful elements in much workplace writing, though the level of detail may sometimes be less than in technical and scholarly writing produced in academic settings.

govern how we write and how we use other people's words. Different communities within our culture interpret plagiarism in their own ways.

- **Academic communities** believe strongly in the individual ownership of ideas, texts, inventions, and other products of research and scholarship. Even though team efforts are common in many academic disciplines, as a student you are participating in a community that thinks of writing as "intellectual property." Thus, almost anything you find written by someone else that you want to use in your own work you must attribute to the original author. You must take care to distinguish precisely between your words and someone else's words—from the first to the last letter.
- **Public communities** tend to have the least concern about the ownership of words, partly because they often produce them without thought of profit and want information to be circulated as widely as possible. No one worries about the plagiarism of flyers announcing public events, for example, and certain civic documents such as bylaws of organizations are freely copied and adapted without concern. At large national conferences, teachers swap classroom strategies and assignments, unconcerned that their documents will be used by oth-

ers without attribution. Health brochures like those you find in a doctor's office often cite the source of research, but sometimes they provide "cloned" information and suggestions without disclosing their origin.

- **Business communities** can be fiercely competitive and territorial; a company will quickly bring a lawsuit against another company that uses its slogans, language, or other representations, partly because the first company sees the act as theft of its identity and products or services. Book publishing as a business enterprise keeps stern watch over plagiarism and the theft of intellectual property. But business communities are also notoriously lax about citing the source of certain *kinds* of text, especially "boilerplate"; there is no financial stake in the specific words of such texts, or the words are so common that no company could be said to have originated them. For example, phrases like "Ideally situated close to shopping and major attractions" appear on hundreds of hotel Web sites and brochures, and no company would try to sue another company by claiming the words are "theirs." Furthermore, in many business settings an individual's work is "owned" not by that person but by the company he or she works for—as is the work produced by teams.

26b Plagiarism in college

Thus, while plagiarism exists in all communities, the standards that apply to the acknowledgment of authors and the citation of sources vary from one context to another. In college, the rules on plagiarism are strict and apply to almost any kind of work done for a course. Not learning and following those rules can lead you to a failing grade for a paper or an entire course, a special plagiarism notation on your transcript, or expulsion from your college or university. Very serious plagiarism, especially at higher levels of research and scholarship, can result in lawsuits and damage judgments that ruin a person's academic or professional career.

According to the Council of Writing Program Administrators (WPA), plagiarism in an academic setting "occurs when a writer deliberately uses someone else's language, ideas, or original (not common-knowledge) material without acknowledging its source" (<www.wpacouncil.org>). Thus, turning in someone else's paper as your own, taking someone's original idea or analysis from a book and passing it off as yours, and copying passages or even sentences from a source into your paper without saying where they came from—all represent plagiarism. Technically, turning in work that you had previously written isn't plagiarism, but by not producing something new, or a substantially reworked version of the original paper, you are violating certain requirements of your school and your courses and denying yourself the chance to learn.

26c The problem of intention

Figure 26.1 is a representation of plagiarism from the perspective of the writer and a reader or teacher. At the top of this figure, cases of plagiarism are conscious and deliberate: you know exactly what you're doing, you know it's wrong, and you take the risk. Toward the bottom of the figure, plagiarism becomes increasingly unconscious—these are cases in which the writer doesn't document sources well, perhaps because he or she has never learned all the elements of proper documentation or comes from a culture where such practices differ. For most honest writers, the problem of plagiarism begins somewhere in the bottom of Figure 26.1, as they try to acknowledge sources but do so clumsily or incorrectly.

According to the WPA statement cited in 26b, cases at the bottom of the figure—at least in school situations—are technically not plagiarism because the writer is not intentionally thieving text or misrepresenting the source of words or ideas. Although plagiarism gradually loses its maliciousness and severity as you move from top to bottom of Figure 26.1, it's important for you to realize that *for many readers and teachers, your naiveté makes no difference at all*, as you can see from the right side of the figure. The result *looks* like plagiarism, and you may still be found guilty of academic misconduct, whether you were conscious of it or not, ill-intentioned, or just uninformed about how to cite sources.

The difference between your intentions and your reader's or teacher's interpretations won't matter at all beyond your campus. But if you were to publish a book or article that improperly incorporated someone else's ideas without crediting them, it would make no difference that you pled innocence on the basis of ignorance. Legally, the evidence is in your text. In many col-

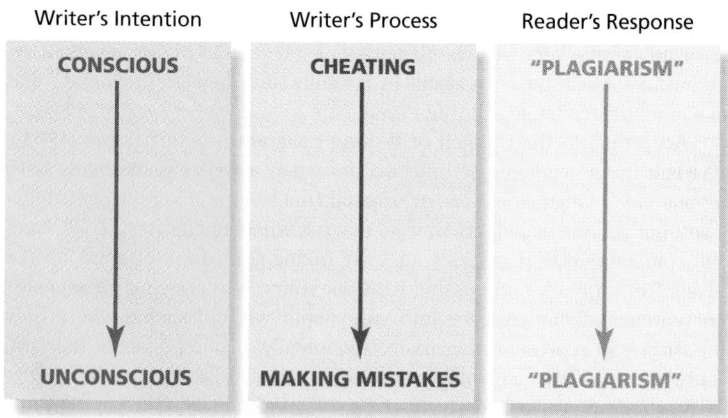

FIGURE 26.1 Plagiarism as seen by the writer and by the reader

lege classrooms, the same principle will apply. Teachers don't know what you know, and they may suspect that you have plagiarized when you simply didn't know any better. In writing classes, however, you have the opportunity to learn good source work and the conventions of attribution, so that you won't find yourself in a position of having to defend yourself.

Little can be said about cases toward the top of Figure 26.1. If you choose to plagiarize consciously and deceptively, your plagiarism will hurt everyone—including you: it cheats you out of your learning opportunity, it robs your parents and the taxpayers who may be funding your education, it subverts and complicates the work of teachers who are trying to help you learn, it slows social progress by undermining the achievement of higher standards of education and work, and it assaults those who put the time and energy into producing the work you're stealing. But you can learn how to cite sources carefully and responsibly so you won't find yourself in situations represented at the bottom of Figure 26.1.

26d When to document sources

In general, you need to document the words, ideas, and information you draw from another person's work. Keep in mind the three most important reasons for documenting sources.

1. **Add support** to your conclusions and credibility to your explanations by showing that they are based on careful research.
2. **Give credit** to someone for their original work.
3. **Show your readers** where they can obtain the materials you cite (and from there, perhaps others).

Decisions on what needs documenting may vary from audience to audience. If you're writing to a general audience, readers may expect you to cite sources for your discussion of subatomic particles. If you're writing for a physics professor or an audience of physicists, you might fairly assume that such matters are common knowledge. However, in some college classrooms, your teacher may want to know all the works you have consulted in order to see the evidence of your explorations.

You must document

- Word-for-word (direct) quotations taken from someone else's work
- Paraphrases or summaries of someone else's work, whether published or presented informally in an interview or email message
- Ideas, opinions, and interpretations that others have developed and presented, even if they are based on common knowledge
- Facts or data that someone else has gathered or identified if the information is not widely known enough to be considered common knowledge

- Information that is not widely accepted or that is disputed
- Illustrations, charts, graphs, photographs, recordings, original software, performances, interviews, and the like
- Anything from the Internet that you can reasonably cite, including emails from discussion groups, text from blogs and chatrooms, and so forth

You do not document

- Ideas, opinions, and interpretations that are your own
- Widely known ideas and information—the sort you can locate in common reference works or that people writing or speaking on a topic usually present as common knowledge
- Commonly used quotations ("To be, or not to be")

26e Citing responsibly

When you include quotations, paraphrases, and summaries in your writing, you *must* acknowledge their sources. If you don't, you're treating someone else's work as your own.

- Be sure you enclose someone else's exact words in quotation marks.
- Make sure that paraphrases and summaries are in your own words.
- Be sure to cite the source of any ideas or information that you quote, paraphrase, or summarize.

The following paraphrase comes too close to repeating the original to be presented without quotation marks. It would be considered plagiarized, even if the writer had done it without knowing better.

ORIGINAL PASSAGE

> Malnutrition was a widespread and increasingly severe problem throughout the least developed parts of the world in the 1970s, and would continue to be serious, occasionally reaching famine conditions, as the millennium approached. Among the cells of the human body most dependent upon a steady source of nutrients are those of the immune system, most of which live, even under ideal conditions, for only days at a time.
>
> —Laurie Garrett, *The Coming Plague*

POORLY PARAPHRASED VERSION

Garrett points out that malnutrition can give microbes an advantage as they spread through the population. Malnutrition continues to be a severe problem throughout the least developed

```
parts of the world. The human immune system contains cells that
are dependent upon a steady source of nutrients. These cells
may live, even under ideal conditions, for only days at a time.
```

The writer of the poorly paraphrased version made only minor changes in some phrases and "lifted" others verbatim. It's difficult, therefore, to tell which words or ideas are Garrett's and which are the writer's.

APPROPRIATE PARAPHRASE

```
     Garrett points out that malnutrition can give microbes an
advantage as they spread through the population. The human body
contains immune cells that help to fight off various diseases.
When the body is deprived of nutrients, these immune cells will
weaken (Garrett 199).
```

Because this writer's paper focused on the general threat of global disease, he could have simply summarized the passage.

APPROPRIATE SUMMARY

```
     It has been suggested that malnutrition can weaken the
immune system and make people more susceptible to diseases they
would otherwise fight off (Garrett 199).
```

STRATEGY

Inadvertent plagiarism—really a kind of sloppiness in your writing process—often happens when you are working between your source material and your developing paper. You *think* you're using your own words, but the words of your source are so fresh in your mind that they creep in and "become" yours. Whenever you paraphrase or summarize a source, be sure to look back at the source and compare your words with those in the source. If you find phrases or sentences are too close to the original, either quote the material directly and exactly (using quotation marks) or revise your summary or paraphrase so that you're not using the author's words as your own.

26f Sources in context

Academic research usually acknowledges and draws on the work of previous scholars and researchers. Each writer indicates where he or she fits in the tradition of research on a given topic and explains any agreements and disagreements with others' work. In this community, much value is placed on the thorough presentation of data and evidence, along with precise, formal documentation in the style appropriate to the subject matter or academic field (MLA, APA, CMS, CSE—see Chapters 28–31). The following excerpt from Summer Arrigo-Nelson and Jennifer Figliozzi's research report shows their careful integration (and critique) of a research study.

> First, although both questions 1 and 4 looked to determine student alcohol use within the home, a discrepancy appeared between the percentage of people who replied that they were offered alcohol at home and those who said that their parents believed alcohol was only for those over twenty-one years of age. This discrepancy could have arisen if the students in the sample were not thorough in their evaluation of their parents' views, in which case, correlations drawn from this data should not be relied upon (Aas, Jakobsen, and Anderssen 1996).

When you read academic research, you'll find that many of the conventions for citation and for the quoting of material will be relevant to your own papers, which will most often assume a similar academic orientation. Material from other settings, however, may follow somewhat different conventions. Work audiences will expect concise treatment of things they already know and extended summaries, tables, graphs, and illustrations—all carefully documented with a recognizable citation system (see Chapters 28–31). Material designed for general public consumption may cite sources in a somewhat informal fashion; texts with many footnotes or academic-sounding references can confuse or put off some public audiences.

The following paragraph is excerpted from a publication of the "Exxon Valdez Oil Spill Trustee Council" at <http://www.oilspill.state.ak.us>, which contains documents of public interest with special focus on the Exxon Valdez cleanup effort and that oil spill's impact on the Alaskan shoreline environment. Notice how the writer condenses several important and scientifically complex studies into a research synthesis that is readily understandable by a reasonably educated public audience, but does not overwhelm the reader with complex references.

> Winter surveys from 1995–1998 found that adult female survival [of harlequin ducks] was lower in oiled versus unoiled areas, and a similar survival scenario is suggested from data collected in 2000 to 2002. Oil remained in the subsurface of the intertidal zone through 2001, including under some mussel beds where harlequin ducks could be feeding. Biopsies from harlequin and Barrow's goldeneye ducks continue to show differences in an enzyme indicative of exposure to hydrocarbons between birds from oiled versus unoiled parts of the sound. These differences are consistent with the possibility of continued exposure to spill-derived hydrocarbons in the western sound. The biological effect of this possible exposure has not been established, but

> the declining trend of female survivability in the oiled areas may be continuing. Although this result cannot be attributed unequivocally to oil exposure, there is reason for concern about possible oil exposure and reduced survival for harlequin ducks in the western sound.

In contrast, consider an excerpt from another document concerning the same oil spill site, a document that is clearly intended for researchers and scholars with technical backgrounds, such as academics in marine biology departments at research universities and members of the Environmental Protection Agency who monitor coastal pollution. Notice especially how careful the authors are to cite the sources of their information.

> The composition, distribution, abundance, and productivity of plant and animal plankton communities in the GOA have been reviewed by Sambrotto and Lorenzen (1986); Cooney (1986); Miller (1993); and Mackas and Frost (1993). In general, dramatic differences are observed between pelagic communities over the deep ocean, and those found in shelf, coastal, and protected inside waters (sounds, fjords, and estuaries). Specifically, the euphotic zone seaward of the shelf edge is dominated year round by very small phytoplankters—tiny diatoms, naked flagellates, and cyanobacteria (Booth 1988). Most are smaller than 10 microns in size, and their combined standing stocks (measured as chlorophyll concentration) occur at very low and seasonally stable levels. It was originally hypothesized that a small group of large oceanic copepods (*Neocalanus spp.* and *Eucalanus bungii*) limited plant numbers and open ocean production by efficiently controlling the plant stocks through grazing (Heinrich 1962). More recent evidence, however, indicates the predominant grazers on the oceanic flora are not the large calanoids (Dagg 1993), but instead abundant populations of ciliate protozoans and heterotrophic microflagellates (Miller et al. 1991a, 1991b, Frost 1993).

Exercise 1

Choose a passage from one of your secondary sources and write a summary and paraphrase of it. Then embed a quotation from the source into a sentence of your own.

26g Integrating sources for specific purposes

Although your research paper is an original contribution to a subject area—something *you* create through your methodical search for information and your particular way of pulling information together and presenting it for others to learn from—it's also about *other people's* work. It's your way of representing what a community of scholars, researchers, and commentators has said about a topic or how this community has tried to answer a question.

Weaving other people's words and ideas into your paper can accomplish many specific purposes. How you integrate outside material into your writing often depends on what you're trying to *do* with the source. Being clear about the reasons for citing someone's work can help you to structure a more effective research paper.

STRATEGY

- As you gather and read your source material, make notes about the possible purposes it might serve in your paper.
- As you write the paper (see Chapter 27), refer to your notes when you make strategic decisions about what to incorporate at different points in the paper.
- Avoid trying to "force" a quotation to fit a purpose it doesn't serve. If an author has objectively cited or described a controversial position, it could misrepresent that author to imply that he or she holds that position as well.
- Be willing to scrap a source or citation if it serves no purpose in your paper.
- Avoid the "display for teacher" syndrome—putting in quotations and referencing sources just to show your instructor that you have collected some information. Research papers can't be developed by merely stringing together quantities of material just because you took the time to gather it.

1 Introducing a topic and providing background

At the beginning of your paper, you may want to use sources to establish a context, to introduce the general area of your topic, or to give a history of activity or thought on the subject. Be careful not to rely too much on sources in your introduction, however; you need to establish your own voice and to explain what you will do in the paper. Your sources should support your own words, not overwhelm them.

In a paper on conspiracy theories, Sam Roles decided to use sources to provide background on why conspiracy theories are so hard to refute. (Here and elsewhere in this chapter, material from Roles's paper follows MLA style in documenting sources; see Chapter 28.)

> Conspiracy theories arise, according to scholars, for a number of reasons: political fragmentation and suspicion of difference (Pipes); something to occupy the imagination of a bored subculture (Fenster); and fear of more powerful groups (Johnson). For example, in the 1950s and 1960s, communism provided a . . . .

2 Summarizing prior research

In some cases, your research paper may explore an area, a specific focus, or a relationship that many others have written about. Instead of providing lots of references, use some of your sources selectively to give a brief summary before moving into your specific focus.

Sam Roles found large amounts of information about conspiracy theory, and he wanted to acknowledge the scope of his topic before focusing on the Roswell Incident as a case study of the concept. Notice how he selects representative references in each category.

> Conspiracy theories are studied within several disciplines. Psychologists, for example, consider the relationship between conspiracy theories and disorders such as paranoia (Edmunds). Sociologists examine the formation and spread of conspiracy theories within a culture or group, and its underlying causes (Haskins). Political scientists focus on the way that political ideologies can lead to the creation of beliefs about leaders' motives (Argyle). And experts in anthropology consider the cultural bases of myth creation, fear of persecution, or the construction of alternative realities (Lizaro). In my . . . .

3 Providing examples and cases

As you make general statements about your topic or question, you will want to provide specific examples or cases to illustrate your points. Sometimes you will summarize them (see 21g-1, 26h-2) because you don't want a lengthy example to overwhelm your paper or divert you from your discussion. You could also refer briefly to several cases to show how your general statement is manifested.

As Sam Roles researched the Roswell Incident, he began to see possible political causes of the theory that for fifty years the government has covered up the discovery of an alien spacecraft in New Mexico. In one paragraph he illustrates his general statement (in red) with three examples (in blue). Notice how each example comes from a different source.

> Many conspiracy theories surround political figures or political events. The Apollo moon missions, for example, are now questioned by conspiracy theorists as having been staged by the government in a studio (Adams). For decades, it has been thought that Jack the Ripper was actually Prince Albert Victor Christian Edward ("Prince Eddy"), the Duke of Clarence (Evans and Skinner). And theories of who assassinated President John F. Kennedy abound (Posner).

4 Showing evidence or support

As you create specific points or make claims and arguments in your research paper, the words of experts can support your ideas. At times your research will help you to formulate your opinions, and you can then cite that research as support.

In his paper on conspiracy theory, student Sam Roles wanted to present both sides of the debate over the claim a UFO was discovered in New Mexico in the 1940s and that this discovery was covered up by the government. Roles decided to incorporate a quotation from a book on the Roswell Incident to begin laying out opposition to the alien theory.

> But were these sightings really UFOs? As Berlitz and Moore have pointed out, New Mexico in the late 1940s was "the site of the major portion of America's postwar defense efforts in atomic research, rocketry, aircraft and missile development, and radar-electronics experimentation" (18). Such activity, such as flashes of light in the sky, could have been mistaken for the presence of UFOs.

In his notes on his sources, Roles wrote the following. Notice how he has found a specific purpose for the material that relates to his broader plan for his paper.

Use to begin showing disagreement with UFO claim.

5 Expanding an idea

As you develop an idea, you can use your sources to extend, refine, and elaborate on that idea. This approach is especially useful as you make transitions from one part of your paper to the next.

To move from his discussion of the Roswell Incident to the main focus of his paper (how the incident represents a case study of the concept of conspiracy theory), Sam needed to show that the argument about the truth or falseness of the alien accounts was not really the point, that it simply illustrates the social nature of conspiracy theories. He decided to use a block quotation (see 26h-1) to accomplish this purpose.

26g plag

> Joltes points out how difficult it is to change the views of conspiracy theorists even when there is overwhelming evidence and rational explanation to account for a phenomenon:
>
> > Likewise, when the US Air Force discloses the existence of a weather balloon experiment that offers a rational explanation for the "Roswell incident" a

conspiracy buff will claim that records were faked, witnesses bought off or silenced, or whatever was necessary to conceal evidence of alien contact. The aliens really do exist, but all the evidence has been suppressed, destroyed, or altered . . . therefore the conspiracy theorist has had to work diligently to reconstruct what really happened, often producing "evidence" that is obviously contrived and illogical. But this matters not as long as it fits the theory.

6 Taking issue with a claim

In your paper, you may want to argue against what someone else has said or what some group (of scholars or people) believes (see 11c). After clearly explaining and referencing the opinion or belief, you can use other references to refute or "answer" the original claim. In this way, a section of your paper becomes a kind of conversation among scholars or commentators. Your artful use of sources can show weaknesses in one line of reasoning, or it can advance your own theory or position.

After Sam Roles had summarized the story of the Roswell Incident and included plentiful evidence from those who believe in the truthfulness of the alien version, he needed to disprove those accounts in order to move on to his analysis of why conspiracy theories arise. He decided to use the strongest quotation he could find in his sources to argue against the alien theory while starting to introduce his main focus, the nature and causes of conspiracy theories.

In summarizing his report of a carefully coordinated 1994 investigation of the Roswell Incident, Col. Richard M. Weaver says "the Air Force research did not locate or develop any information that the 'Roswell Incident' was a UFO event." Records did indicate, however, that the government was engaged in a "top secret balloon project, designed to attempt to monitor Soviet nuclear tests, known as Project Mogul." Tests of these balloons are the only plausible explanation of numerous UFO sightings and of the desert debris assumed to be an alien spacecraft.

Exercise 2

Make a list of the sources you have collected for your research paper, leaving several lines after each source. For each source, think of one or more purposes it might serve in your paper. Consider the list of purposes discussed in 26f. What could you use the source to *do*? (In some cases, you may not be ready to answer this question completely until your paper is further developed; yet even tentative notes at this point will help you to think about the potential role of your sources and help you to know their contexts more clearly.)

26h Quotations, summaries, facts, and visuals

You can integrate sources into your paper in several ways: as quotations, or as summaries and paraphrases. (You may also want to include visuals such as charts, pictures, graphs, and screen shots.)

1 Quotations

Quoting someone's words means putting them into your paper or oral presentation in the *exact* way that they appeared in the original text (this is why it's so important that you be accurate in taking notes during your research). Avoid stringing quotations together or setting off many long quotations in blocks (it may look like padding). Instead, use direct quotations

- to show that you're accurately representing ideas that you want to challenge, modify, or extend;
- to preserve an especially stylish, persuasive, or concise way of saying something;
- to show vividly and dramatically what other people think;
- to provide a change of pace or a jumping-off point for your thoughts.

You can quote entire sentences from a source and let them stand on their own, with proper attribution.

> Yet alcohol awareness campaigns have seen only moderate success. "Although heavy drinking and monthly and daily alcohol use among high school seniors have declined since the 1980s, the decline is less among college-bound seniors, and binge drinking is a widespread problem on college campuses" (Bradley and Miller 1).

You can use an **embedded quotation** if it is less than a line or two.

> Yet a 1994 government investigation of the Roswell Incident "located no records at existing Air Force offices that indicated any 'cover-up' by the USAF or any indication of such a recovery" of alien debris (Weaver 1).

A **block quotation** is a longer passage from a source, set off from your own prose because of its length (more than four sentences). Remember that readers expect you to *do* something with block quotations, not just insert them.

> Some psychologists believe that conspiracy theories have their origins in the public's trust in authority. If that "authority" is not fully credentialed but appears to be, the public may formulate beliefs that are not supported by evidence, a point made by Robyn M. Dawes in an analysis of why people believe in epidemic cases of child sexual abuse and the presence of satanic cults:
>
>> Asking people to doubt the conclusions concerning widespread childhood sexual abuse and satanic cults is asking them not only to reject the usual bases of authority and consensus for establishing reality, but in addition to accept principles that violate foundations of everyday functioning. Now in point of fact we do ask people to accept such principles, and they do. Few people, for example, believe that the world is flat, even though it appears to be, or believe that cigarettes and alcohol are good for them, even though both may have very pleasant effects. We return once more to the efficacy of authority. People who have no direct experience of the curvature of the earth believe that it is not flat, and even the greatest devotees of tobacco and alcohol believe that these drugs are harming them. We accept what we have been told by "reputable authorities." (We even accept what has been communicated by very minor authority figures, such as the person who draws a map that shows the Suez Canal to be longer than the Panama Canal.) (<http://www.fmsfonline.org/dawes.html>)

26h plag

2 Summaries and paraphrases

To make your writing smoother and more sophisticated, be selective in using quotations. Usually, you can summarize, even combining several sources, or paraphrase, putting a passage in your own words, rather than quote sources directly. (See 21g-1 on summarizing and 21g-2 on paraphrasing.)

Yet at first, government officials denied they had any tests underway in New Mexico. Many officials were as baffled as the general public, including Captain Tom Brown, AAF information officer, who told reporters that he and his colleagues were as mystified as everyone else about the phenomena. (Albuquerque Journal)

3 Facts, details, and statistics

You can build entire paragraphs around facts, details, and statistics drawn from sources as long as you indicate those sources clearly. You may retain some of the emphasis of a source in using it; more likely, you'll integrate the details into prose that reflects your own purposes.

4 Visuals

Visuals (drawings, photos, graphs, and the like) can sometimes present or emphasize data better than words can. If you copy a visual from a print source or download it from an electronic source, you'll need to cite the source, and you may need permission to use it. Whether you create a visual yourself or draw it from your research, make sure it adds to the written text and doesn't simply substitute for it. Visuals that add to or extend a text imaginatively can increase the credibility and effectiveness of your writing. (See Chapter 12 and 13e.)

STRATEGY

- Place the visual as near the relevant text as you can without disrupting the flow of the text or distorting the visual.
- Don't interrupt the writing in ways that make it hard to read.
- Make sure your visuals are of good quality and are an appropriate size for the page.
- Ask one or more readers whether your visuals are easy to understand and whether they add to the text's ideas and effectiveness.
- Label each visual (*Figure 1, Figure 2; Table 1, Table 2*).

Exercise 3

Below is a paragraph from Sam Roles's research on the Roswell Incident; it comes from a Web site that shows problems with the Air Force's conclusion that the Roswell Incident was not the crash of an alien spacecraft. Consider Roles's lead-in to this information; then incorporate the material into the text by (1) quoting it directly; (2) summarizing it; and (3) paraphrasing it.

ROLES'S LEAD-IN

In keeping with the processes of building a conspiracy theory, detractors of the Air Force report about the incident try to poke holes in specific versions of the historical record. For example, the Air Force report indicates that the testimony of Frank Kaufman, who was stationed in Roswell, was ignored. Seizing on this omission, Mark Rodeghier, writing for the J. Allen Hynek Center for UFO Studies, argues that

PASSAGE TO INCORPORATE (EXACT WORDS FROM THE SOURCE)

Kaufman claims to have been involved with the recovery of the alien bodies, and he was in the military stationed at Roswell. His claims have never been convincingly refuted. His testimony should have been included in the report. It was, most likely, not included because it is impossible to suggest that Kaufman could be confused about events in which he participated and for which he took written notes. (<http://www.cufos.org/airforce.htm>)

26i Common knowledge

In every field, researchers share certain kinds of knowledge. Everyone in medicine, biology, and related sciences knows what a "double helix" is, recognizes the terms "luteinizing hormone" and "metastasis," and knows that Dr. Christian Barnard performed the world's first heart transplant. If they were to include any of this information in a research article, they would not find it necessary to cite someone as having provided it, any more than you would cite someone for the statement that "it is legal, subject to prior background checks, for Americans to own handguns." Such information is called **common knowledge.**

When you're working in a topic area or discipline that is unfamiliar to you, however, you may not know what counts as "common knowledge." Everything will seem equally specialized and worthy of citation. How will you know when to include a source for information you put in your paper and when it's appropriate to assume information is common knowledge?

The answer to this question depends on your intended audience and the community of writers and readers you're working in. Because this relationship can become tricky, you should pay attention to it as you write and revise your paper.

STRATEGY

- For any information you have gathered from other sources (that is, information that is not your own informational contribution), assess whether this information is widely shared by typical educated readers. If it's not, *cite the source.*
- Consider your instructor as a primary audience. Usually, instructors in writing courses and general education courses want to know that you have learned from your sources. From this perspective, it's better to include citations for what might be considered common knowledge in a specialized field.
- Before making a final decision, ask several people whether they know a piece of information you're not sure whether to credit to a source.
- Use yourself as a litmus test: if you didn't know the information, cite the source.
- When in doubt, *cite.* It's much easier in the revision process to cut a reference than to have to find it again in your notes.

In deciding whether to provide a reference for information he included in his introduction, Sam Roles realized that the information had not come from any one of his sources but represented a frequently repeated assertion. Because it also seemed to be "understood" by most readers, he chose not to provide a reference.

> At some point, virtually every American suspects that our freely elected government is deliberately withholding information from the general public about some highly controversial or sensitive event. Most of the time, the suspicion fades and we go on with our lives. In some cases, however, the suspicion continues to grow, and groups of citizens begin joining forces to explore it. When this happens, a conspiracy theory is born.

CHAPTER 27
Writing, Revising, and Presenting Research

How do you know when to begin *writing* your informative or persuasive research paper? Actually, there's no set time. When you've gathered enough material to create a solid draft of your paper, you can begin writing. But instead of launching into the first word of the first line, think strategically about the nature and shape of your task.

You began your work with a clear research question or thesis (21e–f), and you developed it as you consulted sources and took notes. Nonetheless, you still have decisions to make. This is the time for second thoughts, too. Do you still want to present and *explain* detailed information, or is your goal now to *persuade* readers to share the strong feelings and opinions you developed in the course of your research? Is your original topic still worth the time and effort, or have you arrived at a new set of questions to answer for readers? Has your research changed your outlook and your thesis, too?

27a Planning and drafting

You started out with a goal for your paper:

INFORMATIVE PAPER

I'm going to tell readers about the three kinds of depression that may afflict college students—"the blues," common depression, and clinical depression.

PERSUASIVE PAPER

I want readers to agree with me that hunting is an acceptable activity when not excessive.

PERSUASIVE PAPER WITH PROBLEM-SOLUTION EMPHASIS

I have a three-step solution to the problem of people's downloading music without paying for it.

You also began with a plan, perhaps a formal outline, a set of notes, or a statement of goals for each section of your paper (see Chapter 2 for a discussion of planning).

DeLeo Covington created the following purpose structure for his paper on addressing the problem of sleep deficits among high school students.

PRESENTING RESEARCH IN THREE COMMUNITIES

ACADEMIC SETTINGS	PUBLIC SETTINGS	WORK SETTINGS
Academic audiences will expect you to present your interpretation, conclusion, argumentative proposition, or outlook (your thesis) clearly and to focus on developing and supporting it throughout your paper. They will expect clear and detailed support and explanation. They may expect you to present complicated information in tables or graphs.	Public audiences will look for a clear statement of your position on an issue or a direct statement of the need you are addressing in your presentation of information. They will look for sufficient support and reasoning to explain your position—support that takes into account the concerns of your audience. Visual presentations including *PowerPoint*, graphs, and illustrations can be particularly effective with public audiences.	Workplace audiences will expect you to address directly and concisely the problem or challenge you are discussing and to present solutions or proposed actions in specific but not excessive detail. This audience will appreciate visuals (including *PowerPoint*) that help them understand the situation you are addressing and that will help them remember and implement your proposals or solutions.

BEGINNING Explain what sleep deficits are and how studies show that most high school students' schoolwork suffers because they have sleep deficits. Argue that the solution to the problem is to begin the school day later.

FIRST MIDDLE Explain the problem: High school students need more sleep than most people suppose; the early beginning of the high school day robs them of sleep they need.

SECOND MIDDLE Explain that the high school day begins early because the buses have to be used by elementary, middle, and high school students; most districts can't afford more buses. Show that most school administrators believe it's OK for high school students to get up early in the morning.

THIRD MIDDLE Argue that changing starting times is important despite the difficulties. Tell how high schools that have moved to later beginning times show improvement in student performance linked to overcoming sleep deficits. Explain that they claim the change has been worth the cost.

FOURTH MIDDLE Outline the cost-effective strategies that districts having made the change came up with. Argue that these strategies can be adopted by almost all school districts and that they should do so to help solve the problem.

END *Summarize the solution; encourage readers to take action within their school districts.*

Now is the time to revisit early decisions and revise or refine them.

1 Think about your goal—again!

Think about your general goals (to inform, to persuade) as well as your specific goals (to get a committee to adopt a policy; to show that your interpretation is the most plausible one; to explain the possibilities created by a new technology). Now write out your goals so that you can consider them more thoroughly, critique them, and perhaps revise them. Ask yourself how you want readers to react to your paper as a whole and to its individual parts. Ask if your primary goal is informative, persuasive, or a combination of the two.

For most writing, you should expect some overlap in purpose. To persuade readers to adopt a particular policy on campus alcohol use, for example, you may need to explain the background of the issue or problem and provide details of the regulations and actions you propose. To encourage readers to accept your explanation of the healthiness (or unhealthiness) of the new menus at fast-food restaurants, you must provide nutritional information in a manner that readers will find convincing.

STRATEGY

A **purpose structure** is a series of statements that describe briefly what you intend to do in each section of a paper and that help you visualize the finished product (3b-1). Create a purpose structure as you review your notes and research questions. DeLeo Covington's planning notes on pages 394 and 395 are an example of a purpose structure.

2 Review your research questions

The research questions you formulated to focus and guide your research (21e) should have evolved as you worked, reflecting your developing knowledge of your subject. Use the latest versions of your research questions and arrange them in a logical order. Ask yourself in what sequence you want to address the questions in your essay or report. Add any further questions that you now think you ought to address. Develop this list as a tentative guide for drafting. The sequence you create at this point may change as you become more deeply involved with the details of your writing.

3 Redevelop your thesis

If you began with a tentative thesis statement as a way of focusing your research (21f), take this opportunity to restate it in view of what you have learned in doing your research. Revisiting your thesis enables you to envision your paper as a means of supporting your thesis and persuading readers.

Consider using your thesis statement as an organizing strategy for drafting your paper. Create a **persuasive structure** for your writing by stating your thesis, breaking it into parts, and developing related supporting statements arranged in a series that helps you focus on a persuasive purpose for each section of your paper.

4 Revise your plan and begin drafting

The moment you begin your research, you're planning your project. When you've collected most of the information you need, it's time to focus more sharply on the organization and content of your paper.

Create a working outline. A traditional outline (2d-3) may be too detailed for a long research essay or report because writers were determined to fit into the outline every bit of information they gathered—information that won't always prove useful when the writers begin drafting. Consider making a **working outline** that shows only the general sequence of information and the relationships between segments of information.

STRATEGY

Build an *informal working outline* following these steps.

1. Summarize in a sentence or two each of the main parts of your paper.
2. Write detailed transitions between the parts.
3. Focus on the largest units of your paper, then repeat the process for smaller organizational chunks (sections, paragraphs, groups of paragraphs).
4. Assemble the summaries and transitions into an informal outline.

This process will give you a clear sense of how the parts of your paper might fit together, a useful guide for drafting.

Cluster information. Clustering or grouping your information (2c-1–2) is a useful tactic when you have many bits of information but no clear idea of how they can be related.

STRATEGY

1. Describe on pieces of paper the clusters of information (major points from your sources, informal summaries or paraphrases, thoughts and ideas) you want to include.

2. Arrange the pieces of paper in relation to one another. As you begin to see patterns emerge, you may think of additional information that fits into one grouping or another.

Cut and paste. If you've been keeping a research journal to record and reflect on your research, you may already have the segments of your draft. Instead of spending a lot of time writing, try moving around the pieces you've already sketched to create a skeleton for your paper.

If you've written on both sides of your journal pages or you don't want to cut up the original, photocopy the relevant pages and cut out the individual entries. Arrange the entries to reflect a cohesive relationship, and compose transitions. Depending on how extensive your journal entries are, by the time you finish cutting and pasting, you may have most of your rough draft.

You can easily cut and paste using a word-processing program. Choose relevant passages from your notes or journal and paste them into a new file. Print out the results from time to time to see the overall pattern emerging.

Focus on the introduction and conclusion. Sometimes writing your introduction and conclusion first helps you envision a plan for the whole. In preparing the introduction and conclusion, you'll need to consider your readers' interests and their familiarity with your topic and to signal your paper's design and goals. Your research question(s) and tentative thesis will help you develop your introduction and conclusion.

STRATEGY

In writing the introduction:

- Ask yourself, "How can I engage readers from the start and make them want to read on?"
- Think of interesting ways to begin; even formal academic papers needn't have dull openings.
- Write different versions of the opening, experimenting with style and content.

In writing the conclusion:

- Ask yourself, "How can I make my readers want to keep thinking about the topic?"
- Don't hide behind a quotation.
- Avoid sentimental or patriotic clichés, and don't merely summarize.
- Try several versions.

You can present your research in many different formats; for information on the options, see section 27d.

27b An informative research paper

It's true—but only part of the story—to say that an informative research paper follows the shape of its subject. The other parts of the story are (1) the need to take into account your readers' expectations, knowledge, and values, and (2) the need to make sure readers understand your insights and conclusions. Here are strategies that may be especially helpful for informative writing.

1 Identify the parts

At the beginning of your research, you looked for topics (clusters of information and ideas) within your chosen subject and then focused on one or two of them. Do something similar now.

List. Working from memory, make a list of what you think are the principal elements of your topic, trying to include all those you consider necessary for readers to arrive at an understanding of the topic. In this way, you will draw on the overall understanding you have been developing throughout the research process and begin connecting it to the ways your readers are likely to approach the topic.

Don't stop with an overview, however. Go back to the details and reconsider your topic. Read through your research notes and make a second list of the elements of your topic as they appear in your notes.

Combine the lists. Combine the list drawn from memory with the list derived from your notes, highlighting the elements that come from one source only and combining overlapping categories. The combined list will help you identify areas in which you have gathered significant source material and those in which you need to do further research.

Rank the items. Number the items on your combined list according to what you think are the most important, most interesting, or most useful to readers. Your rankings should reflect your specific goals for writing, whether to provide a general understanding of the topic, to provide detailed advice, or to highlight recent developments and discoveries.

2 Consider readers

Readers may be interested in your topic for the same reasons you are—or maybe not. Perhaps you started your research paper in response to a *National Geographic* television special on the explorations in the Black Sea by the underwater archaeologist Robert Ballard. You may have always been curious about this kind of exploration, or about past civilizations in Eastern Europe, but chances are many of your readers won't share this curiosity. Try to identify the reasons your readers might have for being interested in your topic. Or think of how you might convince them that your topic is worth their attention.

Exercise 1

To help bring your readers and your research together, write down five reasons why readers *might* or *ought to be* interested in your topic. Then try a bit harder and write down five more reasons. Next, identify those aspects of your topic you think are most likely to interest readers or to be of use to them. The aim of this activity is to help you see your topic from a reader's perspective as well as your own.

Draw on all three lists as you plan your paper and prepare an introduction designed to lead readers into your paper. Create an informal outline of the information and ideas you plan to discuss, arranging them in an order that reflects both your interests and those of your readers.

3 Look for a pattern

The information and ideas in your research notes should suggest ways to organize your writing. Review your notes to see if they answer any of the following questions in depth and in detail. If so, make the answers a significant part of your writing.

QUESTIONS	PATTERN
What are the clusters or categories of ideas and information?	Classification
What are the differences or similarities among the concepts, activities, outlooks, situations, or subjects?	Comparison/Contrast
Are there surprising similarities between one subject and another, seemingly very different subject?	Analogy
How does it work? How can it be done?	Process
Why did it happen? What is likely to happen in the future?	Cause/Effect
What are the important concepts and how are they defined?	Definition
What are the features (physical, emotional, relational) of the subject?	Description
What happened? To whom? When? Where? Why? How?	Narration

4 Consider familiar plans

If you don't yet have an overall plan in mind, consider building your writing around one (or more) of these familiar informative plans.

- Describe a surprising or puzzling phenomenon, then provide an explanation.
- Outline a challenging task or goal, then suggest ways to accomplish it.
- Explain a common way of looking at events or situations, then suggest a new perspective.
- Focus on relationships, events, or objects that many people think are unimportant and explain why, to the contrary, they are very important.
- Compare the customs, values, or beliefs of one social or cultural group to those of another; or explain them to people unfamiliar or perhaps unsympathetic to those customs or beliefs.
- Start with a phenomenon about which people have offered many different, less than satisfactory explanations; then offer your own explanation, presenting it in detail and indicating why you think it more satisfactory.

5 Focus on conclusions and insights

Informative research writing isn't simply a presentation of information from sources. If it were, you would simply stitch together your notes. But effective research writing offers, above all, *your* explanations, conclusions, and insights and *your* selection and arrangement of information.

In creating informative research writing, therefore, make sure you can recognize your own insights and conclusions and include them in your writing in ways that enable readers to recognize them also. These strategies include thesis statement, topic sentences, and other direct statements; section headings; and paragraphs that summarize and discuss your interpretations or insights.

Here is the opening paragraph of an essay on animal behavior that ends with the author's conclusions—a sentence that acts as a thesis statement for the essay that follows.

> Scientists who work on animal behavior are occupationally obliged to live chancier lives than most of their colleagues, always at risk of being fooled by the animals they are studying or, worse, fooling themselves. Whether their experiments involve domesticated laboratory animals or wild creatures in the field, there is no end to the surprises that an animal can think up in the presence of an investigator. Sometimes it seems as if animals are genetically programmed to puzzle human beings, especially psychologists.
>
> —Lewis Thomas, "Clever Animals"

27c A persuasive research paper

A persuasive research essay advances, supports, and defends a thesis. The thesis may be a stand on an issue (an argumentative proposition), a proposed policy or a solution to a problem, or an interpretation of a subject. What sets persuasive research writing apart is the presence of alternative opinions, policies, interpretations. Thus, your planning needs to account not only for the reasons and evidence that support your thesis but also for grounds for preferring it to the alternatives.

1 Key elements

To be successful, persuasive writing needs to do the following.

- **Explain the issue, problem, or object of interpretation.** Persuasion responds to a situation in which readers have a choice among various opinions related to an issue or disagreement; among competing solutions to a problem; or among different interpretations of an object, event, or phenomenon. You need to make sure readers understand the issue itself—the focal point of differing opinions or interpretations.
- **Make clear your opinion (argumentative proposition), solution, or interpretation.** Readers will look for a thesis statement and other clear indications of your perspective.
- **Acknowledge and summarize other points of view and demonstrate why yours is preferable.** If you don't deal directly with other perspectives, most readers will think of them anyway—and you'll miss the chance to demonstrate why your outlook is preferable.

2 Plan your reasoning and support

Persuasive writing offers readers a chain of reasons (see 8b) that add up to a case in favor of the writer's thesis. Begin your planning by writing down all the major reasons you have for readers to agree with you, drawing on your research notes as you do. Then arrange these statements in an order that you consider logical and likely to persuade. Remember to include alternative points of view. (Having someone else look at your list is a good idea, too, because others can often spot slips in logic or a need for further reasons that you might overlook in reviewing your own work.)

Next, summarize the evidence and further reasons you can offer to persuade readers to agree with your line of reasoning. Write out your summaries under each of the corresponding major reasons from your earlier list, drawing on your research notes. The result will be an informal outline to guide your drafting.

3 Arrange statements and evidence in persuasive order

As you create your plan and begin writing, consider the procedures that many writers and readers have found effective in persuasion. Some of them are detailed in 11a–h; here are three more that are appropriate for persuasive research writing:

- **Present alternatives.** Begin by discussing the issue or problem. Then discuss the alternatives in detail, indicating why each is lacking in whole or in part. End with an extensive presentation of your own perspective, which may incorporate parts of the alternatives. This strategy is useful when your research has identified extensive arguments in favor of other opinions or solutions.
- **Summarize the scholarship.** Begin with a detailed analysis of other interpretations (in academic writing) or other solutions and policies (in public writing). Indicate why this prior work is flawed or inadequate, then offer your own solution or interpretation.
- **Take a middle ground.** Begin by outlining other opinions, interpretations, or solutions that take extreme positions, none of which is fully satisfactory. Then present your own perspective that takes a reasonable middle ground, avoiding the extremes of other outlooks.

27d Presentation strategies

Perhaps you envision a research paper or report as the outcome of your efforts: a stack of neatly laid out pages emerging from your computer printer. But is this your *only* option or your *best* choice? What if you submitted a disk with an electronic document or created a multimedia presentation? What fresh ways of presenting and explaining information do these choices offer? Can they help make your writing more persuasive? How will your readers react to such presentations? (And will your instructor accept presentations in such forms?)

1 Printed document

We are all familiar with the conventions of printed or word-processed documents. The sentences line up neatly across the page, left to right, top to bottom. The writer controls the order of presentation, choosing the sequence of sections and the arrangement of ideas and information. Readers can approach a paper in any manner, yet they usually choose to proceed from beginning to end, leaping backward or forward only to check details or to reread for clarification.

Because printed documents are linear, effective writers use strategies that help readers understand information and ideas by presenting them in a step-by-step manner with summaries, section headings, topic sentences, and organizing or transitional statements. In addition, printed documents introduce material from sources in a restricted number of ways, primarily through summary, paraphrase, synthesis, and quotation (see 26h).

Chapter 13, on document design, suggests alternative ways of varying type appearance and page layout to highlight and convey ideas. It also describes strategies for incorporating information through visuals such as pictures, charts, graphs, and clip art. As an example, student Jenny Latimer (see Chapter 21) wanted readers to be surprised by the number and kinds of everyday snack foods that contain hydrogenated oils. She first thought of listing examples in the text, but she realized that putting them in columns would call readers' attention to them more effectively. She liked the effect of the columns, but she still wanted to link the items in the list more directly to readers' everyday experience. To do this, she included thumbnail pictures of products that readers would recognize immediately.

2 Electronic document

Electronic documents can take two forms: word-processing documents and documents created through a presentation program like *PowerPoint*. Both can be submitted on disk or as an attachment to email. Both must be read on a computer to take full advantage of the format.

Word-processed documents are similar to traditional print documents except that they can incorporate source material in ways other than by using paraphrases, summaries, and quotes—particularly in the forms of streaming video and audio clips. If your research paper is an interpretation of a film or of several performances of a Shakespeare play on film, you may be able to include clips from the film or short examples of different actors playing the same scene from *Hamlet*. If you are drawing on interviews as a primary source of information, you may be able to include audio clips from an interview as an alternative way of quoting a source.

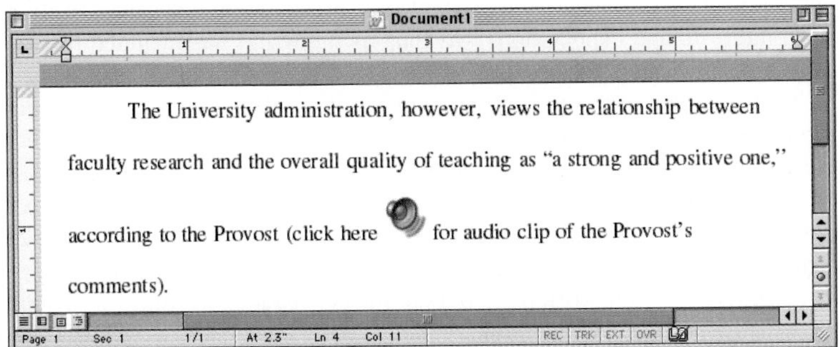

To insert sound clips, follow the directions in your word-processing program.

Presentation programs like *PowerPoint* enable you to arrange information in graphic ways that emphasize relationships and highlight key ideas.

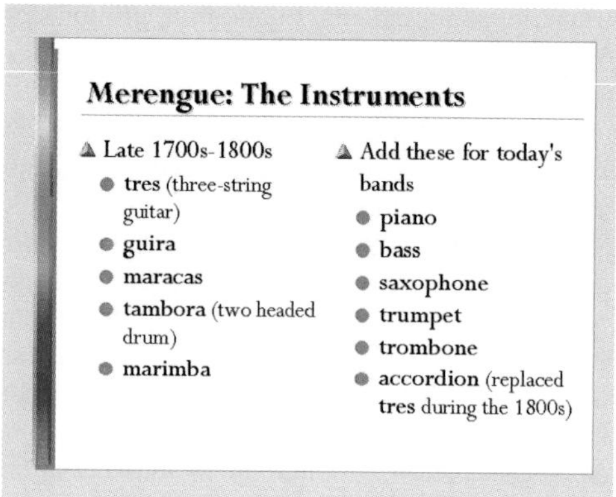

FIGURE 27.1 *PowerPoint* presentation within a document

They can also incorporate action sequences like arrows linking statements or fades from one piece of text (or a visual) to another. Because *PowerPoint* and similar programs do not allow for the extensive presentation of text, they work best when incorporated within word-processed documents (see Figure 27.1 above).

3 Webbed document

A **webbed document,** a Web page or a file written in HTML or a similar language used to create Web pages, allows readers to move around at will within a document. It also includes links that readers can use to move to related documents or source material. Thus, in a webbed document, readers can control the sequence and content of a presentation according to their own interests and expectations—as long as the writer has included the options necessary for such control.

If you plan to create such a document, you will need to write each section so that it can be understood more or less on its own, for some readers may choose to read it as a free-standing statement.

In addition, you will need to add links to your paper in ways that serve your purposes. For instance, you can include links to the full texts of research articles you have summarized or paraphrased, giving readers a chance to test the accuracy of your work or to pursue further reading. Or you can include links to supporting evidence and arguments that allow readers to view added support about points on which they need further reasons for agreeing with you.

In an argument for a vegetarian lifestyle, student Naomi Roth included links to vegetarian menus and recipes and to famous people who are committed vegetarians as a way of answering potential objections to her arguments.

```
Misperception #3 Nobody really important is a vegetarian.
    On the contrary, famous people ranging from the actor
Keenan Ivory Wayans to the actress Reese Witherspoon to the
power lifter Pat Reeves to the late comedian Milton Berle
(lived to 93) were either vegetarians or vegans. Want to learn
about others? Try this link for famous vegetarians and vegans
(with some biographies) and this link for vegetarians and
vegans both past and present.
```

4 Multimedia presentation

Some computer programs (such as Macromedia *Dreamweaver*) enable you, with very little expertise or training, to create presentations incorporating text, audio, still visuals, and action video. The result can be presentations similar to television documentaries, with the option of adding extensive text offering detailed information, references, and documentation.

In a multimedia presentation, you control the choice of information, the techniques, and the sequence, much as a television or film director does. Indeed, the finished product can have many of the techniques you are familiar with in films: fades, blurring, closeups, quick cuts from scene to scene, and the like.

The amount of print information and discussion you can incorporate in a multimedia document is limited, though the voice track can provide a relatively specific and detailed account of your research and reasoning. You can, however, present significant amounts of visual data. An environmental presentation can contain closeups of a polluted site, with arrows highlighting specific features and a voiced commentary providing further data. Or a research project drawing on ethnographic observation and interview can allow subjects to speak for themselves, as printed text on the screen provides comments and conclusions from the writer.

The key to a successful multimedia presentation is to resist the temptation to create a flashy image and to provide readers with the detailed discussion of information and ideas they expect from traditional research writing.

PART 6

Documenting Sources

CHAPTER 28 MLA Documentation

Modern Language Association (MLA) documentation style calls for in-text (parenthetical) references and a list of works cited. This chapter discusses MLA style and provides models for the most common kinds of entries you will use.

MLA IN-TEXT (PARENTHETICAL) FORMATS

MLA WORKS CITED MODEL ENTRIES

1. BOOKS AND WORKS TREATED AS BOOKS

PARENTHETICAL During World War II, government posters often portrayed homemakers "as vital defenders of the nation's homes" (Honey 135).

2. Author's name as part of discussion

You can make the author's name (or the title and other information as well) part of the discussion.

AUTHOR NAMED IN DISCUSSION According to Maureen Honey, government posters during World War II often portrayed homemakers "as vital defenders of the nation's homes" (135).

3. Placement of parenthetical citations

In general, put parenthetical citations close to the quotation, information, paraphrase, or summary you are documenting. Place the parenthetical citation either at the end of a sentence (before the final punctuation) or at a natural pause in the sentence.

> Wayland Hand reports on a folk belief that going to sleep on a rug made of bearskin can relieve backache (183).

If the citation applies to only part of the sentence, put it after the borrowed material at the point least likely to disrupt the sentence.

> The folk belief that "sleeping on a bear rug will cure backache" (Hand 183) is yet another example of a kind of magic in which external objects produce results inside the body.

4. General reference

A **general reference** enables you to refer to the main ideas in a source or to information presented throughout the work, not in a single place. You need not provide page numbers for a general reference.

PARENTHETICAL Many species of animals have developed complex systems of communication (Bright).

The statement summarizes one of the work's main points, so the reference cites the work as a whole, not a specific page or pages.

AUTHOR NAMED IN DISCUSSION According to Michael Bright, many species of animals have developed complex systems of communication.

5. Specific reference

A **specific reference** enables you to document words, ideas, or facts appearing in a particular place in a source.

> People have trouble recognizing sound patterns dolphins use to communicate. Dolphins can perceive clicking sounds "made up of 700 units of sound per second," yet "in the human ear the sounds would fuse together in our minds at 20-30 clicks per second" (Bright 52).

The page number gives the specific location of the quotation.

> According to Michael Bright, dolphins recognize patterns consisting of seven hundred clicks each second, yet such patterns begin to blur for people at around twenty or thirty clicks each second (52).

The page number cites the specific source of information in the summary.

STRATEGY

Use the following questions to help decide whether to make in-text citations general or specific and whether to make them parenthetical or part of the discussion.

- Am I trying to weave broad concepts into my own explanation or argument (general), or am I looking for precise ideas and details to support my conclusions (specific)?
- Will this part of my paper be clearer and more effective if I draw on the author's own words (specific) or if I merely point out that the author's text as a whole presents the concepts I am discussing (general)?
- Do I wish to highlight the source by naming the author (part of discussion), or to emphasize the information itself (parenthetical)?
- Will this passage be more concise, emphatic, or effective if I put the author's name in parentheses or if I work it into the discussion?
- Do I wish to refer to more than one source without distracting readers (parenthetical), or do the several sources I am citing need individual attention (part of discussion)?

6. Two or three authors

Give the names of all the authors in parentheses or in the discussion.

PARENTHETICAL By the time Elizabeth I died, Francis Bacon had amassed considerable debt (Jardine and Stewart 275).

If the book had three authors, the citation would read (Jardine, Stewart, and Ringler 275).

AUTHOR NAMED IN TEXT Jardine and Stewart provide a partial list of Francis Bacon's debts from the year Elizabeth I died (275).

7. Four or more authors

Supply the first author's name and the phrase *et al.* (meaning "and others") within parentheses. To introduce the citation as part of the discussion, use a phrase like "Chen and his colleagues point out. . . ."

More funding would encourage creative research of complementary medicine (Chen et al. 82).

If you give all the authors' names rather than *et al.* in the works cited list (Entry 3, see p. 422), then give all the names in the in-text citation.

8. Organization or group as author

If an organization or government agency is named as the author, use its name (shortened, if cumbersome) in the citation.

Concerns over the quality of local news programs led to a proposed system of standards ("benchmarking") for raising the quality of journalism (Project for Excellence 189-91).

Project for Excellence is the shortened name of Project for Excellence in Journalism.

9. More than one work by the same author

When the list of works cited includes more than one work by the same author, add the title in shortened form to your citation.

The members of some Protestant groups in the Appalachian region view the "handling of serpents" during worship "as a supreme act of faith" (Daugherty, "Serpent-Handling" 232).

"Serpent-Handling" is a shortened version of "Serpent-Handling as Sacrament." In a parenthetical citation, add a comma between the author's name and the title.

10. Authors with the same last name

When the authors of different sources have the same last name, identify the specific author by giving the first initial (or the full first name, if necessary).

Medical errors remain a major problem (D. Adams 1); however, new information systems may help reduce them (J. Adams 309).

11. No author given

When no author's name is given, use the title instead (in a shortened version if it is long). Begin the abbreviated title with the word used to alphabetize the work in the list of works cited.

On January 1, 1993, the former state of Czechoslovakia split into two new states, the Czech Republic and the Slovak Republic (Baedeker's 67).

The shortened title refers to *Baedeker's Czech/Slovak Republics*, a book for which no author is given.

12. Indirect source ("quoted in")

When your source provides you with a quotation (or paraphrase) taken from yet another source, you need to include the phrase *qtd. in* (for "quoted in") to indicate the original source.

For Vitz, "art, especially great art, must engage all or almost all of the major capacities of the nervous system" (qtd. in Feuch 65).

Feuch is the source of the quotation from Vitz.

When referring to an indirect source, you should generally include in your discussion the name of the person from whom the quotation is taken. If the same information were presented in a parenthetical citation—(*Vitz, qtd. in Feuch 65*)—some readers might mistakenly look for Vitz rather than Feuch in the list of works cited.

13. Summary or paraphrase

When your summary or paraphrase (see pp. 311–313) provides the author's name, your parenthetical citation should provide only the page number(s) of your source. Otherwise, name the source in the citation.

SUMMARY

Bauerlein argues that important conservative thinkers like Friedrich von Hayek and Russell Kirk receive little attention in college courses (B5-B7).

PARAPHRASE

Lauren Hillenbrand says she came across Red Pollard, the jockey for Seabiscuit, when she was examining papers about the well-known thoroughbred horse (111).

14. Long quotation

The citation in parentheses comes at the end of a long quotation set off as a block (quotation not enclosed in quotation marks) (see pp. 388–389). Put the citation after the end punctuation, with a space before the parentheses.

> Cricket, as played in India, has taken a path of commercialization similar to that of American football and basketball.
>
> > Like other sports figures in the capitalist world, the best-known Indian cricket stars are now metacommodities, for sale themselves while fueling the circulation of other commodities. The sport is increasingly in the hands of advertisers, promoters, and entrepreneurs, with television, radio, and print media feeding the national passion for the sport and its stars. (Appadurai 106)

15. Short quotation

The citation in parentheses comes after the quotation marks that close the quotation. If the quotation ends with an exclamation point or question mark, put it inside the quotation marks. If the material you are quoting contains quotation marks, use double quotation marks to enclose the quotation as a whole and single quotation marks to enclose the interior quotation.

> According to Dubisch, "Being a 'healthfood person' involves more than simply changing one's diet or utilizing an alternative medical system" (61).

16. Two or more sources in a single citation

When you use a parenthetical citation to refer to more than one source, separate the sources with a semicolon.

> Differences in the ways people speak, especially differences in the ways men and women use language, can often be traced to who has power and who does not (Tannen 83-86; Tavris 297-301).

17. Selection in anthology

If your source is a reprint of an essay, poem, short story, or other work appearing in an anthology, cite the work's author (not the editor of the anthology), but refer to the page number(s) in the anthology.

John Corry argues that pornographic material is not really available "with just the click of a button" (114).

The selection appears on page 114 of the anthology *Pornography: Opposing Viewpoints.*

18. Multivolume work

Give the volume number followed by a colon and a space, then the page number: (*Franklin 6: 434*). When referring to the volume as a whole, use a comma after the author's name and add *vol.* before the volume number: (*Franklin, vol. 6*).

In 1888, Lewis Carroll let two students call their school paper Jabberwock, a made-up word from Alice's Adventures in Wonderland (Cohen 2: 695).

The author is Cohen, the volume number is 2, and the page number is 695.

19. Literary work

When you refer to a literary work, consider including information that will help readers find the passage you are citing in any of the different editions of the work. Begin by giving the page number of the particular edition followed by a semicolon; then add the appropriate chapter, part, or section numbers.

In Huckleberry Finn, Mark Twain ridicules the exaggerated histrionics of provincial actors through his portrayal of the King and the Duke as they rehearse Hamlet's famous soliloquy: "So [the duke] went to marching up and down, thinking, and frowning horrible every now and then; then he would hoist up his eyebrows; next he would squeeze his hand on his forehead and stagger back and kind of moan; next he would sigh, and next he'd let on to drop a tear" (178; ch. 21).

Note that there is a semicolon after the page number, followed by *ch.* (for "chapter"). If you also include a part number, use *pt.* followed by a comma and the chapter number, as in (*386; pt. 3, ch. 2*). For a play, note the act, scene, and line numbers, if needed, as in this reference to *Hamlet*: (*Ham. 1.2.76*). For poems, give line numbers (*55–57*) or, if there are part divisions, both part and line numbers (*4.220–23*).

20. Web site or other electronic (nonprint) source

Provide the name of the author, the title, or any other information readers need to find the appropriate entry in your list of works cited. You need not include a page number for electronic sources of a single page or without page numbering. For numbered paragraphs, give the number and use the abbreviation *par(s)*, and for screens or sections, use *screen* or *sec.*

WEB SITE WITHOUT PAGE NUMBERING

According to the Royal College of Psychiatrists Web site, one problem with using alcohol to get to sleep "is that you will usually wake up half-way through the night."

WEB SITE .PDF FILE WITH PAGE NUMBERING

According to the Royal College of Psychiatrists Web site, one problem with using alcohol to get to sleep "is that you will usually wake up half-way through the night" (4).

WEB SITE WITH SCREEN NUMBERING

Offspringmag.com summarizes current research on adolescent behavior (Boynton, screen 2).

FILM

In contrast, the heroine's mother in the film Clueless died in an ironic and contemporary fashion: the victim of an accident during liposuction.

21. Visual in text

In your discussion, refer to the visual as a *figure* (abbreviated *fig.*). Include citation information in the caption for the visual.

TEXT

Satellite photos (fig. 2) give some idea of the damage flooding from Hurricane Katrina caused in New Orleans.

FIGURE CAPTION

Fig. 2. Extent of flooding on September 8, 2005 (National Aeronautics and Space Administration).

22. Bible, Koran, or other religious text

Give book, chapter, and verse for the Bible, Koran, or other religious text. MLA style uses a period between the chapter and verse numbers (*Mark 2.3–4*). For parenthetical citations, use abbreviations for names of five or

more letters, as in the case of Deuteronomy: (*Deut. 16.21–22*) or (Holy Bible New International Version *Num. 5.5-8*).

> God's instructions to Moses also cover issues of guilt, forgiveness, and restitution (Num. 5.5-8).

23. Email, interview, or personal communication

Direct readers to the information in your Works Cited list (pp. 432–433) by giving the name of the writer or the person being interviewed.

> One of the director's assistants recalls that staging the show for the first time was "an experiment in chaos and misunderstanding" (Shiels).

24. Numbered paragraphs or screens

If a source contains numbered paragraphs or screens, use *par(s)*. or *screen(s)* to identify the location of information or a quotation, preceded by a comma.

> In "Life Without Principle," he asks us to "consider the way in which we spend our lives" (Thoreau, par. 3).

25. More than one reference to a source in a sentence or paragraph

If you refer to a source more than once in a passage, you may be able to combine references.

> Anthony Giddens views contemporary society as "a runaway world" in which belief in the powers of reason or rationality may be outmoded but "a world of multiple possibilities" is open to us (Bryant and Jary 263, 264).

The first page number is for the first quotation and the second for the second quotation.

or

> Anthony Giddens views contemporary society as "a runaway world" (Bryant and Jary 263). He argues that belief in the powers of reason or rationality may be outmoded but that a "world of multiple possibilities" is open to us (264).

The second page number clearly refers to the Bryant and Jary source.

28c Informative footnotes and endnotes

At times you may wish to comment on the usefulness or reliability of a source, provide some additional background details, or discuss a specific point at length. You recognize, however, that doing so would disrupt the flow of the discussion and would be useful for only a few readers. Informative footnotes (or endnotes) offer a solution. Place a number (raised slightly above the line of the text) at a suitable point in your discussion. Then provide the note itself, labeled with a corresponding number at the bottom of a page (for a footnote) or at the end of the paper before the list of works cited on a page titled "Notes" (for an endnote).

> [1]Anyone still inclined to question the intricacy of video games and the conceptual challenges they pose might consider investigating the numerous publications devoted to strategies for games and the imaginative, detailed worlds the programmers create for the games.

28d Works Cited list

In an alphabetized list titled "Works Cited," placed on a new page that follows the last page of your paper or report, provide readers with detailed information about the sources you have cited in the text. To indicate all the works you consulted, even if you did not cite them all, you may provide a list titled "Works Consulted."

In your list of works cited, alphabetize the entries by the author's last name or by last and first names for authors with the same last name. If a source does not identify an author, alphabetize by the first word in the title (other than *A*, *An*, or *The*).

1 Books and works treated as books

MODEL FORMAT FOR BOOKS AND WORKS TREATED AS BOOKS

period + space (after Author(s).) · period + space (after Title of Work.) · colon + space (after Place of Publication:)

```
Author(s). Title of Work. Place of Publication:
     Publisher, Year Published.
```

indent five spaces · comma + space (after Publisher,) · period (after Year Published.)

- **Author(s).** Give the author's last name first, followed by the first name (spelled out unless the author uses initials), any middle name or initial, and a period. Do not include titles like *M.D.* or *SJ*, but include other parts of a name, like *III* or *Jr.*, placing them at the end of the name preceded by a comma: *Valantasio, Louis, Jr.* (See Entries 2 and 3 for sources with more than one author.)
- **Title of work.** Give the title of the work, including any subtitle. (Use a colon to introduce a subtitle unless the primary title ends with a question mark, dash, or exclamation point.) Capitalize the main words, and end with a period unless the title ends with some other mark of punctuation. Underline the title, but not the period.
- **Publication information.** After the title, provide the city where the work was published, followed by a colon and a single space. If not obvious, add the country (abbreviated, as in *Dover, Eng.*). If more than one place of publication appears in the work, use the first one in your citation. Then give the publisher's name (followed by a comma) and the year of publication (followed by a period). Omit unnecessary words such as *Publisher, Inc.*, and *Co.* (For example, use just *McGraw*, not *McGraw-Hill, Inc.*) Substitute the letters *U* and *P* for the words *University* and *Press* where they appear in the publisher's name (for example, *U of Chicago P*). If any of the basic publication information is missing, use *n.p.* ("no place" or "no publisher") or *n.d.* ("no date").
- **Spacing.** Double-space all entries, and indent five spaces for the second and any additional lines in each entry. Leave spaces between each of the major elements in an entry (author's name, title of work, and publication information).

1. One author

Hockney, David. Secret Knowledge: Recovering the Lost Techniques of the Old Masters. New York: Viking Studio, 2001.

2. Two or three authors

Give the first author's name, starting with the last name, followed by the other names in regular order. Use commas to separate the names, and introduce the second of two names or the third name with *and*.

Kress, Gunther, and Theo van Leeuwen. Reading Images: The Grammar of Graphic Design. London: Routledge, 1996.

3. Four or more authors

Use the first author's name and then the phrase *et al.* (meaning "and others"). You may choose to give all the names, but if you do, you must list all of them in any parenthetical citations (see p. 415).

Bellah, Robert N., et al. Habits of the Heart: Individualism and Commitment in American Life. Berkeley: U of California P, 1985.

All authors listed: Bellah, Robert N., Richard Madsen, William M. Sullivan, Ann Swidler, and Steven M. Tipton.

4. Organization or group as author

Treat the corporation, organization, or government agency as the author, alphabetizing by the first main word of the organization's name. If the organization is also the publisher, repeat its name again, abbreviated if appropriate.

United Nations Educational, Scientific, and Cultural Organization. A Short Internet Guide. New York: UNESCO, 2001.

5. No author given

List the work alphabetically according to the first main word of its title.

Guide for Authors. Oxford: Blackwell, 1985.

6. More than one book by the same author

List multiple works by an author alphabetically by the first main word of the title. For the first entry, include the full name(s) of the author(s). For additional entries, use three hyphens in place of the name, followed by a period and a space, but only if the author or authors are *exactly* the same for each work. If the authorship differs in any way, include the name(s) in full.

Tannen, Deborah. The Argument Culture: Moving from Debate to Dialogue. New York: Random, 1998.

---. You're Wearing That? Understanding Mothers and Daughters in Conversation. New York: Random, 2006.

7. One or more editors

Begin with the editor's name followed by a comma and the abbreviation *ed.* or *eds.*

Achebe, Chinua, and C. L. Innes, eds. African Short Stories. London: Heinemann, 1985.

8. Author and an editor

Begin with either the author's or the editor's name depending on whether you are using the text itself or the editor's contributions.

Leonardo da Vinci. Leonardo on Painting. Ed. Martin Kemp. New Haven: Yale UP, 1989.

9. Translator

Refer to the book by its author, not its translator, even though the English words are the translator's. Abbreviate the translator's title as *Trans.*

Baudrillard, Jean. Cool Memories II: 1978-1990. Trans. Chris Turner. Durham: Duke UP, 1996.

10. Edition other than the first

Give the edition number (*3rd ed.*) or description (*Rev. ed.* or *1998 ed.*, for example) after the title.

Coe, Michael D. The Maya. 7th ed. New York: Thames, 2005.

11. Reprinted book

Supply the original publication date after the title. If pertinent, include the original publisher or place of publication. Then follow with the publication information from the work you are using.

Kerouac, Jack. On the Road. 1957. New York: Viking, 1997.

12. Multivolume work

Indicate the total number of volumes after the title (or after the editor's or translator's name).

Tsao, Hsueh-chin. The Story of the Stone. Trans. David Hawkes. 5 vols. Harmondsworth, Eng.: Penguin, 1983-86.

If you are citing a particular volume instead of the whole work or several volumes from the whole work, supply only the particular volume number and publication information. Indicate the total number of volumes at the end of the entry.

Tsao, Hsueh-chin. The Story of the Stone. Trans. David Hawkes. Vol. 1. Harmondsworth, Eng.: Penguin, 1983. 5 vols.

13. Book in a series

Give the series name and any item number after the title of the work. Use abbreviations for familiar words in the name of the series (such as *ser.* for *series*).

Grover-Friedlander, Michal. Vocal Apparitions: The Attraction of Cinema to Opera. Princeton Stud. in Opera. Princeton: Princeton UP, 2005.

14. Book published before 1900

For books published before 1900, include the publisher's name only if it is relevant to your research. Use a comma rather than a colon after place of publication.

Darwin, Charles. Descent of Man and Selection in Relation to Sex. New York, 1896.

15. Book with a publisher's imprint

For a book issued with a special imprint name, give the imprint name first, followed by a hyphen and the main publisher's name.

Sikes, Gini. 8 Ball Chicks: A Year in the Violent World of Girl Gangs. New York: Anchor-Doubleday, 1997.

16. Anthology or collection of articles

To refer to an anthology or a collection of scholarly articles as a whole, supply the editor's name first, followed by *ed.*, and then the title of the collection.

Silver, Alain, and James Ursini, eds. Horror Film Reader. Pompton Plains, NY: Limelight, 2001.

To cite a selection within an anthology or collection, see Entries 35 and 36 on page 431.

17. Government document

Begin with the government or agency name(s) or the author, if any. Start with *United States* for a congressional document or a report from a federal agency; otherwise, begin with the name of the government and agency or the name of the independent agency. For congressional documents, write *Cong.* (for *Congress*), identify the branch (*Senate* or *House*), and give the number and session (for example, *101st Cong., 1st sess.*). Include the title of the specific document and the title of the book in which it is printed. Use *GPO* for *Government Printing Office*.

United States. Office of Juvenile Justice and Delinquency Prevention. Promising Strategies to Reduce Gun Violence. By David I. Sheppard and Shay Bilchik. Washington: GPO, 1999.

United States. Cong. Senate. Committee on Commerce, Science, and Transportation. Internet Filtering Systems. 105th Cong., 2nd sess. Washington: GPO, 1998.

18. Title within a title

When a book title contains another work's title, do not underline the title of the second work. If the second title would normally be enclosed in quotation marks, add them and underline the entire title.

Weick, Carl F. Refiguring Huckleberry Finn. Athens: U of Georgia P, 2000.

19. Pamphlet

Use the same form for a pamphlet as for a book.

Vareika, William. John La Farge: An American Master (1835-1910). Newport: Gallery of American Art, 1989.

20. Published dissertation

Treat a published doctoral dissertation as a book. Include the abbreviation *Diss.*, the school for which the dissertation was written, and the year the degree was awarded.

Said, Edward W. Joseph Conrad and the Fiction of Autobiography. Diss. Harvard U, 1964. Cambridge: Harvard UP, 1966.

21. Unpublished dissertation

Use quotation marks for the title; include the abbreviation *Diss.*, the school for which the dissertation was written, and the date of the degree.

Pennell, Michael. "English in the 'Hurricane Winds of Change': Labor Market Intermediaries in Two Indiana Counties." Diss. Purdue U, 2005.

22. Conference proceedings

Begin with the title unless an editor is named. Follow with details about the conference, including name and date.

Childhood Obesity: Causes and Prevention. Symposium Proc., 27 Oct. 1998. Washington: Center for Nutrition Policy and Promotion, 1999.

23. Bible, Koran, or other religious text

Identify the version, the editor or translator (if indicated), and the publication information.

Zondervan NIV Study Bible. Grand Rapids: Zondervan, 2006.

2 Articles and selections from books

MODEL FORMAT FOR ARTICLES AND SELECTIONS

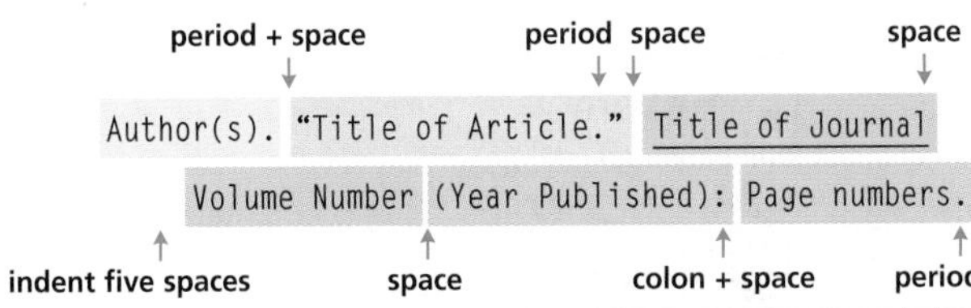

- **Author(s).** Give the author's last name first, followed by the first name, any initial, and a period. If the piece has more than one author, give subsequent names in regular order separated by commas with *and* preceding the final name.
- **Title of article.** Give the article's full title in quotation marks, concluding with a period unless the title ends with a question mark or an exclamation point.
- **Title of journal, periodical, or book.** Give the publication's title, underlined, but not including an opening *The*, *A*, or *An*. Do not end the title with a period.
- **Publication information.** Supply the volume number (and sometimes the issue number), the year of publication (in parentheses), and the page numbers for the full article or selection. The volume number is always found on the publication's cover or title page; even if it is in Roman numerals, use Arabic numerals for your entry. For a scholarly journal, you don't need to include the month or season (e.g., Winter). Introduce the page numbers with a colon.
- **Spacing.** Double-space all entries, and indent five spaces for the second and any additional lines in each entry. Leave a space between each of the major elements in an entry (author's name, article or selection title, and journal title along with publication information). Leave a space between the colon and the page numbers and also after the journal title and the volume number.

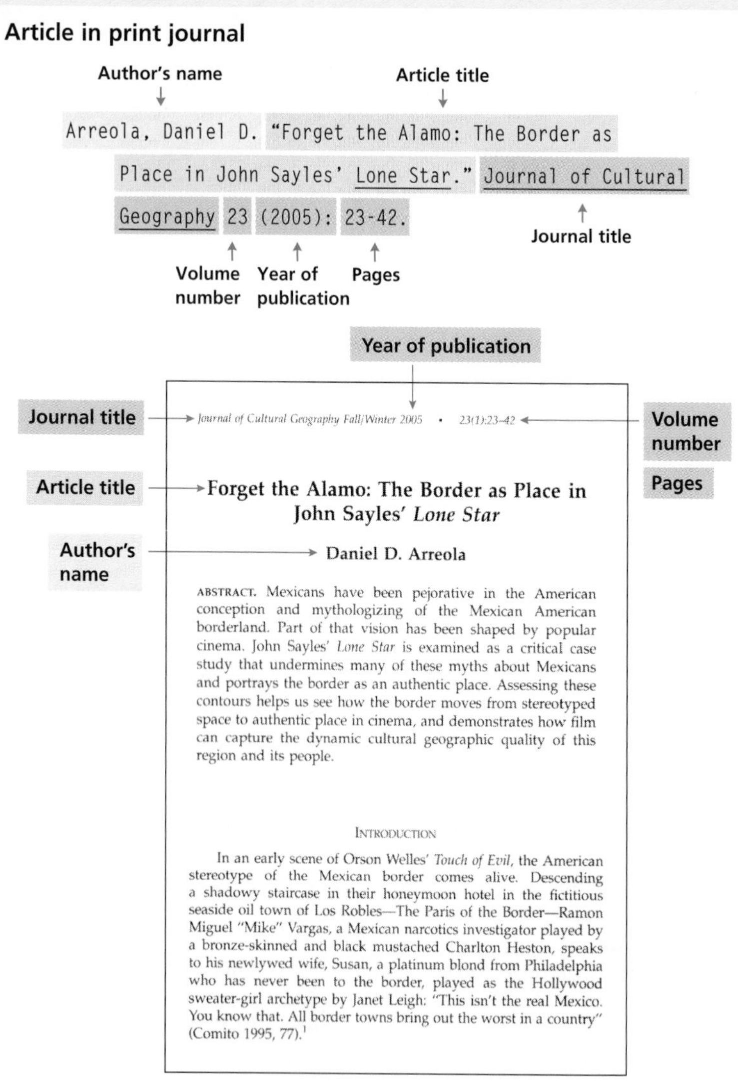

Article in print journal
Author's name
Article title
Arreola, Daniel D. "Forget the Alamo: The Border as
Place in John Sayles' Lone Star." Journal of Cultural
Geography 23 (2005): 23-42.
Journal title
Volume number
Year of publication
Pages
Year of publication
Journal title
Volume number
Pages
Article title
Author's name
Journal of Cultural Geography Fall/Winter 2005 • 23(1):23–42
Forget the Alamo: The Border as Place in John Sayles' Lone Star
Daniel D. Arreola
ABSTRACT. Mexicans have been pejorative in the American conception and mythologizing of the Mexican American borderland. Part of that vision has been shaped by popular cinema. John Sayles' Lone Star is examined as a critical case study that undermines many of these myths about Mexicans and portrays the border as an authentic place. Assessing these contours helps us see how the border moves from stereotyped space to authentic place in cinema, and demonstrates how film can capture the dynamic cultural geographic quality of this region and its people.
INTRODUCTION
In an early scene of Orson Welles' Touch of Evil, the American stereotype of the Mexican border comes alive. Descending a shadowy staircase in their honeymoon hotel in the fictitious seaside oil town of Los Robles—The Paris of the Border—Ramon Miguel "Mike" Vargas, a Mexican narcotics investigator played by a bronze-skinned and black mustached Charlton Heston, speaks to his newlywed wife, Susan, a platinum blond from Philadelphia who has never been to the border, played as the Hollywood sweater-girl archetype by Janet Leigh: "This isn't the real Mexico. You know that. All border towns bring out the worst in a country" (Comito 1995, 77).[1]

24. Article in journal paginated by volume

Each volume consists of several issues, paginated continuously; that is, each issue begins where the preceding issue left off—at page 354, for example. Give the volume number after the journal's title.

Eagleton, Terry. "Political Beckett?" New Left Review 40 (2006): 67-74.

25. Article in journal paginated by issue

The issues making up a volume are paginated separately. Give the volume number first, followed by a period and the issue number.

Adams, Jessica. "Local Color: The Southern Plantation in Popular Culture." Cultural Critique 42.1 (1999): 171-87.

26. Article in weekly magazine

Put the day first, then the month (abbreviated except for May, June, and July), and then the year followed by a colon. Give inclusive page numbers. If the pages are not consecutive, give the first page with a plus sign (for example, *23+*). (Treat biweekly magazines in a similar fashion.)

Conlin, Michelle. "Unmarried America." Business Week 20 Oct. 2003: 106+.

27. Article in monthly magazine

Treat a monthly or bimonthly magazine as a weekly magazine (Entry 26), but without listing the day.

Jacobson, Doranne. "Doing Lunch." Natural History Mar. 2000: 66-69.

28. Unsigned article in magazine

Begin with the title (ignoring *A*, *An*, and *The* when alphabetizing).

"The Obesity Industry." Economist 27 Sept. 2003: 64+.

29. Article in newspaper

Treat a newspaper as a weekly magazine, including citation of pages (see Entry 26), but include the section number or letter with the page number. Omit *A*, *An*, or *The* at the beginning of a newspaper's name. For a local newspaper, give the city's name in brackets after the title unless the city is named in the title.

Willis, Ellen. "Steal This Myth: Why We Still Try to Re-create the Rush of the 60s." New York Times 20 Aug. 2000, Late Ed., Sec. 2: AR1+.

30. Editorial

Supply the title first for an unsigned editorial and the author's name first for a signed editorial. Identify with the word *editorial*.

"A False Choice." Editorial. Charlotte Observer 16 Aug. 1998: 2C.

31. Letter to the editor

Use the word *letter* to identify a letter to the editor.

Hogner, Lindon. Letter. "Mandate Time Off for Fatigued Doctors." USA Today 18 Dec. 2006: 20A.

32. Interview—published

Treat the person interviewed, not the interviewer, as the author. For untitled interviews, include the word *Interview* (without underlining or quotation marks) in place of a title.

Stewart, Martha. "'I Do Have a Brain.'" Interview with Kevin Kelly. Wired Aug. 1998: 114.

33. Review

Give the title after the name of the reviewer. Cite an unsigned review by its title.

Muñoz, José Esteban. "Citizens and Superheroes." Rev. of The Queen of America Goes to Washington City, by Lauren Berlant. American Quarterly 52 (2000): 397-404.

For a review with no title, give the name of the reviewer followed by *Rev. of* ("Review of"), the work's title, a comma, the word *by*, and the author of the work.

Asante, Molefi Kete. Rev. of Race and the Writing of History: Riddling the Sphinx, by Maghan Keita. Journal of Black Studies 31 (2001): 699-701.

34. Article from encyclopedia or reference volume

Begin with the author's name or with the article's title if no author is named. You need not include the publisher or place of publication for a common reference work or series; instead, note the edition and the date. If entries are arranged alphabetically, you need not note the volume or page(s).

Oliver, Paul, and Barry Kernfeld. "Blues." The New Grove Dictionary of Jazz. Ed. Barry Kernfeld. New York: St. Martin's, 1994.

"The History of Western Theatre." The New Encyclopaedia Britannica: Macropedia. 15th ed. 1987. Vol. 28.

35. Selection in anthology or chapter in edited book

List the author of the selection or chapter and give the title in quotation marks (but underline titles of novels, plays, and other works first published on their own). Next, provide the underlined title of the book containing the selection or chapter. If the collection has an editor, follow with the abbreviation *Ed.* and the name(s) of the editor(s) in regular order. Conclude with publication information and the selection's inclusive page numbers.

Atwood, Margaret. "Bluebeard's Egg." Bluebeard's Egg and Other Stories. New York: Fawcett-Random, 1987. 131-64.

After citing in full the original source for a selection reprinted in a collection, use the phrase *Rpt. in* ("Reprinted in") followed by information about the source you consulted.

Atwood, Margaret. "Bluebeard's Egg." Bluebeard's Egg and Other Stories. New York: Fawcett-Random, 1987. 131-64. Rpt. in Don't Bet on the Prince: Contemporary Feminist Fairy Tales in North America and England. Ed. Jack Zipes. New York: Methuen, 1989. 160-82.

36. More than one selection from anthology or collection (cross-reference)

When you cite two or more works from an anthology or collection, include an entry for the collection and provide cross-references for individual selections.

Hooper, Glenn, and Colin Graham, eds. Irish and Postcolonial Writing: History, Theory, Practice. London: Palgrave-Macmillian, 2002.

Entry for collection.

Mustafa, Shakir. "Demythologizing Ireland: Revisionism and the Irish Colonial Experience." Hooper and Graham 66-86.

Individual selection.

Innes, Lyn. "Orientalism and Celticism." Hooper and Graham 142-56.

Individual selection.

37. Preface, foreword, introduction, or afterword

Indicate whether the selection is a preface, foreword, introduction, or afterword. Give the title of the work and the name of its author, preceded by the word *By*.

Tomlin, Janice. Foreword. The Complete Guide to Foreign Adoption. By Barbara Brooke Bascom and Carole A. McKelvey. New York: Pocket, 1997.

38. Letter—published

Treat the letter writer as the author. Indicate the date or the collection number of the letter if the information is available.

Garland, Hamlin. "To Fred Lewis Pattee." 30 Dec. 1914. Letter 206 of Selected Letters of Hamlin Garland. Ed. Keith Newlin and Joseph B. McCullough. Lincoln: U of Nebraska P, 1998.

39. Dissertation abstract

For an abstract of a dissertation published in *Dissertation Abstracts International* (*DAI*) or *Dissertation Abstracts* (*DA*), follow the author's name and the title with the abbreviation *Diss.* (for "Dissertation"), the institution's name, and the date of the degree. Conclude with publication information for the particular volume of abstracts.

Hawkins, Joanne Berning. "Horror Cinema and the Avant-Garde." Diss. U of California, Berkeley, 1993. DAI 55 (1995): 1712A.

40. Unpublished essay

Give the author's name, the title, the words *Unpublished essay,* and the date the essay was written.

Solokov, Yvor. "From Theory to Practice in the Coming Century." Unpublished essay, 2007.

3 Field resources and other printed resources

Use the following formats for sources other than books or articles.

41. Interview—unpublished

Give the name of the person interviewed. Indicate the type of interview: *Personal interview* (you did the interview in person), *Telephone interview* (done over the telephone), *Email interview* (done by email), or *Interview* (someone else conducted the interview, perhaps on a radio or television program). If a recorded or broadcast interview has a title, give it in place of the word *Interview*. Give the date of the interview or appropriate citation information for a broadcast or address (URL) for electronic source.

Coppola, Francis Ford. Interview with James Lipton. Inside the Actors Studio. Bravo. 10 July 2001.

Schutt, Robin. Personal interview. 7 May 2007.

42. Survey or questionnaire

MLA does not specify a form for these field resources. When citing your own field research, you may wish to use the following format.

Arrigo-Nelson, Summer, and Jennifer Emily Figliozzi. Questionnaire on Student Alcohol Use and Parental Values. U of Rhode Island, Kingston. 15-20 Apr. 2004.

43. Observations

MLA does not specify a form for this type of field research. You may wish to use the following form to cite your notes on field observations.

Williams, Keyshawn. Observations of ATM Patrons. Aurora, CO. 11 Mar. 2006.

44. Letter or memo—unpublished

Give the author's name, a brief description (for example, *Letter to Jane Cote*), and the date of the document. For letters addressed to you, use the phrase *Letter to the author*; for letters between other people, give the name and location of any library holding the letter in its collection.

Hall, Donald. Letter to the author. 24 Jan. 1990.

45. Performance

Following the title of the play, opera, dance, or other performance, supply the name of the composer, director, writer, theater or place of presentation, and city where the performance took place as well as the date (include actors when relevant).

The Producers. By Mel Brooks and Thomas Meehan. Dir. Susan Stroman. St. James Theatre, New York. 8 July 2001.

46. Oral presentation

Identify speaker, title or type of presentation, and details of the meeting, sponsoring group, location, date; include electronic address, if any.

Dunkelman, Martha. "Images of Salome in Italian Renaissance Art." The Renaissance Woman, II. Sixteenth Century Studies Conf., Adams Mark Hotel, St. Louis. 11 Dec. 1993.

47. Map or chart

If the source is electronic, conclude with its address (URL).

Arkansas. Map. Comfort: Gousha, 1996.

48. Cartoon

Provide the cartoonist's name and the title, if any. Include the word *Cartoon* and publication information (or electronic address).

Cochran, Tony. "Agnes." Comic strip. Denver Post 18 Apr. 2007: 13F.

49. Advertisement

Begin with the name of the subject of the advertisement (product, company, or organization). Include the electronic address (URL), if any.

Toyota. Advertisement. GQ July 2001: 8.

4 Media resources

50. Film or videotape

Alphabetize according to the title of the work. The director's name is almost always necessary; names of actors, producers, writers, musicians, or others are needed only if they are important to identification or to your discussion. Include the distributor, the date, and other relevant information including the URL for electronic sources.

Super Size Me. Prod. Morgan Spurlock. Perf. Morgan Spurlock. Samuel Goldwyn Films, 2004.

For a videotape, filmstrip, DVD, or similar resource, indicate the medium—*videocassette*, *videodisc*, and so forth. If the date of the original version is important, add this just before the description of the medium.

Rosencrantz and Guildenstern Are Dead. Dir. Tom Stoppard. Perf. Gary Oldman, Tim Roth, and Richard Dreyfuss. Videocassette. Buena Vista Home Video, 1990.

51. Television or radio program

Begin with the episode title, and use it to alphabetize the entry. Give the program's name and, if they are pertinent to the discussion, include names for writer, director, actors, or others. Use abbreviations for their roles; for example, *Writ.*, *Dir.*, *Prod.*, *Perf.*, *Cond.*, *Introd.*, or *Narr.* Conclude with the URL for an electronic source, if appropriate.

"Love Comes to the Butcher." All in the Family. Dir. Paul Bogart. CBS. 15 Jan. 1978.

52. Recording

Begin the entry with the title of the recording or with the name of the person whose role in the recording you wish to emphasize, for example, the performer, the composer, the conductor, or the speaker. Underline the title of the compact disc, tape, or record. Put the name of a specific work in quotation marks unless the piece is identified by key, form, or number, such as *Symphony in A minor, no. 41*. Continue with performers or others involved, the manufacturer, and the year when the recording was issued. Indicate the medium if it is anything other than a compact disc (for example, *audiocassette*, or *LP* for a record).

The Goo-Goo Dolls. Dizzy Up the Girl. Warner, 1998.

Mozart, Wolfgang Amadeus. Symphony no. 40 in G minor. Vienna Philharmonic. Cond. Leonard Bernstein. Audiocassette. Deutsche Grammophon, 1984.

53. Artwork

Give the name of the artist, the title of the work, and the location of the work. Because many museum and gallery names are similar, indicate the city.

Uccello, Paolo. Saint George and the Dragon. National Gallery, London.

5 Online (Web) articles and documents and CD-ROM resources

The following models demonstrate the guidelines for citing electronic sources according to the 2003 *MLA Handbook for Writers of Research Papers*. The MLA recommends the following general conventions.

- **Publication dates.** For sources taken from the Internet, include the date the source was posted or last updated or revised; give also the date the source was accessed.
- **Uniform resource locator.** Include a full and accurate **URL** for any source taken from the Internet (with access-mode identifier—*http*, *ftp*, *gopher*, or *telnet*). Enclose the URL in angle brackets < >. When a URL continues from one line to the next, break it only after a slash. Do not add a hyphen.
- **Page numbering.** Include page or paragraph numbers when given by the source.

Journal article (online)

Brown, Stuart. "Student Affairs and Podcasting: The New Frontier?" Student Affairs On-Line 7.2 (2006). 14 Mar. 2007 <http://www.studentaffairs.com/ejournal/Summer_2006/StudentAffairsandPodcasting.html>.

Author's name · Article title · Journal title · Volume and issue number · Year of publication · Date of access* · URL

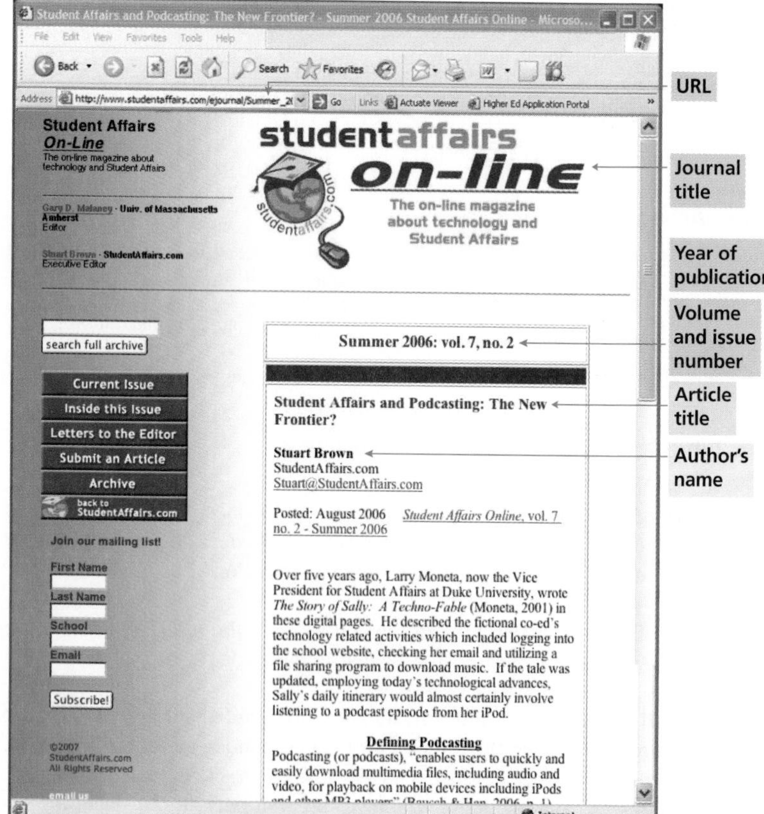

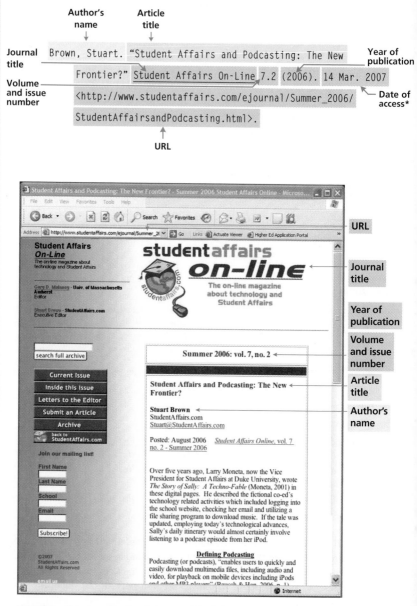

*For date of access, use the date you visited the source.

54. Web site

History of the American West, 1860-1920. 25 July 2000. Denver Public Library. 1 Dec. 2006 <http://memory.loc.gov/ammem/award97/codhtml>.

55. Personal or professional Web site

Give the name of the person who created the site, a title or description such as *Home page*, and any sponsor. If the name given as author of the Web site is not the real name and if you know the real name, give it in brackets following the name from the site.

Baron, Dennis. Home page. 20 Apr. 1999. Dept. of English, U of Illinois, Urbana-Champaign. 1 Dec. 2006. <http://ww2.english.uiuc.edu/Baron/Default.htm>.

56. Course home page

Give the instructor's name and the course title or the title of the site. Provide inclusive dates of the course, the department name, and the school name. (If the site has no name, use the course name and number from the institution's course catalog.)

Brown, Rebecca M. Introduction to Art History. Course home page. 21 Jan.-8 May 2003. Dept. of Art and Art History, St. Mary's College of Maryland. 20 Feb. 2003 <http://newton.uor.edu/FacultyFolderrebecca_brown/old/arth100/index.html>.

57. Blog

Give the name of the author, then the title of the posting or entry in quotation marks, followed by *Weblog posting.* Next provide the name of the blog (underlined), the date of the posting, the date of access, and the URL.

Ramsey, Doug. "Zoot, Red, Lorraine." Weblog posting. Rifftides. 5 Mar. 2007. 10 Mar. 2007 <http://www.artsjournal.com/rifftides/>.

58. Podcast

"You Are Getting Sleepy. . . ." The Loh Down on Science. Perf. Sandra Tsing Loh. KPCC/Natl. Public Radio. 12 Mar. 2007. <http://www.scpr.org/programs/perspectives/lohscience.html>.

59. Book (online)

Include the author's name and the title; the name(s) of any editor, compiler, or translator (if relevant); information about print publication (if any); electronic publication information (sponsoring organization and date of publication if the online text has not been published before); the scholarly project containing the work (if any) and date posted (see following example); date of access; and URL.

London, Jack. The Iron Heel. New York: Macmillan, 1908. The Jack London Collection. 10 Dec. 1999. Berkeley Digital Library SunSITE. 15 July 2006 <http://sunsite.berkeley.edu/London/Writing/IronHeel/>.

60. Selection from book (online)

Muir, John. "The City of the Saints." Steep Trails. 1918. 17 Apr. 2007 <http://encyclopediaindex.com/b/sttrl10.htm>.

61. Journal article (online)

Give the author; the title of the article (if any); the name of the periodical; details about the volume, issue, and item number; and date of publication (in parentheses). If the number of pages or paragraphs is available, place a colon after the parentheses containing the date and give the number. Finally, give your access date and add the electronic address in angle brackets.

Dugdale, Timothy. "The FAN and (Auto)Biography: Writing the Self in the Stars." Journal of Mundane Behavior 1.2 (2000). 19 Apr. 2007 <http://www.mundanebehavior.org/issues/v1n2dugdale.htm>.

62. Magazine article (online)

Supply the same information required for an online journal article.

Wright, Laura. "My, What Big Eyes. . . ." Discover 27 Oct. 2003. 11 Nov. 2006 <http://www.discover.com/web-exclusives/big-eyed-trilobite1027>.

63. Newspaper article (online)

When citing an editorial, a review, or a letter to the editor, indicate it as you would a similar print source. See Entries 30 and 33 for examples.

Otherwise supply the author's name, the title of the article, the name of the online version of the newspaper followed by the date of publication, and the date of access and electronic address.

Colker, David. "Seven Days of Spam." Los Angeles Times 3 May 2001. 12 Jan. 2007 <http://www.latimes.com/tech.../la0000371/17/1Jun30.story?coll=la%2Dfeaturees%2Dtechnolog>.

64. Government document (online)

United States. Dept. of Commerce. Bureau of the Census. Census Brief: Disabilities Affect One-Fifth of All Americans. Dec. 1997. 18 July 2006 <http://www.census.gov/prod/3/97pubs/cenbr975.pdf>.

65. Editorial (online)

"Mall Mania/A Measure of India's Success." Editorial. StarTribune.com Minneapolis-St.Paul 31 Oct. 2003. 9 Sept. 2006 <http://www.startribune.com/stories/1519/4185511.html>.

66. Letter to the editor (online)

Hadjiargyrou, Michael. "Stem Cells and Delicate Questions." Letter. New York Times on the Web 17 July 2001. 18 Jan. 2007 <http://www.nytimes.com/2001/07/18/opinion/L18STEM.html>.

67. Interview (online)

Payan, Victor. Interview with David Riker. San Diego Latino Film Festival. May 1999. 20 Jan. 2007 <http://www.sdlatinofilm.com/video.html#Anchor=David=64709>.

68. Review (online)

Harvey, De. Rev. of Bossa Nova, dir. Bruno Barretto. Film Monthly 1.10 (2000). 28 Aug. 2006 <http://freehosting2.at.webjump.com/84f640...Playing/Articles/BossaNova/BossaNova.htm>.

69. Abstract (online)

Prelow, Hazel, and Charles A. Guarnaccia. “Ethnic and Racial Differences in Life Stress Among High School Adolescents.” Journal of Counseling & Development 75.6 (1977). Abstract. 6 Apr. 2004 <http://www.counseling.org/journals/jcdjul197.htm#Prelow>.

70. Posting (online)

Provide the name of the author and, in quotation marks, the title of the posting or the subject line, followed by *Online posting*. Give the date of the post, the name of the list or discussion group, the date of access to the posting, and the electronic address.

Palmer, Megan. “Global Warming.” Online posting. 15 May 2001. Environmental Science Bulletin Board. 18 July 2001 <http://www.escribe.com/science/es/bb/index.html?bID=29>.

For a forwarded posting, give the writer, title, and date of the document, then the phrase *Fwd. by* and the name of the person forwarding it, followed by the phrase *Online posting*, the date of the posting, name of the forum, and electronic address.

Many discussion groups maintain archives. For your readers' convenience, cite archived versions whenever possible.

Sawyer, Nede. “Electric Cars.” Online posting. 1 Mar. 1999. ENVIRON. 18 July 2001 <http://gimli.worc.mass.edu/scripts/wa.exe?A2=ind9903&L=environ&F=&S=&P=507>.

When citing a Usenet newsgroup, give the information on author and title, the phrase *Online posting*, and the date of posting. Give the date of access. Next, in angle brackets, give the name of the newsgroup, with the prefix *news*.

Jarvilehto, Timo. “How Far Can Unity of the Organism-Environment System Be Maintained?” Online posting. 18 Dec. 1998. 19 Dec. 1998 <news:sci.journals.psycoloquy>.

Again, citing an archived posting from a newsgroup is preferable. In that case, give the name of the group after the date of posting and follow the access date with the electronic address.

Jarvilehto, Timo. "How Far Can Unity of the Organism-Environment System Be Maintained?" Online posting. 18 Dec. 1998. PSYCOLOQUY. 19 Dec. 1998 <http://x2.dejanews.com/=liszt/getdoc.xp?AN=424430517.1&CONTEXT=915464904.1241448542&hitnum=0&>.

71. Email

Begin with the writer's name and the title of the communication (in quotation marks), a description of the message including recipient, and the date.

Smithee, Alan. "The Director Confesses." E-mail to the author. 17 Sept. 2006.

Note that *e-mail* is spelled with a hyphen in MLA citations.

72. Synchronous communication

When citing material from a MUD, MOO, or other form of synchronous communication, begin with the speaker's name if you are citing only one. Give a description of the event, its date, its forum (e.g., *CollegeTownMOO*), and the date of access. End with the prefix *telnet://* and the electronic address in angle brackets.

Finch, Jeremy. Online debate "Can Proust Save Your Life?" 3 Apr. 1998. CollegeTownMOO. 3 Apr. 1998 <telnet://next.cs.bvc.edu.7777>.

For your readers' convenience, cite an archived version of material from a synchronous communication forum when possible. Provide the same information as above, but substitute the electronic address of the archived version for the electronic address of the forum at the end.

73. CD-ROM, diskette, or magnetic tape

Databases containing information or texts come in portable forms (such as CD-ROM) or online. Begin entries with author and title, provide publication information about the printed source (if any); give the title of the database or service (underlined), the medium (e.g., *CD-ROM*, *Online*), the name of the vendor or computer service, and the publication date (for CD-ROM) or date of access (for online sources).

Shakespeare, William. All's Well That Ends Well. William Shakespeare: The Complete Works on CD-ROM. CD-ROM. Abingdon, Eng.: Andromeda Interactive, 1994.

74. CD-ROM abstract

For abstracts, include information about an article being summarized, the electronic version, and any printed version of the abstract.

Straus, Stephen. Interview with Claudia Dreifus. "Separating Remedies from Snake Oil." New York Times 3 Apr. 2001: D5+. Abstract. CD-ROM. InfoTrac. 19 July 2006.

6 Online databases

75. General entry (online database)

For databases available on online subscription services (such as EBSCOhost or LexisNexis) provided by libraries, begin with information about print publication, if any, according to the kind of document (book, magazine article, or newspaper article, for example). Give the name of the database (underlined), the name of the service, the name of the library or library system, and the date of access. Then give the URL. If it is too long, give the URL of the search page for the site. Include page numbers as you would for a print entry; if the service gives only the starting page number of the printed text, give it followed by a hyphen, a space, and a period, for example: *223–* .

76. Journal article (online database)

FULL TEXT

Stillman, Todd. "McDonald's in Question: The Limits of the Mass Market." American Behavioral Scientist 47 (2003): 107-18. Academic Search Premier. EBSCOhost. U of Rhode Island Lib. 15 Nov. 2006 <http://0-ejournals.ebsco.com>.

ABSTRACT

Lewis, David A., and Roger P. Rose. "The President, the Press, and the War-Making Power: An Analysis of Media Coverage Prior to the Persian Gulf War." Presidential Studies Quarterly 32 (2002): 559-71. Abstract. America: History and Life. ABC/CLIO. U of Rhode Island Lib. 1 Nov. 2006 <http://0-serials.abc-clio.com>.

Journal article from a subscription database (HTML format)

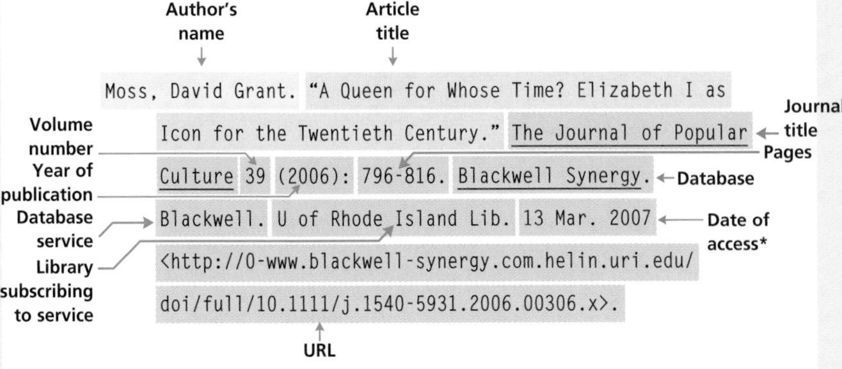

Database

URL

Library subscribing to service

Journal title

Year of publication

Volume number

Pages for print original (no page numbers in online HTML text)

Article title

Author's name

Database service

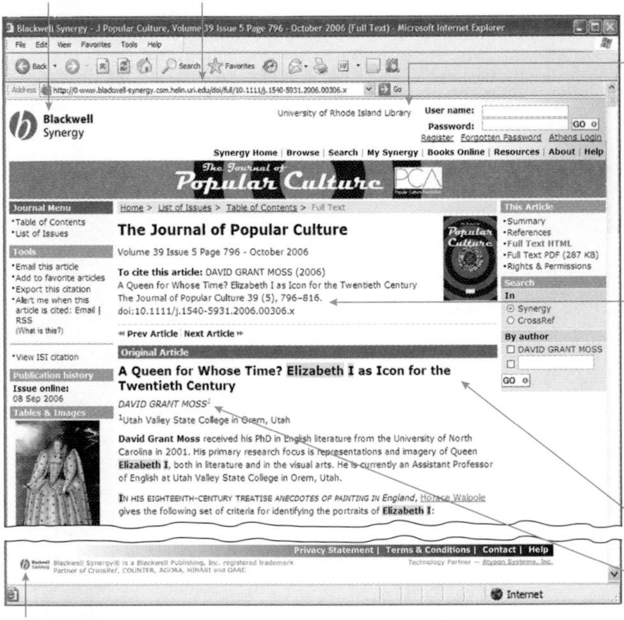

*For date of access, use the date you visited the source.

Journal article from a subscription database (PDF version)

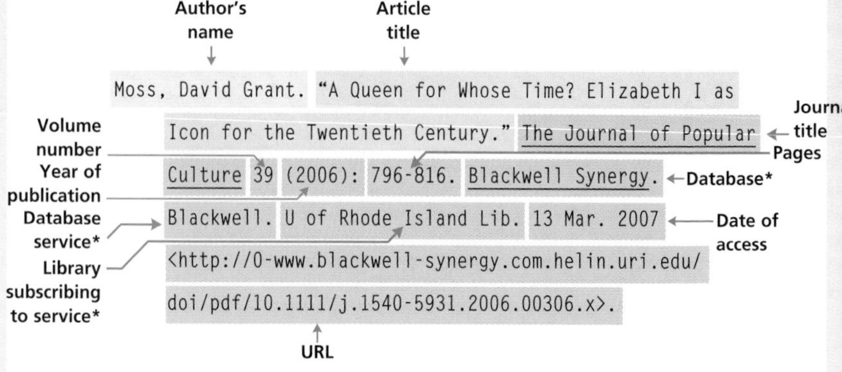

URL → http://0-www.blackwell-synergy.com.helin.uri.edu/doi/pdf/10.1111/j.1540-5931.2006.00306.x - Windows Internet Explorer

Article title → A Queen for Whose Time?
Elizabeth I as Icon for the Twentieth Century

Author's name → DAVID GRANT MOSS

IN HIS EIGHTEENTH-CENTURY TREATISE *ANECDOTES OF PAINTING IN England,* Horace Walpole gives the following set of criteria for identifying the portraits of Elizabeth I:

> A pale Roman nose, a head of hair loaded with crowns and powdered with diamonds, a vast ruff, a vaster fardingale, and a bushel of pearls, are the features by which every body knows at once the pictures of Queen Elizabeth. (150)

And this is how Elizabeth is portrayed when she is presented in the popular media of the twentieth century. The ruff, the hair, the pearls, and the elaborate dresses are the cues by which people recognize her. Indeed, in the British comic television series *Blackadder II*, Miranda Richardson's Elizabeth is never referred to by name; her appearance is more than enough to indicate who she is.

Richardson's appearance, like that of so many other screen Elizabeths, is that of the Ditchley portrait (which fits Walpole's description particularly well). The Ditchley portrait (Figure 1) has in effect become the standard image of her in popular culture. In Shekhar Kapur's film *Elizabeth* (1998), the film ends with Elizabeth transformed by wig, makeup, and costume into a stiff, pale, statuesque icon in white; Kapur's Elizabeth becomes the Ditchley painting even though the film purports to end in 1563, almost thirty years before the painting was completed.[1]

Journal title, Volume number, Year of publication → *The Journal of Popular Culture*, Vol. 39, No. 5, 2006
© 2006, Copyright the Authors
Journal compilation © 2006, Blackwell Publishing, Inc.

796

1 of 21

Done — Unknown Zone

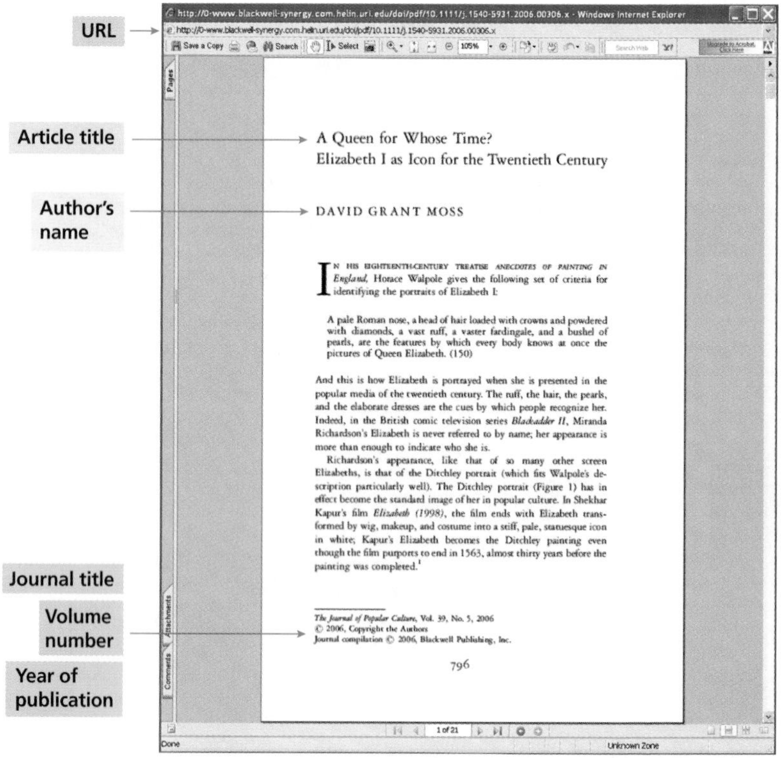

*Database, database service, and library subscribing to service are not provided in the PDF version. Obtain this information from the database screen shown on page 443.

77. Magazine article (online database)

Barrett, Jennifer. "Fast Food Need Not Be Fat Food." Newsweek 13 Oct. 2003: 73-74. Academic Search Premier. EBSCOhost. U of Rhode Island Lib. 31 Oct. 2006 <http://0-ejournals. ebsco.com>.

78. Newspaper article (online database)

Lee, R. "Class with the 'Ph.D. Diva.'" New York Times 18 Oct. 2003: B7. InfoTrac OneFile. Thompson Gale. Providence Public Lib., RI. 31 Oct. 2006 <http://infotrac.galegroup.com/menu>.

79. Summary of research (online database)

ERIC Clearing House on Higher Education. "ERIC Digest: Early Decision Programs." ED470540. 2002. ERIC Digests. Educational Resources Information Center. U of Rhode Island Lib. 7 Nov. 2006 <http://www.ericfacility.net/ericdigests/ed470540.html>.

80. Collection of materials (online database)

"Combating Plagiarism." CQ Researcher 9 Sept. 2003. CQ P. U of Rhode Island Lib. 12 Nov. 2003 <http://0-library.cqpress.com.helin.uri.edu:80/cqresearcher/>.

Collection of articles and documents on a specific topic.

81. Personal subscription service (online database)

Some personal subscription services allow you to retrieve resources by using keywords or by following a series of topics. Specify the path you followed by writing *Keyword* or *Path*.

"Deciphering the Origin, Travels of Iceman." NationalGeographic.com. 30 Oct. 2003. America Online. 31 Oct. 2003. Keyword: Anthropology.

"Moldova." Country Watch. 2003. CountryWatch.com. America Online. 14 Nov. 2003. Path: Research and Learn; Maps and Geography; Countries; Moldova; Profile.

7 Online media resources

82. Videotape or film (online)

Coppola, Francis Ford, dir. Apocalypse Now. 1979. Film.com. 17 July 2006 <http://ramhurl.filmcom/smildemohurl.ram?file=screen/2001/clips/apoca.smi>.

83. Television or radio program (online)

Edwards, Bob. “Adoption: Redefining Family.” Morning Edition. Natl. Public Radio. 28-29 June 2001. 17 July 2006 <http://www.npr.org/programs/morning/features/2001/jun/010628.cfoa.html>.

84. Recording (online)

Malcolm X. “The Definition of Black Power.” 8 Mar. 1964. Great Speeches. 2000. 18 July 2006 <http://www.chicago-law.net/speeches/speech.html#lm>.

85. Artwork (online)

Elamite Goddess. 2100 BC (?). Louvre, Paris. 8 Apr. 2007 <http://www.louvre.fr/llv/commun/home_flash.jsp>.

86. Map or chart (online)

“Beirut [Beyrout] 1912.” Map. Perry-Castaneda Library Map Collection. 16 July 2000 <http://www.lib.utexas.edu/maps/historical/beirut2_1912.jpg>.

87. Cartoon or comic strip (online)

Auth, Tony. “Spending Goals.” Cartoon. Slate 7 Sept. 2006. 16 Oct. 2001 <http://cagle.slate.msn.com/politicalcartoons/pccartoons/archives/auth.asp>.

88. Advertisement (online)

Mazda Miata. Advertisement. 16 July 2001 <http://www.mazdausa.com/miata/>.

89. Other media sources (online)

When citing electronic sources other than those explained above (such as a photo, work of art, film, or interview), adapt MLA models for their nonelectronic equivalents. Include the date of access and electronic address.

NASA/JPL. "Martian Meteorite." Views of the Solar System: Meteoroids and Meteorites. Ed. Calvin J. Hamilton. 12 Mar. 2005 <http://spaceart.com/solar/eng/meteor.htm#views>.

Exercise

A. Rewrite the following sentences to include MLA-style in-text citations.

1. The article concludes that "a 10-percent permanent increase in the price of cigarettes reduces current consumption by 4 percent in the short run and by 7.5 percent in the long run."

   The quotation is from page 397 of an article by Gary S. Becker, Michael Grossman, and Kevin M. Murphy. It appeared in *American Economic Review*. The volume number was 84, the year was 1994, and the article ran from page 396 to page 418.

2. The original release of Neil Young's concert film *Rust Never Sleeps* in 1979 was a major event in the history of rock and roll and popular music. According to one critic, the DVD release provides continued evidence of its importance.

   The reference is to a review by LC Smith in *Rolling Stone* magazine titled "My, My, Hey, Hey: A Neil Young Treasure Resurfaces." The date is 10/17/2002 and it appears on page 39. It was accessed on 14 November 2003 through Academic Search Premier, an EBSCO database, through the University of Rhode Island Library: http://0-web11.epnet.com.helin.uri.edu/citation.asp?tb=1&_ug=dbs+0+ln+en%2Dus+sid+D0695035%2D68B1%2D42F6%2DAABC%2D8963F3EC6024%40sessionmgr3%2Dsessionmgr4+699B&_us=bs+San++Francisco++And+++sleep+db+0+ds+San++Francisco++And+++sleep+dstb+ES+fh+0+hd+0+hs+0+or+Date+ri+KAAACBTB00365969+sm+ES+ss+SO+302E&cf=1&fn=1&rn=6

3. In Samoa during the 1930s, girls separated socially from their siblings at about age seven and began to form close and lasting relationships with other girls their age.

The reference is to Margaret Mead's Discussion in *Coming of Age in Samoa*, originally published in 1928 and reprinted in 1961 by Morrow Publishers in their Morrow Quill paperback series. It cites the general discussion in Chapter 5, "The Girl and Her Age Group," on pages 59 through 73 of the 1961 edition.

B. Create a list of works cited using MLA style, and include the following items:

1. A book by Peter Brazaitis titled *You Belong in a Zoo!* It was published in 2003 by Villard Books in New York.
2. A poem by Jorie Graham titled "Self-Portrait as Apollo and Daphne," available in her *The Dream of the Unified Field: Selected Poems, 1974–1994*. The book was published in 1995 by Ecco Press, and the poem appeared on pages 70–73.
3. A review in the online magazine *Salon.com*. The title of the review is "The Matrix Revolutions," and it was written by Andrew O'Hehir. It was accessed on November 5, 2003, at http://salon.com/ent/movies/review/2003/11/5/matrix_revolutions/index_np.html. The date of publication is also November 5, 2003.
4. An abstract of an article titled "Understanding Sleep Disorders in a College Student Population." The article was written by Dallas R. Jensen. It appeared in the *Journal of College Counseling* in the Spring 2003 issue on pages 25–34. The abstract appeared in a research database, Academic Search Premier, created and maintained by EBSCO. It was accessed on November 15, 2003, through the University of Rhode Island Library at the URL http://0-search.epnet.com.helin.uri.edu:80/direct.asp?an=9744711&db=aph. It was first included in the database in 2003.
5. A book of 280 pages by Vera Rosenbluth titled *Keeping Family Stories Alive.* The subtitle is *A Creative Guide to Taping Your Family Life and Lore.* It was published in 1990 by Hartley and Marks, a publisher in Point Roberts, Washington.

28e Sample MLA paper

The following paper was written by a student using the MLA documentation style. The *MLA Handbook* recommends beginning a research paper with text on the first page, using the format shown on Kimlee Cunningham's page one. Because her teacher required a title page, she prepared this too. In the margins of the paper is a running commentary on the elements of the paper, from considerations of audience and purpose to organizational strategy, style, and format.

Title page optional

Place title one-third of the way down the page

Title catches readers' attention

Disney's Magic Mirror

Reflects Traditions of Old

Center and double-space all lines

by

Kimlee Cunningham

Double-space twice between groups of lines

Professor N. Reynolds

English 201

21 Dec. 2006

Note format of date

½"

1" from top of page

½" from top

Cunningham 1

Kimlee Cunningham

Professor N. Reynolds

English 201

21 Dec. 2006

Heading format without a title page

Double-spaced heading and paper

1" margin on each side

Title reflects key ideas and catches readers' attention

Disney's Magic Mirror Reflects Traditions of Old

¶ indented 5 spaces

Introduces key ideas to be developed

Gives back-ground

1 Since Disney Studio's first animated feature, Snow White and the Seven Dwarfs (1937), the portrayal of female characters has changed in some obvious ways but has also remained the same in some key respects. By contrasting Snow White and the Seven Dwarfs with the recent animated features Beauty and the Beast (1991) and Aladdin (1992), we can see the leading female characters becoming more independent and assertive. At the same time, a comparison of the three movies reveals the studio's continuing appeal to its audiences' sense of feminine physical beauty.

Synthesizes varied points of view

Omits page numbers for 1-page (Showalter) and electronic (Hoffman) sources

2 It is probably an exaggeration to say that a character like Belle in Beauty and the Beast is a lot like a contemporary feminist, as one critic suggests (Showalter). However, we should not simply ignore an interpretation like this. Even if many people view a film like Beauty and the Beast (or Aladdin) as a simple love story (Hoffman), the films nonetheless grow out of the complicated values and roles that shape relationships today. Disney's contemporary portrayal of women characters shows a willingness to change with the times but also a reluctance to abandon traditional values and stereotypes.

1" margin at bottom

Cunningham 2

3 Nearly sixty years separates Snow White and the Seven Dwarfs from Beauty and the Beast and Aladdin. During this time of great social change, the roles of women have expanded. The shift has been from American women as housewives to American women as workers, college students, and corporate executives. By contrasting the main female character in Snow White with those in Beauty and Aladdin, we can see that they reflect both their own times and the social changes separating the different time periods.

Repeats and develops key ideas while indicating method of analysis; refers to films listed in Works Cited

4 In Snow White and the Seven Dwarfs, Snow White is portrayed as a homemaker when she and her furry and feathered companions in the forest come upon the Dwarfs' cabin. Her first reaction upon seeing the inside of the cabin is "We'll clean the house and surprise them. Then maybe I can stay." Snow White also becomes a mother to the Dwarfs. Before dinner, she checks their hands and sends them out to wash. Later in the evening, she calls out, "Bedtime! Right upstairs to bed." Visually, Snow White looks like an adolescent girl with wide doe eyes, tiny mouth, and pure ivory skin (Allan 161) instead of looking like a woman.

Supplies supporting evidence

Explains values implied in portrait of Snow White

Identifies details of appearance

Reaches conclusion

5 Though Snow White is certainly not a feminist in contemporary terms, she is portrayed in ways that were probably viewed as at least partly progressive at the time the film was created. As Terri Martin Wright points out, "Disney's Snow White parallelled the popular heroines of the 1930s. . . . These women were

Cunningham 3

Electronic version cited here does not contain page numbers

resourceful individuals who not only survived but found a measure of freedom and independence in spite of their second-class status in a patriarchal society." Wright draws further parallels by pointing out that "Popular Hollywood films of the 1930s commonly included the motif of a heroine taking refuge in the living quarters of men to avoid an unpalatable destiny arranged by others." Nonetheless, Snow White's way of speaking and her appearance certainly differ markedly from those of the later characters.

Introduces both *Beauty* and *Aladdin*

Contrasts appearances of other characters

Supplies supporting detail

Leads into discussion of contrasting values and characters

6 The facial features of both Belle in Beauty and the Beast and Jasmine in Aladdin are more realistic and womanly. Instead of looking like porcelain figurines, both Belle and Jasmine look like vigorous young women. Their skin has a realistic tone, their cheeks are not as artificially rounded as Snow White's, and their eyes are still wide but are not exaggerated. Their roles and personality traits are also very different from Snow White's.

More on ¶ 3 discussion of Belle's personality, actions, and implied values

7 Beauty and the Beast is an unusual fairy tale in which the woman is the hero (McKenna A13). Belle's intelligence allows her to defeat her enemy, Gaston. Gaston, her would-be suitor, offers a masculine parallel to Belle's beauty but no equivalent to her intelligence. Gaston, the brawny, bluff beefcake figure, is nothing short of brainless. Wisely, Belle cannot be wooed by looks alone, and Gaston's words would disappoint any intelligent woman. Gaston also

Cunningham 4

manages to alienate Belle when he criticizes her zest for reading and books by saying, "It's not right for a woman to read. Soon she starts getting ideas and thinking."

Leads to start of next ¶

8 While Snow White has to wait passively for a man, her prince, to release her from her imprisonment in an unnatural sleep, Belle is an active agent in her fate. Belle's compassion is her father's salvation from death and the Beast's salvation from his curse. To release her father from the Beast's imprisonment, Belle offers her own eternal freedom in return for her father's. This action is also the first step toward the Beast's salvation from himself and the curse.

9 The curse that has been placed upon the Beast has severely altered his appearance, turning a handsome prince into a hairy creature mixing the features of a lion and a buffalo. In order for the spell to be broken, someone must be able to see past this appearance and love the Beast for his inner qualities before the last petal of an enchanted rose falls. It is Belle, through her compassion and understanding, who changes the spirit of the man who has been turned into a beast. He learns to control his temper and becomes kind and forbearing. Belle conquers adversity with her quick wit, compassion, understanding, and love. This is truly a refreshing contrast to the familiar "battle or conquest" approach of most heroes (McKenna A13).

Summarizes preceding discussion

Uses source to support conclusion

Cunningham 5

Picks up theme that concludes ¶ 9

Develops idea introduced in quotation

Summarizes events

Could have added quotations

10 Jasmine of Aladdin has been acclaimed by some critics as the "most independent-minded Disney heroine yet" (Rosenberg). The rebellious spirit within causes her to do things that would be considered daring and bold for a princess. She escapes from her father's palace walls to assert her freedom by exploring the streets of Agrabah, but most significantly, she refuses to marry for politics or the tradition that the sultan's daughter must marry a prince. Jasmine rejects her princely suitors by saying that they lack character and that she does not love them. Jasmine's desire for true love is nothing new to Disney films; Snow White desires a true love as well, but in Aladdin the terms of love are dictated by the female character. She is someone to be wooed, but not a prize to be won. It is she who makes the real choice.

Supplies transition to discussion of similarities

Might have developed key element of appearance in more detail

Mentions selected details from all three films

Reaches strong conclusion that seems to undermine earlier assertions of independence

11 At the same time, by comparing Snow White with Beauty and Aladdin, we can see how Disney films still try to preserve some traditional attitudes. Although Snow White, Belle, and Jasmine may have different appearances, they all appeal to our culture's traditional sense of physical beauty. They are fragile and thin with perfect skin, hair, and teeth. Their figures are also proportioned in traditionally attractive ways. Snow White's looks draw a kiss from a prince; Belle's beauty (as the name itself implies) is part of her power to change the Beast; and Jasmine's looks are an essential part of her power, as

Cunningham 6

illustrated by her ability to distract the evil vizier Jafar while Aladdin attempts to steal back the lamp.

12 None of the heroines is active or involved in any modern sense. Snow White cooks, cleans, and hums; Belle buries her nose in a book and takes care of her father; Jasmine sits in her father's palace and mopes, rejecting suitor after suitor. Their lives take a positive or active turn only when they are introduced to the men they will come to love. Regarding Beauty and the Beast as "a liberated love story for the '90s" (Showalter) seems to miss the film's balance of contemporary and traditional values.

Could discuss further, though interpretation is consistent with main idea

13 Disney has frequently been criticized for its powerful ability to adapt reality to fit its own purposes (Baudrillard). But perhaps Disney's retention of stereotypes of feminine beauty and passivity reflects our culture's reluctance to let go of traditions. Many men and women are still trying to define their priorities in life, especially in terms of work and relationships. For many, this struggle becomes a battle between family and work. Like many people, Americans may need to focus on traditional values when they believe that their culture and their lives are undergoing painful change and potential disorder. Could it be possible that Beauty and Aladdin reflect the need of many in their audiences to retain certain traditional values and behavior patterns while simultaneously endorsing new roles and perspectives?

Broadens focus to look at films in culture

Returns to ideas introduced in opening ¶s

Raises question tentatively answered at end of paper

Cunningham 7

14 Despite the fact that Snow White and the Seven Dwarfs was made roughly sixty years earlier than Beauty and the Beast and Aladdin, many things in the movies remain the same. There is a formula that Disney animators seem to follow in creating the appearance of female characters, one of conventional feminine beauty. The writers have also chosen fairy tale patterns for the story lines with such familiar features as the "happily-ever-after ending" and the image of a woman swept away by a man's love. What is different is that Beauty and the Beast and Aladdin weave themes of independence, intelligence, and action into the stories, centering them on the female characters. In contrast, the character and actions of Snow White emphasize themes of innocence, naiveté, and motherliness. While the continuing popularity of Snow White reveals at the very least a nostalgia for these themes, the shift to the more contemporary themes of Beauty and Aladdin is probably a sign of Disney's accurate perception of a society endorsing change yet looking for reassurance.

Restates opening observations, then summarizes key points

Answers question raised in ¶ 13

1" from top of page

½" from top

Cunningham 8

Page numbers continue

Works Cited

Heading centered

Aladdin. 1992. Videocassette. Walt Disney, 1993.

Allan, Robin. "Fifty Years of Snow White." Journal of Popular Film and Television 24 (1988): 155-63.

Baudrillard, Jean. "Disneyworld Company." Trans. Francois Debrix. CTHEORY 27 Mar. 1996. 15 Dec. 2006 <http://www.ctheory.com/e25-disneyworld_comp.html>.

Beauty and the Beast. 1991. Videocassette. Walt Disney, 1991.

Hoffman, Loreen. "Feminism in a Disney Film." Online posting. 2 Feb. 1998. 21 Nov. 2006 <wysiwyg://22/http://faculty.ucr.edu/wcb/s...t/master/2/forums/forum2/messages/7.htm>.

McKenna, M. A. J. "Film Provides 'Beauty'-ful Role Models." Boston Herald 1 Dec. 1991: A13+.

Rosenberg, Scott. "The Genie-us of Aladdin." San Francisco Examiner 25 Nov. 1992: B2.

Showalter, Elaine. "Beauty and the Beast: Disney Meets Feminism in a Liberated Love Story for the '90s." Premiere Oct. 1997: 66.

Snow White and the Seven Dwarfs. 1937. Videocassette. Walt Disney, 1994.

Wright, Terri Martin. "Romancing the Tale." Journal of Popular Film and Television 25 (1997): 98-108. Academic Search Premier. EBSCOhost. U of Rhode Island Lib. 19 Dec. 2006 <http://0-web2.epnet. com.helin.uri.edu>.

Sources from paper listed alphabetically

All lines double-spaced

First line of each entry not indented

Additional lines indented 5 spaces (½")

CHAPTER 29 APA Documentation

American Psychological Association (APA) documentation style calls for in-text (parenthetical) references and a reference list. This chapter discusses APA style and provides models for the most common kinds of entries you will use.

APA IN-TEXT (PARENTHETICAL) FORMATS

APA REFERENCES FORMATS

1. BOOKS AND WORKS TREATED AS BOOKS

The in-text documentation style developed by the APA (American Psychological Association) identifies the source of information, ideas, or quotations by providing the author's name and the date of publication for the source within parentheses. For this reason, APA style is often called a name-and-date style. The information in the parenthetical citation enables readers to locate more detailed information about the source in a **reference list** at the end of a paper or report.

Many writing situations call for either APA style or a name-and-date style loosely based on APA style but adapted to the needs of specific audiences. APA style can be easily modified and lends itself to informal uses; as a result, it is an important resource for writers looking for a direct, simple documentation system that does not disrupt the reading of a text with detailed information or require readers to turn to a footnote or endnote.

APA documentation style makes the year of publication part of an in-text citation, as in (*Kitwana, 2002*), and gives the date right after the author's name in a reference list to which the in-text citation refers.

Kitwana, B. (2002). *The hip hop generation: Young blacks and the crisis in African American culture.* New York: Basic*Civitas*.

For more detailed discussion of this documentation style, consult the *Publication Manual of the American Psychological Association* (5th ed., 2001) or check for updates online at <http://www.apastyle.org>.

29a In-text (parenthetical) citations

The APA system provides parenthetical citations for quotations, paraphrases, summaries, and other information in the text of a paper. For advice on what to document and what not to document, see 26d. For an APA in-text citation, include the author's name and the year of publication, separating these items with a comma. You may choose to name the author (and give the date) either within the parenthetical citation or within your text.

29b Content footnotes

Occasionally you may wish to expand on information presented in the text or discuss a point further without making the main text of your paper more complicated or harder to follow. A content footnote allows you to do this, but you should use such footnotes sparingly because too many footnotes or long footnotes can distract your readers.

To prepare a content footnote, place a number slightly above the line of your text that relates to the footnote information. Make sure that you number the footnotes in your paper consecutively.

TEXT OF PAPER I tape-recorded all the interviews and later transcribed the relevant portions.[1]

On a separate page at the end of your paper, below the centered heading "Footnotes," present the notes in the order in which they appear in your text. Begin each note with its number, placed slightly above the line. Indent five to seven spaces, the same as a paragraph, for the first line only of each footnote, and double-space all notes.

FOOTNOTE [1]Sections of the recordings were hard to hear and understand because of problems with the tape recorder or background noises. These gaps did not substantially affect information needed for the study.

Your instructor may prefer that you type any footnote at the bottom of the page with the text reference.

29c In-text (parenthetical) citation examples

1. Author's name inside parentheses

Include the author's name and the year of publication inside parentheses, separating these items with a comma. When you are documenting the source of a quotation, follow the date with a comma, *p.* or *pp.*, and the page number or numbers on which the quoted material appears in the source.

One recent study argues that "the fan's link to the star--or the team, the favorite composer, the game, the genre, the style--is emotional, visceral" (Gitlin, 2001, p. 129).

To indicate the specific location of information or the source of paraphrased or summarized material, give the page number of the source.

In the mid-1960s, Tom Wolfe began writing unconventional and insight-filled essays about American popular culture.

Despite his Ph.D. in American Studies from Yale, Wolfe and his work were at first ignored by most intellectuals, both inside and outside universities, who viewed serious or high-brow culture as far more important than popular culture (Aronowitz, 1993, p. 198).

2. Author's name as part of discussion

When you make an author's name part of the discussion, give the date of the source in parentheses after the name. For quoted or paraphrased material, provide the page number in the source within parentheses following the quotation or paraphrase.

As Gitlin (2001) argues, "the fan's link to the star--or the team, the favorite composer, the game, the genre, the style--is emotional, visceral" (p. 129).

When you supply the author's name and the date in your text or in an in-text citation, your readers will be able to identify a source in the list of references you provide at the end of your paper.

3. One author

Supply the author's last name and the date of the publication in parentheses, separated by a comma and a space. If the author's name appears in the text, give only the date in parentheses. If both the name and the date are included in the text, no other information need be cited.

Mau's 2001 study of gender differences on the SAT, ACT, and college grades confirmed observations of test results made earlier (Arbeiter, 1985) as well as Young's (1994) study of gender differences in college grades.

4. Two authors

Include both names in citations. In a parenthetical reference, separate the names by an ampersand (&); in the text, use the word *and*.

Given evidence that married men earn more than unmarried men (Chun & Lee, 2001), Nakosteen and Zimmer (2001) investigate how earnings affect spousal selection.

5. Three to five authors

Include all the authors' names, separated by commas, for the first citation. For parenthetical citations use an ampersand (&) rather than *and*.

> Biber, Conrad, and Reppen (1998) point out that "the language you use to write a term paper is different from the language you use when talking to your roommate" (p. 135).

In the second and other following citations, give only the first author's name followed by *et al.* and the date (for example, "Biber et al. (1998) present evidence that . . .").

An exception to this would occur when two or more citations, after being shortened, become identical. In that case, cite more than one author, separated with commas, to differentiate the references, providing the minimum number of authors necessary to prevent ambiguity, followed by *et al.* and the date.

6. Six or more authors

Give the name of the first author followed by *et al.* and the date in all citations: (*Gold et al., 2000*). An exception to this would occur when two or more citations, after being shortened, become identical. In that case, cite more than one author, separated with commas, to differentiate the references, providing the minimum number of authors necessary to prevent ambiguity, followed by *et al.* and the date.

Supply the names of the first six authors in the reference list at the end of your report. For more than six authors, list the first six and shorten any remaining authors to *et al.*

7. Organization or group author

Spell out the name of an association, corporation, or government agency for the first citation, following with an abbreviation of a cumbersome name within brackets. You may use the abbreviation for later citations.

FIRST CITATION Besides instilling fear, hate crimes limit where women live and work (National Organization of Women [NOW], 2001).

LATER CITATION Pending legislation would strengthen the statutes on bias-motivated crimes (NOW, 2001).

8. No author given

Give the title or the first few words of a long title (*The Great Utopia: The Russian and Soviet Avant-Garde, 1915–1932* might appear in a citation as *Great Utopia)* and the year.

> Art and design in 1920s Russia mixed aesthetically startling images with political themes and an endorsement of social change (*Great Utopia*, 1992).

When the word *Anonymous* designates the author, use it in the citation: (*Anonymous, 2002*).

9. Specific page or section

Indicate the part of the work you are citing: *p.* (for "page"); *chap.* ("chapter"), *fig.* ("figure"), for example. Spell out any words that may be confusing.

> Time management is more important than leisure activities in its effect on academic stress among college students (Mesia & McKean, 2000, Table 2).

10. Work cited more than once

When you cite the same source more than once in a paragraph, repeat the source as necessary to clarify a specific page reference or to show which information comes from one of several sources. If a second reference is clear, do not repeat the date.

> Personal debt has become a significant problem in the past decade. Much of the increase can be linked to the lack of restraint in spending people feel when using credit cards (Schor, 1998, p. 73). The problem is so widespread that "about one-third of the nation's population describe themselves as either heavily or moderately in financial debt" (Schor, p. 72).

11. Authors with the same last name

When your reference list contains works by two different authors with the same last name, provide each author's initials for each in-text citation, both for works by a single author and for works by several authors.

> Scholars have looked in depth at the development of African American culture during slavery and reconstruction (E. Foner, 1988). The role of Frederick Douglass in this process has also been examined (P. Foner, 1950).

12. Two or more sources in a citation

If you are summarizing information found in more than one source, include all the sources—names and years—within the citation. Separate the authors and years with commas; separate the sources with semicolons. List sources alphabetically by author (as in your list of references; see the example that follows—Binghamr before Griffin), then oldest to most recent for several sources by the same author, separating the dates with commas.

Several researchers have investigated personal and organizational reasons for job satisfaction (Binghamr, Valenstein, Blow, & Alexander, 2002; Griffin, 2001, 2006).

13. Personal communications, including interviews and email

In your text, cite letters, memos, interviews, email, telephone conversations, and similar personal communications by giving the initials and last name of the person, the phrase *personal communication*, and the date. Readers probably will have no access to such sources, so you need not include them in your reference list.

AUTHOR NAMED IN TEXT According to J. M. Hostos, the state has begun cutting funding for social services duplicated by county agencies (personal communication, October 7, 2006).

PARENTHETICAL REFERENCE The state has begun cutting funding for social services duplicated by county agencies (J. M. Hostos, personal communication, October 7, 2006).

14. Work cited in another source

Include the phrase *as cited in* as part of a parenthetical citation for a source you did not use directly but drew from another source.

Writing in the late 1800s about Halloween customs, William Shepard Walsh lamented that "gangs of hoodlums throng the streets, ringing the door-bells or wrenching the handles from their sockets, and taking gates from off their hinges" (as cited in Skal, 2002, pp. 33-34).

15. Electronic source

In general, treat an electronic source in the same way as a print source, giving the writer's name and date of publication. If the document is a .pdf file with page numbers, give them as if the source were in print form. If the paragraphs are numbered, use *para.* or ¶ (instead of *p.*) followed by the number of the specific part of the document you are citing. If the source has neither page numbers nor paragraph numbers, give the heading and paragraph number under the heading for the location of specific information or a quotation.

Body builders sometimes suffer from muscle dysmorphia, an obsessive-compulsive disorder similar to anorexia (Lee, 2006, What is dysmorphia? para. 4).

16. Sacred text or classical text

Give the name or number of the book, section, or part along with the name of the particular version or translation you are citing, using standard abbreviations and part numbering. Cite the source in the body of your text only.

```
Aristotle argues that liberty is a fundamental element of
democracy (Politics, VI.I.6).
```

17. Two or more works by the same author in the same year

If you use works published in the same year by the same author or author team, add letters after the year to distinguish the works.

```
Gould (1987a, p. 73) makes a similar point.
```

29d Reference list

Immediately after the last page of your paper, you need to provide a list of references to enable readers to identify and consult the sources you have cited in your report.

- **Page format.** One inch from the top margin of a separate page at the end of your report's text (before notes or appendixes), center the heading "References" without underlining or quotation marks.
- **Alphabetizing.** List works cited in the report alphabetically by author or by the first main word of the title if there is no author. Arrange two or more works by the same author from the oldest to the most recent according to year of publication.
- **Spacing.** Double-space all entries and between entries.
- **Indentation.** Do not indent the first line, but indent five to seven spaces for the second and additional lines.

1 Books and works treated as books

MODEL FORMAT FOR BOOKS AND WORKS TREATED AS BOOKS

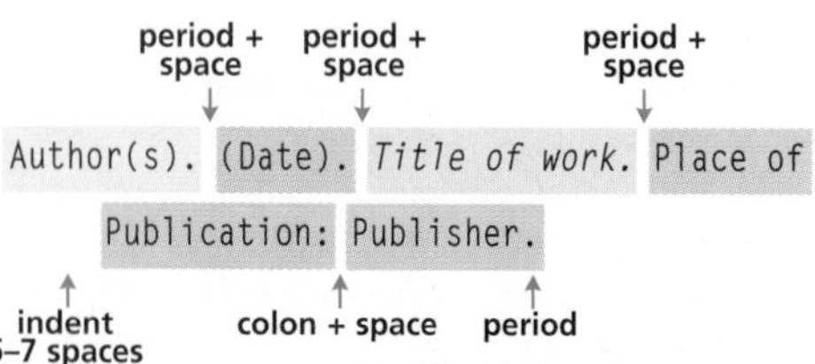

29d APA

- **Author(s).** Give the author's last name followed by a comma and the initials of the first and middle names. For a book with more than one author, use the same inverted order for each author. Separate the names with commas, using an ampersand before the final name.
- **Date.** Provide the year of publication (in parentheses) followed by a period.
- **Title of work.** Give the title in italics (or underlined) followed by a period. (Underlining must continue under the period that follows the title.) Use a capital only for the first word of the main title, the first word of any subtitle, and any proper nouns.
- **Publication information.** For U.S. publishers, give the city and state followed by a colon and a space; then supply the publisher's name, leaving out unnecessary words such as *Inc.* or *Publishers*. Abbreviate the name of the state using the standard postal abbreviation. You do not need to name the state for the following familiar publishing locations: Baltimore, Boston, Chicago, Los Angeles, New York, Philadelphia, and San Francisco. For publishers outside the United States, give the city and the abbreviated name of the country. No country is needed for these familiar locations: Amsterdam, Jerusalem, London, Milan, Moscow, Paris, Rome, Stockholm, Tokyo, and Vienna.
- **Spacing.** Double-space all entries, and indent five to seven spaces, the same indentation that you choose for paragraphing, for the second and any additional lines.

1. One author

Ortner, S. B. (2003). *New Jersey dreaming: Capital, culture, and the class of '58.* Durham, NC: Duke University Press.

2. Two or more authors

List each author's last name first, followed by first and middle initials.

Biber, D., Conrad, S., & Reppen, R. (1998). *Corpus linguistics: Investigating language structure and use.* Cambridge, England: Cambridge University Press.

For a book with more than six authors, name the first six, followed by a comma, then add *et al.* to indicate the rest.

3. Organization or group author

Treat the organization or agency responsible for the work as an individual author, and alphabetize by the first main word. When author and publisher are the same, give the word *Author* following the place of publication instead of repeating the name.

Amnesty International. (2001). *Annual Report 2001.* [Brochure]. London: Author.

4. No author given

Give the title first, then the date. Use the first significant word of the title to alphabetize the entry. If the word *Anonymous* is used for the author, designate the author with it and alphabetize under *anonymous.*

Boas anniversary volume: Anthropological papers written in honor of Franz Boas. (1906). New York: Stechert.

5. More than one work by the same author

List works in chronological order. Include the author's name in each entry.

Aronowitz, S. (1993). *Roll over Beethoven: The return of cultural strife.* Hanover, NH: Wesleyan University Press.

Aronowitz, S. (2000). *From the ashes of the old: American labor and America's future.* New York: Basic Books.

If the same lead author has works with different coauthors, alphabetize these entries based on the last names of the second authors.

6. More than one work by the same author in the same year

List in alphabetical order works appearing in the same year by the same author. Add lowercase letters after dates (e.g., *1992a, 1992b*). Alphabetize by the first main word in the title. For in-text citations, provide both the date and the letter (*Gould, 1987b*).

Gould, S. J. (1987a). *Time's arrow, time's cycle: Myth and metaphor in the discovery of geological time.* Cambridge, MA: Harvard University Press.

Gould, S. J. (1987b). *An urchin in the storm: Essays about books and ideas.* New York: Norton.

Alphabetized under *urchin*, not *An*.

7. One or more editors

Include (*Ed.*) or (*Eds.*) after the name(s) of the editors.

Bowe, J., Bowe, M., & Streeter, S. C. (Eds.). (2001). *Gig: Americans talk about their jobs.* New York: Three Rivers Press.

8. Translator

Include the translator's name, in normal order, followed by *Trans.*, in parentheses after the title.

Bourdieu, P. (1990). *In other words: Essays towards a reflexive sociology* (M. Adamson, Trans.). Stanford, CA: Stanford University Press.

9. Edition other than the first

Include information about the specific edition in parentheses after the title (for example, *Rev. ed.* for "revised edition" or *3rd ed.* for "third edition").

Groth-Marnat, G. (1996). *Handbook of psychological assessment* (3rd ed.). New York: Wiley.

10. Reprint

Butler, J. (1999). *Gender trouble.* New York: Routledge. (Original work published 1990)

11. Multivolume work

Include the names of the editors or authors, making sure you indicate if they are editors. Then provide the inclusive years of publication. If the work is a revised edition or has a translator, give this information after the title. Then identify in parentheses the volumes you are using for your paper.

Strachey, J., Freud, A., Strachey, A., & Tyson, A. (Eds.). (1966-1974). *The standard edition of the complete psychological works of Sigmund Freud* (J. Strachey et al., Trans.) (Vols. 3-5). London: Hogarth Press and the Institute of Psycho-Analysis.

12. Anthology or collection of articles

Give the name of the editor(s) first, followed by the abbreviation *Ed.* or *Eds.* in parentheses.

Appadurai, A. (Ed.). (2001). *Globalization.* Durham, NC: Duke University Press.

Ghosh, A., & Ingene, C. A. (Eds.). (1991). *Spatial analysis in marketing: Theory, methods and applications.* Greenwich, CT: JAI.

13. *Diagnostic and Statistical Manual of Mental Disorders*

The manual known in short form as the *DSM-IV* is widely cited in fields such as psychology, social work, and psychiatry because its definitions and guidelines often have legal force and determine patterns of treatment. Because of the volume's importance, the APA *Publication Manual* recommends the following specific form for the entry.

American Psychiatric Association. (1994). *Diagnostic and statistical manual of mental disorders* (4th ed.). Washington, DC: Author.

In your text, following an initial full citation, you may use the standard abbreviations for this work: *DSM-III* (1980), *DSM-III-R* (1987), *DSM-IV* (1994), or *DSM-IV-TR* (2000).

14. Encyclopedia or reference work

Winn, P. (Ed.). (2001). *Dictionary of biological psychology.* London: Routledge.

15. Dissertation (unpublished)

Conrad, S. (1996). *Academic discourse in two disciplines: Professional writing and student development in biology and history.* Unpublished doctoral dissertation, Northern Arizona University, Flagstaff.

16. Government document

Select Committee on Aging, Subcommittee on Human Services, House of Representatives. (1991). *Grandparents' rights: Preserving generational bonds* (Com. Rep. No. 102-833). Washington, DC: U.S. Government Printing Office.

17. Report

Begin with the name of the author, whether an individual or a group or government agency. If the agency also publishes the report, use the word *Author* in the publication information instead of repeating the group's name.

> Advisory commission to study the Consumer Price Index. (1996). *Toward a more accurate measure of the cost of living.* Washington, DC: Senate Finance Committee.

If the report has a number, give it in parentheses after the title with no punctuation between the title and parentheses. When several numbers are listed in the report, choose the one most likely to help readers obtain the document.

> Dossey, J. A. (1988). *Mathematics: Are we measuring up?* (Report No. 17-M-02). Princeton, NJ: Educational Testing Service. (ERIC Document Reproduction Service No. ED3000207).

2 Articles and selections from books

MODEL FORMAT FOR ARTICLES AND SELECTIONS

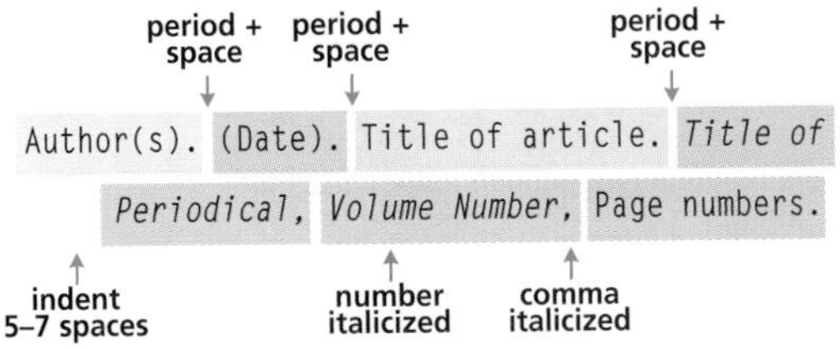

- **Author(s).** Give the author's last name and initials followed by a period and a space.
- **Date.** Supply the date in parentheses followed by a period and a space.
- **Title of article.** Give the article title, capitalizing only the first word (and the first word of any subtitle along with any proper names). Do not use quotation marks with the title. End with a period and a space.
- **Title of journal, periodical, or book.** Give the journal title in italics (or underline) with all main words capitalized, the volume number (also in italics or underlined), and the page numbers. Use commas to separate these. If you choose to underline, make sure you also underline any punctuation within or immediately following the title and volume number.
- **Spacing.** Double-space all entries, and indent five to seven spaces, the same indentation that you choose for paragraphing, for the second and any additional lines.

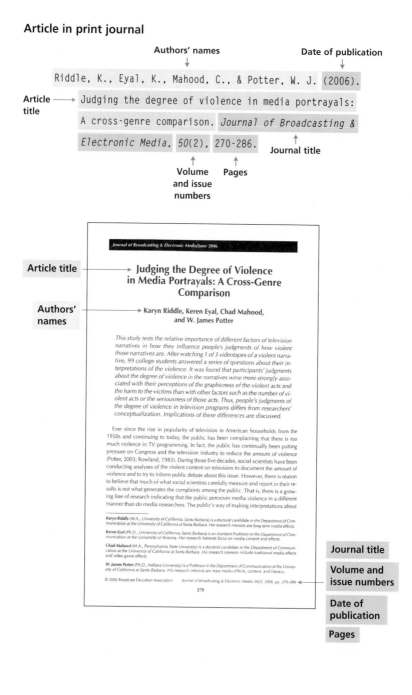

Article in print journal

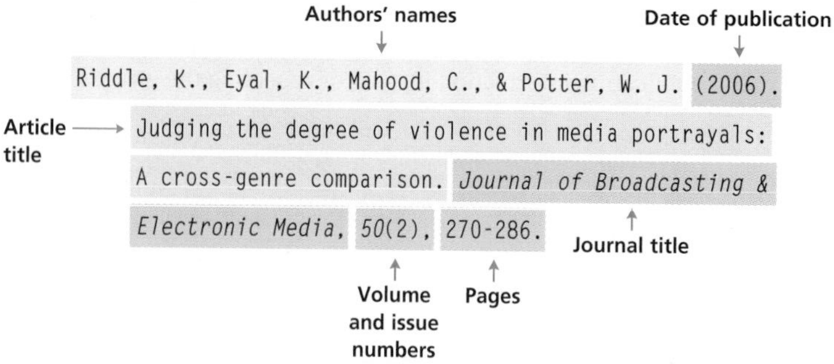

Article title
Authors' names

Journal of Broadcasting & Electronic Media/June 2006

Judging the Degree of Violence in Media Portrayals: A Cross-Genre Comparison

Karyn Riddle, Keren Eyal, Chad Mahood, and W. James Potter

This study tests the relative importance of different factors of television narratives in how they influence people's judgments of how violent those narratives are. After watching 1 of 3 videotapes of a violent narrative, 99 college students answered a series of questions about their interpretations of the violence. It was found that participants' judgments about the degree of violence in the narratives were more strongly associated with their perceptions of the graphicness of the violent acts and the harm to the victims than with other factors such as the number of violent acts or the seriousness of those acts. Thus, people's judgments of the degree of violence in television programs differs from researchers' conceptualization. Implications of these differences are discussed.

Ever since the rise in popularity of television in American households from the 1950s and continuing to today, the public has been complaining that there is too much violence in TV programming. In fact, the public has continually been putting pressure on Congress and the television industry to reduce the amount of violence (Potter, 2003; Rowland, 1983). During those five decades, social scientists have been conducting analyses of the violent content on television to document the amount of violence and to try to inform public debate about this issue. However, there is reason to believe that much of what social scientists carefully measure and report in their results is not what generates the complaints among the public. That is, there is a growing line of research indicating that the public perceives media violence in a different manner than do media researchers. The public's way of making interpretations about

Karyn Riddle *(M.A., University of California, Santa Barbara) is a doctoral candidate in the Department of Communication at the University of California at Santa Barbara. Her research interests are long-term media effects.*

Keren Eyal *(Ph.D., University of California, Santa Barbara) is an Assistant Professor in the Department of Communication at the University of Arizona. Her research interests focus on media content and effects.*

Chad Mahood *(M.A., Pennsylvania State University) is a doctoral candidate in the Department of Communication at the University of California at Santa Barbara. His research interests include traditional media effects and video game effects.*

W. James Potter *(Ph.D., Indiana University) is a Professor in the Department of Communication at the University of California at Santa Barbara. His research interests are mass media effects, content, and literacy.*

 Journal of Broadcasting & Electronic Media 50(2), 2006, pp. 270–286

270

Journal title
Volume and issue numbers
Date of publication
Pages

18. Article in journal paginated by volume

You do not have to include the particular issue number because page numbers run continuously through the issues making up a volume.

Iran-Nejad, A., McKeachie, W. J., & Berliner, D. C. (1990). The multisource nature of learning: An introduction. *Review of Educational Research, 60,* 509-515.

Klein, R. D. (2003). Audience reactions to local TV news. *American Behavioral Scientist, 46,* 1661-1672.

For references with up to six authors, supply the names of all the authors in the reference list entry. For more than six authors, list the first six and shorten the remaining authors to *et al.*

All in-text citations for references having two authors should include both authors. For three to five authors, list all authors at the first citation; thereafter, give only the name of the first author followed by *et al.*, as in (*Albertini et al., 1986*). For six or more authors, cite the first author's surname followed by *et al.* and the date for all citations, including the first.

19. Article in journal paginated by issue

When each issue of a journal begins with page 1, include the issue number in parentheses immediately (with no space) after the volume number. Do not italicize the issue number.

Wurzbacher, K. V., Evans, E. D., & Moore, E. J. (1991). Effects of alternative street school on youth involved in prostitution. *Journal of Adolescent Health, 12*(7), 549-554.

20. Special issue of journal

Begin with the special issue's editor (if other than the regular editor); otherwise, place the title at the beginning, then the date. Indicate in brackets that it is a special issue. You need not include page numbers.

Balk, D. E. (Ed.). (1991). Death and adolescent bereavement [Special issue]. *Journal of Adolescent Research, 6*(1).

21. Article in popular magazine (weekly or biweekly)

Supply the same information as you would for an article in a monthly magazine (see Entry 22), but add the specific date.

Adler, J. (1995, July 31). The rise of the overclass. *Newsweek, 126*, 33-34, 39-40, 43, 45-46.

When an article is continued, list all the pages, separated by commas.

22. Article in popular magazine (monthly)

Include the month and year of the magazine. Spell out months. Add the volume number and pages. If there is no author, put the title first, before the date.

Dold, C. (1998, September). Needles and nerves. *Discover, 19*, 59-62.

23. Article with no author given

Begin the entry with the article's title, and alphabetize using the first main word in the title.

Large TADS study hopes to determine best treatments for teenage depression. (2001, February). *Brown University Child & Adolescent Psychopharmacology Update, 3*(1), 4-7.

24. Article in newspaper

Use *p.* or *pp.* to introduce the section and page numbers for newspaper articles. If no author is given, put the title first.

Murtaugh, P. (1998, August 10). Finding a brand's real essence. *Advertising Age*, p. 12.

25. Letter to the editor or editorial

Treat a letter to the editor like another newspaper article, but label it in brackets.

Ellis, S. (2001, September 7). Adults are problem with youth sports [Letter to the editor]. *USA Today*, p. A14.

26. Interview—published

Although APA does not specify a form for published interviews, you may wish to employ the following form, which is similar to other APA references.

Dess, N. K. (2001). The new body-mind connection (John T. Cacioppo) [Interview]. *Psychology Today, 34*(4), 30-31.

29d APA

27. Review with a title

Following the title of the review, indicate in brackets the kind of work (*book, film, video program, television program,* and so on) and the title (italicized) of the work being reviewed.

McMahon, R. J. (2000). The Pentagon's war, the media's war [Review of the book *Reporting Vietnam: Media and military at war*]. *Reviews in American History, 28,* 303-308.

28. Review without a title

Begin with the name of the reviewer. If the review article does not have a title, substitute a description in brackets consisting of the phrase *Review* followed by the type of material and the title of the book, motion picture, television show, or other topic of the review.

Verdery, K. (2002). [Review of the book *The politics of gender after socialism*]. *American Anthropologist, 104,* 354-355.

29. Article from encyclopedia or reference work

If no author is identified, begin with the title of the article. Use *In* before the work's title, and follow it with the volume and page numbers.

Chernoff, H. (1978). Decision theory. In *International encyclopedia of statistics* (Vol. 1, pp. 131-135). New York: Free Press.

30. Chapter in edited book or selection in anthology

For a selection from an anthology, begin with the author's name, the year the book was published, and the title of the selection. Following the word *In*, cite the editors, the title of the collection, and the page numbers.

Chisholm, J. S. (1999). Steps to an evolutionary ecology of mind. In A. L. Hinton (Ed.), *Biocultural approaches to the emotions* (pp. 117-150). Cambridge, England: Cambridge University Press.

31. Dissertation abstract

Yamada, H. (1989). American and Japanese topic management strategies in business conversations. *Dissertation Abstracts International, 50* (09), 2982B.

If you consult the dissertation on microfilm, give the University Microfilms number at the end of the entry in parentheses: (*UMI No. AAC–9004751*).

3 Field resources

32. Unpublished raw data

When you use data from field research, including field observations or a survey, briefly describe its topic within brackets, and end with *Unpublished raw data.*

Molochevic, V. (2007). [Survey of response to proposed changes in Social Security benefits]. Unpublished raw data.

33. Interview—unpublished

To refer to an interview you have conducted yourself, provide the information only as part of an in-text citation: (V. Friedman, personal communication, November 14, 2003). (See Entry 34.)

34. Personal communication (including email)

Letters, email, telephone conversations, and similiar communications cannot be consulted by your readers, so do not include them in your reference list. Instead, cite them in text. (See p. 465 and Entry 33 for examples.)

35. Paper presented at a meeting

For an unpublished paper presented at a conference or symposium, include the month as well as the year, and list both the name and location of the meeting.

Nelson, J. S. (1993, August). *Political argument in political science: A meditation on the disappointment of political theory*. Paper presented at the annual meeting of the American Political Science Association, Chicago, IL.

4 Media resources

36. Videotape or film

Begin with the name or names of the people primarily responsible for the work, and indicate each person's role (for example, *Director* or *Producer*) in parentheses following the name. Italicize the title (or underline), and then indicate the medium (for example, *Motion picture* or *Slides)* in brackets. At the end of the entry, within parentheses, indicate the location and name of the distributor (for example, *WGBH, Boston*). If the distributor is not well known, supply the address. For motion pictures, give the country of origin and the name of the studio.

Simon, T. (Producer), & LeBrun, N. (Writer). (1986). *Atocha: Quest for treasure* [Motion picture]. (Available from Columbia Tristar Home Video, 3400 Riverside Drive, Burbank, CA 91505-4627)

Coen, E. (Producer), & Coen, J. (Director). (2000). *O brother, where art thou?* [Motion picture]. United States: Universal Pictures.

37. Television or radio program

Begin the entry for a series of programs with the name of the script writer, the producer, the director, or any other person whose role you wish to indicate. Give the title of the program or series (italicized) followed by *Television series* in brackets. Conclude with the location and name of the network or channel responsible for the broadcast.

Surnow, J., & Cochran, R. (Creators). (2001-2007). *24* [Television series]. Los Angeles: Fox Broadcasting.

A specific episode in a series is treated much like an anthology. List the script's writer as you would an author, then the name of the director, with each of these followed by his or her function in parentheses. Follow the episode title with *Television series episode* in brackets, then indicate the producer in the editor position, before the italicized title of the series.

Moyers, B. A. (Writer), & Grubin, D. (Director). (1993). A life together [Television series episode]. In D. Grubin (Producer), *Bill Moyers' journal*. New York: WNET.

38. Recording

Begin by giving the name of the writer and the date of copyright (in parentheses). Following the song title, supply the name of the recording artist in brackets, if this is someone other than the writer. Indicate the medium in brackets after the album title; include a number for the recording within the brackets if one is necessary for identifying the recording and obtaining a copy.

Give the location, followed by a colon and the name of the recording label. Include the recording date, if different from the copyright date, in parentheses, with no period after the final parenthesis.

Freeman, R. (1994). Porscha [Recorded by R. Freeman & The Rippingtons]. On *Sahara* [CD]. New York: GRP Records.

5 Internet, Web, and electronic resources

Journal article (online)

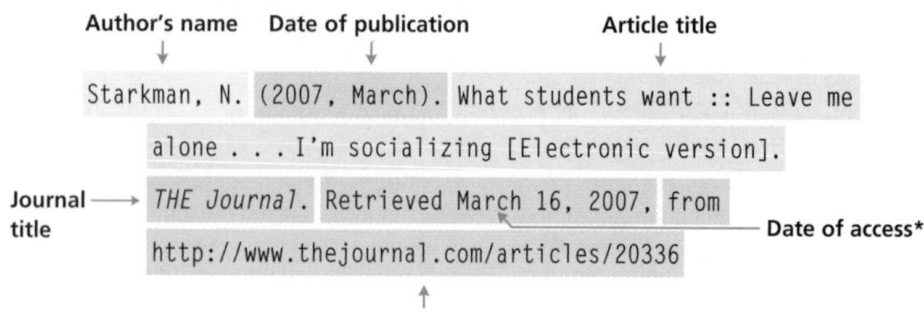

Starkman, N. (2007, March). What students want :: Leave me alone . . . I'm socializing [Electronic version]. *THE Journal*. Retrieved March 16, 2007, from http://www.thejournal.com/articles/20336

URL

Journal title

Article title

Author's name

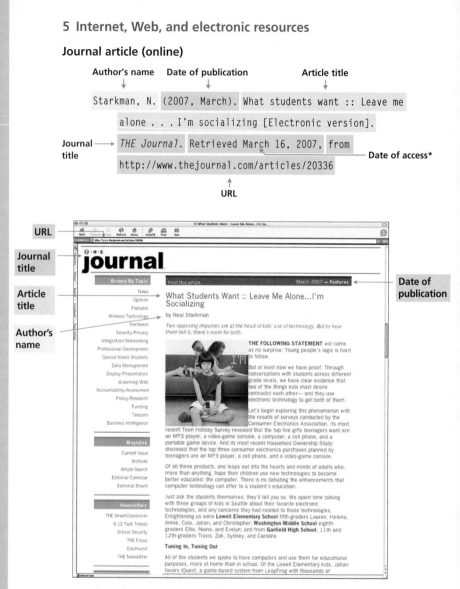

Date of publication

THE journal

Browse By Topic

News
Opinion
Features
Wireless Technology
Hardware
Security/Privacy
Integration/Networking
Professional Development
Special Needs Students
Data Management
Display/Presentation
eLearning/Web
Accountability/Assessment
Policy/Research
Funding
Telecom
Business Intelligence

Magazine

Current Issue
Archives
Article Search
Editorial Calendar
Editorial Board

Newsletters

THE SmartClassroom
K-12 Tech Trends
School Security
THE Focus
EduHound
THE Newsletter

Print this article — March 2007 — Features

What Students Want :: Leave Me Alone...I'm Socializing

by Neal Starkman

Two opposing impulses are at the heart of kids' use of technology. But to hear them tell it, there's room for both.

THE FOLLOWING STATEMENT will come as no surprise: Young people's logic is hard to follow.

But at least now we have proof. Through conversations with students across different grade levels, we have clear evidence that two of the things kids most desire contradict each other— and they use electronic technology to get both of them.

Let's begin exploring this phenomenon with the results of surveys conducted by the Consumer Electronics Association. Its most recent Teen Holiday Survey revealed that the top five gifts teenagers want are an MP3 player, a video-game console, a computer, a cell phone, and a portable game device. And its most recent Household Ownership Study disclosed that the top three consumer electronics purchases planned by teenagers are an MP3 player, a cell phone, and a video-game console.

Of all these products, one leaps out into the hearts and minds of adults who, more than anything, hope their children use new technologies to become better educated: the computer. There is no debating the enhancements that computer technology can offer to a student's education.

Just ask the students themselves; they'll tell you so. We spent time talking with three groups of kids in Seattle about their favorite electronic technologies, and any concerns they had related to those technologies. Enlightening us were **Lowell Elementary School** fifth-graders Lauren, Helena, Annie, Cole, Jahari, and Christopher; **Washington Middle School** eighth-graders Ellie, Naina, and Evelyn; and from **Garfield High School**, 11th and 12th-graders Travis, Zak, Sydney, and Caroline.

Tuning In, Tuning Out

All of the students we spoke to have computers and use them for educational purposes, more at home than in school. Of the Lowell Elementary kids, Jahari favors iQuest, a game-based system from LeapFrog with thousands of

*For date of access, use the date you visited the source.

39. Web site

Include the information specified in Entry 42.

Ringertz, N. (1998, December 2). Alfred Nobel's health and his interest in medicine. Retrieved December 31, 1998, from The Electronic Nobel Museum Project Web site: http://www.nobel.se/alfred/ringertz/index.html

40. Online book or document

For texts lacking a publication date, use *n.d.* ("no date").

Frary, R. B. (n.d.). *A brief guide to questionnaire development.* Retrieved August 8, 1998, from http://ericae.net/ft/ tamu/upiques3.htm

41. Selection from online book or document

Lasswell, H. D. (1971). Professional training. In *A pre-view of policy sciences* (chap. 8). Retrieved May 4, 2002, from http://www.policysciences.org/spsresources.htm

42. Article in online journal

Begin with the author(s) and the date of posting. Add the title, list the source with the volume and issue numbers, and list the page numbers if given. Provide retrieval date and electronic address.

Sheridan, J., & McAuley, J. D. (1998). Rhythm as a cognitive skill: Temporal processing deficits in autism. *Noetica, 3*(8). Retrieved December 31, 1998, from http://www.cs.indiana.edu/Noetica/OpenForumIssue8/McAuley.html

43. Online article identical to print version

If online and print articles are identical, you may use the print format but identify the online version you used. If you have viewed the article online only, add the words *Electronic version* in brackets after the article. Retrieval date and electronic address should be included when there is a possibility that the material has been changed from its printed form.

Epstein, R. (2001). Physiologist Laura [Electronic version]. *Psychology Today, 34*(4), 5.

44. Newsletter article (online)

Cashel, J. (2001, July 16). Top ten trends for online communities. *Online Community Report.* Retrieved October 18, 2001, from http://www.onlinecommunityreport .com/features/10/

45. Newspaper or news service article (online)

Begin with as much information as possible that would be provided for a printed source. Give the date of retrieval, a comma, and the electronic address.

Sonner, S. (1998, December 31). Psychologist ponders horse killer. *Washington Post Online.* Retrieved December 31, 2003, from http://search.washingtonpost.com/ wp-rv/WAPO/19981231/V000412-123198-idx.html

46. Organization or agency document (online)

Arizona Public Health Association. (n.d.). *Indigenous health section.* Retrieved September 6, 2006, from http:// www.geocities.com/native_health_/AzPHA.htm

47. Government document (online)

U.S. Department of Labor, Women's Bureau. (2001). *Women's jobs 1964-1999: More than 30 years of progress.* Retrieved September 7, 2005, from http://www.dol.gov/dol/wb/public/ jobs6497.htm

48. Document from academic site (online)

Cultural Studies Program. (n.d.). Retrieved September 9, 2001, from Drake University, Cultural Studies Web site: http://www.multimedia.drake.edu/cs/

49. Report (online)

Amnesty International. (1998). *The death penalty in Texas: Lethal injustice.* Retrieved September 7, 2006, from http://www.web.amnesty.org/ai.nsf/index/AMR510101998

50. Report from academic site (online)

Vandell, D. L., & Wolfe, B. (2000). *Child care quality: Does it matter and does it need to be improved?* (Special Report No. 78). Available from University of Wisconsin, Institute for Research on Poverty Web site, http://www.ssc.wisc.edum/irp/sr/sr78.pdf

51. Abstract (online)

For an abstract, give the source of the original work and the location of the abstract.

Globus, G. (1995, August). Quantum consciousness is cybernetic. *PSYCHE, 2*(12). Abstract retrieved January 8, 2004, from http://psyche.cs.monash.edu.au/v2/psyche-2-12-curran.html

52. CD-ROM abstract

Schroeder, E. (1988). Therapy for the chemically dependent family [CD-ROM]. *Journal of Chemical Dependency, 2,* 95-129. Abstract retrieved May 17, 1994, from SilverPlatter File: PsycLIT Item 76-37924.

53. Journal article from online database

Piko, B. (2001). Gender differences and similarities in adolescents' ways of coping. *Psychological Record, 51*(2), 223-236. Retrieved August 31, 2001, from InfoTrac Expanded Academic database.

54. Newspaper article from online database

Sappenfield, M. (2002, June 24). New laws curb teen sports drugs. *The Christian Science Monitor*. Retrieved June 26, 2002, from America Online: News Publications database.

55. Presentation from virtual conference

Brown, D. J., Steward, D. S., & Wilson, J. R. (1995). *Ethical pathways to virtual learning.* Paper presented at the Center

Journal article from a subscription database (HTML format)

Authors' names

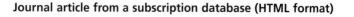

Buboltz, W. C., Jr., Soper, B., Brown, F., & Jenkins, S. (2002). Treatment approaches for sleep difficulties in college students. *Counselling Psychology Quarterly, 15*(2), 229-237. Retrieved March 12, 2007, from Academic Search Premier database.

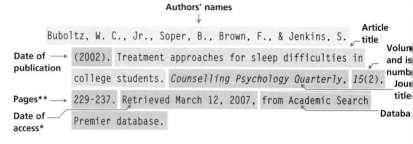

Date of publication — Article title — Volume and issue number — Journal title — Pages** — Date of access* — Database

Database

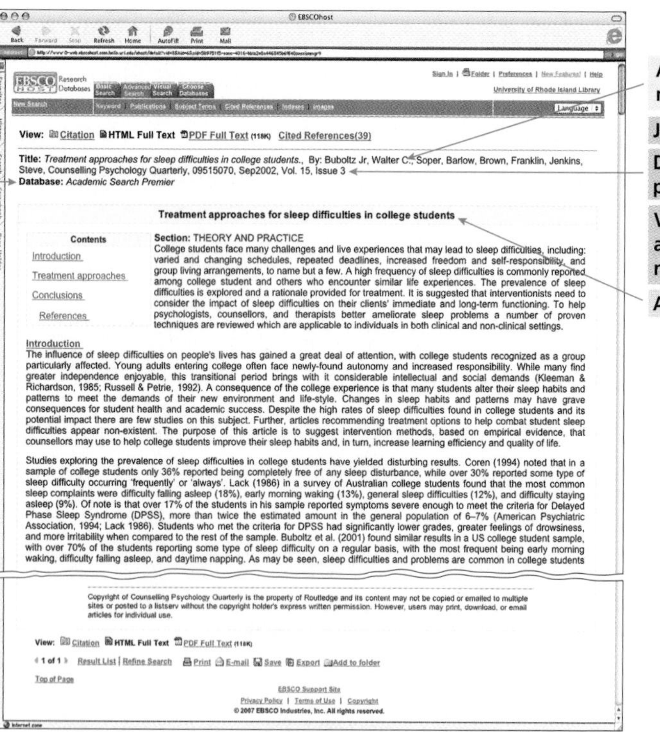

EBSCOhost

Sign In | Folder | Preferences | New Features! | Help

University of Rhode Island Library

View: Citation HTML Full Text PDF Full Text (118K) Cited References(39)

Title: *Treatment approaches for sleep difficulties in college students.*, By: Buboltz Jr, Walter C., Soper, Barlow, Brown, Franklin, Jenkins, Steve, Counselling Psychology Quarterly, 09515070, Sep2002, Vol. 15, Issue 3
Database: *Academic Search Premier*

Treatment approaches for sleep difficulties in college students

Contents
Introduction
Treatment approaches
Conclusions
References

Section: THEORY AND PRACTICE
College students face many challenges and live experiences that may lead to sleep difficulties, including: varied and changing schedules, repeated deadlines, increased freedom and self-responsibility, and group living arrangements, to name but a few. A high frequency of sleep difficulties is commonly reported among college student and others who encounter similar life experiences. The prevalence of sleep difficulties is explored and a rationale provided for treatment. It is suggested that interventionists need to consider the impact of sleep difficulties on their clients' immediate and long-term functioning. To help psychologists, counsellors, and therapists better ameliorate sleep problems a number of proven techniques are reviewed which are applicable to individuals in both clinical and non-clinical settings.

Introduction
The influence of sleep difficulties on people's lives has gained a great deal of attention, with college students recognized as a group particularly affected. Young adults entering college often face newly-found autonomy and increased responsibility. While many find greater independence enjoyable, this transitional period brings with it considerable intellectual and social demands (Kleeman & Richardson, 1985; Russell & Petrie, 1992). A consequence of the college experience is that many students alter their sleep habits and patterns to meet the demands of their new environment and life-style. Changes in sleep habits and patterns may have grave consequences for student health and academic success. Despite the high rates of sleep difficulties found in college students and its potential impact there are few studies on this subject. Further, articles recommending treatment options to help combat student sleep difficulties appear non-existent. The purpose of this article is to suggest intervention methods, based on empirical evidence, that counsellors may use to help college students improve their sleep habits and, in turn, increase learning efficiency and quality of life.

Studies exploring the prevalence of sleep difficulties in college students have yielded disturbing results. Coren (1994) noted that in a sample of college students only 36% reported being completely free of any sleep disturbance, while over 30% reported some type of sleep difficulty occurring 'frequently' or 'always'. Lack (1986) in a survey of Australian college students found that the most common sleep complaints were difficulty falling asleep (18%), early morning waking (13%), general sleep difficulties (12%), and difficulty staying asleep (9%). Of note is that over 17% of the students in his sample reported symptoms severe enough to meet the criteria for Delayed Phase Sleep Syndrome (DPSS), more than twice the estimated amount in the general population of 6–7% (American Psychiatric Association, 1994; Lack 1986). Students who met the criteria for DPSS had significantly lower grades, greater feelings of drowsiness, and more irritability when compared to the rest of the sample. Buboltz et al. (2001) found similar results in a US college student sample, with over 70% of the students reporting some type of sleep difficulty on a regular basis, with the most frequent being early morning waking, difficulty falling asleep, and daytime napping. As may be seen, sleep difficulties and problems are common in college students

Copyright of Counselling Psychology Quarterly is the property of Routledge and its content may not be copied or emailed to multiple sites or posted to a listserv without the copyright holder's express written permission. However, users may print, download, or email articles for individual use.

View: Citation HTML Full Text PDF Full Text (118K)

1 of 1 Result List | Refine Search Print E-mail Save Export Add to folder

Top of Page

EBSCO Support Site
Privacy Policy | Terms of Use | Copyright
© 2007 EBSCO Industries, Inc. All rights reserved.

Authors' names

Journal title

Date of publication

Volume and issue numbers

Article title

*For date of access, use the date you visited the source.
**Pages are for print original. No page numbers are provided in online HTML text.

Journal article from a subscription database (PDF format)

Authors' names

Buboltz, W. C., Jr., Soper, B., Brown, F., & Jenkins, S. (2002). Treatment approaches for sleep difficulties in college students. *Counselling Psychology Quarterly, 15*(2), 229-237. Retrieved March 12, 2007, from Academic Search Premier database.

Date of publication — (2002).
Article title — Treatment approaches for sleep difficulties in college students.
Journal title — *Counselling Psychology Quarterly*
Volume and issue numbers — *15*(2)
Pages — 229-237.
Date of access* — Retrieved March 12, 2007
Database** — from Academic Search Premier database.

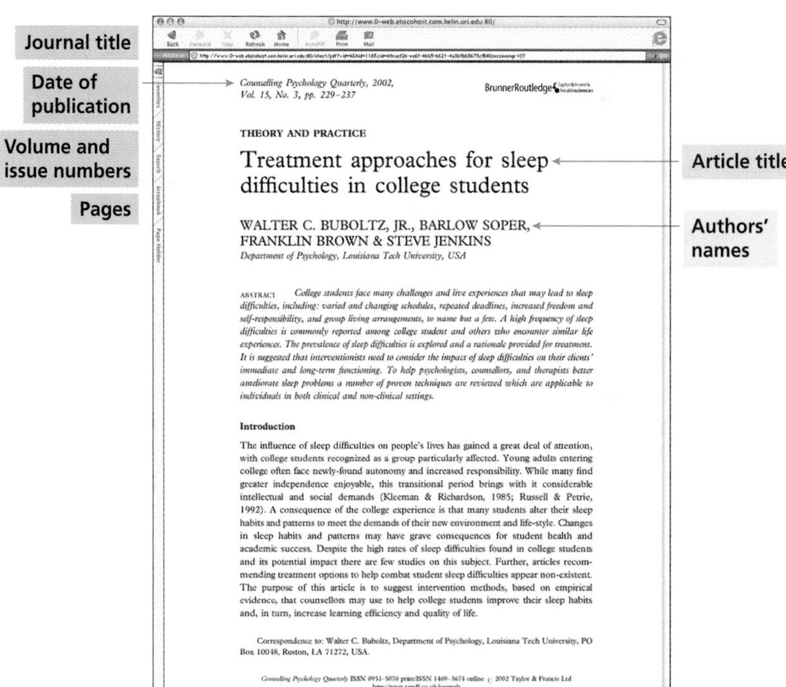

Counselling Psychology Quarterly, 2002,
Vol. 15, No. 3, pp. 229–237

BrunnerRoutledge

THEORY AND PRACTICE

Treatment approaches for sleep difficulties in college students

WALTER C. BUBOLTZ, JR., BARLOW SOPER, FRANKLIN BROWN & STEVE JENKINS
Department of Psychology, Louisiana Tech University, USA

ABSTRACT *College students face many challenges and live experiences that may lead to sleep difficulties, including: varied and changing schedules, repeated deadlines, increased freedom and self-responsibility, and group living arrangements, to name but a few. A high frequency of sleep difficulties is commonly reported among college student and others who encounter similar life experiences. The prevalence of sleep difficulties is explored and a rationale provided for treatment. It is suggested that interventionists need to consider the impact of sleep difficulties on their clients' immediate and long-term functioning. To help psychologists, counsellors, and therapists better ameliorate sleep problems a number of proven techniques are reviewed which are applicable to individuals in both clinical and non-clinical settings.*

Introduction

The influence of sleep difficulties on people's lives has gained a great deal of attention, with college students recognized as a group particularly affected. Young adults entering college often face newly-found autonomy and increased responsibility. While many find greater independence enjoyable, this transitional period brings with it considerable intellectual and social demands (Kleeman & Richardson, 1985; Russell & Petrie, 1992). A consequence of the college experience is that many students alter their sleep habits and patterns to meet the demands of their new environment and life-style. Changes in sleep habits and patterns may have grave consequences for student health and academic success. Despite the high rates of sleep difficulties found in college students and its potential impact there are few studies on this subject. Further, articles recommending treatment options to help combat student sleep difficulties appear non-existent. The purpose of this article is to suggest intervention methods, based on empirical evidence, that counsellors may use to help college students improve their sleep habits and, in turn, increase learning efficiency and quality of life.

Correspondence to: Walter C. Buboltz, Department of Psychology, Louisiana Tech University, PO Box 10048, Ruston, LA 71272, USA.

Counselling Psychology Quarterly ISSN 0951-5070 print/ISSN 1469-3674 online © 2002 Taylor & Francis Ltd
http://www.tandf.co.uk/journals
DOI: 10.1080/09515070210151788

*For date of access, use the date you visited the source.
**Database is not provided in the PDF version. Obtain this information from the database screen shown on page 482.

on Disabilities 1995 virtual conference. Retrieved September 7, 2001, from http://www.csun.edu/cod/95virt/0010.html

56. Online posting or archived discussion list

Give the name of the author and in parentheses the date the message was posted, followed by a period. Next write the title of the message from the subject line and in brackets any identifier for the message. Finally, write the words *Message posted to* and the Uniform Resource Locator (URL), or electronic address.

When listing URLs, do not allow your word processor to hyphenate at the right margin. Instead, break lines either before a period or after a slash. (This can be accomplished with most word processors by inserting an extra space where you want the line to break.) Do not use a period after URLs.

Morrison, A. (1998, September 11). Chlorambucil [Msg 1]. Message posted to http://www.acor.org/lists/cancer/ws/98/09/0078.html

57. Computer program

You need not reference standard, off-the-shelf software. However, if the software is in limited distribution, identify the source as computer software or computer programming language after the title. If the program's author owns specific rights to it, begin the entry with the author's name. Otherwise, begin with the name of the material. Give the location and name of the organization producing the program. Add any version number or retrieval information at the end in parentheses unless it is part of the title.

Checkmate [Computer software]. (1993). Memphis, TN: Psych Development Software. (Windows version)

58. Blog

Baron, D. (2006, October 26). I found it on Wikipedia, the eBay for facts. *The Web of language*. Retrieved December 20, 2006, from http://webtools.uiuc.edu/blog/view?blogId=25&topicId=298&count=&ACTION=TOPIC_DIALOGS&skinId=286

59. Podcast

Malakoff, D. (Speaker). (2007, April 30). Your questions: Carbon power [Podcast]. In *Climate connections*.

Washington, DC: National Public Radio and National Geographic Society. Retrieved May 6, 2007, from http://www.npr.org/rss/podcast/podcast_directory.php

Exercise

A. Turn to Exercise A in Chapter 28. Rewrite the sentences supplied there to add in-text citations in APA style.

B. Turn to Exercise B in Chapter 28. Rewrite the items supplied there to create a list of references in APA style.

C. Working with a partner or a small group, compare your answers to Exercises A and B above. Correct any errors in your answers, using your handbook or your instructor's advice to resolve any differences of opinion.

29e Sample APA paper

Number title page and all others using short title

Body Esteem 1

Supply abbreviated title (50 characters maximum) for heading

Running head: BODY ESTEEM

Center title and all other lines

Body Esteem in Women and Men

Sharon Salamone

University of Rhode Island

Supply name and institution

Double-space twice between groups of lines

Professor Robert Schwegler

Writing 233

Section 2

April 30, 2003

Ask your instructor if instructor's name, course name, and date are necessary

Use short title and page number Body Esteem 2

Center heading Abstract

Summarize paper in one ¶, no more than 120 words

Double-space abstract and rest of paper

Undergraduate students, male and female, were asked to complete a Body Esteem Survey to report attitudes toward their bodies (body images). Responses to the survey provided an answer to the question of whether the men or the women had a higher body esteem. The mean of the responses for women and men indicated a higher level of body esteem among men, with the difference in the means being statistically significant. Because the sample was limited to college undergraduates and displayed little variety in ethnicity (predominantly white), the conclusions of the study are somewhat limited. Prior research on ethnicity and body image suggests that a more ethnically varied sample might produce different results.

[Besides the abstract, typical sections in an APA paper are Introduction, Method, Results, and Discussion]

1" from top of new page

Body Esteem 3

Body Esteem in Women and Men

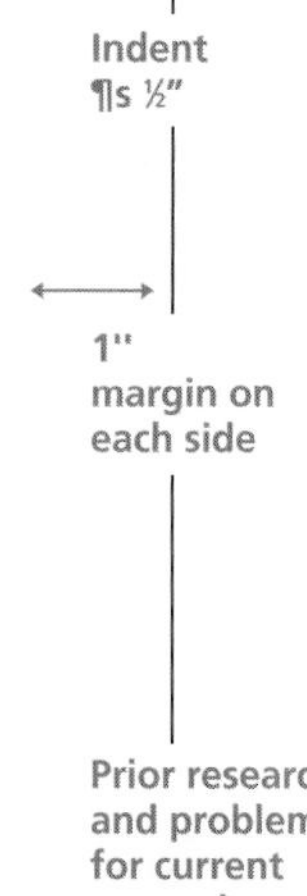

1 The concept of beauty has changed over the years in Western society, especially for women. In past centuries the ideal was a voluptuous and curved body; now it is a more angular and thin shape (Monteath & McCabe, 1997). Lean, muscular bodies are currently held up as ideals for men, too. Ideals of physical appearance and attractiveness play an important role in the lives of people. People considered attractive are often preferred as working partners, as dating partners, or as job candidates (Lennon, Lillethun, & Buckland, 1999). Media images endorse particular body ideals as well; for example, “media in Western countries have portrayed a steadily thinning female body ideal” (Monteath & McCabe, 1997, p. 711).

2 Most of us assume that women are quite concerned about their weight and appearance--their body images--and that they often lack positive body esteem, perhaps as a result of media images and other cultural influences (Rodin, Silberstein, & Striegel-Moore, 1984; Polivy & Herman, 1987; Wilcox & Laird, 2000). But what about men? Are they concerned as well? Is their level of body esteem higher or lower than women’s or about the same? In this paper I report on a study I undertook with a group of college undergraduates to compare the attitudes of men and women toward their bodies. In particular, I wanted to determine whether or not the men had a higher body esteem than the women had.

Multiple sources in one citation

Research questions

1" margin at bottom

Center subheading

Literature Review

Review of earlier studies

3 Thinness is prized in contemporary society, especially for women. In our culture, thinness, a statistical deviation, has become the norm, leading millions of women to believe their bodies are abnormal. Therefore, it is reasonable for women to be concerned about their appearance and to compare themselves to others on the basis of what they believe to be the norm (Lennon et al., 1999). As Lennon et al. point out, “Comparison with such images may be related to negative outcomes such as low self-esteem (Freedman, 1984), dissatisfaction with appearance (Richens, 1991), eating disorders (Peterson, 1987; Stice et al., 1994), and negative body image (Freedman, 1984).”

Citations part of passage being quoted

Body image defined for women

4 Body image is basically made up of two important components; one’s perception and one’s attitude toward body image. Social factors can play a large role in determining both components (Monteath & McCabe, 1997). Given the cultural pressures on women to be thin, we might expect many women to have somewhat negative body images. As Kathy Wilcox and James Laird (2000) put it, “To many observers, the media appear to be unwittingly engaged in a campaign to make women feel badly about themselves” (p. 279).

Male body image defined

5 On the other hand, some researchers suggest that “men seem less obsessed with and disturbed by being or becoming fat: thus, the occurrence of pathogenic values related to eating and body size is extremely low among

men" (Demarest & Allen, 2000, p. 465). Although there has been some research, "the literature on body image perception in men is far more limited" than that on women (Pope, Gruber, Mangweth, Bureau, deCol, Jouvent, & Hudson, 2000). Thus there are reasons to suspect that men also suffer from distorted perceptions of body image. This has been evident in two recent studies. First, men with eating disorders believe that they are fatter than men of normal weight are. Also, recent studies have shown that athletes perceive themselves to be small and frail when they are, in fact, large and muscular (Pope et al., 2000). Moreover, in one particular study, men indicated that they would prefer to have a body with twenty-seven pounds more muscle than they actually have (Pope et al., 2000). Thus it seems reasonable to ask whether men and women have clearly different levels of body esteem.

Method

6 To measure differences between men's and women's levels of body esteem, I administered a Body Esteem Scale (BES) (Franzoi & Shields, 1984). Participants in my study were a sample consisting of 174 undergraduate college students from a state university. I approached them and asked them to complete the BES. I asked each willing participant to read and sign an informed consent form before participating. This form states that the participant may stop at any point if he or she feels uncomfortable answering a particular question or

Describes methods for the study

group of questions and reassures each person that he or she will remain anonymous.

Participants

7 The majority of the participants, between the ages of 18 and 59, were White, making up 81% of the sample. Blacks and African Americans made up 6.3%; Asian/Pacific Islanders made up 3.4%; Latino/Latina, mixed race, and all others made up 2.9% each; and Native Americans made up .6% of the sample. The sample was equally divided between men and women.

Detailed discussion of questionnaire

8 The Body Esteem Scale (BES) consists of general questions (see Appendix) followed by three components (BES 1, BES 2, and BES 3). BES 1 makes up the Physical/Sexual Attractiveness part of the scale, focusing primarily on elements of the body; BES 3 consists of the Physical Condition component of the scale, covering such matters as stamina, physical condition, and strength. BES 1 and BES 3 have different forms and questions for women and men. For BES 2, the women's questionnaire constitutes the Weight Concern component of the scale while the men's questionnaire constitutes the Upper Body Strength component of the scale.

Results and Discussion

Results presented in detail

9 I recorded the results from the questionnaires into an Excel spreadsheet. In order to determine whether women or men had higher levels of body esteem as measured by the BES, I calculated the average score for each group (statistical mean). The mean for women was lower than for men: for women, M = 3.2304; for men,

M = 3.6514. From this I arrived at my preliminary conclusion that for this particular sample of college students, the men had clearly higher body esteem than did the women, by .4211, or approximately .4 on a scale of 1-5.

10 I realized, however, that results can occur by chance and that there are statistical procedures for determining the likelihood that chance was responsible for the difference between the two groups. To determine whether the results were statistically significant (not occurring by chance), I had the spreadsheet program calculate an ANOVA (univariate analysis of variance) to compare the two body esteem indexes. The results indicated that the differences were significant, F (1.172) = 28.05, p <.05.

11 I conducted this study in order to determine whether men had higher, lower, or similar levels of body esteem than women had, at least for the group of people (university undergraduates) I was studying. For this group, it is clear that men had higher levels of body esteem.

Presents conclusion

12 Comparing men's and women's body esteem is not as simple as this study might seem to suggest, however. The body esteem scales for men and women are certainly comparable, but they do not measure exactly the same things. According to Franzoi and Shields (1984), body esteem for women appears to consist of three primary components: sexual attractiveness, weight concern, and physical condition. The sexual attractiveness subscale

Discusses limitations of the study and its conclusions

consists of physical attributes that cannot generally be changed through exercise, but only through cosmetics. The physical appearance subscale includes body parts that can be altered through exercise or the control of food intake. The third subscale pertains to qualities such as stamina, agility, and strength. For men, the first subscale measures facial features and some aspects of the physique. The second subscale is composed of upper body parts and functions that can be altered through exercising. The third subscale is similar to the woman's physical subscale, consisting of stamina, agility, and strength.

Possibilities for future research

13 As social attitudes and values change, perhaps men's and women's versions of the BES may need to change too. As sports and physical strength become more important to women, parts of the BES may possibly need to be revised to be more parallel to the men's. Right now, however, the BES seems to provide some understanding of the different levels of bodily self-esteem held by women and men.

Discusses findings in detail

14 The great pressure on women in our society to be thin and physically attractive according to standards that do not represent a normal range of body types and sizes probably accounts for the difference between the women's and men's results. Franzoi and Shields (1984) make a comment that helps explain the higher body esteem of the males: "It appears that men associate these body parts and functions, not with how they and

others assess them as static objects, but with how they will help or hinder physical activity."

15 My results are consistent with other research. For example, "In studies of body-shape perception, men typically have more positive body images than women do, regardless of their weight" (Demarest & Langer, 1996, p. 466). Overall, men are generally satisfied with their body size, although they misjudge what women think to be attractive (Demarest & Allen, 2000).

16 Gender is not the only factor that influences body image. Ethnicity is also very important, especially among women. In interviews conducted by Lopez, Blix, and Blix (1995) and by Rosen and Gross (1987), Black women seem to have more positive body images and less desire to be thin than White or Hispanic women (Demarest & Allen, 2000). When compared to Black women, White women showed greater body dissatisfaction at lower body weights (Demarest & Allen). It has also been found that Black men were less likely than White men to refuse a date with a woman because she was overweight. According to Demarest and Allen, among the female participants, Black women have a more accurate view of the perception of men, whereas White women have a more distorted perception.

17 In my study, the majority of the sample consisted of White participants. This may have affected my results and my conclusions. Because ethnicity is important in a study such as this, a more varied sample would lead to stronger conclusions.

Begin on new page

References

Demarest, J., & Allen, R. (2000). Body image: Gender, ethnic, and age differences. *Journal of Social Psychology 140,* 465-471.

Demarest, J., & Langer, E. (1996). Perception of body shape by underweight, average-weight, and overweight men and women. *Perceptual and Motor Skills 83,* 569-570.

Franzoi, S. L., & Shields, S. A. (1984). The body esteem scale: Multidimensional structure and sex differences in a college population. *Journal of Personality Assessment, 407,* 173-178.

Lennon, S. J., Lillethun, A., & Buckland, S. S. (1999). Attitudes toward social comparison as a function of self-esteem: Idealized appearance and body image. *Family & Consumer Science Research Journal, 27,* 379-406.

Lopez, E., Blix, G., & Blix, A. G. (1995). Body image of Latinas compared to body image of non-Latina white women. *Health Values, 19,* 3-10.

Monteath, S. A., & McCabe, M. P. (1997). The influence of societal factors on female body image. *Journal of Social Psychology, 137,* 708-727.

Polivy, J., & Herman, C. P. (1987). The diagnosis and treatment of abnormal eating. *Journal of Consulting Clinical Psychology 55,* 635-644.

Pope, H. G., Gruber, A. J., Mangweth, B., Bureau, B., deCol, C., Jouvent, R., et al. (2000). Body image perception among men in three countries. *American Journal of Psychiatry, 157*, 1297-1301.

Rodin, J., Silberstein, L., & Striegel-Moore, R. (1984). Women and weight: a normative discontent. In T. B. Sonderegger (Ed.), *Nebraska symposium on motivation: Psychology and gender.* Lincoln: University of Nebraska Press, 267-307.

Rosen, J. C., & Gross, J. (1987). Prevalence of weight reducing and weight gaining in adolescent boys and girls. *Health Psychology, 6*, 131-147.

Wilcox, K., & Laird, J. D. (2000). The impact of media images of super-slender women on women's self-esteem: Identification, social comparison, and self-perception. *Journal of Research in Personality, 34*, 278-286.

Appendix

Begin on new page

Body Esteem Scale for Adolescents and Adults

General Questions

Instructions: Indicate how often you agree with the following statements: ranging from "never" (0) to "always" (4). Circle the appropriate number beside each statement

Never = 0 Seldom = 1 Sometimes = 2 Often = 3 Always = 4

1. I like what I look like in pictures. 0 1 2 3 4
2. Other people consider me good looking. 0 1 2 3 4
3. I'm proud of my body. 0 1 2 3 4
4. I am preoccupied with trying to change my body weight. 0 1 2 3 4
5. I think my appearance would help me get a job. 0 1 2 3 4
6. I like what I see when I look in the mirror. 0 1 2 3 4
7. There are lots of things I'd change about my looks if I could. 0 1 2 3 4
8. I am satisfied with my weight. 0 1 2 3 4
9. I wish I looked better. 0 1 2 3 4
10. I really like what I weigh. 0 1 2 3 4
11. I wish I looked like someone else. 0 1 2 3 4
12. People my own age like my looks. 0 1 2 3 4
13. My looks upset me. 0 1 2 3 4
14. I'm as nice looking as most people. 0 1 2 3 4
15. I'm pretty happy about the way I look. 0 1 2 3 4
16. I feel I weigh the right amount for my height. 0 1 2 3 4
17. I feel ashamed of how I look. 0 1 2 3 4
18. Weighing myself depresses me. 0 1 2 3 4
19. My weight makes me unhappy. 0 1 2 3 4
20. My looks help me to get dates. 0 1 2 3 4
21. I worry about the way I look. 0 1 2 3 4
22. I think I have a good body. 0 1 2 3 4
23. I'm looking as nice as I'd like to. 0 1 2 3 4

CHAPTER 30
CMS Documentation

The Chicago Manual of Style (CMS) offers several methods of documentation, one of which calls for footnotes/endnotes and a bibliography. This chapter discusses CMS style and provides models for the most common kinds of entries you will use.

CMS FORMATS FOR NOTES

CMS BIBLIOGRAPHY FORMATS

CMS style, the documentation style outlined in *The Chicago Manual of Style* (15th ed., 2003), provides references in the form of endnotes or footnotes. Endnotes or footnotes are signaled by a superscript numeral in the text (for example,[1]) and a correspondingly numbered reference note at the end of the paper (an endnote) or, less often, at the bottom of the page (a footnote). A bibliography at the end of the paper provides a list of all the sources in alphabetical order by author. Endnotes and footnotes are less compact than parenthetical references, yet they offer you a chance to cite a source in full and to include brief explanatory material. Readers especially interested in your sources will find themselves repeatedly turning away from the text itself to consult the notes, however.

30a Endnotes and footnotes

To indicate a reference in the body of your text, insert a number slightly above the line[2], making sure you number the references consecutively. Insert a number to indicate a reference to the source of a quotation, to alert readers to specific information and ideas borrowed from a source, or to specify the source of paraphrased or summarized material. At the end of the paper (in an endnote) or at the bottom of the page (in a footnote), provide detailed information about the source. To create notes, use the footnote/endnote generator in your word-processing program.

TEXT OF PAPER To emphasize how isolated and impoverished his childhood neighborhood was, Wideman describes it as being not simply on "the wrong side of the tracks" but actually "under the tracks, if the truth be told--in a deep hollow between Penn and the abrupt rise of Bruston Hill."[1]

NOTE 1. John Edgar Wideman, *Brothers and Keepers* (New York: Penguin Books, 1984), 39.

1 Select endnotes or footnotes

When pages contain many footnotes or long footnotes, you may find it hard to place the notes on the same pages as the material to which they refer. Multiple or long notes at the bottom of a page can also draw readers' attention away from the text to the notes. For these reasons, even though it may be a bit easier for readers to look at the bottom of the page for a note than to turn to the end of the paper, you should generally employ endnotes. Most readers mark the page containing the endnotes so they can refer to notes with a minimum of disruption. Because readers may sometimes skip consulting a note unless they are particularly interested in your sources, you should make sure that you place all information necessary for understanding your argument or explanation in the body of your paper and not in the notes.

2 Content and explanatory notes

At times you may wish to supplement your text with material that may interest only a few readers. Notes are an appropriate place to do this, but don't make notes so detailed that they distract readers from the main text of the paper. You can also combine explanation with a source reference, though you need to make sure that a long and detailed discussion does not obscure the reference.

TEXT OF PAPER Did some famous artists begin their paintings by tracing using a *camera obscura*? The answer is probably "yes," and the process can be understood this way.

> If a small hole is made in the wall of a darkened room, an image of the scene outside can be formed by light rays passing through the hole. The image may appear on a wall opposite the hole, or can be observed on a sheet of paper or other screen placed in front of the hole.[2]

NOTE

2. Philip Steadman, *Vermeer's Camera* (Oxford: Oxford University Press, 2001), 4. In an electronic age, we often forget that complex effects can be created by simple devices such as the *camera obscura*.

30b Note examples

After you have placed a number slightly above the line of text[3] to indicate the presence of an endnote or footnote and have made sure that your numbering system maintains consecutive order, you need to prepare the note. A typical note provides the author's name in regular order, the title of the work being cited, publication information, and the page number(s).

Place endnotes at the end of a paper, after appendixes but before a bibliography. Supply notes on a separate page with the centered heading "Notes." Your word-processing footnote/endnote program should indent the first line. If not, indent it .5" or five spaces. Start the note with the number, followed by a period and a space. Do not indent the second line or any others that follow. Double-space for ease of reading.

1 Books and works treated as books

MODEL FORMAT FOR BOOKS AND WORKS TREATED AS BOOKS

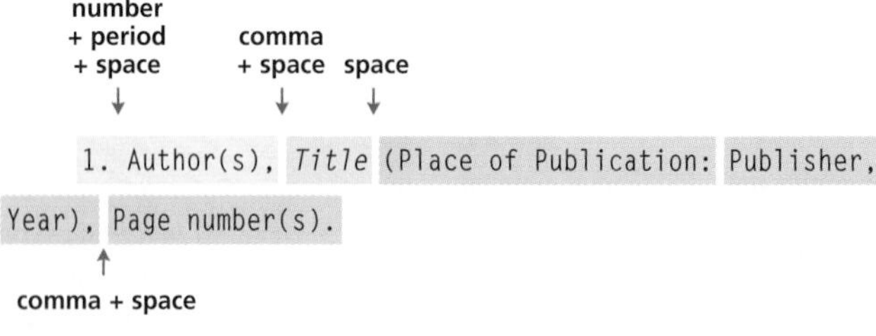

- **Author(s).** Give the name of the author(s) in regular order followed by a comma and a space.
- **Title.** Give the title of the work being cited. Italicize the title of a book and follow the title with a space. (See 54c on capitalization of titles.)
- **Publication information.** Give all publication information within parentheses. Start with the city of publication, followed by a comma

and an abbreviation for the state or country if this information is necessary to avoid confusion between two cities with the same name or to identify little-known places. Add a colon and a space, then give the publisher's name followed by a comma, a space, and the date of publication. Place a comma followed by a space after the closing parenthesis mark.

- **Page number(s).** Conclude with the specific page numbers containing the information being cited or the passage being quoted, paraphrased, or summarized.

1. One author

1. Bobby Bridger, *Buffalo Bill and Sitting Bull: Inventing the Wild West* (Austin: University of Texas Press, 2002), 297.

2. Two or three authors

Separate the names of two authors with *and*. Separate those of three authors with commas as well as *and* before the name of the third author.

2. Canter Brown Jr. and Barbara Gray Brown, *Family Records of the African American Pioneers of Tampa and Hillsborough County* (Tampa: University of Tampa Press, 2003), 129.

2. Michael Wood, Bruce Cole, and Adelheid Gealt, *Art of the Western World* (New York: Summit Books, 1989), 206-10.

3. Four or more authors

For works with more than three authors, give the name of the first author followed by *and others*. (Generally, all the names are supplied in the corresponding bibliography entry.)

3. Bernadette Casey and others, *Television Studies: The Key Concepts* (London: Routledge, 2002), 81.

4. No author given

If the author is not known, begin the entry with the title.

4. *The Great Utopia: The Russian and Soviet Avant-Garde, 1915-1932* (New York: Guggenheim Museum, 1992), 661.

5. Editor

When a work has an editor, translator, or compiler (or some combination of them), give the name or names after the title preceded by a comma and the appropriate abbreviation, for example, *ed.*, *trans.*, or *comp.*

5. Mahatma Gandhi, *Gandhi in India: In His Own Words,* ed. Martin Green (Hanover, NH: University Press of New England, 1987), 261.

Gandhi is the author, and Green has prepared the particular selection of the writings.

If you wish to emphasize the role of the editor, translator, or compiler, give his or her name at the beginning of the entry.

5. Donald M. Scott and Bernard Wishy, eds., *America's Families: A Documentary History* (New York: Harper & Row, 1982), 177.

The editors are responsible for assembling materials from a variety of sources.

5. Robert H. Ferrell, ed., *Dear Bess: The Letters from Harry to Bess Truman 1910-1959* (New York: W. W. Norton, 1983), 71-2.

The word *by* with the author's name (*Harry S Truman*) would be appropriate following the title, but it is not necessary because the author's name appears in the title.

6. Edition other than the first

Use an abbreviation following the title to indicate the particular edition, for example, *4th ed.* ("fourth edition") or *rev. and enl. ed.* ("revised and enlarged edition").

6. Thomas E. Skidmore and Peter H. Smith, *Modern Latin America*, 5th ed. (New York: Oxford University Press, 2001), 243.

For a work that has been reprinted or appears in a special paperback edition, give information about both the original publication and the reprint.

6. Henri Frankfort and others, *The Intellectual Adventure of Ancient Man* (1946; repr., Chicago: University of Chicago Press, 1977), 202-4. Citations are to the reprint edition.

7. Multivolume work

A multivolume work can consist of volumes all by a single author (sometimes with different titles for each) or of works by a variety of authors with an overall title. If you are referring to the whole multivolume work, include the number of volumes after the title. To indicate volume and page number for a specific volume, use volume and page numbers separated by a colon and no space. Give the volume number and name for separately titled volumes after the main title and omit the volume number in the page reference.

7. Sigmund Freud, *The Standard Edition of the Complete Psychological Works of Sigmund Freud,* trans. James Strachey (London: Hogarth Press, 1953), 11:180.

2 Articles and selections from books

MODEL FORMAT FOR ARTICLES AND SELECTIONS

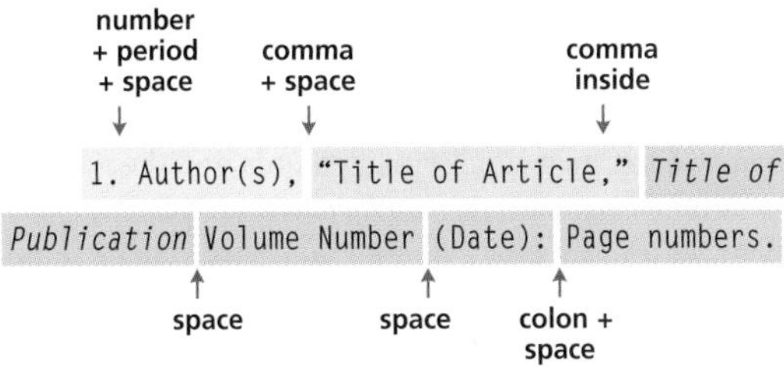

- **Author(s).** Give the author's name in regular order.
- **Title.** Put the title of the article or selection in quotation marks. Put a comma inside the closing quotation mark, and leave a space after the quotation mark.
- **Publication information.** Next give the title of the journal or book, italicized, and leave a space after it with no punctuation. Supply the volume number and then the date of publication in parentheses, varying the information and style for different types of publications. Place a colon after the final parenthesis, and leave a space.
- **Page number(s).** Supply the page numbers for the pertinent part of the article or selection.

8. Article in journal paginated by volume

When the page numbers run continuously through the individual issues that make up a volume, give the volume number but do not include the month, season, or number of the individual issue containing the article. Give specific page numbers for the part of the article you are citing. If you wish to refer to the article as a whole, give inclusive page numbers for the entire article, for example, *98–114*.

8. Lily Zubaidah Rahim, "The Road Less Traveled: Islamic Militancy in Southeast Asia," *Critical Asian Studies* 35 (2003): 224.

9. Article in journal paginated by issue

If each issue of a journal begins with page 1, give the volume number followed by a comma, the abbreviation *no.* (for "number"), and the issue number. If the issue is instead identified by month or season, include information just before the year and within the same set of parentheses, for example (*Winter 1994*) or (*February 1996*). Give page numbers for the specific part of the article you are citing or inclusive page numbers for the entire article if you are referring to it as a whole.

9. Steven High, "Deindustrializing Youngstown: Memories of Resistance and Loss Following 'Black Monday,' 1977-1997," *History Workshop Journal* 54 (Autumn 2002): 101-21.

10. Article in popular magazine

Follow the name of the magazine with a comma and the date. Use this order for the date if it includes the day: *25 November 1995*. Place a comma at the end of the date before the page number, and give a page number for the specific part of the article you are citing or inclusive page numbers for the entire article if you are referring to it as a whole.

10. Edward Hoagland, "The American Dissident: Individualism as a Matter of Conscience," *Harper's*, August 2003, 35.

11. Article in daily newspaper

Identify newspaper articles by date (rather than volume number) following the title of the article and the name of the newspaper. Present the date in this order: *February 4, 1996*. When the sections of a newspaper are separately paginated, provide the section number or letter and the page number—for example, *sec. B, p. 3*—using *p.* or *pp.* to introduce the page number(s).

11. Mark Brennock,"55% of Young Know of Peer Suicide Attempts," *The Irish Times* (Dublin), September 20, 2003, sec. A, p. 1.

When an American newspaper's title does not include the city's name, give it at the start of the title (underlined). For less-known newspapers, for those outside North America with the city not mentioned in the title, and for those from places easily confused with well-known cities, give the name of the state or country after the title or after the name of the city in the title: Westerly (RI) Sun; Times (*London*).

12. Chapter in book or selection from anthology

For a selection from an anthology or for a book chapter, give the name of the selection or chapter in quotation marks followed by *in* and the name of the book. If the book has an editor, follow the book's title with *ed.* and the editor's name.

12. Robert Glennon, "The Future of Water: Tourism and Grand Canyon National Park," in *Water Follies: Groundwater Pumping and the Fate of America's Fresh Waters* (Washington, DC: Island Press, 2002), 195.

Chapter in a book.

12. W. E. B. Du Bois, "The Call of Kansas," in *W. E. B. Du Bois: A Reader*, ed. David Levering Lewis (New York: Henry Holt, 1995), 173.

Selection from an edited collection of one writer's works.

12. John Matviko, "Television Satire and the Presidency: The Case of *Saturday Night Live*," in *Hollywood's White House: The American Presidency in Film and History*, ed. Peter C. Rollins and John E. O'Connor (Lexington: University of Kentucky Press, 2003), 341.

Selection from an edited collection of essays.

3 Field resources

13. Unpublished interview

For unpublished interviews done by someone else, begin with the name of the person interviewed followed by a comma; then give the phrase *interview by*, the name of the interviewer, the date (in this order: *May 2, 2001*), any file number, the medium (*tape recording* or *transcript*, for example), and the place where the interview is stored (such as *Erie County Historical Society, Buffalo, New York*). For interviews you conduct, provide the name of the person interviewed, the phrase *interview by author*, a description of the kind of interview, the medium, and the place and date of the interview.

13. LeJon Williams, interview by author, tape recording, San Diego, CA, October 11, 2006.

13. Lenelle Chu, telephone interview by author, transcript, Hinsdale, IL, June 5, 2006.

4 Media and electronic resources

14. Article in journal (online)

Use the form for *article in journal paginated by volume* (Entry 8), but add the URL and the date of access. If you are referring to a particular section of the article, include the page (if available) or some other locator such as a heading.

14. Anthony B. Pinn, "DuBois' *Souls*: Thoughts on 'Veiled' Bodies and the Study of Black Religion," *The North Star: A Journal of African American Religious History* 6, no. 2 (2003), under "Music and the 'Style' of Life," http://northstar.vassar .edu/volume6/pinn.html (accessed October 7, 2006).

15. Magazine article (online)

Use the form for *article in popular magazine* (Entry 10), but add the URL and the date of access.

15. Alexander Barnes Dryer, "Our Liberian Legacy," *The Atlantic Online*, July 30, 2003, http://www.theatlantic.com/ unbound/flashbks/liberia.htm (accessed October 24, 2006).

16. Newspaper article (online)

Use the form for *article in daily newspaper* (Entry 11), but add the URL and the date of access.

16. Joshua Klein, "Scaring Up a Good Movie," *Chicago Tribune Online Edition*, October 28, 2003, http://www .chicagotribune.com/ (accessed October 28, 2006).

17. Book (online)

Include the kinds of information required in Entries 1–7. Indicate the URL and the date of access.

17. Sharon Marcus, *Apartment Stories: City and Home in Nineteenth-Century Paris and London* (Berkeley: University of California Press, 1999), http://ark.cdlib.org/ark:13030/ ft0d5n99jz/ (accessed October 15, 2006).

For older works, use the following format.

17. Charles Darwin, *On the Origin of Species by Means of Natural Selection, or the Preservation of Favoured Races in the Struggle for Life* (1859; Project Gutenberg 1998), ftp://sailor .gutenberg.org/pub/gutenberg/etext98/otoos10.txt (accessed November 1, 2006).

18. Web site

Provide the author of the content, the title of the site, the owner or group responsible for the site, the URL, and the date of access.

18. Smithsonian Center for Folklife and Cultural Heritage, "2002 Smithsonian Folklife Festival: The Silk Road,"

Smithsonian Institution, http://www.folklife.si.edu/CFCH/festival2002.htm (accessed October 27, 2006).

19. Post to electronic mailing list

Provide the name of the writer, an indication of the kind of document, the name of the list, date of the posting, URL, and date of access. You need not include this information in your bibliography.

19. Justin M. Sanders, e-mail to alt.war.civil.usa, February 15, 2002, http://groups.google.com/groups?q=civil+war&hl=en&lr=&ie=UTF-8&selm=civil-war-usa/faq/part2_1013770939%40rtfm.mit.edu&rnum=1 (accessed October 21, 2006).

20. Audio or video recording

Start with the title unless the recording features a particular individual. Give the names and roles (if appropriate) of performers or others. Add any recording number (audio) after the company name.

20. *James Baldwin*, VHS, directed by Karen Thorson (San Francisco: California Newsreel, 1990).

5 Multiple sources and sources cited in prior notes

21. Multiple sources

When you wish to cite more than one source in a note, separate the references with semicolons and give the entries in the order in which they were cited in the text.

21. See Greil Marcus, *Mystery Train: Images of America in Rock 'n Roll Music* (New York: E. P. Dutton, 1975), 119; Susan Orlean, "All Mixed Up," *New Yorker*, June 22, 1992, 90; and Cornel West, "Learning to Talk of Race," *New York Times Magazine*, August 2, 1992, 24.

22. Work cited more than once

The first time you provide a reference to a work, you need to list full information about the source in the note. In later notes you need to provide only the last name of the author(s), a shortened title, and the page(s). Separate these elements with commas.

22. Macklin, *Mortal*, 161.

22. Wood, Cole, and Gealt, *Art*, 207.

If a note refers to the same source as the note before, you can use a traditional scholarly abbreviation, *ibid.* (from the Latin for "in the same place"), for the second note. *Ibid.* means that the entire reference is identical, but if you add a new page reference, the addition shows that the specific page is different.

23. Tarr, "'A Man,'" 183.

24. Ibid.

25. Ibid., 186.

30c Bibliography

At the end of your paper you need to provide readers with an alphabetical list of the sources cited in your notes. CMS style calls for this list to be titled "Bibliography" or "Works Cited." If it includes all the works you consulted, you might call it "Works Consulted."

Place your bibliography on a separate page at the end of your paper, and center the title two inches below the upper edge. Continue the page numbering used for the text. Double-space entries for ease of reading. Do not indent the first line, but indent the second line and any subsequent lines five spaces. Alphabetize the entries according to the authors' last names or the first word of the title, excluding *A*, *An*, and *The*, if the author is unknown.

1 Books and works treated as books

MODEL FORMAT FOR BOOKS AND WORKS TREATED AS BOOKS

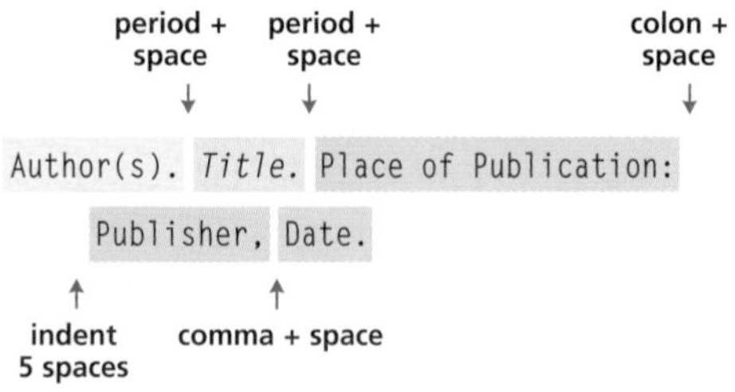

- **Author(s).** Give the author's last name followed by a comma, then the first and any middle names or initials followed by a period and a space.
- **Title.** Give the title of the work, italicized, ending with a period and space. Capitalize the main words of the title and any subtitle. Do not capitalize *a*, *an*, *the*, coordinating conjunctions (such as *and*, *or*, and *but*), and prepositions. Always capitalize the first and last words of any title or subtitle.

30c CMS

- **Place of publication.** Give the city where the work was published, followed by a comma and an abbreviation for the state or country if necessary to avoid confusion between cities with the same name or to identify little-known places. End with a colon and a space.
- **Publisher.** Give the publisher's name followed by a comma and a single space.
- **Date.** Give the date of publication followed by a period.

1. One author

Bridger, Bobby. *Buffalo Bill and Sitting Bull: Inventing the Wild West*. Austin: University of Texas Press, 2002.

2. Two or three authors

Brown, Canter Jr., and Barbara Gray Brown. *Family Records of the African American Pioneers of Tampa and Hillsborough County*. Tampa: University of Tampa Press, 2003.

Wood, Michael, Bruce Cole, and Adelheid Gealt. *Art of the Western World*. New York: Summit Books, 1989.

3. Four or more authors

Casey, Bernadette, Neil Casey, Ben Calvert, Liam French, and Justin Lewis. *Television Studies: The Key Concepts*. London: Routledge, 2002.

4. No author given

The Great Utopia: The Russian and Soviet Avant-Garde, 1915-1932. New York: Guggenheim Museum, 1992.

5. Editor

Gandhi, Mahatma. *Gandhi in India: In His Own Words*. Edited by Martin Green. Hanover, NH: University Press of New England, 1987.

Scott, Donald M., and Bernard Wishy, eds. *America's Families: A Documentary History*. New York: Harper & Row, 1982.

Ferrell, Robert H., ed. *Dear Bess: The Letters from Harry to Bess Truman 1910-1959*. New York: W. W. Norton, 1983.

6. Edition other than the first

Skidmore, Thomas E., and Peter H. Smith. *Modern Latin America*. 5th ed. New York: Oxford University Press, 2001.

Frankfort, Henri, H. A. Frankfort, John A. Wilson, Thorkild Jacobsen, and William A. Irving. *The Intellectual Adventure of Ancient Man.* Chicago: University of Chicago Press, 1946. Reprint, Chicago: University of Chicago Press, 1977.

7. Multivolume work

Freud, Sigmund. *The Standard Edition of the Complete Psychological Works of Sigmund Freud.* Translated by James Strachey. Vol. 11. London: Hogarth Press, 1953.

2 Articles and selections from books

MODEL FORMAT FOR ARTICLES AND SELECTIONS FROM BOOKS

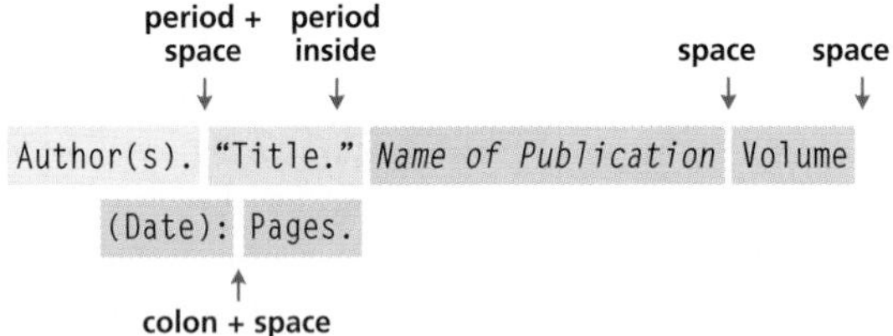

- **Author(s).** Give the author's last name followed by a comma, then the first and any middle names or initials followed by a period and a space.
- **Title.** Give the title of the article within quotation marks, and capitalize the main words of the title and of any subtitle. Do not capitalize *a*, *an*, *the*, coordinating conjunctions (such as *and* and *or*), and prepositions. Always capitalize the first and last words of any title or subtitle. If the article's title contains the title of a work that needs to be italicized or underlined, use underlining; if it contains a title that requires quotation marks, use single quotation marks to enclose the interior title.
- **Name of publication.** Give the title of the journal or magazine containing the article, and italicize it.
- **Volume.** Give the volume number of the periodical; separate it from the name of the publication by a space without a comma or any other punctuation. Include the issue number only for certain kinds of publications.
- **Date.** Provide the year in which the article was published (within parentheses), but indicate the month or season only for certain kinds of publications.
- **Pages.** Follow the parentheses containing the date with a colon and a space; then give the inclusive pages on which the article appears.

8. Article in journal paginated by volume

Rahim, Lily Zubaidah. "The Road Less Traveled: Islamic Militancy in Southeast Asia." *Critical Asian Studies* 35 (2003): 209-32.

9. Article in journal paginated by issue

High, Steven. "Deindustrializing Youngstown: Memories of Resistance and Loss Following 'Black Monday,' 1977-1997." *History Workshop Journal* 54 (Autumn 2002): 101-21.

10. Article in popular magazine

Hoagland, Edward. "The American Dissident: Individualism as a Matter of Conscience." *Harper's*, August 2003, 33-41.

11. Article in daily newspaper

Brennock, Mark. "55% of Young Know of Peer Suicide Attempts." *The Irish Times* (Dublin), September 20, 2003, sec. A, p. 1.

12. Chapter in book or selection from anthology

Glennon, Robert. "The Future of Water: Tourism and Grand Canyon National Park." In *Water Follies: Groundwater Pumping and the Fate of America's Fresh Waters*, 195-207. Washington, DC: Island Press, 2002.

Du Bois, W. E. B. "The Call of Kansas." In *W. E. B. Du Bois: A Reader*, edited by David Levering Lewis, 101-21. New York: Henry Holt, 1995.

Matviko, John. "Television Satire and the Presidency: The Case of *Saturday Night Live*." In *Hollywood's White House: The American Presidency in Film and History*, edited by Peter C. Rollins and John E. O'Connor, 341-60. Lexington: University of Kentucky Press, 2003.

3 Field resources

13. Unpublished interview

Williams, LeJon. Interview by author. Tape recording. San Diego, CA, October 11, 2006.

Chu, Lenelle. Telephone interview by author. Transcript. Hinsdale, IL, June 5, 2006.

4 Media and electronic resources

14. Article in journal (online)

Include the page range, if available.

Pinn, Anthony B. "DuBois' *Souls*: Thoughts on 'Veiled' Bodies and the Study of Black Religion." *The North Star: A Journal of African American Religious History* 6, no. 2 (2003). http://northstar.vassar.edu/volume6/pinn.html (accessed October 7, 2006).

15. Magazine article (online)

Dryer, Alexander Barnes. "Our Liberian Legacy." *The Atlantic Online*, July 30, 2003. http://www.theatlantic.com/unbound/flashbks/liberia.htm (accessed October 24, 2006).

16. Newspaper article (online)

Klein, Joshua. "Scaring Up a Good Movie." *Chicago Tribune Online Edition,* October 28, 2003. http://www.chicagotribune.com/ (accessed October 28, 2006).

17. Book (online)

Marcus, Sharon. *Apartment Stories: City and Home in Nineteenth-Century Paris and London.* Berkeley: University of California Press, 1999. http://ark.cdlib.org/ark:13030/ft0d5n99jz/ (accessed October 15, 2006).

Darwin, Charles. *On the Origin of Species by Means of Natural Selection, or the Preservation of Favoured Races in the Struggle for Life*. 1859; Project Gutenberg 1998. ftp://sailor.gutenberg.org/pub/gutenberg/etext98/otoos10.txt (accessed November 1, 2006).

18. Web site

Smithsonian Center for Folklife and Cultural Heritage. "2002 Smithsonian Folklife Festival: The Silk Road." Smithsonian Institution. http://www.folklife.si.edu/CFCH/festival2002.htm (accessed October 27, 2006).

30c CMS

19. Audio or video recording

James Baldwin. VHS. Directed by Karen Thorson. San Francisco: California Newsreel, 1990.

5 Multiple sources

20. Multiple sources

When a note lists more than one source, list each one separately in your bibliography, integrating them in alphabetical order among your other sources.

Exercise

A. Turn to Exercise A in Chapter 28. Rewrite the sentences supplied there to add note numbers in CMS style. Then prepare the corresponding notes for these items.

B. Turn to Exercise B in Chapter 28. Rewrite the items supplied there to create a list of works cited in CMS style.

C. Working with a partner or a small group, compare your answers to Exercises A and B above. Correct any errors in your answers, using your handbook or your instructor's advice to resolve any differences of opinion.

30d Student CMS Paper

Center title

Begin one-third of the way down the page

STUDY DRUGS: THE NEW DRUG CRAZE AMONG COLLEGE STUDENTS

Center and double-space all lines

JENNA IANUCILLI

DR. SCHWEGLER

WRT 106

MARCH 2, 2007

1" ½"

1

1 Have you ever had to stay up all night to cram for a bio exam? Have you ever had to write three papers in one night because you put them all off until the last night? Ever felt like you could use something that could make you focus on your work during an all-night study session? Many people think they have found an effective strategy in the newest drug craze to sweep college campuses: drugs to increase academic performance.

¶ indented ½"

Double-space

Introduces topic

2 The drugs they use are normally prescribed for attention deficit hyperactivity disorder (ADHD), with the most common drugs being Ritalin and Adderall. The drugs are usually prescribed to people suffering from ADHD to allow them to reach normal functioning level by stimulating the frontal lobes of the brain, areas that monitor task performance;[1] college students, however, often use the drugs as study aids. Dr. Eric Heiligenstein, a psychiatrist at the University of Wisconsin who studies substance abuse, points out that when taken by people with normal brain function, "The drugs can give healthy people an almost superhuman ability to focus for long periods."[2]

1" 1"

Superscript numbers refer to endnotes

Two ¶s provide background and explain the problem

3 The drugs are stimulants, in the class of cocaine, caffeine, amphetamines, and methamphetamines, so the result in normal people is to feel like they are on "speed." They will have huge amounts of energy and will require less sleep. That can be a useful feeling

1"

2

when it is almost midnight and one has to cram in lots of studying for an organic chemistry exam at eight o'clock the next morning, yet side effects can include emotional and physical strains and anxiety and, in some cases, addiction or dependence.

Focus on danger

4 In a survey of 13,500 college students conducted by the American College Health Association, 94 percent of respondents reported feeling overwhelmed by everything they had to do at school.[3] College life creates increased stress. Extracurricular activities that build résumés for graduate schools create strain. Students sleep less than normal. They worry more than ever about financial, social, and academic pressures.

Writer draws on own field research

CMS does not require note, but her instructor did

5 In a survey I conducted, all the students believed that the competitiveness of college life might cause someone to choose to take drugs to improve academic performance.[4] The students also agreed that parents, peers, relatives, and teachers were other sources of pressure. Jobs are yet another cause of stress. Some college students work a substantial number of hours every week, not just for extra spending money but also to lighten some of the heavy debt load of student loans they will have once they graduate. For many, it is easier to pop a pill to aid concentration than to have to struggle to fit more sleep time into a full schedule of classes, extracurricular activities, parties,

3

and work. Such students are at risk for misusing or abusing study drugs.

6 According to a 2002 Johns Hopkins University study, up to 20 percent of college-age students have regularly used drugs to enhance academic performance, and another study at the University of Wisconsin confirmed this.[5] Dr. Tim Wilens of Massachusetts General Hospital reports that a quarter of college-age students have tried stimulants such as Ritalin or Adderall without prescriptions.[6] These are staggering figures, which show the great lengths to which students will go to gain an edge.

Article cited in footnote summarizes studies at Johns Hopkins and Wisconsin

Problem is widespread

7 Where do the drugs come from, and how do they work? The drugs were developed to treat attention deficit hyperactivity disorder (ADHD), a condition that begins appearing in children in their preschool years. Between 30 and 70 percent of children with the disorder will continue to exhibit symptoms in their adult years. The principal characteristics of ADHD are inattention, hyperactivity, and impulsivity.[7]

8 Medications are one of the main treatments for ADHD. The most effective medications are stimulants such as Adderall and Ritalin. For many people afflicted with ADHD, the stimulants dramatically reduce hyperactivity and impulsivity and improve the ability to focus, work, and learn.[8]

How the drugs work

9 They have similar effects for college students, allowing them to work more efficiently while

Discussion of Adderall

requiring less sleep. Adderall stimulates the central nervous system (the brain and nerves) by increasing the amount of certain chemicals, such as dopamine and norepinephrine, in the brain. These chemicals or neurotransmitters help the brain send signals between nerve cells. Adderall helps restore the balance of these neurotransmitters to the parts of the brain that control the ability to focus and pay attention.[9] "Think of a staticky radio signal," says Anthony Rostain, Professor of Psychiatry and Pediatrics at the University of Pennsylvania School of Medicine. "You turn the dial, and you get a better signal--the focusing and concentration are better."[10]

Discussion of Ritalin

10 Ritalin is a mild stimulant to the central nervous system. The exact way that it works is unknown. The U.S. Drug Enforcement Administration states that the medication produces the same effects as cocaine and amphetamines.[11] Adderall prescriptions have grown greatly, overtaking the once-popular medication Ritalin as the leader in treating ADHD. Adderall is the most common study drug as well.[12]

Negative effects of the drugs

11 These seemingly innocuous academic-enhancing drugs can have serious and long-lasting side effects. For normal, healthy people who take them, the drugs can cause emotional and physical strain.[13] Side effects of Ritalin include insomnia, nervousness, drowsiness, dizziness, headache, blurred vision, tics, abdominal pain, nausea, vomiting, decreased appetite or

5

weight loss, and slower weight gain. More serious side effects include irregular or fast heartbeat, confusion, and liver damage.[14] Side effects of Adderall include irregular heartbeat, very high blood pressure, hallucinations, abnormal behavior, and confusion. Other side effects include restlessness or tremor, anxiety or nervousness, headache, dizziness, insomnia, dryness of the mouth or unpleasant taste, diarrhea or constipation, and impotence or changes in sex drive.[15] Dr. John D. Hall, an addiction psychiatrist working in student mental health services at the University of Florida, says, "If you don't have ADHD, Adderall or Ritalin can cause significant anxiety."[16]

12 Users of study drugs are also at risk for dependence or addiction; users may become addicted to the energy the drug gives them.[17] With continued use of Adderall, a person can develop a tolerance and need for a higher dose to achieve the same effects. Physical and psychological dependence can also occur. Ritalin can produce physical dependence as well.[18] There is also a risk of overdose, especially when the drug is obtained through a friend's prescription. Adderall or Ritalin dosage is carefully determined by height, weight, and symptoms. Another person's dosage can be dangerous, particularly if the person is bigger.[19]

More negative effects

13 In a society where the notion of popping a pill to solve problems is encouraged by advertisements

6

suggesting that you "ask your doctor if Drug X is right for you," it seems logical for students to look for something that will help them stay alert longer and concentrate harder, especially if there are no obvious side effects. These seemingly innocuous and academically beneficial drugs can have serious side effects, however.

Final warning

14 Though there have been no reported overdoses of study drugs, their use is still a serious problem, on a par with the use of performance-enhancing drugs in sports. The side effects of the drugs outweigh any academic advantage, and their use raises ethical questions as well in that it gives some students an unfair advantage. Dr. Hall, the addiction psychiatrist, offers simple advice: "Don't depend on a pill to get you through the pressures of exam week. The long-term solution is to plan ahead, do as well as you can in your exams, and take life as it comes."[20]

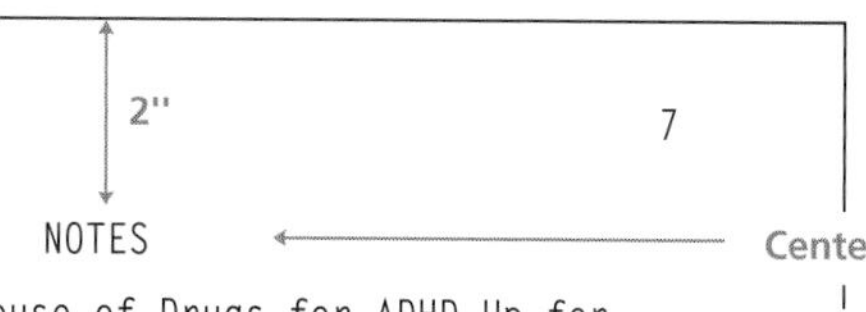

NOTES

1. Deborah Chun, "Abuse of Drugs for ADHD Up for Finals," *GainesvilleSun.com,* April 29, 2004, http://www.psychiatry.ufl.edu/Gainesvillesun_com2.htm (accessed January 20, 2007).

2. William Campbell Douglass, "College-Age Students Use ADHD Drugs to Make the Grade," *Real Health Breakthroughs*, January 14, 2005, http://www.healthiernews.com/dailydose/dd200501/dd20050114.html (accessed February 12, 2007).

3. Richard Kadison, "Getting an Edge--Use of Stimulants and Antidepressants in College," *The New England Journal of Medicine* 353 (2005): 1089.

4. Jenna Ianucilli, Survey of students' attitudes on academic-enhancing drugs, unpublished raw data, University of Rhode Island, 2007.

5. Kadison, "Getting an Edge," 1090.

6. New York University Health Center, "Health Promotion and Wellness--Study Drugs," New York University, http://www.nyu.edu/nyuhc/studydrugs (accessed January 31, 2007).

7. National Institute of Mental Health, *Attention Deficit Hyperactivity Disorder* (Baltimore: National Institute of Mental Health, 2003), 5.

8. Michael I. Reiff, *ADHD: A Complete and Authoritative Guide* (Chicago: American Academy of Pediatrics, 2004), 23.

9. Ibid., 15.

10. As quoted in Reiff, 24.

11. New York University Health Center, "Health Promotion and Wellness."

12. National Institute of Mental Health, *Attention Deficit Hyperactivity Disorder,* 7.

13. Kadison, "Getting an Edge," 1090.

Center

Double-space between entries

Indent ½"

Endnotes listed in order in which they appear in the paper

Subsequent references to the same source include author's last name, shortened title, and page numbers

Ibid. **is used for a subsequent reference to the same source when there are no intervening references**

8

14. New York University Health Center, "Health Promotion and Wellness."

15. Ibid.

16. Chun, "Abuse of Drugs."

17. Kadison, "Getting an Edge," 1091.

18. New York University Health Center, "Health Promotion and Wellness."

19. Chun, "Abuse of Drugs."

20. Ibid.

2"

9

BIBLIOGRAPHY ← Center

Chun, Deborah. "Abuse of Drugs for ADHD Up for Finals." *GainesvilleSun.com*, April 29, 2004. http://www.psychiatry.ufl.edu/Gainesvillesun_com2.htm (accessed January 20, 2007).

Douglass, William Campbell. "College-Age Students Use ADHD Drugs to Make the Grade." *Real Health Breakthroughs*, January 14, 2005. http://www.healthiernews.com/dailydose/dd200501/dd20050114.html (accessed February 12, 2007).

Ianucilli, Jenna. Survey of Students' Attitudes on Academic-Enhancing Drugs. Unpublished raw data, University of Rhode Island, 2007.

Kadison, Richard. "Getting an Edge--Use of Stimulants and Antidepressants in College." *The New England Journal of Medicine* 353 (2005): 1089-91.

National Institute of Mental Health. *Attention Deficit Hyperactivity Disorder*. Baltimore: National Institute of Mental Health, 2003.

New York University Health Center. "Health Promotion and Wellness--Study Drugs." New York University. http://www.nyu.edu/nyuhc/studydrugs (accessed January 31, 2007).

Reiff, Michael I. *ADHD: A Complete and Authoritative Guide*. Chicago: American Academy of Pediatrics, 2004.

1" 1"

Double-space

First line of each entry is flush with the left-hand margin; subsequent lines are indented ½"

CMS does not provide a form for this kind of entry; writer provides key information

Entries are listed alphabetically according to the author's last name

CHAPTER 31 CSE Documentation

The Council of Science Editors (CSE) endorses two styles for documentation, one that numbers each source and one that provides names and dates for each source. This chapter discusses both styles and provides models for in-text references and for a reference list.

CSE REFERENCES FORMATS

You are preparing a paper in a course in engineering, the sciences, or a technical field. You ask the instructor, "What documentation style should I use for references?" The answer is likely to be either "Use a scientific style" or "Look at the professional journals you've been consulting and follow the style they recommend."

This doesn't sound like much guidance, but it is if you can do three things.

1. Recognize situations calling for scientific or engineering documentation (see below).
2. Recognize the general elements of scientific and engineering style (see 31a).
3. Analyze and understand the documentation style used in a particular scientific, engineering, or technical publication (see 31b).

Students are not the only people who need these skills. Scientists, engineers, technicians, and technical writers also need to be able to choose a documentation style appropriate for a writing situation. Fortunately, some resources are available, though their influence is not as widespread nor as uniform as that of the manuals outlining MLA and APA styles (see Chapters 28 and 29).

The manual published by the Council of Science Editors outlines a general scientific style known as CSE style: *Scientific Style and Format: The CSE Manual for Authors, Editors, and Publishers* (7th ed., 2006). (See also the CSE Web site at <http://www.councilscienceeditors.org>.) The style endorsed by the American Chemical Society is used or adapted widely in engineering, technical, and scientific publications: *The ACS Style Guide: A Manual for Authors and Editors*, edited by Janet S. Dodd (2nd ed., 1997). Some widely used engineering style guides include the following.

ASCE [American Society of Civil Engineers] *Author's Guide to Journals, Books, and Reference Publications*

"Information for IEEE Transactions and Journal Authors," <http://www.ieee.org/organizations/pubs/authors.html>

31a Elements of scientific and engineering styles

As is the case with other documentation styles, including MLA (Chapter 28) and APA (Chapter 29), scientific and engineering styles contain those kinds of information important for locating a source and identifying it in ways appropriate to a particular discipline or kind of publication.

1 In-text citations

In-text references in scientific and engineering writing take two forms. With the **number method,** numbers, either within parentheses (7) or as superscript figures raised above the line,[7] refer to numbered items in a reference list at the end of the text. The number method saves space (always at a premium in scientific and engineering publications, which are often expensive to publish). It does not disrupt reading, unless the reader decides to turn to the reference list to identify the source. It allows a writer to cite multiple sources (a common practice) in a brief space, for example, (1–3,5,7). Yet the number system does not enable readers to identify the author or recency (date) of a source without interrupting their reading.

With the **name-and-date method,** the name of the author or authors appears in the text along with the date of publication (both generally in parentheses, but not always; see 31b). Without stopping to consult the reference list, therefore, readers can identify how recent the source is and may recognize the particular source from the author's name if they are familiar with work in the field. Name-and-date citations take more space, however, and they can disrupt reading, especially when a citation refers to two or more sources.

2 Reference list

Coming at the end of a text, a reference list provides information necessary to identify a source. This information generally includes the following.

- Author(s) name(s)
- Title of work or article
- Title of publication containing an article
- Publication information (for books—city, publisher, and date of publication; for articles—date, volume and issue number, and page numbers)
- Number of pages (total) (for books) or specific pages used as source
- Electronic address and date of access (for electronic sources)

Entries in a reference list are arranged either alphabetically (to correspond with name-and-date citations) or according to the order of citation in the text (to correspond with number citations).

The form and order of the elements in a reference list may vary slightly according to documentation style.

CSE

BOOK Simpson HN. Invisible armies: the impact of disease on American history. Indianapolis (IN): Bobbs-Merrill; 1980. 239 p.

ARTICLE Yousef YA, Yu LL. Potential contamination of groundwater from Cu, PB, and Zn in wet detention ponds receiving highway runoff. J Environ Sci Hlth 1992;27:1033-1044.

ACS

BOOK Dresselhaus, M.S.; Dresselhaus, G.; Eklund, P.C. *Science of Fullerenes and Carbon Nanotubes;* Academic: New York, 1996; pp 126-141.

ARTICLE Hill, M.; Fott, P. Kinetics of gasification of Czech brown coals. *Fuel* **1993,** *72,* 525-529.

31b Analyzing the documentation style of a publication

Many research publications in science and engineering include guidelines for authors preparing manuscripts for submission, generally with titles like "Information for Authors" or "Editorial Policy and Manuscript Preparation Guidelines." These sections usually contain detailed advice about presenting citations and references, including examples, which you can supplement by looking for examples in the publication itself.

Here is particularly detailed and helpful advice published in the *Journal of the Air & Waste Management Association.*

> References must be formatted according to the first reference style listed in the *ACS Style Guide* on p. 173; that is, in consecutive order as they are cited within the text, using Arabic numeral superscripts (do not use the author-date format). Do not use an automatic footnoting or referencing function in word processing. Do not use "et al." in references unless there are more than 10 authors; rather, list all authors for each reference. At a minimum, all references should include author, title, publisher, place, year, volume and issue number, and page numbers. Examples of reference styles include the following:
>
> 1. Carson, M.A.; Atkinson, K.D.; Waechter, C.J. An Analysis of Leachate in Groundwater; *J. Biol. Chem.* **1982,** *257*, 8115-8121.
> 2. Bockris, J.O.; Reddy, A.K.N. *Modern Electrochemistry;* Plenum: New York, 1970; Vol. 2, p 132.
> 3. Geactinov, N.E. In *Polycyclic Hydrocarbons and Carcinogenesis;* Harvey, R.G., Ed.; ACS Symposium Series 283; American Chemical Society: Washington, DC, 1985; pp 12-45.
> 4. Kanter, H. Ph.D. Dissertation, University of Arizona, December 1984.
> 5. U.S. Environmental Protection Agency. *Quality Control for Pesticides and Related Compounds;* EPA-600/1-79/008; U.S. Government Printing Office: Washington, DC, 1979.
> 6. Roe, A.B. *J. Pharm. Sci.*, in press. [this means that the article has been accepted for publication but has not yet been published]
> 7. Roe, A.B. *J. Pharm. Sci.*, submitted for publication.
> 8. Urdal, K.; Fallon, J.D. Structure and Reactivity of Surfaces. In *Proceedings of the 80th Annual Meeting of the A&WMA*, Denver, CO, June 5-8, 1994; pp 173-204.
>
> Authors should look to previous issues of the *Journal*, as well as *The ACS Style Guide*, for reference styles not listed above.

For books, technical reports, and documents not providing guidelines, or for articles photocopied from a journal, consult the text itself for examples of citation and reference style. The following examples are from an article in

IEEE Transactions on Knowledge and Data Engineering titled "Main Memory Database Systems: An Overview" by Hector Garcia-Molina and Kenneth Salem.

> IMS, one of the earliest database systems, recognized these access differences, and has provided two systems in one for many years: Fast Path [9] for memory resident data, and conventional IMS for the rest. A recent paper by Stonebraker [25] also discusses some of the issues involved in multilevel database systems and data migration.
>
> References
>
> [9] D. Gawlick and D. Kinkade, "Varieties of concurrency control in IMS/VS Fast Path," *Data Eng. Bull.*, vol. 8, no. 2, pp. 3-10, June 1985.
>
> [25] M. Stonebraker, "Managing persistent objects in a multi-level store," in *Proc. ACM SIGMOD Conf.*, Denver, CO, May 1991, pp. 2-11.

31c Scientific in-text citations

This section and the next, covering a scientific reference list, provide examples in CSE style. For examples in ACS style, see 31b.

1 Using the name-and-date method

With this method, you include the name of the author or authors along with the publication date of the text. If you do not mention the author's name in the paper itself, include both the name and the year in parentheses; if you do mention the name, include only the year.

PARENTHETICAL REFERENCE

```
Decreases in the use of lead, cadmium, and zinc in industrial
products have resulted in a "very large decrease in the large-
scale pollution of the troposphere" (Boutron et al. 1991).
```

AUTHOR NAMED IN TEXT

```
Boutron et al. (1991) found that decreases in the use of lead,
cadmium, and zinc in industrial products have resulted in a
"very large decrease in the large-scale pollution of the
troposphere."
```

If you cite several works by the same author, all of which appeared in a single year, use letters (*a*, *b*, and so forth) after the date to distinguish them.

ONE OF SEVERAL APPEARING IN THE SAME YEAR

```
Decreases in the use of lead, cadmium, and zinc in industrial
products have resulted in a “very large decrease in the large-
scale pollution of the troposphere” (Boutron et al. 1991a).
```

2 Using the number method

With this method, you use numbers instead of names of authors. The numbers can be placed in parentheses in the text or raised above the line as superscript figures. The numbers correspond to numbered works in your reference list. There are two ways to use the number method. In one style, you number your in-text citations consecutively as they appear in your paper and arrange them accordingly on the reference page.

```
Decreases in the use of lead, cadmium, and zinc in industrial
products have reduced pollution in the troposphere (1).
```

In the second style, you alphabetize your references first, number them, and then refer to the corresponding number in your paper. Since only the number appears in your text, make sure you mention the author's name if it is important.

31d Scientific reference list

You may use “Cited References,” “References,” or “Bibliography” as the heading for your reference list. If your instructor asks you to supply references for all your sources, not just the ones cited in your text, prepare a second list called “Additional References” or “Additional Reading.”

The order of the entries in your reference list should correspond to the method you use to cite them within your paper. If you use the name-and-date method, for example, alphabetize the references according to the last name of the main author and by date of publication for works by the same author(s).

If you use the consecutive number method, the reference list will not be alphabetical but will be arranged according to which work comes first in your paper, which second, and so forth. If you use the alphabetized number method, arrange your list alphabetically, and then number the entries.

Following are some examples of the most commonly used formats for entries. Refer to *Scientific Style and Format: The CSE Manual* for further examples of documentation.

1 Books and works treated as books

Formats for entries for the name-and-date method and the number method are the same except for the location of the year. The sample entries for a reference list follow the style for the number method, but model formats are shown for both methods.

MODEL FORMAT FOR BOOKS AND WORKS TREATED AS BOOKS

NAME-AND-DATE METHOD

period + space ↓ period + space ↓ period + space ↓

```
Author(s). Date. Title of work. Place of
Publication: Publisher. Total pages.
```

↑ colon + space ↑ period + space

NUMBER METHOD

period + space ↓ period + space ↓ period + space ↓

```
1. Author(s). Title of work. Place of
   Publication: Publisher; Date. Total pages.
```

↑ colon + space ↑ semicolon + space ↑ period + space

- **Author(s).** Give the author's name in inverted order, beginning with the last name and followed by *the initials only* (without periods or spaces) of the first and middle names, concluding with a period and a space. For more than one author, follow the same pattern for each author, and separate the names with a comma followed by a space. (Some scientific publications use full names for authors; check if this style is required for your paper.) If no author is given, begin with the word *Anonymous* in brackets.
- **Title of work.** Give the title followed by a period and a space. Do not underline the title, and capitalize only the first word and proper nouns or adjectives. Do not capitalize the subtitle following a colon.
- **Publication information.** Indicate the city, publisher, and date of publication. Put a colon after the city and a semicolon after the publisher. Conclude with a period. To avoid confusion between two cities with the same name or to identify cities likely to be unfamiliar, leave a space after the city and include in parentheses the abbreviated name of the state or the country.
- **Total pages.** Supply the total number of pages in the work, including the index, but do not add in any preliminary pages with Roman numerals.
- **Spacing.** Double-space your entries. For the name-and-date method, do not indent any lines. For the number method, begin the second and

any later lines underneath the beginning of the opening word in the first line. If your instructor gives you other spacing directions, follow them carefully.

1. One author

1. Bishop RH. Modern control system analysis and design using MATLAB. Reading (PA): Addison-Wesley; 1993. 239 p.

2. Two or more authors

List each author's last name first, and use commas to separate the authors.

2. Freeman JM, Kelly MT, Freeman JB. The epilepsy diet treatment: an introduction to the ketogenic diet. New York: Demo; 1994. 180 p.

3. Organization or group author

Treat an organization or government agency responsible for a work as you would an individual author. If the author is also the publisher, include the name in both places. You can use an organization's acronym in place of the author's name if the acronym is well known.

3. Intergovernmental Panel on Climate Change. Climate change 1995: the science of climate change. Cambridge: Cambridge University Press; 1996. 179 p.

4. Editor

Identify the editor(s) by including the word *editor(s)* (spelled out) after the name.

4. Bandy AR, editor. The chemistry of the atmosphere: oxidants and oxidation in the earth's atmosphere. Cambridge: Royal Society of Chemistry; 1995. 437 p.

5. Translator

Give the translator's name after the title, followed by a comma and the word *translator*. If the work has an editor as well, place a semicolon after the word *translator* and then name the editor and conclude with the word *editor*. Give the original title at the end of the entry after the words *Translation of* and a colon.

5. Jacob F. The logic of life: a history of heredity. Spillmann BE, translator. New York: Pantheon Books; 1982. 348 p. Translation of: Logique du vivant.

6. Conference proceedings

Begin with the name of the editor(s) and the title of the publication. Indicate the name, year, and location of the conference, using semicolons to separate the information. Include the total number of pages at the end. You need not name the conference if the title does so.

6. Witt I, editor. Protein C: biochemical and medical aspects. Proceedings of the International Workshop; 1984 Jul 9-11; Titisee, Germany. Berlin: De Gruyter; 1985. 195 p.

7. Technical report

Treat a report as you would a book with an individual or corporate author, but include the total number of pages after the publication year. If the report is available through a particular agency—and it usually is—include the information a reader would need to order it. The report listed here can be obtained from the EPA department mentioned using the report number EPA/625/7-91/013. Enclose a widely accepted acronym for an agency in brackets following its name.

7. Environmental Protection Agency (US) [EPA]. Guides to pollution prevention: the automotive repair industry. Washington: US EPA; 1991; 46 p. Available from: EPA Office of Research and Development; EPA/625/7-91/013.

2 Articles and selections from books

MODEL FORMAT FOR ARTICLES AND SELECTIONS

NAME-AND-DATE METHOD

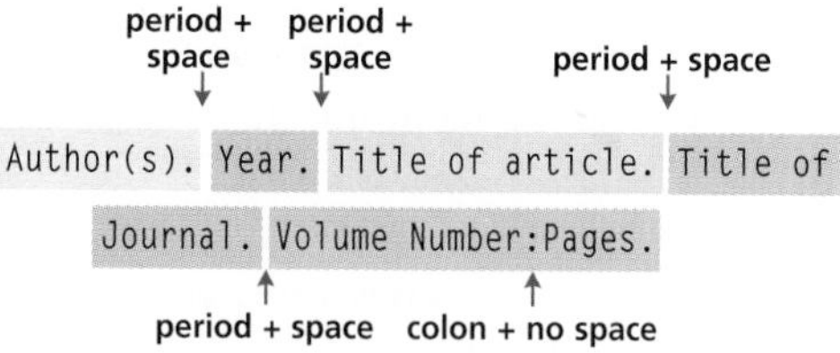

NUMBER METHOD

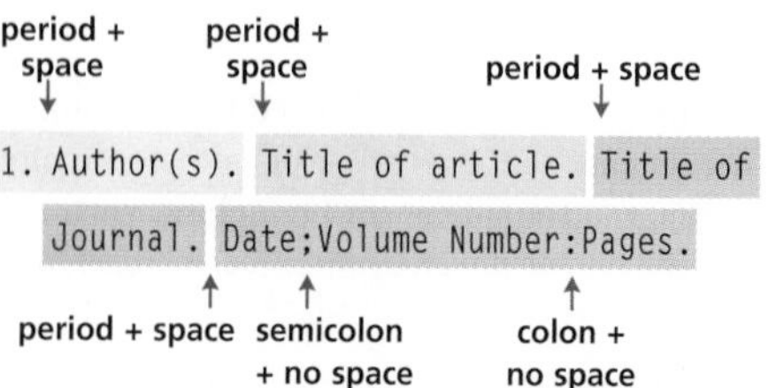

31d CSE

- **Author(s).** Give the author's name in inverted order, beginning with the last name and followed by the initials only (without periods or spaces) of the first and middle names, concluding with a period and a single space. For more than one author, follow the same pattern for each author, and separate the names with a comma followed by a space. If no author is given, begin with *Anonymous*, placed in brackets.

- **Title of article and publication information.** Give the article name, journal name, date, volume number and issue number (in parentheses), and page numbers. Do not enclose the article title in quotation marks or underline the journal title. Capitalize only the first word and any proper nouns in an article's title; do not capitalize the first word in a subtitle. For journal titles, follow regular capitalization rules, but use abbreviations standard in the field. Conclude the title of the article with a period and a space. Place a space but no punctuation between the title of the journal and the date. Do not include a space before or after the colon separating the volume number from the page numbers or between volume and issue numbers.
- **Pages.** Include the specific pages of the article or chapter.
- **Journal title (abbreviated).** Always abbreviate a journal title unless it is a one-word title. To find out how to abbreviate titles, notice the abbreviations used in your sources and ask your instructor which book lists abbreviations for your field.
- **Spacing.** Double-space all entries. Do not indent the first line or any subsequent lines (name and year); align second and later lines under the beginning of the initial word of the first line.

8. Article in journal paginated by volume

```
8. Yousef YA, Yu LL. Potential contamination of groundwater
   from Cu, Pb, and Zn in wet detention ponds receiving
   highway runoff. J Environ Sci Hlth. 1992;27:1033-1044.
```

9. Article in journal paginated by issue

Give the issue number within parentheses immediately (with no space) after the volume number.

```
9. Boutron CF. Decrease in anthropogenic lead, cadmium and
   zinc in Greenland snows since the late 1960s. Nature.
   1991;353(6340):153-155, 160.
```

10. Article with organization or group author

Treat the corporate or group author as you would any author. If a person's name is part of the corporation, as in this example, do not transpose the first and last names. Alphabetize by the first main word in the corporation name, even if it is a first name.

```
10. Derek Sims Associates. Why and how of acoustic testing.
    Environ Eng. 1991;4(1):10-12.
```

11. Entire issue of journal

Include the title of the main editor or compiler of the specific issue, because this person will often be a guest editor.

11. Savage A, editor. Proceedings of the workshop on the zoo-university connection: collaborative efforts in the conservation of endangered primates. Zoo Biol. 1989;1(Suppl).

12. Figure from article

Include the title of the figure (or table, chart, or diagram) and its number, as well as the page on which it appears. Use *p* in this context.

12. Kanaori Y, Kawakami SI, Yairi K. Space-time distribution patterns of destructive earthquakes in the inner belt of central Japan. Engng Geol. 1991;31(3-4):209-230. Table 1, p. 216.

13. Selection in anthology or collection

The first name and title refer to the article; the second name and title refer to the book from which the article is taken. Include the page numbers of the article at the end of the citation.

13. Moro M. Supply and conservation efforts for nonhuman primates. In: Gengozian N, Deinhardt F, editors. Marmosets in experimental medicine. Basel: S. Karger AG; 1978. p. 37-40.

3 Electronic resources

14. Patent from database or information service

The sample below, from the inventors' names through the date, illustrates how to cite a patent. In this instance, information about electronic access is added at the end.

14. Collins FS, Drumm ML, Dawson DC, Wilkinson DJ, inventors; Method of testing potential cystic fibrosis treating compounds using cells in culture. United States patent 5,434,086. 1995 Jul 18. Available from: Lexis/Nexis/ Lexpat library/ALL file.

15. Article (online)

15. Grolmusz V. On the weak mod m representation of Boolean functions. Chi J Theor Comp Sci [Internet] 1995 [cited 1996 May 3];100-5. Available from: http://www.csuchicago.edu/ publication/cjtcs/articles/1995/2/contents.html

16. Book (online)

16. Darwin C. On the origin of species by means of natural selection, or the preservation of favoured races in the struggle for life [Internet]. London: Down, Bromley, Kent; 1859. Available from: ftp://sailor.gutenberg.org/pub/gutenberg/etext98/otoos10.txt via the World Wide Web. Accessed 2002 Feb 12.

17. Abstract (online)

Use a form similar to that for journal articles, but give the word *abstract* in brackets following the title.

17. Smithies O, Maeda N. Gene targeting approaches to complex genetic diseases: atherosclerosis and essential hypertension [abstract]. Proc Natl Acad Sci USA [Internet]. 1995 [cited 1996 Jan 21]; 92(12):5266-5272. 1 screen. Available from: Lexis/Medline/ABST.

18. CD-ROM abstract

Indicate the medium (*CD-ROM*) in brackets following the title. Close the entry with the phrase *Available from*, followed by information about the source and retrieval number.

18. MacDonald R, Fleming MF, Barry KL. Risk factors associated with alcohol abuse in college students. Am J Drug and Alc Abuse [CD-ROM];17:439-449. Available from: SilverPlatter File: PsycLIT Item: 79-13172.

Exercise

A. Turn to Exercise A in Chapter 28. Rewrite the sentences supplied there to add either form of in-text citations in CSE or ACS style. Prepare a corresponding list of references.

B. Turn to Exercise B in Chapter 28. Rewrite the items supplied there to create a list of references following either form used in CSE or ACS style.

C. Working with a partner or a small group, compare your answers to Exercises A and B above. Correct any errors in your answers, using your handbook or your instructor's advice to resolve any differences of opinion.

31e Student CSE paper

Begin one-third of the way down the page

Center title

Title indicates that paper will report on a scientific research project

Predator Occurrence at Piping Plover Nesting Sites

in Rhode Island

Center and double-space all lines

Anne S. Bloomfield

University of Rhode Island

WRT 333

Professor Robert A. Schwegler

17 April 2006

Abstract

During the spring of 2006, I recorded predator occurrence based only on animal tracks on two beaches in Rhode Island. The main objective of the study was to predict the occurrence of potential predator species on piping plover (*Charadrius melodus*) nesting grounds in the area. I quantified the spatial distribution of predators at both beaches. Predators showed a preference for an area that was easily accessible to a salt pond from the barrier beach ($P < 0.05$ Table 1). Predator species present included gulls (*Laridae*), striped skunk (*Mephitis mephitis*), muskrat (*Ondatra zibethicus*) and red fox (*Vulpes vulpes*). This method was simple and low cost, but I found flaws in the experimental design that should be addressed in future studies.

Abstract provides concise summary of content

Table 1. Chi-squared analysis showing preference of predators for a given area on a piping plover nesting site at Moonstone Beach, Rhode Island, spring 2006.

Actual Segment	Sign	No Sign
0-500	1	9
501-1000	1	9
1001-1500	1	9
1501-2000	11	7
Expected Segment	**Sign**	**No Sign**
0-500	2.917	1.458
501-1000	2.917	1.458
1001-1500	2.917	1.458
1501-2000	5.250	12.750

$P < 0.001$

Last name, one space, and page number

Focuses on specific topic and problem

Specific phenomenon being studied

Potential usefulness of research

States two closely related research questions

Literature review—little prior work on the subject

Bloomfield 1

1 In Rhode Island, the threatened piping plover (*Charadrius melodus*) prefers to breed on open beaches and sandflats.[1] Habitat destruction due to development of beaches and predation are contributing factors to the birds' decline.[2] For most ground-nesting bird species, the primary cause of nesting mortality is due to egg predation.[3] I investigated the spatial distribution and abundance of potential predators. This information, coupled with information on plover nesting success, could be used to better manage the species.

2 The main objectives of my research were to discover what types of predators occur at potential breeding sites and their spatial distribution along the beach. I was also interested in which species occurred most often. My data were collected solely based on mammalian and avian tracks on sites at the breeding grounds. Information on such studies has not been easily located in peer-reviewed literature. This approach was low cost, as the researcher only needs to visually search the beach for tracks. No restraint techniques or cameras were used to capture live predators physically or on film. A pen and paper were the only materials needed to collect data on site.

3 The results of my study will help wildlife biologists to implement the proper management strategies for predator control on the beaches. If the species predating the nests are better understood, then management strategies can be tailored to a specific species or a specific area.

Study Area

Center headings if used

Describes location for the study

4 I conducted fieldwork at Moonstone Beach at Trustom Pond National Wildlife Refuge (NWR) and East Beach at Ninigret NWR. The study was focused at Moonstone Beach, but additional data were collected at Ninigret. These areas are important seasonal nesting areas for the piping plover. Both areas are barrier beaches with grassy dunes, bordering large coastal salt ponds. Moonstone Beach had a particular section which measured about 62 m that was free of vegetation and dunes. This area of the beach supplied a direct path from Trustom Pond to the beach area and coastal waters. This type of habitat was not present at my study site at Ninigret. These areas are managed by the U.S. Fish and Wildlife Service (USFWS) for piping plovers. Moonstone Beach is annually closed to the public, for this reason, beginning on April 1. After April 1, I conducted fieldwork only at Ninigret NWR.

Methods

Describes specific time, place, and technique (method) of study

5 During my research, I based the occurrence of predators on the presence of their tracks in the sand. At Moonstone Beach a 610 m stretch of beach was searched. This area was searched on 24 March and 29 March for two hours each day. The beach was marked in 30.5 m (100 ft) sections by PVC pole markers on the foredune.

6 During each study period I recorded any factors on the beach that would disrupt or bias data collection. This mainly included human and domestic dog (*Canis familiaris*)

Bloomfield 3

tracks on the beach. I searched for tracks in each 30.5 meter section. When a track was located, the species was recorded. In addition to the species, I recorded the quality of the track on a 1-3 scale (1 being poorest). I also noted whether the track was found in wet or dry sand. To limit identification error, I always carried a tracking text with me which included photographs, diagrams, and measurements. The same method was used at Ninigret, with the exception of the 30.5 m markers.

Describes method used to understand the data

7 I used a chi-squared test to assess the spatial distribution of predator tracks on the beach. This test was only done for Moonstone Beach because the tracks and beach quality at Ninigret were very poor during the study period. Also, figures were constructed to show the frequency of track occurrence, number of species per section, and number of tracks per section at Moonstone Beach. The data from Ninigret could only be used qualitatively to indicate which species were present.

Notes a limitation

Results

Summarizes data

8 The only predatory species present at Ninigret NWR was gulls (*Laridae*). At Moonstone Beach, the spatial distribution of predators was not uniform ($P < 0.001$), with more tracks present on the section of beach extending from pole 15 to pole 20 (Table 1). The numbers of species per section and number of tracks recorded were greatest in this area as well (Figures 1 and 2). This was particularly true in section 17, which was located in the

Conclusions

Bloomfield 4

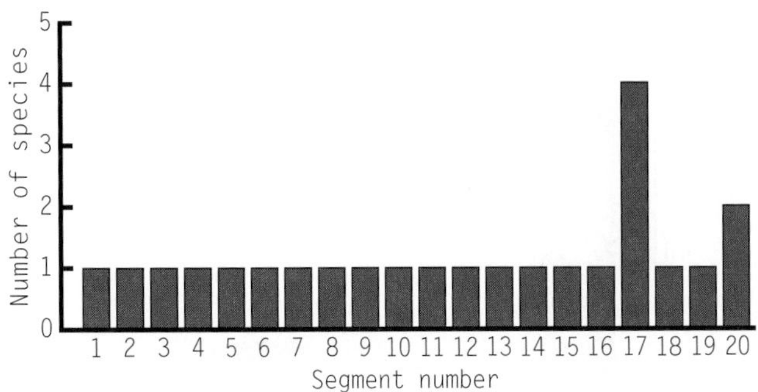

Figure 1. Number of species present at Moonstone Beach is highest in segment 17, Rhode Island, spring 2006.

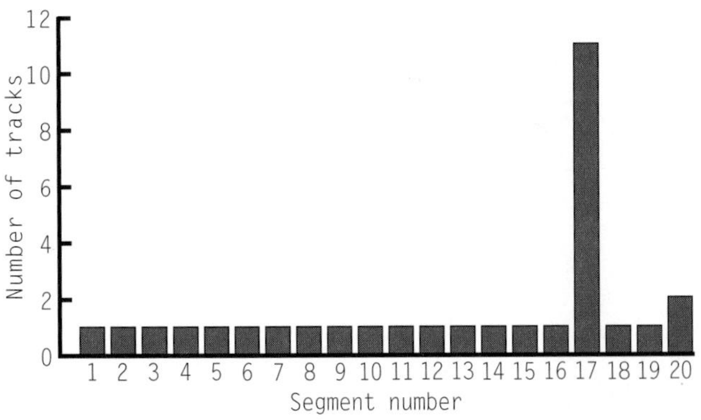

Figure 2. Sets of tracks were counted at Moonstone Beach, Rhode Island, spring 2006 and section 17 showed the greatest number of total tracks overall.

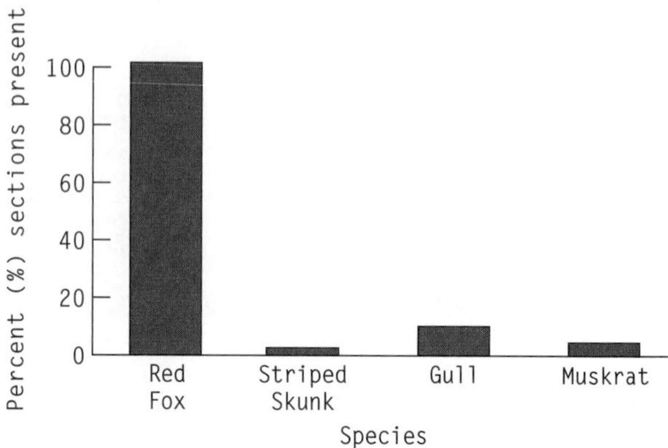

Figure 3. Occurrence of species across entire beach shows the red fox is present all along the shore of Moonstone Beach, Rhode Island, spring 2006.

area with immediate access to the pond from the beach. Red fox (*Vulpes vulpes*) covered the largest distance over the study area, occurring in all 20 sections during both study periods (Figure 3). The tracks always ran in a straight path parallel to the shore all the way across the study site and beyond.

Discussion

9 Using tracks to determine the presence of predators on the beach is a low-cost method which has the potential to yield promising results. Although this method was low-cost and a simple way to collect data, I found that there were many flaws in the experimental design that should be

addressed in further studies. Public use and roping of the beaches were two of the greatest difficulties I encountered during my study.

10 The condition of East Beach at Ninigret NWR was so poor that the data had to be almost entirely discredited. Human and domestic dog tracks were so abundant at the site that detecting other tracks seemed almost impossible. Ninigret also lacked the PVC poles to mark every 30.5 m. The quality of the data made them unusable for statistical and quantitative analysis. It is also important to note that one study suggested that in areas of beach open to domestic dogs, nests not protected by exclosures were all lost to dogs.[4] Keeping dogs off the beach or leashed is very important to the birds' survival.

11 The areas at Ninigret that were not overrun with human and dog tracks were roped off for the piping plovers. I tried to view tracks over the ropes with binoculars but decided this was not a very accurate technique. In the future, observers should be uniformed volunteers with USFWS so they can go behind roped areas. Letting the public know about the study would cut back on the amount of "clutter" to sort through on the beach.

Suggestions for future studies

12 Although ghost crabs (*Ocypode quadrata*) are more of a problem in southern areas, it is relatively unknown how large an impact they have on piping plover nest failure rates. Crab predation in Rhode Island is something my study did not address. Their tracks in the

More limitations

sand would have been impossible to find with all of the human disturbance. One study documented a ghost crab predating a piping plover chick. The research indicates that more studies must be done to determine if it was an isolated incident or if ghost crabs really are frequent predators of the piping plover.[5] Another study examined a beach with high piping plover mortality rates and abundant ghost crabs. The results showed a correlation, not necessarily a causation. Their data, at the same time, seemed to suggest that adult plovers would avoid bringing their chicks to forage in areas of abundant ghost crabs. They indicated that this could possibly indirectly lead to higher mortality rates of the chicks.[6]

Prior research

Further limitations

13 My research neglected to account for small mammal predation. Maier and DeGraff discovered, in 2000, that captive wild-caught white-footed mice (*Peromyscus leucopus*) were capable of consuming house sparrow eggs (*Passer domesticus*) in laboratory trials. They also noted that the effectiveness of the white-footed mouse as a significant predator of ground-nesting birds appears to be questionable.[7] While my study did not address crab or small mammal predation, it appears that the relevant literature does not show strong evidence for these animals as important nest predators.

Prior research

Conclusions

14 Based on the results (Table 1, Figures 1-3), I would expect the highest predation levels to be in segment 17 near the salt pond. More research must be done though,

Bloomfield 8

because according to Golden and Regosin, plover broods with access to a salt pond habitat experienced higher fledgling success than broods limited to an ocean beachfront habitat.[1] Further research must be done to figure out how the birds can have higher fledgling success rates near salt ponds if predator occurrence also appears to be higher near salt ponds.

Cites first reference again

15 Predator exclosures are one way to reduce predation rates. A previous study[8] found that daily survival rates of pectoral sandpiper (*Calidris melanotos*) nests, behavioral responses to exclosures, and the fact that no protected nests were predated suggested that exclosure was effective at deterring predators. The authors suggest that this method may be used for other shorebirds as well. In addition, 9 out of 13 nests had attempted predation by Arctic fox (*Alopex lagopus*), but all of these nests remained successful. The exclosures had an effective anchoring system and mesh wire.

Possible applications

16 Some exclosures can actually cause the plovers to abandon their nests. Research was done to determine what conditions and types of exclosures resulted in nest abandonment. The data suggested that exclosure construction, size, shape, mesh size, and fence height were not significantly related to nest abandonment, but covered exclosures were.[9]

17 My data could be useful to people interested in nest exclosures because if a biologist can predict what

Bloomfield 9

Applications set

predators are in the area, an exclosure can be tailored to meet specific needs. Different designs could be implemented based on whether the predators are mainly diggers or mostly avian. My data could also be used to reduce nest abandonment related to exclosures. If biologists know where the predators are distributed along the beach, they can predict exactly where an exclosure is needed. If there is a low occurrence of predators in an area, then there is little or no need for an exclosure. In addition, knowing where predators occur could make it easier for biologists to trap predators in the area.

18 In summary, exclosures are a good way to protect nests if done correctly. Predator occurrence by tracking needs to be further researched to improve accuracy but appears to be a cost-effective way to sample for predators on beaches. This technique is only useful if the volunteer trackers are very skilled at tracking in sand. In addition, it was only efficient to collect data under ideal conditions when there was little or no human disturbance on the beaches. If the techniques are further developed and the problems addressed, this method has great potential to be a low-budget and easy way to determine presence of predators on piping plover nest sites.

Bloomfield 10

References

1. Goldin MR, Regosin JV. Chick behavior, habitat use, and reproductive success of piping plovers at Goosewing Beach, Rhode Island. J Field Ornith. 1998;69:228-234.
2. Haig SM. Piping plover. In: Poole A, Stettenheim PS, and Gill F, editors. The birds of North America. Washington (DC): American Ornithologists' Union; 1992. p. 1-18.
3. Skutch AF. A breeding bird census and nesting success in Central America. Ibis. 1996;108:1-16.
4. Nol E, Brooks RJ. Effects of predator exclosures on nesting success of killdeer. J Field Ornith. 1982;53:263-268.
5. Loegering JP, Fraser JD, Loegering LL. Ghost crab preys on piping plover chick. Wilson Bulletin. 1995;107:768-769.
6. Wolcott DL, Wolcott TG. High mortality of piping plovers on beaches with abundant ghost crabs: correlation, not causation. Wilson Bulletin. 1999;111:321-329.
7. Maier TJ, DeGraaf RM. Predation on Japanese quail vs. house sparrow eggs in artificial nests: small eggs reveal small predators. Condor. 2000;102:325-332.
8. Estelle VB, Mabee TJ, Farmer AH. Effectiveness of predator exclosures for pectoral sandpiper nests in Alaska. J Field Ornith. 1996;67:447-452.

Center heading

Indent references from number; no other indentation needed (number system)

Number sources (number method) or list references alphabetically (name & year system)

Bloomfield 11

9. Vaske JJ, Rimmer DW, Deblinger RD. The impact of different predator exclosures on piping plover nest abandonment. J Field Ornith. 1994;65:201-209.

PART 7

Grammar

CHAPTER 32
Sentence Elements and Patterns

To create a sentence, you do not need to name its parts. Most of the time, however, you do need a fundamental understanding of grammatical concepts and terms to spot difficulties in your writing, to correct them, or to find helpful information in a handbook. Discussions in this handbook generally avoid technical language. Yet some technical knowledge is essential, and this chapter provides a basic introduction.

32a Words

Sentences contain different types of words, the *parts of speech:* nouns, pronouns, verbs, adjectives, adverbs, prepositions, conjunctions, and interjections.

1 Recognizing nouns and articles

This familiar definition can help you: A **noun** is a word naming a person, place, idea, or thing.

Rosemary Wells employs **humor** in her **books** for **children.**

Nouns often require an **article:** *the*, *a*, or *an* (*a* before consonants, *an* before vowels).

A report proposes **an** administrative solution to **the** problem.

Most nouns add *-s* to the singular form to make the plural: *cow* + *s* = *cows.* Some nouns ending with *s*-like sounds (*s, z, j, x, ch, sh*) add *-es* for the plural: *gas* + *es* = *gases; base* (silent *e*) + *es* = *bases; fax* + *es* = *faxes.* Some nouns have irregular plurals: child/children, deer/deer, goose/geese, mouse/mice, ox/oxen.

Count nouns name items that can be *counted* (e.g., two *chairs*, four *cups*). **Mass (noncount) nouns** indicate material that can't be counted (e.g., *flour, water, steel*). **Collective nouns** generally take singular form but refer to a unit of more than one (e.g., *group* or *board of directors*), and may be singular or plural in meaning.

Proper nouns refer to specific people, places, titles, or things. They are capitalized: *Miss America; Tuscaloosa, Alabama; Tierra del Fuego;* and *Microsoft.* All others are **common nouns** and are not capitalized (see 54b). Nouns indicating possession (**possessive nouns**) are easy to identify because they usually add an apostrophe and *-s* (see 35a): school (common); Tollgate High (proper); school's, Tollgate High's (possessive).

ESL ADVICE: THE ARTICLES *A, AN,* AND *THE*

For the **indefinite articles** *a* and *an* or the **definite article** *the*, follow the rules and guidelines but also pay attention to the many exceptions. Remember: your sentence's basic meaning will be communicated even if you choose the wrong article or forget to use one.

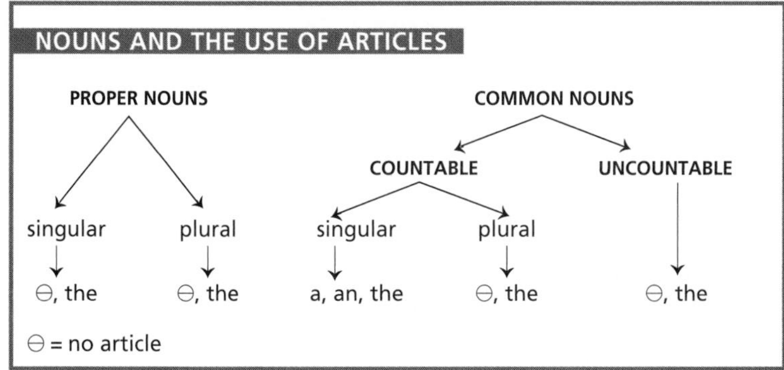

Singular proper nouns generally use no article, and **plural proper nouns** usually use *the.*

SINGULAR **Rosa Parks** was important to the civil rights movement.

PLURAL **The Everglades** have abundant wildlife and tropical plants.

Singular **count nouns** use *a*, *an*, or *the.* They cannot stand alone.

The pig is an intelligent animal.

Plural count nouns use either no article (to present a generalization) or *the* (to refer to something specific).

Books are the best teachers. (generalization)

The books on his desk are from the library. (specific)

Noncount (mass) nouns use either no article or *the*, but never use *a* or *an*. **General noncount (mass) nouns** sometimes stand alone. **Specific noncount (mass) nouns** use *the*.

INCORRECT A laughter is good medicine.

CORRECT **Laughter** is good medicine. (general)

INCORRECT Laughter of children is good medicine.

CORRECT **The laughter** of children is good medicine. (specific)
The prepositional phrase makes the noun specific.

- Use *a* or *an* when you are not talking about a specific person or thing (a nonspecific, singular count noun).

  You need **an identification card** to cash a check.
  [nonspecific, *any* identification card]

- Use *the* when talking about a specific, singular noun, meaning you know the exact person or thing.

  You need **the university identification card** to borrow books.
  [a specific, known card]

- Use no article with plural nouns because most plural and mass nouns do not require one.

COUNT **Airline tickets** to Florida are at half price.

MASS **Information** about flights to Florida is available.

- Use *the* when a plural noun is followed by a modifier because plural count and mass nouns are specific when followed by modifiers.

COUNT **The** airline tickets that you bought are at half price.

MASS **The** information that you received has changed.
The modifying clause makes the noun specific.

2 Recognizing pronouns

A **pronoun,** like *them, she, his,* or *it* takes the place of a noun or pronoun, playing the same role in the sentence as the word to which it refers—the **antecedent.**

antecedent pronoun
Jean presented **her** proposal to the committee.

(For help making pronoun-antecedent links clear, see 35c and 39a–b.)
Pronouns can also modify a noun or another pronoun.

pronoun noun pronoun pronoun
This part has been on order for a week, **that** one for twenty days.

Pronouns change form for the **number** (singular or plural) or **gender** (masculine, feminine, or neuter) of the noun to which they refer. They also change form according to their role in a sentence—subject, object, or possessive (see 34a).

Personal pronouns designate persons or things and change form according to their role in a sentence (singular: *I, me, you, he, him, she, her, it;* plural: *we, us, you, they, them;* see 34a).

A **possessive pronoun** shows ownership (singular: *my, mine, your, yours, her, hers, his, its;* plural: *our, ours, your, yours, their, theirs;* see 34a).

The **relative pronouns** *who, whom, whose, which,* and *that* introduce subordinate clauses (**relative clauses**) that modify or add information to a main clause (see 31d). They answer the questions "What kind of?" and "Which one?" *Who* takes different forms depending on its role (see 31d).

The **interrogative pronouns** *who* and *which* introduce questions.
Intensive pronouns (*-self, -selves*) add emphasis.

They did all the work on the new barn **themselves.**

Reflexive pronouns make the subject or doer also the receiver of an action.

He paid **himself** for the work.

Indefinite pronouns refer to people, things, and ideas in general rather than to specific antecedents. They include *all, any, anybody, anything, anyone, another, both, each, every, everybody, everyone, everything, either, few, fewer, many, neither, nothing, nobody, no one, none, one, several, some, somebody, someone,* and *something.*

Demonstrative pronouns or **demonstrative adjectives**—*this, that, these,* and *those*—point out or highlight an antecedent or sum up an entire phrase or clause.

That copier breaks down about once a week.

She was late for the meeting. **This** surprised me because she is usually punctual.

Reciprocal pronouns (*one another, each other*) refer to individual parts of a plural antecedent.

The two kinds of birds compete, destroying **each other's** nests.

Exercise 1

A. Underline each noun in the following selection *once* and each pronoun *twice.*

Seconds later the Help Desk received a call from another user with the same problem. The switchboard lit up. There were callers from all over the company, all with the same complaint: their computers were making odd noises. It might be a tune, one of the callers added helpfully, coming from the computer's small internal speaker. The sixth caller recognized the melody. The computers were all playing tinny renditions of "Yankee Doodle."

—Paul Mungo and Bryan Clough, "The Bulgarian Connection"

B. Exchange papers in progress with another writer, and identify all the nouns and pronouns in a relatively long paragraph of your partner's work. Then return the essay and point out where you agree or disagree with your partner's identification of nouns and pronouns (or lack of identification).

3 Recognizing verbs

Verbs express actions (*jump, build*), occurrences (*become, happen*), and states of being (*be, seem*). You change a verb's form to signal relationships in time (**tense**), **person,** and **number.**

TENSE	They **prepare** invoices.	They **prepared** invoices.
PERSON	He **restores** antique cars.	They **restore** antique cars.
NUMBER	The copier **makes** noise.	The copiers **make** noise.

Differences in **voice** (active or passive; see 33e) and **mood** (33g) also require changes in form.

ACTIVE VOICE	The filter **cleans** the water.
PASSIVE VOICE	The water **is cleaned** by the filter.

You may employ a **main** verb on its own or with one or more **helping** (or **auxiliary**) **verbs,** including forms of *be, do,* and *have* (main verb + helping verb = **verb phrase**). You may use **modal auxiliary verbs** (*will/would, can/could, shall/should, may/might, must,* and *ought to*) as helping verbs, though never as main verbs. (See 33b.)

helping verb / main verb

The tourist agency **is planning** to make a video of the local attractions.

modal / main verb

They **might decide** to include the old courthouse.

A **verb phrase** consists of a main verb plus a helping verb.

verb phrase / verb phrase

I **am hoping** that the renovations **can be done** in time.

Use **action verbs** for an action or activity (e.g., *swim, analyze, dig, turn, negotiate).* Use **linking verbs** (or **state-of-being verbs**) for a state of being or an occurrence: *is, seems, becomes, grows* (see 32b-2). A linking verb links a subject with a complement that renames or describes it.

ACTION The company and the union **negotiated** a new contract.

LINKING Flowers **remain** my favorite gift.
subject verb complement renames subject

The flowers **smelled** musky.
subject verb complement describes subject

Phrasal verbs consist of a verb plus a word that seems like a preposition but is known as a **particle,** as in *run along* (depart), *run down* (exhaust), or *look up* (improve). The meaning of phrasal verbs differs considerably from the meanings of the separate words.

PHRASAL VERB	VERB + PREPOSITION
I **looked up** the word in the dictionary. or I **looked** the word **up** in the dictionary.	I **looked up** the hill.
Profits are **falling off.**	My cousin **fell off** the deck.

Exercise 2

A. In the following sentences, underline each main verb once and each helping verb twice.

EXAMPLE

The new construction in Maple Valley has created some problems.

1. The power company's engineers began studying a map of the area.
2. They had thought about using underground cables.
3. A field test revealed a large rock ledge, so the engineers decided that underground lines would be too expensive.
4. They proposed cutting a path through the woods for the power lines, but the contractor claimed that potential homebuyers might not like the effect on the scenery.

5. They strung the power lines on poles along the main road into the development.

B. Exchange papers in progress with a fellow student. Choose a relatively long paragraph and underline all main verbs once and helping verbs twice.

---

4 Recognizing adjectives

Adjectives can modify nouns, pronouns, or word groups acting as nouns. They answer questions like "How many?" "What kind?" and "Which one?"

HOW MANY?	The **three** meetings will last all day.
WHICH ONE?	Our report was the **longest** one.
WHAT KIND?	Their proposal was **unacceptable.**

Adjectives come in three degrees of comparison: *high, higher, highest; crooked, more crooked, most crooked* (see 36c).

ESL ADVICE: ADJECTIVE FORMS

Adjectives in English never use a plural form.

NOT APPROPRIATE	Santo Domingo is renowned for beautifuls beaches.
CORRECT	Santo Domingo is renowned for beautiful beaches.

5 Recognizing adverbs

Adverbs modify verbs, adjectives, other adverbs, and entire sentences. Use them to answer such questions as "When?" "Where?" "Why?" "How often?" "Which direction?" "What conditions?" and "What degree?"

WHEN?	Our committee met **yesterday.** [modifies verb *met*]
WHAT DEGREE?	We had a **very** long meeting. [modifies adjective *long*]
HOW OFTEN?	I attend school board meetings **quite frequently.** [modifies adverb *frequently*, which modifies verb *attend*]

Many adverbs consist of an adjective plus *-ly: quickly, blindly, frequently, efficiently.* Others do not take this form, including *very, too, tomorrow, not, never, sometimes, well,* and *so.* In addition, some adjectives end in *-ly*, including *neighborly, slovenly,* and *lovely.* The surest way to distinguish an adverb from an adjective, therefore, is to see whether the word modifies a noun or pronoun (it's an adjective) or a verb, adjective, or adverb (it's an adverb). By adding *more, less, most,* or *least* to many adverbs, you can describe three comparative levels: *quickly, more quickly, most quickly; clearly, less clearly, least clearly* (see 36c).

Conjunctive adverbs, such as *however, moreover, thus,* and *therefore,* indicate logical relationships. (See 38b-4.)

Exercise 3

A. In the following passage, underline all adjectives once and all adverbs twice.

> Back in Chicago, Sereno's analysis of his new dinosaur's skeleton convinces him it is indeed more primitive than *Herrerasaurus.* It lacks a flexible jaw that let *Herrerasaurus* and later carnivores snag and trap struggling prey. Thus Sereno believes this new creature is the closest fossil we have to the first dinosaur.
>
> "I call it 'Eoraptor,' " he says. "Eos was the Greek goddess of dawn. Raptor means thief. It was a light-bodied little rascal. And it may have been a thief, dashing in to grasp scraps of someone else's kill."
>
> —RICK GORE, "Dinosaurs"

B. Expand the following sentences by adding details and information in the form of adjectives and adverbs.

EXAMPLE

generally deep, extended

The term *coma* ^ refers to a ^ state of unconsciousness.

1. Accidents leave people in comas.
2. Comas are serious medical problems.
3. Newspapers contain reports of people awakening from comas.
4. Long comas are dangerous.
5. They cause irreversible damage.

---

6 Recognizing prepositions

A **preposition** is a word like *on, over, for,* or *with;* followed by a noun or pronoun, it becomes a **prepositional phrase.** Prepositional phrases can add detailed and precise information to sentences.

> A faint smell of grilled onions (adjective) came through the window (adverb) and mixed with the musty air (adverb) of the dungeon (adjective).
>
> —JIMMY BUFFETT, *Where Is Joe Merchant?*

COMMON PREPOSITIONS

about	at	despite	near	to
above	before	down	of	toward
across	behind	during	off	under
after	below	except	on	until
against	beneath	for	out	up
along	between	from	outside	upon
among	beyond	in	over	with
around	by	into	past	within
as	concerning	like	through	without

Exercise 4

A. Underline all the prepositions in the following sentences. Circle all the prepositional phrases.

EXAMPLE

At eighteen minutes after one o'clock, the emergency number received a call from Mrs. Serena Washington.

1. From its station near city hall, the rescue truck drove to Briar Brook Avenue.
2. Along the way, it narrowly missed colliding with a bread truck that failed to pull to the side of the road.
3. Despite the near accident, the rescue team arrived at the Washingtons' home in less than five minutes.
4. Mr. Washington was complaining of pain in his chest and back and displaying other symptoms of a heart attack.
5. By its quick response to the emergency call, the rescue team may have saved a life.

B. For each of the following word groups, create two sentences, one using the words as a verb plus preposition, the other using the words as a phrasal verb (see 32a-3). Then rewrite the sentence that contains the phrasal verb, substituting another word or words for the phrasal verb.

EXAMPLE: TEAR OUT

Brian tore out the door.

Brian tore out the old shelving.

Brian removed the old shelving.

cut down	hang around	run up
fill in	put up with	call up

ESL ADVICE: PREPOSITIONS

PREPOSITIONS OF TIME

Use *at* for a specific time; *on* for days and dates; and *in* for nonspecific times during a day, month, season, or year.

Brandon was born **at** 11:11 a.m., **on** Monday, **in** the morning.

PREPOSITIONS OF PLACE

Use *at* for specific addresses, *on* for the names of streets, and *in* for large areas of land—counties, states, countries, and continents.

He works **at** 99 Tinker Street but lives **on** Chance Avenue, **in** Portland.

Follow this order: **prepositional phrase of place + prepositional phrase of time.**

place time
The runners will be starting **in the park on Saturday.**

PREPOSITIONS OF PLACE: *IN, AT, ON,* AND NO PREPOSITION

IN	AT	ON	NO PREPOSITION
the bedroom	the bottom of the stairs	a bicycle	downstairs
the car	home	the ceiling	downtown
a mirror	the office	the floor	inside
the newspaper	a party	the horse	outside
a picture	school*	the plane	upstairs
school*	work	the train	uptown

*You may sometimes use different prepositions for these locations.

Going to a place. Use the preposition *to*.

I am going **to** work; she is going **to** the office.

Use no preposition in the following cases.

I am going home. They are going downstairs (downtown, inside).

Time expressions. Use *for* with an amount of time (minutes, hours, days, months, and years); use *since* with a specific date or time.

The housing program has been in operation **for** many years.

The housing program has been in operation **since** 1974.

Combinations. Some nouns, verbs, and adjectives are typically associated with specific prepositions.

noun + preposition
He has an **understanding of** global politics.

verb + preposition
Vegetarians often **care about** animal rights.

adjective + preposition
Life in your country is **similar to** life in mine.

NOUN + PREPOSITION COMBINATIONS

approval of	fondness for	need for
awareness of	grasp of	participation in
belief in	hatred of	reason for
concern for	hope for	respect for
confusion about	interest in	success in
desire for	love of	understanding of

VERB + PREPOSITION COMBINATIONS

apologize for	jump into	step into
ask about	look at	study for
ask for	look for	talk about
belong to	look into	think about
care for	participate in	trust in
come out of	pay for	walk away from
go by	prepare for	work for
grow into	refer to	worry about

ADJECTIVE + PREPOSITION COMBINATIONS

afraid of	fond of	proud of
angry at	happy about	similar to
aware of	interested in	sorry for
capable of	jealous of	sure of
careless about	made of	tired of
familiar with	married to	worried about

7 Recognizing conjunctions

Conjunctions join words and word groups, signaling relationships.

Use the **coordinating conjunctions** (*and*, *but*, *or*, *nor*, *for*, *yet*, and *so*) to link grammatically equal elements.

WORDS	analyze **and** discuss
PHRASES	determined to cut costs **yet** worried about quality of service
CLAUSES	They surveyed the wetland, **and** they prepared a positive report.

Use **subordinating conjunctions** such as *because, although, while, if,* or *since* to create a subordinate or modifying clause (see 32c-5; see 44c for a list of conjunctions). The clause created by a subordinating conjunction is a modifier, so it cannot stand on its own as a sentence; attach it to a **main** (or **independent**) **clause** that it qualifies or limits.

main clause — subordinate clause

The equipment still works, **although** it needs routine maintenance.

Correlative conjunctions come in pairs, including *not only . . . but also, either . . . or, neither . . . nor, both . . . and, whether . . . or,* and similar combinations. Use them to join grammatically equal sentence elements. (See 43b-2 on parallelism.)

8 Recognizing interjections

You can use an **interjection** to convey a strong reaction or emotion, such as surprise (*Hey!*) or disappointment (*Oh, no!*). Interjections often stand on their own or are loosely linked to the rest of a sentence.

Exercise 5

A. Underline all the conjunctions in the following passage. Indicate whether each is a coordinating, subordinating, or correlative conjunction.

Thirty-five years ago, E. R. Guthrie and G. P. Horton described an experiment in which cats were placed in a glass-fronted puzzle box and trained to find their way out by jostling a slender vertical rod at the front of the box, thereby causing a door to open. What interested these investigators was not so much that the cats could learn to bump into the vertical rod, but that before doing so each animal performed a long ritual of highly stereotyped movements, rubbing their heads and backs against the front of the box, turning in circles, and finally touching the rod. The experiment has ranked as something of a classic in experimental psychology, even raising in some minds the notion of a ceremony of superstition on the part of cats: before the rod will open the door, it is necessary to go through a magical sequence of motions.

—Lewis Thomas, "Clever Animals"

B. Working with a group, rewrite the passage in Exercise 5A by employing different conjunctions (or kinds of conjunctions) than those in the original. Try to retain the general sense of the original, but feel free to add your own emphasis or perspective in the revision. Reword as necessary.

32b Subjects and predicates

Sentences need a **subject,** naming the doer or thing talked about, and a **predicate,** indicating an action or a relationship, conditions, and consequences.

1 Creating sentence subjects

A **simple subject** consists of one or more nouns (or pronouns) naming the doer or the topic. A **complete subject** is the simple subject *plus* all its modifying words or phrases.

simple subject
Cellophane was originally made from wood fiber.

complete subject
Clear plastic wraps used today are petroleum products.

A subject may be singular, plural, or compound (linked by *and* or *or*).

Subject-verb order. In most sentences, the subject comes before the verb.

subject verb
Homeless people camped in this area during the summer.

You can delay the subject until after the verb by beginning sentences with expletive constructions such as *there is* (*are*) or *here is* (*are*) (see 10a).

verb subject
There **were homeless people** camping in this area during the summer.

You can also alter the position of subject and verb by inverting sentence structure for emphasis or dramatic effect (see 10c).

verb subject
In this valley, eons ago, **grew plants** whose leaves are now fossils.

Questions frequently place the subject between the helping verb and the main verb (see 32a-3).

helping verb subject main verb
Did dinosaurs live in this valley millions of years ago?

The subject *you* is generally implied, not stated, in an imperative sentence (a request or command): [*You*] slide the liner under the ledge.

2 Creating sentence predicates

A sentence **predicate** indicates the action or relationship expressed in the sentence and may also specify the consequences or conditions. A **simple predicate** consists of a verb (*met*) or a verb phrase (*might meet*) (see 32a-3).

The verb may be single (*slipped*) or compound (linked by *and* or *or*, e.g., *slipped* and *fell*).

A **complete predicate** consists of a verb or verb phrase *plus* any modifiers and words or word groups receiving the action or completing the verb.

Object patterns. With a *transitive verb*, you can include in the predicate a **direct object** that tells *who* or *what* receives the action.

subject predicate
The bank officer approved the loan application.
verb direct object

The sentence can also include an **indirect object,** a noun or pronoun letting readers know *to whom* or *for whom* the action is undertaken.

subject verb indirect object direct object
The Marine Corps Reserve gives needy children toys.
to whom?

You can add information to a predicate with an **object complement,** a word (noun or adjective) that renames or describes the direct object.

ADJECTIVE Critics judged the movie **inferior.**

NOUN His coworkers elected Jim **project leader.**

Subject complement patterns. A sentence built around a linking verb, such as *is*, *seems*, or *feels* (see 32a-3), allows you to include a **subject complement,** "completing" the verb by describing the subject or renaming it.

subject verb subject complement
The new store seems successful.

subject verb subject complement
The plan is too complicated.

Intransitive verb patterns. An intransitive verb does not take either an object or a complement; the verb's meaning is complete without them, for example, Our team **lost;** Last week, the ferryboat **sank.**

FIVE BASIC PREDICATE STRUCTURES

1. **Subject + intransitive verb**
   The bus crashed.
2. **Subject + transitive verb + direct object**
   A quick-thinking passenger called the police.
3. **Subject + transitive verb + indirect object + direct object**
   The paramedic gave everyone blankets.
4. **Subject + transitive verb + direct object + object complement**
   Officials found the driver negligent.
5. **Subject + linking verb + subject complement**
   The quick-thinking passenger was a hero.

Exercise 6

A. In each of the following sentences, circle the complete subjects and draw a wavy line under the complete predicates.

EXAMPLE

Stories about Mount Everest often mention people known as Sherpas.

1. The Sherpas are well-known guides for mountain-climbing expeditions in the Himalayas.
2. They are a group of about 35,000 people who live in the country of Nepal.
3. The Sherpas, who are primarily Buddhists, live in a country dominated by Hindus.
4. Before the early 1900s, most Sherpas did not attempt to scale the mountains in their homeland.
5. In the early part of this century, however, Westerners wishing to climb the mountains gave many Sherpas jobs as guides and laborers.

B. Exchange papers in progress with another writer. Choose two paragraphs, and identify which of the five predicate patterns (listed in the chart in 32b-2) the writer uses in each sentence. Then suggest revisions that vary the predicate patterns in order to provide appropriate emphasis and variety. When you finish, work together to identify those suggested revisions most likely to improve each paper.

32c Phrases and clauses

A **main clause** (also called an **independent clause**) is a word group that includes a subject and a verb and can act as a complete sentence (see 32b). A **phrase** is a word group that lacks one or more elements needed to make a complete sentence. (For example, the phrase *will be climbing* lacks a subject; *the man running across the field* lacks a predicate; and *under the sink* lacks both.) A **subordinate clause** contains both a subject and a predicate yet cannot stand on its own as a sentence because it begins with a subordinating word such as *because, since, although, which,* or *that* (see 32a-7).

1 Recognizing prepositional phrases

A prepositional phrase has two parts: a **preposition** (a word like *at, for, in, to, according to,* or *under;* see 32a-6), and the **object of the preposition**—the noun, pronoun, or word group that follows the preposition.

You can use a prepositional phrase as an adjective, almost always following the noun or pronoun it modifies.

The coupons **in the newspaper** offer savings **on groceries.**

When you use a prepositional phrase as an adverb, place it next to the verb being modified or elsewhere in the sentence.

Her electronic wristwatch started beeping **during the meeting.**

During the meeting, her electronic wristwatch started beeping.

2 Recognizing absolute phrases

An **absolute phrase** includes (1) a noun, a pronoun, or a word group acting as a noun; (2) a present or past participle and any modifiers (*the deadline approaching quickly*). You can use an absolute phrase to modify a sentence as a whole as well as a word or element within the sentence.

Their lungs burning from the acrid smoke, the firefighters pressed ahead into the burning building.

3 Recognizing appositive phrases

An **appositive** renames a noun to add information to a sentence. An **appositive phrase** is an appositive (generally a noun) plus its modifiers.

Ken Choi, **my classmate,** won an award for packaging design.

He used "environmentally conscious" materials, **for example, recycled paper and soy-based ink.**

4 Recognizing verbal phrases

The verb parts called **verbals** (**infinitives**, **present** and **past participles,** and **gerunds**) act as nouns, adjectives, or adverbs, but cannot act alone as verbs. A verbal plus its modifiers, object, or complements is a **verbal phrase.**

present participle — object — adverb
sanding the tabletop with care

infinitive — object — modifying (prepositional) phrase
to bury the roots under an inch of soil

Participial phrases. You build a **participial phrase** around the *-ing* (present participle) or *-ed/-en* (past participle) forms of a verbal. You can use it as an adjective to modify a noun or pronoun.

Everyone **watching the show** failed to notice the smoke.

The chef chose a cake **flavored with orange peel.**

Gerund phrases. You build a **gerund phrase** around the *-ing* form of a verbal, and you can use it as a noun in a subject, object, or subject complement.

sentence subject — object of preposition
Closing the landfill will keep it from **polluting the groundwater.**

Infinitive phrases. You can create an **infinitive phrase** using the *to* form of a verbal and use it as an adjective, adverb, or noun.

noun (sentence subject)
To live in the mountains of Montana was his goal.

adverb
He used several books on organic farming **to help plan his garden.**

Exercise 7

A. First, identify all the phrases in the following passage, and tell whether each is a prepositional, verbal, absolute, or appositive phrase.

Without electricity, we would perish. We could learn to do without the flow of electrons that power VCRs and food processors, but the currents inside our bodies are vital. The brain needs electricity to issue its commands from neuron to neuron. When these signals reach a muscle, they set up a wave of electrical excitation in the fibers, which in turn triggers the chemical reactions that make the fibers contract or relax. The most important muscle is the heart; it shudders under a wave of electricity about once each second.

—CARL ZIMMER, "The Body Electric"

Next, combine the following sentences to create a paragraph that might follow the one above. Try to create a variety of phrases.

The heart has an electric field. The field radiates into the chest cavity. The field sends clues. The clues are about the heart's function. The clues go toward the skin. Cardiologists can get a peek at the heart. They are taping electrodes. The electrodes are taped to a person's torso. Each electrode produces a familiar squiggle. The squiggles are on an electrocardiogram. The electrocardiogram shows how the voltage changes at that single point. The point is on the body. Cardiologists spend years learning. They learn to infer heart function from these signals. They learn to recognize the telltale signs. The signs are in EKG readings. The signs tell of dangerous heart conditions.

B. Share your revised paragraph from Exercise 7A with a group of fellow writers in order to decide which versions are the most effective.

ESL ADVICE: GERUNDS AND INFINITIVES

Gerunds (base form of verb + *-ing*) and infinitives (base form of verb + *to*) are verbals (see 32c-4).

VERBS FOLLOWED BY EITHER GERUNDS OR INFINITIVES

You can use a gerund or infinitive after some verbs.

Developers prefer **working** [gerund] with local contractors.

Developers prefer **to work** [infinitive] with local contractors.

COMMON VERBS TAKING EITHER GERUNDS OR INFINITIVES		
begin	intend	regret
can't stand	learn	remember
continue	like	start
forget	love	stop
hate	prefer	try

The meaning of some verbs (such as *remember*, *forget*, and *stop*) will change depending on whether you use a gerund or an infinitive.

GERUND I **remembered** meeting your friend.
I recall an event in the past.

INFINITIVE I **remembered** to meet your friend.
I did not forget to do something in the past.

GERUND I never **forget** visiting the Statue of Liberty.
I recall a past event.

INFINITIVE I never **forget** to study for exams.
I remember to do something.

GERUND I **stopped** smoking.
I do not smoke anymore.

INFINITIVE I **stopped** to smoke.
I paused to smoke.

VERBS FOLLOWED BY GERUNDS

After some verbs you can use only a gerund (and not an infinitive).

subject + verb + gerund
GERUND Children enjoy **reading** fairy tales.

COMMON VERBS TAKING GERUNDS

admit	deny	mind
anticipate	discuss	miss
appreciate	dismiss	postpone
avoid	enjoy	practice
can't help	finish	quit
consider	imagine	recommend
delay	keep	suggest

You *must* use gerunds with some idiomatic expressions.

- After the word *go* (in any tense): I **go** shopping. I **went** hiking.
- After the expression *spend time*: Researchers **spend** a lot of **time** preparing reports.
- After the expression *have* + noun: Young children **have difficulty** following directions.
- After a preposition: Physicians' assistants are trained **in** treating routine cases.

In the following examples, the phrase beginning with *to* is not an infinitive. *To* acts like a preposition in each sentence and must be followed by a gerund ending in *-ing*.

I am looking **forward** to living abroad.

Managers are **accustomed** to receiving frequent updates.

Patrons are **used** to viewing complex exhibits.

VERBS FOLLOWED BY INFINITIVES

After some verbs, you must use an infinitive instead of another verb form.

INFINITIVE Some students need **to work** part time.

COMMON VERBS TAKING INFINITIVES

agree	hope	pretend
ask	intend	promise
choose	manage	refuse
decide	need	seem
expect	offer	venture
fail	plan	want

You must use an object and then the infinitive to follow some verbs.

subject + verb + object + infinitive
Doctors often **advise** their patients to eat well.

COMMON VERBS TAKING AN OBJECT + INFINITIVE

advise	convince	force	teach
allow	encourage	permit	tell
ask	expect	persuade	urge

When *make*, *let*, and *have* suggest "cause" or "forced," they follow a different model using the infinitive without *to* (the base form).

subject + verb + object + base form
She **made/let/had** me clean my room.

Use infinitives after certain adjectives.

I	**am**	delighted	to meet you.
The report	**is**	easy	to understand.
The volunteers	**are**	pleased	to help.

5 Recognizing subordinate clauses

A **main** clause (or **independent clause**) contains a subject and a verb; it can stand on its own as a complete sentence. A **subordinate clause** also contains both a subject and a complete verb, yet cannot stand on its own as a complete sentence because it begins with a subordinating word. This word (usually a subordinating conjunction like *because, although,* or *if,* or a relative pronoun like *who, which,* or *that;* see 32a-2 and 32a-7) signals that the clause is merely a sentence element—modifying the main clause to which it is attached. Subordinate clauses are sometimes called **dependent clauses.**

SUBORDINATE CLAUSE **because** I was very busy.

AS PART OF A SENTENCE **Because I was very busy,** I forgot to call.

Subordinate clauses as modifiers. You can modify a noun or a pronoun with a subordinate clause. Use a **relative pronoun** (*who, which, that, whom, whose*) or a **relative adverb** (*when, where*) as the subordinating word.

Many people **who live in Foxwood Estates** came to the meeting.

They asked about the industrial park **that the county plans to create.**

You can also use subordinate clauses as adverbs. An adverb clause begins with a subordinating conjunction such as *because, although, since,* or *while* (see 32a-7) and modifies verbs, adjectives, or adverbs.

As the workshop proceeded, many of Jeanelle's questions were answered.
The clause is an adverb answering the question "When?"

Subordinate clauses as nouns. Noun clauses begin with *who, whom, whose, whoever, whomever, what, whatever, when, where, why, whether,* or *how.* They can play the same roles as nouns: subject, object, or complement.

SENTENCE SUBJECT	**Whoever is interested in a career in accounting** ought to attend.
DIRECT OBJECT	You should pack **what you need for the weekend.**

Exercise 8

A. Underline all subordinate clauses in the following passage.

Because the tax laws have gotten more complex recently, we have published a guide to tax preparation that highlights new features of the tax code. In addition, the guide provides step-by-step instruction for tax forms, which should be helpful even if a person has considerable experience filling out the forms. Anyone who plans to file taxes for a small business will be interested in the special section on business tax laws. Although many professionals and businesspeople rely on accountants when tax time arrives, they will nonetheless find that the guide provides money-saving advice.

B. Working with another writer, revise the passage in Exercise 8A by combining ideas and word groups in different ways and by using different supporting words. Retain the general sense of the passage, but feel free to add your own ideas and perspective.

ESL ADVICE: ADJECTIVE, ADVERB, AND NOUN CLAUSES

ADJECTIVE CLAUSES

Adjective clauses (also called **relative clauses**) modify or add more information to nouns. To form a relative clause, use a relative pronoun: *who, whom, that, which,* or *whose. Who, whom, that,* and *whose* are used to modify people. *That, which,* and *whose* are used to modify animals, places, and things.

Place the relative clause as close as possible to the noun (the antecedent) that it modifies.

DRAFT	The attorney is excellent **who advises on product liability.**
REVISED	The attorney **who advises on product liability** is excellent.

You may choose to drop the relative pronoun if it is not the subject of the clause.

INCLUDED	The apartment **that** we rented was very lovely.
OMITTED	The apartment we rented was very lovely.

When a relative pronoun is the subject of an adjective clause, you can change it to an **adjective phrase.** To change a clause with a *be* verb, omit the relative pronoun and the *be* verb.

CLAUSE (WITH *BE*)	He is the man **who is studying German**.
PHRASE	He is the man **studying German.**

To change a clause with another verb to a phrase, omit the relative pronoun and change the verb to the present participle form (see 33b).

CLAUSE (WITHOUT *BE*)	He is the man **who wants to study German.**
PHRASE	He is the man **wanting to study German.**

ADVERB CLAUSES

Adverb clauses give information about time, reason, contrast, and condition, acting like adverbs to modify verbs.

TIME	**When** the season changes, clients want to see new colors.
REASON	Last year's clothes seem dated **because** the color palette has changed.
CONTRAST	**Although** many clients want the new colors, some choose the old palette.
CONDITION	We may have cost overruns **unless** we move the inventory.

SOME WORDS TO INTRODUCE ADVERB CLAUSES

TIME		REASON	CONTRAST	CONDITION
while	when	because	although	if
before	whenever	since	though	even if
since	as soon as	as	even though	only if
until	after	now that	while	unless
once	as		whereas	provided that
				as long as

NOUN CLAUSES

Noun clauses work in the same way as nouns in the sentence: subject, object, object of preposition, and complement of an adjective.

SUBJECT	**What she said** was interesting.
OBJECT	We don't know **where the ambassador is going.**
OBJECT OF PREPOSITION	His parents were concerned about **how safe the car was.**

COMPLEMENT OF ADJECTIVE They are confident **that he will pass the test.**

SOME WORDS TO INTRODUCE NOUN CLAUSES

who	where	however
whom	why	how much
whose	whether	how many
what	that	how long
when	which	how often

You may also use noun clauses to report information questions. Word order in *wh-* question noun clauses may vary.

- The word order changes when the question includes a form of *be* and a subject complement.

  QUESTION Who **are** your friends?

  NOUN CLAUSE I wonder who your friends **are.**

- The word order changes when the question includes a modal.

  QUESTION How **can** I meet them?

  NOUN CLAUSE Please tell me how I **can** meet them.

- The word order changes when the question includes the auxiliary *do, does*, or *did*.

  QUESTION When **do** you plan to introduce us?

  NOUN CLAUSE Let me know when you [do] plan to introduce us.

- The word order changes when the question includes the auxiliary *have, has*, or *had*.

  QUESTION How **have** you met so many people?

  NOUN CLAUSE I'm interested in how you **have** met so many people.

Sometimes the word order remains the same as the word order in the original question.

QUESTION Who discovered the fire?

NOUN CLAUSE Do you know **who discovered the fire?**

QUESTION What started the fire?

NOUN CLAUSE Did anyone see **what started the fire?**

QUESTION	How much damage was caused?
NOUN CLAUSE	The company knows **how much damage was caused.**
QUESTION	Which firefighters came to help?
NOUN CLAUSE	He knows **which firefighters came to help.**

32d Sentence types

Sentences vary in structure according to the kind and number of clauses they include.

1 Recognizing sentence structures

A **simple sentence** is a sentence with one main (independent) clause and no subordinate (dependent) clauses.

The community development program sponsors construction projects.

A **compound sentence** is a sentence with two or more main (independent) clauses and no subordinate (dependent) clauses.

main clause / main clause
Most people liked the plans, yet some wanted more detail.

A **complex sentence** is a sentence with one main (independent) clause and one or more subordinate (dependent) clauses.

subordinate clause
Because people complained about the lack of green space, the
main clause / subordinate clause
architect revised the plans when he returned to the office.

A **compound-complex sentence** has two or more main (independent) clauses and one or more subordinate (dependent) clauses.

subordinate clause / subordinate clause
Because he wanted to make sure that work on the extension did not
main clause
damage the existing building, the architect asked the contractor to
main clause
test the soil for stability, and he then proceeded with the plans.

2 Recognizing sentence purposes

You can create various kinds of sentences according to the relationship you want to establish with readers. A **declarative sentence** makes a statement. An **interrogative sentence** poses a question. An **imperative sentence** makes a request or command. An **exclamatory sentence** makes an exclamation.

DECLARATIVE	The motor is making a rattling noise.
INTERROGATIVE	Have you checked it for overheating?
IMPERATIVE	Check it again.
EXCLAMATORY	It's on fire!

CHAPTER 33 Verbs

Readers may forgive a spelling mistake or two, but as soon as you write "The Dolphins done real good in the playoffs" or "The polio vaccine could have brang about some forms of cancer," readers are likely to lose confidence in your ideas. Irregular verb forms may be accepted in many communities, especially in speech, yet when they appear in academic, work, or public writing, they undermine a writer's credibility. Editing verb problems in your writing is therefore an important skill.

33a Simple present and past tense

You can put a verb into the **present tense** for action occurring now or the **past tense** for action that has already occurred. Most verbs form their past tense by adding *-ed* to the present tense form, also called the **base form.** Depending on the particular verb, this addition can be pronounced as *-t* (*baked*), *-d* (*called*), or *-ed* (*defended*). You need no special ending to mark the present tense *except* in the third person singular form (with *he*, *she*, or *it* or a singular noun).

> The trucks **wait** in line until the border crossing **opens.**

1 Using present and past tense in academic settings

Academic and professional readers may expect you to use the present and past tenses in special ways. When discussing a piece of literature, a film, an essay, a painting, or a similar creative production, use the present tense. Treat events, ideas, characters, or statements within such works as if they exist in an ongoing present tense.

> In Louise Erdrich's *Love Medicine*, Albertine **returns** to the reservation.

In the social and natural sciences, use the present tense to discuss the results and implications of a current study or experiment, but use the past tense to review the findings of earlier researchers.

> Although Maxwell (1991) **identified** three crucial classroom interactions, the current survey **suggests** two others as well.

2 Pay attention to the endings of past tense verbs

When you write the past tense of a regular verb, you usually add *-ed* to its base form. Sometimes you may incorrectly leave off the *-ed* because you don't "hear" it, particularly when a word beginning in *d* or *t* follows the verb.

DRAFT The company **use** to provide dental benefits.

EDITED The company **used** to provide dental benefits.

3 Watch for irregular verbs

About sixty or seventy common English verbs are exceptions to the "add *-ed*" rule for past tense. Most of these irregular verbs change an internal vowel in the simple past tense, such as *run* (present) and *ran* (past).

The following chart of the principal parts of common irregular verbs should help you as you edit. Check a dictionary for verbs not included in the list.

COMMON IRREGULAR VERBS

PRESENT	PAST	PAST PARTICIPLE
arise	arose	arisen
am/is/are	was/were	been
bear	bore	borne
begin	began	begun
bite	bit	bitten/bit
blow	blew	blown
break	broke	broken
bring	brought	brought
buy	bought	bought
catch	caught	caught
choose	chose	chosen
come	came	come
creep	crept	crept
dive	dived/dove	dived
do	did	done
draw	drew	drawn
dream	dreamed/dreamt	dreamt
drink	drank	drunk
drive	drove	driven
eat	ate	eaten
fall	fell	fallen
fight	fought	fought

(*continued*)

COMMON IRREGULAR VERBS *(continued)*

PRESENT	PAST	PAST PARTICIPLE
fly	flew	flown
forget	forgot	forgotten
forgive	forgave	forgiven
freeze	froze	frozen
get	got	got/gotten
give	gave	given
go	went	gone
grow	grew	grown
hang (object)	hung (object)	hung (object)
hang (person)	hanged/hung (person)	hanged/hung (person)
know	knew	known
lay	laid	laid
lead	led	led
lie	lay	lain
light	lit/lighted	lit
lose	lost	lost
pay	paid	paid
prove	proved	proved/proven
ride	rode	ridden
ring	rang	rung
rise	rose	risen
run	ran	run
see	saw	seen
seek	sought	sought
set	set	set
shake	shook	shaken
sing	sang/sung	sung
sink	sank/sunk	sunk
sit	sat	sat
speak	spoke	spoken
spring	sprang	sprung
steal	stole	stolen
sting	stung	stung
strike	struck	struck
swear	swore	sworn
swim	swam	swum
swing	swung	swung
take	took	taken
tear	tore	torn
throw	threw	thrown
wake	woke/waked	woken/waked/woke
wear	wore	worn

33b Participles: Recognizing and editing

When you provide the main verb in a sentence with a **helping,** or **auxiliary, verb** (such as *is* or *has*) and also change the form of the main verb, you create complex verb forms conveying important aspects of past, present, or future time, as in the following sentences.

> After **having eaten** up all the cake, little Jennifer **would have begun** to feel guilty **had it not been** for her father's unexpected treat—a box of delicious parfaits for the family.
>
> Assuming he **would be going** on the trip, Terry **had started** packing when to his surprise the whole apartment **began** to tremble from a small earthquake that **will be remembered** as the July Surprise.

But how can you be sure you are using the correct verb forms when creating sentences like these?

The form a verb takes when it's linked to a helping verb is called a **participle,** which itself can take two forms: **past participle** and **present participle.** When writers have problems with complex tenses, they typically use the wrong participle.

To form the present participle, add *-ing* to the base form of the verb (the form with no endings or markers).

HELPING VERB	PARTICIPLE (MAIN VERB)
He will be	loading the truck.

> Chan is **greeting** the jugglers at the airport as we speak.

To form the past participle of most verbs, just use the simple past tense.

HELPING VERB	PAST PARTICIPLE (MAIN VERB)
Mike has	rented the truck.

> Chan has **greeted** the jugglers every year for the past five years.

Some participial forms are irregular, however, involving an internal vowel change or an *-en* ending. (See the list of common irregular verbs on pp. 577–578.)

INCORRECT	Louise lost the pie-eating contest because she **had drank** three glasses of lemonade just before it began.
EDITED	Louise lost the pie-eating contest because she **had drunk** three glasses of lemonade just before it began.

ESL

33b verb

Most verbs are formed from one or more helping verbs plus a main verb (see 32a-3). The main verb plus any helping verb is called a **verb phrase.**

	verb phrase
ONE HELPING VERB	I **was walking** to school during the snowstorm.
TWO HELPING VERBS	I **have been walking** to school for many years.

Exercise 1

A. In each of the following sentences, a correct or incorrect irregular verb form appears in parentheses. Edit each sentence to make it correct, or indicate that it's already correct. If necessary, consult the list on pp. 577–578 or look in a dictionary for the principal parts of a particular verb.

EXAMPLE

had fallen

The rain (~~*had falled*~~) all night.

1. Jeremy (*had chose*) to work along the levee as part of the volunteer corps.
2. The floodwater (*had rised*) rapidly during the night.
3. The work team (*had heaved*) sandbags on top of the levee for almost twenty-four hours.
4. Jim O'Connor and Rebecca Gomez (*had hung*) plastic sheeting up to plug a leak.
5. By eight o'clock in the morning, people (*had woke*) up to find that the river (*had fell*) by six inches and the town was safe.

B. Review the list of irregular verbs on pp. 577–578. Compose five sentences in which you correctly or incorrectly use the past or past participle form of an irregular verb. In a small group, exchange lists and edit your sentences. Discuss the changes you made or did not make.

ESL ADVICE: VERB FORMS

THIRD PERSON *-S* OR *-ES* ENDING

Be sure to add *-s or -es* to verbs that are third person singular.

SUBJECT	VERB	SUBJECT	VERB + -S
I/you/we/they	write	he/she/it (animal, thing, concept)	**writes**

SIMPLE PRESENT AND SIMPLE PAST

These two tenses add no helping verbs to form the verb, except for the negative and interrogative forms. No other verb forms can stand alone!

SIMPLE PRESENT	They **live** in the dormitory this semester.
SIMPLE PAST	They **lived** in an apartment last semester.

PRINCIPAL PARTS OF VERBS IN ENGLISH

BASE FORM	PAST	PRESENT PARTICIPLE	PAST PARTICIPLE
REGULAR VERBS			
live	lived	living	lived
want	wanted	wanting	wanted
IRREGULAR VERBS			
eat	ate	eating	eaten
run	ran	running	run

HELPING VERBS

Most verbs combine one or more helping verbs with a main verb to form a **verb phrase.** Helping verbs include *am, is, are, will, would, can, could, have, has, had, was, were, should, might, may, must, do, does,* and *did.* Sometimes these words work in combination, as in *have been, has been, had been, will be, will have,* and *will have been.*

VERB FORMS AND HELPING VERBS FOR COMMONLY USED VERB TENSES

PROGRESSIVE FORM

	subject + *was/were* + present participle
PAST	I **was** working in my studio yesterday.
	subject + *am/is/are* + present participle
PRESENT	I **am** working in my studio right now.
	subject + *will* (modal) + *be* + present participle
FUTURE	I **will be** working in my studio tomorrow.

PERFECT FORM

	subject + *had* + past participle
PAST	I **had** tried to call you all day.
	subject + *have/has* + past participle
PRESENT	I **have** tried to call you all day.
	subject + *will* (modal) + *have* + past participle
FUTURE	I **will have** called you by midnight.

33c Progressive and perfect tenses: Editing

The **present, past,** and **future progressive** show an action in progress at some point in time. When you attach a helping verb to a main verb in the **progressive tense,** the main verb must take the *-ing* ending. In the future tense, the progressive must also include the verbal element *be.*

PRESENT PROGRESSIVE	Sales **are increasing** this quarter.
PAST PROGRESSIVE	At this time last year, we **were working** for improvement.
FUTURE PROGRESSIVE	I **will be discussing** the results at the meeting.

Note that irregular main verbs are not affected in any unique way by the progressive tense; all consist of the base form plus *-ing.*

The **perfect tenses** are used to show the order in which events take place. The **past perfect tense** allows you to indicate that something had already happened before something else happened. The form consists of *had* plus the past participle (see 33b for participle forms).

> The general practitioner **had treated** the patient for six months before the specialist took over the case.

The **present perfect tense** works much like the past perfect, but the action is something that has recurred or that the writer insists has already occurred.

> I **have reported** the burglary already.

The present perfect also presents something begun in the past and continuing into the present. It differs from the simple past, which indicates an action already completed or specified in time.

PRESENT PERFECT	I **have lived** in St. Louis for three weeks.
SIMPLE PAST	I **lived** in St. Louis in 2001.

The **future perfect tense** shows that something will have happened by the time something else will be happening. This form consists of the helping verb *will* plus *have* plus the past participle of the main verb.

> The technician **will have finished** by the time the dentist is ready.

1 Check the helping verb in progressive tenses

Most errors in progressive tense occur when you either use the wrong form of the helping verb or omit part of it. Look over sentences in a progressive tense carefully to see if you have used the correct form of the helping verb or have omitted part of it (as is common in some dialects).

DRAFT The interview **starting** five minutes late.

EDITED The interview **is starting** five minutes late.

DRAFT The employees **was running** for the elevator.

EDITED The employees **were running** for the elevator.

2 Check the form of the past participle in the past perfect tense

Writers sometimes set out to use the past perfect tense but mistakenly substitute a simple past tense form for the past participle.

DRAFT Pierre **had rode** for six years before he got injured in a rodeo.

EDITED Pierre **had ridden** for six years before he got injured in a rodeo.

ESL ADVICE: SIMPLE PRESENT AND PRESENT PROGRESSIVE TENSES

Use the **simple present** tense to describe factual or habitual activities. These activities occur in the present, but they are not necessarily in progress.

subject + verb (with *-s* if third person singular)

SHOWS FACT The planets **revolve** around the sun.

SHOWS HABIT The museum **offers** summer programs for children.

COMMON TIME EXPRESSIONS FOR PRESENT TENSE HABITUAL ACTIVITIES

all the time	every holiday	every year	rarely
always	every month	frequently	sometimes
every class	every semester	most of the time	usually
every day	every week	often	never

Use the **present progressive** tense to describe activities in progress.

subject + *am/is/are* + present participle

Santiago **is testing** the revised formula.

Santiago **is testing** the revised formula **this month.**

COMMON PROGRESSIVE TIME EXPRESSIONS FOR ACTIVITIES IN PROGRESS

at the moment	this afternoon	this month	this year
right now	this evening	this morning	today

CHOOSING BETWEEN SIMPLE PRESENT AND PRESENT PROGRESSIVE

When you choose between the simple present and present progressive tenses, think about which time expression best describes the activity. Is it happening only at the moment (present progressive) or all the time as a fact or habit (simple present)?

NOT APPROPRIATE All people are communicating in some language.

CORRECT All people communicate in some language.
This is a fact, so the correct tense must be simple present tense.

NOT APPROPRIATE The students are speaking their own languages in class.

CORRECT The students speak their own languages in class.
This is a habitual activity that occurs all the time, so the correct tense is simple present.

VERBS THAT CAN BE TROUBLESOME IN PROGRESSIVE TENSES

VERB	EXAMPLE	OTHER USAGES AND MEANINGS
SENSES		
see	I **see** the beauty.	Also: I **am seeing** the consultant. (meeting with, visiting, dating)
hear	I **hear** the birds.	Also: I **have been hearing** about the problem for a while. (receiving information)
smell	The flowers **smell** strong.	Also: I **am smelling** the flowers. (action in progress)
taste	The food **tastes** good.	Also: The cook **is tasting** the soup. (action in progress)
POSSESSION		
have	We **have** many friends.	Also: We **are having** a lot of fun. (experiencing)
own	They **own** many dogs.	
possess	She **possesses** much knowledge.	
belong	The book **belongs** to me.	
STATES OF MIND		
be	I **am** tired.	
know	I **know** the city well.	

VERB	EXAMPLE	OTHER USAGES AND MEANINGS
STATES OF MIND		
believe	She **believes** in God.	
think	LaShonda **thinks** it is true. (knows, believes)	Also: LaShonda **is thinking** about relocating. (having thoughts about)
recognize	His dog always **recognizes** him. (knows)	
understand	The social worker **understands** the problem.	
mean	I **don't mean** to pry. (don't want)	Also: I **have been meaning** to visit you. (planning, intending)
WISH OR ATTITUDE		
want	We **want** peace.	
desire	He **desires** his freedom.	
need	We **need** rain.	
love	Children **love** snow.	Also: I **have been loving** this book. (enjoying)
hate	Cats **hate** getting wet.	
like	He **likes** skiing.	
dislike	Patients **dislike** waiting.	
seem	The office **seems** efficient.	
appear	He **appears** tired. (seems to be)	Also: He **is appearing** at the theater. (acting, performing)
look	He **looks** tired. (seems to be)	Also: We **are looking** at the revised maps. (action of using eyes) I **am looking** it up in a dictionary. (consulting, investigating)

33d Troublesome verbs (*lie, lay, sit, set*)

Even for experienced writers, a few verbs can be tricky. Until you can remember their correct forms, you should identify these verbs when you edit your drafts and then check them by reviewing this section. Here are the verbs most often confused.

VERB	PRESENT	PAST	PARTICIPLE
lie (oneself)	lie	lay	lain
lay (an object)	lay	laid	laid

VERB	PRESENT	PAST	PARTICIPLE
sit (oneself)	sit	sat	sat
set (an object)	set	set	set

1 Check *lie* and *lay*

When you use the verb *lie* to mean "lie down," you may confuse it with the verb *lay*, which means to put something down, as in "Lay the book on the table." *Lie* is an intransitive verb—it can't be used with a **direct object** (see 32b)—whereas *lay* must be used with a direct object.

DRAFT I **laid** down yesterday afternoon for a nap. I **have laid** down at around 2 p.m. each day for over a year now.

EDITED I **lay** down yesterday afternoon for a nap. I **have lain** down at around 2 p.m. each day for over a year now.

DRAFT Dr. Parsons **lay** the cadaver on the table and began the autopsy.

EDITED Dr. Parsons **laid** the cadaver on the table and began the autopsy.

2 Pay attention to *sit* and *set*

The verb *sit* means to place oneself on or in something, such as a chair. *Set*, however, means to place an object, such as a book, on a surface. You can figure out which form to use by asking yourself whether there is a direct object in your sentence. *Sit* can't be used with a direct object, but *set* must be.

DRAFT First Erica and Steve **sat** the projector down on the table. Then they **set** down and listened to the chairperson's speech.

EDITED First Erica and Steve **set** the projector down on the table. Then they **sat** down and listened to the chairperson's speech.

Exercise 2

A. For each sentence, circle the appropriate verb from the choices within parentheses.

EXAMPLE

A fire last Saturday (*lead*, *led*) to Sandy's first big assignment as a reporter.

1. Sandy (*laid/lay*) the article for the newspaper on her editor's desk.
2. To get information for the article, she (*sat/set*) in the waiting room of the fire commissioner's office for three days.
3. During the interview, she (*layed/lay/laid*) on his desk a copy of the report criticizing the fire department's performance during the Brocklin Warehouse fire.

4. The commissioner looked the report over and then (*sat/set*) it next to the other report, which praised the department's performance.
5. After she had (*lead/led*) the three-hour discussion with the commissioner, Sandy was convinced that the department had done an adequate job at the fire.

B. Write four or five sentences in which you use *incorrect* forms of *sit, set, lie,* and *lay.* Exchange your sentences in a small group, edit them, and then discuss your changes.

EXAMPLE

Mrs. Jones sat the tuna salad dangerously close to Puff, her Siamese cat.

33e Active and passive voice

Verbs in the **active voice** appear in sentences in which the doer of an action is the subject of the sentence.

	DOER (SUBJECT)	ACTION (VERB)	GOAL (OBJECT)
ACTIVE	The car	hit	the lamppost.
ACTIVE	Dana	distributed	the fliers.

To rewrite an active sentence in the **passive voice,** add a form of *be* as a helping verb and use the participial form of the verb. Place the subject (or doer) into the object position after the word *by.* (A prepositional phrase states the doer and is optional.)

	GOAL (SUBJECT)	ACTION (VERB)	[DOER] [PREPOSITIONAL PHRASE]
PASSIVE	The lamppost	**was hit**	[by the car].
PASSIVE	The fliers	**were distributed**	[by Dana].

The active voice and passive voice versions of a sentence create different kinds of emphasis. In addition, a passive sentence can eliminate any mention of the doer.

ACTIVE VOICE	The city council banned smoking in restaurants.
PASSIVE VOICE	Smoking in restaurants was banned by the city council.
AGENT ELIMINATED	Smoking in restaurants was banned.

(For a discussion of use and misuse of the passive voice, see 10c-3.)

ESL ADVICE: THE PASSIVE VOICE

All transitive verbs in English may be written in the passive voice *except* the progressive forms of the present perfect, past perfect, future, and future perfect. The verb *make* in the passive voice, unlike in the active voice, is followed by the infinitive.

ACTIVE VOICE The council member made us **wait.**

PASSIVE VOICE We were made **to wait** by the council member.

Exercise 3

A. Edit the following passage by rewriting unnecessary uses of the passive voice into the active voice. In rewriting passive voice sentences that do not indicate an agent (doer), fill in the names of the person(s) or thing(s) you consider responsible for the action.

Having cash registers full of change was found to increase the likelihood of a late-night robbery. In one example, a store clerk was held up at gunpoint. It was decided by management that requiring full payment for gasoline in advance of a purchase would minimize the risk of further holdups. This course of action had been voted on by the board of directors prior to implementation. The decision was posted at each location. Following implementation, it was discovered that holdups were not minimized unless large signs indicating the clerk's lack of available cash were placed in plain view. Once this was done, fewer holdups were experienced, and the turnover of late-night personnel was decreased.

B. Compare your rewritten version of the passage in Exercise 3A with those produced by other students. Be sure you explain why you have decided to let any sentences remain in the passive voice. Working with several other students, produce one version of the passage reflecting group agreement on the best way to rewrite the sentences.

33f Clear tense sequence

In conversation, we often shift from verb tense to verb tense indiscriminately, sometimes moving from past to present and back again with little warning or planning. In writing, however, such tense shifts can be annoying to readers who expect consistency. You need to maintain a clear **tense sequence** in your writing, indicating the time relationships of events and ideas. In the following passage, the shift from past to present is logical and clear.

LOGICAL In the 1950s, great ocean liners still **offered** an attractive way to travel. Nowadays, people **prefer** jet travel.

When changes in tense do not reflect clear relationships in time or do so inconsistently, your readers may become confused.

INCONSISTENT The author **begins** by giving a factual account of the storm. He **said** that if people had heeded the warnings, many lives would have been saved.

EDITED The author **begins** by giving a factual account of the storm. He **says** that if people had heeded the warnings, many lives would have been saved.

You can shift tenses inside a sentence without creating confusion as long as you make the tense sequence logical.

LOGICAL Although my mother and father both **loved** (past) cats, I **dislike** (present) them.

LOGICAL People **forget** (present) that four serious candidates **ran** (past) in the 1948 presidential election.

LOGICAL I **will accept** (future) your recommendations; they **seem** (present) reasonable.

LOGICAL The accountant **destroyed** (past) evidence because the police **had forgotten** (past perfect) to warn him of the files' importance.

LOGICAL None of the expedition's crew **had recognized** (past perfect) that food stored in cans sealed with lead solder **is** (present) poisonous.

Putting *is poisonous* in the present tense is appropriate because the phrase is a generally true (or widely applicable) statement.

Use the present tense to discuss events, ideas, and statements in a piece of literature, a film, an essay, a painting, or a similar creative production.

INCORRECT In *The Mating Season*, the main character **described** an unpleasant relative as a person "who chews broken bottles and kills rats with her teeth."

CORRECT In *The Mating Season*, the main character **describes** an unpleasant relative as a person "who chews broken bottles and kills rats with her teeth."

33g Subjunctive mood

Sentences can be classified according to **mood,** a term that highlights the speaker's or writer's attitude as reflected in the statement. Most of your sentences will be in the **indicative mood** (characterizing statements intended as truthful or factual) or the **imperative mood** (characterizing statements like "Stop!" or "Watch out!" which function as commands).

Because it is not used frequently in ordinary speech, you may have trouble with the **subjunctive mood** in your writing. The subjunctive mood is used to express uncertainty—supposition, prediction, or possibility.

Were the deadline today, our proposal would not be ready.

The subjunctive mood has faded from most casual speech and even some writing, but it is still used on occasion, particularly in formal writing. Whenever you create sentences that express desires or wishes, whether positive or negative, the subjunctive may be required.

DRAFT — Jacqueline wished the news **was** not true.

EDITED (SUBJUNCTIVE) — Jacqueline wished the news **were** not true.

Many **conditional statements,** expressing the improbable or hypothetical and often beginning with *if*, require the subjunctive.

DRAFT — If Sandy **was** a person who always wore a helmet, his family would be much less worried about his riding motorcycles.

EDITED (SUBJUNCTIVE) — If Sandy **were** a person who always wore a helmet, his family would be much less worried about his riding motorcycles.

Finally, some clauses with *that* require a subjunctive verb when they follow certain verbs that make demands or requests. The common error in such cases is to use the incorrect form of the main verb, which should be the same as for the past participle (see 33c-2).

DRAFT — Parents desire that their child **shows** respect.

EDITED — Parents desire that their child **show** respect.

DRAFT — The judge asked that the eyewitnesses **be swore** in before testifying.

EDITED — The judge asked that the eyewitnesses **be sworn** in before testifying.

When you write conditional sentences (with *if*), be careful not to add the auxiliary *would* to the *had* + *verb* structure in the conditional clause. This error is common, in part because the clause after the conditional often does correctly contain that structure.

DRAFT If Sandy **would have worn** his helmet on the night of the party, he **would have hurt** himself less seriously.

EDITED If Sandy **had worn** his helmet on the night of the party, he **would have hurt** himself less seriously.

Exercise 4

A. Decide whether the complex verb forms highlighted in the following sentences are correct. Edit those that are not; explain why you left any as they appear.

EXAMPLE

The team leader **is planning** to ask for reports just after the production meeting ~~**will begin.**~~ begins.

1. Kamal **is finished** testing the circuit board by the time the production meeting **had started.**
2. The team members **will ask** Kamal if he **was planning** to test the remainder of the circuit boards.
3. As I prepare this report on the project, Michelle **is assembling** the prototype using the circuit boards.
4. The other people **will assemble** the extra machines as soon as the delivery van **arrived.**
5. If our customers **will be able** to recognize the advantages of our product, they **would order** more of the machines.

B. Compose five sentences with correct and incorrect subjunctive mood or tense shifts. Edit each other's sentences in a small group; then discuss the changes you made.

Exercise 5

A. Rewrite each of the following sentences in the tense or mood indicated in brackets by substituting appropriate main verb forms and any necessary helping verbs for the verb in parentheses.

EXAMPLE

The airplane assembly plant ~~(*fail*)~~ has been failing for several years. [present perfect progressive]

1. First, the recession (hurt) the market for small airplanes. [past perfect]
2. Then a new management team announced, "We (*close*) the plant unless productivity increases." [future]
3. At the same time, the company (*lose*) a product liability lawsuit. [past progressive]
4. This week, the company president (*announce*), "Unless we get some new orders in a few days, we (*declare*) bankruptcy." [simple past; future progressive]
5. If the plant (*be*) closed, three hundred workers would lose their jobs. [past subjunctive]

B. Write five sentences of your own, three using different complex tenses and two employing the subjunctive mood. Exchange sentences with a fellow writer and check that your partner has used the tenses and the subjunctive mood correctly.

ESL ADVICE: CONDITIONALS

Conditional statements may be (1) *true* in the present, true in the future, or possibly true in the future; (2) *untrue* or contrary to fact in the present; or (3) *untrue* or contrary to fact in the past. Each includes an *if* clause and a result clause that combine different verb tenses.

TYPE I: TRUE IN THE PRESENT

***IF* CLAUSE**	**RESULT CLAUSE**
• Generally true as a habit or as a fact	
if + subject + present tense verb	subject + present tense verb
If Rafi drives to school every day,	he gets to class on time.
• True in the future as a one-time event	
if + subject + present tense verb	subject + future tense verb
If Rafi drives to school today,	he will get to class on time.
• Possibly true in the future as a one-time event	
if + subject + present tense verb	subject + modal + base form verb
If Rafi drives to school today,	he may/might/could/should get to class on time.

TYPE II: UNTRUE IN THE PRESENT

IF CLAUSE	RESULT CLAUSE
if + subject + past tense verb	subject + *would/could/might* + simple form of verb
If Rafi drove to school,	he would/could/might arrive on time.

With Type II statements, the form of *be* in the *if* clause is always *were:* If she *were* president, she would reform tax laws.

TYPE III: UNTRUE IN THE PAST

IF CLAUSE	RESULT CLAUSE
if + subject + past perfect tense	subject + *would/could/might* + *have* + past participle
If Rafi had driven to school,	he would not have been late.

CHAPTER 34
Nouns and Pronouns

You use changes in pronoun form to guide your audience through sentences. In the following sentence, for example, the forms of pronouns change, helping people understand your meaning.

> Aretha Franklin started making recordings in the 1960s, and **she** has kept on releasing **them** during the five decades of **her** career.

As you read the pronouns in this sentence, you probably noticed, quickly and unconsciously, that *she* indicates the sentence's subject, *them* indicates the object of the action, and *her* indicates possession.

For the most part, you choose appropriate pronoun forms as quickly and unconsciously as you recognize them while reading or listening. At times, however, you may have to decide between *we* and *us*, *she* and *her*, and *who* and *whom* to avoid misleading your audience.

CONFUSING Dr. Landova criticized the report. The other team members liked it better than **her.**

READER'S REACTION: *Her* makes the sentence say that the team members liked the report more than they liked Dr. Landova. It's possible that the writer means this, but I don't think so.

EDITED Dr. Landova criticized the report. The other team members liked it better than **she.**

They liked the report better than *she* liked it.

Some errors are likely to irritate your audience and create a negative image of you.

INCORRECT **Him** and **me** will make a strong management team.

READER'S REACTION: *Him and* me sounds careless and uneducated. It's a lot easier to trust the judgment and leadership of someone who writes more carefully and precisely.

EDITED **He** and **I** will make a strong management team.

34a Pronoun forms

Because a pronoun's form can signal its role in a sentence, you need to choose those that accurately reflect your meaning.

1 Recognizing pronoun case

Pronouns acting as subjects take subjective form (**subjective case**). Those acting as objects take objective form (**objective case**). Those indicating possession or ownership take possessive form **(possessive case**).

SUBJECTIVE CASE **He** designs furniture for Herman Miller Company.

OBJECTIVE CASE The modular furniture we are using was designed by **him.**

POSSESSIVE CASE **His** design team created the work spaces in the sales office.

When your sentences follow a familiar order, such as subject-verb-object (see 32b-1–2), pronoun case merely highlights roles that will also be obvious to readers from the sentence's arrangement. When you use complicated sentence structures, your readers will depend on pronoun case to help grasp your meaning.

> With Jim, **her,** and Susan, **you** have hired three people **who** are better able to work together than **we.** In addition, as engineers, **they** pay attention to a product's ease of assembly as well as **its** appearance.

2 Recognizing forms of personal pronouns

I, we, he, she, it, you, and *they,* the **personal pronouns,** take additional forms to impart other kinds of information. **First person** pronouns (*I, we*) tell who is speaking. **Second person** (*you*) tells who is being spoken to. And **third person** pronouns (*he, she, it, they*) tell who or what is being spoken about. Pronouns can also indicate **number** (*I, we, he, she, they*) and **gender** (*he, she, it*).

Other kinds of pronouns (**relative, interrogative,** and **indefinite** types; see 32a-2) change form only to indicate case. Because nouns in English vary in form only for the possessive case—*the study/the study's conclusions*—the present chapter looks primarily at pronoun variation.

3 Choosing subjective forms

When a pronoun is a sentence subject, deciding to use a pronoun's subjective form is relatively easy (e.g., *She* ordered the test equipment).

Often, however, you need to choose the subjective case for pronouns playing other roles. (See 32b for discussion of these roles.)

FORMS OF PRONOUNS

PERSONAL PRONOUNS

	SUBJECTIVE		OBJECTIVE		POSSESSIVE	
	SINGULAR	**PLURAL**	**SINGULAR**	**PLURAL**	**SINGULAR**	**PLURAL**
FIRST PERSON	I	we	me	us	my mine	our ours
SECOND PERSON	you	you	you	you	your yours	your yours
THIRD PERSON	he/she/it	they	him/her/it	them	his/her/ hers/its	their/ theirs

RELATIVE AND INTERROGATIVE PRONOUNS

SUBJECTIVE	OBJECTIVE	POSSESSIVE
who	whom	whose
whoever	whomever	whosever
which	which	
that	that	
what	what	

INDEFINITE PRONOUNS

SUBJECTIVE	OBJECTIVE	POSSESSIVE
anybody	anybody	anybody's
everyone	everyone	everyone's

STRATEGY

As you edit, check whether a pronoun is acting as a subject within some part of a sentence. Check also whether it renames or restates a subject. If it plays either role, use the subjective form.

subject of subordinate clause

Because **they** were unable to get a loan, the business failed.

subject of relative clause

Atco Manufacturers will be hiring people **who** are willing to work the night shift.

subject of implied verb

I attend class more regularly than **he** [does].

complement renames subject

The new auditor is **he,** the person at Sandi's desk.

appositives rename subject

Two of the people in the group, **she** and **I,** have experience with desktop publishing.

4 Choosing objective forms

When you make a pronoun the direct (or indirect) object of an entire sentence, use the objective form.

indirect object direct object
The company bought **her** **an antivirus program.**

In addition, objective forms for pronouns play a number of object roles in a sentence. (See 32b for definitions of object roles.)

STRATEGY

As you edit, check whether a pronoun is acting as an object within some part of a sentence. Check also whether it renames or restates an object. If it plays either role, choose the objective form.

object of preposition
The rest of **them** had to wait several months for the software.

object in relative clause
An accountant **whom** the firm hired helped her out.

object in gerund phrase
Mr. Pederson's research for the report included interviewing **them.**

object in participial phrase
Having interviewed **us,** too, Mr. Pederson had a lot of material to summarize.

The report contained interviews with the two dissatisfied workers,
appositive renames object
her and him.

Pronouns used with infinitive phrases can be tricky, so keep the following example in mind.

Mr. Pederson asked **us** to read the summaries of the interviews.

You might be tempted to treat *us* as the subject of the phrase *to read the summaries of the interviews. Us* is the direct object of the sentence, however (*Mr. Pederson asked* us), and the objective form is correct.

5 Choosing possessive forms

When you use a pronoun to show possession, choose the possessive case. The form you choose depends on whether you use the pronoun *before a noun* or *in place of a noun.*

BEFORE NOUN	The Topeka office requested a copy of **her** report.
IN PLACE OF NOUN	**Hers** was the most thorough and up-to-date study available.

You should also use the possessive form before a gerund.

gerund
Their requesting a copy of the report pleased the project supervisor.

CHOOSING POSSESSIVE FORMS

BEFORE A NOUN		IN PLACE OF A NOUN
my problem	=	mine
your problem	=	yours
her problem	=	hers
their problem	=	theirs
our problem	=	ours
BUT		
his problem	=	his
its problem	=	its

Do not use an apostrophe with a possessive pronoun. Readers will notice the error. (See 50a.) Use *it's* only as a contraction meaning *it is*.

INCORRECT	your's, her's, it's, their's
CORRECT	yours, hers, its, theirs

Form possessive nouns with an apostrophe: *Luis's, cat's, government's.*

Exercise 1

A. In each of the following sentences, choose the correct pronoun from the pair within parentheses. Then name the case of the pronoun you have chosen.

EXAMPLE

Ruth and (*I*/*me*) are planning to open a children's clothing store.
subjective

1. The design for the new store was prepared by (*she/her*).
2. The city requires (*we/us*) to submit plans for remodeling the store we plan to rent.
3. Having interviewed Ruth and (*I/me*) about our marketing plan, the bank's officer approved our loan.

4. The person who will choose the stock for our store is (*she/her*).
5. I will supervise the salespeople (*who/whom*) we hire.

Next, revise the following sentences by correcting any errors in pronoun case.

EXAMPLE

The foundation sent copies of the grant proposal to ~~she~~ her and me.

1. Her and three other people worked for three weeks preparing the grant proposal.
2. The original grant-writing team included two other people, Kristen and she.
3. Because I spent more time working on the grant, I think I ought to get more credit for its success than him.
4. It is me who will have to supervise research work done under the grant.
5. Responsibility for budgeting the grant money is your's.

B. Working with a group of writers, choose a draft paper one of the group has written and examine two paragraphs carefully. Identify all pronouns in the subjective, objective, and possessive cases, and check to see that they are used correctly. Then suggest revisions for the paragraphs, drawing on some of the sentence and pronoun patterns illustrated in 34a–b.

34b Common problems with pronouns

We all struggle at times with pronoun forms. Many of our troubles are likely to occur at predictable places in a sentence; pay attention, therefore, to the following troublesome sentence constructions.

1 Pay attention to compound subjects and objects

When you use a compound such as *the committee and I* or *Jim and me*, you need to decide on the proper form for the pronoun. The rule is simple enough: Use the same case for pronouns in compounds that you would use for single pronouns playing the same role.

COMPOUND SUBJECT	Denise or (*he/him*) should be responsible for creating the new database.
USE SUBJECTIVE CASE	Denise or **he** should be responsible for creating the new database.

COMPOUND OBJECT	The coach selected (*she and him/her and him*) as team representatives.
USE OBJECTIVE CASE	The coach selected **her and him** as team representatives.

STRATEGY

To choose the correct pronoun form in compound subjects and objects, use the **focus-imagine-choose strategy.**

- **Focus** on the pronoun for which you need to choose the appropriate form.

  UNEDITED Anne-Marie and **me** will develop videotapes for the sales presentation.
  I or *me*?

- **Imagine** each possible choice for the pronoun as a singular subject (or object) in a sentence.

  Me will develop videotapes for the sales presentation.

  I will develop videotapes for the sales presentation.

- **Choose** the correct form, and use it in the compound subject (or object). If the correct form is not immediately apparent to you, refer to the chart on page 596. (Choosing the form that "sounds right" can be a misleading strategy with compounds.)

  EDITED Anne-Marie and **I** will develop videotapes for the sales presentation.

An incorrect pronoun form may pass without much notice in conversation because it "sounds right."

SPOKEN This is a private agreement between you and **I.**

Readers are more likely than listeners to notice the faulty choice of pronoun form.

EDITED This is a private agreement between you and **me.**

As you edit, pay special attention to pronoun forms that sound "wrong" or "unusual." Some of them may actually be correct.

CORRECT Responsibility for keeping the coffee room clean is shared between **them** and **us.**

2 Watch for *we* or *us* with a noun

When you pair *we, us,* or other pronouns with nouns, make sure the pronoun form—*we, they* (subjective) or *us, them* (objective)—matches the role played by the noun (subject or object).

CORRECT **We taxpayers** ought to demand that the city fill the potholes on Pine Avenue.

CORRECT The award went to the coach, but it really belonged to **us team members** who worked so hard during the season.

CORRECT If a customer returns to our store because of the quality of the service, the credit belongs to **you salespeople.**

STRATEGY

Check for a correct match of pronoun and noun by imagining a sentence in alternative versions without the noun.

SENTENCE The teaching evaluation should be conducted by (*us? we?*) students, not by the faculty or administration.

VERSION 1 (INCORRECT) The teaching evaluation should be conducted by **we**. . . .

VERSION 2 (CORRECT) The teaching evaluation should be conducted by **us**. . . .

EDITED The teaching evaluation should be conducted by **us** students, not by the faculty or administration.
Us **is the object of a preposition and takes the objective form (see 34a-2).**

3 Be alert for subject complements

When you follow a form of the verb *be* (*is, am, are, was, were*) with a pronoun renaming the subject, you create a **subject complement** (see 32b-2). You choose the subjective form because you are restating the subject.

CORRECT The last pharmacy graduates to get jobs at Upstate Medical Center were Rebecca Soares and **I.**

In speaking, the objective form is often acceptable. Moreover, in writing, the correct form may seem stilted and call for rewriting.

CONVERSATION The new traffic reporter is **him.**

STILTED The new traffic reporter is **he.**

REWRITTEN **He** is the new traffic reporter.

4 Check appositives

When you rename a preceding noun or pronoun in an appositive phrase (see 32c-3), match the case of the word being renamed.

CORRECT As an investment, the two sisters, **she** and her twin, bought a small chain of dry cleaners.

> **STRATEGY**
>
> Check for the correct pronoun form in an appositive by imagining alternative versions in which you leave out the noun (or pronoun) that was renamed in the original sentence.
>
> SENTENCE The two children's book illustrators on the panel, (*she? her?*) and (*I? me?*), discussed all the questions asked by the audience.
>
> VERSION 1 (INCORRECT) **Her and me** discussed all the questions asked by the audience.
>
> VERSION 1 (CORRECT) **She and I** discussed all the questions asked by the audience.
>
> EDITED The two children's book illustrators on the panel, **she and I,** discussed all the questions asked by the audience.
> **The pronouns rename the subject, so the subjective forms are correct.**

5 Be careful with comparisons using *than* or *as*

When using *than* or *as* followed by a pronoun, make sure the pronoun form you choose accurately signals the information left out. A pronoun in the subjective case acts as the subject of the implied statement; a pronoun in the objective case acts as the object.

SUBJECTIVE Josie located the resources more quickly than **he** [did].

OBJECTIVE Josie located the resources more quickly than [she located] **him.**

You can leave out part of a sentence containing the comparison so long as your readers can fill in the missing part easily and accurately.

CLEAR I earned a better grade in chemistry than she [did].

Rewrite sentences that may be ambiguous or confusing even though they employ correct pronoun forms.

POTENTIALLY AMBIGUOUS I like working with Aisha better than she.

READER'S REACTION: **Does this mean you prefer to work with Aisha? Or that you like to work with Aisha better than someone else does?**

REWRITTEN She doesn't like working with Aisha as much as I do.

6 Consider using possessive forms with gerunds

When you use the *-ing* form of a verb as a noun (a *gerund*, see 32a-4), use the possessive for a noun or pronoun that comes before it as a modifier.

CORRECT **My** skidding across the wet floor frightened me.

Why is using the possessive case important? Versions of a sentence with and without the possessive may differ considerably in meaning.

WITH POSSESSIVE We were surprised by the principal's golfing.

He was golfing, and we were surprised that he had taken up the sport (or that he was so good at it).

WITHOUT POSSESSIVE We were surprised by the principal golfing.

We were golfing, and he came up to us unexpectedly.

Correct use of the possessive may make some sentences hard to read. Rewrite them.

INCORRECT The new store manager was surprised by virtually **everybody** in town showing up for the sale.

READER'S REACTION: **Does this writer mean that *virtually everybody* managed to surprise the new manager? Wasn't it the number of people who showed up that was so surprising?**

AWKWARD The new store manager was surprised by virtually **everybody** in town's showing up for the sale.

REWRITTEN The new store manager was surprised **that virtually everybody in town showed up for the sale.**

7 Be cautious when using *myself* and other reflexive pronouns

People sometimes use *myself*, *yourself*, and other **reflexive pronouns** (see 32a-2) inappropriately as sentence subjects or objects.

INCORRECT The Nucor project led to some major disagreements between Stan and myself.

CORRECT The Nucor project led to some major disagreements between Stan and **me.**

34c
pron

Exercise 2

A. Correct any errors in pronoun case in the following sentences.

EXAMPLE

Denise and ~~her~~ joined the Disney film group in our class.

1. The rest of us team members decided we should use recent animated movies as the subject of our project.
2. Because their parents own a video store, her brother and her brought in tapes of the movies we planned to study.
3. Bill and I decided to take notes on *Aladdin;* Pat and her chose to study *Beauty and the Beast.*
4. I thought the notes we took were more detailed and better than they.
5. Writing the final paper led to disagreements between the other members and myself.

B. Working with a group, create a brief story involving three or four characters. Use at least five of the troublesome pronoun case patterns discussed in 34b, avoiding problems in their use.

34c *Who* and *whom*

Many people find it hard to choose between *who* and *whom.* They will be inclined to forgive an occasional misuse of *who, whom, whoever,* and *whomever.* Nonetheless, the places where you are most likely to have trouble with these forms are places where they can affect the meaning of a sentence substantially.

1 Choosing between *who* and *whom in* relative clauses

You often use the pronouns *who* and *whom, whoever* and *whomever* to begin the subordinate clauses known as **relative clauses** or **adjective clauses** (see 32c-5). Choose *who* and *whomever* when you use the pronouns as subjects; choose *whom* and *whomever* when you use them as objects (see 34a-1–2).

SUBJECT The artist **who creates a painting or sculpture** ought to benefit from its sale.

OBJECT The proceeds benefit **whomever** the artist designates.

You need to choose the appropriate form according to the role the pronoun plays *within the relative clause.* You need to ignore the role the clause plays *within the sentence.*

INCORRECT The fine must be paid by **whomever** holds the deed to the property.

Although the whole relative clause is the object of the preposition *by*, within the clause the pronoun acts as a subject, not an object.

EDITED The fine must be paid by **whoever** holds the deed to the property.

If you are in doubt about either the use of *whom* or its appropriateness, try rewording to avoid making the choice.

EDITED The person with the deed to the property must pay the fine.

2 Choosing between *who* and *whom* in questions

Use *who* at the beginning of a question when the pronoun is the sentence subject; use *whom* when the pronoun is an object. (See 34a-1–2.)

SUBJECT **Who** is most likely to get the reader's sympathy at this point in the novel, Huck or Jim?

OBJECT **Whom** can Cordelia trust for counsel about her dilemma?

CASE OF *WHO* AND *WHOEVER*

	SUBJECTIVE	OBJECTIVE	POSSESSIVE
FIRST, SECOND, AND THIRD PERSON	who	whom	whose
	whoever	whomever	whosever

Exercise 3

A. Correct any errors in pronoun case in the following sentences.

EXAMPLE

~~Whomever~~ [Whoever] has taken an IQ test probably remembers the score.

1. In the past, psychologists assumed that whomever scored well on IQ tests was likely to succeed at school and work.
2. Recent studies of IQ tests have produced evidence of them being unable to predict success.
3. A test of constructive thinking skill may tell more about your or mine ability to meet challenges.
4. Reporting on research conducted by he and two of his colleagues, Robert Sternberg points out that "the ability to sell" is an important part of practical intelligence.

5. Other psychologists claim that personal qualities like self-confidence and optimism may by theirselves have as much to do with our mental abilities as IQ does.

B. Working with fellow writers, identify the pronouns in the following passage and correct any mistakes in case. Keep a record of those identifications and corrections you found most difficult, and be ready to try to explain why you found them difficult.

For we humans, yawning is a familiar activity. You and me probably yawn when we stretch, though not always. Boredom is also a likely cause for us yawning. People often think that no one yawns as much as them, but this is seldom true. We all yawn frequently during a day. We may even start yawning ourselves when we notice someone else whom is yawning.

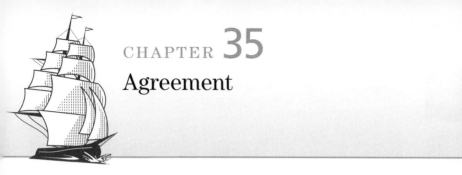

CHAPTER 35
Agreement

What's wrong with the following sentence?

INCORRECT The Citizenship Institute and the Civic Program focuses on social justice.

READER'S REACTION: I assumed the sentence was about two things—the Citizenship Institute and the Civic Program—until I came to the word *focuses.* I know *focuses* is *singular* in form, so it can't refer to more than one thing.

EDITED The Citizenship Institute and the Civic Program **focus** on social justice.

Readers expect you to make the parts of a sentence fit together grammatically. Especially important are **agreement** between a subject and a verb and agreement between a pronoun and the word to which it refers (its **antecedent**). By failing to align the parts of a sentence, you create inconsistency and confusion.

INCONSISTENT Project status reports should address the needs and values of its audience.

CLEAR **A project status report** should address the needs and values of **its audience.**

CLEAR **Project status reports** should address the needs and values of **their audiences.**

SERIOUS ERROR 35a Subject-verb agreement (simple)

To make subjects and verbs agree, make sure they are aligned in two ways: **number** (singular or plural) and **person** (first, second, or third). Keeping them aligned helps your sentences convey consistent, clear meaning.

SINGULAR The **worker** tears down the platform.

NOTE: Present tense verbs add *-s* when the subject is in the third person even though the subject and verb are both singular.

PLURAL The **workers** tear down the platform.

FIRST PERSON **I** operate the air compressor.

We operate the air compressor.

SECOND PERSON **You** operate the air compressor.

THIRD PERSON **He** (**she, it**) operates the air compressor.

They operate the air compressor.

To identify (and edit) **subject-verb agreement**, look for a subject, identify its *number* (singular or plural) and *person* (first, second, or third), and make sure the verb agrees with it in grammatical form.

INCORRECT The clients is impatient.

CORRECT The **clients** are impatient.

CORRECT The **client** is impatient.

(For help in identifying number and person, see pages 620–621.)

Pay special attention to plurals. Subjects plural in both form and meaning need plural verbs, but recognizing and choosing the right verb forms can be tricky.

STRATEGY

1. **Find the subject.** Look for *-s* or *-es* endings indicating a plural subject. Look for plural pronouns such as *they* and *we*. (*Exceptions*: nouns with irregular plurals such as *person/people*, *child/children*, or *louse/lice* as well as nouns with the same form for singular and plural, such as *moose/moose*.)
2. **Identify the verb.** Locate the verb and check that its form is also plural. Remember, in contrast to subjects, present tense verbs become *singular* with the addition of *-s* or *-es*. (*Exceptions:* Verbs with irregular forms, including *be* and *have*, see 33b.)
3. **Edit.** If the subject is plural but the verb singular (or vice versa), edit to make them agree.

   SINGULAR The dam prevent**s** flooding.

   PLURAL The dam**s** prevent flooding.

4. **Check again.** Check if the verb contains more than one word (a verb phrase, see 32a-3). If you find a main verb *plus* a helping verb, remember this: the helping verb *sometimes* changes form for singular and plural, while the main verb always remains the same.

	HELPING VERB CHANGES FORM	HELPING VERB DOES NOT CHANGE FORM
SINGULAR	The **park** does seem safer.	The **park** might seem safer.
PLURAL	The **parks** do seem safer.	The **parks** might seem safer.

Exercise 1

A. Fill in the blanks in the following sentences with verbs that agree in number and person with their subject.

EXAMPLE
Every day I __walk__ past the Valois Cafeteria.

1. The retired men in the neighborhood ______ lunch at the cafeteria.
2. The cafeteria's motto, "See What You Eat," ______ on the sign above the entrance.
3. The restaurant ______ run down.
4. Nonetheless, it ______ a clean and safe place.
5. A sociologist has studied the ways people of different races and cultures ______ with each other at the cafeteria.

B. Copy a paragraph from one of your papers or a book, but replace the verbs with blanks (as in Exercise 1A). Exchange paragraphs with a partner and fill in the blanks in that paragraph. Work together to check your answers.

ESL ADVICE: SUBJECT-VERB AGREEMENT WITH TROUBLESOME VERBS

Some troublesome verbs change form according to person or tense. Select the correct form so that subject and verb agree.

- *Be* (present and past): I **am, was**. You (sing., pl.)/We/They **are, were.** He/She/It **is, was.**
- Helping verb *be* (present progressive and past progressive)

  Present Progressive: I **am** talking. You/We/They **are** talking. He/She/It **is** talking.

  Past Progressive: I/He/She/It **was** talking. We/You/They **were** talking.

- *Have* (present): I/You/We/They **have** a new home. He/She/It **has** a new home.
- Helping verb *have* (present perfect and present perfect progressive)

ESL

35b agree

Present Perfect: I/You/We/They **have** lived here for years. He/She/It **has lived** here for years.

Present Perfect Progressive: I/You/We/They **have** been living here since May. He/She/It **has** been living here for a long time.

- *Do* or *Does* to show emphasis: I/You/We/They **do** want the contract! He/She/It **does** want the contract!
- *Doesn't* or *Don't* to show the negative: I/You/We/They **don't** exercise enough. He/She/It **doesn't** exercise enough.

In English, many nouns, called **mass** or **noncount nouns** (see 32a-1), use the singular form and need a singular verb.

Her **clothing** was made by hand.

Rush-hour **traffic** is always heavy.

35b Subject-verb agreement (complex)

The usually simple process of checking for subject-verb agreement sometimes becomes more complex. Certain kinds of words and sentence structures pose special problems for writers seeking to match subject and verb forms. Keeping all the "rules" in mind as you write can be distracting. The best solution is to remember the kinds of words and structures likely to cause problems, and then be ready, if necessary, to look up strategies for editing the problems.

- Plural words with singular meanings (for example, *politics* and *statistics*)
- Collective nouns (for example, *audience, crew, herd*)
- Subjects linked by *and, or,* and *nor* (compound and alternative subjects), sometimes accompanied by the word *each*
- Word groups coming between subject and verb (often beginning *as well as* or *along with*)
- Unusual word order and sentences beginning *There is* or *There are*
- Words like *all, everybody, none, who, which, that, is,* and *seems*

1 Watch for plural forms with singular meanings

Subjects plural in form (*shoes, filters, children, mathematics, we, they*) generally need a plural verb—but not always.

Subjects with plural forms and singular meanings. Words like *politics, statistics, linguistics, news, physics, mumps,* and *athletics* have the *-s* ending of plural nouns but are singular in meaning—and need singular verbs.

Mathematics is an increasingly popular field of study.

STRATEGY

Try the **pronoun test.**

Choose a pronoun that can accurately replace the subject: *he*, *she*, or *it* (singular); *they* (plural). Read the sentence with the replacement and edit the verb to agree.

DRAFT The **news** about the job market ______ surprisingly good.

PRONOUN TEST: Replace "The news" with "it" to read "It is surprisingly good."

EDITED The **news** about the job market **is** surprisingly good.

The pronoun test is especially useful for two special kinds of subjects.

- **Measurements or numbers**
  A measurement or figure (even one ending in *-s*) may still be singular if it names a quantity or unit as a whole. When it refers to individual elements, however, treat it as plural.

  Four years is the amount of time Dr. Santiago spent studying the effects of stress.
  PRONOUN TEST: "It is the amount of time Dr. Santiago spent. . . ."

  One-third of the job trainees **leave** the program after three weeks.
  PRONOUN TEST: They [plural] leave the program individually.

- **Titles and names**
  When the title of a work or a company's name is the subject, choose a singular verb even if the name or title is plural.

  New West Logistics **pays** high wages and **has** excellent benefits.
  PRONOUN TEST: "It [the company] pays high wages. . . ."

  The White Roses **is** second on the best-seller list this month.
  PRONOUN TEST: "It [the book] is second. . . ."

2 Be alert for collective nouns

A **collective noun** is singular in form yet identifies a group of individuals (*audience*, *crew*, *troop*, or *tribe*). When a group acts as a single unit, choose a singular verb; when its members act individually, choose a plural verb.

The **staff** is hardworking and well trained.

The **staff** have earned the respect of our clients.

If a plural verb makes a sentence awkward, rewrite using a plural subject.

35b agree

AWKWARD The congregation react to Reverend Cullen's sermons in different ways.

REWRITTEN **Members** of the congregation react to Reverend Cullen's sermons in different ways.

3 Check subjects linked by *and, or,* and *nor*

And creates a **compound subject;** *or* and *nor* create **alternative subjects.** As you edit, look for subjects containing these words.

Compound subjects joined by *and.* By joining two or more subjects with *and* or *both*, you create a **compound subject.** Because *and* makes the subject plural even if one or all of the individual parts are singular, you generally need to choose a plural verb.

> **Aaron and the rest of the staff** were responsible for the display.
>
> **Both rain and condensation** cause damage to the frame.

However, if the parts should be taken as a unit or if the parts designate a single person, thing, or idea, you need to choose a singular verb.

UNIT (SINGULAR) **Ham and eggs** is still my favorite breakfast.

TWO ELEMENTS (PLURAL) **Ham and eggs** are the main ingredients in this casserole.

ONE PERSON **My fellow art teacher and friend** also has paintings in the show.

TWO PEOPLE **My fellow art teacher and my friend** also have paintings in the show.

Depending on where you place the words *each* or *every*, you can give a compound subject a singular or plural meaning.

EACH BEFORE COMPOUND SUBJECT

compound subject singular verb

Each shift manager and unit manager **reviews** the progress logs daily.

EACH AFTER COMPOUND SUBJECT

compound subject plural verb

The shift managers and unit managers **each review** the progress logs daily.

Alternative subjects joined by *or*. When you use *or* or *nor* (*either . . . or*, *neither . . . nor*) to link alternative elements of a subject, make the verb agree with the closer part. Putting the plural element closer to the verb generally makes a sentence less awkward.

PLURAL CLOSE TO VERB — The auditor or **the staff accountants** review each report.

SINGULAR CLOSE TO VERB — False records or **late reporting** weakens the review process.

When parts of a subject differ in person and therefore need different verb forms (for example, *I have*, *he has*), make the verb agree with the part of the subject closer to it.

AWKWARD — Either the other new residents or **I** am going to file a complaint.

REWRITTEN — Either the other new **residents** are going to file a complaint or **I** am.

4 Pay attention to separated subjects and verbs

When you insert words or even a whole phrase between the subject and verb of a sentence, you may be tempted to make the verb agree with one of the intervening words rather than the actual subject.

FAULTY AGREEMENT — The new trolley system, with its expanded routes and lower fares, are specially popular with senior citizens.
The words *routes* and *fares* are not the subject of the sentence.

EDITED — The new trolley **system**, with its expanded routes and lower fares, **is** especially popular with senior citizens.

To identify possible problems with subject-verb agreement, be alert for phrases like *as well as*, *in addition to*, *together with*, and *along with*, or any other clusters of words between a subject and a verb.

UNEDITED — A regular tune-up, *along with* frequent oil **changes**, prolong the life of your car.

To recognize faulty agreement, identify the real subject by imagining the sentence without the intervening phrase, then check that the subject and verb agree.

FAULTY AGREEMENT — A regular **tune-up** . . . prolong the life of your car.

EDITED — A regular **tune-up,** along with frequent oil changes, prolongs the life of your car.

Because phrases like *as well as* can be easily mistaken for *and*, you may unintentionally treat a singular subject as a compound (plural) subject.

MISTAKEN The university's **provost**, as well as the deans, have issued new guidelines emphasizing teaching.

EDITED The university's **provost,** as well as the deans, has issued new guidelines emphasizing teaching.

If you mean *and*, use the word itself.

REWRITTEN The university's provost **and** the deans have issued new promotion guidelines emphasizing teaching.

Exercise 2

A. In each of the following sentences, choose the word inside the parentheses that creates subject-verb agreement.

EXAMPLE

The mayor, as well as members of the city council, (*has*/*have*) been searching for better ways to fund the zoo.

1. Several large lizards and an eight-foot python (*makes/make*) up the main attractions in the reptile building of the tiny zoo.
2. The displays as well as the building itself (*appears/appear*) well designed and well maintained.
3. The animals each (*displays/display*) good health and behavior.
4. Neither the zoo's overseers nor its director (*is/are*) satisfied with the reptile building and the number of animals on display.
5. Of the zoo's visitors, three-quarters (*says/say*) that the collection should be enlarged.
6. This year the Cajun and Bluegrass Festival (*features/feature*) several new bands.
7. The group *Beausoleil* (*appears/appear*) twice on the program.
8. The Cajun food, along with more familiar snacks, (*does/do*) draw many people to the refreshment tent.
9. The festival staff (*wears/wear*) buttons saying "Ask me for help."
10. Both the dancing lessons and the crafts display (*occupies/occupy*) the same tent.

B. Make up five sentences like those in Exercise 2A on any topic of your choice. Give them to a partner to complete, and work on those your partner has created.

ESL ADVICE: PAIRED CONJUNCTIONS AND SEPARATED SUBJECTS AND VERBS

Both . . . and always needs a plural verb.

Both the president **and** her advisor are in Tokyo this week.

Both the president **and** her advisors are in Tokyo this week.

Either . . . or, neither . . . nor, and *not only . . . but also* may take either a singular or plural verb. The subject closer to the verb determines the verb's form.

Either the president **or** her advisor is in Tokyo.

Neither the president **nor** her advisors are in Tokyo.

Check agreement when phrases or clauses come between a subject and verb.

PHRASES

NOT APPROPRIATE A person with sensitive eyes have to wear sunglasses.

CORRECT A **person** with sensitive eyes **has** to wear sunglasses.

CLAUSES

NOT APPROPRIATE A person whose eyes are sensitive have to wear sunglasses.

CORRECT A **person** whose eyes are sensitive **has** to wear sunglasses.

5 Recognize unusual word order

When you invert typical word order to create emphasis or ask a question, make sure the verb still agrees with the subject.

verb subject

QUESTION Are **patient satisfaction and increased efficiency** possible at the New Rockville Medical Clinic?

EMPHASIS Following landslide victories comes **overconfidence** for many politicians.

SERIOUS ERROR

6 Watch for *there is, there are*

There is/are, *it is/are*, and *here is/are* help you reverse the usual subject-verb sentence order so you can present the subject *after* the verb. As a result, you need to make the verb agree with the subject *following* it.

	verb subject
SINGULAR	There **is opportunity** for people starting new service industries.

	verb subject
PLURAL	There **are** many new **opportunities** for service industries.

Although it is strictly grammatical to use *there are* with a compound subject, you may use *there is* if the first part of this subject is singular.

> There is **a guard and an alarm system** protecting the warehouse.

7 Pay attention to *is, appears, feels,* and other linking verbs

When you build a sentence around *is*, *appears*, *feels*, or another linking verb (see 32a-3), make sure the verb agrees with the subject. You may be tempted to make it agree with the noun or pronoun renaming the subject (the complement—see 32b-2), but edit carefully to avoid this problem.

	subject verb complement
INCORRECT	The chief **obstacle** to change are the **mayor and her political allies.**
EDITED	The chief **obstacle** to change is the mayor and her political allies.

8 *All, everybody, none; who, which, that*—using special subjects

All, *everybody*, *none* (and other indefinite pronouns) do not refer to specific ideas, people, or things. Most have clearly singular meanings and require singular verbs.

> **Someone** is preparing the pamphlet.
>
> **Everybody** has the right to appeal a zoning decision.

You can treat a few pronouns, such as *all*, *any*, *most*, *none*, and *some*, as either singular or plural according to meaning.

STRATEGY

To decide whether to choose a singular or plural verb for words like *all, any,* or *none,* start by identifying the noun or pronouns to which they refer, then use the following test.

- Does the pronoun refer to something that *cannot be counted*? Choose singular.

SINGULAR **All** of the food is for the elderly lunch program.
all = singular noun
food = food in general (not countable)

- Does the pronoun refer to two or more elements of something that *can be counted*? Choose plural.

PLURAL **All** of the food supplies are for the elderly lunch program.
all = plural noun
supplies = many different kinds of supplies (countables) such as flour, meat, and canned vegetables

Who, which, and *that* (relative pronouns—see 32a-2) do not have singular and plural forms, yet the words to which they refer (antecedents) generally do have separate singular and plural forms. Choose a verb for *who, which,* or *that* so that it matches the number of the antecedent.

SINGULAR He prefers **a program** that awards grants to individuals.

PLURAL I support **programs** that distribute funds to community groups.

Make a habit of noticing the phrases *one of* and *the only one of.* They can create agreement problems when they come before *who, which,* or *that.*

Dr. Gotari is **one** of those professors who help students succeed.
Who refers to the plural *professors;* consequently the verb, *help,* is plural. There are other professors like Dr. Gotari.

Dr. Gotari is **the only one** of the professors who helps students succeed.
Who refers to the singular *Dr. Gotari;* consequently, the verb, *helps,* is singular. Dr. Gotari is the only supportive instructor.

9 Pay special attention to titles and names

When you use the title of a work or the name of a company as a sentence subject, choose a singular verb even if the name or title is plural.

35b agree

New West Consultants **pays** high wages and **offers** excellent benefits.
Think to yourself: The company pays . . .

The White Roses **is** second on the best-seller list.
Think to yourself: The book is . . .

"Tall ships" **is** the name given to the largest sailing ships.

Exercise 3

A. For each of the following sentences, give the correct present tense form of the infinitive verb indicated in parentheses.

EXAMPLE

None of the department heads (~~*to have*~~ has) the same administrative style.

1. Frieda O'Connor is one of those managers who (*to lead*) by example.
2. All the other department heads (*to respect*) her leadership ability.
3. She knows each of the employees who (*to work*) in her department.
4. Each year, Alberti and Campos Design Associates (*to give*) a plaque and a bonus to the employee with the highest rating on a peer survey.
5. The award, both the plaque and the money, (*to be*) given to Frieda almost every other year.

B. Working with another student, correct the errors that have been introduced into the following passage from Thomas R. McDonough's "Is Anyone Out There?" Not all the sentences contain an error, and some may have more than one. If correcting an error results in an awkward sentence, rewrite, but do not do so simply to avoid dealing with an agreement problem. When finished, compare your corrections with those of another pair of students, and explain the differences.

Each of the scientists involved in the search are pretty sure something is out there. A lot of numbers, some high and some low, is thrown around to express the probability of intelligent life somewhere else in the universe. Here is some figures that are middle-of-the-road. There is an estimated four hundred billion stars in the Milky Way. Planets may be fairly common, so you can figure one out of every ten of these stars have planets, which equals forty billions stars with planets. But how many of these places seems suitable for life? Neither too hot nor too cold is the conditions needed for life forms similar to our own. An atmosphere along with some water are also necessary. In our solar system only Earth qualifies, though Mars and Venus each comes close. Let us be conservative and estimate that only one of each solar system's planets fit the pattern. That's still forty billion habitable planets.

SERIOUS ERROR

ESL ADVICE: WORDS AFFECTING SUBJECT-VERB AGREEMENT

QUANTIFIERS

A quantifier—like *each*, *one*, or *many*—indicates the amount or quantity of a subject.

expressions followed by a plural noun	+	a singular verb
Each of/Every one of/One of/None of		the ESL **students** lives on campus.

expressions followed by a plural noun	+	a plural verb
Several of/Many of/Both of		the **students** live off campus.

In some cases, the noun after the expressions determines the verb form.

expressions followed by either a singular or a plural verb — noncount noun + singular verb

Some of/Most of/All of/A lot of the **produce** is fresh.

plural noun + plural verb

Some of/Most of/A lot of/All of the **vegetables** are fresh.

MUCH AND ***MOST*** (NOT ***MUCH OF*** OR ***MOST OF***) WITH NONCOUNT AND PLURAL NOUNS

NONCOUNT NOUN **Much traffic** occurs during rush hour.

PLURAL NOUN **Most Americans** live in the cities or suburbs.

OTHER, OTHERS, AND ***ANOTHER*** AS PRONOUNS OR ADJECTIVES

PRONOUNS

Others **+ plural verb:** adds points about a topic; there may be more points.

I enjoy Paris for many reasons. Some reasons are the beautiful architecture and gardens; **others are** the wonderful people, culture, and language.

The others **(plural) + plural verb;** ***the other*** **(singular) + singular verb:** adds the last point or points about the topic; there are no more.

Some hikers favor Craig's plan; **the others want to follow Tina's.**

ADJECTIVES

Another **+ singular noun:** adds an idea; there may be more ideas.
Other **+ plural noun:** adds more ideas; there may be more ideas.

One strength of our engineering team is our knowledge of the problem. **Another strength** is our experience. **Other strengths** include our communication skills, our teamwork, and our energy.

The other **+ singular or plural noun:** adds the final point or points to be discussed.

Of the two most important sights to see in Paris, one is the Louvre Museum and **the other** is the Cathedral of Notre Dame.

One of the major sights in Paris is the Louvre Museum. **The other** major sights are the Eiffel Tower, the Champs-Elysees, the Cathedral of Notre Dame, and the Arc de Triomphe.

35c Pronoun-antecedent agreement

A pronoun takes its meaning from another word to which it refers (its **antecedent**).

antecedent — pronoun
Campers should treat **their** tents with a mildew-preventing spray.

pronoun — antecedent
Its preference for damp fabric makes **mildew** a major problem.

Matching pronoun and antecedent (either a noun or another pronoun) in *gender*, *person*, and *number* helps link the two by creating pronoun-antecedent agreement. **Number** refers to singular or plural forms. **Person** refers to the speaker or the subject spoken to/about. **Gender** refers to masculine, feminine, or neuter qualities generally associated with a noun or pronoun.

NUMBER, PERSON, AND GENDER

NUMBER

Number shows whether words are singular or plural in meaning.

SINGULAR — This **community** needs its own recreation center.

PLURAL — Local **communities** need to share their facilities.

SINGULAR WORDS

1. Nouns naming individual people, animals, ideas, and things
2. *I, you, he, she, it* (personal pronouns referring to individuals)
3. *Each, someone* (indefinite pronouns) or *who, which, that* (relative pronouns) when they refer to singular nouns or pronouns
4. Verbs in their singular forms (I *am*, she *is*; I *analyze*, she *analyzes*)

PLURAL WORDS

1. Nouns naming more than one person, animal, idea, or thing
2. *We, you, they* (personal pronouns referring to more than one individual)
3. *All, none* (indefinite pronouns) or *who, which, that* (relative pronouns) when they refer to plural nouns or pronouns
4. Verbs in their plural forms (we *are*, they *are*; we *analyze*, they *analyze*)

PERSON

Person indicates the speaker or the subject being spoken to or about

First person (speaker): *I, we*

I operate the compressor. **We** operate the compressor.

Second person (spoken to): *you*

You operate the forklift.

Third person (spoken about): *he, she, it, they;* nouns naming things, people, animals, ideas

He/she/it operates the drill. **They** operate the drill.

GENDER

Gender refers to the masculine, feminine, or neuter character generally attributed to a noun or pronoun.

MASCULINE/FEMININE

While the father printed the document on **his** computer, his daughter completed the financial report on **hers.**

NEUTER

Despite **its** income from sales, the company has yet to show a profit.

Masculine wording: *he,* nouns indicating males, and pronouns (*everyone, somebody, who, which, that*) when they refer to males

Feminine wording: *she,* nouns indicating females, and pronouns (*everyone, somebody, who, which, that*) when they refer to females

Neuter wording: *it,* nouns indicating places, things, and ideas, and pronouns (*everything, something, which, that*) when they refer to places, things, and ideas

1 Recognize antecedents joined by *and, or,* and *nor*

When you wish to make a pronoun refer to several things (Luis *and* Jennifer, for example, or the other students *and* I), the pronoun form you choose should depend, to a great extent, on the word that links the elements of the antecedent: *and*, *or*, or *nor*.

Identify the antecedent and the word used to link its parts: *and*, *or* (*either . . . or*), or *nor* (*neither . . . nor*)

- **And** (compound antecedent)
  Choose a plural pronoun (such as *they*) even if one or more of the antecedent's parts are singular.

  Luis and Jennifer said that the tests they ran on the groundwater were conclusive.

  The other students and I admit that the tests we ran were not conclusive.

  Exception: A compound antecedent can refer to a single person, thing, or idea. When it does, use a singular pronoun.

  My colleague and coauthor is someone skilled at analyzing soil samples.

  You can place *each* and *every* before a compound antecedent to single out the individual elements. When you do, use a singular pronoun.

  Each of the soil and water samples is brought to the lab in **its** own sterile container.

  Every soil and water sample brought to the lab undergoes **its** own three tests.

- **Or** and **Nor** (alternative antecedent)
  Choose a pronoun that agrees with the part of the antecedent that is closer to it.

  Neither the project manager **nor** the engineers submitted their accident reports on time.

  Editing advice: If one part of a subject is singular and the other part plural, consider putting the plural element second or rewriting to avoid an awkward or confusing sentence.

  CONFUSING Either Jamal and Alan or **Richard** will include the sales projections in his report.

  READER'S REACTION: Does this mean that Jamal and Alan may be putting things in Richard's report? Or does it mean that there will be two reports, Richard's plus Jamal and Alan's, one of which will contain the projections?

  EDITED Either Richard or **Jamal** and **Alan** will include the sales projections in their report.

REWRITTEN Either Richard will include the sales projections in his report, or Jamal and Alan will include the projections in theirs.

2 Pay attention to *everyone, any, something* (indefinite pronouns) as antecedents

Many words like *somebody* and *each* (indefinite pronouns) are singular. Make sure that the pronouns you use to refer to them are also singular.

Somebody on the staff left his or her confidential data disks in the lunchroom.

Each member of the women's basketball team has her own training regimen.

Sometimes you may use an indefinite pronoun to mean *many* or *all*. In formal writing or speaking, your audience may prefer a plural antecedent.

INFORMAL Everyone on the research team handed in their sections of the report.

EDITED **Members** of the research team handed in their sections of the report.

To avoid sexist language (see 47a), many publishers and communities of writers accept a plural pronoun with a singular antecedent; when in doubt, however, use *both* a plural pronoun and a plural antecedent.

SEXIST Everybody should include charts and slides in his sales talk.

INFORMAL/ SOMETIMES ACCEPTABLE **Everybody** should include charts and slides in their sales talks.

SAFEST **All presenters** should include charts and slides in their sales **talks.**

3 Watch for collective nouns as antecedents

A noun such as *team, group, clan, audience, army,* or *tribe* (collective noun) can act as a singular or plural antecedent, depending on whether it refers to the group as a whole or to the members acting separately.

SINGULAR The **subcommittee** submitted its revised version of the report.

PLURAL The **subcommittee** brought their different suggestions for a revised report to the meeting for discussion.

ESL ADVICE: DEMONSTRATIVE ADJECTIVES OR PRONOUNS

In addition to subjects and verbs, other elements in a sentence must agree. **Demonstrative adjectives** or **pronouns** (*this*, *that*, *these*, and *those*) must be either singular or plural, depending on the noun being modified. (See also 32a-2.)

INAPPROPRIATE This agencies conduct outreach programs in local schools.

APPROPRIATE **These agencies** conduct outreach programs in local schools.

INAPPROPRIATE Those agency conducts outreach programs in local schools.

APPROPRIATE **That agency** conducts outreach programs in local schools.

Exercise 4

A. Correct any errors in pronoun-antecedent agreement in the following sentences. You may need to change other parts of a sentence besides the pronoun or the antecedent. Each sentence can be corrected in more than one way.

EXAMPLE

People like
~~A person~~ who ~~likes~~ camping should no longer feel they are unusual.

1. In any circle of friends, several are likely to say that he or she enjoys camping.
2. Everyone who goes camping needs to pay attention to their equipment.
3. All hikers should select good shoes and socks to protect your feet.
4. A camper or a hiker needs to choose their clothing carefully, paying attention to comfort, durability, and protection as well as style.
5. Both regular campers and occasional campers should be willing to put his or her money into well-designed tents, sleeping bags, and cooking equipment.
6. Each store or chain of stores in the retail camping industry meets the needs of their customers in a different way.
7. A store catering to campers and the hiker usually offers him or her a wide choice of equipment at different prices.
8. Eddie Bauer or L.L. Bean provides mail-order service to his customers.
9. A camping supplies and athletic equipment store may provide a narrower range of choices to their customers because of the need to stock sporting goods as well as camping equipment.

10. Nonetheless, any of these businesses should be able to provide you and their other customers with good, safe camping equipment.

B. Working with a group of students, compare your corrections for the sentences in Exercise 4A. Make note of any differences, and decide which version (if any) is preferable and why.

CHAPTER 36
Adjectives and Adverbs

If you use the wrong forms of some familiar words, your readers will be likely to notice the errors.

DRAFT The new medication acts **quick.**

EDITED The new medication acts **quickly.**

DRAFT They **hadn't never** implemented the cost-saving program.

EDITED They **had never** implemented the cost-saving program.

Admittedly, not all mistaken forms are likely to irritate or confuse your readers. Some readers, for example, may not notice the difference in meaning between the following two sentences.

The fumes from the mixture smelled **bad.**

The fumes from the mixture smelled **badly.**

Others, however, will notice that the second sentence says the fumes themselves have a sense of smell, but one that isn't working well.

36a What adjectives and adverbs do

Adjectives and adverbs **modify** other words, adding to, qualifying, focusing, limiting, or extending their meaning. Because the *-ly* ending does not appear on all adverbs, and because some familiar adjectives do end in *-ly* (such as *friendly*, *lonely*), you may sometimes have to determine whether a word is an adjective or adverb by looking at how it is used in sentences or by looking it up in a dictionary.

FEATURES OF ADJECTIVES AND ADVERBS

ADJECTIVES

- Modify nouns and pronouns
- Answer the questions "How many?" "What kind?" "Which one (or ones)?" and "What size, color, or shape?"

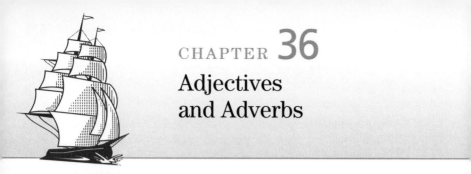

- Include words like *blue, complicated, good,* and *frightening*
- Include words created by adding endings like *-able, -ical, -less, -ful,* and *-ous* to nouns or verbs (such as *controllable, sociological, seamless, careful, nervous*)

ADVERBS

- Modify verbs, adjectives, and other adverbs
- Modify phrases (*almost* beyond the building), clauses (*soon after* I added the last ingredients), and sentences (*Remarkably,* the mechanism was not damaged)
- Answer questions such as "When?" "Where?" "How?" "How often?" "Which direction?" "What degree?"
- Consist mostly of words ending in *-ly,* like *quickly, carefully,* and *smoothly*
- Include some words that do not end in *-ly,* such as *fast, very, well, quite,* and *late*

36b Avoiding confusion between adjectives and adverbs

Much of the time you will have little trouble deciding whether to use the adjective or adverb form of a word. Nonetheless, a recent trend in informal speech has been the dropping of *-ly* in the adverb form of some words. In addition, some pairs of words, such as *good/well,* and some common sentence patterns need special attention.

1 Figure out what a modifier does in a sentence

If you can't tell which modifier to use, analyze what the word will do in your sentence. (See "Features of Adjectives and Adverbs," pp. 626–627.)

DRAFT Write **careful** so the directions are clear.
Write *how*? It answers an adverb question.

EDITED Write **carefully** so the directions are clear.

STRATEGY

Try drawing an arrow to the word that is modified. If this word acts as a noun or pronoun, modify it with an adjective; if it acts as a verb, adjective, or adverb, modify it with an adverb.

DRAFT The rubber insulation underwent **remarkable** quick deterioration.

CORRECTION: *Remarkable* modifies *quick* (and answers the adverb question "How quick?"). *Quick* in turn modifies *deterioration* and answers the adjective question "What kind of deterioration?"

EDITED The rubber insulation experienced **remarkably** quick deterioration.

2 Be alert for verbs like *look, feel, prove,* and *is*

Verbs such as *look, feel,* and *prove* can show both states of being (**linking verbs**) and activities (**action verbs**). The verb *is* always acts as a linking verb. Choose an adjective for a state of being or an adverb for an activity. (The adjective following a linking verb is called a **complement,** see 32b-2.)

SUBJECT	LINKING VERB	COMPLEMENT (ADJECTIVE)
The room	smelled	musty.
The procedure	proved	unreliable.

ADJECTIVE (BEING) The motor's metal cover turned **hot.**

ADVERB (ACTION) The large wheel turned **quickly.**

ADJECTIVE The movement grew **rapid.** [The motion became quick.]

ADVERB The movement grew **rapidly.** [The group got bigger, and its ideas spread rapidly.]

3 Pay special attention to *real/really, sure/surely, bad/badly,* and *good/well*

Some common uses of words like *bad/badly*—especially *sure* for *surely*—may be acceptable in informal speech or writing, but not in other settings.

4 Check the words that complete direct objects

When you add a word right after or before a direct object to complete (or complement) its meaning, make sure you choose an adjective.

The review panel considered the researcher **objective.**

Objective completes *researcher* by indicating the person's qualities.

CHOOSING BETWEEN *BAD/BADLY, GOOD/WELL, REAL/REALLY,* AND *SURE/SURELY*

BAD/BADLY

Use *bad* (adjective) with linking verbs such as *is, seems*, or *appears*.	I feel **bad** that our group isn't working well together. (not *badly*)
Use *badly* (adverb) with action verbs.	The expensive new breathing apparatus works **badly.** (not *bad*)

GOOD/WELL

Use *good* (adjective) with linking verbs.	The chef's new oil and garlic dressing tastes **good.** (not *well*)
Use *well* (adverb) with action verbs, unless it refers to health.	The new pump works **well.** (not *good*)

REAL/REALLY

Use *really* (adverb) to modify an adverb like *fast, efficient*, or *hot*	Lu Ming is **really** efficient. (not *real*)

SURE/SURELY

Use *surely* (adverb) to modify adjectives like *misleading, outdated,* or *courageous.*	This drawing of the mechanism is **surely** misleading. (not *sure*)

You can place an adverb after the object, but it will modify the verb.

> The review panel considered the researcher **objectively.**
> *Objectively* describes their manner in evaluating the researcher.

Unlike adjectives completing a direct object, adverbs can usually appear at other places in a sentence.

ADJECTIVE	The agency judged her artwork **competent.**
ADVERB	The agency judged her artwork **competently.**
ADVERB	The agency **competently** judged her artwork.

Exercise 1

A. Rewrite the following sentences to eliminate any problems in adjective or adverb use.

EXAMPLE

I thought the band sounded ~~badly~~ bad, though many of my friends enjoyed the music.

1. Many scholars have begun studying some real surprising subjects such as rock music.
2. At first, they had trouble persuading many people to take their work serious.
3. Now they produce careful researched studies of musicians like the Beatles as well as biographies of influential figures like Sid Vicious, Joey Ramone, and Courtney Love.
4. Remember, just because a piece of rock music sounds well does not mean that it is worth careful study.
5. At a time when the careers of many rock musicians are going bad, rock is doing quite good on campus.

B. Working in a group, decide which piece of advice in sections 36a and b applies to the particular problem in adjective or adverb use illustrated by each of the following sentences. Make a note of each relevant section of the discussion, and rewrite the sentence to eliminate the problem.

EXAMPLE

Some dead rock musicians have ~~surprising~~ surprisingly large and active fan clubs.

1. Over the past year, the number of books devoted to rock groups or rock stars has grown remarkable.
2. The writer Greil Marcus has produced several high-regarded books that praise Elvis Presley as an artist and person.
3. The title of one of Marcus's books, *Dead Elvis: A Chronicle of a Cultural Obsession*, may suggest that he views Elvis "sightings" and memorabilia as humorously.
4. Some of the events he describes are undoubted weird.
5. Nonetheless, he feels surely that Elvis and his music really deserve respect.

ESL ADVICE: ADJECTIVES IN A SERIES

Place two or more adjectives in a series in correct order.

DETERMINER	QUALITY	PHYSICAL DESCRIPTION	NATIONALITY	MATERIAL	QUALIFYING NOUN	MAIN NOUN
that	expensive	smooth black	German	fiberglass	racing	car
our	friendly	big old	English		hunting	dog
four	little	round white		plastic	Ping-Pong	balls
several	beautiful	young red	Japanese		maple	trees

36c Comparatives and superlatives: Correct forms

You can use most adjectives and adverbs in three forms: positive, comparative, and superlative. Choose the form appropriate for your purpose.

POSITIVE (NO COMPARISON)	COMPARATIVE (COMPARE TWO THINGS)	SUPERLATIVE (COMPARE THREE OR MORE THINGS)
quick	quicker	quickest
	less quick	least quick
quickly	more quickly	most quickly
	less quickly	least quickly

POSITIVE This is a **quick** route.

Rainha drove **quickly** through the circuit.

COMPARATIVE This is a **quicker** route.

Rainha drove **more quickly** through the circuit.

SUPERLATIVE This is the **quickest** route.

Rainha drove **most quickly** through the circuit.

IRREGULAR COMPARATIVES AND SUPERLATIVES

POSITIVE	COMPARATIVE	SUPERLATIVE
ADJECTIVES		
bad	worse	worst
good	better	best
ill (harsh, unlucky)	worse	worst
a little	less	least
many	more	most
much	more	most
some	more	most
well (healthy)	better	best
ADVERBS		
badly	worse	worst
ill (badly)	worse	worst
well (satisfactorily)	better	best

1 Watch out for illogical comparatives

Some adjectives and adverbs cannot logically take comparative or superlative form. These include *unique, impossible, pregnant, infinite, dead, gone, perfectly,* and *entirely.*

ILLOGICAL	Gottleib's "Nightscape" is a **most unique** painting.
	READER'S REACTION: *Unique* means "one of a kind." How can a thing be *more* or *most* if it is the only one?
LOGICAL	Gottleib's "Nightscape" is a **unique** painting.

2 Look for imprecise use of comparatives

In conversation, people often use comparative forms loosely, knowing listeners will still grasp the intended meaning of a phrase like "She is my oldest daughter" even though the speaker has only two daughters. In writing, you need to be more precise, especially if you are presenting facts and figures.

INACCURATE	The survey covered four age groups: 20–29, 30–44, 45–59, and 60+. The people in the older group smoked the least.
	READER'S REACTION: Did the people in the older *groups* smoke the least or did the people in the *oldest* group smoke the least?
PRECISE	The survey covered four age groups: 20–29, 30–44, 45–59, and 60+. The people in the **oldest group** smoked the least.

3 Check for double comparatives

Most readers will not accept double comparatives or superlatives.

INCORRECT	The temperature dropped, and the weather became **more foggier.**
EDITED	The temperature dropped, and the weather became **foggier.**
INCORRECT	Jorge is the **most agilest** athlete on the team.
EDITED	Jorge is the **most agile** athlete on the team.

36d Avoiding double negatives

Negative words include *no, none, not, never, neither, hardly, scarcely, barely,* and words like *haven't* and *don't* (formed with *n't*, the abbreviation for *not*). In general, negative words do not become more forceful when more than one appears in a sentence (a **double negative**). Readers may view the negatives as canceling each other out.

DOUBLE NEGATIVE	The highway department hasn't done nothing about the dangerous exit ramp.
	READER'S REACTION: If the department hasn't done nothing, maybe it *has* done *something*.

EDITED The highway department hasn't done anything about the dangerous exit ramp.

Exercise 2

A. Revise the following sentences to eliminate any incorrect use of adjectives or adverbs.

EXAMPLE

I think the real difference between Necco Wafers and Skittles is that Necco Wafers last ~~longest~~ longer.

1. Of the three candy bars, Snickers, Three Musketeers, and Baby Ruth, which is older?
2. Which of the two kinds of gummy bears is more sweeter?
3. Broccoli-flavored candy had even badder sales than chocolate-dipped carrots.
4. Trying to create a candy bar that pleases everyone's taste is a most impossible task.
5. Some people can't hardly bear the taste of sour-flavored candy.

B. Working in a group, create two different correct versions of each of the following sentences. Then decide as a group which version of each sentence you prefer and why.

1. Surveys of customers' preferences are the most costliest method of market research.
2. They are not unlikely to be a waste of money.
3. One survey showed that consumers find a blend of hazelnuts and raspberries a most tastier combination.
4. The company wanted a more unique combination, however.
5. By adding marshmallows to the blend, the company eventually turned the bar into a most complete marketing success.

PART 8

Sentence Problems

CHAPTER 37
Sentence Fragments

To treat a cluster of words as a sentence, start with a capital letter and put a period at the end, but make sure you include essential elements such as a subject and a verb; otherwise, you may confuse readers by leaving out crucial information.

SUBJECT MISSING — Began pumping water out of the basement.

READER'S REACTION: Who was pumping, or what was doing the pumping?

EDITED — **The fire truck** began pumping water out of the basement.

VERB MISSING — The insurance company responsible for the costs.

READER'S REACTION: What did the company do?

EDITED — The insurance company **became** responsible for the costs.

A cluster of words punctuated as a sentence but lacking a crucial element that enables it to stand alone as a sentence is called a **sentence fragment.** Another kind of fragment consists of a group of words acting as a modifier but mistakenly asked to stand on its own as a sentence. Such fragments make readers do the writer's job, forcing them to reattach mentally a word group to a nearby sentence.

FRAGMENT — They were able to get the pump started again. **By replacing the gas filter.**

The second statement is a modifying phrase detached from the preceding sentence.

EDITED — They were able to get the pump started again **by replacing the gas filter.**

Fragments that confuse readers or make them do extra, unnecessary work are serious errors. On occasion, an **intentional fragment** (also called a **partial sentence,** see 37c) may effectively create emphasis or a change of pace. For the most part, however, academic, business, and professional readers will judge a piece of writing (and its writer) harshly when they encounter a fragment.

37a Sentence fragments: Recognizing

Some sentence fragments are easy to recognize, others less so. Watch for word groups falling into one of these three general categories.

- Word groups lacking a subject or a verb
- Modifying word groups detached from sentences
- Troublesome constructions, such as *for example* fragments or verbal phrases

37a frag

1 Look for a subject and a verb

If a word group punctuated as a sentence lacks either a subject or a complete verb, expressed or implied, it is a fragment (see 32b).

STRATEGY

- **Ask *Who* (or *what*) *does?* or *Who* (or *what*) *is?*** If a word group does not answer "Who?" or "What?" then it *lacks a subject* and is a sentence fragment.

FRAGMENT Yet also needs to establish a family counseling program.

READER'S REACTION: This doesn't say who (or what) needs to establish the program.

EDITED Yet **Community Health Clinic** also needs to establish a family counseling program.

If a word group does not answer "Does?" or "Is?" then it lacks a verb and is a sentence fragment.

FRAGMENT The new policy to determine scholarship size on the basis of grades rather than on the basis of need.

READER'S REACTION: This doesn't indicate anything about what the new policy *does* or *is*.

EDITED The new policy **determines** scholarship size on the basis of grades rather than on the basis of need.

In trying to identify the "Who" in a passage, remember that in commands, the subject *you* is understood: [**You**] Use the spectrometer to test for the unknown chemical ingredient. Some familiar sentence patterns also use a clearly implied verb: John went to Stanford, Regina [**went**] to UCLA.

- **See if you can turn a word group into a question that can be answered *yes* or *no*.** If it can be, it is a sentence.

WORD GROUP They bought a van to carry the new equipment.

QUESTION: Did they buy a van to carry the new equipment?

CONCLUSION The word group is a sentence.

SERIOUS ERROR

37a frag

To decide whether a subject or a verb is missing, see if you need to add or alter an element to create a question.

WORD GROUP Bought the building to use as a warehouse.

QUESTION: Did ______ buy the building to use as a warehouse?

CONCLUSION The question does not have a subject, so the word group is a fragment lacking a subject.

EDITED **Johnson Manufacturing** bought the building to use as a warehouse.

WORD GROUP The company providing repairs for our computers.

QUESTION: Does the company providing repairs for our computers?

CAUTION: Do not begin the questions with *is/are* or *has/have*. In doing so you may unintentionally provide a verb for the word group you are testing.

CONCLUSION The word *providing* cannot act as the verb in its present form. The word group is a fragment lacking a verb.

EDITED The company **is** providing repairs for our computers.

In checking for fragments, be careful not to mistake a verbal for a verb. Verbals include words like *testing*, *tested* (participles), *to test* (infinitives), and *testing* (gerunds). A verbal alone cannot act as the verb in a sentence. (See 37a-3.)

Exercise 1

Indicate which of the following word groups are sentence fragments and which are complete sentences. Correct sentence fragments by supplying any information necessary to make complete sentences.

EXAMPLE

is

Our job ^ to find a new head for nursing services.

1. Several people applying for the job.
2. The job description in the newspaper asks for someone who is a good administrator and also an innovator.
3. Is able to convince fellow workers to develop their own innovative staffing plan and present it to the hospital administration.
4. Julie Kim, the prior head of nursing services responsible for so much turmoil during her time in the job and also so many improvements in the way nurses interact with patients and physicians.
5. A study suggesting that nursing administrators develop in-service programs to create improved morale among the professional staff and also better patient care.

2 Look for *although, because, that, since,* and other subordinating words

Pay attention to word groups containing a subject and a verb but beginning with subordinators such as *although, if, because,* or *that.* Subordinators tell readers to regard the word group that follows as part of a larger statement.

Look for a word group beginning with a subordinating conjunction such as *after, although, if, because, unless,* or *since* (see 44c) or with a relative pronoun (*that, what, which,* or *who*). Then check whether this word group is attached to a main clause (see 32c)—a cluster of words that can stand on its own as a sentence. If the word group is unattached, then it is a fragment.

FRAGMENT Most residents love the friendly, unspoiled nature of the town. **Which has led to rapid population growth and a rise in property values.**

EDITED Most residents love the friendly, unspoiled nature of the town, which has led to rapid population growth and a rise in property values.

FRAGMENT Many experts think that the SAT and the ACT are somewhat biased. **Although they also consider most criticism of the tests overblown.**

EDITED Many experts think that the SAT and the ACT are somewhat biased, although they also consider most criticism of the tests overblown.

EDITED Many experts think that the SAT and the ACT are somewhat biased yet also consider most criticism of the tests overblown.

Exercise 2

A. Indicate which of the following word groups are sentence fragments and which are complete sentences. Correct all the sentence fragments by supplying any information necessary to make complete sentences or attaching a fragment to an adjacent main clause.

EXAMPLE

Although many people think that afternoon sleepiness is caused by a heavy lunch. Researchers say this is not true.

1. People such as interns and truck drivers often feel drowsy. Even though they are aware of a need to stay awake and alert.
2. Having an afternoon nap can greatly increase your alertness. Whether or not you got enough sleep the night before.
3. Almost accidentally, researchers started becoming aware of the importance of naps while they were mapping cycles of drowsiness and alertness we each go through during an entire day.
4. Almost everyone experiences sleepiness and a decline in mental alertness during the afternoon. Because our internal clocks tell us it is time to nap and get out of the sun's strongest rays.
5. Despite a widespread belief that siestas and naps are cultural customs. They actually have a biological base.

B. Working with a group, look through one or more popular magazines, focusing on either the advertising or the articles. Identify ten sentence fragments and list them. Indicate which fragments lack a subject or a verb (or both), and indicate which fragments are modifying clauses that contain a subject and a verb but are controlled by a subordinating word.

3 Look for troublesome constructions

Watch for structures often incorrectly treated as complete sentences: *for example* fragments, split predicates, and disconnected verbal phrases.

***For example* fragments.** Word groups beginning with phrases like *for example, such as,* and *for instance* are sometimes disconnected from sentences and mistakenly made to stand on their own. You can identify such fragments by looking for one of the phrases at the beginning of a word group and then checking whether the word group is either (1) attached to a main clause or (2) contains all the elements needed to act as a complete sentence.

FRAGMENT	We are trying to hire a new staff member who has skills that none of us possess. **For example, knowledge of computer-aided design.**
EDITED (SEPARATE SENTENCE)	We are trying to hire a new staff member who has skills that none of us possess. For example, **we need** someone with knowledge of computer-aided design.
FRAGMENT	Very few people are aware of the familiar species that are suffering from pollution or mismanagement. **Such as the striped bass and the snook.**
EDITED (ATTACHED TO MAIN CLAUSE)	Very few people are aware of the familiar species, **such as the striped bass and the snook,** that are suffering from pollution or mismanagement.

SERIOUS ERROR

37a frag

Split predicate. A sentence can contain two or more complete verbs (for example, "I *unfastened* the seat and *removed* it."). Writers sometimes mistakenly split off the second (or last) element as a separate sentence, perhaps unconsciously assuming that the subject in the opening section is still present in the later one. To recognize a fragment of this type, look for a word group whose verb comes near the beginning (often following a word like *and*, *yet*, or *but*) and whose subject is nearby—but in another sentence.

FRAGMENT	Beethoven's work as a composer began in a style similar to that of Mozart. **But soon took on its own unique style.**
CORRECTED (SUBJECT ADDED)	Beethoven's work as a composer began in a style similar to that of Mozart. But **his work** soon took on its own unique style.
CORRECTED (REATTACHED)	Beethoven's work as a composer began in a style similar to that of Mozart **but** soon took on its own unique style.

Disconnected verbal phrases. To identify a disconnected verbal phrase, you need to be aware of the difference between verbs and verbals. Verbals are similar in form to verbs, but play different roles: participles (*analyzing*, *analyzed*), infinitives (*to analyze*), and gerunds (*analyzing*). (See 32c-4.) When combined with a helping verb (such as *is*, *has*, *can*, or *should*—see 32a-3), a verbal can be part of a complete verb (*was analyzing*, *should analyze*). Often, verbal phrases (verbal plus object and modifiers) are detached from adjacent sentences or related to them as modifiers.

FRAGMENT (PARTICIPIAL PHRASE)	**Frustrated by the meager offerings in journalism.** She decided to transfer to another university.
EDITED (ATTACHED TO MAIN CLAUSE)	Frustrated by the meager offerings in journalism, she decided to transfer to another university.

FRAGMENT (INFINITIVE PHRASE)	Divorcing parents should seek advice from a counselor. **To help lessen emotional problems for their children.**
EDITED (ATTACHED TO MAIN CLAUSE)	Divorcing parents should seek advice from a counselor to help lessen emotional problems for their children.

FRAGMENT (GERUND PHRASE)	**Introducing competing varieties of crabs into the same tank.** He did this in order to study aggression.
EDITED (REWRITTEN)	He **introduced** competing varieties of crabs into the tank in order to study aggression.

Exercise 3

A. Correct each of the fragments in the following passages in two different ways.

EXAMPLE

Some innovative rock groups have been touring this year. Drawing large crowds.

Some innovative rock groups have been touring this year. They have been drawing large crowds.

Some innovative rock groups have been touring this year, drawing large crowds.

1. Realizing that musical tastes are probably changing. Many record companies have decided to explore new and newly rediscovered kinds of music.
2. Some formerly popular musical artists no longer have recording contracts. Their sales of CDs having dropped drastically.
3. In recent campus concerts, jazz artists have attracted large and enthusiastic audiences. Because of their innovative melodies and sounds.
4. The rhythm section of one group consists of a single unusual instrument. An electronic instrument making sounds like a drum but looking like a guitar.
5. Undecided about whether to sign new groups to long-term contracts. Some companies agree to produce and sell a single CD with an option for future recordings.

B. Instead of doing Exercise 3A on your own, work with another person and create *three* correct versions of each passage, rewriting extensively if necessary. Note the ways each of you prefers to correct fragments, especially any differences between your choices.

37b Sentence fragments: Editing

You can correct sentence fragments in four ways.

1. **Supply** the missing sentence element.

FRAGMENT (LACKS VERB) Several arguments favor enabling adopted children to contact their birth parents. **Among the most important the need to find out about any hereditary diseases.**

EDITED Several arguments favor enabling adopted children to contact their birth parents. Among the most important is the need to find out about any hereditary diseases.

2. **Attach** the fragment to a nearby main clause. Rewrite if necessary.

FRAGMENT (SUBORDINATE CLAUSE) Modern trauma centers are equipped to give prompt care to heart attack victims. **Because rapid treatment can minimize damage to heart muscles.**

EDITED Modern trauma centers are equipped to give prompt care to heart attack victims because rapid treatment can minimize damage to heart muscles.

3. **Drop** a subordinating word so the subordinate clause can act as a complete sentence (main clause).

FRAGMENT **Although** several people argued strenuously against the motion. It passed by a considerable majority nonetheless.

EDITED Several people argued strenuously against the motion. It passed by a considerable majority nonetheless.

4. **Rewrite** a passage to eliminate the fragment.

FRAGMENT Some sports attract large numbers of participants in their fifties, sixties, and even seventies. **For example, tennis and bowling.**

EDITED Some sports, **such as tennis and bowling,** attract large numbers of participants in their fifties, sixties, and even seventies.

Exercise 4

A. Correct each of the fragments in the following passages in two different ways.

EXAMPLE

Living and working in another country creates many challenges for families. For example, arranging for children's schooling.

Living and working in another country creates many challenges for families. Arranging for children's schooling is one such challenge.

1. The armed forces run elementary and secondary schools around the world. To provide education for dependents.
2. Japanese executives working in North America worry about educating their children in the Japanese language. And worry about whether they will fit into Japanese culture when they are adults.
3. Americans and Canadians working outside North America often look for schools conducted in English. To make sure their children will be prepared to attend college when the families return home.
4. The modern world makes many demands on parents. Who must spend considerable time and energy educating their children.
5. Whoever grows up with knowledge of two different cultures. I think that person will have some distinct advantages.

B. Working with a group, identify the fragments in the following word groups. Then combine word groups to form a paragraph consisting of complete sentences. Feel free to alter wording or add information necessary to make the paragraph interesting and clear.

1. One store chain asks people to provide an address when cashing a check. And uses the information to create a mailing list for its advertising.
2. As a result, people who buy two pairs of pants and a few blouses are going to be receiving something in the mail each week for the next few months. For instance, a colorful flyer about home furnishings or automobile accessories.
3. Some people resent this marketing strategy. And complain to the post office or the company itself.
4. Lots of people consider advertising brochures fun to read. And a way to make shopping easier.
5. I think they are one of the many small irritations we encounter every day. Such as free samples of useless products and computerized telephone calls.

37c Partial sentences

In writing of all kinds, you are likely to encounter sentence fragments used correctly and effectively, called **partial sentences.** Used sparingly, partial sentences call attention to details, provide special emphasis for ideas, heighten contrasts, or create powerful images, as in the following passage.

> Our house stood apart. A gaudy yellow in a row of white bungalows. We were the people with the noisy dog.
>
> —RICHARD RODRIGUEZ, "Aria"

GUIDELINES FOR CREATING PARTIAL SENTENCES

1. Have a clear purpose, such as highlighting details and ideas or providing strong emphasis and contrast.
2. Make sure readers will recognize the purpose and not mistake the fragment for a detached modifier or word group missing an important element.
3. Take care that readers will be easily able to understand the fragment and any connections among it and other word groups.

Exercise 5

If you have not already completed Exercise 2B, do so now, making a copy of each fragment you locate. Working with a group, share your different sets of fragments. Identify those fragments you consider effective partial sentences. Explain how each effective fragment fits the criteria in 37c, and tell what purpose each one fulfills.

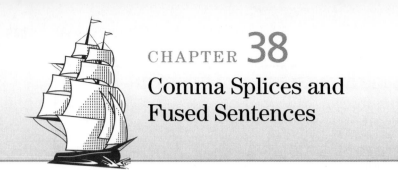

CHAPTER 38
Comma Splices and Fused Sentences

You can easily confuse and annoy readers if you inappropriately join two or more sentences using either a comma only (comma splice) or no punctuation at all (fused sentence). Readers may have to look over a sentence containing a comma splice several times to be sure of its meaning because the sentence does not clearly specify the relationship between the clauses making it up.

COMMA SPLICE — CBS was founded in 1928 by William S. Paley, his uncle and his father sold him a struggling radio network they had bought to advertise their La Palina cigars.

READER'S REACTION: At first I thought CBS had three founders: Paley, his uncle, and his father. Then I realized that the sentence probably means Paley founded CBS after buying the radio network from his relatives.

EDITED — CBS was founded in 1928 by William S. Paley; his uncle and his father sold him a struggling radio network they had bought to advertise their La Palina cigars.

Even after a close examination, however, readers may find it difficult to understand a fused sentence, two sentences joined with no punctuation at all.

FUSED SENTENCE — The city had only one swimming pool without an admission fee the pool was poorly maintained.

READER'S REACTION: I can't decide if the *single* swimming pool in the town is poorly maintained or if the only swimming pool that does not charge a fee is in bad shape.

EDITED — The city had only one swimming pool, **but** without an admission fee, the pool was poorly maintained.

38a Comma splices and fused sentences: Recognizing

When you link two sentences *by a comma alone*, you create a **comma splice** (see also 32c).

COMMA SPLICE — Eight inches of rain fell in twenty-four hours, all the creeks swelled rapidly.

READER'S REACTION: I had to read the sentence twice because at first I couldn't tell where one part ended and the next began.

EDITED Eight inches of rain fell in twenty-four hours**,** **and** all the creeks swelled rapidly.

When you provide *neither a punctuation mark nor a connecting word* to show where one main (independent) clause ends and the next begins, you create a **fused sentence** (often called a **run-on sentence**).

FUSED SENTENCE That night the river overflowed its banks and spread over the lowlands thousands of people were left homeless by the time the waters receded.

READER'S REACTION: When I first read that the river "spread over the lowlands thousands of people," I imagined a mass of people being pushed over the land.

EDITED That night the river overflowed its banks and spread over the lowlands**;** **as a result,** thousands of people were left homeless by the time the waters receded.

1 Look for sentences with more than one word group

As you edit, look for sentences containing more than one word group that could stand on its own as a sentence. (Consider marking such word groups in some way, such as drawing a line, in order to focus your attention on them.) Take note of those word groups that are joined by a comma alone (comma splice) or that are joined without any punctuation at all (fused sentence).

COMMA SPLICE In a typical Navajo family, the husband serves as trustee,/the mother and her children are the real owners of the family's property.

WRITER'S REACTION: When I drew a line to separate the two word groups that could stand alone, I noticed I had created a comma splice by joining them with only a comma.

FUSED The engineering and social work programs get the most public attention/the medical technology and marketing programs get the largest enrollments.

WRITER'S REACTION: Putting a line between the word groups that could be sentences on their own helped me see how the lack of any punctuation between them makes the sentence hard to read.

Pay attention to writing likely to contain comma splices or fused sentences. When you are drafting quickly, adding idea to idea and clause to clause, you may sometimes use commas to string word groups together, creating comma splices—or you may leave out punctuation entirely.

Pay attention to long sentences. Fused sentences can occur in sentences of any length, but as you edit, pay special attention to long sentences without internal punctuation. Check to see if they contain freestanding (main) clauses joined without punctuation. (Look at the commas in long sentences, too, in order to identify any that are creating comma splices.)

38a
cs/fs

STRATEGY

As you edit, ask, "How many statements are there in this sentence?" A fused sentence is not a single unit but two (or more) units whose relationship is not clearly signaled to readers. If a sentence appears to contain more than one statement, check for appropriate punctuation and connecting words.

FUSED SENTENCE — The scientists had trouble identifying the fossil skeleton it resembled both that of a bird and that of a lizard.

COMMENT: The sentence makes two statements: one about the troubles encountered by scientists and one about the nature of the skeleton.

EDITED — The scientists had trouble identifying the fossil skeleton **because** it resembled both that of a bird and that of a lizard.

2 Notice sentence patterns that may lead to comma splices and fused sentences

By joining sentences, you can emphasize their relationship. Some kinds of related sentences follow patterns that lead to more than their fair share of comma splices and fused sentences, however. Pay attention to the following patterns as you edit.

- **Sentences (main clauses) with the same subject**

COMMA SPLICE — **The ice cream cake** had begun to melt, **it** was dripping onto Grandmother's lace tablecloth.

EDITED — The ice cream cake had begun to melt, **and** it was dripping onto Grandmother's lace tablecloth.

- **One sentence (main clause) illustrated by another**

FUSED SENTENCE — Children with Down syndrome feel the same emotions as the rest of us they get sad, puzzled, and playful.

EDITED — Children with Down syndrome feel the same emotions as the rest of us; they get sad, puzzled, and playful.

- **Balanced sentences (main clauses) with contrasting ideas**

COMMA SPLICE The engineering and social work programs get the most public attention, the medical technology and marketing programs get the largest enrollments.

EDITED The engineering and social work programs get the most public attention**;** **nonetheless,** the medical technology and marketing programs get the largest enrollments.

SERIOUS ERROR

38a cs/fs

- **Sentences (main clauses) with related ideas**

FUSED SENTENCE Health costs are rising rapidly solutions to the problem are not clear.

EDITED Health costs are rising rapidly**;** **moreover,** solutions to the problem are not clear.

Exercise 1

A. First, use the strategies discussed in 38a to identify the comma splices in the following passage.

The subarctic region provides little variety in food, therefore, Eskimo diet includes large quantities of meat such as seal and caribou. The cold weather and the available materials determine dressing habits, a loose shirt with a hood, trousers, stockings, and mittens (often made of caribou skin and fur) are a common outfit for men, women, and children alike. Social affairs are important in Eskimo communities, favorite gatherings include carnivals, Christmas parties, and feasts of game brought in by hunters. Children in Eskimo communities begin school at the age of five or six, most quit by the time they are twelve in order to go to work. Boys usually go hunting with their fathers, girls learn to sew and cook.

Next, draw a double vertical line between each of the independent (main) clauses making up the following fused sentences.

EXAMPLE

Casinos used to operate legally in only a few states // they are now springing up all over the country as states make casino gambling legitimate.

1. The gaming industry is one of the fastest-growing industries in some areas it is a major employer.
2. Legalized gambling takes many forms bingo, lotteries, casinos, and video games are run under government supervision in many states.
3. State lotteries are popular they may also encourage people to gamble unwisely.

4. The economic and law enforcement objections to legalized gambling get the most public attention the moral and psychological objections may deserve the most attention.
5. Legalized gambling now goes beyond people in casinos betting on roulette or sports events it includes people playing bingo at a charity event or playing video poker in a family restaurant.

B. Working in a group, decide which, if any, of the sentences in the first passage in Exercise 1A follow sentence patterns likely to lead to comma splices or fused sentences, and identify the patterns.

38b Comma splices and fused sentences: Editing

Here are six strategies for correcting comma splices and fused sentences. As you revise, choose a strategy that brings your ideas into sharper perspective, creates emphasis, and highlights relationships.

1. Create separate sentences.
2. Join main clauses with a comma plus a coordinating conjunction (*and, but, or, for, nor, so*, or *yet*).
3. Join main clauses with a semicolon.
4. Join main clauses with a semicolon plus a conjunctive adverb or transitional expression (*however, moreover, for example, in contrast*, and similar words or phrases).
5. Subordinate one of the clauses.
6. Join main clauses with a colon.

1 Create separate sentences

When the ideas in main clauses are loosely related, you can generally express them best in separate sentences.

COMMA SPLICE AND FUSED SENTENCE: Costa Rica's political life has been relatively free of damaging conflict, the same cannot be said of its neighbors El Salvador and Nicaragua, in particular, have long histories of civil unrest.

EDITED: Costa Rica's political life has been relatively free of damaging conflict**.** **The** same cannot be said of its neighbors**.** **El Salvador** and Nicaragua, in particular, have long histories of civil unrest.

2 Join main clauses with a comma plus a coordinating conjunction

When main clauses convey ideas or information of approximately equal importance, consider linking the clauses with a comma plus a coordinating conjunction (*and, but, or, for, nor, so*, or *yet*) marking their relationship.

COMMA SPLICE The experienced teams use complicated strategies for offense and defense, the inexperienced teams concentrate on the basics.

EDITED The experienced teams use complicated strategies for offense and defense, **but** the inexperienced teams concentrate on the basics.

FUSED SENTENCE Schizophrenia is a mental illness its causes may be physical.

EDITED Schizophrenia is a mental illness, **yet** its causes may be physical.

Three or more closely related clauses can be punctuated as a series in order to emphasize their relationship. Be sure to include the conjunction before the last item.

We collected the specimens, we cleaned them with a mild detergent, **and** we measured them.

3 Join main clauses with a semicolon

You can use a semicolon to emphasize the similar importance of two main clauses.

COMMA SPLICE During flight an airplane tends to drift up or down, left or right because of air turbulence. An autopilot is a device that detects and corrects drift, the system senses changes in the aircraft's motion and reacts accordingly.

EDITED During flight an airplane tends to drift up or down, left or right because of air turbulence. An autopilot is a device that detects and corrects drift; the system senses changes in the aircraft's motion and reacts accordingly.

4 Join main clauses with a semicolon plus a conjunctive adverb or transitional expression

However, nonetheless, therefore, consequently, moreover, thus, and similar words (conjunctive adverbs) specify relationships between word groups. Transitional expressions such as *for example, in contrast,* and *in addition* have similar purposes. Use them following a semicolon.

FUSED SENTENCE Commercially raised animals such as chickens or beef cattle can reach marketable size within a matter of months or a year the American lobster must grow for an average of six to eight years before it reaches the proper size.

EDITED — Commercially raised animals such as chickens or beef cattle can reach marketable size within a matter of months or a year**;** **in contrast,** the American lobster must grow for an average of six to eight years before it reaches the proper size.

Words like *however, nonetheless*, and *thus* and expressions like *for example* and *on the other hand* can appear *within* a second main clause as well as at the beginning. Wherever they appear, the words must be set off with a comma(s) and the clauses themselves joined by a semicolon.

38b cs/fs

AT BEGINNING — The Great Lakes once supported a thriving fishing industry; **however,** in recent decades pollution has reduced the catch.

IN MIDDLE — The Great Lakes once supported a thriving fishing industry; in recent decades**, however,** pollution has reduced the catch.

AT END — The Great Lakes once supported a thriving fishing industry; in recent years pollution has reduced the catch, **however.**

5 Subordinate one of the clauses

Subordinators such as *although, while, when, because, since*, and *unless* and relative pronouns such as *who, which*, or *that* enable you to specify a wide range of relationships (see 44c).

COMMA SPLICE — Margaret Atwood is best known for her novels, her essays and poems are also worth reading.

EDITED — **Although** Margaret Atwood is best known for her novels, her essays and poems are also worth reading.

6 Join the clauses with a colon

When a clause summarizes, illustrates, or restates a preceding clause, you can join the two with a colon (see 49b).

FUSED SENTENCE — Foreign study calls for extensive language preparation vaccinations and a passport are not enough.

EDITED — Foreign study calls for extensive language preparation**:** vaccinations and a passport are not enough.

Exercise 2

A. Identify and edit in *two* ways each of the following comma splices and fused sentences. Use the methods of revision indicated in brackets after each sentence.

EXAMPLE

Children often fight among themselves, these conflicts pose many challenges for parents. [comma plus coordinating conjunction; semicolon]

Children often fight among themselves, and these conflicts pose many challenges for parents.

Children often fight among themselves; these conflicts pose many challenges for parents.

1. Some parents refuse to become involved in their children's squabbles, they fear the children will resent the interference. [subordination; semicolon]
2. Siblings have special reasons to fight competing for space and playthings or for attention from a parent can turn playmates into rivals. [colon; semicolon plus transitional phrase]
3. Sibling fights offer an opportunity for children to become sensitive to the feelings of others, the arguments pose dangers as well. [comma plus coordinating conjunction; semicolon plus conjunctive adverb]
4. Bickering is common and normal excessive fighting can be a sign of more serious trouble. [semicolon plus conjunctive adverb; separate sentences]
5. By adolescence, most children have worked out compatible relationships with their siblings, they may still occasionally argue. [subordination; comma plus coordinating conjunction]

B. Working with a group, edit each of the following sentences in two ways, using strategies discussed in 38b. You may need to make changes in wording or punctuation.

1. One group claims that cattle raising is hard on the environment another group argues that raising wheat and other cereal grains causes water pollution and destroys topsoil.
2. In Central Florida, cattle waste has polluted Lake Okeechobee runoff from fertilizer has greatly increased the growth of algae in the lake.
3. The waters of Long Island's south shore are also polluted the main culprit is lawn fertilizer.
4. In my state, pesticides from potato farming have polluted the groundwater pig and chicken farming have caused problems.
5. Our large population makes a massive farming industry necessary we are going to have to deal with the problems caused by large-scale farming and livestock raising.

CHAPTER 39
Pronoun Reference

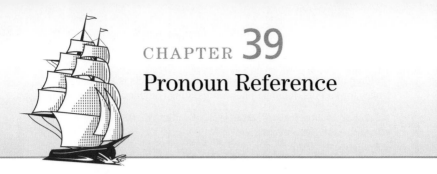

Words like *they, it, she, who,* and *which* (pronouns) help you make sentences less repetitive and easier to understand, while linking ideas.

> **Freud** made **the claim** that slips of the tongue reveal subconscious thoughts and desires, yet **he** offered no real evidence to support **it.**

For this linking process (called **pronoun reference**) to work, readers must recognize the word to which a pronoun refers, known as its **headword** (or **antecedent**). When the relationship is not clear, readers may be confused.

CONFUSING Much of my supposedly glamorous life with the circus consisted of leading the elephants from their cages and hosing **them** down.

READER'S REACTION: What got hosed down? the elephants? the cages? both?

By creating clear pronoun reference, however, you can tie sentences and ideas together and guide your readers.

CLEAR Much of my supposedly glamorous life with the circus consisted of hosing the **elephants** down after leading **them** from **their** cages.

39a Unclear pronoun reference: Recognizing and editing

As long as your readers can clearly identify the word or words acting as a single antecedent, pronoun reference will help you tie statements together.

> **Calvin Klein, Liz Claiborne,** and **Donna Karan** started out as clothing designers. **They** now head major corporations bearing their names.

1 Watch for pronouns with several possible antecedents

Look for passages containing a pronoun and two or more words or word groups to which it might *possibly* refer. If your readers cannot easily identify the appropriate antecedent, they will have trouble understanding the meaning.

AMBIGUOUS REFERENCE — Detaching the measuring probe from the glass cylinder is a delicate job because **it** breaks easily.

READER'S REACTION: Which is especially fragile, the probe or the cylinder?

STRATEGY

You can correct passages with **ambiguous reference** in two ways.

1. **Replace** the troublesome pronoun with a noun.

   Detaching the measuring probe from the glass cylinder is a delicate job because **the probe** breaks easily.

2. **Reword** the sentence.

   Because the measuring probe breaks easily, detaching it from the glass cylinder is a delicate job.

In addition, watch for pronouns that can refer to each of two or more subjects in earlier sentences.

AMBIGUOUS REFERENCE — Robespierre and Danton disagreed over the path the French Revolution should take. **He** was convinced that the Revolution was endangered by its internal enemies; **his opponent** believed the Revolution had been won.

EDITED (ADD NOUNS) — Robespierre and Danton disagreed over the path the French Revolution should take. **Robespierre** was convinced that the Revolution was endangered by its internal enemies; **his opponent** believed the Revolution had been won.

When you use *said* or *told* to report in a general way what someone has said (**indirect quotation**), you may sometimes create confusion.

AMBIGUOUS — When the project was completed, Jennifer's supervisor said **she** needed a few days off because she had been working so hard.

READER'S REACTION: Who needs the time off, Jennifer or her supervisor?

Edit this problem by (1) reporting the person's words exactly (**direct quotation**) or (2) rewriting with nouns rather than pronouns.

DIRECT QUOTATION When the project was completed, Jennifer's supervisor said, "**You** need a few days off because **you** have been working so hard."

REWRITTEN WITH NOUN When the project was completed, her supervisor said that **Jennifer** needed a few days off because **she** had been working so hard.

SERIOUS ERROR

2 Pay attention to pronouns widely separated from their antecedents

When you place a pronoun at a distance from its antecedent, your readers may have a hard time recognizing the connection—even though no other possible referent comes between them.

REMOTE REFERENCE
James Van Allen designed an instrument that the first American space satellite used to detect what are now known to be two doughnut-shaped rings of high-energy particles extending from between several hundred to fifty thousand kilometers above the earth. The belts were eventually named for **him.**

To edit for this problem, either bring the pronoun closer to its antecedent or rename the noun or pronoun to which it refers.

EDITED (RENAMED)
James Van Allen designed an instrument that the first American space satellite used to detect what are now known to be two doughnut-shaped rings of high-energy particles extending from between several hundred to fifty thousand kilometers above the earth. They were eventually named **the Van Allen belts after the man instrumental in their discovery.**

3 Pay attention to the location of *who, which,* and *that*

Keeping pronouns and antecedents close together is especially important for word groups beginning with *who*, *which*, and *that* (relative pronouns). Avoid confusion by placing the pronoun right after its antecedent.

CONFUSING As I lay on the carpet in my old bedroom, I noticed two stale pieces of bubble gum under **the dresser that I loved to chew as a boy.**

EDITED As I lay on the carpet in my old bedroom, I noticed under the dresser two stale pieces of **the bubble gum that I loved to chew as a boy.**

Exercise 1

A. Rewrite each of the following sentences to create clear pronoun reference.

EXAMPLE

Someone needs to pick up the weekend shipment ~~at the airport~~ that may arrive [at the airport] late Saturday night.

39a pr ref

1. Both Carlo and Andy agree that he will be responsible for getting the cartons of replacement parts from the air terminal.
2. The accountant has told his client that he will be answerable for any problems with billing.
3. Airfreight offers weekend shipment and is cheaper, which means that work doesn't have to stop on Monday morning while workers wait for delivery of the replacement parts.
4. The van used to pick up shipments is the old one the company's owner purchased right after her divorce which is covered with rust spots.
5. The sales projections used to order supplies are often inaccurate because the sales manager calculates them using a formula on a spreadsheet that is overly optimistic.

B. Working with a group of fellow students, compare the choices each of you made in editing the sentences in Exercise 1A.

4 Create clear reference chains

You can guide readers through a passage using a chain of pronouns to connect sentences. A **reference chain** begins with an antecedent stating the topic linked to pronouns (or nouns) later in the passage.

1. State the antecedent clearly in the opening sentence.
2. Link the antecedent to pronouns in sentences that follow.
3. Make sure other possible antecedents do not interrupt links in the chain.
4. Do not interrupt the chain and then try to pick it up after several sentences.
5. Call attention to the links by giving the pronouns prominent positions (usually the beginnings of sentences); vary their positions only slightly.

SERIOUS ERROR

UNCLEAR

Sand paintings were a remarkable form of Pueblo art from the Southwest and Southern California. An artist would sprinkle dried sand of different colors, ground flower petals, corn pollen, and similar materials onto the floor to create **them.** The sun, moon, and stars as well as animals and objects linked to the spirits were represented in the figures **they** contained. **Their** purpose was to encourage the spirits to send good fortune to humans.

Because the pronouns *them* and *they* are buried at the ends of sentences in the middle of the paragraph, readers can easily lose sight of the paragraph's topic, sand paintings.

EDITED TO CREATE A REFERENCE CHAIN

Sand paintings were a remarkable form of Pueblo art from the Southwest and Southern California. To create **them,** an artist would sprinkle dried sand of different colors, ground flower petals, corn pollen, and similar materials onto the floor. **They** contained figures representing the sun, moon, and stars as well as animals and objects linked to the spirits. **Their** purpose was to encourage the spirits to send good fortune to humans.

Exercise 2

A. Revise the following sentences so that they form a reference chain giving appropriate emphasis to information provided in the passage. You should emphasize some ideas and details more than others.

When it comes to reading material, Americans have some clear favorites. In terms of circulation, the top five newspapers in the country are *The Wall Street Journal*, *USA Today*, the *New York Daily News*, the *Los Angeles Times*, and the *New York Times*. Sales of softbound books far outnumber sales of hardbound books. Our favorite subject areas for books are medicine, history, fiction, sociology and economics, religion, and technology. The top three magazines in terms of revenue are *Time*, *Sports Illustrated*, and *People*. More people subscribe to *Modern Maturity* and the *AARP Bulletin* than to any other magazines, including *Reader's Digest*, which is number three on the subscription list. *1,001 Home Ideas* and *The Elks Magazine* have larger paid circulations than *Vogue*, *Rolling Stone*, and *Mademoiselle.*

B. Working with a group of writers, share your versions of the passage in Exercise 2A. Choose two versions that give the information different emphases. Identify the ways each writer has created a reference chain, and indicate which ideas and details have been highlighted and which have been moved to the background.

39b Nonspecific pronoun reference: Recognizing and editing

39b pr ref

If readers say they "get lost" reading your work or "can't quite figure out what you are saying," part of the problem may be pronoun reference that is not specific. **Specific pronoun reference** points out for readers the precise relationships among statements. When pronouns refer to antecedents that are implied rather than stated, however, or when pronouns refer too broadly to a preceding passage, readers become confused.

1 Use *it, which, this,* and *that* with care

It, which, this, and *that* are useful words but easy to misuse. Used carefully, the words can help you refer effectively to an entire idea, as does the writer of the following pair of sentences.

> Every few million years an extremely large asteroid collides with the earth. **This** has not happened in historic times, so we have no experience of the consequences of **that** event.
>
> —Robert Jastrow, *Journey to the Stars*

Such **broad pronoun reference** can help you sum up ideas in order to comment on them, as in the preceding example. On the other hand, **overly broad reference** can easily confuse readers by failing to make clear the *specific* antecedent of *it, which, that,* or *this.*

OVERLY BROAD REFERENCE
Redfish have been heavily harvested for years, but in the last decade they have been subjected to oil pollution and to the destruction of their mangrove swamp habitat by waterfront building. **That** has led to a recent and rapid decline in the redfish population.

READER'S REACTION: Does *that* refer to the destruction of habitat, to oil pollution, to overfishing, or to some combination?

Look for the words *it, which, this,* and *that.* See if you have provided a specific word or group of words to which the pronoun clearly refers. If not, edit by specifying, replacing, or rewording.

- **Specify.** Right after *this, that,* or another troublesome word, add a word or phrase stating the pronoun's referent.

EDITED (SPECIFIES)
Redfish have been heavily harvested for years, but in the last decade they have been subjected to oil pollution and to the destruction of their mangrove swamp habitat.

That **combination** has led to a recent and rapid decline in the redfish population.

EDITED (EXPLAINS) Redfish have been heavily harvested for years, but in the last decade they have been subjected to oil pollution and to the destruction of their mangrove swamp habitat. That **increasingly serious set of challenges** has led to a recent and rapid decline in the redfish population.

39b
pr ref

- **Replace.** Drop the pronoun; use a noun or noun phrase in its place.

VAGUE One test conducted by the Mars lander discovered some evidence of life on Mars, but the other uncovered no evidence whatsoever. This led many scientists to conclude that there is no life on the planet.

REPLACED One test conducted by the Mars lander discovered some evidence of life on Mars, but the other uncovered no evidence whatsoever. **The reliability of the second test** led many scientists to conclude that there is no life on the planet.

- **Reword.** Rewrite so that the pronoun is no longer needed.

REWORDED One test conducted by the Mars lander discovered some evidence of life on Mars, but the second and more reliable test uncovered no evidence whatsoever, leading many scientists to conclude there is no life on the planet.

2 Look for *it* used in more than one sense

You can employ *it* in many ways to convey your meaning.

REPLACING A NOUN
I threw the blender out after **it** broke for the third time.

WAY OF POSTPONING SUBJECT
It is the lack of sunshine in winter that often causes depression.

IDIOMATIC EXPRESSION
It is raining.

But you may confuse readers if you use *it* in more than one sense in a sentence or short passage.

CONFUSING When I was young, I always found **it** surprising that my father would come home from a hard day at his job and go out to the garden to work in **it,** even when **it** was raining.

EDITED When I was young, I was always surprised when my father came home from a hard day at his job and went out to work in the garden, even when **it** was raining.

3 Watch for antecedents that are implied rather than directly stated

Often, writers have an antecedent in mind but fail to communicate it to readers.

IMPLIED In the West, **they** often prefer Japanese cars; in the center of the country, **they** drive mostly Detroit-made autos; and in the Northeast and Southeast, **they** often choose European models.

READER'S REACTION: I am guessing that *they* means "people in general." But it could mean rich people, people under forty, or some other group.

By stating an antecedent directly, you eliminate both guessing and possible misunderstanding.

EDITED In the West, **people under forty** prefer Japanese cars; in the center of the country, they drive mostly Detroit-made autos; and in the Northeast and Southeast, they often choose European models.

***They* or *it* without an antecedent.** During conversation, listeners can usually figure out the meaning of *they* or *it*. Writing, especially academic writing, needs to provide precise and clear statements, so make sure your readers can identify an antecedent in the text itself.

IMPLIED In February, frost damaged most of the citrus groves in the state, but **it** has not been determined.

READER'S REACTION: I can't be sure what *it* is.

EDITED In February, frost damaged most of the citrus groves in the state, but **the extent of the loss** has not been determined.

***You* without an antecedent.** When you intend to address the reader directly ("you, the reader"), *you* is acceptable in most writing.

ACCEPTABLE In implementing the recommendations, **you** may find your staff resisting the report's suggestions. These statistics should help **you** convince them the new procedures are useful.

When *you* refers indefinitely to experiences, situations, and people in general, it often leads to confusing and wordy sentences.

MISLEADING In Brazil, you pay less for an alcohol-powered car than for a gasoline-powered one.

READER'S REACTION: Who is *you*? After all, I'm not likely to be buying a car in Brazil.

EDITED In Brazil, alcohol-powered cars cost less than gasoline-powered ones.

EDITED In Brazil, consumers pay less for an alcohol-powered car than for a gasoline-powered one.

Possessive as antecedent. Remember to pair possessive nouns with possessive pronouns: *Kristen's . . . hers.*

UNCLEAR The **company's** success with a well-known jazz fusion artist led **it** to contracts with other musicians.

EDITED The **company's** success with a well-known jazz fusion artist led to **its** contracts with other musicians.

When readers encounter the following pattern in academic writing, they will consider it inappropriate because the pronoun refers to the possessive form of a noun. (This pattern is more acceptable in informal writing.)

INAPPROPRIATE In William Faulkner's *The Sound and the Fury*, he presents the first part of the story from the point of view of a mentally disabled person.

William Faulkner, not *William Faulkner's* should be the antecedent of *he*.

EDITED In *The Sound and the Fury*, William Faulkner presents the first part of the story from the point of view of a mentally disabled person.

Modifier mistakenly treated as antecedent. A modifier (like *experimental*) may *suggest* an antecedent (like *experiment*) without directly stating it. If you mistakenly rely on an implied antecedent of this sort, you force readers to guess at your intentions.

CONFUSING A product's successful marketing may depend on how many demographic studies were conducted. As a result, people trained in it often get good jobs in major corporations.

READER'S REACTION: What field do the people get training in? *demographic*? That's not the name of a field.

EDITED A product's successful marketing may depend on how many demographic studies were conducted. As a result, people trained in **demography** often get good jobs in major corporations.

Antecedent implied by another word. If you make a pronoun refer to a word that is not actually in a sentence but merely implied by some other word, your sentence is likely to be clumsy or hard to understand.

CLUMSY Growing up in the Southwest, Alice dreamed of studying oceanography, though she had never seen **one.**

EDITED Growing up in the Southwest, Alice dreamed of studying oceanography, though she had never seen **an ocean.**

UNCLEAR Rosalind Franklin participated in the discovery of DNA's molecular structure, yet she seldom gets credit for **it.**

READER'S REACTION: For what should she receive credit: the discovery? the structure? her participation?

EDITED Rosalind Franklin participated in the discovery of DNA's molecular structure, yet she seldom gets credit for **her contributions.**

Exercise 3

A. Revise the following sentences to eliminate vague pronoun reference and provide specific antecedents.

EXAMPLE

The committee's report

~~In the committee's report it~~ ^ points out that students generally benefit from participating in a music program.

(*or* In its report, the committee points out . . .)

1. Many people study a musical instrument in high school though few students intend to become one.
2. At most secondary schools they offer a variety of music programs.
3. Last February, the town began investigating the quality of its high school band program, but it has not yet been completed.
4. In many regional high schools in the West, the band's large size mirrors the role it plays in the school's social life.
5. In the Northwest you quickly get used to marching and playing in the rain.

B. Compare your revised versions of the sentences in Exercise 3A with those of other writers. As a group, choose the best version of each sentence and state the reasons for your choice.

39c Matching *who, which,* and *that* to antecedents

Who refers to people or to animals with names. *Which* refers to animals and things (including ideas). *That* refers to animals, to things, and to anonymous people or people viewed collectively.

WHO Branford and Wynton Marsalis, **who** are brothers, rank among the top contemporary jazz musicians.

WHICH Quantum theory, **which** includes the work of Einstein, Planck, and Bohr, was the chief contribution of early twentieth-century physics.

THAT Rheumatoid arthritis is a disease **that** affects the entire body, and the patients **that** this clinic serves get extended therapy for the disease.

Some readers will expect you to use *which* or *who* with **nonrestrictive clauses** and *that, which,* or *who* with **restrictive clauses** (see 48c for discussion of these two kinds of modifiers). Other readers may pay little attention to the distinction. In formal writing, however, you should generally pay attention to the difference.

RESTRICTIVE (ESSENTIAL, LIMITS MEANING)
Drugs **that** limit tissue rejection are necessary for the survival of transplant recipients.

NONRESTRICTIVE (NONESSENTIAL)
The license, **which** will cost you thirty dollars, permits you to fish anywhere in the state for seven days.

Exercise 4

A. Revise the following sentences to correct inappropriate pronoun references. Indicate which sentences, if any, contain appropriate pronoun reference.

EXAMPLE

who
Many scholars ~~which~~ are interested in Buddhism have begun to study Tibetan religious practices.

1. The gathering was addressed by the Dalai Lama, a man which is one of the spiritual leaders of Tibetan Buddhism.
2. Tibetan Buddhism is characterized by large monastic organizations who practice yoga and other spiritual and intellectual rituals.
3. It is also true that this form of Buddhism retains features that it inherited from the folk religions of Tibet.

4. Up until the recent Chinese invasion, that occurred in 1959, Tibetan life was dominated by religious practices.
5. Although Lamaism has its greatest influence in Tibet and in countries who are nearby, such as Nepal and Mongolia, it is beginning to spread its influence in the West, including North America.

B. At a library, find a magazine with somewhat complicated, information-filled articles. Choose an article that interests you, and identify several paragraphs in which the author uses some of the pronoun reference patterns discussed in this chapter. Make copies of these paragraphs to share with a group of classmates. As a group, identify each of the pronoun reference strategies and decide why the author used each one.

CHAPTER 40

Misplaced, Dangling, and Disruptive Modifiers

The following sentences leave readers with questions.

MISPLACED MODIFIER When I was at the store I only looked at the DVD player.

READER'S REACTION: *Only* is confusing. Do you mean you just looked and didn't try the DVD player out? You didn't have time to look at other equipment? You were the only person who looked at the DVD player?

DANGLING MODIFIER Rushing to get to the post office before it closed, my bicycle nearly hit an unwary young woman.

READER'S REACTION: Who was rushing to the post office—I, the bicycle, or the young woman?

The relationship between a modifier and the word(s) it modifies needs to be clear to readers. If it is unclear, it will result in unanswered questions and confusion.

A **misplaced modifier** is not placed closely enough to the word(s) it is intended to modify and appears to modify something else. A **dangling modifier** appears in a sentence that contains no word or phrase to which the modifier can be reasonably linked.

A **disruptive modifier** separates closely connected elements such as a subject and a verb, making a sentence difficult to read and understand.

DISRUPTIVE MODIFIER The chief accountant, **even though her assistant first uncovered evidence that the company president had been embezzling funds,** assumed the responsibility of reporting the crime.

Careful editing can make clear the relationship between a modifier and the word(s) being modified.

EDITED When I was at the store I looked only **at the DVD player.**

EDITED Rushing to get to the post office before it closed, **I** nearly hit an unwary young woman while riding my bicycle.

EDITED Even though her assistant first uncovered evidence that the company president had been embezzling funds, **the chief accountant** assumed the responsibility of reporting the crime.

40a Misplaced modifiers: Recognizing and editing

Misplaced modifiers take many forms, yet you can readily develop your ability to recognize them by using these techniques.

RECOGNIZING MISPLACED MODIFIERS

- Look for a *word that fails to modify the word(s) you intend* and instead appears to modify some other word or group of words.
- Pay attention to a modifier's *location*.
- Pay attention to limiting modifiers such as *only, hardly,* and *exactly.*
- Pay attention to squinting modifiers that appear to modify *both* the word *before* and the word *after*.
- Pay attention to groups of words beginning with *who, which,* or *that.*

Editing misplaced modifiers involves either moving the modifier or rewriting the sentence.

- *Move* the modifier closer to the word(s) it should modify.

MISPLACED MODIFIER — After you have installed the fan, follow the directions for the wiring connections on the back of the cover plate.

READER'S REACTION: Are the wiring connections on the back of the cover plate?

MOVED — After you have installed the fan, follow the directions **on the back of the cover plate** for the wiring connections.

- *Rewrite* or *modify* a sentence so that the connection between modifier and words to be modified is clear.

MISPLACED MODIFIER — People who abuse alcohol frequently have other problems.

READER'S REACTION: Does *frequently* refer to the rate of alcohol abuse or the likelihood of problems?

REWRITTEN — People who abuse alcohol tend to have other problems as well.

1 Pay attention to a modifier's location

You can word a sentence many different ways to create emphasis and meaning. Don't be surprised if you position a modifier inappropriately on the first try. As you edit, check that modifiers come close enough to the word(s) they are intended to modify so that the relationship is clear.

DRAFT After a divorce, toddlers demand to be fed often instead of feeding themselves.

READER'S REACTION: **I think this could be read as a statement that *all* toddlers regress, not just that this happens *often*.**

EDITED After a divorce, toddlers **often** demand to be fed instead of feeding themselves.

Look at the end of sentences. During drafting, you may occasionally add new ideas and details to the end of a sentence, modifying a word you do not actually intend to modify.

MISPLACED MODIFIER The wife believes she sees a living figure behind the wallpaper in the story by Charlotte Perkins Gilman, which contributes to her sense of entrapment.

READER'S REACTION: **This sounds as if the story itself causes a feeling of entrapment.**

EDITED (MODIFIER MOVED) The wife **in the story by Charlotte Perkins Gilman** sees a living figure behind the wallpaper, which contributes to her sense of entrapment.

Check the order of modifying phrases. You may sometimes draft sentences that present modifying phrases in confusing order. (Pay special attention to prepositional and participial phrases—see 32c-1 and 32c-4.)

CONFUSING It was not a good idea to serve food to the guests standing around the room on flimsy paper plates.

READER'S REACTION: **Surely the guests were not standing on their plates!**

EDITED (MODIFIER MOVED) It was not a good idea to serve food **on flimsy paper plates** to the guests standing around the room.

Exercise 1

Identify and correct the misplaced modifiers (words or phrases) in the following sentences. You may decide either to move the modifier or to rewrite the entire sentence.

EXAMPLE

in pet store windows

Puppies^ spend a lot of time staring at people ~~in pet store windows~~.

1. They decided to buy the beagle puppy confused by the many exotic breeds of dogs.
2. This dog would replace the one killed by a truck running across a busy highway.

3. They forgot to buy a dog bed distracted by the crowd of people in the store.
4. Hurriedly, John sighed and began tearing up newspapers in order to begin house-training the puppy.
5. The parents could hear the children playing outside with the dog yelling and laughing.

ESL ADVICE: CHOOSING THE POSITION OF A MODIFIER

In some languages, the form of a modifier determines its meaning and its role in a sentence. In English, the position of a modifier can be the determining factor. The discussions in this chapter will help you choose a position for a modifier that enables you to communiicate your meaning precisely.

2 Pay attention to *only, simply, even,* and other limiting modifiers

You can alter the meaning of a sentence considerably by moving around words like *only, almost, hardly, just, scarcely, merely, simply, exactly,* and *even* (called **limiting modifiers**). As you edit by moving a modifier or rewriting, remember that a limiting modifier generally applies to the word that immediately follows, though not always.

> During difficult economic times, **only** charities for disabled children maintain their normal levels of support.
> They are the sole charities able to maintain normal levels.

> During difficult economic times, charities for disabled **only** children maintain their normal levels of support.
> The charities are for disabled children from families with one child.

> During difficult economic times, charities for disabled children **only** maintain their normal levels of support.
> They do not increase the levels of support.

3 Be alert for squinting modifiers

When readers encounter a modifier that appears to modify *both* the word(s) before and the word(s) after, they become understandably confused. To identify such **squinting modifiers,** read your sentences with attention not just to the meaning you intend but also to other possible readings that a reasonable reader might notice. To edit, ask yourself which word or word group you intend to modify, then move the modifier into a position that repairs the ambiguity.

SQUINTING MODIFIER People who enjoy listening to Aaron Copland's music **often claim** that he was the finest American composer of the twentieth century.

READER'S REACTION: Does this mean that they *listen often* to the music or that they *often claim* something about Copland?

EDITED People who enjoy **listening often** to Aaron Copland's music also tend to claim that he was the finest American composer of the twentieth century.

EDITED People who enjoy listening to Aaron Copland's music **will often** claim that he was the finest American composer of the twentieth century.

Exercise 2

A. Each of the following sentences contains either ambiguity caused by a squinting modifier or a limiting modifier that can be moved to different positions. Indicate the type of problem in each sentence.

EXAMPLE

Adults over age thirty who return to college frequently complete both undergraduate and advanced degree programs. *(squinting modifier)*

1. Adults entering college after working or raising a family officially are classified "nontraditional students" by many colleges.
2. "Nontrads" defer college entry often until after a major life event.
3. Following divorce or job loss, returning to college temporarily provides a boost to self-esteem.
4. Experts report that nontraditional students earn high grade point averages easily exceeding those of traditional students.
5. Nonetheless, failing to take into account the special needs of "nontrads" causes them to drop out frequently.

B. Working with a group of other writers, edit the sentences in Exercise 2A by rewriting each in two different ways.

4 Pay attention to clauses beginning with *who, which*, and *that,* or other subordinators

You should generally place a modifying clause beginning with *who*, *which*, or *that* right after the word(s) it is intended to modify. (See 32c-5.)

MISPLACED MODIFIER The environmental engineers discovered another tank behind the building that was leaking toxic wastes.

READER'S REACTION: I know a building can leak, but I'll bet the writer meant to identify the tank as the culprit.

EDITED Behind the building, the environmental engineers discovered another tank that was leaking toxic wastes.

Modifying clauses that begin with other subordinators, such as *when*, *although*, *because*, and *while* (see 32a-7), allow more flexibility in placement. Nonetheless, you still need to check that they convey your intended meaning.

SERIOUS ERROR

MISPLACED MODIFIER The company switched from the old health plan to one offered by a competing insurance company because premiums were rising.

EDITED **Because premiums were rising,** the company switched from the old health plan to one offered by a competing insurance company.

Exercise 3

A. Revise the following sentences to avoid any misplaced modifiers.

EXAMPLE

Sliding into second base, ~~my leg~~ I broke my leg.

1. The coach tossed out the practice balls to the players, wet and soft from yesterday's rain.
2. They worked on hitting and catching for fifteen minutes before the first game which was the only practice time they had.
3. The coach who was known as a strict disciplinarian of the championship Little League team invented a rigorous new set of conditioning exercises.
4. A proposal to follow the infield fly rule was defeated by the coach's committee which no one understood.
5. The coach is unable to present the award given in memory of Father Baker because he is sick.

B. Compare your edited versions of the sentences in Exercise 3A with those of other students. As a group, decide which versions you prefer and why you prefer them.

40b Dangling modifiers: Recognizing and editing

Pay attention to modifying words or phrases at the beginning of sentences. If the modifier does not mention the person, idea, or thing being modified, readers will expect you to name it immediately following as the subject of the main clause. If neither the modifier nor the subject of the main clause mentions clearly what you intend to modify, then the modifier is a **dangling modifier.** Often vague, illogical, or unintentionally humorous, dangling modifiers can needlessly distract readers or leave out important information.

DANGLING MODIFIER — Leaking in several places, the scouts abandoned their tents for the dry cabin.

EDITED — **Their tents leaking in several places,** the scouts decided to spend the night in the dry cabin.

EDITED — The scouts decided to spend the night in the dry cabin **because their tents were leaking in several places.**

Remember, even if you can find the word(s) to which a modifier should refer somewhere else in a sentence (in some position other than as the sentence's subject), the result will still be a dangling modifier.

DANGLING MODIFIER — Jumping into the water to save the drowning swimmer, the crowd cheered the lifeguard.

EDITED — Jumping into the water to save the drowning swimmer, **the lifeguard** was cheered by the crowd.

A modifier in the body of a sentence can dangle, too, when there is no word or phrase to which it can reasonably refer.

DANGLING MODIFIER — The emergency repairs were completed by noon, having become aware of the problem only at ten o'clock.

READER'S REACTION: **Who became aware of the problem?**

EDITED — The emergency repairs were completed by noon, **the telephone company** having become aware of the problem only at ten o'clock.

STRATEGY

To correct a dangling modifier, take *one* of the following steps.

1. **Add** a subject to the modifier.

DANGLING — While shopping for a birthday gift for my brother, the stuffed alligator caught my eye.

EDITED — While **I was** shopping for a birthday gift for my brother, the stuffed alligator caught my eye.

2. **Change** the subject of the main clause.

DANGLING Trying to decide where to hold the fundraiser, the new restaurant was attractive.

EDITED Trying to decide where to hold the fundraiser, **the committee** was attracted to the new restaurant.

3. **Rewrite** the entire sentence.

DANGLING After debating new regulations for months without a decision, the present standards were allowed to continue.

EDITED The commission debated new regulations for months without a decision, then allowed the present standards to continue.

Exercise 4

A. Rewrite each of the following sentences in the *two* ways indicated in brackets, in order to eliminate dangling modifiers.

EXAMPLE

Marion designed her research poorly.

Unable to meet with an advisor, ~~Marion's research was poorly designed.~~ [change subject of main clause; rewrite]

Because Marion was unable to meet with an advisor, she designed her research poorly.

1. Because of a failure to gather enough data, her study was incomplete. [rewrite; add subject to modifier]
2. Lacking the money to pay skilled interviewers, minimally trained volunteers were relied upon. [change subject of main clause; rewrite]
3. Many subjects were not asked appropriate questions because of poor training. [add subject to modifier; change subject of main clause]
4. Anxious and tired, the two-day attempt to write the research report was unsuccessful. [add subject to modifier; change subject of main clause]
5. After spending over twenty hours writing at the computer, the report was still not satisfactory. [rewrite; add subject to modifier]

B. Compare your edited versions of the sentences in Exercise 4A with those of another student, and decide which versions are best and why.

40c Disruptive modifiers: Recognizing and editing

Readers generally expect sentence elements like subjects and verbs to stand close to each other. The same is true for verbs and the sentence elements that follow them (objects or complements). Modifiers that come between such elements may be disruptive, making a sentence difficult to understand.

DISRUPTIVE MODIFIER — The researcher, **because he had not worked with chimpanzees before and was therefore unaware of their intelligence,** was surprised when they purposely undermined the experiment he was trying to conduct.

1 Pay attention to separated subjects and verbs

Some modifiers placed between subject and verb are disruptive; others are not. How can you recognize the difference?

- **Disruptive.** Modifiers providing information related to both the subject and the verb.
- **Not disruptive** (generally). Modifiers providing information related to the subject alone.

DISRUPTIVE — Work on the building (subject), **due to problems with the construction permits,** (modifier) was completed (verb) three months late.

NOT DISRUPTIVE — The electronics mall (subject) **that opened last month** (modifier) has drawn (verb) crowds of customers.

Move a potentially disruptive modifier from between subject and verb.

DISRUPTIVE MODIFIER — Contractors, **because house building is a boom-or-bust business,** should be ready to do home repairs when housing starts are down.

EDITED — **Because house building is a boom-or-bust business,** contractors should be ready to do home repairs when housing starts are down.

2 Pay attention to separations between verbs and objects (or complements)

Edit by moving the disruptive modifier.

CLUMSY Joanne began collecting, **with special attention to survey results,** data for her study of dating preferences.

EDITED **With special attention to survey results,** Joanne began collecting data for her study of dating preferences.

3 Be alert for split infinitives or verb phrases

Look for words that come between the parts of an infinitive (*to* plus a verb, as in *to run* or *to enjoy*), making it hard for readers to understand the relationship between the parts. Edit by moving the intervening words.

UNCLEAR The office designer tried **to** respectively **address** each of the workers' concerns.

EDITED The office designer tried **to address** each of the workers' concerns **respectively.**

Even when a **split infinitive** is easy to understand, you might consider revising it because some readers find split infinitives irritating. At times, however, a split infinitive is the clearest and most concise alternative.

Our goal is to more than halve our manufacturing errors.
The alternatives are more wordy and complicated—for example, "Our goal is a rate of manufacturing error less than half the present rate."

You will usually cause no difficulty for readers if you separate the parts of a verb phrase (helping verb plus main verb, as in *had been digging*) by adding one or more adverbs.

CLEAR The archaeologists had been **carefully** digging at the site for three years.

Longer word groups within a verb phrase may be disruptive, however.

DISRUPTIVE The archaeologists had been, **because of initial discoveries made during construction of a new house,** digging at the site for three years.

CLEAR **Because of initial discoveries made during construction of a new house,** archaeologists had been digging at the site for three years.

Exercise 5

A. Rewrite each of the following sentences to eliminate disruptive modifiers and to make the sentence easier to read and understand.

EXAMPLE

B
~~The architect,~~ because she was unfamiliar with eighteenth-century in-
the architect
terior design and furnishings, had to do some research before completing the project.

1. The overall design of a building and its interior decoration ought to thoughtfully and harmoniously work together.
2. Furniture design has at least for the past several centuries been greatly influenced by a handful of designers, including Hepplewhite, Chippendale, Sheraton, and, most recently, Eames.
3. Design in Colonial America, because of economic limitations and social customs, was generally simple and practical.
4. Americans had, by the early 1800s in what is now known as the Federalist period, developed more refined and expensive tastes.
5. Today, magazines like *Architectural Digest* and *House Beautiful* illustrate the tendency for styles in interior design to rapidly change and to add considerably to the cost of a home.

B. Working with a group of fellow writers, compare your revisions of the sentences in Exercise 5A. Decide which versions you prefer and why.

40d Using absolute phrases effectively

An **absolute phrase** consists of a noun or pronoun, a participle, and modifiers (for example, *the water level having risen* and *her view of market conditions changing almost daily*). It modifies an entire sentence rather than a specific word or group of words. Absolute phrases can add variety and flair to your writing; nonetheless, many people avoid them for fear of creating dangling modifiers. However, an absolute phrase provides its own noun or pronoun subject, so it does not dangle.

The water level having risen, people in the valley feared that the dam was about to burst.

The absolute phrase sets the scene for the rest of the sentence.

The stockbroker began pelting her clients with urgent and sometimes contradictory advice, **her view of market conditions changing almost daily.**

CHAPTER 41
Shifts

In the course of writing, you are likely to ask readers to shift their attention many times—from events in the past to plans for the future, for example, or from what you are saying to what other people have said. As long as such shifts are signaled clearly, your readers should have little trouble following them. Inconsistent and confusing shifts may cause readers to wonder about your meaning, however.

INCONSISTENT **I** am thinking of taking out a two-year certificate of deposit because **you** can get a high interest rate on it.

READER'S REACTION: **I don't think the writer means that *she* may buy the certificate of deposit because *someone else* can get a good interest rate.**

EDITED **I** am thinking of taking out a two-year certificate of deposit because **I** can get a high interest rate on it.

41a Person and number

Person refers to the ways you can use words like pronouns and nouns to shape the relationships among you, your readers, and your subject.

FIRST PERSON (*I, WE*)

- Use *I* to refer to yourself as the writer or as the subject of an essay.
- Use *we* when more than one person is author or subject.
- Use *we* for both yourself and your readers when discussing shared experiences or understandings.
- Use *we* in some academic fields such as the study of literature ("In this part of the poem we begin to see . . .") but not in others (for example, chemistry or engineering).

SECOND PERSON (*YOU*)

- Use *you* to refer directly to the reader.
- Do not use *you* in most kinds of academic and professional writing unless called for by the situation, as in a set of instructions.

THIRD PERSON (*HE, SHE, IT, THEY; ONE, SOMEONE, EACH,* AND OTHER INDEFINITE PRONOUNS)

- Use third person for the ideas, things, and people you are writing about.
- *People* and *person* are third person nouns, as are names of groups of things, ideas, and people (for example, *students, teachers, doctors*).

1 Pay attention to shifts in person

Look for shifts in person. In particular, watch for inconsistencies created by illogical shifts between **I** and **you** or between **you** and **he, she, it** (or a noun in the third person).

INCONSISTENT If a **person** is looking for an even higher interest rate, **you** might consider a corporate bond.

EDITED If **you** are looking for an even higher interest rate, **you** might consider a corporate bond.

2 Pay attention to shifts in number

Look for shifts in number, especially with words that identify groups or members of a group, such as *business executives* or *a student*, or with words like *person* or *people*. Remember: *person* is singular and *people* is plural. Check that pronouns and their antecedents agree in number (see 35c).

SHIFTED When **a business executive** is looking for a new job, **they** often consult a placement service.

READER'S REACTION: I think this writer had business executives in mind as a group, even though the sentence mentions only one *business executive*.

EDITED When **business executives** are looking for **new jobs, they** often consult a placement service.

SHIFTED If **a person** has money to invest, **they** should talk to a financial consultant.

EDITED If **people have** some money to invest, **they** should talk to a financial consultant.

READER'S REACTION: I know that *a person . . . he or she* would also be correct, but it seems more complicated than necessary.

Exercise 1

A. Rewrite the following sentences to make them consistent in person and number.

EXAMPLE

Each person has ~~their~~ a favorite fast-food restaurant.

1. A would-be restaurant owner often fails to carefully consider the competition they will face from other restaurants of all kinds, both fancy and informal.
2. Good franchise chains survey competition, tell potential owners how much money they will need to open the business, and help you with the many problems a restaurant owner faces.
3. Admittedly, running a doughnut shop or a pizza place gives one less prestige than you get from owning a gourmet restaurant.
4. I would still rather run a successful business than one where you lose money.
5. Not all franchise arrangements are good ones, so people should do some research before he or she decides to open a franchised restaurant.

B. Working with a group of fellow students, write a brief paragraph on a topic of general interest. Choose a topic about which the group members have some knowledge—for example, finding a good summer job or buying good clothing cheaply. Then rewrite the paragraph so it contains several nouns and pronouns that do not agree in person and number. Give a copy of the faulty paragraph to another group as a "quiz." Correct the paragraph they have created, in turn, for you.

41b Tense and mood

By changing verb **tense** within a sentence or group of sentences, you signal a change in time and the relationship of events (see 33a, 33c, and 33f). When you choose a particular verb **mood,** you indicate an aim or attitude (see 33g).

1 Pay attention to shifts in tense

As you edit, watch out for unnecessary, illogical shifts in verb tense that can mislead readers and contradict your meaning.

ILLOGICAL Paleontologists **discovered** nests and clutches of eggs that **indicate** how some dinosaurs **take care** of their young.

Indicate (present tense) is appropriate because the scientists interpret the evidence in the present. *Take care* (present tense) is inappropriate because the dinosaurs clearly acted in the past.

LOGICAL Paleontologists **discovered** nests and clutches of eggs that **indicate** how some dinosaurs **took care** of their young.

Watch especially for any narration of events in the past tense that shifts suddenly to the present tense.

TENSE SHIFT We **had been digging** at the site unsuccessfully for several weeks when suddenly Tonia **starts yelling,** "Eggs! I think I've found fossil eggs!"

EDITED We **had been digging** at the site unsuccessfully for several weeks when suddenly Tonia **started yelling,** "Eggs! I think I've found fossil eggs!"

2 Watch for tense shifts in indirect quotation

In an **indirect quotation** you *report* what someone has said, rather than quoting word for word as in **direct quotation.** Reserve the past tense for indirect quotations.

DIRECT A report says that in 2008, "The region will face increased environmental problems over the next ten years."

INDIRECT A report **says** that in 2008, the region **will** encounter an increase in the damage to the air, water, and land caused by pollution.

INCONSISTENT A report **said** that in 2008 the region **would** encounter an increase in the damage to the air, water, and land caused by pollution.

Use the present tense when you summarize or comment on a written work, film, television show, or similar source.

INCONSISTENT In the novel's opening, Ishmael **arrives** at New Bedford with the intention of shipping out on a whaler, which he soon **did.**

CONSISTENT In the novel's opening, Ishmael **arrives** at New Bedford with the intention of shipping out on a whaler, which he soon **does.**

3 Be alert for shifts in mood

Choose the *mood* of a verb according to your purpose: to make a command or request (**imperative mood**), to present a statement or question (**indicative mood**), or to offer a conditional or hypothetical statement (**subjunctive mood**). (See 33g.)

INCONSISTENT It is essential that our company **cut** (subjunctive) costs and **increases** (indicative) revenue.

EDITED It is essential that our company **cut** [subjunctive] costs and **increase** [subjunctive] revenue.

When you are giving directions, use the imperative consistently so your directions will be less wordy and easier to understand.

INCONSISTENT To reduce costs, **order** refilled cartridges for printers, and **you should** encourage employees to use email in place of paper memos.

CONSISTENT To reduce costs, **order** refilled cartridges for printers and **encourage** employees to use email in place of paper memos.

Exercise 2

A. Rewrite the following sentences to make them consistent in tense and mood.

EXAMPLE

I went to the video store last week, and after half an hour I still ~~can't~~ couldn't figure out which movies I ~~want~~ wanted.

1. The video store manager said that if I bought two DVDs I will get a third one free, and then he tells me about his favorite DVDs.
2. In the movie *Sacrifice for Glory*, set in World War II, a British Mosquito bomber crashes in the jungle, and only the copilot managed to survive the long walk through the jungle back to civilization.
3. The hot sun beat on the shoulders of the copilot as he wades through the waist-deep, crocodile-infested swamp.
4. In *The Phantom Menace*, Anakin is a child with the power of the Force, but later in the series he turned to the Dark Side as Darth Vader.
5. In *Ghoulish Lunch*, the main character was reaching into the refrigerator around the guacamole dip for the last piece of apple pie when suddenly a cockroach crawls out from under the crust.

B. In a newspaper or magazine, locate a brief review of a movie, performance, book, or recording. Make sure the review contains numerous shifts in tense and mood. Make a copy of the review to share with a group of fellow students. After looking over all the reviews brought in by the group, choose one with particularly complex shifts. As a group, identify each shift and describe its nature. Continue working through as many reviews as you can.

41c Voice

To recognize a verb in the **active voice,** see if the *doer* (or *agent*) of the action acts as the sentence's subject. To recognize a verb in the **passive voice,** see if the *goal* of the action acts as the sentence's subject. (See 33e.)

ACTIVE — The lava flow (subject; doer) **destroyed** (verb; action) twelve houses (object; goal).

PASSIVE — Twelve houses (subject; goal) **were destroyed** (verb; action) [by the lava flow] ([doer]).

Note that mentioning the doer is optional in the passive.

In general, stick to either active or passive voice within a sentence, and be alert as you edit for unwarranted shifts.

INCONSISTENT — Among the active volcanoes, Kilauea **erupts** (active) most frequently, and over 170 houses **have been destroyed** since 1983.

READER'S REACTION: **The first part of the sentence focuses on Kilauea, but the second part doesn't mention it, leading me to wonder if some of the other volcanoes share responsibility.**

EDITED — Among the active volcanoes, Kilauea has erupted most frequently in recent years, and **it has destroyed** over 170 houses since 1983.

Occasionally, you may need to shift between active and passive voice to highlight a sentence's subject or emphasize your meaning.

> Hawaii **was built** (passive) by volcanic activity, and the island still **has** (active) active volcanoes.
>
> The shift between passive and active keeps Hawaii as the sentence's focus.

When you write instructions, shifts between active and passive voice can make your directions hard to follow.

CONFUSING — **You can purchase** hiking clothes from an outdoor equipment store, and picks, specimen bags, and other rock-collecting equipment **may be obtained** from a geological supply Web site.

EDITED — **You can purchase** hiking clothes from an outdoor equipment store, and **you can obtain** picks, specimen bags, and other rock-collecting equipment from a geological supply Web site.

Exercise 3

A. Rewrite the following sentences to make them consistent in voice.

EXAMPLE

We enjoyed the expedition, ~~and much was~~ learned about fossils. [handwritten edit: "and" and "much" inserted]

1. In the morning we dug in the base of the ravine, and during the afternoon the walls were explored.
2. The team found fossils of trilobites, and other fossils were also found at the site.
3. Team members learned many things about the science of paleontology, and much was learned about the geological history of our area as well.
4. A chart helped in identifying fossilized animals, and we also learned useful identifying strategies from the lecture given by Bill Gonzales, the team leader.
5. After you fill out the application for next month's dig, the form should be given to Bill or sent to his office.

B. Working in a group, use the sentences in Exercise 3A as the basis for a brief narrative telling the story of the "dig." Add sentences to fill in the information needed to make the story believable and interesting. Make your narrative consistent in voice.

41d Direct and indirect quotation

In **direct quotation** you present a speaker's or writer's exact words, set off by quotation marks. Through **indirect quotation** you present the substance of what was said, but in your own words and without quotation marks. Try to avoid mixing direct and indirect quotation within sentences.

MIXED Writing about the Teenage Mutant Ninja Turtles, Phil Patton names cartoonists Peter Laird and Kevin Eastman as their creators and says, "They were born quietly in 1983, in the kitchen of a New England farmhouse."

EDITED Writing about the Teenage Mutant Ninja Turtles, Phil Patton says, "Cartoonists named Peter Laird and Kevin Eastman dreamed up the characters," who "were born quietly in 1983, in the kitchen of a New England farmhouse."

Be especially alert for sentences mixing indirect and direct quotations without quotation marks to indicate the difference.

CONFUSING

Before we set out on the hike, the guide told us to stay in line and you should obey all orders immediately.

EDITED TO INDIRECT QUOTATION

Before we set out on the hike, the guide told us to stay in line and to follow every order right away.

EDITED TO DIRECT QUOTATION

Before we set out on the hike, the guide told us, "You should stay in line and obey all orders immediately."

Exercise 4

A. Rewrite each of the following sentences twice. First use direct quotation consistently, then use indirect quotation consistently. (Feel free to invent direct quotations in order to complete the exercise. Be sure to change direct quotations into your own words when you present them as indirect quotations.)

EXAMPLE

The article began by saying, "People often fear bees" and that this fear is a result of ignorance.

The article began by saying, "People often fear bees, and this fear comes from ignorance."

The article began by saying that the widespread fear of bees is caused by ignorance.

1. I once heard a beekeeper claim that unless beekeeping becomes more popular as a hobby, "I believe that agriculture in this country may suffer."
2. At a meeting last night, the county agriculture commissioner argued that increased beekeeping would aid agriculture in our area and "We should be willing to provide beekeepers with financial support for their efforts."
3. Having eaten honey every day for sixty years, my grandfather says, "I may not look as good as I did when I was younger," but that he feels just as good.
4. My grandfather also says that he has stayed mentally alert because "I manage a large beekeeping and honey business."

5. My neighbor told me, if you are too busy to sell your honey at a roadside stand I should see if the supermarket in town would sell it for me.

B. Share your edited sentences from Exercise 4A with a group of classmates. Decide which versions of each sentence are best and why.

CHAPTER 42
Mixed and Incomplete Sentences

When someone you are talking with switches topics abruptly, you can ask for an explanation. When you are reading, however, you can't ask the author to explain a confusing topic shift that comes in the middle of a sentence.

SHIFTED TOPIC	One **skill** I envy is **a person** who can study despite noise and other distractions. Clearly, a *skill* is not a *person*.
EDITED	One **skill** I envy is **the ability** to study despite noise and other distractions.

Just as confusing are sentences that begin with one grammatical pattern then shift to another.

SHIFTED STRUCTURE	Because the new television show did poorly in the ratings **explains why** programming executives decided to move it to a slot between two hit shows.
EDITED	Because the new television show did poorly in the ratings, **programming executives** decided to move it to a slot between two hit shows.

Sentences with confusing shifts (called **mixed sentences**) mislead readers by undermining patterns they rely on as they read. An **incomplete sentence** that omits wording necessary to make a logical and consistent statement does the same. For example, if you start by writing "*X* is larger," you should be ready to complete the comparison: "*X* is larger *than Y*."

INCOMPLETE	When they are first introduced, electronic products are likely to cost three times as much. READER'S REACTION: Are the new products likely to cost more when they are first introduced than they will cost later? Or are they likely to cost more than products being sold now?
EDITED	When they are first introduced, electronic products are likely to cost three times as much **as the most expensive products currently available.**

(Fragments are incomplete sentences lacking grammatical completeness. See Chapter 37.)

42a Mixed sentences: Recognizing and editing

Mixed sentences shift topics or grammatical structures without warning and for no clear reason. They throw readers off the track and make illogical statements.

1 Recognizing topic shifts

Keep this basic sentence pattern in mind: The subject *announces a topic*, and the predicate comments on or renames *the same topic*.

subject | predicate
The Old PC Network publishes a newsletter about outdated computers.
topic | comment

subject | predicate
The Apple IIe is an out-of-date but still beloved computer.
topic | topic renamed

You create confusion if you mistakenly make each part of a sentence address a *different* subject. (The resulting problem is sometimes called a **topic shift** or **faulty predication.**)

SHIFTED TOPIC — The **presence** of ozone in smog is the **chemical** that causes eye irritation.

Presence is not a chemical, though that is what the sentence says.

EDITED — The **ozone** in smog is the **chemical** that causes eye irritation.

STRATEGY

To identify shifted topics, try asking the question "Who does what?" or "What is it?" If the answer is illogical, the sentence needs editing.

SHIFTED — In this factory, **flaws** in the product noticed by any worker **can stop** the assembly line with the flip of a switch.

Who does what? Certainly flaws can't stop the line or flip a switch.

EDITED — In this factory, **any worker** who notices flaws in the product **can stop** the assembly line with the flip of a switch.

SHIFTED	An **actuary** is the **process** of determining insurance risks and premiums. What is it? An actuary is a person, not a process.
EDITED	An **actuary** is a **person** who determines insurance risks and premiums.

2 Editing topic shifts

In general, you can eliminate problems with topic shifts by making sure the topic in both parts of a sentence, subject and predicate, is the same. You can also use some simple techniques to edit some common patterns of topic shifting.

Rename the subject. When you build a sentence around the verb *be* (*is, are, was, were*) you may choose to have the predicate rename the subject in order to create a definition. When you do, make sure the topics on each side of the verb are roughly equivalent.

SHIFTED TOPIC	**Irradiation** is **food** that is preserved by the use of radiation. READER'S RESPONSE: Irradiation is a process of preservation, not the food itself.
EDITED	**Irradiation** is a **process** that can be used to preserve food.

Cut *is when* or *is where*. The phrases *is when* and *is where* make it impossible to balance the topics in a definition built around the verb *is*. Cut them and rewrite to create balance and eliminate a shift in topic.

NOT BALANCED	**Blocking** is **when** a television network schedules a less popular program between two popular ones.
EDITED	**Blocking** is the **practice** of scheduling a less popular television program between two popular ones.

Omit *the reason . . . is because.* In conversation, the phrase *the reason . . . is because* causes little confusion. In writing, however, readers will recognize that it creates an illogical statement. Why? A phrase opening with *because* is a modifier that cannot logically rename the topic (subject) of the first part of a sentence.

NOT LOGICAL	One **reason** for research into alternative fuels **is because** of the need to reduce air pollution.
EDITED	One **reason** for research into alternative fuels is **the need** to reduce air pollution.

Rewriting a sentence to eliminate *the reason . . . is because* is an obvious editing strategy, yet this approach may occasionally prove to be surprisingly difficult. When it does, try either of the following techniques.

- Drop *the reason . . . is.*

INCORRECT **The reason** he took up figure skating **is because** he wanted something to do during the long winter.

EDITED He took up figure skating **because** he wanted something to do during the long winter.

- Change *because* to *that.*

EDITED **The reason** he took up figure skating **is that** he wanted something to do during the long winter.

Edit for intervening words. Watch for words and phrases coming between a subject and a verb. You may sometimes mistakenly treat these intervening words as the sentence's topic.

SHIFTED TOPIC Programming **decisions** by television executives generally keep in mind the need to gain audience share.

READER'S REACTION: I know that network executives can keep an audience in mind, but according to this sentence it is programming decisions that are thinking about the viewers.

EDITED **Television executives** making programming decisions generally **keep** in mind the need to gain audience share.

Exercise 1

A. Rewrite the following sentences to eliminate topic shifts.

EXAMPLE

Hides ~~that are~~ treated with tanning chemicals turn ~~them~~ into leather.

1. Tanning is when animal hide is made supple and resistant to decay.
2. The first step is when the hides are thoroughly scraped and cleaned.
3. The use of diluted acid is the substance that pickles the hides to prepare them for tanning.
4. The reason leather is supple is because it is lubricated with oil after pickling, then dried and impregnated with resins.
5. The final steps are when the leather is dyed and given a shiny surface through compression.

B. Compare your edited sentences for Exercise 1A with those produced by classmates. Decide which versions you prefer and why you prefer them.

3 Recognizing shifts in grammatical pattern

Occasionally, you begin a sentence with one grammatical pattern in mind and shift to another partway through. The result confuses readers.

SHIFTED PATTERNS

Because of the rebellious atmosphere generated by protests against the Vietnam war helps explain the often outrageous fashions of the time.

READER'S REACTION: When I encounter a word like *because*, I expect it to be attached to some main statement and to add to (modify) the core statement in a sentence. But that doesn't happen here. The sentence simply says the same thing twice: *because* and *helps explain*.

EDITED (MAIN CLAUSE ADDED)

Because of the rebellious atmosphere generated by protests against the Vietnam war, **fashions of the time became outrageous.**

EDITED (REWRITTEN)

The rebellious **atmosphere** generated by protests against the Vietnam war **helps explain** the often outrageous fashions of the time.

STRATEGY

Shifts in grammatical constructions are hard to identify because they take so many forms. These techniques may help.

- **Focus on the meaning** by checking that all the elements, especially subjects and predicates, stand in clear and reasonable relationships to each other. Read aloud sentences that seem potentially confusing.
- **Ask** "What is the topic of this sentence, and how does the rest of the sentence comment on or rename the topic?"
- **Check** that the sentence clearly indicates *who does what to whom.*

SHIFTED By wearing bell-bottom pants, love beads, long hair, and tie-dyed T-shirts was how many young people expressed their opposition to mainstream values.

READER'S REACTION: I can puzzle out the meaning, but this sentence really doesn't make clear who did what to whom.

EDITED By wearing bell-bottom pants, love beads, long hair, and tie-dyed T-shirts, many young people expressed their opposition to mainstream values.

4 Editing shifts in grammatical pattern

Sentences can mix grammatical patterns in many different ways. You may have to study a sentence with an inappropriate shift very carefully in order to decide how to edit it. The following four kinds of grammatical shifts are quite common.

- Sentences that begin twice
- Whole sentences used as subjects
- Adverb phrases used as subjects
- Subordinating clauses used as subjects

Sentences that begin twice. When you try to give more emphasis to a topic than the structure of a sentence allows, you may mistakenly start the sentence over again, treating the sentence's object as a second subject.

To edit sentences that begin twice, rewrite the sentence, moving most or all of the information in one of the two main clauses to a modifying phrase or clause.

MIXED PATTERNS — **The new procedures for testing cosmetics, we** designed them to avoid cruelty to laboratory animals.

READER'S REACTION: It seems that the writer starts this sentence again with the word *we*.

EDITED — **We** designed **the new procedures for testing cosmetics** to avoid cruelty to laboratory animals.

EDITED — **The new procedures for testing cosmetics** were designed to avoid cruelty to laboratory animals.

Whole sentences used as subjects. Another way you may mistakenly give emphasis to a topic is to put it in a complete sentence (main clause), which you then use incorrectly as the subject of another sentence.

Rewrite so that most (or all) of the information in one of the two main clauses appears instead in a modifying phrase or clause.

MIXED PATTERNS

In 1872, Claude Monet exhibited the painting *Impression, Sunrise* was the source of the term *Impressionism.*

EDITED (PHRASE CREATED)

The source of the term *Impressionism* was the painting *Impression, Sunrise,* **exhibited by Claude Monet in 1872.**

EDITED (CLAUSE CREATED)

In 1872, Claude Monet exhibited the painting *Impression, Sunrise,* **which was the source of the term *Impressionism.***

Adverb phrase used as subject. When readers encounter a phrase like "By designing the questionnaire carefully" at the beginning of a sentence, they expect it to be followed by the sentence's subject. They do not expect it to act as the subject.

To edit, either add a new subject or alter the form of the phrase so that it can act as a subject.

adverb phrase

MIXED PATTERNS **By designing the questionnaire carefully** made Valerie's psychology study a success.

EDITED By designing the questionnaire carefully, **Valerie made** her psychology study a success.

EDITED The **careful design** of the questionnaire **made** Valerie's psychology study a success.

Adverb clause used as subject. When readers encounter a word like *when, because, if, while, as,* or *despite* (subordinating conjunction) at the head of a clause beginning a sentence (adverb clause), they expect it to be followed by a main clause, not to act itself as the sentence's subject.

To edit, either add a subject or rewrite the sentence by dropping the subordinating word and turning the introductory clause into a subject.

MIXED

subordinate clause

Even if an audition gets off to a bad start does not mean giving up hope of getting the part.

EDITED (SUBJECT ADDED)

Even if an audition gets off to a bad start, **you** should not give up hope of getting the part.

EDITED (SUBORDINATING WORD DROPPED)

An audition that gets off to a bad start does not mean you should give up hope of getting the part.

Exercise 2

A. Rewrite the following sentences to eliminate shifts in grammatical pattern.

EXAMPLE

~~Many people used to die from infectious diseases was why~~ scientists worked hard to develop vaccinations. because many people used to die from infectious diseases.

(handwritten: S over "scientists")

1. By observing that farm workers who had cowpox were resistant to smallpox led Jenner to develop an inoculation for smallpox in the 1790s.
2. Paying attention to Jenner's methods was why Pasteur was able to develop vaccines for chicken pox, rabies, and human anthrax.

3. Vaccinations produce antibodies are the sources of immunity.
4. Because they are not effective against all infections means that vaccinations are not a perfect solution for diseases.
5. Making sure your vaccinations are up to date, you need to do this during your regular medical checkup.

B. In a group, compare your edited sentences for Exercise 2A with those produced by other writers. Identify those edited versions you consider correct, consistent, and clear.

42b Incomplete sentences: Recognizing and editing

Sentences that fail to complete an expected logical pattern, such as a comparison, or that leave out words necessary to meaning or logic are called **incomplete sentences.** They make readers do extra, unnecessary work. (Sentences missing a *grammatical* element are fragments; see Chapter 37.)

1 Recognizing and avoiding incomplete or illogical comparisons

When readers encounter a comparison, they expect to learn something about the relationship, for example that *X* is *greater/lesser* than *Y*. You will confuse readers if you leave out one element (*X* is *larger*) or if the things you try to compare are not logically comparable.

Recognize missing elements and supply them. Check that you have included both of the items being compared. Omitting one creates an **incomplete comparison.** To edit, supply the missing element.

INCOMPLETE The picture quality of the DVDs is much better.

READER'S REACTION: The picture quality is better than what? Than the quality on DVDs used to be? Than the quality was on analog (VHS) tapes?

EDITED The picture quality of the DVDs is much better than **it was on VHS tapes.**

Look also for places where you have omitted a word or words necessary to complete a comparison or make it clear, and then supply them.

AMBIGUOUS The most experienced members of the maintenance staff respect the new supervisor more highly than their fellow workers.

READER'S REACTION: Do the experienced staff members respect the supervisor more than they respect their fellow workers, or do they respect the supervisor more than their fellow workers do?

CLEAR The most experienced members of the maintenance staff respect the new supervisor more highly **than do** their fellow workers.

CLEAR The most experienced members of the maintenance staff respect the new supervisor more highly **than they respect** their fellow workers.

Occasionally, you can omit part of the wording of a comparison when the meaning is clear without it or can be easily inferred.

42b inc

CLEAR Most customers like dealing with a bank teller better than [dealing with] a machine.

The second *dealing with* can be left out because the sentence has only one possible meaning.

Watch for illogical comparisons (especially within and between groups). As you review comparisons, ask, "Can these things be reasonably compared?" If a comparison seems to be illogical, consider using either of these strategies: (1) fill in the missing words or (2) use the possessive.

ILLOGICAL

Even a small hamburger's fat content is higher than a skinless chicken breast.

READER'S REACTION: The writer probably wants to compare the fat content of two foods, but the sentence actually compares one *kind* of food (chicken breast) to the *fat content* of the other.

EDITED (WORDS PROVIDED)

The fat content of even a small hamburger is higher than **that of** a skinless chicken breast.

EDITED (POSSESSIVE USED)

Even a small **hamburger's** fat content is higher than a skinless chicken **breast's**.

Groups pose special problems for comparisons. When you are comparing items belonging to the *same group*, you need to distinguish each item (for example, field hockey) from other members of the class to which it belongs (all *other* team sports). Otherwise, your comparison will be illogical.

The word *other* serves to keep the two things separate by marking off the group as a whole from one of its members.

Field hockey has a higher percentage of women players than does any **other** team sport.

Therefore, if you leave out the word *other* when comparing members of a group or class, your comparison will be illogical.

ILLOGICAL At times, more cargo was loaded onto ships docked at New Orleans than at **any** city in North America.

READER'S REACTION: **Do you mean that New Orleans is not a city in North America?**

EDITED At times, more cargo was loaded onto ships docked at New Orleans than at **any other** city in North America.

For *different groups*, however, a comparison using the word *other* is inappropriate and illogical.

ILLOGICAL Though he wrote in the 1800s, Dickens painted as vivid a picture of oppressive government and society as **any other** author writing today.

READER'S REACTION: **Do you mean that Dickens is still writing even though he is dead?**

EDITED Though he wrote in the 1800s, Dickens painted as vivid a picture of oppressive government and society as **any** author writing today.

2 Recognizing appropriate and inappropriate omissions

Leaving out repeated words or phrases can often make sentences easier to read, yet careless omissions have the opposite effect.

Repeated words and phrases. Look for sentences containing repeated words and phrases. So long as omitting these repetitions does not undermine meaning or confuse readers, you should consider cutting them to create **elliptical constructions** that make writing concise and effective.

LEFT IN Some presidents spend much time mastering the facts before making a major decision; others spend little **time mastering the facts before making a major decision.**

OMITTED BUT CLEAR Some presidents spend much time mastering the facts before making a major decision; **others spend little.**

You can also frequently eliminate the word *that* from sentences where it introduces a noun clause after a verb: "Artists know [that] there is a difference between oil and acrylic paints."

Careless omissions. Beware of careless omissions (of articles, prepositions, pronouns, or parts of verbs) whenever you are writing hurriedly or are focusing on the information and ideas rather than on the details of your writing. Careful editing (including reading passages aloud) is normally the best way to identify such omissions.

INCOMPLETE A corporation issues common stock a way raising money.

EDITED A corporation issues common stock **as** a way **of** raising money.

Exercise 3

A. Rewrite the following sentences to eliminate any incomplete or illogical constructions.

EXAMPLE

Both Shannon and Bill like tennis more than any ^other game.

1. His tennis serve has more speed and accuracy than Bill.
2. He also has better sense of where an opponent is going hit ball.
3. Bill's commitment to tennis is greater than his family.
4. He has more fun playing tennis.
5. Like many exercise-addicted people, Bill would be exercising than eating, and he would rather be playing tennis than doing anything else.

B. In a small group, compare the effectiveness of your edited sentences in Exercise 3A with those of your fellow writers. Make sure the members of your group agree on what is incomplete or illogical in the original version of each sentence.

CHAPTER 43 Parallelism

Parallelism is the expression of similar or related ideas in similar grammatical form, as in the following sentence.

I furnished my first apartment

with **purchases** | **from department stores,**
items | **from the want ads,**
and **gifts** | **from my relatives.**

Parallelism enables you to present ideas concisely while highlighting their relationships.

Parallelism can also offer pleasure and surprise. You can use it to create intriguing sentence rhythms while highlighting unexpected images and contrasts.

> According to **how** and **when** you said it, zydeco meant either **the kind of music itself,** or **the kind of two-step touch-dancing that you did at parties to the music.** In theory, this meant that you could **zydeco** to **zydeco** at the **zydeco.**
>
> —SUSAN ORLEAN, *Saturday Night*

43a Building parallelism

Readers generally find a sentence with parallel elements easy to read and understand. They also appreciate the touch of style parallelism can bring even to everyday sentences.

In deciding which elements to make parallel and where to place them, you should consider each sentence's message as well as the emphasis you wish to create within an entire passage. In the following selection, the poet Nikki Giovanni uses parallel structures to point out similarities between people who often see themselves as different from one another.

> The true joy, perhaps, of being a Black American is that we really have no home. **Europeans bought** us; but the **Africans sold.** If we are to be human we must forgive **both . . . or neither.** It has become acceptable, in the last decade or so, for intellectuals to concede

> Black Americans **did not come here** out of our own volition; yet, I submit that just as **slavery took away our choice, so also did** the overcrowded, disease-ridden cities of Europe; **so also did** religious persecution; **so also did** the abject and all but unspeakable Inquisition of the Spanish; **so also did** starvation in Italy; **so also did** the black, rotten potatoes lying in the fields of Ireland. **No one came** to the New World in a cruise ship. **They all came** because they had to.
>
> —Nikki Giovanni, "Pioneers: A View of Home"

43b Problems with parallelism: Recognizing and editing

Once you begin a parallel pattern in your writing, you need to complete it. Incomplete or **faulty parallelism** disappoints readers' expectations and may make sentences confusing and hard to read. The following common writing strategies will help you to employ parallelism.

- **Series**
- **Paired elements,** including those created by words such as *and, or, either . . . or,* and *neither . . . nor,* as well as comparisons and contrasts
- **Lists**

To create parallelism with words, phrases, or clauses, you need to make sure all the elements employ the same grammatical form. To recognize lack of parallelism, look for shifts in grammatical form.

FAULTY PARALLELISM	Consider swimming if you are looking for exercise that **aids** cardiovascular fitness, **overall** muscle strength, and probably **will not cause** injuries.
PARALLEL	Consider swimming if you are looking for exercise that **aids** cardiovascular fitness, **develops** overall muscle strength, and **causes** few injuries.

1 Check for parallelism in a series

When you place items in a series, check that they are parallel in grammatical form. A series without this consistency can seem clumsy and distracting.

To check for parallelism in a series, first identify a series: . . . *x, y, and z* (the series may have more than three elements). Then mentally isolate each element and check that each takes the same grammatical form.

NOT PARALLEL	patient, tactful, and **to display tolerance**
PARALLEL	patient, tactful, and **tolerant**

Remember, the elements in a series can be words, phrases, clauses—even a series of separate sentences.

To edit, put the elements in similar grammatical form. You don't have to create word-for-word parallels. Sentence elements that differ somewhat in length and wording can still be parallel as long as they have the same structure.

WORDS (NOT PARALLEL)	To get along with their parents, teenagers need to be patient, tactful, and **to display tolerance.**
WORDS (PARALLEL)	To get along with their parents, teenagers need to be patient, tactful, and **tolerant.**
PHRASES (NOT PARALLEL)	The singer Jim Morrison is remembered for his innovative style, his flamboyant performances, and **for behavior that was self-destructive.**
PHRASES (PARALLEL)	The singer Jim Morrison is remembered for his innovative style, his flamboyant performances, and **his self-destructive behavior.**
CLAUSES (NOT PARALLEL)	In assembling the research team, we looked for engineers whose work was innovative, **with broad interests, and who had boundless energy.**
CLAUSES (PARALLEL)	In assembling the research team, we looked for engineers whose work was innovative, **whose interests were broad, and whose energy was boundless.**

The final position in a series often receives the greatest emphasis from writers and the most attention from readers. You can create sentences with a strong cumulative effect, directing attention to the final element.

> When VG Industries moved, the town was left with abandoned buildings, unused rail lines, and **thousands of unemployed workers.**

2 Decide which words to repeat

In creating parallelism, make sure you repeat all words necessary to the meaning of a sentence, including all the words called for by grammatical structures or idiomatic expressions. You need not repeat a lead-in word, however, if it is the same for all elements in a series.

> Mosquitoes can breed in puddles, ~~in~~ ponds, and in swimming pools.

If the lead-in words differ, you must include them.

> You need to **chop** the cilantro, **grind** the coconut, and **grate** the nutmeg.

43b
//

STRATEGY

As you edit, pause when you encounter a series. Read it carefully with the structure of the full sentence in mind so you can decide what words are necessary to the meaning.

INCOMPLETE	The main character from the novel *Tarzan of the Apes* has appeared on television, films, and comic books. READER'S REACTION: **Do you really mean to say he appeared *on* films and *on* comic books?**
EDITED	The main character from the novel *Tarzan of the Apes* has appeared *on* television, *in* films, and *in* comic books.

Exercise 1

A. Underline the parallel structures in each of the following sentences.

1. We've told you about the bombs, the fires, the smashed houses, and the courage of the people.

   —EDWARD R. MURROW, "From London, September 22, 1940"

2. She looked at a man because she liked the way the hair was tucked behind his ears, or she liked the question-mark line of a long torso curving at the shoulder and straight at the hip.

   —MAXINE HONG KINGSTON, "No Name Woman"

3. But far below, in the warren of passages on the starboard side forward, in the forward holds and boiler rooms, men could see that the *Titanic*'s hurt was mortal.

   —HANSON W. BALDWIN, "R.M.S. *Titanic*"

4. In that context three groups of wounded soldiers are identified: those whose survival depends on their receiving immediate treatment; those who need medical attention but will survive even if they do not get it immediately; and those who are hurt so badly they would not survive even with medical attention.

   —RUTH MACKLIN, *Mortal Choices*

5. For in each American marriage there is a special code, developed from the individual pasts of the two partners, put together out of the accidents of honeymoon and parents-in-law, finally beaten into a language that each understands imperfectly.

   —MARGARET MEAD, *Male and Female*

B. Working in a group, rewrite the following sentences to correct faulty parallelism and create appropriate emphasis. Include all necessary words. If a sentence can be rewritten in several ways, choose the version the group considers most effective.

1. What kind of job would be appropriate for a person who enjoys sailboarding, skiing, and to skydive?
2. The college's career counselor suggested that Rosalie write out her personal goals, read some materials on choosing a profession, or that she might take a career test.
3. Optimism, stamina, and being a good thinker are three traits of a good sales representative.
4. If you wish to choose a career at which you can succeed, you might start by making a list of the things you like to do, anything you are very good at, and also jobs or experiences you always try to avoid.
5. You can locate possible jobs in newspaper ads, friends, and employment agencies.

---

3 Pay attention to parallelism with paired sentence elements

When you are creating paired sentence elements to emphasize similarities and heighten contrasts, you will call attention to the relationship if you use parallelism—and readers will expect you to present the paired elements in parallel form.

And, but, or, for, nor, so,* and *yet. Take notice of sentence elements you have joined with *and, but, or, for, nor, so,* and *yet* (**coordinating conjunctions**). In general, present the words, phrases, or clauses in parallel form, to direct your readers' attention to the relationship of the elements and make the sentence easier to read.

WORDS NOT PARALLEL

A well-trained scientist learns to keep a detailed lab notebook and make the entries accurately.

PARALLEL

A well-trained scientist learns to keep a **detailed and accurate** lab notebook.

PHRASES NOT PARALLEL

First-year chemistry courses are supposed to teach students how to take notes on an experiment and the ways of writing a lab report.

PARALLEL

First-year chemistry courses are supposed to teach students **how to take notes on an experiment** and **how to write a lab report.**

CLAUSES NOT PARALLEL

Because she is interested in science and organizing complex information intrigues her, Lynn has decided to become a technical writer.

PARALLEL

Because she is interested in science and intrigued by organizing complex information, Lynn has decided to become a technical writer.

Both . . . and, not only . . . but also, either . . . or, neither . . . nor,* and *whether . . . or. When you wish to call special attention to a relationship or a contrast, you may choose to employ pairs of connectors such as *both . . . and, not only . . . but also, either . . . or, neither . . . nor,* or *whether . . . or* (**correlative conjunctions**). If you use these connectors, check to make sure you also use parallel forms for the elements you are joining.

Our dilemma is clear: **either** we must reduce manufacturing costs **or** we must file for bankruptcy.

The items you link with correlative conjunctions should be clearly related in meaning and similar in grammatical form. If the elements following the first and second connectors do not match, the sentence may be hard to follow or unclear in meaning.

AMBIGUOUS

Leon Blum's election represented a significant change in French politics and society because he was not only the first Socialist premier but also the first Jew.

PRECISE (PARALLELISM ADDED)

Leon Blum's election represented a significant change in French politics and society because he was not only the **first Socialist premier but also the first Jewish premier.**

Comparison and contrast. Be alert for places in your writing where you are comparing or contrasting items, and use parallel forms to help call attention to them.

DRAFT — This new ingredient will reduce the calories in our frozen yogurt, and the yogurt will have more taste.

EDITED — This new ingredient in our frozen yogurt **will reduce the calories** and **improve the taste.**

When you use *who(m), which,* or *that* (relative pronouns) to begin two parallel clauses, check that you use the same word to begin both. If you do not, the clauses will lack parallelism because they will not have the same grammatical form.

LACKS PARALLELISM The sailor embarking on hazardous voyages and who wore one earring of his lover's matched pair believed he would always be reunited with her.

PARALLEL The sailor **who** embarked on hazardous voyages and **who** wore one earring of his lover's matched pair believed he would always be reunited with her.

Exercise 2

A. Rewrite the following sentences to eliminate faulty parallelism.

EXAMPLE

In choosing a career, you should plan carefully and ~~also~~ *do* some research *.* ~~is needed.~~

1. Anthony could not decide whether he wanted to be a lawyer or if investment banking was a more promising career.
2. His friends thought Anthony's career plans were not suited to his abilities and his interests didn't fit the plans either.
3. After thinking about his goals, Anthony realized that the two things he wanted most from a career were stability and an income that was reasonable.
4. The counselor suggested that he might consider either working for the federal government or a job with a large, stable corporation.
5. Anthony had been reading about corporations in financial trouble and which had been laying off employees, so he decided to look carefully at government jobs.

B. Working with a group of fellow students, gather a number of pamphlets offering advice. Campus offices, libraries, clinics, banks, and similar places usually provide pamphlets on all kinds of subjects, from health care and home safety to job hunting. Choose one of the pamphlets, identify those places where parallelism is used effectively with paired sentence elements, and edit to correct any faulty parallelism. Enhance the parallelism when appropriate in order to highlight ideas and their relationships.

43c Creating parallelism beyond the sentence

As you write and revise, you can create parallelism beyond the sentence level to organize clusters of sentences and even paragraphs. Parallelism of this sort can clarify complicated information or highlight the overall pattern of an argument or explanation.

1 Creating parallel sentence clusters

By adding parallelism to groups of sentences, you call attention to **sentence clusters,** groups of sentences that develop related ideas or information. The parallel elements can link related items or guide readers through an explanation or argument.

One way to draw readers' attention to a sentence cluster is through parallel sentence openers, as in the following passage, which also uses parallel elements to reinforce the writer's opening point about conflicting values.

> Each of us probably belongs to several organizations whose values are in conflict. **You may belong to** a religious organization that **endorses restraint** in alcohol use or **in** relationships between the sexes while at the same time **you belong to** a social group whose activities seem to endorse a contrasting set of values. **You may belong to** a sports team **that endorses** conflict and winning and a club **that promotes** understanding among people and conflict resolution. **You may belong to** a political club whose platform contradicts the policies of your professional organization.

2 Creating parallel paragraphs

By creating paragraphs that are parallel in structure and wording, you can reinforce the overall pattern of a report or essay and alert readers to your line of argument or explanation. The parallel element can be as simple and unobtrusive as parallel opening phrases for a series of paragraphs.

> **One reason for acting** on this recommendation is that the flooding gets worse every spring. . . .
>
> **A second reason for action** is that the city currently has a budget surplus that could be spent on drainage improvement. . . .
>
> **A third, and most important, reason for taking immediate steps** is that the health and safety of city residents is endangered by the floods.

Exercise 3

A. Underline all examples of parallelism in the following passage.

> Large computers have some essential attributes of an intelligent brain: they have large memories, and they have gates whose connections can be modified by experience. However, the thinking of these computers tends to be narrow. The richness of human thought depends to a considerable degree on the enormous number of wires, or nerve fibers, coming into each gate in the human brain. A gate in a computer has two, or three, or at most four wires entering on one side,

and one wire coming out the other side. In the human brain, a gate may have as many as 100,000 wires entering it. Each wire comes from another gate or nerve cell. This means that every gate in the human brain is connected to as many as 100,000 other gates in other parts of the brain. During the process of thinking, innumerable gates open and close throughout the brain. When one of these gates "decides" to open, the decision is the result of a complicated assessment involving inputs from thousands of other gates. This circumstance explains much of the difference between human thinking and computer thinking.

—Robert Jastrow, "Brains and Computers"

B. Working in a group, decide what each example of parallelism in Exercise 3A contributes to the effectiveness of the individual sentence or the entire passage. Note any differences of opinion, and discuss whether these differences reveal alternative ways of viewing the meaning or purpose of the passage.

43d Parallelism in lists

Lists can summarize key points, instructions, or stages in a process. To avoid confusing readers, make sure the elements in lists are as nearly parallel as possible.

UNEDITED (CONFUSING)

The early 1960s were characterized by the following social phenomena.

1. A growing civil rights movement
2. Kennedy pursued a strongly anticommunist foreign policy.
3. An emphasis on youth in culture and politics
4. Taste in music and the visual arts was changing.
5. Government support for scientific research increased greatly.

EDITED (CLEAR)

The early 1960s were characterized by the following social phenomena.

1. **A growing** civil rights movement
2. **A strongly** anticommunist foreign policy (encouraged by President Kennedy)
3. **A youthful** emphasis in culture and politics
4. **A changing** taste in music and the visual arts
5. **A marked** increase in government support for scientific research

If you present every item in a list in a different grammatical form, readers must shift expectations often and will find it difficult to concentrate on the differences and similarities between the items. Parallelism makes it easy for readers to pay attention to the ideas and information in the list, and it encourages readers to compare the items covered in the list.

Exercise 4

A. Arrange the following materials into a list whose elements maintain parallel form.

The awards for arts and entertainment for 1985 offer an interesting picture of American culture in the middle of the decade.

Academy Award: *Out of Africa* (Best Picture); William Hurt, *Kiss of the Spider Woman* (Best Actor); Geraldine Page, *The Trip to Bountiful* (Best Actress); Don Ameche, *Cocoon* (Best Supporting Actor); Anjelica Huston, *Prizzi's Honor* (Best Supporting Actress).

The Emmy Awards went to *The Golden Girls* (Outstanding Comedy Series), *Cagney & Lacey* (Outstanding Drama Series), William Daniels and Sharon Gless (Outstanding Lead Actor/Actress in a Drama Series), and Michael J. Fox and Betty White (Outstanding Lead Actor/Actress in a Comedy Series).

Tony Awards for Broadway Theater. Best Play: *As Is* by William Hoffman. Best Musical: *Big River* by Roger Miller.

MTV Video Music Awards. Best Video: Don Henley, "The Boys of Summer." Best Male Video: Bruce Springsteen, "I'm on Fire." Best Female Video: Tina Turner, "What's Love Got to Do with It?" Best Group Video: USA for Africa, "We Are the World."

B. Compare your list for Exercise 4A with the lists of several other students. Note any differences in the ways your lists are organized.

CHAPTER 44
Coordination and Subordination

You are asked to revise the following passage, which is filled with short, choppy sentences that fail to emphasize the connections among ideas.

> California's farmers ship fresh lettuce, avocados, and other produce to supermarkets. They never send fresh olives. Fresh olives contain a substance that makes them bitter. They are very unpleasant tasting. Farmers soak fresh olives in a solution that removes oleuropein, the bitter-tasting substance. They make sure just enough is left behind to produce the tangy "olive" taste.

You might decide to **coordinate** the sentences, linking them in ways that show how the sentences are related while giving equal emphasis to each statement. (Resources for **coordination:** words like *and* and *but*; words like *however*; and punctuation marks like the semicolon.)

> COORDINATED
>
> California's farmers ship fresh lettuce, avocados, and other produce to supermarkets, **but** they never send fresh olives. Fresh olives contain a substance that makes them bitter, **so** they are very unpleasant tasting. Farmers soak fresh olives in a solution that removes oleuropein, the bitter-tasting substance; **however,** they make sure just enough is left behind to produce the tangy "olive" taste.

Or you might try specifying the relationships and relative importance of ideas by using **subordination:** making some of the sentences modify others by employing subordinating words (such as *because*, *although*, and *since*) and attaching the subordinated sentences to the others.

> SUBORDINATED
>
> California's farmers ship fresh lettuce, avocados, and other produce to supermarkets, **though** they never send fresh olives. **Because** fresh olives contain a substance that makes them bitter, they are very unpleasant tasting. **When** farmers soak fresh olives in a solution that removes oleuropein, the bitter-tasting substance, they make sure just enough is left behind to produce the tangy "olive" taste.

44a Creating coordination

When you want to link words or groups of words, the techniques of coordination enable you to give equal weight to the different elements.

WORDS	trims **and** shapes
CLUSTERS OF WORDS	in the shallow water, near the islands, **or** in the middle of the main channel
MAIN CLAUSES	The winter freeze prevents boats from sailing; **however,** the residents are still able to fish through holes in the ice.

To recognize coordination, look for the words and punctuation marks used to create it (listed below).

CREATING COORDINATION

JOINING WORDS AND CLUSTERS OF WORDS (PHRASES)

1. **Use *and, but, or, nor,* or *yet* (coordinating conjunctions).**

   cut **and** hemmed   smooth **or** textured   intrigued **yet** suspicious

2. **Use pairs like *either . . . or, neither . . . nor,* and *not only . . . but also.***

   either music therapy **or** pet therapy
   not only a nursing care plan **but also** a psychological treatment program

JOINING MAIN (INDEPENDENT) CLAUSES

1. **Use *and, but, or, for, nor, so,* or *yet* (coordinating conjunctions) preceded by a comma.**

   The students observed the responses of shoppers to long lines, **and** they interviewed people waiting in line. Most people in the study were irritated by the checkout lines, **yet** a considerable minority enjoyed the wait.

2. **Use a semicolon** (see 49a).

   The wait provoked physical reactions in some people**;** they fidgeted, grimaced, and stared at the ceiling.

3. **Use words like *however, moreover, nonetheless, thus,* and *consequently* (conjunctive adverbs) preceded by a semicolon.**

   Store managers can take simple steps to speed up checkout lines**; however,** they seldom pay much attention to the problem.

4. **Use a colon** (see 49b).

   Tabloids and magazines in racks by the checkout counters serve a useful purpose**:** they give customers something to read while waiting.

By creating effective coordination you can specify and highlight relationships among ideas.

RELATIONSHIPS NOT SPECIFIED	Cats have no fear of water. They do not like getting their fur wet and matted. Cats like to feel clean and well groomed.
CLEAR RELATIONSHIPS	Cats have no fear of water, **but** they do not like getting their fur wet and matted**;** they like to feel clean and well groomed.
CHOPPY	Cats are able to swim. A hungry cat will gladly jump into water to catch a fish. House cats are usually well fed. They are not willing to get soaked for an extra bite to eat.
SMOOTHER	Cats are able to swim, **and** a hungry cat will gladly jump into water to catch a fish. House cats are usually well fed**; therefore,** they are not willing to get soaked for an extra bite to eat.

Exercise 1

A. Combine each of the following pairs of sentences into a single sentence using coordination. Make sure you use each of the strategies listed in the preceding table for joining main clauses, and do not use any particular conjunction (such as *and* or *however*) more than once. Rewrite the sentences if necessary to avoid awkwardness or confusion.

EXAMPLE

Winter weather makes outdoor exercise difficult. Winter has its own forms of exercise.

1. Ice skating can be enjoyable. It is also physically demanding.
2. Recreational skaters need to be in good shape physically. They should exercise to increase their fitness.
3. Skaters who are not in good shape get tired quickly. These skaters are also more likely to pull a muscle or fall.
4. To get in shape for skating, try a program of regular exercise for at least several weeks. Pay special attention to exercises focusing on knees and ankles.
5. Other areas to exercise are hip and leg muscles. Exercises aimed at each muscle group are best.

B. Working with a group of fellow writers, prepare a brief paragraph (five to seven sentences) offering advice on some subject: fitness, cooking, appliance repair, gardening, or the like. Make sure all but one or two of the sentences are compound sentences containing at least two main clauses. Connect the clauses using a variety of strategies for coordination, making sure they are appropriate for your subject and purpose.

44b Problems with coordination: Recognizing and editing

Problems with coordination generally take two forms: excessive use of a strategy, and illogical linking of ideas and sentence elements.

1 Look for excessive coordination

If you use words like *and*, *so*, or *but* merely to string together groups of loosely related sentences, you risk boring readers with excessive coordination.

These approaches may help you spot excessive coordination.

- **Look for sentences that make several statements (usually three or more) and also contain several connectives like *and* or *so*.** When you have identified a sentence like this, read it carefully to see if it contains too much coordination and too many conjunctions so that the result is a "stringy," hard-to-follow sentence.

STRINGY — The toy was designed in Japan, **but** its parts are made in Brazil, **and** it is assembled in Mexico, **so** what is the country of origin for tax purposes?

EDITED — The toy was designed in Japan, **but** its parts are made in Brazil, **and** it is assembled in Mexico. What is the country of origin for tax purposes?

- **Pay attention to *when* and *how* you wrote a passage**. Often during drafting when you write quickly, the result is excessive coordination. Remember which passages you drafted quickly, look them over, and edit to complete the job of specifying relationships.

DRAFT — Ripe fruit spoils quickly, **and** the fresh grapefruit for sale in supermarkets is picked before it matures to avoid spoilage, **and** it can taste bitter, **but** the grapefruit in cans is picked later, **and** it tastes sweeter.

EDITED — Ripe fruit spoils quickly. The fresh grapefruit for sale in supermarkets is picked before it matures, **so** it can taste bitter. The grapefruit in cans is picked later; **consequently,** it tastes sweeter.

Try arranging three or more coordinated main clauses as a series in order to create emphasis. Place a conjunction only before the last clause.

The lawyers drew up the contract, the accountants checked it for accuracy, **and** we signed it in good faith.

2 Check for illogical coordination

Check that clauses you have linked (or plan to link) by coordination are related closely enough to deserve equal emphasis within a single sentence. To identify loosely related elements (illogical coordination), take on a reader's perspective and question the relationship, perhaps asking "How are these two elements linked?" To correct illogical coordination, try adding information to a sentence or changing its emphasis.

ILLOGICAL Antarctica is a remote continent with an unusually harsh climate, and scientists are now studying its unique animal life in detail.

READER'S REACTION: **What do the remoteness and the climate have to do with either the scientists or the animals?**

EDITED Antarctica's remoteness and harsh climate **have made exploration difficult,** and scientists are **only now beginning detailed study** of its unique animal life.

Exercise 2

A. Revise the following passage to eliminate excessive or illogical coordination. Use coordination to combine short sentences when appropriate, to clarify relationships, and to eliminate choppiness.

Working for someone else can be unrewarding, and this is also true of working for a large corporation, so many people in their early thirties decide to open businesses of their own, but they often do not have very original ideas, so they open restaurants or small retail stores, for these are the small businesses they are most familiar with, yet they are also the ones that are most likely to fail, and they face the most competition. Franchises are small businesses, and they often provide help to people getting into business on their own for the first time. Enterprising people can own the local office of an armored car service, or they can run a regional unit of a nationwide cleaning service for commercial buildings, and they can open hardware stores with the name of a national chain over the front door.

B. Work with a group of fellow writers to produce two versions of the passage in Exercise 2A, each with a different emphasis.

44c Creating subordination

When you want to help readers understand links between ideas or information, you can use **subordination,** in which one clause modifies or comments on another. In using subordination, you create a sentence with unequal elements: one presenting the central idea (main clause), and one or more beginning with a subordinating word like *because*, *although*, *who*, *which*, or *that* and acting as a modifier (subordinate clause).

MAIN CLAUSES Most first-time home buyers are people in their late twenties or early thirties. They have tired of paying rent.

SUBORDINATED Most first-time home buyers are people in their late twenties or early thirties **who** have tired of paying rent.

READER'S REACTION: **The information after *who* adds to the statement presented at the beginning of the sentence and ties the ideas together.**

SUBORDINATED Sales of single-family homes are up, **although** sales of the more expensive homes are still depressed.

READER'S REACTION: **The clause following *although* not only qualifies the meaning of the opening statement—it also takes the sentence in a new direction.**

SUBORDINATED I am saving money **so that** I can make a down payment **as soon as** I find an affordable house.

READER'S REACTION: **I like the way the subordinate clauses add more and more focus to the opening statement.**

CREATING AND RECOGNIZING SUBORDINATION

MEANING	SUBORDINATOR
Time	before, while, until, since, once, whenever, whereupon, after, when
Cause	because, since
Result	in order that, so that, that
Concession or Contrast	although, though, even though, as if, while, as though
Place	where, wherever
Condition	if, whether, provided, unless, rather than
Comparison	as
Identification	that, which, who

Subordination enables you to put some information in the foreground (in a main clause) and other information in the background (in a subordinate clause). Thus, you help readers distinguish primary statements from secondary statements, new ideas from old, and important information from background.

SECONDARY/PRIMARY **Although** energy costs are increasing, costs for raw materials have dropped more than 30 percent in the past six months.

OLD/NEW **Though** most biographies of Charles Dickens have spent much time examining his childhood, his latest biographer pays little attention to this period.

IMPORTANT/BACKGROUND Raymond Carver, **who** died in 1990, created a stir with his "minimalist" short stories.

You can also vary the meaning of a sentence considerably, depending on the subordinating conjunction you choose.

As soon as the copier is repaired, we can print the newsletter.

Whenever the copier is repaired, we can print the newsletter.

If the copier is repaired, we can print the newsletter.

Short, choppy sentences can become smooth and graceful through careful subordination.

CHOPPY For each moon, the Seneca have a name. They draw the name from the season. The sixth moon is called the Strawberry Moon. Strawberries ripen in June.

EDITED For each moon, the Seneca have a name **that** they draw from the season. **Because** strawberries ripen in June, the sixth moon is called the Strawberry Moon.

LOCATING AND PUNCTUATING SUBORDINATION

SUBORDINATING CONJUNCTIONS

You can use a subordinating conjunction such as *although, because*, or *since* (see list on page 712) to create a subordinate clause at the beginning or end of a sentence (see 5h).

PUNCTUATION WITH SUBORDINATING CONJUNCTIONS

Use a comma *after* an introductory clause that begins with a subordinating conjunction. At the end of a sentence, do not use commas if the clause is *essential* to the meaning of the main clause (restrictive); use commas if the clause is *not essential* (nonrestrictive). (See 48c.)

BEGINNING **Once she understood the problem**, she had no trouble solving it.

END Radar tracking of flights began **after several commercial airliners collided in midair.**
Essential

(continued)

LOCATING AND PUNCTUATING SUBORDINATION *(continued)*

END	The present air traffic control system works reasonably well, **although accidents still occur.** Nonessential

RELATIVE PRONOUNS

You can use a relative pronoun (*who, which, that*) to create a relative clause (also called an adjective clause) at the end or in the middle of a sentence. (See 5h.)

PUNCTUATION WITH RELATIVE PRONOUNS

If the modifying clause contains information that is *not essential* to the meaning of the main clause, the modifying clause is nonrestrictive and you should set it off with commas. If the information is *essential*, the modifying clause is restrictive and you should not set it off with commas. (See 48c.)

RESTRICTIVE	The anthropologists discovered the site of a building **that early settlers used as a meetinghouse.**
NONRESTRICTIVE	At one end of the site they found remains of a smaller building, **which may have been a storage shed.**
RESTRICTIVE	The people **who organized the project** work for the Public Archaeology Lab.
NONRESTRICTIVE	A graduate student, **who was leading a dig nearby,** first discovered signs of the meetinghouse.

Exercise 3

A. Use subordination to combine each of the following pairs of sentences. Choose appropriate subordinating conjunctions, and create emphasis consistent with each sentence's meaning. Rewrite the clauses if necessary to produce effective sentences.

EXAMPLE

Newspapers often contain reports of car accidents. ~~The accidents~~ [that] were preventable.

1. The comedian Sam Kinison died in a car crash. A pickup truck swerved across the road and hit his car.
2. Kinison was not wearing a seat belt. A seat belt might have saved his life.
3. Driving quickly off the road to the right is one thing you can do. This will help you avoid collisions.
4. Drive a large car. Big, heavy cars and passenger vans are much safer in crashes.

5. Buying a car with front and side impact air bags is an excellent way to reduce your chances of getting injured or dying. These cars cost more money.

B. Working with a group of fellow students, conduct research to determine which subordinating words are widely used. Each person should locate a five- to seven-paragraph segment of a magazine article and make a list of all the subordinating words in it, tallying the number of times each word appears. (The list on page 712 and a dictionary can help you decide whether a word is a subordinator.) Pool your lists, and determine how often the various words appear in the articles you sampled.

44d Problems with subordination: Recognizing and editing

Problems with subordination generally take two forms: illogical or unclear relationships and excessive use of a strategy.

1 Be alert for illogical or unclear relationships

Sometimes the subordinating word you choose may not specify a clear relationship, or it may indicate an illogical relationship.

To identify **illogical subordination,** state a sentence's meaning to yourself with slightly different wording.

- Ask yourself, "Does the original sentence convey my intended meaning?"
- Ask yourself, "Can the subordinating word I have chosen convey several conflicting meanings?"

If your answer to either question reveals a problem, revise the sentence by choosing a more appropriate subordinator (see page 712 for alternatives).

UNCLEAR EMPHASIS — Since she taught junior high school, Jean developed keen insight into the behavior of adolescents.

READER'S REACTION: I'm not sure whether *since* here means she developed insights *because* she was a teacher or *after* she quit teaching.

EDITED — **Because** she taught junior high school, Jean developed keen insight into the behavior of adolescents.

To identify **unclear subordination,** look for sentences that confuse readers by presenting key ideas in a subordinate clause and secondary ideas in a main clause. Correct this problem by making sure the main clause presents the most important statement.

FAULTY His training and equipment were inferior, although Jim was still able to set a record throwing the discus.
READER'S REACTION: **Isn't Jim's achievement the key point?**

EDITED **Although** his training and equipment were inferior, Jim was still able to set a record throwing the discus.

2 Be careful with troublesome subordinators: *as/while, and which, but that, and who*

When you use the following coordinators, be especially careful, for they can be especially ambiguous, confusing, or irritating to readers: (1) *as* and *while*, and (2) *and which*, *but that*, and *and who*.

As, while. You can use *as* correctly to create a comparison, or you can use it to indicate simultaneous events.

COMPARISON Our team spent **as much** time on the accounting problems **as** the other, less successful teams did.

TIME They began interviewing students **as** the semester was coming to an end.

However, if you use *as* to point out a cause-effect relationship, you will probably confuse some readers. Other readers may consider this use of *as* unacceptable in standard written English.

AMBIGUOUS **As** the level of achievement in the two classes differed, the researchers looked for possible explanations.
READER'S REACTION: **Does *as* mean "while" or "because"?**

EDITED **Because** the level of achievement in the two classes differed, the researchers looked for possible explanations.

Do not use *as* in place of *whether* or *that*. This substitution is always incorrect in writing and formal speaking.

INCORRECT They were not sure **as** the differences in achievement were significant.

EDITED They were not sure **whether** the differences in achievement were significant.

EDITED They were not sure **that** the differences in achievement were significant.

While can indicate events occurring at the same time. *While* can also signal a concession.

SIMULTANEOUS EVENTS I can get some work done at home **while** the children are at school.

CONCESSION **While** she thinks the speech was a success, I am not so sure.

Nonetheless, *while* may be ambiguous in some sentences, and you may need to replace it with another, clearer subordinator.

UNCLEAR **While** they interviewed the students, the researchers did not come to any conclusions.

READER'S REACTION: Does *while* mean "although" or "when"?

EDITED **When** they interviewed the students, the researchers did not come to any conclusions.

EDITED **Although** they interviewed the students, the researchers did not come to any conclusions.

In addition, *while* is never an acceptable replacement for *but* or *and.*

INCORRECT One researcher claimed that teachers in the morning classes were more effective than those in the afternoon, **while** the other researcher disagreed.

CORRECT One researcher claimed that teachers in the morning classes were more effective than those in the afternoon, **but** the other researcher disagreed.

And which, but that, and who. When you place *and* or *but* at the head of a clause along with *which, that,* or *who,* you add an unnecessary word and confuse readers by obscuring the relationship signaled by the subordinator.

CONFUSING The research was funded by the Champlin Foundation, **and which** also published the results.

EDITED The research was funded by the Champlin Foundation, **which** also published the results.

3 Watch out for excessive subordination

When you use too much subordination in a sentence, you create a pattern of relationships so intricate that it overloads readers. To clear up such confusion, separate your ideas into several sentences, and rewrite them so that readers can grasp your meaning more easily.

CONFUSING The election for mayor will be interesting this year because the incumbent has decided to run as an independent while his former challenger for the Democratic nomination has decided to accept the party's endorsement even though the Republican nominee is her former campaign manager who switched parties last week.

EDITED The election for mayor will be interesting this year. The incumbent has decided to run as an independent. His former challenger for the Democratic nomination has decided to accept the party's endorsement even though she will have to run against her former campaign manager. He switched parties last week to become the Republican nominee.

Exercise 4

A. Revise the following sentences to eliminate illogical, incorrect, or excessive subordination. When appropriate, combine short sentences through subordination to clarify relationships and eliminate choppiness.

EXAMPLE

Because

~~Since~~ my doctor said I need more exercise, I have been looking for a sport I might enjoy.

1. As I am not particularly good at athletics, I want a sport that is not too demanding. I would also like a sport that is fun.
2. I enjoy volleyball, although it is a serious, highly competitive sport demanding considerable quickness and coordination. Volleyball is not the answer.
3. Since I have played tennis, I have thought about trying out for the tennis team. I have also thought about talking this idea over with the tennis coach.
4. Some of my friends think I should give the tennis team a try while others think the idea is laughable.
5. What I really want to find is a brand-new sports program, and which will give me the training I need, because I don't have the experience necessary to succeed in established sports, although I am willing to work as hard as I need to in order to bring my skills up to a competitive level.

B. Working in a group, share your revisions of the sentences in Exercise 4A. Decide which versions of the sentences are the best, and be ready to explain and defend your choices.

ESL ADVICE: GRAMMATICAL STRUCTURES FOR COORDINATION AND SUBORDINATION

Use both coordinators and subordinators, but avoid mixing the two.

MIXED **Although** frogs can live on land and in water, **but** they need to breathe oxygen.

This sentence has a subordinator, *although*, and a coordinator, *but*. Use one pattern, but not both.

CONSISTENT COORDINATION Frogs can live on land and in water [main clause], **but** they need to breathe oxygen [main clause].

CONSISTENT SUBORDINATION **Although** frogs can live on land and in water [subordinate clause], they need to breathe oxygen [main clause].

PART 9

Words and Style

CHAPTER 45
Wordiness

As a writer, you can state similar thoughts in different ways to achieve different effects on your readers. For example, you can create a short, direct sentence.

Incentive pay improves work quality.

You can then add words to anticipate readers' reactions and guide the effect of the sentence.

Incentive pay **often encourages** work **of higher** quality.

Or you can bury the message with unnecessary language that clogs the meaning and frustrates or bewilders your reader.

> **There is evidence that the use of** pay **as an** incentive **can be a contributing or causative factor** in the improvement **of the** quality **of** work.

Wordy writing includes words not necessary to the meaning or desired effect of a passage. Of course, even the best writing often starts out wordy. While drafting, you may pay more attention to exploring ideas than to writing concisely. Most rough drafts contain sentences that need pruning.

Avoiding **wordiness** does not always mean using the fewest words possible. It means including all the words appropriate for your meaning, purpose, and audience, but no more. Defining every medical term in an article on a rare skin disorder might seem wordy to specialists in the field but be appropriate for general readers. Other aspects of wordiness are more universal, such as redundancy or overblown vocabulary. To make sure your final drafts are concise, you need to learn how to edit for wordiness.

45a Common types of wordiness

Redundancy can creep into your writing when you use everyday phrases and patterns of expression. Their familiarity disguises their wordiness.

1 Eliminate empty words and phrases

Empty phrases like *at this point in time, totally overcome, due to the fact that,* and *each and every* add length but little meaning. Cut them.

WORDY **At this particular juncture**, the fire damage **makes it incumbent** upon us to decide whether **or not** to rebuild the old plant.

READER'S REACTION: What exactly is a "particular juncture"? What does "incumbent upon" mean? Doesn't deciding "whether" imply "or not"?

CUT The fire damage **now** forces us to decide whether to rebuild the old plant.

Reduce redundant pairs. English is rich in pairs (and larger groups) of synonyms and near-synonyms. Because they say the same thing twice, **redundant pairs** are always candidates for editing.

above and beyond	free and clear	questions and problems
aid and abet	full and complete	ready and willing
any and all	kith and kin	various and sundry
around and about	one and only	way, shape, or form
each and every	part and parcel	will and testament

WORDY To encourage innovation, the manager spoke with **each and every individual** team assigned to the project. Team One made a complex task manageable by dividing it into **bits and pieces.**

CUT To encourage innovation, the manager spoke with **each** team assigned to the project. Team One made a complex task manageable by dividing it into **pieces.**

REPHRASED To encourage innovation, the manager spoke with **each** team assigned to the project. Team One made a complex task manageable by **splitting it up.**

Shorten wordy phrases. You can shrink many familiar phrases to just one or two words. The shorter versions are easier to read and more effective.

WORDY Carbon 14 can be used to date a site only **in the event that** organic material has survived. **In a situation in which** rocks need dating, potassium-argon testing is appropriate.

CUT Carbon 14 can be used to date a site only **if** organic material has survived. **When** rocks need dating, potassium-argon testing is appropriate.

COMMON WORDY PHRASES

PHRASE	REPLACEMENT
as a result of being that due to the fact that for the reason that on account of on the grounds that	because, since
has the capability of is able to possesses the ability to	can
at the present moment at this juncture at this point in time within the current time frame	now
a considerable proportion of a large number of the greater number of the substantial majority of	many, most
a case in point is an example of this would be in regard to in the case of with attention to	for example
it is evident that it should be obvious that	clearly, obviously
concerning the matter of	about
circumstances dictate that it is imperative that it is incumbent upon it is of great importance that there is a need for	should, must
at a time which during an occasion when in a situation in which on the occasion of	when
despite the conditions that even taking into consideration the fact that	although

PHRASE	REPLACEMENT
even though regardless of the fact that	although
at all times	always

Cut intensifying phrases. **Intensifying phrases** meant to add force (*for all intents and purposes*, *in my opinion*, and *all things considered*, for example) carry little meaning. Readers will find your sentences more effective without them.

WORDY **As a matter of fact,** most archaeological discoveries can be dated accurately.

CUT Most archaeological discoveries can be dated accurately.

Shorten or rewrite redundant phrases. **Redundant phrases** say the same thing twice, adding unnecessary words. *True facts*, *free gifts*, and *final outcomes* are redundant because by definition facts are true, gifts are free, and outcomes are final.

added bonus	baby puppies	each individual
end result	fresh news	future plan
necessary requirements	past history	terrible tragedy
unintentional mistake	cheap bargain	unexpected surprise

Similar repetition occurs in redundant verb phrases (*completely finished*, *totally overcome*, and *revert back*).

Some redundancies occur when you use a specific word that implies a more general term you've used with it. *Blue*, for example, clearly implies the category *color*, so it is redundant to state both (*blue in color*).

aggressive ~~by nature~~	circle ~~around~~
consensus ~~of opinion~~	curved ~~in form~~
expensive ~~in cost~~	first ~~in order~~
handsome ~~in appearance~~	~~in a~~ clumsy ~~manner~~
~~in a~~ grumpy ~~mood~~	old ~~in age~~
plans ~~for the future~~	small ~~in size~~

WORDY Because it was sophisticated **in nature** and tolerant **in style,** Kublai Khan's administration aided the development of China in the late 1200s.

CUT Because it was **sophisticated and tolerant,** Kublai Khan's administration aided the development of China in the late 1200s.

Edit all-purpose words. They sound important, yet **all-purpose words** like *factor, aspect, situation, type, range, thing, nature,* and *character* are often fillers. Eliminating them makes sentences easier to understand.

WORDY — Viewed **from a** sociological **perspective,** the president's popularity **factor** might be **a type of** result of the changing **nature of** our attitude toward authority.

EDITED — Viewed sociologically, the president's popularity might be a result of our changing attitude toward authority.

All-purpose modifiers include *very, totally, major, central, secondary, unlikely, peripheral, great, really, surprisingly, definitely, absolutely, marginal, quite, superlative,* and similar terms. They are appropriate when used precisely and sparingly but can easily become clutter.

WORDY — In the short story, Young Goodman Brown is so **totally** overwhelmed by **his own** guilt that he becomes **extremely** suspicious of the people around him and **absolutely** destroys his relationships. [*30 words*]

EDITED — In the short story, Young Goodman Brown is so overwhelmed by guilt that he becomes suspicious of the people around him and destroys his relationships. [*25 words*]

REWRITTEN — In the short story, Young Goodman Brown's **overwhelming** guilt makes him suspicious **of everyone** and destroys his relationships. [*18 words*]

Exercise 1

A. Edit the following sentences to make them more concise. Use one of the three editing options for wordiness: cut unnecessary words, substitute better words, or rewrite the sentence entirely. Keep track of your changes.

EXAMPLE

~~In spite of the fact that~~ Although most ~~ordinary~~ middle-aged people ~~say they generally~~ feel ~~physically~~ healthy, ~~and in good shape, severe physical~~ catastrophes such as ~~debilitating~~ strokes ~~and~~/or heart attacks can strike ~~suddenly~~ at any time.

1. As a matter of fact, my uncle had just come back from playing nine holes of golf when he suffered the terrible tragedy of his heart attack.
2. We all thought my aunt was absolutely in the very best of health, but she also died extremely suddenly.

3. For me, the end result of these experiences has been regular periodic visits to the doctor to check on my health.
4. On account of my last visit to the doctor, I have actually started exercising on a regular basis.
5. A regular exercise program really helps me to a better kind of feeling about myself.

B. In a small group, compare your revised versions of the sentences in Exercise 1A. Create a "best" version of each sentence by pooling the changes in your group. Try to base your decisions on which version gets the writer's point across most concisely.

---

2 Edit wordy and repetitive sentences

Some sentence patterns encourage wordiness, which will annoy your readers. Treat them as likely candidates for cutting and rewriting.

Rewrite sentences with expletive constructions. Beginning a sentence with a construction like *there is, there are,* or *it is* allows you to hold off announcing the subject—sometimes creating emphasis or surprise. You should use this technique sparingly, however (see 7b). Using strong verbs in place of expletive constructions can yield shorter, more forceful sentences.

OVERUSED **It was** between 1346 and 1350 **that** the bubonic plague struck swiftly and horribly. **There were** over 20 million deaths from the plague—one-fourth of Europe's population. **It is** not surprising that records from the period are confusing and incomplete.

REWRITTEN Between 1346 and 1350, one-fourth of Europe's population—about 20 million people—died swiftly and horribly from the bubonic plague. Not surprisingly, records from the period are confusing and incomplete.

Substitute active for passive constructions. Sentences in the active voice often strike readers as livelier and more direct than their passive counterparts. (See 7c-3) This impression may come from the presence of a strong verb closer to the beginning of the sentence, tied to the subject or doer of the action. Favor the active voice in your writing unless you have good reason to use the passive.

PASSIVE Even more unanswered questions **are posed** by Mercury, the smallest planet. Pictures of Mercury **were taken** from within 300 kilometers.

ACTIVE Mercury, the smallest planet, **poses** even more unanswered questions. ***Mariner X* took** pictures of Mercury from within 300 kilometers.

Substitute verbs for nominalizations. A **nominalization** is a verb transformed into a noun or an adjective.

VERB	NOMINALIZATION
analyze	analysis
combine	combination
fail	failure
move	movement
propose	proposition
recognize	recognition
vary	variable

Some professions and disciplines heavily nominalize their prose. However, you can create shorter, livelier sentences if you turn nominalizations into verbs.

NOMINALIZED The committee held **a discussion of** the new regulations for airplane safety. **A limitation on** flammable seat materials now is necessary.

EDITED The committee **discussed** the new regulations for airplane safety. Airlines now **must limit** flammable seat materials.

Turn clauses into phrases and phrases into words. You can often shorten clauses and phrases or reduce them to single words. Look for clauses beginning with *which*, *who*, or *that* and phrases beginning with *of*.

CLAUSES The Comstock Lode, **which was a vein of high-quality silver ore,** was named after Henry T. P. Comstock, **who staked one of the first claims.**

CUT TO PHRASES The Comstock Lode, **a vein of high-quality silver ore,** was named after Henry T. P. Comstock, **one of the first claimants.**

CLAUSES A driver **who has been drinking too much** can turn a car into a weapon **that is potentially lethal.**

CUT TO WORDS An **intoxicated** driver can turn a car into a **potentially lethal** weapon.

PHRASES Bridge joints **covered with paint** cannot flex to relieve pressure or to avoid **fatiguing of the metal.**

CUT TO WORDS **Painted** bridge joints cannot flex to relieve pressure and avoid **metal fatigue.**

Eliminate unnecessary repetition. When you write quickly, you may become repetitive. Such careless repetition will tire and annoy your readers. As you revise and edit, look for ideas *already stated or implied* elsewhere in your sentence or paragraph.

WORDY GPS is a **navigation** system that helps sailors and pilots **navigate.** By getting information **about their position** from **orbiting** satellites, travelers can pinpoint their **global** position **on a chart.**

EDITED GPS is a system that helps sailors and pilots navigate. By getting information from satellites, travelers can pinpoint their position.

REPETITIVE **Our proposal** outlines a **three-step** program for **converting the building** into a **research center** for the study of literature, film, and culture. Each of the **three steps** discussed in **our proposal** should be complete in six months. We expect that **the building** will be **converted** to its new use as a **research center** eighteen months from the time work is begun.

CUT Our proposal outlines a **three-step** program for **converting the building** into a center for the study of literature, film, and culture. Each **step** should be completed in six months. We expect that **the building** will be **converted** to its new use eighteen months from the time work is begun.

REWRITTEN We propose **three steps** for **converting the building** into a center for the study of literature, film, and culture. At six months per **step,** the project should be completed in eighteen months.

45a wordy

Exercise 2

Rewrite the following sentences to make them less wordy.

EXAMPLE

My attracted me to

~~It was an~~ interest in ancient cultures ~~that first sparked my interest in~~ ~~an~~ anthropology course~~, taught by~~ Professor Donaldson's.

1. There is much information and detail in this informative course about the civilizations of the pre-Columbian Americas.
2. Anthropologists have spent a great deal of time studying and investigating Machu Picchu, which was the center point of an advanced culture high in the Andes Mountains.

3. There are many excavations in the area that have received support from American universities.
4. It seems to be true that the ruins are a really breathtaking sight.
5. Proposals for further exploration are now being made to funding organizations by several groups of anthropologists.

45b Clichés, generalizations, and overblown language

Many writers in college choose language that is either overused (clichéd) or stuffy or complicated. They may do this because they're unfamiliar with a specialized topic or think they must sound "smart" to their reader, a teacher with considerable knowledge. But most teachers are more irritated than impressed by such language.

1 Omit clichés and vague generalizations

Much wordiness stems from a lack of tough, careful attention to language. **Clichés** and **vague generalizations** are empty of meaning until the reader plugs in some concrete association. But it's a serious mistake to assume that your reader will do your work for you.

CLICHÉD In **today's modern world**, college graduates **stumble across a startling discovery** before they **strike out on their own.** The best jobs are not necessarily the ones that give you a **shot at big money** but the ones that **turn you on** personally.

EDITED Almost before they have received their diplomas, today's college graduates begin to rethink the idea of employment. The glamour of high-salary positions soon wears thin, replaced by hopes of happiness, job security, and friendly colleagues.

A passage with vague generalizations may be short but still wordy because it offers relatively little information. To revise, *add specific details* or *combine sentences* to eliminate repetition and highlight relationships.

WORDY Glaciers were of central importance in the shaping of the North American landscape. They were responsible for many familiar geological features. Among the many remnants of glacial activity are deeply carved valleys and immense piles of sand and rock.

COMBINED Glaciers carved deep valleys and left behind immense piles of sand and rock, shaping much of the North American landscape in the process.

DETAILS ADDED Glaciers carved deep valleys and left behind immense piles of sand and rock, shaping much of the North American landscape in the process. Cape Cod and Long Island are piles of gravel deposited by glaciers. The Mississippi River and the Great Lakes were left behind when the ice melted.

2 Edit overblown language

Overblown language consists of words too formal or technical for your purpose and audience. Rein in your formal diction and technical words, using them only when they contribute directly to your point.

OVERBLOWN Under the **present conditions of** our society, marriage **practices** generally **demonstrate a high degree of** homogeneity.

APPROPRIATE In our culture, people tend to marry others like themselves.

3 Eliminate excessive writer's commentary

In certain contexts, talking directly to readers can be an acceptable strategy. If you use such **writer's commentary,** do so cautiously. You can occasionally use phrases like *as previously stated* or *I intend to demonstrate* to remind your readers of a point you made earlier or to set the stage for what's to come, but such phrases can become superfluous if you use them too often.

IRRITATING **As I have already shown,** considerable research suggests that placebos (pills with no physical effect) can sometimes lead to improvements or a cure. However, **my paper documents the tendency of** experts in medical ethics to question the ethics of placebo use, calling it a form of lying. **I intend to show** that the effects of placebos (**mentioned above**) overcome any moral concerns **such as the one I have just described.**

EDITED Considerable research has shown that placebos (pills with no physical effect) can sometimes lead to improvements or a cure. Experts in medical ethics, however, question the ethics of placebo use, calling it a form of lying. **This paper** will argue that the effects of placebos overcome any such moral concerns.

TOO OVERT **The thesis of my paper is that** American culture associates the pursuit of knowledge with social ineptitude and the denial of emotion. **I have chosen to focus on** Mr. Spock from the *Star Trek* series as an exemplar of this unfortunate public attitude toward education.

EDITED American culture associates the pursuit of knowledge with social ineptitude and the denial of emotion. This unfortunate public attitude toward education is well represented in the character of Spock, the brilliant but only half-human Vulcan in the *Star Trek* series.

Exercise 3

A. Rewrite the following passage to eliminate overblown language, unnecessary commentary, vague generalizations, and clichés. As you revise, make the passage more concise.

The social psychologist and student of human behavior Peter Marsh several years ago published a tome entitled *Tribes* in which he set forth the challenging, and for many readers, downright revolutionary, conception that the denizens of our modern world perpetuate the primitive form of social organization known as a tribe. According to Marsh in his book, as a reaction against the tendency of our modern society to break up the social networks characteristic of the more rural lifestyles of earlier decades and centuries, many people form formal and informal groups based on their preferences in food, clothing, recreation, and work. Some of these groupings are of remarkably short duration, consisting of what we might call fads. Let me point out that, in my opinion, Marsh is trying to be critical of many of these groups, particularly those that seek to raise the social status of members by excluding nonmembers from certain privileges. Yet I think that a careful reading of Marsh's book would also indicate that he is favorably predisposed toward the tendency of modern people to form tribes.

B. In a small group, compare your revisions of the passage in Exercise 3A. What specific changes did you and your peers make that were especially effective?

CHAPTER 46
Style, the Dictionary, and Vocabulary

Consider the following sentence.

Dr. Parsippani [*caused to die*] Mr. Rollet.

Now, ask yourself what word will best express your intended meaning. Several words meaning "caused to die" could fill the slot, including *killed*, *slaughtered*, *assassinated*, and *murdered*. Choosing the appropriate word means first avoiding incorrect or inaccurate choices. *Assassinate* is usually reserved for important political figures; *slaughtered* usually applies to livestock; and *murdered* indicates foul play. If you meant none of these more specific meanings, *killed* might be the simplest and most precise choice.

Choosing the right words also means choosing words appropriate to your intended purpose, audience, and context. Your choice of words and phrases, your **diction,** should include terms and a level of formality appropriate to your task as well as language enabling you to write as (un)emotionally, amusingly, objectively, or persuasively as you wish.

46a Style and community

Consider these examples.

Ideally located in Manhattan's Murray Hill neighborhood . . . , the *Park South* is a beautifully restored historic 1906 building. Combining the design elements of a classic New York-style hotel with the latest high-tech amenities, contemporary decor and a boutique ambiance, our 141 rooms feature refined, relaxing common areas and stylishly furnished guestrooms, ranging from standard to superior, each outfitted with state-of-the-art technology. http://parksouthhotel.com/new/frames.htm

A recent wave of research promotes the idea that anonymity or deindividuation precipitates collective behavior. Specifically, anonymous individuals are more likely to participate in collective behavior events than people among friends and acquaintances. To reconsider this recent resurgence of a more contemporary contagion theory, we replicate and expand among Aveni's study of crowd behavior. (Neal, D. M. "A further examination of anonymity, contagion, and deindividuation in crowd and collective behavior." *Sociological Focus*, 26.2 (1993): 93–107.)

Clearly, the style of the writing in these excerpts is about the same as apples and oranges: the first is written in a punchy, visually descriptive style with lots of adjectives and adverbs (*ideally, beautifully, classic, high-tech, contemporary, relaxing, stylishly*). The second is peppered with academic terms and phrases not in general use among the public (*deindividuation, contagion theory, collective behavior events*). The language is dense and, unlike the hotel description, sounds scholarly and serious.

The styles of these excerpts are largely determined by the *communities* their authors speak to and are located in. The hotel Web site speaks to a broad public interested in places to stay in lower Manhattan. Its community of readers ranges widely but is bound together by interests in travel and tourism. The sociology journal article's community is much narrower: specialists in social psychology and related fields, mostly scholars and teachers, and perhaps some who are studying social phenomena in work settings such as social services to better understand why people in crowds sometimes behave in ways that differ from "who they really are."

You need to adjust the style of your writing to the expectations of the communities you are writing in and for. Otherwise your readers may become confused or lose faith in your ability to speak to them.

1 Study texts in the community you're addressing

If you are not already an "insider" in a community you're writing to or for, try to get a general sense of its expectations. Look at the kinds of words members of the community use. Consider the way that sentences are structured, and how larger pieces of text are organized. Are paragraphs long and complex, or short and punchy? What information is assumed to be "common knowledge" in the community? Remember also that even within a specific community, these features will differ according to certain kinds of text with certain purposes. Other information at the hotel site above, for example, may sound more legalistic, such as the policies on the cancellation of a reservation.

2 Try out your writing on a trusted member of the community

If you already know and trust a specific member of a community, see how well a draft of your writing works by asking him or her for helpful commentary. Graham Nichols did this with a commentary he had written about plans for a veteran's memorial park nearby; he had been asked to serve on the planning board.

ORIGINAL I guess the thing that I'm thinking about is the history center in the park. The memorial will celebrate veterans, right? But if the history center shows all sides of war, couldn't it sort of wreck the take on the vets' role?

ADVICE Because this document goes to ten people on the board and will be archived for the wider community, it's a little informal for its purpose. You should probably delete the "right?", and revise the "I guess the thing that I'm thinking" to something more formal.

46b Word choice, readers' needs, and writers' purposes

Whenever you choose specific words while you draft and revise, you base your decisions on your purpose, audience, context, and persona (the image of yourself that you project in your writing).

1 Adjust your diction to your readers' needs

The characteristics of your readers should play a major role in your choice of words (see Chapter 3). When you write for college audiences, maintain a fairly high level of formality (the exceptions being deliberately informal notes, responses, journal entries, and quoted speech).

TOO INFORMAL The stock market **crash** didn't seem to **faze** many of the investors with **dollars stashed** in property assets.

READER'S REACTION: This seems really colloquial; I'm not sure I trust the writer's authority.

EDITED The stock market's fall did not significantly affect investors with extensive property assets.

2 Adjust your diction to your purpose

Your *purpose* plays an important role in determining your diction (see Chapter 3). In much academic writing, your aim will be to inform readers, providing a balanced, detailed assessment of a topic. Using highly emotional, unreasoned, or outrageous language will subvert your purposes.

BIASED Most proponents of rock-music censorship grew up listening to pablum and thinking even wimpy bands like the Beach Boys were a bunch of perverts.

READER'S REACTION: **I thought this was a paper weighing the sides of the rock-music censorship debate. This seems too biased and emotional.**

EDITED Proponents of rock-music censorship may unfairly stereotype all of rock-and-roll culture as degenerate or evil.

3 Adjust your diction to your persona

Through your choice of words, you can sound like a mean-spirited, unyielding demagogue or a reasonable, open-minded arbiter of conflicting opinion. Your **persona** as a writer refers to the public role or character you assume.

Use words that help you create an appropriate persona. For example, your persona in a clinical experiment will be objective and detached; too many personal references may call into question the accuracy of the experiment. But clinical diction may be too cold and unfeeling for other occasions.

ROBOTLIKE The river having been reached, it was decided to portage to the campsite. A camp was set, and dinner was prepared and eaten. The sunset was observed at the lake. Then eight hours of sleep ensued.

READER'S REACTION **This narrative lacks vitality. The characters seem like robots.**

EDITED When we reached the river, we decided to portage to the campsite. There we set camp, cooked dinner, enjoyed the sunset at the lake, and slept for eight hours.

4 Use specialized diction appropriately

If you're writing in a specific field or discipline, you need to adjust your diction to your context. In a history course, for example, readers of your papers will expect certain terms and language that might not be appropriate in a physics course.

Many specialized terms eventually find their way into general usage, two examples being *ego* from Freudian psychology and *modem* (*mo*dulator-*dem*odulator) from computer science. When you write for general audiences, your readers will find highly specialized language inappropriate. If you use diction too general for readers in a specialized field, however, your writing may seem naive *in that context*. Revise your drafts to include specific terms used in the field (if you actually understand those terms, and if they improve accuracy and economy).

TOO GENERAL [*in an analysis of a painting for an art history course*] Tiepolo's *Apotheosis of the Pisani Family* (1761) is a lively painting with lots of action going on in it, with nice colors, and typical of the period when it was painted.

READER'S REACTION: **The diction seems too general for a specialized analysis in my field of art history.**

EDITED Tiepolo's *Apotheosis of the Pisani Family* (1761) shows affinities with typical rococo frescoes of the period, including bright colors with characters in various highlighted actions set against dark border accents.

When you learn new words in one field, you may inadvertently use those words in another field in which they are inappropriate.

TOO COMPLEX [*in an economics paper on the influence of sexuality in the marketplace*] Ego gratification, originating in the neo-erotic domains of the pleasure principle, remains one of the chief factors influencing the attractiveness of sexuality in marketing.

READER'S REACTION: **I'm an economics major, not a Freudian psychoanalyst. Talk in my language, please.**

EDITED Freudian theory can help us to explain why sexuality sells in the American marketplace. According to Freud, humans are biologically caught in a kind of sexual rhythm. This rhythm causes us to seek certain kinds of gratification not always explicitly sexual.

Exercise 1

A. Assume that the following paragraph is part of a brochure on dental hygiene found in a dentist's office. Examine the passage, and circle words and phrases you find inappropriate. Write a paragraph explaining the problems in diction that you identified in the passage. Consider its intended audience, purpose, context, and persona.

Brushing and flossing of human dentin has been shown to be instrumental in the systematic reduction of invasive caries. When brushing, it is advisable to rotate the cusp of the preventive maintenance tool at alternating angles during upward and downward motion. When flossing, it is advisable to insert and retract the flossing material several times between the dentitial spaces.

B. In a group, compare your responses to Exercise 1A. Which choices of diction did everyone find inappropriate? As a group, try editing the passage.

46c Precise diction

Because you may draft more fluently when you're not weighing every word, you'll find it helpful to work with diction as you edit. Think of this process as adjusting your prose to match your intended meaning.

1 Choose specific words

Try whenever possible to edit for more specific, accurate words.

TOO VAGUE [*in a do-it-yourself brochure describing bathroom remodeling*] Note: Do not place flooring over uneven floor or with wood rot. Remove damaged area first.

READER'S REACTION: **The language is vague and imprecise. What do I do with a "damaged area"?**

EDITED Note: Do not install any new flooring over existing floors that are weak or uneven or show signs of wood rot. Replace any damaged flooring material before installing new flooring.

2 Choose words with appropriate connotations

English is full of **synonyms,** words identical or nearly identical in meaning. When choosing among words, consider the words' **connotations**—"shades" of meaning, or associations that words acquire over time. When editing, look for inappropriate connotations in your choice of words.

IMPRECISE The senator **retreated** from the gathering.

READER'S REACTION: **Did the senator feel attacked, bewildered, or overcome? Or did she just leave?**

EDITED The senator **left** the gathering.

3 Edit for stuffy language

Borrowings from Latin and Greek entered the English language centuries ago, adding to its range and richness. Yet too many of these and similar terms can make your writing unnecessarily complicated and indirect. As you edit, consider the many simple alternatives (see Chapter 7).

PLAIN WORD	LATIN-BASED
bathroom	lavatory
bickering	disputatious
die	expire
drunk	intoxicated
graveyard	cemetery

PLAIN WORD	LATIN-BASED
split	bifurcate
stingy	penurious
think	cogitate

In general, use simple, direct diction unless the context of your writing calls for specialized language or a more abstract term better reflects your intended meaning.

4 Edit for archaic words and neologisms

The English language changes constantly. Some words are doomed to become obsolete. New words enter the vocabulary by the hundreds. Still others shift their meanings, as in the case of *gay*, which used to mean "carefree" but now almost exclusively means "homosexual."

Most **archaic words**—words that are rarely used any more but are still found in older literature—will be labeled as such in the dictionary. In general, use them only for special reasons. **Neologisms**—words coined very recently—may not be in the dictionary at all. Whenever you suspect that a term is too new to be acceptable in writing, identify it as new and define it, or else avoid it altogether.

ARCHAIC/ NEOLOGIC — Good reviews of our previous play had been scarce (**save** in *Fanfare*), and this time around we had to **forfend** attacks from the critics again.

READER'S REACTION: *Save* and *forfend* seem old-fashioned.

EDITED — Good reviews of our previous play had been scarce (**except** in *Fanfare*), and this time around we had to **defend ourselves against** the critics' attacks again.

5 Edit for idiomatic and trite expressions

Idioms are words and phrases whose meanings have changed, usually to something quite different from their literal definitions. These terms often have "forgotten histories." Here are some common idioms.

IDIOM	MEANING
bust a gut	work extremely hard
get in the fast lane	be ambitious, rise up; lead a fast-paced, self-destructive lifestyle
lose your marbles	go insane
meet your maker	die
pack it in	quit, resign
take a spin	go for a ride
wipe the slate clean	start over

In most academic writing, idioms are too informal or have become trite from overuse. Replace them with precise words.

IDIOMATIC The winning team was **placed high upon a pedestal,** while the losers, **wallowing in a slough of despond,** reminded themselves of what a **dog-eat-dog** world it is in sports.

EDITED The winning team was idolized and cheered by fans, while the losers, despondent and humorless, consoled themselves over their defeat.

Exercise 2

A. Read the following paragraph and identify as many cases as you can of inappropriate diction. Look for imprecise, misused, stuffy, or trite words, checking in a dictionary if you need to. Then edit the passage by replacing the misused words or expressions with more appropriate ones.

The inaugural time I witnessed someone parachuting from a plane was when I was in college. The parachuting establishment was located in the desert of Arizona. First we apprised ourselves on the diminutive single-prop plane and shackled ourselves into the seats. Three employees of a local business were the jumpers. We circled around until we reached the pinnacle for jumping, about 6,000 feet up. The first customer was about to detort but became lugubrious with fear and couldn't jump. The second man faced us with his back to the open side of the plane and a verecund expression on his face, then fell back deliberately and dejected himself from the craft, spinning downward toward the verdurous desert.

B. In a small group, compare your edited versions of the passage in Exercise 2A. Discuss all your choices, and then try to reach consensus on the best substitutions.

46d Editing for diction

Having a wide-ranging vocabulary—not just *knowing* lots of words, but knowing how to use them appropriately—is clearly helpful for editing your diction. But even the most experienced writers will tell you that when it comes to choosing words, they always search for just the right flavor. Use the following strategies when you think common sense isn't enough.

1 Use the dictionary

Dictionaries give you precise definitions as well as usage notes. When editing your work, circle any words that you have learned fairly recently or have not used often; then look them up to be sure you've used them correctly.

IMPRECISE Employees should know that their contracts may be terminated if they deliberately abrogate their work hours.

READER'S REACTION: **The term *abrogate* means to abolish or nullify, usually by some formal means. Do you really mean this?**

EDITED Employees should know that their contracts may be terminated if they miss work.

ESL ADVICE: USING DICTIONARIES

Sometimes you want to express an idea or concept in writing, but you do not know what word or words would express it in English. Bilingual dictionaries are usually a good starting point to find a possible translation. However, for every word, they list several options. It is important that you consult an English dictionary to ensure that you choose the most appropriate word. These dictionaries contain definitions and examples that can help you decide which word best matches your intended meaning and your diction.

2 Use a thesaurus

A thesaurus provides lists of synonyms useful when you're editing diction and want to replace an existing word. But be careful. Be sure you're familiar with a synonym and its connotations before simply substituting it, or you could fall prey to "thesaurusese." This condition may lead you to reject good, common words, choosing instead to pepper your prose with sophisticated-sounding but inappropriate synonyms.

When using a thesaurus, ask yourself whether your new word choice captures your meaning more accurately, gives more flavor, or avoids redundancy more effectively than your original choice. When in doubt, stick with words you know.

ORIGINAL She was **angered** to the point of frustration.

WRITER'S REACTION: **I'm not satisfied with *anger*. My thesaurus suggests the alternatives *vexed, irritated, exasperated, infuriated, inflamed, miffed,* and *enraged*.**

IMPRECISE She was **enraged** to the point of frustration.

WRITER'S REACTION: **This word is too strong and does not convey the woman's true feelings.**

EDITED She was **irritated** to the point of frustration.

3 Use the slash/option technique

Sometimes you have several alternatives in mind for a particular word, but stopping to weigh the alternatives may break your train of thought. Write down the alternative words and separate them with slashes. Later, as you revise and edit, choose the word that most accurately fits your intended meaning.

4 Fight insecurity with simplicity

The problem of overblown, deliberately complex diction—diction intended to puff up your writing with "sophisticated" language—often has its roots in insecurity. Professionals in advanced fields have earned the right to use words with *specialized* meanings. They sound sophisticated because, in their fields, they *are*. But using overly complex prose out of a fear of sounding naive only makes you sound *more* naive.

Whenever you have the slightest urge to puff up your prose with jargon or needlessly complicated diction, *stop*. Then return to your draft. Be direct; choose concrete, lively words.

Exercise 3

A. Locate a short passage in a newspaper or magazine article. Rewrite the passage, substituting words that are inappropriate or inaccurate.

B. Make several copies of your original passage and the changed version in Exercise 3A. In a group, work on each other's passages to "repair" the damage. Then compare your edited versions with the original passages. How close did you come to the originals? What differences can you see between your "repaired" versions and the originals?

46e Choosing and using dictionaries

As you work with your writing, you will need different kinds of dictionaries for different purposes, even beyond the typical need to check on the correct spelling, pronunciation, and definition of a word. Here are common questions writers ask about dictionaries and their use.

- *What's the best kind of all-purpose dictionary I can get?*
  Desk dictionaries, often called *college dictionaries*, are suitable for most routine academic and professional tasks. Although they don't pretend to give an exhaustive list of English vocabulary, they are substantial reference works.

- *What if I don't want to lug around a huge book when I'm working on my writing away from home?*

  Most people use a **pocket dictionary** for quick checks on spelling or syllable division. Pocket dictionaries are **abridged dictionaries,** meaning that they contain far fewer words and much less information than standard dictionaries.
- *What's a good place to get really full information on a word? What's the most authoritative source?*

  If your desk dictionary doesn't answer your questions or contain the word you're looking up, you can consult much more comprehensive **unabridged dictionaries,** which are found in most libraries and schools. These dictionaries contain many more words than desk and pocket dictionaries. They usually provide detailed information about words, including specialized terms, and notes on usage as well as complete etymological information.
- *Sometimes I feel that I use the same words over and over. Is there a book that can help me to find alternatives?*

  A **thesaurus** is a dictionary of **synonyms** and **antonyms**—words related or opposite in meaning to each other. A thesaurus is useful when you want to find an alternative to a word you've already considered, or perhaps to remember a word that has temporarily slipped your mind. Under the word *funny,* for example, *Webster's Collegiate Thesaurus* lists the synonyms *laughable, comic, comical, droll, farcical, gelastic, ludicrous, ridiculous,* and *risible.*
- *What if I just want to check on correct spelling?*

  Spelling dictionaries are dictionaries without definitions. They provide spellings and information on word division (**syllabification**). If you own a good desk dictionary, you probably won't need a spelling dictionary unless you're a frequent misspeller or do a good deal of your writing away from your desk.
- *I've often needed to know the complete history of a specific word. What reference should I use?*

  Most good dictionaries include etymological information, and research dictionaries, especially the *Oxford English Dictionary* (OED), will give you very complete accounts. **Etymological dictionaries,** however, specialize in the history of words (**etymology**) and will often give fuller histories of some words.
- *I've noticed that some words just aren't in the standard dictionary. How can I find their proper spellings and meanings?*

  Most formal dictionaries don't include every word that might be heard in casual conversation, much less the sort of jargon found among computer enthusiasts, avid sports fans, surfers, and the like. Dictionaries of colloquialisms, slang, idioms, and informal usage fill the gaps.

- *In some of my classes, I hear words that I can't find in the dictionary, probably because they're specialized. Where can I look them up to make sure I understand them and can use them correctly?*

  Many disciplines use and require complex vocabularies that sound like a foreign language to the average person. To ensure the precise use of specialized terms, these disciplines have their own academic and professional dictionaries. It's a good idea to ask a librarian or teacher to help you locate such dictionaries for your field of study.

Exercise 4

A. Conduct a brief "anatomy exam" of your own dictionary by answering the following questions.

1. What kinds of information does your dictionary give for each word?
2. How complete are the entries?
3. How have the definitions been determined?
4. How many separate entries does the dictionary include? (A good reference dictionary should contain at least 150,000 words.)
5. Are variant uses, definitions, and spellings given?
6. Does the dictionary contain acronyms (such as SIDS, ARC, NATO, FDA)?
7. Does it contain abbreviations?
8. Does it include often-used foreign words such as *tête-à-tête*, *pied-à-terre*, *calzone*, *karate*, and *kibosh*?
9. Does the dictionary show when to *italicize* words such as *cogito ergo sum* or *mea culpa?*
10. What is contained in the introduction or preface? Is there an appendix? Are there any special features?

B. Compare your notes from Exercise 4A (and your dictionaries) with those of other students.

46f Electronic resources

Dictionaries and dictionary-like programs are readily available for computers and can be accessed online. Those used most often are simple spell checkers. Most spell checkers don't contain definitions or guides to usage. A few programs, however, do. Software and online versions of major dictionaries contain definitions, notes on correct usage, hyphenation information, and spelling correctors. Some have accompanying thesauruses. These programs can provide acronyms, synonyms, antonyms, contrasted words, compared words, and related words.

Computerized dictionaries have several advantages over typical printed dictionaries: they are far less bulky, they can be upgraded more easily and more quickly than a book can be, and you can personalize many computer dictionaries, adding your own special words to the dictionary's memory.

Computerized dictionaries also have their limitations. It's more difficult to browse through them. They may cost three or four times more than a good college dictionary. If you like to write in different locations, you won't be able to use your dictionary without a computer.

46g Building vocabulary

A rich, varied vocabulary is the mark of an educated person, and it is essential to effective writing and reading. Clearly, the better your vocabulary, the more easily you'll recognize words as a reader and listener, and the more able you'll be to choose effective words as a writer and speaker.

1 Vocabulary and the writing process

If you don't give yourself many options for word choice, you put a stranglehold on your prose, limiting its variety, its accuracy, and its metaphoric potential. Consider the six versions of one line written by Johanna Vaughan in her paper about food-shelf programs.

> Without the help of local and state government, the food-shelf program in Seattle will become **ineffective.**
>
> Without the help of local and state government, the food-shelf program in Seattle will become **obsolete.**
>
> Without the **beneficence** of local and state government, the food-shelf program in Seattle will **die.**
>
> Without the beneficence of local government, the food-shelf program in Seattle will die **of starvation.**
>
> Without the **financial nurturing** of local government, Seattle's food-shelf program will die of **nutritional neglect.**
>
> Without the financial **sustenance** of local government, Seattle's food-shelf program will **slowly** die of starvation.

Many of Vaughan's changes depend on more than the substitution of individual words, but it's hard to overlook the role her vocabulary plays in her writing process. She can revise more effectively *because she has more options*—she can experiment with words like *sustenance*, *beneficence*, and *obsolete*.

Although it can become tedious to keep moving between your emerging sentences and that 1,500-page dictionary on your desk, there is something to be said for some modest vocabulary development during the process of completing each of your writing assignments. Especially while revising, take time to consider alternatives to some of your words, perhaps circling those that seem repetitive or bland, then listing alternatives or using a dictionary or thesaurus.

2 Vocabulary and the reading process

Every time you pick up a book or newspaper, you're exposed to new words. If you're like most people, you probably pass over them, as long as you're not hopelessly confused without knowing their meaning. In many cases, the mere exposure to these words, in their contexts, helps you to acquire them as part of your vocabulary. But a few deliberate techniques can help.

- Each day, select one word from something you've read, look up its definition, and check its etymology. Then, without sounding too unnatural, try incorporating the word into your speech at least three times during the day. If that's not possible, just make up sentences on your own, and say them silently to yourself.
- Keep an ongoing list of unfamiliar words, look them up, and review them periodically, crossing them out when they've become part of your vocabulary. The words on your list should come directly from material you're reading and studying, from the daily newspaper to the most complex textbook chapters.
- Every time you look up a word for its meaning, check its etymology. Most English words have Anglo-Saxon, Latin, Greek, or French origins. When you look up a word's roots, you further develop your vocabulary.

Exercise 5

A. To practice studying the etymologies of words, look up the following examples in a full-length (unabridged) dictionary. (The best source will be the *Oxford English Dictionary* in your college library.) Look for anything unusual or interesting about the history of these words.

EXAMPLE: KANGAROO

The OED says that the word probably comes from an indigenous aboriginal language of Australia and meant "I don't know" or "I don't understand," the response given to visitors who asked the aborigines the name of the animal.

barbecue	guillotine	mesmerize	sadist
blimp	juke (box)	muscle	sandwich
blurb	ketchup	OK or okay	serendipity
dollar	laser	robot	voodoo

B. In a group, compare your etymologies for the words in Exercise 5A. What surprised you about the origins of these words?

CHAPTER 47
Appropriate and Respectful Language

What is **sexist language?** People disagree about some common terms. For example, *seminal* is widely used to mean "highly original and influencing future events or developments"—but the literal meaning of the word is "pertaining to, containing, or consisting of semen." As such, it represents a potentially sexist usage: why should originality and creativity be associated with maleness? Some people think the term should be dropped in favor of words like *important* or *influential;* others argue that it's perfectly acceptable.

No matter how you feel about specific issues, as a writer you *must* be concerned with the reactions of readers to the way you represent men and women and members of minority groups. You don't want to alienate your readers, prejudice people against your ideas, or perpetuate unhealthy attitudes.

47a Home and community language varieties

Every language in the world is spoken in a variety of ways called *dialects.* English has hundreds of dialects, which vary in obvious ways between different countries, like England and the United States, but also within these countries. The American English spoken in Natchez, Mississippi, differs considerably from the American English spoken in Bar Harbor, Maine, and speakers in Fort Wayne, Indiana, don't, as a group, share the same dialect as Hoosiers who live just a few hours south in Bloomington or Evansville. Dialects can also vary by culture, ethnicity, and nationality. Not only do Cuban Americans and Puerto Rican Americans speak different dialects of American English in New York City, but their dialects may vary between the Bronx and Brooklyn. Similar people may have different dialects even though they live just a few miles from each other—or a few blocks.

1 Learn to see dialect variations as "rules"

Linguists point out that all dialects have rules. What conforms to a rule in one dialect may break a rule in another. This is how all language works—the "rules" are the structures and conventions that people within a group unconsciously agree to use in their speech. Pronouncing the word *pen* to rhyme with *hen* is a rule of Northern and much Midwestern speech, but the rule in large parts of the South is to rhyme *pen* with *tin*. Many British speakers pronounce the *t* in the word *butter* but leave off the *r* at the end ("buttah"), whereas Americans generally turn the *t* into a *d* and pronounce the *r* ("budder")—except in the South and in parts of New England. Who's right? Each group follows the rules of its own community. To break them is to be seen as an outsider.

2 Understand standard English as a function of power and social prestige

If every community has its own language rules, then who's to say that the so-called standard language is the "better" language? Why *should* it be any more correct to say "There isn't anyone who can tell me anything about what I haven't seen" than to say "Ain't no body gon' tell me nuffin' bout what I ain't see"? After all, double negatives are acceptable in hundreds of languages around the world, so there is no logical reason why they should be incorrect in English. In fact, they were once perfectly acceptable and were used by Chaucer and Shakespeare.

The answer to this question doesn't come from something in the nature of the language; it comes from something about the people who speak it. Around the world, each language has a prestige dialect that is thought to be more "correct" or "proper" than other dialects. How this dialect came to be preferred is almost always a matter of historical, political, and social forces. Some group of people came into power. They used language in a certain way. Because they had power, they also controlled things like schools, information, and books. Before long, their language variety became associated with correctness; grammarians then simply described that form of the language *as* correct, and people who wanted to be thought powerful or educated had to learn its rules.

If your home dialect differs from the standard, you may be unfairly stereotyped or discriminated against by people in positions of power. Even unbiased people may not listen to you—because they can't: they aren't part of your dialect group; you're leaving them out of the conversation. Before deciding what, if anything, you want to do about differences between your community dialect and the standard, it's important to reflect on this issue of power. Some people believe that our society must begin accepting more varieties of language. Others believe that if such acceptance occurs, it will happen very slowly, but people will still discriminate against certain language varieties in the meantime. If that's true, people without power will remain powerless if they can't communicate in the language of the powerful. But if they can gain positions of power, maybe they can then help to change public prejudices about language and culture.

Exercise 1

A. Briefly describe any features of your own home or community language that you're aware of in your speech or writing habits. What kinds of features are they: words? accent? grammar? What are their sources? Have you ever felt stereotyped or discriminated against because of your home or community language, or felt awkward in a situation in which your speech differed from that of others? Is there disagreement within your own community about what's correct? How do you feel about the issue of language authority? Do you want to hold on to your community language? Or do you want to get rid of all traces of that language? If you did, how do you think people in your home community would respond?

B. In a group, compare your reflections from Exercise 1A. Focus specifically on the problems of power, prestige, and language prejudice.

3 Recognize the difference between accents and written variations

Different *accents* get stigmatized all the time, yet they're more likely to be accepted than differences in *grammar.* While Americans don't usually mind differences in our leaders' accents, most people would balk at a president who said, "Them senators ain't ready for this-here veto" or "The First Lady, she all d'time be givin' me good advice on foreign policy."

In writing, the most glaring (and least forgiven) variations are *grammatical,* followed by *lexical* differences (word choice, including slang, jargon, and the like). People form unfair stereotypes on the basis of these language features, thinking that they're signs of ignorance or laziness. To avoid such negative stereotypes and to succeed in your most important goal—having your readers listen to and respect your ideas—you'll need to recognize and edit any instances of home or community language variations that may not be shared by a wider reading public. Paying attention to these differences will make you a more flexible communicator, able to move effectively between a home or community dialect and a broader public form of language.

4 Learn how to code-shift

One way speakers adjust their language to meet the expectations of particular communities is through what's called **code-shifting.** Some situations compel you to talk in ways that meet the expectations of your home or community language variety, while other situations—less personal or more broadly public—beg for a different kind of speech. In other words, you have to talk the talk and walk the walk.

Code-shifting is also a characteristic of writing. Many people write in a home or community language to their friends, but they shift into formal language in an essay, a letter to an elected official, or a corporate report. University of Pittsburgh assistant dean Barbara Mellix, for example, describes her own code-shifting in an essay, "From Outside, In." Annoyed by her daughter's persistent interruptions while she's writing, she tells her, "Looka here, Allie, you are too old for this kind of carryin' on. I done told you this is important. You wronger than dirt to be in here haggin' me like this and you know it. Now git outta here and leave me off before I put my foot all the way down." Yet, to make her points about language difference, Mellix feels compelled to use a different code in her writing.

> Now that I know that to seek knowledge, freedom, and autonomy means always to be in the concentrated process of becoming—always to be venturing into new territory, feeling one's way at first, then getting one's balance, negotiating, accommodating, discovering one's self in ways that previously defined "others"—I sometimes get tired.
>
> —BARBARA MELLIX, "From Outside, In"

In some formats—such as personal letters or journals designed to help you think about course material (see 2b)—you should feel at ease writing in a home or community variety. In other, typically more formal situations, where home or community variations can be stigmatized, most writers play it safe and adopt a style for their writing that will work across many different communities. In the United States, this variety is often called standard edited American English.

5 Become aware of the grammatical variations in your home dialect

Grammatical variations in your home or community dialect can be tricky to notice in your writing; after all, they may not look the least bit odd or problematic—to you. But someone who isn't a member of your dialect community will see them right away.

HOME VARIETY Miss Brill know that the lovers making fun of her, but she act like she don't care.

EDITED Miss Brill knows that the lovers are making fun of her, but she acts as if she doesn't care.

HOME VARIETY The FDA guy said to Dougherty could he borrow him the test kit, but Dougherty said he would bring it with.

EDITED A representative of the FDA asked whether Dougherty could lend him the test kit, but Dougherty said he would bring it with him.

HOME VARIETY The minutes of the last meeting state that unless if RayCorp had ordered the resistors, the shipment was sent out on accident.

EDITED The minutes of the last meeting state that unless RayCorp had ordered the resistors, the shipment was sent out accidentally.

If you can see variations in your home or community language as rules or patterns, it may be easier for you to match them up against the rules of a standard. What are the rules of your community language? Keep a list in a notebook. First, record examples of rules specific to your community language; then write down the corresponding examples in standard English. Then try to write an explanation of the differences in your own terms, as in the following example written by a student from Kentucky.

Rule in my part of Kentucky: The lawn needs mowed.
Rule elsewhere: The lawn needs to be mowed.

Everyone in my part of Kentucky leaves out the *to be* and just puts in the verb after *needs.* It's always seemed natural to me, but I learned that it is only done in certain parts of the United States. I can use the "search" function on my computer to look for the word *needs* and then make sure I fix the mistake.

Exercise 2

A. Consider the following excerpt from *Their Eyes Were Watching God*, a novel by the African American author Zora Neale Hurston. This conversation between two characters, Phoeby Watson and Janie Stark, represents the language variety used in the characters' home and community and is therefore the most expressive way for them to relate to each other.

[Phoeby] found [Janie] sitting on the steps of the back porch with the lamps all filled and the chimneys cleaned.

"Hello, Janie, how you comin'?"

"Aw, pretty good, Ah'm tryin' to soak some uh de tiredness and de dirt outa mah feet." She laughed a little.

"Ah see you is. Gal, you sho looks *good.* You looks like youse yo' own daughter." They both laughed. "Even wid dem overhalls on, you shows yo' womanhood."

"G'wan! G'wan! You must think Ah brought yuh somethin'. When Ah ain't brought home a thing but mahself."

"Dat's a gracious plenty. Yo' friends wouldn't want nothin' better."

—Zora Neale Hurston, *Their Eyes Were Watching God*

The second passage is a letter requesting that a local YWCA suspend the writer's membership until she is able to exercise again. The passage contains features of the writer's home community dialect that are not considered standard. The letter is aimed at a general reading public, because the YWCA may employ people who do not share the writer's language variety.

Dear Mrs. Voit,

Like I explain to you when I call last week, I ain't been use my YWCA membership since November because I am pregnant and my doctor be telling me not to work out. Please stop my membership now and I call you when I want it start up again.

Sincerely,

Loretta Saunders

Edit both passages to make them conform to standard written English. Now reflect on the consequences of your changes. Has anything been lost from either passage? Has anything been gained through editing? How appropriate are the changes made to each passage?

B. In a group, compare your changes and your reflections from Exercise 2A. What does this exercise suggest about the principle of standard English and the idea of flexibility?

47b How dialects influence writing

Along with dialect differences, all speakers of English also use differences in **register** in both their speaking and their writing. Register is the form that language takes in a particular context. The variations can be in pronunciation, grammar, or word choice. You might use a *formal* register when being interviewed for an important job, an *informal* register at a ball game, a *technical* register when explaining to a colleague how a piece of electronic equipment works, or a *simplified* register when talking with a toddler.

In writing and formal speaking occasions, you want to be sure to use the right register. Your choice of register will depend on your intended audience or readers and their knowledge, your context, and your **persona,** or who you want to "be" in your writing. You may need to shift registers if aspects of your home or community language are generally thought to be too informal for broader or more formal settings. (See also 47a-5.)

1 Become aware of oral language influences

Most of the language we produce is spoken. If you haven't been an avid reader, there may be expressions, terms, and constructions that you've *heard* often but haven't *seen* much in print. Your knowledge of the sound can trick you into making an error when you turn that sound into print.

Consider one of the most common mistakes in writing: spelling the phrase *a lot* as one word (*alot*). Why do so many people do this? Partly because they're smart: spoken, this phrase really does sound like one word, with little or no pause between *a* and *lot*. Or they may not have noticed *a lot* spelled again and again as two words. These sorts of transcription errors show up often in unedited prose.

I should of signed the check	for	*I should have signed the check*
excetera	for	*et cetera*
Atom and Eve	for	*Adam and Eve*
It's a doggy-dog world	for	*It's a dog-eat-dog world*
expresso	for	*espresso*

The way language sounds in your home or community variety can also end up in your writing, and this may unfortunately (and often unfairly) lead your reader to judge you negatively or doubt your credibility or intelligence. In the first example below, the omission of *-ed* from *ask* is clearly an intelligent mistake: the *-ed* of *asked* is pronounced as a *t*, and the *t* of *Trish* swallows it in speech. In the second example, illustrating the influence of Spanish, *this* sounds like *these* to the writer, leading to another intelligent mistake, while the repetition of *either* is a common feature of the Chicano English of Southern California.

DRAFT The personnel department ask Trish Walters could she expedite the request.

READER'S REACTION: **Why is *ask* in the present tense? Also, when I get to *could,* I'm thrown off track. The writer seems careless.**

EDITED The personnel department asked Trish Walters whether she could expedite the request.

DRAFT Either the character cause all this events, or either they are coincidental.

EDITED Either the characters cause all these events, or they are coincidental.

2 Consider your word choices

Usually, writers consciously choose their words to make them appropriate for the occasion—formal or informal, complex or simple. Sometimes, however, writers unknowingly use words that are part of their home or community language but are not shared by a broader community of readers. In such cases, readers may think the text is too informal because it uses "local" words. These words can usually be spotted with a careful editorial eye and the help of a good dictionary.

DRAFT Our interoffice mail is consistently slow because the mailboy has to schlep the large packages along with the memos and letters.

READER'S REACTION: **"Schlep?" Is that some sort of corporate term?**

EDITED Our interoffice mail is consistently slow because the mailboy has to carry the large packages along with the memos and letters.

DRAFT Some of the budget surplus should be used on our public parks, which need new play areas and working bubblers.

READER'S REACTION: **What's a bubbler?**

EDITED Some of the budget surplus should be used on our public parks, which need new play areas and drinking fountains that work.

3 Distinguish between slang and dialect

Words that are part of a dialect have usually been around in that dialect for some time. People of all ages may use them, and they are known by much or most of the dialect community. Sometimes these words even become part of the standard language—for example, the word *jazz*.

When groups within a dialect community (often young people) create new words that aren't shared by the entire community, those words will be considered **slang.** Many older members of a dialect community express negative attitudes toward the use of slang by younger people, even though all of them may be using a language variety considered to be nonstandard. Although slang is an important way to show membership in a group and is often very creative, you should avoid using it in writing (except perhaps in informal journals or learning logs). Some people may not understand it; others may feel alienated from your prose. Still others, both within and beyond your language community, may not trust your ideas or take them seriously.

SLANG The battle scenes in The Iliad are phat. Just when Agamemnon chill, someone diss him or jack something up and he wage another war.

(For more on word usage, see Chapter 46.)

4 Recognize hypercorrection

People who use a nonmainstream or stigmatized dialect may become aware of certain language habits that are not considered the norm. When they shift registers in formal situations, they may consciously or unconsciously try to "repair" their speech. Sometimes they may unwittingly create a new error in trying to be correct. Linguists call this phenomenon **hypercorrection.**

In speech, for example, some New Englanders who don't pronounce their *rs* at the end of words after vowels (*mothuh*, *fathuh*, and *cah* for *mother*, *father*, and *car*) may hypercorrect themselves by putting an *r* at the end of a word where it doesn't belong. Some Cockney speakers in London incorrectly put *hs* at the beginning of words with vowels (*howl* for *owl* or *hasked* for *asked*) in formal situations, because they tend to drop the *h* from words that should have it (*'e* for *he*, *'asn't* for *hasn't*, *'ad* for *had*).

Certain kinds of hypercorrection can affect writers, especially in the area of grammar. Writers create hypercorrection because they're *trying* to be formal. In an urge to be correct, the writer guesses that a construction is wrong and ironically substitutes an error for it.

HYPERCORRECT Stuart will give the petitions to Mary and I.

EDITED Stuart will give the petitions to Mary and me.

The concept of hypercorrection can also apply to the style and structure of your sentences. If you try too hard to be formal and sophisticated, you may end up writing tangled prose. Don't be fooled into thinking that complex words and sentences alone will create an "impressive" register; your readers won't be impressed, just frustrated.

CONVOLUTED That the girl walks away, and the showing of the parrot to the restaurant owner who, having closed shop, is not about to let her inside, is indicative of that which characterizes the novel throughout, i.e., denial and deception.

EDITED The central theme of denial and deception is illustrated when the girl tries to show the parrot to the restaurant owner and is turned away.

Hypercorrection can also affect the use and spelling of words. For example, when a writer spells the phrase *Adam and Eve* as *Atom and Eve*, she's assuming that the *d* in *Adam* works like the *ts* in *writer* or *batter* (which are pronounced like *ds*), so she hypercorrects the word to *Atom*.

47c Sexist language: Recognizing and editing

As you edit your writing, try to read what you've written from the perspective of a person of the opposite gender or another culture. Be especially sensitive when you're characterizing groups, discussing occupational roles, or referring to all human beings.

1 Avoid demeaning characterizations of women

Your readers are likely to object to language that demeans women or plays into negative stereotypes of women's behaviors, roles, and attributes.

DEMEANING Two undergraduates and **a co-ed** were jointly awarded the prize for the research project.

READER'S REACTION: I'm angered by the implication that women aren't real students.

EDITED **Three undergraduates** were jointly awarded the prize for the research project.

DEMEANING Driving **like a typical woman,** Susan backed her car into the shopping cart.

READER'S REACTION: This unfairly stereotypes women as incompetent.

EDITED Susan **inadvertently** backed her car into the shopping cart.

2 Avoid gender-stereotyping roles and occupations

Our use of language has not entirely kept pace with social changes in men's and women's roles, especially in the area of occupation. Be on the lookout for unfair or inaccurate stereotyping.

STEREOTYPED The most important thing **a mother can do** to facilitate language growth in **her** child is to read aloud to **him** as much as possible.

READER'S REACTION: I'm the father of a little girl. I object to the implications that only mothers can care for children and that all children are boys.

EDITED The most important thing **parents can do** to facilitate language growth in **their children** is to read aloud to **them** as much as possible.

3 Beware of male terms used generically

The most common form of sexist language uses *mankind* or *men* for humankind; *he*, *his*, or *him* for all people; and a host of words that imply male roles for occupations (*fireman*, *policeman*, and the like). Most cases are easily edited: *police officer* for *policeman, garbage collector* for *garbageman.* Editing out the generic *he*, however, may prove more difficult. When possible, try first to make the construction plural. For example, you can substitute *their* for *his* or for the clumsy *his or her.*

SEXIST Every child should bring **his** lunch money to school with **him** each day.

AWKWARD Every child should bring **his or her** lunch money to school with **him or her** each day.

BETTER All children should bring **their** lunch money to school with **them** each day.

SEXIST The Alejandro Restaurant serves **man-sized** portions of paella.

EDITED The Alejandro Restaurant serves **heaping** portions of paella.

Some nonsexist style manuals suggest avoiding the use of generic *he* by making a pronoun plural even if it does not agree in number with the subject (see 35c). Some readers, however, object more strenuously to the error in agreement than to the sexist language. The solution is to avoid both problems whenever possible.

ORIGINAL **Everyone** has at one time or another squandered **his** money at a casino.

PROBLEMATIC **Everyone** has at one time or another squandered **their** money at a casino.

BETTER **Everyone** has at one time or another squandered money at a casino.

Exercise 3

A. The following list of words and proposed replacements ranges from the obviously sexist (and therefore inflexible and in need of revision) to the highly debatable and even absurd. For each word, decide whether you would accept the alternative term, and explain why. (Tip: Consult a dictionary when in doubt.)

1. *Persondible* for *mandible*
2. *People-eating tiger* for *man-eating tiger*
3. *Personic depressive* for *manic depressive*
4. *Face-to-face talk* for *man-to-man talk*
5. *Sanitation employee* for *garbageman*
6. *Actor* for both *actor* and *actress*
7. "*Our parent, who art in heaven . . .*" for "*Our Father, who art in heaven . . .*"

8. *Chair* or *chairperson* for *chairman*
9. *Waitperson* or *waitron* for *waiter* and *waitress*
10. *Flight attendant* for *steward* and *stewardess*

B. Compare your responses to Exercise 3A with those of your fellow writers. (And, while you're at it, add *fellow* to your list in Exercise 3A.)

---

4 Avoid implying sexist views

Whenever you revise your prose, pay special attention to the ways you characterize men and women and their roles and relationships. Avoid making offhand remarks that could be interpreted as sexist.

SEXIST **Being a girl,** Sondra was chosen to be at the top of the cheerleading pyramid.

READER'S REACTION: I'm not comfortable with what's being implied about girls' abilities here.

EDITED **Being the lightest person on the team,** Sondra was chosen to be at the top of the cheerleading pyramid.

SEXIST **Naturally,** Mike wrestled with the flat tire while Natasha **tried to seduce someone into pulling over and helping.**

READER'S REACTION: This stereotypes men as inherently strong and capable and women as sex objects.

EDITED Mike **struggled to change the tire** while Natasha **tried to flag down a car for help.**

5 Avoid making unwarranted claims

Much sexism finds its energy in misunderstandings about the biological and intellectual nature of men and women. Men are assumed to be stronger, more agile, and more aggressive. Women are assumed to be weaker, worse at math and science but better at language, and less able to manage and negotiate. Many of these assumptions are either unfair or unsubstantiated. In your writing, avoid reinforcing such unfair and incorrect notions.

STEREOTYPED The anti-abortion protest became more heated when several people appealed to the **instinctive nurturing emotion of the women** in the crowd.

READER'S REACTION: Aren't men nurturers too?

EDITED The anti-abortion protest became more heated when several people appealed to the **feelings of nurture among the parents** in the crowd.

STEREOTYPED **Behaving like a wimp,** Roger chose to stay home and read instead of playing football with his friends.

READER'S REACTION: **This attaches negative stereotypes to men who engage in intellectual activities.**

REVISED Roger chose to stay home and read instead of playing football with his friends.

Exercise 4

A. Examine the following paragraph. Then revise its sexist language. Add to the original if you wish.

Preschool programs for children in poor families have always been underfunded and at best only a stopgap measure for more permanent educational reform. This was the message delivered by the man-and-wife team, Dr. and Mrs. Herbert Kline, Ph.D.s, at the Eleventh Regional Conference on Preschool Education. About seven hundred elementary school teachers came to the conference to hear the Klines debunk some old wives' tales about education. The Klines also focused on what the future holds for those interested in becoming public school teachers, including the need to balance work with attending to one's husband and family. Every teacher of young children, Mrs. Herbert Kline pointed out, must not only practice her craft well but also keep abreast of new theory and research which she can then integrate into her classroom in a way rewarding to her and to her students.

B. In a small group, compare your responses to Exercise 4A. What strategies did you use to revise the sexist language?

47d discrm

47d Discriminatory language: Recognizing and avoiding

Members of minority groups often suffer from discriminatory practices, especially those that are manifested in language. Most readers won't tolerate racism, and as soon as they encounter **discriminatory language,** they'll stop reading or throw the material away.

1 Avoid derogatory terms

You may be used to hearing certain derogatory terms and epithets in others' speech. Make sure that they don't appear in your writing, or you may anger and alienate your readers.

RACIST The economic problems in the border states are compounded by an increase in the number of **wetbacks** from Mexico, some of whom are illegally trying to rip off jobs from good, taxpaying citizens.

READER'S REACTION: I object to characterizing a group of people this way. This derogatory name is offensive.

EDITED The economic problems in the border states are compounded by an increased number of illegal immigrants from Mexico, some of whom are able to get jobs in this country.

HOMOPHOBIC The talk show included a panel of **fags** who spoke about what it's like to be a **homo.**

READER'S REACTION: Using emotionally loaded names for people doesn't encourage reasonable discussion. You'll have to be more objective than this if you want me to pay attention to your ideas.

EDITED The talk show included a panel of gay and lesbian guests who shared their thoughts about homosexuality.

DEROGATORY In a typically **white-male** fashion, the principal argued against the schoolteachers' referendum.

READER'S REACTION: The fact that white men are in the majority doesn't give you permission to stereotype all white males negatively.

EDITED The principal argued against the schoolteachers' referendum.

DISCRIMINATORY The Johnsons **welshed on** their response.

READER'S REACTION: What made you think that you could say this without offending people of Welsh descent? Casual stereotyping is just as offensive as deliberate insults.

EDITED The Johnsons were not true to their word.

2 Revise unfair stereotypes

Some racial and cultural stereotypes are so ingrained in our society that you may not notice them at first. Try to maintain a critical consciousness about these stereotypes, and edit sentences or words that run the risk of unfairly stereotyping groups. Don't rely on your intentions here; think first about how your reader *might* construe your words.

RACIST/ELITIST The streets in St. Paul are so confusing that they must have been planned by a bunch of **drunken Irishmen.**

READER'S REACTION: I object to the off-hand acceptance of this stereotype and the condescending attitude toward a group of people.

EDITED The streets in St. Paul are so confusing that no one appears to have done any planning.

DEMEANING My paper focuses on the **weird** courtship rituals of a **barbaric** Aboriginal tribe living in southwestern Australia.

READER'S REACTION: **Your paper already sounds biased. How can you fairly inform me about this topic if you don't speak respectfully about this tribe yourself?**

EDITED My paper focuses on the unusual courtship rituals of an Aboriginal tribe living in southwestern Australia.

In attempts to create an ideally just world, some social critics have proposed new names and terms for various groups, such as the homeless, the physically and mentally disabled, and even the short or the fat. The terms *vagabond*, *bum*, and *tramp*, for example, are no longer acceptable; *homeless* is now generally preferred. More questionable, however, are the terms *differently abled* for *disabled*, *vertically challenged* for *short*, and *pre-woman* for *girl*. Debates about such proposed substitutions don't seem likely to subside in the near future. The best advice on this matter is to test your choices on your readers and keep up with changes in the language.

3 Choose appropriate group names and terms

Just as the issue of sexism in language continues to evolve, the representation of various groups, especially minorities, cannot be seen as "finally" corrected. Making informed decisions about how to identify different groups may require some thought or consultation. The term *American Indian* is still widely accepted, but a preferred form, *Native American*, has entered the vocabulary. Some Native American groups prefer their tribal names (*Hopi*, *Navajo*, *Havasupai*). In the 1960s, the word *Negro* gradually gave way to *black*, but not without considerable overlap in usage and much debate in both the black and white communities, including whether the terms should be capitalized. The term *colored* has been out of use for some time, but *people of color* is now preferred for members of any "nonwhite" minority group. (Many people also object to the term *nonwhite*.) *African American* itself has been gaining popularity in place of *black*, though even African Americans do not agree on which is preferred. Terms for people of Hispanic descent can also be confusing, from *Chicano* (and its feminine form, *Chicana*) for Mexicans to *Latino* and *Latina* for people from South and Central America more generally.

How, then, should you decide what terms to use to describe members of various groups?

1. Whenever possible, use the term preferred *by the group itself*.
2. When there is disagreement within the group itself about the preferred name or term, choose the *most widely accepted term* or the one favored by a majority of the group's members.

Exercise 5

A. The chief editor of a large city newspaper received several complaint letters from readers about a sportswriter's use of the word *niggardly* to characterize the owner of a major football team who was reluctant to pay the salary asked by a new superstar player. In a column, the chief editor explained that the word *niggardly* means "stingy" or "cheap" (from Old Norse) and has absolutely no etymological connection with any racial terms. Yet some readers were offended. And, he argued, as long as they were simply *reminded* of a more offensive word, he had a duty to avoid it. He subsequently asked all reporters and editors to use alternative words. In your judgment, did the chief editor do the right thing? What issues are at stake here? Write a position statement.

B. Share your position statement from Exercise 5A with your classmates.

PART 10

Punctuation, Mechanics, and Spelling

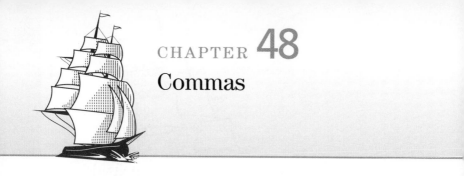

CHAPTER 48 Commas

Of all the punctuation marks in the English language, the comma is probably the one writers most often misuse. Perhaps because at some places in a sentence, commas are mandatory; at others, they are optional. Following is a sentence that uses no commas.

> During interviews avoid dominating the discussion because doing so especially with reticent subjects can affect whatever they say cut off the free flow of their ideas and contaminate your data.

Clearly, it's difficult to read. Where should you use commas? In the following version, they are correctly used and make the sentence easier to read and understand.

> During interviews, avoid dominating the discussion because doing so, especially with reticent subjects, can affect whatever they say, cut off the free flow of their ideas, and contaminate your data.

48a Joining sentences

Whenever you wish to use *and*, *but*, *or*, *for*, *nor*, *so*, or *yet* (coordinating conjunctions) to link two word groups that can stand alone as sentences (main clauses—see 32c), you need to use a comma before the conjunction.

> The air was cold, **and** he could see his breath.
>
> He heard the dog barking on the other side of the field, **so** he decided to investigate.
>
> The ground was rough, **yet** the dog still ran quickly through the grass.

Remember that a comma alone isn't enough; join main clauses with a comma *plus* a coordinating conjunction. If you join the clauses with only a comma, you create a comma splice, a serious sentence error that can distract or irritate readers (see 38a).

If the main clauses you plan to join are quite short or there is no danger of misreading, you can sometimes omit the comma.

The temperature dropped **and** the snow began falling.

A comma is appropriate even with short clauses, however.

When you use a comma plus a coordinating conjunction to join main clauses, make sure you do not distract readers by adding commas at the following inappropriate places.

- Coming after *and, but, or, nor, so, yet,* or *for* linking main clauses rather than before.

  INCORRECT I coated the table with varnish **and,** I sanded it again.

  EDITED I coated the table with varnish**,** **and** I sanded it again.

- Coming between sentence elements other than main clauses—words, phrases, or clauses—that are linked by a coordinating conjunction.

  INCORRECT We sanded**,** and stained the old oak table.
  The comma splits parts of a compound verb that belong together.

  EDITED We sanded and stained the old oak table.

  INCORRECT I bought a wood stain that was inexpensive**,** and that cleaned up easily.
  The comma comes between subordinate clauses, not main clauses.

  EDITED I bought a wood stain that was inexpensive and that cleaned up easily.

SERIOUS ERROR

48a ^,

Exercise 1

A. Combine each of the following sentence pairs into a single sentence, using commas and coordinating conjunctions.

EXAMPLE

Shopping by mail can be convenient~~. It~~, and it sometimes helps save money.

1. Jim wanted to buy paper for his copier. He went to all the office supply stores in town.
2. The stores had plenty of paper. It cost more than Jim was willing to pay.
3. Jim then heard about a mail-order office supply company. He called the company for a catalog.
4. The catalog contained more than fifty different kinds of reasonably priced copier paper. The paper was available in packs of one thousand sheets. For an even greater discount, the paper came in bulk orders of five thousand sheets.
5. He ordered five thousand sheets of medium-quality paper. It lasted for three months.

B. Compare your versions of the sentences in Exercise 1A with those produced by a group of classmates. Decide which versions are the most effective and why.

48b Setting off introductory phrases

A comma can help your readers sort sentence parts that might otherwise run together and create confusion. The simplest sentences need no comma.

noun verb phrase
Jessica mowed the lawn.

When you add another layer to this basic sentence—a word or a word group—you may need to signal the addition with a comma.

Tirelessly, Jessica mowed the lawn.

On Saturday, Jessica mowed the lawn.

After running five miles, Jessica mowed the lawn.

In spite of the throbbing pain in her ankle, Jessica mowed the lawn.

Place a comma after an introductory sentence element when the comma makes the sentence easier to read and understand.

48a ^,

CONFUSING Forgetting to remove the hose Jessica mowed the lawn.

EDITED Forgetting to remove the hose, Jessica mowed the lawn.
The comma lets readers know where the introductory word group ends and the main sentence begins.

In contrast, the following sentences are easy to understand without a comma.

CLEAR By noon Jessica will be finished mowing the lawn.

CLEAR Suddenly it started raining and Jessica quit mowing.

In general, you need to put a comma at the end of a long introductory element to let readers know where the main sentence begins.

CONFUSING When Ruane came home and saw the chopped pieces of hose she was furious at Jessica.

CLEAR When Ruane came home and saw the chopped pieces of hose, **she** was furious at Jessica.

You should also use a comma with a short introductory element that might otherwise briefly confuse readers.

CONFUSING By six boats began showing up.

EDITED By six, boats began showing up.

You can insert a comma to tell readers which of two possible meanings you intend.

Curious, George went deeper into the cave.

Curious George went deeper into the cave.
Curious George is a character in a series of children's books.

Well, over there was where I saw him, officer.

Well over there was where I saw him, officer.
Well over there is a location.

1 Use a comma after an introductory clause beginning with *because, although, if,* and similar words

When you open a sentence with a clause that begins with a word such as *since*, *although*, *because*, or *when*, place a comma after the clause to mark the beginning of the main sentence. (See 44c on subordinate clauses and subordinating words.)

Although I am healthy, I see a physician for a regular checkup.

When I need to see my doctor because I feel ill, I can usually schedule an appointment within a day.

2 Use a comma after an introductory phrase

Phrases lack one or more elements necessary to form a complete sentence, such as a subject, a predicate, or both (see 32b). When you start a sentence with a phrase, you generally add a comma to signal the boundary between the phrase and the main sentence.

During the past decade, Dr. Bandola worked for an HMO.

Having grown tired of the HMO's management, she decided last year to open her own medical practice.

Worried about the costs of a new office, she consulted a real estate broker specializing in medical and dental offices.

To furnish her waiting room, she went to a discount office furniture company.

Her office now furnished, she is ready to begin seeing patients.

3 Use a comma after introductory words like *however* or transitional phrases like *for example*

Set off words like *however*, *nonetheless*, and *moreover* (**conjunctive adverbs;** see 32a-6) when they begin a sentence. Do the same with *for example*, *in addition*, *in contrast*, and similar word groups (**transitional expressions**).

> **Nonetheless,** I do not think we should ban all chemical pesticides.
>
> **In contrast,** a group of organic farmers has been urging us to rely entirely on natural methods of pest control.

You may occasionally wish to open a sentence with an interjection, such as *yes*, *no*, *well*, or *oh*. When you do, follow it with a comma unless an exclamation mark is more appropriate as a way to express strong emotion.

> **Yes,** I cleaned the beakers and the test tubes.
>
> **No!** I do not want to attend any more meetings on the problem.

Exercise 2

A. Edit the following sentences by placing commas after introductory elements where necessary.

EXAMPLE

In the past, mailboxes usually had simple designs.

48b

1. In contrast mailboxes today come in many surprising designs.
2. Occasionally people in the suburbs choose an unusual mailbox, but residents of small towns generally display the most imagination.
3. On a recent trip through rural Iowa I noticed mailboxes in the shape of log cabins, igloos, Eiffel Towers, cows, cats, and even parrots.
4. One morning I drove down a block on which each mailbox took the shape of a different kind of fish, including bass, trout, bluegill, shark, pike, and salmon.
5. Whenever you start thinking that people in big cities or suburbs are more creative than people in small towns remember the mailboxes.

B. Working in a group, combine each of the following pairs of sentences by making one an introductory element for the other. Insert commas when appropriate.

EXAMPLE

Because
~~The~~ the morning was gray and foggy, ~~Many~~ many people woke up late.

1. People felt sleepy. They still had to go to their offices and plants for a full day's work.
2. People were trying to get to work on time. They jammed the highways and commuter trains.
3. Avi felt rested and alert. The gloomy weather did not bother him.
4. Avi worked hard throughout the afternoon. The other people in Avi's office were exhausted by two o'clock in the afternoon.
5. Avi still felt awake at seven o'clock in the evening. He went to see a movie.

48c Setting off nonrestrictive modifiers

Restrictive and nonrestrictive modifiers are common midsentence elements. You use a **restrictive modifier** to present information that is essential to the meaning of a passage. You use a **nonrestrictive modifier** to add information that is interesting or useful but that is not essential to the meaning (see 39c).

1 Recognize nonrestrictive and restrictive modifiers

As you edit, you need to recognize nonrestrictive modifiers and set them off with commas. You also need to be able to recognize restrictive modifiers, which require no commas to set them off.

Because of the difference between restrictive and nonrestrictive modifiers, you can change the meaning of a sentence considerably by deciding whether to set off a modifier with commas.

When the information in a modifier adds to a passage but is not essential to its meaning, set it off with commas so that readers will regard it as providing helpful but not necessary detail.

NONRESTRICTIVE The charts, **drawn by hand**, were hard to read.

READER'S REACTION: This sentence says that all the charts were hard to read. It adds the detail that the charts were hand-drawn but doesn't indicate that this was necessarily related to the problem with legibility.

When the information in a modifier is essential to the meaning of a passage, present it without commas so that readers will regard it as a necessary, integral part of the sentence.

RESTRICTIVE The charts **drawn by hand** were hard to read.

READER'S REACTION: This sentence implies that other charts, presumably computer-generated, were easier to read than the hand-drawn ones.

STRATEGY

To identify a nonrestrictive modifier, try eliminating the modifier from a sentence. If you can do so without altering the sentence's essential meaning, then the modifier is nonrestrictive and you should use commas with it.

UNEDITED SENTENCE — Their band **which performs primarily in small venues like clubs** has gotten many fine reviews for its music.

WITHOUT MODIFIER — Their band has gotten many fine reviews for its music.
The meaning is retained, though the sentence does not offer as much interesting information. The modifier is nonrestrictive.

EDITED — Their band, **which performs primarily in small venues like clubs**, has gotten many fine reviews for its music.

If eliminating a modifier changes a sentence's meaning, the modifier is restrictive. Do not set it off with commas.

UNEDITED SENTENCE — Executives, **who do not know how to cope with stress**, are prone to stress-related illness.

WITHOUT MODIFIER — Executives are prone to stress-related illness.
The intended meaning of the original sentence is that *some* executives are susceptible to stress-related problems; the shortened sentence says *all* are. The modifier is restrictive.

SERIOUS ERROR

EDITED — Executives **who do not know how to cope with stress** are prone to stress-related illness.

2 Understand the use of commas with nonrestrictive modifiers

If a nonrestrictive modifier appears in the middle of a sentence, enclose it with commas. Place a comma after one coming at the beginning of a sentence and before one coming at the end.

main clause begins, nonrestrictive modifier, main clause ends
The public hearing, scheduled for 7 p.m., will gather responses to cable TV rates.

nonrestrictive modifier, main clause
Unable to meet their rising costs, the cable companies have requested a rate hike.

main clause, nonrestrictive modifier
Many oppose the hike, which is larger than last year's.

3 Pay special attention to modifying clauses, phrases, and appositives

In recognizing nonrestrictive (and restrictive) modifiers as you edit, keep in mind that they can be clauses, phrases, or words (see 39c).

Look for modifying clauses beginning with *who* and *which*. Pay special attention to clauses beginning with *who, which, that, whom, whose, when,* or *where* (see 32c-5 and 39c), and decide whether or not they should be set off with commas. These common modifying elements can appear in the middle or at the end of a sentence.

NONRESTRICTIVE Preventive dentistry, **which is receiving greater emphasis**, reduces the number of times each of us has to visit a dentist's office.

NONRESTRICTIVE At the heart of preventive dentistry are toothbrushing, flossing, and rinsing, **which are all easily done.**

RESTRICTIVE Dentists **who make a special effort to encourage good oral hygiene** often provide helpful pamphlets and samples of toothbrushes and floss.

48c

Watch for modifying phrases. Be alert as well for phrases (word groups lacking a subject, a predicate, or both) that are nonrestrictive and should be marked with commas. These modifying elements can appear at the beginning, middle, or end of sentences.

NONRESTRICTIVE **Occupying the daily headline of the local newspaper for the last two weeks**, our city's budget crisis now threatens to spread to the state budget.

NONRESTRICTIVE The governor has called for a conference of the people most directly involved in trying to solve the budget problem, **including the mayor, state legislators, and the city's budget director.**

RESTRICTIVE City services **popular with voters** are seldom cut from the budget.

Look for appositives. An **appositive** is a noun or pronoun that renames or stands for a preceding noun. Since most appositives are nonrestrictive, you generally need to set off appositives with a comma. Be on the lookout for an occasional restrictive appositive, however, and do not use commas with it.

NONRESTRICTIVE Amy Nguyen, **a poet from Vietnam**, recently published her second collection of verse.

NONRESTRICTIVE An athletic performance drink, **a concoction of electrolytes, vitamins, minerals, and fructose**, contributed to Jose's endurance in the marathon.

NONRESTRICTIVE Stump grinding, **a method for removing old tree roots with a special machine**, is much easier than digging the roots out with a shovel.

RESTRICTIVE The well-known executive **Louis Gerstner** went from heading RJR Nabisco to the top job at IBM.

RESTRICTIVE The terms ***cognitive* and *neural pathways*** are familiar to anyone involved in brain research.

Exercise 3

A. Edit the following sentences to set off all nonrestrictive modifiers with commas and to eliminate any commas that unnecessarily set off restrictive modifiers.

EXAMPLE

My mother, who is ninety, lives in the retirement residence, called South Bay Manor.

1. Fifty years ago, a residence that served retired people, was called an old folks' home.
2. These homes which provided few services for residents were apartment buildings with dining rooms.
3. A retirement residence today offers many things to do including recreational activities, fitness programs, trips, classes, and social events.
4. The image of infirm people, sitting in rocking chairs, has been replaced by one of senior citizens, who are vigorous and involved.
5. Retirement residences often known as retirement communities are small towns, where people go to lead active lives.

B. Have each member of a small group bring in a paragraph from a magazine article, both in original form and rewritten to eliminate the commas setting off all nonrestrictive modifiers. Working as a group, first restore the commas to the rewritten versions, then check the originals to see if you agree with their punctuation.

48d Setting off parenthetical expressions

The basic structure of a sentence can be interrupted with all sorts of words and word groups that add information or modify the sentence's various elements. Use commas to set off words like *however* and *moreover* (see

32a-6, 38b). Do the same with transitional expressions like *on the other hand* and *for example* and with parenthetical remarks like *in fact* and *more important* (sometimes called **interrupters**).

TRANSITIONAL EXPRESSION	The hailstorm last week, **in contrast,** caused severe damage.
INTERRUPTER	**In fact,** the hailstorm was so powerful that it broke a dozen priceless stained glass windows on the west side of the church.
CONJUNCTIVE ADVERB	We should not be surprised, **therefore,** if someone takes up a collection for the windows' repair.

You should also use commas to set off tag questions, statements of contrast, and words indicating direct address.

TAG QUESTIONS	We should be ready to contribute to the cause even if we don't attend the church, **shouldn't we?**
STATEMENT OF CONTRAST	The windows' beauty touched all of us in the community, **not just the church members.**
DIRECT ADDRESS	Please remember, **friends of beauty,** that your contribution will help restore the windows to their former magnificence.

Exercise 4

Edit the following sentences to add or delete commas as appropriate.

EXAMPLE

Scheduling may be, in fact, the toughest job any manager faces.

1. Project schedules need to be arranged so that the job gets done on time of course.
2. Moreover meetings need to be set up so they do not interrupt people's work, unnecessarily.
3. Most staff members are cooperative however, and may even offer suggestions for scheduling.
4. Management training programs should, I think offer instruction in scheduling techniques.
5. Remember your staff's time is too valuable to be wasted.

48e Using commas in a series

Whenever you list items in a series and give each roughly equal status, you should separate the items with commas. In one sense, commas take the place of a repeated *and*, which appears only before the last item in the series.

HARD TO READ Harvey's favorite novels are *Moby-Dick* **and** *The Awakening* **and** *Jane Eyre* **and** *Things Fall Apart.*

EDITED Harvey's favorite novels are *Moby-Dick*, *The Awakening*, *Jane Eyre*, **and** *Things Fall Apart.*

Placing a comma before the *and* that introduces the last item in a series helps avoid confusion. Many readers prefer this practice, especially in academic and professional writing. Editors of newspapers and some magazines, however, do not use this comma.

CONFUSING The ingredients for the casserole are peas, potatoes, ham, caramelized sugar and bread crumbs.

READER'S REACTION: **Does *caramelized sugar* and *bread crumbs* refer to some special mixture, or are they two separate ingredients?**

EDITED The ingredients for the casserole are peas, potatoes, ham, caramelized sugar, and bread crumbs.

A numbered or lettered list that is part of a sentence should be punctuated as a series.

> To make sure your analysis is complete, you should (1) check the bottom of the container for residue, (2) measure the salinity of the water, (3) weigh any organic waste in the filter, and (4) determine the amount of dissolved oxygen in the water.

48f ^,

If the items in a list are long and complex or if they contain commas, separate the items with semicolons rather than commas (see 49a).

CONFUSING The company is marketing a line of jigsaw puzzles of cities, like San Antonio, Texas, states, like Michigan and Montana, and countries, like Mexico, Japan, and France.

EDITED The company is marketing a line of jigsaw puzzles of cities, like San Antonio, Texas; states, like Michigan and Montana; and countries, like Mexico, Japan, and France.

48f Separating coordinate adjectives

In a pair of **coordinate adjectives,** each adjective modifies a noun on its own. Thus, you need to separate coordinate adjectives with commas.

COORDINATE (EQUAL) These drawings describe a **quick**, **simple** solution to the drainage problem.

With **noncoordinate adjectives,** the first adjective modifies the entire noun phrase formed by the next adjectives plus the noun. Usually, noncoordinate adjectives are of different categories. For example, one adjective may describe a quality and another a nationality, as in the phrase *friendly Dutch student* (see 36a). Do not separate noncoordinate adjectives with a comma. In the following example, the adjective *flexible* modifies *plastic pipe.*

NONCOORDINATE (UNEQUAL) We can use **flexible plastic** pipe to carry water away from the building.

In place of a comma, you can connect coordinate adjectives with *and* or *but.*

COORDINATE These drawings describe a **quick and simple** solution to the drainage problem.

STRATEGY

If the answer to either of the following questions is *yes*, the adjectives are coordinate and should be separated with a comma.

- Can you place *and* or *but* between the adjectives?

COORDINATE Through irrigation, the region's farmers have turned dry infertile [*dry and infertile?—yes*] land into orchards.

EDITED Through irrigation, the region's farmers have turned dry, infertile land into orchards.

NOT COORDINATE Five percent of the budget goes to new telecommunications [*new and telecommunications?—no*] equipment.

- Can you easily invert the adjectives without creating an awkward sentence?

COORDINATE We moved from our small cramped [*cramped small?—acceptable*] apartment.

EDITED We moved from our small, cramped apartment.

NOT COORDINATE We moved to a small Manhattan [*Manhattan small?—awkward*] apartment.

Exercise 5

A. Edit the following sentences so that any series and any coordinate adjectives are correctly punctuated. Let any correct sentence stand.

EXAMPLE

McDonald's, Burger King, and Wendy's are worldwide symbols of American culture.

1. McDonald's and the others offer quick appetizing meals and clean pleasant surroundings.
2. In the late 1940s, the McDonald brothers opened a restaurant serving a limited inexpensive menu, including fifteen-cent hamburgers french fries and shakes.
3. The brothers did not want to expand their modestly successful restaurant into a chain.
4. Ray Kroc, a manufacturer of milkshake machines, recognized the potential of the brothers' innovations joined their business to help it expand and, frustrated by their lack of ambition, eventually bought them out.
5. Kroc continued to develop innovative imaginative ways to serve customers, and these fast efficient practices have come to characterize today's fast-food restaurants.

B. Working with a partner, exchange your current papers. Edit your partner's draft so that all series and coordinate adjectives are correctly punctuated.

48g Dates, numbers, addresses, place names, people's titles, and letters

Separate the elements in dates, place names, long numbers, and addresses according to conventional practice. Separate the elements whether or not they appear in sentences.

1 Dates

Put a comma between the date and the year and between the day of the week and the date.

The first computer in this office arrived on August 17, 1985.

The workshop will begin on Wednesday, September 23.

In the middle of a sentence, follow the year with a comma when you are giving the full date.

On February 4, 1961, the woman destined to be my mother was born in the middle of a snowstorm.

Use no commas when giving only month and year or a month and a day.

A test version of the software will be available in January 2005. The regular version will be shipped to stores on June 1.

Likewise, do not use commas with dates stating a season and a year.

The fall 2004 issue of the magazine arrived late.

Do not use commas with the elements of a date in inverted order (MLA style): 5 July 2006.

2 Numbers

To help readers understand long numbers, use commas to create groups of three, beginning from the right. With four digits, you may choose whether or not to use the comma, but keep your practice consistent.

During the livestock census on the ranch, we counted 1,746 sheep, 835 beef cattle, and 3,589 chickens.

The combined income for people in our rural town is $8,543,234.

The best high-speed server costs $3,525 at Electronics World.

Omit commas in addresses and all page numbers.

18520 South Kedzie Drive page 2054

ESL ADVICE: NUMBERS

Use commas to create groups of three. Periods are used only to indicate decimals.

1.000 = one 1,000 = one thousand

3 Addresses and place names

Separate names of cities and states with commas. Within a sentence, place a comma between all elements *except* the state and zip code.

Kansas City, Missouri, is a larger town than Kansas City, Kansas.

You can order the zucchini and carrot seeds from Fredelle and Family, Seed Brokers, Box 389, Holland, Michigan 30127.

Do not place a comma after the zip code unless the punctuation of some other sentence element requires one.

NO COMMA Send the bill to Mr. Robert Mfume at 82 Nassau Avenue, Kenmore, New York 11327-8501 for a full refund.

COMMA NEEDED The pamphlet can be obtained from Bradley Hospital, Veterans Memorial Parkway, East Providence, Rhode Island 02915, a children's psychiatric center.

4 People's names and titles

Place a comma before a title or initials that come after a person's name.

The report on possible lung damage among plant employees was prepared by **Luis Aguayo, M.D.**

If the name and title come at the beginning of a sentence or in the middle, use a comma after the title as well.

We hired **Crystal Bronkowski, A.I.A.,** to design the new building.

When you give a person's surname (last name) first, separate it from the first name with a comma: **Shamoon, Linda K.**

5 Salutations and closings of letters

Use a comma after the salutation of personal or informal letters.

Dear Tiffany, Dear Volleyball Players,

Use a colon after the salutation in business and formal letters.

Dear Specialty Metals Customers: Dear Sir or Madam:

Use a comma after a letter's closing, just before the signature.

Sincerely, Best wishes, With affection, Regards,

Exercise 6

A. Edit the following sentences by adding or eliminating commas as appropriate.

EXAMPLE

My mother remembers assembling her first jigsaw puzzle in autumn, 1985, several months before my birth on January 22, 1986.

1. Puzzles have fascinated me for the last thirty years, and last year I spent exactly $2479.83 on them.
2. For my birthday this year, one cousin gave me a map of Chicago Illinois in the form of a jigsaw puzzle, and another cousin gave me a puzzle of a seventeenth-century print from the Beinecke Library at Yale University New Haven Connecticut.
3. I have ordered a puzzle map of Atlanta Georgia from Buffalo Games, Inc. P.O. Box 85 601 Amherst Street Buffalo New York 14207 and a puzzle of Edward Hopper's painting, *Nighthawks* from Galison Books 36 West 44th Street New York New York 10036.
4. From January through June 2001, I assembled one puzzle a week, with the puzzles ranging from 500 to 1250 pieces each for a total of somewhere between 10500 pieces and 26250 pieces.
5. I am planning to have a business card made up with both my official and unofficial titles, Jessica Montoya Ph.D. Puzzle Assembler.

B. Working in a group, share copies of magazine or newspaper articles that contain numbers, addresses, people's names and titles, or openings and closings of letters. Check the articles to see whether they follow the same conventions for comma use as those described in 48g. If not, or if the author uses commas inconsistently, edit each article so that it agrees with the recommendations for comma use covered in 48g.

SERIOUS ERROR

48h Commas with quotations

When you introduce or conclude a quotation by indicating its source, separate your explanation and the quotation itself by using commas.

At the grand opening, he said, "This facility is dedicated to the physical and mental health of the citizens of Oakdale."

"Some books are meant to be chewed," said Francis Bacon, "and others to be digested."

Because the explanatory words interrupt the quotation, the first part ends with a comma.

"The fire doors need to be replaced before the school can be reopened," the commissioner wrote.

When a quotation ends with a question mark or an exclamation point, keep this punctuation even if your sentence continues.

"We can't afford the $30,000 to replace the doors right away!" the schoolboard president responded angrily.

"Why can't you understand the paramount importance of fire safety?" the commissioner retorted.

If your explanation ends with *that* just before the quotation, do not include a comma.

> Lorene Cary begins her story by saying that "they had just come home from Woolworth's, where they both worked at the cheap-and-greasy fountain on Friday nights and Saturdays in a town they and their friends called 'Tacky' Darby."

When you quote a person's words indirectly (rather than word for word in quotation marks), do not use a comma after *that*.

FAULTY He testified that, he did not damage the machinery as a protest during the strike.

EDITED He testified that he did not damage the machinery as a protest during the strike.

Exercise 7

A. Edit the following passages by adding, deleting, or moving commas so that quotations are appropriately punctuated.

"Ice cream is virtually the only food we eat frozen, which means that its flavor, which we define as a composite of taste and smell, is only fully released upon melting" explains Arun Kilara, a 43-year-old professor of food science at Penn State and one of the world's acknowledged authorities on ice cream.

Not surprisingly, few true ice cream connoisseurs are fond of the industry's use of fat substitutes, such as the complex protein found in NutraSweet's Simplesse. "The search for the perfect fat substitute" Kilara says "is like a contemporary version of alchemy—lots of useful discoveries, but they'll never turn lead into gold." While some protein-based fat substitutes approximate fat's texture, or "mouth feel" he explains, they cannot dissolve flavor compounds in the same way.

"The smaller the ice crystals, the smoother the ice cream" says Kilara. "You get the smallest crystals when the drop in temperature is the most rapid and when agitation is most vigorous."

"There's one basic truth about ice cream—its quality begins deteriorating from the moment it is made" Kilara concludes. "Over the product's lifetime, ice cream's air escapes, its fat clumps, its ice melts, and its water freezes."

—LAWRENCE E. JOSEPH, "The Scoop on Ice Cream"

B. Working in a group, write a paragraph that presents information drawn from a newspaper or magazine article. Include several quotations from the article in your paragraph. Indicate the source or context for the quotations, and use commas appropriately to introduce or conclude the quoted material.

SERIOUS ERROR

48i Commas to make your meaning clear

Even if no rule specifies a comma, you may still include one in a sentence if it is necessary to make your meaning clear to readers, to remind them of deleted words, or to add emphasis.

CONFUSING When food is scarce, animals that can expand their grazing territory at the expense of other species.

EDITED When food is scarce, animals that can, expand their grazing territory at the expense of other species.

HARD TO READ Anyone who can afford to buy this high-speed file management program should.

EDITED Anyone who can afford to buy this high-speed file management program, should.
The comma reminds readers that should means "should do so."

UNEMPHATIC Stocks go up and down.

EMPHATIC Stocks go up, and down.
The comma emphasizes the contrast.

SERIOUS ERROR

48j Commas that do not belong

When they are not sure precisely where to put commas, some writers insert them at every possible point. The result is confusing and irritating to readers. If you are not sure whether to add a comma, leave it out until you have checked to make sure one is required.

1 Do not insert a comma after words like *although* and *because* that introduce a clause

Words like *although*, *when*, and *since* (subordinators; see 44c-2) introduce an entire subordinate clause and should not be set off with commas.

INCORRECT **Although**, Jim had just started to learn how to ski, we took him to the most expert slope on his first trip up the mountain.

EDITED **Although** Jim had just started to learn how to ski, we took him to the most expert slope on his first trip up the mountain.

2 Do not insert a comma between a subject and a predicate

Don't insert a comma between subjects and predicates unless they are separated by a modifying clause (see 48c-3).

INCORRECT Cézanne's painting *Rocks at L'Estaque*, hangs in the Museu de Arte in São Paulo, Brazil.

EDITED Cézanne's painting *Rocks at L'Estaque* hangs in the Museu de Arte in São Paulo, Brazil.

3 Do not overuse commas

Today readers generally prefer a style in which commas are not used heavily. Whenever possible, avoid sentence structures that call for a large number of commas. If necessary, edit and rewrite.

TOO MANY COMMAS Samantha, always one, like her mother, to speak her mind, loudly protested the use of force, as she called it, by two store detectives, who had been observing her while she, looking for bargains, absentmindedly slipped a pair of gloves into her jacket pocket.

SERIOUS ERROR

EDITED Always one to speak her mind, like her mother, Samantha loudly protested what she considered the use of force by two store detectives who saw her absentmindedly slip a pair of gloves into her jacket pocket while she was looking for bargains.

48j

Exercise 8

A. Edit each of the following sentences in two ways: (1) by removing any unnecessary commas and (2) by rewriting to create sentence structures that contain fewer commas, all of which are necesssary.

EXAMPLE

When, they realized they had no job prospects, the five friends, formed, a company, which they called Home Restorers, Inc.

When they realized they had no job prospects, the five friends formed Home Restorers, Inc.

1. Because, she likes the outdoors, Sandy, a devoted gardener, takes care of landscaping, grass cutting, and outdoor cleanup.
2. Strong, tireless Jun, does roofing, paving, and similar work.
3. Interior design was, Padmaja's major, so she, everyone agrees, is the person best qualified to do interior decorating.

4. Having painted, her parents' house one summer, Rachael was, chosen, by her partners, as the company's painting supervisor.
5. Desperate, for a place in the company, Joel decided that, marketing, because it would draw on his undergraduate work in sociology, was the best thing for him to do.

B. Exchange draft papers with another writer, and edit each other's work to eliminate unnecessary commas. When you encounter a sentence that might be rewritten to reduce the number of commas, underline it. When your partner returns your paper, check over the editorial changes and consider rewriting any underlined sentences.

CHAPTER 49
Semicolons and Colons

Semicolons and colons help you connect words, word groups, or sentences in useful and varied ways.

> On April 12, 1861, at 4:30 a.m., one of Beauregard's batteries fired upon Fort **Sumter. The** Civil War had begun.
>
> On April 12, 1861, at 4:30 a.m., one of Beauregard's batteries fired upon Fort **Sumter; the** Civil War had begun.
>
> On April 12, 1861, at 4:30 a.m., one of Beauregard's batteries fired upon Fort **Sumter: the** Civil War had begun.

Each example encourages readers to take a different perspective. In the first, there is no *necessary* connection between the two sentences. Readers may choose whether to view them as simple statements of fact or as the presentation of a dramatic moment. In the second, however, the *semicolon* connects the two statements and encourages readers to link the firing of a gun battery to the beginning of the Civil War. In the third version, the *colon* provides even more direction. It focuses on the guns' firing as a dramatic and significant moment: the beginning of the Civil War.

49a Using semicolons

A semicolon joins two word groups (main clauses) that could act as complete sentences on their own. The semicolon indicates that the clauses are linked logically; at the same time, it creates a brief reading pause between them.

1 Try joining two sentences with a semicolon

You can use a semicolon to join two complete sentences (main clauses; see 32c-2) into a single unit. Think of a semicolon as an alternative to using a period and starting a new sentence.

TWO SENTENCES The demand for paper products is at an all-time high. Businesses consume millions of tons of paper each year.

ONE SENTENCE The demand for paper products is at an all-time high; businesses consume millions of tons of paper each year.

You signal the relationship between main clauses by joining them with a semicolon, though you do not specify the logical link as you might by joining them with a word such as *and*, *but*, or *yet* (see 44a). A semicolon can highlight the close relationship of ideas or dramatically emphasize a contrast.

> The city council wants more parks, an expanded recreation program, and a civic center; the mayor wants to cut expenses and limit services.

When you join such units with a semicolon, make sure readers will be able to recognize the relationship without having to puzzle over the sentence.

STRATEGY

Check for correct use of a semicolon by making sure the units on either side of the semicolon can stand on their own as sentences.

INCORRECT The demand for recycled paper has also increased greatly; with manufacturers looking for new supplies of scrap paper.

TEST The demand for recycled paper has also increased greatly.
The first clause is a complete sentence.

With manufacturers looking for new supplies of scrap paper.
The second part is a sentence fragment.

CORRECT The demand for recycled paper has also increased greatly; manufacturers are looking for new supplies of scrap paper.

2 Use a semicolon with words such as *however, on the other hand*

When you use a semicolon by itself to link sentences, you ask readers to recognize the relationship on their own; in contrast, when you use a word like *however* or an expression like *on the other hand*, you specify the relationship. The effect on readers is something like the following.

assertion	→	semicolon (*pause*)	→	transition (*consider relationship*)	→	assertion
I like apples assertion		; pause		**however**, contrast		I hate pears. assertion

To specify the link, you can choose a **conjunctive adverb** such as *however, moreover, thus*, or *therefore* (see 44b-2) or a **transitional expression** like *for example, in contrast*, or *on the other hand*. The linking words can appear between the units (just after the semicolon), within a clause, or at the end of a clause. If it comes right after a semicolon, it must be followed by a comma; if it comes within a clause, it must be enclosed by commas; if it comes at the end of a clause, it must be preceded by a comma.

BETWEEN	Joe returned from the Arctic; **however**, Alan was never found.
WITHIN	Joe returned from the Arctic; Alan, **however**, was never found.
AT END	Joe returned from the Arctic; Alan was never found, **however.**

Consider joining a series of short to medium-length sentences with semicolons when (1) the sentences are logically linked; (2) as a group, the unlinked sentences seem choppy or disconnected; and (3) commas do not separate the elements enough to encourage readers to consider each one fully.

CHOPPY	The shelty took first prize. The German shepherd took second. The poodle walked away in third place.
BETTER	The shelty took first prize, the German shepherd took second, **and** the poodle walked away in third place.
MOST EFFECTIVE	The shelty took first prize; the German shepherd took second; and the poodle walked away with third.

49a ;

3 Use a semicolon with deleted structures

There are exceptions to the rule that semicolons must join units that can stand on their own as sentences (main clauses). In some cases, you can delete elements in a second clause if they "match" elements in the first. You can join them with a semicolon even though the second clause cannot stand on its own as a sentence.

ELEMENTS INCLUDED	In winter, **the hotel guests enjoy** the log fire in the dining room; in summer, **the hotel guests enjoy** the patio overlooking the river.
ELEMENTS DELETED	In winter, **the hotel guests enjoy** the log fire in the dining room; in summer, the patio overlooking the river.

4 Use a semicolon with a complex series

Most of the time, you can use commas to separate elements in a series, with no risk of confusion (see 48e). When some of the items themselves contain commas, however, readers may struggle to decide which mark series parts and which belong within items.

CONFUSING For the project, I interviewed Debbie Rios, my roommate, Liza Marron, my former employer, and my calculus instructor.

READER'S REACTION: **How many people were interviewed? three, four, or five?**

To avoid confusion, put semicolons between elements in a series when one or more of the elements contain commas or some other internal punctuation such as a dash, parentheses, or a colon.

EDITED For the project, I interviewed Debbie Rios, my roommate; Liza Marron, my former employer; and my calculus instructor.

Exercise 1

A. The following passage contains some semicolons used correctly and some used incorrectly. It also contains sentences that might be more effective if joined with semicolons and others that would be better as separate sentences. Rewrite the passage, adding or eliminating semicolons and making any other changes necessary to create a more effective piece of writing.

The Grateful Dead came back into my life recently; largely because of my children's interest. My daughter has been *associated* with the group; I find it difficult to apply the common description of a fan as a Deadhead; since she was fifteen. Her school band; the Cosmic Country Sound, was patterned after the Grateful Dead; she was its lead singer and tambourine player.

I had no idea that my son, four years younger; had any interest in the group. His room is decorated with posters of Boris Becker and Albert Einstein. But then a year ago he let his hair grow into a mane; started wearing beaded necklaces and rope wristlets, and, sure enough; turned up one day at my study door to announce, "Dad; there's this concert I'd like to go to. . . ."

Both of my children have urged me to go to a Grateful Dead concert. I hadn't taken them up on the offer until this summer; when by chance I met someone way up in the band's hierarchy who gave me not only some tickets to a concert at the Meadowlands in New Jersey; but also a backstage pass. I told my son. His eyes widened at the news. He invited three of his friends. His sister; with a job on the West Coast, was devastated that she couldn't be on hand.

—Adapted from GEORGE PLIMPTON, "Bonding with the Grateful Dead"

B. The passage in Exercise 1A can be rewritten in many ways, depending on the focus and stylistic effect a writer wishes to create. Share your version of the passage with a group of fellow students. Each group member should be ready to explain the reasons for his or her choices when they differ from those of other writers in the group. As a group, rewrite the passage, and share that version with the class.

49b Using colons

You can use a colon to introduce or set up an example, illustration, list, or quotation. By calling attention to what follows, a colon seems to say "Here is . . ." or "Pay attention to this." In most cases, the words coming *before* a colon form a complete sentence while those coming after take the form of a dependent clause, a phrase, or even a single word.

WORDS	Bring these things with you**:** paintbrushes, a drop cloth, and gloves.
WORDS, PHRASES, AND CLAUSES	Each year the river claims something that optimistic humans have built on its banks**:** part of a yard, a toolshed, a driveway edged with bushes, or a house that people admired for its dramatic view from the bluff.

Sometimes, however, you may wish to use a colon to join two sentences, the first providing a relatively broad statement and the second a sharper focus, summary, or change in direction.

> After searching through the house most of the day, she finally admitted the obvious**:** her grandmother's ring was lost.

1 Use a colon to introduce examples, statements, and lists

You can use colons to introduce examples and concluding generalizations. Commonly, a colon comes after the first part of a sentence, which offers a statement or generalization that the remainder of the sentence (following the colon) illustrates, explains, or makes concrete and particular.

> Mulholland said the growing city at the desert's edge would need another source of water**:** the Owens Valley, several hundred miles away.

> Remember this important selling guideline**:** Know your customer!

By asking readers to pause partway through a sentence, a colon calls attention to the second half and avoids the run-together effect a comma may create.

RUN TOGETHER After saving for eleven years, the Cranes finally had enough money to get what they wanted, a ranch in Wyoming where they could live out their own version of self-reliance.

EDITED After saving for eleven years, the Cranes finally had enough money to get what they wanted: a ranch in Wyoming where they could live out their own version of self-reliance.

A colon can also introduce a more formal series or list.

> Though baseball doesn't reign in England, the British enjoy a wide variety of sports: soccer, rugby, cricket, tennis, croquet, polo, and billiards, to name just a few.
>
> The prosecutor introduced into evidence the following exhibits: a nine-inch knife, a piece of clothing belonging to the victim, and a blood-stained rag from the suspect's car.

When a complete sentence follows a colon, you can choose to begin it with either a capital or a lowercase letter. Stick to one style or the other throughout an essay.

CORRECT The airline lost my insulated jacket, pants, and boots: **our** long-awaited winter hike in the Rockies was ruined.

ALSO CORRECT The airline lost my insulated jacket, pants, and boots: **Our** long-awaited winter hike in the Rockies was ruined.

When the word group following a colon is not a sentence, begin it with a lowercase letter.

LOWERCASE The symptoms are as follows: **sore** throat, joint pain, fever, and headache.

2 Use a colon to introduce quotations

You can use a colon as a convenient way to introduce quotations, either short ones that you integrate into your own words or longer ones that you set off from the body of your text (see Chapter 26). The word group before the colon must be a complete sentence; if it is not, use a comma instead.

> Ms. Johnson responded to criticism of the sales campaign: "For a program launched in the middle of a recession, sales were quite strong."

3 Use a colon to separate titles and subtitles

Colons separate main titles from their subtitles.

Ballroom Dancing for the Absolute Novice: An Introduction

Freddie's Dead: The Final Nightmare

Alcohol Policy: A Major Problem on Today's Campuses

The title of your own paper should not be italicized.

Colons are also used in separating hours from minutes (10:32); in certain chapter and verse notations, such as those in the Bible (John 8:21–23); and in some reference styles (see Chapters 28–31).

4 Use a colon to join sentences

Use a colon to join complete sentences (main clauses) when the second sentence focuses, sums up, or illustrates the first (see 38b).

Hearing a sound like rushing water and ripping cloth, she knew it was too late to abandon her house: The mud slide had begun.

In the middle of a week filled with heavy rain and mud slides, Joel thought of the bushes and grasses now sprouting: Next summer the hillside might be on fire.

5 Avoid overuse and misuse of colons

Because colons add emphasis to examples and assertions, you may be tempted to use them often. Don't. Vary your style.

COLON OVERUSED — Suzanne had an obsession for books: there were bookshelves in her kitchen, her bathrooms, and even her closets. She read voraciously: in the morning, at lunch, after dinner, and late at night. And she liked everything: classics, mysteries, pulp romances, autobiographies.

EDITED — Suzanne had an obsession for books. There were bookshelves in her kitchen, her bathrooms, and even her closets. She read voraciously **from morning to** late at night. And she liked everything: classics, mysteries, pulp romances, autobiographies.

You can use a colon to introduce a list at the end of a complete sentence. When you introduce a list with a word group other than a complete sentence, however, do not use a colon.

INCORRECT — Her three favorite activities were: jogging, volunteering at the local homeless shelter, and cooking.

EDITED Her three favorite activities **were jogging,** volunteering at the local homeless shelter, and cooking.

EDITED **She had three favorite activities:** jogging, volunteering at the local homeless shelter, and cooking.

The colon and the words introduced by it should appear only at the end of a sentence, not in the middle.

INCORRECT Keep in mind these elements: introduction, body, and conclusion, while preparing your presentation.

EDITED Keep in mind these **elements—**introduction, body, and conclusion**—while** preparing your presentation.

Exercise 2

A. Edit the following sentences by deleting misused or overused colons, adding colons where needed, and retaining any colons that are appropriate. You may need to rewrite some of the sentences.

EXAMPLE

For the Hirsches: retirement meant a trip to France.

1. They prepared for the trip by: first looking for inexpensive hotels in Paris.
2. The Residence Rivoli seemed like a good value clean, centrally located: private bath.
3. Mr. Hirsch, however, wanted to splurge: He argued that an upper-bracket hotel would be so much more enjoyable: a shining marble bath, plush dining room, and elegant meals. There would be parking as well: essential for anyone with a car.
4. But Mrs. Hirsch wasn't impressed: the expensive hotels would be comfortable, but she wanted atmosphere: and small, charming hotels would have that in abundance.
5. Finally, they reached a compromise; they would: stay in a chateau near the Loire, which would be cheaper than a fancy Paris hotel but afford plenty of atmosphere. Then they could: drive into Paris; enjoy the sights; and have a peaceful night: all without driving more than an hour or so each way.

B. Share your edited versions of the sentences in Exercise 2A with a group of classmates. For each sentence, choose one version the group considers correct and effective. Then share your chosen sentences with other groups to see how often you have made similar and different choices.

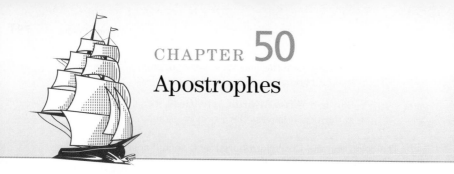

CHAPTER 50
Apostrophes

Like the dot above the *i*, the apostrophe may seem trivial. But without the help of apostrophes, your readers would stumble over your sentences. Misplaced apostrophes are also distracting.

MISUSED OR LEFT OUT — James horse cant canter, but two months rest and his leg's will heal, and then well see him in race's at Blueberry Down's again.

No doubt you had difficulty reading this sentence. You weren't sure which words were possessives, which were contractions, and which were plurals; the omitted and misplaced apostrophes misled you into putting some words into the wrong categories. Try reading it again.

CORRECTED — **James's** horse **can't** canter, but two **months'** rest and his **legs** will heal, and then **we'll** see him in **races** at Blueberry **Downs** again.

50a Marking possession

A noun that expresses ownership is said to be a **possessive noun.** In writing, you must mark possessive nouns to distinguish them from plurals. A reader encountering the phrase *the cats meow*, for example, will assume it is a sentence: *cats* is the subject and *meow* the verb.

An apostrophe changes the meaning: cat's.

Without a way of distinguishing between the plural and the possessive in writing, readers would be misled and frustrated.

1 Add an apostrophe plus -*s* to mark possession in singular nouns

In general, when you write a singular possessive noun, you will follow it with an apostrophe plus -*s*.

Bill'**s** coat   the dog'**s** collar   New Mexico'**s** taxes

When a noun ends with -*s*, showing possession may be tricky. Writers follow two different conventions in such circumstances (and editors will usually adopt one of them and stick to it).

1. Add an apostrophe and another *-s*, just as you would do with any other noun. This is the more common and preferred method.

   Chris's car Elliott Ness's next move

2. Alternatively, simply add an apostrophe to the final *-s*.

   Chris' car Elliott Ness' next move

For nouns ending in *-s*, choose one of these conventions and stick to it throughout an essay.

INCONSISTENT After driving closer to the **lioness'** cub, we discovered that **Hess's** camera had no film.

EDITED After driving closer to the **lioness's** cub, we discovered that **Hess's** camera had no film.

To avoid awkward possessives for nouns ending in *-s* ("the pass**'s** success"), try revising the construction: ("the success of the pass").

Be careful with personal pronouns. You may be tempted to add an apostrophe plus *-s*, but they're already possessive.

INCORRECT If the car was **your's,** why did you tell Jose that it was Lida's and then take **her's** and dent **it's** fender?

EDITED If the car was **yours,** why did you tell Jose that it was Lida's and then take **hers** and dent **its** fender?

50a
'
v

Be especially wary of confusing *it's* and *its*. Practice expanding the contraction *it's* (*it* + *is*) whenever you use it in writing, and you'll locate such slips more easily.

DRAFT **Its** not the muffler shop employees who were responsible for the fraud, but **its** managers.

EXPANDED **It is** not the muffler shop employees who were responsible for the fraud, but **it is** managers.

EDITED **It's** not the muffler shop employees who were responsible for the fraud, but **its** managers.

2 Add an apostrophe to mark possession in plural nouns

Most plural nouns end in *-s* or *-es*. Add an apostrophe after the *-s*.

POSSESSIVE The **Solomons'** house had its lead paint removed.

POSSESSIVE The **roses'** petals had begun to wither.

Some irregular nouns form their plurals differently (*mice, children, fish*). Mark possession by adding an apostrophe plus *-s* to the plural, even if the word does not change in the plural (*deer/deer, fish/fish*).

PLURAL The livestock show included several **oxen.**

PLURAL POSSESSIVE The livestock show featured the **oxen's** plowing abilities.

Even though third person singular verbs end in *-s*, remember that these are not possessive nouns, so they don't require an apostrophe.

INCORRECT The *Enterprise* **speed's** out of the galaxy.

EDITED The *Enterprise* **speeds** out of the galaxy.

3 Add an apostrophe plus *-s* or an apostrophe to only the last word in a noun phrase

Hyphenated and **multiple-word nouns** are becoming increasingly common in English. As a general rule, treat the entire noun phrase as a single unit, marking possession on the last word.

SERIOUS ERROR

HYPHENATED NOUN My **father-in-law's** library is extensive.

MULTIPLE-WORD NOUN The **union leaders'** negotiations fell through at the last minute.

50a

With two or more nouns connected by *and* or *or*, you'll need to decide whether these nouns function as separate items or as a single unit.

SEPARATE ITEMS **Billy's and Harold's** lawyers were ruthless.

READER'S REACTION: Billy must have one lawyer and Harold another, since the possessive is marked on both.

SINGLE UNIT **Billy and Harold's** lawyers were ruthless.

READER'S REACTION: Billy and Harold must have shared the same team of lawyers, since the entire noun phrase is marked as possessive.

Exercise 1

A. Edit the possessive forms in the following sentences so that each uses possessive apostrophes correctly. You may also have to add or move apostrophes, but do not change any correct forms.

EXAMPLE

France's longest river, the Loire, has its source in Vivarais and winds its way some six hundred miles to the Atlantic.

1. The rivers name is especially associated with the many chateaux that line its bank's.
2. Serious sightseers visits to the Loire Valley should include tours of several of this regions beautiful castles.
3. The Loires reputation is also founded on its renowned cuisine and its sophisticated wines.
4. Barton and Jone's wine import businesses have flourished in the United States ever since Jones came up with the companys award-winning advertising campaign.
5. Several other companies have found an eager market for Frances excellent wine's.

B. In a small group, compare your corrections to Exercise 1A and discuss any especially difficult cases.

50b Marking contractions and omissions

You can use the apostrophe to indicate omission of one or more letters when two words are brought together to form a **contraction.**

When you want to use contractions, generally in informal settings, follow a simple rule: learn exactly where the apostrophe goes. Most contractions are so common that you've already memorized them. But you still might omit apostrophes from simple words. For example, perhaps you've written *your* (a possessive pronoun) when you really meant *you're* (*you are*).

1 Use an apostrophe to contract a verb form

You can contract pronouns and verbs into a single unit by "splicing" them, eliminating the first part of the verb and substituting an apostrophe. Use the following chart to check your work.

it's	=	it	+	is
who's	=	who	+	is
they're	=	they	+	are
can't	=	can	+	not
you'll	=	you	+	will
you're	=	you	+	are

When writing informally, you can also splice nouns followed by *is.*

INFORMAL **Shoshana’s** going to the ballet, but her **seat’s** in the very last row of the theater.

MORE FORMAL **Shoshana is** going to the ballet, but her **seat is** in the very last row of the theater.

Edit your papers *very* carefully for contractions before turning them in. Take note of these often-confused forms.

they're	=	they + are
there	=	an adverb
their	=	a pronoun
you're	=	you + are
your	=	a possessive pronoun
who's	=	who + is
whose	=	a possessive pronoun
it's	=	it + is
its	=	a possessive pronoun

2 Use an apostrophe to mark plural letters

To make individual letters plural, add an apostrophe plus *-s*.

Mind your **p's and q's.** The **x's** mark the spots.

You can omit the apostrophe in the plurals of numbers.

I'll take two size **5s** and two size **7s.**

They walked out in **twos** and **threes.**

The apostrophe is often omitted from the plural form of abbreviations, especially if it runs the risk of making the word look like a possessive. "I took all my freshman courses from **TAs**" might be just as acceptable as "**TA's**" because the abbreviation is capitalized.

3 Use an apostrophe to abbreviate a year

You can abbreviate years by omitting the first two numbers of the century as long as the century is understood by your reader. Such contractions represent informal usage.

INFORMAL Sam has an **'85** Johnson class M sixteen-foot sailboat for sale.

UNCLEAR Victorian details on houses in our neighborhood remained popular throughout the **'90s.**

READER'S REACTION: Does this mean the 1890s (in the Victorian period)? I'm confused.

EDITED Victorian details on houses in our neighborhood remained popular throughout the **1990s.**

4 Use an apostrophe to show colloquial pronunciation

When quoting people, you can use apostrophes to indicate certain omissions and other features of colloquial speech and dialects.

DIALECT I'm **a-goin'** to the post office first **an'** then home.

Exercise 2

A. The following paragraph contains sentences with some contracted words that require apostrophes and some "lookalikes" that do not. All these words appear in italics. Insert apostrophes where they belong.

Many medical scholars believe that the age of molecular biology *didnt* really begin until April 1953 when Watson and Crick's article on the double helix appeared in a scientific journal. These researchers *werent* sure at that time how influential their ideas would become. *Its* generally thought, for example, that if several important researchers *hadnt* immediately seen the underlying brilliance of the double helix, the whole idea *wouldnt* have gained such a quick following. "*Your* basic educator," Professor Ewell Samuels asserts, "*couldnt* have seen beyond what was already a given in biology. *Its* when *youre* presented with many scholars *whose* ideas agree that things really begin to happen. *Whos* going to argue with a whole field jumping on the bandwagon of a new theory?"

B. In a small group, compare your corrections to the passage in Exercise 2A. After reaching agreement on which cases are actual errors, try to decide as a group which contractions in the passage, if any, are too informal. Would you use no contractions in this passage? some?

CHAPTER 51
Quotation Marks

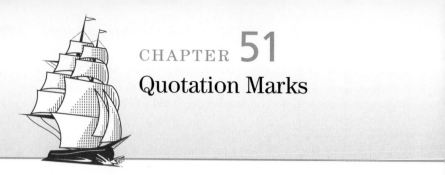

You learn about some of the many uses for quotation marks almost as soon as you begin to read.

> The three soldiers went on to the house of Albert and Louise.
>
> "Could you spare a bit of food? And have you some corner where we could sleep for the night?"
>
> "Oh no," said Albert. "We gave all we could spare to soldiers who came before you."
>
> "Our beds are full," said Louise.
>
> —MARCIA BROWN, *Stone Soup*

You use quotation marks in still other ways when you incorporate other people's words and ideas in your writing.

> As Ruth Macklin points out in *Mortal Choices*, however, "many state laws now permit involuntary hospitalization of mental patients only if they are judged dangerous to themselves or others."

Quotation marks have many important roles, so keeping track of the various conventions for their use is both difficult and necessary.

51a Marking quotations

Use quotation marks whenever you quote someone else's words. Quotation marks tell readers which words are someone else's.

To use quotation marks effectively, you need to know whether you are quoting words directly or indirectly, on their own or within another quotation.

1 Direct quotations

Whenever you quote someone directly, use double quotation marks (" ") both before and after the quotation—unless the quotation is long or needs special emphasis (see 51b). Make sure that the words within the quotation marks are the exact spoken or written words of your source.

DIRECT QUOTATION (SPOKEN)
"The loon can stay beneath the water for several minutes," the park ranger told us as we walked along the shore.

DIRECT QUOTATION (WRITTEN)
Samuel Gross has written that "every generation looks with scorn upon its offspring's own developing culture."

As you edit, check that you have placed quotation marks around all directly quoted material.

QUOTATION NOT FULLY MARKED
"Had it not been for the flight navigator," the pilot said, we wouldn't have been able to make the emergency landing.

READER'S REACTION: The second part of the sentence doesn't have any quotation marks, so at first I didn't notice that it was something the pilot said.

EDITED
"Had it not been for the flight navigator," the pilot said, "we wouldn't have been able to make the emergency landing."

Make sure you use quotation marks within a sentence to separate quoted material from the words you use to introduce or comment on it. This is an especially important practice when your words interrupt a quotation.

SERIOUS ERROR

QUOTATION MARKS MISSING
"I'm grateful, too, commented one passenger dryly, though I would have gladly missed the whole experience."

READER'S REACTION: "Commented one passenger dryly" seems like part of the quotation.

EDITED
"I'm grateful, too," commented one passenger dryly, "though I would have gladly missed the whole experience."

2 Indirect quotations

Whenever you **paraphrase** or **summarize** someone else's speaking or writing, do not use quotation marks.

INDIRECT QUOTE (PARAPHRASE)
The pilot told us that if it hadn't been for the flight navigator, the plane would not have made a safe landing.

INDIRECT QUOTE (SUMMARY)
Samuel Preston believes that after just one generation, the social consequences of a major war have almost completely vanished.

3 Quotations inside quotations

Whenever a direct quotation contains another quotation, use single quotation marks (' ') for the inside quotation and double quotation marks (" ") for the one enclosing it.

> Goddio became interested in searching for the sunken ship *San Diego* after reading an account by De Morga who "wrote of a struggle 'obstinately and bitterly waged on both sides so that it lasted more than six hours,' until the pounding of the battle caused his ship to 'bust asunder at the bows.'"
>
> **Note how the comma is placed inside the single quotation marks and the period is inside both the single and double quotation marks. (See 48h.)**

ESL ADVICE: QUOTATION MARKS

Conventions for using quotation marks vary from language to language, and British conventions vary from American ones. Check the advice in this section carefully and proofread your work to make sure you are using quotation marks correctly.

51b Block quotations

When you quote more than four typed lines of prose, you should use a **block quotation** rather than quotation marks. To create a block quotation, begin on a new line after the sentence preceding the quotation, indent one inch (or ten spaces), and present the quotation double-spaced without quotation marks. Do not indent the opening line of the quotation if you are quoting only one paragraph or part of a paragraph.

> According to Postman, we can no longer ignore the profound effects of technology on all aspects of American life:
>
> > To be unaware that a technology comes equipped with a program for social change, to maintain that technology is neutral, to make the assumption that technology is always a friend to culture is, at this late hour, stupidity plain and simple.

In a longer quotation, indent one-fourth inch (three spaces) for the first line of each full paragraph. In addition, include any quotation marks that appear within the original, but do not add any at the beginning or end of the block quotation.

Clifford Geertz's discussion of cockfights on the island of Bali illustrates the personal, almost informal tone of much contemporary anthropology:

> My wife and I were still very much in the gust-of-wind stage, a most frustrating, and even, as you soon begin to doubt whether you are really real after all, unnerving one, when, ten days or so after our arrival, a large cockfight was held in the public square to raise money for a new school.
>
> Now, a few special occasions aside, cockfights are illegal in Bali under the Republic (as, for not altogether unrelated reasons, they were under the Dutch), largely as a result of the pretensions to puritanism radical nationalism tends to bring with it. The elite, which is not itself so very puritan, worries about the poor, ignorant peasant gambling all his money away, about what foreigners will think, about the waste of time better devoted to building up the country. It sees cockfighting as "primitive," "backward," "unprogressive," and generally unbecoming an ambitious nation. And, as with those other embarrassments--opium smoking, begging, or uncovered breasts--it seeks, rather unsystematically, to put a stop to it.
>
> —Clifford Geertz, "Deep Play: Notes on the Balinese Cockfight"

(See Chapter 28 for a discussion of parenthetical documentation with block quotations; see 49b-3 for the use of colons to introduce block quotations.)

When you are quoting more than three lines of verse, present them in a block quotation, beginning on the next line after an introductory sentence and indented one inch from the left margin. If the verse contains quotation marks, include them, but do not add any of your own at the beginning and end of the quotation.

Donald Hall also uses lines of uneven length and varying rhythm in his poem "The Black-Faced Sheep."

> If one of you found a gap in a stone wall,
> the rest of you--rams, ewes, bucks, wethers, lambs;
> mothers and daughters, old grandfather-father,
> cousins and aunts, small bleating sons--
> followed onward, stupid

```
as sheep, wherever
your leader's sheep-brain wandered to.
My grandfather spent all day searching the valley
and edges of Ragged Mountain,
calling "Ke-day!" as if he brought you salt,
"Ke-day! Ke-day!"
```

51c Dialogue

When writing dialogue, use the conventions for direct quotations (see 51a-1). Whenever a new person speaks, indent as if you're beginning a new paragraph, and begin with new quotation marks.

> Finally the old man woke.
>
> "Don't sit up," the boy said. "Drink this." He poured some coffee in a glass.
>
> The old man took it and drank it.
>
> "They beat me, Manolin," he said. "They truly beat me."
>
> "*He* didn't beat you. Not the fish."
>
> "No. Truly. It was afterwards."
>
> —Ernest Hemingway, *The Old Man and the Sea*

When a character in a written dialogue speaks for more than one paragraph with no interruption, begin each new paragraph with quotation marks, but don't end with them. End only the *last* paragraph with quotation marks.

CORRECT

> "And then that imbecile crowd down on the deck started their little fun, and I could see nothing more for smoke.
>
> "The brown current ran swiftly out of the heart of darkness, bearing us down towards the sea with twice the speed of our upward progress. . . ."
>
> —Joseph Conrad, *Heart of Darkness*

51d Titles of short works

Use quotation marks to enclose titles of short works, such as articles, essays, stories, songs, and short poems; parts of a larger work or series, such as chapters in a book, episodes in a television series, or sections of a musical work; and unpublished works, such as doctoral dissertations or speeches.

QUOTATION MARKS WITH TITLES

ARTICLES AND STORIES	
"TV Gets Blame for Poor Reading"	newspaper article
"A Political Identity Crisis"	magazine article
"The Idea of the Family in the Middle East"	chapter in book
"Baba Yaga and the Brave Youth"	story
"The Rise of Germism"	essay
POEMS AND SONGS	
"A Woman Cutting Celery"	short poem
"Evening" (from *Pippa Passes*)	section of a long poem
"You're Beautiful"	song
EPISODES AND PARTS OF LONGER WORKS	
"The Promise" (from *Cold Case*)	episode of a TV series
"All We Like Sheep" (from Handel's *Messiah*)	section of a long musical work
UNPUBLISHED WORKS	
"Renaissance Men—and Women"	unpublished lecture
"Sources of the Ballads in Bishop Percy's Folio Manuscript"	unpublished dissertation

Never put the title of your own paper in quotation marks. This is a common mistake that irritates many teachers. If your title contains quoted material, place that material, not the entire title, in quotation marks.

INCORRECT "The Theme of the Life Voyage in Crane's 'Open Boat' "

EDITED The Theme of the Life Voyage in Crane's "Open Boat"

51e " "

51e Special meanings of words and phrases

You can use quotation marks to set off words and phrases you are using in a special sense or to indicate terms that are part of a technical vocabulary or that are unusual in some way. In using quotation marks to call attention to words and phrases, remember an important principle: Go lightly to avoid distracting readers with too many highlighted words.

Most disciplines use a host of specialized words that readers *within* the discipline readily recognize. If you are writing for a general audience, however, consider calling attention to specialized terms and phrases by setting them off with quotation marks. Quotation marks can also help you highlight a term you are defining. (Italics can be used for this purpose as well; see 55a-4.)

> The phenomenon that draws each person into the crowd's irrational and often destructive and confrontational behavior is known among social psychologists as "crowd contagion."
>
> The term "FSBO" (sometimes actually pronounced as "fizbo") is generally used in the real estate industry to refer to a home that is "for sale by owner."

When deciding whether to use quotation marks to set off specialized terms, ask yourself whether the term is likely to be known to your readers. Ask also whether the term is unusual enough to require highlighting or will seem clear to readers. In the following sentence, a well-known writer includes quotation marks that most readers will probably consider unnecessary.

UNNECESSARY

> The number of these folds varies from individual to individual and each adult has a characteristic "frown pattern" of one, two, three or four lines.
>
> —DESMOND MORRIS, *Body Watching*

READER'S REACTION: I have no trouble figuring out what a frown pattern is, so for me the quotation marks make the sentence appear cluttered.

Clichés and idioms, perhaps because they seem informal or slang-like, often fool writers into placing them in quotation marks. Doing so, however, only calls more attention to their presence, further weakening the prose. Instead of placing such expressions in quotation marks, simply replace them with stronger words and phrases.

Exercise 1

A. Add quotation marks to the following passage as appropriate.

The shame of illiteracy—or so Robert Cullany puts it—affects millions of adults in the United States alone, but the problem is not nearly as prevalent as innumeracy, Cullany's term that means being unable to use numbers. Cullany writes, illiteracy and innumeracy are a national blight on our intellectual landscape, and cannot be tolerated. He also points out that they cripple our productivity, lead to familial dysfunction (poor family structures), and deny people the ability to become what Cullany calls self-learners. The ALVC, or Adult Literacy Volunteer Corps, is made up of dedicated people who believe they can help this so-called mind plague.

B. Working in a small group, share your edited versions of the passage in Exercise 1A. Which quotation marks did you all agree on? Which ones did members of your group miss or disagree on?

51f Irony, sarcasm, and authorial distance

You can—*sparingly*—use quotation marks to indicate irony or sarcasm or to show a reader that you don't "lay claim" to a specific term or expression.

> To the people who oppose animal rights, the suffering of helpless animals is somehow justified by the "great medical advances" that are encouraged by what they view as "legitimate research" on animals.

This strategy is easy to misuse or overuse, and careful word choice is generally a more effective way of conveying disapproval (see 46c-1 and 2).

Exercise 2

A. Edit the following passage by adding or deleting quotation marks as appropriate. Leave in place any quotation marks that are correctly used.

On April 12, 1633, Galileo was interrogated by the Inquisitor for the Holy Roman and Universal Inquisition. The focus was Galileo's book, the "*Dialogue on the Great World Systems*," in which he posited the theory of a "spinning" earth that "circulated" around the sun. The theory itself was "bad" enough given the Pope's "beliefs," but one of the "characters" in the book's "dialogue" was cast as a "simpleton," and the Pope thought that perhaps it referred to him because he didn't go along with Galileo's "theory." At one point, the Inquisitor asked Galileo, "Did you obtain permission to write the book? To which Galileo replied, I did not seek permission to write this book because I consider that I did not disobey the instruction I had been given. "Did you disclose the Sacred Congregation's demands when you printed the book?" asked the Inquisitor. "I said nothing, Galileo replied, when I sought permission to publish, not having in the book either held or defended opinion. In the end, "Galileo" had to retract his "book," and was also shown instruments of torture "as if" they were going to be used—a "scare tactic," to be sure.

—Adapted from Jacob Bronowski, *The Ascent of Man*

B. Working in a small group, share your edited versions of the passage in Exercise 2A. Discuss each change and note any that gave you trouble. Indicate whether all group members agreed about each change.

CHAPTER 52
Periods, Question Marks, and Exclamation Points

When you speak, you mark boundaries between sentences with changes in pitch or with pauses. When you write, you must mark these divisions with visual symbols because your reader can't "hear" the boundaries. When you want to mark the end of a sentence, you will use one of three symbols: a period, a question mark, or an exclamation point.

52a Periods

Use a period to mark the end of a sentence. Periods can also be used in abbreviations.

1 End a sentence with a period

No matter how long or complicated, all sentences that are *statements* must end with periods. However, sometimes a sentence will contain embedded clauses that appear to be something other than statements. Use a period to end a sentence when the main, or "outer," sentence is a statement.

INCORRECT Ten-year-old Naomi affectionately kissed her little brother on the forehead but wondered whether he really knew that she was sorry for startling him?

READER'S REACTION: The sentence as a whole is a statement; the question in the second half is being reported in the sentence, but the sentence doesn't ask the question.

EDITED Ten-year-old Naomi affectionately kissed her little brother on the forehead but wondered whether he really knew that she was sorry for startling him.

2 Use periods in abbreviations

Periods are also used to punctuate abbreviations and to mark decimal points in numbers. Most abbreviations require periods to let the reader know that something has been eliminated from the word or term.

Dr.	Mrs.	a.m. (or A.M.)
pp.	in.	abbr. (for *abbreviation*)
Jr.	Ph.D.	B.C. (or B.C.E.)

Many common abbreviations, including *a.m.* and *p.m.*, come from Latin and, for brevity, have been "permanently" shortened (it would seem odd to spell out *a.m.* and *p.m.* as *ante meridiem* and *post meridiem*).

Some abbreviations, especially acronyms (see 58a), may not require periods at all. When the entire term is capitalized, periods are generally not used (NASA, EU, NATO). Use of periods in abbreviations varies considerably. When in doubt, use the preferred choice in a dictionary. Remember too that some academic disciplines have their own styles for abbreviations. (See Chapters 28–31.)

When an abbreviation that requires a period occurs at the *end* of a sentence, that period will also end the sentence.

CORRECT Before he became a freelance writer, Richard Rodriguez earned a Ph.D.

If the abbreviated word occurs in the *middle* of a sentence, the period may be followed by another punctuation mark, such as a comma, dash, colon, or semicolon.

INCORRECT Officials from the paper industry testified until **10 p.m,** well before the meeting adjourned.

EDITED Officials from the paper industry testified until **10 p.m.,** well before the meeting adjourned.

52a .

Exercise 1

Edit the following sentences so that periods are used correctly, adding or omitting punctuation as appropriate.

EXAMPLE

Every two years the French department at St. Joseph's College organizes a group trip to a foreign country.

1. On our trip to France, we visited the medieval city of Carcassonne
2. As we approached the inner city, which was surrounded by high walls and a real moat, we wondered whether we were still in the twentieth century?
3. "Have we fallen into a time warp or something" Trish said?
4. As we climbed up to the ramparts at 10 p.m, we decided that the experience was almost as good as watching a N.A.S.A. space shuttle launch.
5. Mr Siefert, the hotel manager, told us that the Bastille Day fireworks would begin at 9:30 p.m.

52b Question marks

A question mark indicates that something has been asked, either directly or hypothetically.

1 End a direct question with a question mark

Always end a direct question with a question mark.

DIRECT When is the train leaving?

DIRECT Considering all the media attention to homestead tax breaks, why aren't more homeowners filing for the exclusion?

When a sentence (like the preceding example) has more than one clause, the main clause will usually determine the proper punctuation. Occasionally, you may embed a direct question within an outer statement, generally using parentheses to set off the embedded question.

EMBEDDED The telephone repair technician arrived only after the electricians had removed the power lines (did they pose a danger?) and disconnected the service box.

End **indirect questions** with a period. These are sentences whose main clause is a statement and whose embedded clause asks a question.

INDIRECT Phil wondered whether to support the department's proposal to create a new program.

INDIRECT Carlos asked if he could see the bid for the new project.

When you present the exact words, your quotation is *direct* rather than *indirect*, and you need to include the question mark.

QUOTED It was Laitan who asked, "Why is the temperature in the solution rising so quickly?"

2 Watch for other uses of question marks

Question marks may appear in writing for more specialized reasons. In various kinds of informational writing, for example, a question mark may signal a date or other fact that is uncertain or that has been questioned.

David Robert Styles, 1632?–1676

Meadville, pop. 2,330?

Occasionally, writers will call attention to other people's statements by including a parenthetical question mark. This device may indicate genuine doubt, lack of information, or sarcasm.

PARENTHETICAL The veterinarian informed us that our Siamese cat had contracted a rare (?) ailment.

SARCASTIC We dispute R & D's finding that the lubricant burns off (?) under high heat.

Such a use of question marks is usually colloquial or informal; in general, try to find other ways to convey the same message in academic writing.

Unless you're writing very informally (in a note to a friend, for example), avoid using more than one question mark for emphasis or combining question marks and exclamation points.

INAPPROPRIATE Can you believe they arrested him for parking in front of the building?! How can they do that?????

EDITED Can you believe they arrested him for parking in front of the building? How can they do that?

Exercise 2

A. Edit the following passage by removing any inappropriate question marks and adding any that are required.

Are you bat-phobic. Although bats have been hated and feared for centuries, most species are harmless to humans and beneficial to the environment. In his article "Are We Batty Over Bats," Harlan Sneed wonders whether our destruction of bats is really justified? Should we be smoke-bombing caves that are breeding places for thousands of bats, just because we are afraid of them. Sneed also gives examples of cultures that are contributing to the extinction of bats not through fear but through excessive trapping—for food; they are a delicacy (!?) in some parts of the world. Sneed ends his article with a reminder: "Environmental protection is as much a matter of the way we think as the way we act. Maybe you have never *acted* against your environment but are you entirely inculpable in your thoughts and attitudes."

B. In a small group, compare your edited versions of the passage in Exercise 2A. Create one collaboratively edited version.

52c Exclamation points

When you use an exclamation point, you make your statement emphatic. You can also use exclamation points to indicate commands or, in quotations, words that are shouted.

1 End an emphatic statement with an exclamation point

Exclamation points are often used to end emphatic statements such as commands or warnings.

EMPHATIC Keep all the camp children away from the precipice!

Avoid overusing exclamation points to do the work that should be assigned to strong, carefully chosen words.

OVERUSED I couldn't believe it! Andrea and I were face to face with a small black bear! We were terrified! I screamed! Andrea jumped back into the tent and buried herself under her sleeping bag! That left me holding an entire bag of delicious corn chips right under the hungry creature's nose!

REVISED Suddenly, I began to realize we were not alone. Out of the shadows, just three feet from the front of our tent, appeared the black nose and sharp, glinting teeth of a small black bear.

Also avoid using more than one exclamation point at the end of any sentence. A single exclamation point is worth exactly as much as a hundred.

INCORRECT The bear was grunting right outside our tent!!!!!

EDITED The bear was grunting right outside our tent!

2 Watch for other uses of exclamation points

Like question marks, exclamation points can be used parenthetically or marginally in casual writing to express dismay, outrage, shock, or strong interest. In formal contexts, look for other ways to add emphasis.

INAPPROPRIATE Emergency rescue workers spent several hours (!) trying to reach the stranded toddler.

EDITED Emergency rescue workers spent several **agonizing** hours trying to reach the stranded toddler.

When you quote people's words directly, you can use exclamation points to indicate emphatic statements or commands.

QUOTED Halfway to the airport, Sybil suddenly shouted, "Oh, no! We forgot the plane tickets!"

Use exclamation points sparingly and realistically in quotations and dialogue. Few people continue to speak emphatically for very long.

Remember that when you use an exclamation point, you are punctuating the end of your sentence. Don't add another mark, such as a comma, when you write an emphatic sentence within an outer sentence. (This same rule applies to the question mark.)

INCORRECT "Stop!," yelled Steve.

EDITED "Stop!" yelled Steve.

Exercise 3

A. Edit the following passage by removing or adding exclamation points to make them correct and stylistically acceptable.

Seventy-five miles (!) from anywhere, Frank's old Buick decided to sputter and stall out on the edge of Route 61. Meanwhile, the temperature had fallen to 16 below!!!! To make matters worse, the wind had whipped up to 30 miles per hour! That's an incredible wind chill of around 75 below zero!!!!! "Hey," yelled Bill, "don't anyone leave this car. If we stay put, maybe the highway patrol will spot us." "Who are you kidding!!??," shouted Frank. "It's 3 a.m.!"

B. In a small group, compare your edited versions of the passage in Exercise 3A. Discuss any differences, and create one collaboratively edited version.

CHAPTER 53
Special Punctuation

Punctuation symbols make up a kind of toolbox for writing. Five "special" punctuation marks—parentheses, brackets, dashes, ellipses, and slashes—can be useful strategies for guiding readers through complex sentences and for providing emphasis appropriate to your purpose for writing.

53a Parentheses

Parentheses *enclose* a word, sentence, or clause: you can't use just one. Whatever you write between two parentheses takes on the quality of an aside—something in a "softer" voice than that of the rest of a sentence. It becomes something presented in the background rather than the foreground.

1 Use parentheses to set off words or sentences

With parentheses, you can set off a word, a group of words, an entire sentence, or groups of sentences from the rest of your text. By using parentheses to place some information in the background, you can direct your readers' attention to the main assertions and details in a passage without having to omit worthwhile (though potentially distracting) secondary material.

INFORMATION SET OFF WITHIN A SENTENCE

Although most of the team always eats a hearty and varied breakfast (if also a little high in fats and cholesterol), Jim feels he performs much better with less food in his stomach. Invariably, this means only one thing: a bowl of Cheerios (without milk).

INFORMATION SET OFF IN A SEPARATE SENTENCE

Consuelo had tried for two years to get a hearing about her immigration status. (Her employer, during this time, had been unsympathetic to her pleas.) Then, in June, she finally received a letter.

Use parentheses sparingly and carefully. Too many parenthetical statements can clutter your sentences and obscure your main assertions.

DISTRACTING Handico, Inc., decided (early in 1993) to use its waste milling chips (which had been warehoused in Detroit) to manufacture pencils (described as "environmentally friendly") to donate to public schools (which gave the company a tax credit).

CLEAR Early in 1993, Handico, Inc., decided to use its waste milling chips (warehoused in Detroit) to manufacture "environmentally friendly" pencils. These they donated to public schools, resulting in a tax credit for the company.

2 Watch for special uses of parentheses

You can use parentheses to present information that is not part of the structure of a sentence. You can also use parentheses in numbered lists.

NUMBERS AND LISTS Harry's Bookstore has a fax number (349-0934) for (1) ordering books, (2) inquiring about the availability of specific items, or (3) requesting publication information.

3 Punctuate parenthetical statements correctly

Don't use a comma *before* a parenthetical statement placed in the middle of a sentence. *After* the closing parenthesis, use whatever punctuation would normally occur at this point in the sentence if the parenthetical statement were not there.

53a ( )

WITHOUT PARENTHESES If you sign up for Telepick by August 15, you are eligible for one hour of free long-distance calls.

WITH PARENTHESES If you sign up for Telepick by August 15 (and list up to four commonly called numbers), you are eligible for one hour of free long-distance calls.

When a parenthetical statement *inside a sentence* comes at the end of the sentence, always place the sentence's end punctuation *after* the closing parenthesis.

INCORRECT People on your Telepick list can also call you at the same discounted rate (as long as they, too, use Coombs Communication as their long-distance carrier.)

CORRECT People on your Telepick list can also call you at the same discounted rate (as long as they, too, use Coombs Communication as their long-distance carrier).

When parentheses enclose an entire freestanding sentence, however, place the end punctuation *inside* the closing parenthesis.

CORRECT You can sign up for Telepick's "Free Hour" program until August 10. (This offer does not include international calls.)

53b Brackets

Use brackets to indicate that you have added words of your own to a quotation, or to act as parentheses within parentheses.

1 Use brackets for interpolations

Sometimes you need to introduce your own words into a quotation to help clarify a word or a statement for readers, or to provide important background information. To indicate that the words are your own, and not those of the writer or speaker being quoted, enclose the **interpolation** in brackets.

INTERPOLATION My friends Paula and Kent decided to have their wedding on a sailboat off Key West. When I asked them if the ceremony would take place at a specific place offshore, Kent said, "It's a surprise even to us. Captain Sims [the boat's owner] has chosen a special place within two hours of Key West."

53c

2 Use brackets within parentheses

When you need to include a parenthetical statement *within* a parenthetical statement, use parentheses first, and then use brackets for the inner statement. Try to limit your use of brackets because they can make your writing seem unnecessarily complex.

You can contact Rick Daggett (Municipal Lumber Council [Violations Division], Stinson County Municipal Center) to report violations of the rules governing logging of old-growth trees.

53c Dashes

You can use dashes, like parentheses, to set off material within a sentence. Dashes call more attention to a word or group of words than parentheses do; use them to create emphasis or indicate a change in tone. Dashes differ in function from hyphens, which are used to connect words or to separate words into parts (see Chapter 56). On keyboards, dashes appear as two unspaced hyphens, with no space before, between, or after them: --. In professional typesetting, the dash is represented by a single line: —. (Some word-processing programs automatically convert two hyphens to a dash, while some provide a choice to insert a dash under "Tools.")

1 Use dashes for emphasis

Use dashes in pairs to highlight a word or group of words in the middle of a sentence.

MATERIAL SET OFF IN THE MIDDLE

After picking out two pet mice**—one brown with white spots and one white with a brown forehead—**the little boy realized he had only enough money to buy one of them.

When the word or words you want to emphasize appear at the *end* of a sentence, however, use one dash to introduce the material. Conclude with the appropriate end punctuation for the sentence.

MATERIAL SET OFF AT THE END

Heartbroken at the thought that someone might buy the mouse, the boy offered his six quarters as a deposit**—along with his Mickey Mouse watch and his school notebook.**

You can use dashes to create contrasts in tone or structure within a sentence. You don't need to make the material within them part of the grammatical structure of the sentence or make it consistent in tone with the rest of the sentence. Inside the following sentence, the dashes enclose another complete sentence.

FULL SENTENCE SET OFF

The mice**—by this time they were fully domesticated—**frolicked in the cedar chips.

Remember that dashes call attention to the material within them. In contrast, enclosing material in commas provides no real emphasis, and using parentheses de-emphasizes the enclosed material.

STRONG EMPHASIS

When the boy**—clutching three weeks' allowance—**returned to the store, it had already closed.

NO SPECIAL EMPHASIS

When the boy, **clutching three weeks' allowance,** returned to the store, it had already closed.

LOSS OF EMPHASIS

When the boy (**clutching three weeks' allowance**) returned to the store, it had already closed.

2 Use dashes to set off introductory and concluding ideas

You can use dashes to set off an idea or a series of items. This is a dramatic way of opening a sentence or calling attention to the assertion it makes.

ITEMS SET OFF IN OPENING

Extended TV hours, better meals, and more physical exercise— these were the inmates' three major demands for prison reform.

You can also use dashes instead of a (nonemphatic) colon to list a series of items at the *end* of an assertion.

ITEMS SET OFF AT THE END

Charles had learned several ways to avoid the effects of long flights**—drinking lots of water, passing up alcohol, and moving around the cabin as much as possible during the flight.**

3 Avoid overuse of dashes

The use of dashes can become addictive, resulting in sentences and paragraphs that seem to be clusters of fragmented statements.

OVERUSED There had been some interest—chiefly by Stockton—in an automated navigation system—a way to track cars by telecommunication and let drivers know if they are going in the right direction—or give them directions.

READER'S REACTION: This sentence highlights so many points with dashes that it is hard to tell what the writer considers the most important point.

MORE EFFECTIVE There had been some interest, chiefly by Stockton, in an automated navigation system—a way to track cars by telecommunication and let drivers know if they are going in the right direction or give them directions.

If you find yourself using too many dashes in your writing, look over a draft and circle the dashes that seem really important—those that help emphasize the key point in an entire section of an essay, for example. Then either replace the other dashes with commas, colons, or parentheses, or create emphasis through word choice and sentence structure. (See 7c for advice on creating emphasis within sentences.)

Exercise 1

A. Some dashes and parentheses have been added to the following paragraph. Edit the paragraph to make it more effective, deciding which of these punctuation marks should stay and which should be replaced. Change sentence structure and strategy if necessary.

The next morning—their donkeys carried them—to the site of the excavation. Carter and his assistant—A. R. Callender—had already begun clearing the stairway (again). As more of the doorway was exposed, the seals (of Tutankhamun) could be seen—in addition to those of the royal necropolis. When all sixteen steps had been cleared (and the entire doorway could be seen), Carter got a jolt—holes had been cut into the (upper) part of the door. The damage had been repaired—and bore the seals of the necropolis, but the question remained—had this tomb, too, been pillaged?

—METROPOLITAN MUSEUM OF ART, *The Treasures of Tutankhamun*

B. Compare your edited version of the passage in Exercise 1A with those created by some of your fellow students. Remember that there will be no single—or "most correct"—answer. Compare the relative strengths and weaknesses of each version.

53d Ellipses

The **ellipsis** (from Greek *elleipsis*, "an omission") is a series of three *spaced* periods telling your reader that something has been left out. You will use ellipses chiefly for two purposes: to omit parts of a quotation and to suggest gaps in a sentence, either in dialogue or in quoted speech.

1 Place and space ellipses correctly

Correct placement and spacing of ellipses can be tricky. The following guidelines should cover most cases.

- Use three spaced periods . . . for ellipses within a single sentence. Occasionally, an instructor may ask you to indicate omitted material by placing brackets around the ellipsis marks. [. . .]
- Use a period before an ellipsis that falls at the end of a sentence. . . .
- Leave a space before the first period . . . and after the last period of all ellipses.
- When another punctuation mark occurs before omitted words, you can eliminate it if it is not necessary to the grammar of the sentence, but you must retain it if it is necessary to the grammar.

EXAMPLE The newspapers reported that "Officer Hatt testified solemnly, . . . often staring at his hands and slowly shaking his head."

2 Use ellipses in quotations with omitted words

Ellipses are especially useful when you want to quote some (but not all) words in a passage. You may wish to omit a portion because it doesn't offer relevant ideas or information, because it makes the quotation too long for your purposes, or because you want to "skip" from one part of a long quotation to the next without including everything between. The following examples from a student's paper on sailing show his original draft, from which he wanted to cut the boldfaced sentence in the block quotation, and his edited draft, in which he has used ellipses to do so.

ORIGINAL Drummond, in his *Complete Guide to Sailing*, blames the instability of the sandbagger on its sail-to-hull ratio:

> Extremely fast, sandbaggers were very wide and shallow. They carried an enormous amount of sail area on an expanded rig. **As a result, when they were raced, they carried twenty-five or more bags of sand in the cockpit as ballast. When a boat came about, a crew of husky men quickly shifted the bags of sand to the windward side.** The boats ran from eighteen to twenty-eight feet in length, and carried a bowsprit almost as long as the hull and a main boom that extended ten feet or more beyond the stern.

EDITED Drummond, in his *Complete Guide to Sailing*, blames the instability of the sandbagger on its sail-to-hull ratio:

> Extremely fast, sandbaggers were very wide and shallow. They carried an enormous amount of sail area on an expanded rig. . . . The boats ran from eighteen to twenty-eight feet in length, and carried a bowsprit almost as long as the hull and a main boom that extended ten feet or more beyond the stern.

You can also eliminate *parts* of a sentence. When you do so, maintain normal sentence structure and grammatical form; don't just rip out words at random. The following example from a student's interview paper shows the original quotation from his notes; the way he incorporated this into his rough draft (with ellipses); and his corrected, edited version.

ORIGINAL QUOTATION "We've always played well against Duke. Year before last, we creamed them. Last year their defense fouled us up, but we still won. This year we've got a deep bench. I bet we'll take them to the cleaners, for sure."

INCORRECT DRAFT

When I pressed him to predict his team's performance, Coach Harms paused for a minute, then said with determination, "We've always played well against Duke. Year before last, we creamed them. Last year . . . but we still won. . . . we'll take them to the cleaners. . . .

EDITED

When I pressed him to predict his team's performance, Coach Harms paused for a minute, then said with determination, "We've always played well against Duke. Year before last, we creamed them. Last year . . . we still won. This year . . . we'll take them to the cleaners. . . ."

3 Use ellipses for other gaps

Occasionally you may want to indicate a pause or a gap in your own writing, not just in quoted material. In fiction and personal narrative, for example, ellipses are often used to show suspense, hesitation, or uncertainty, or to suggest continuing action.

FOR SUSPENSE

When we returned to our campsite, we were stunned. The tent was in a shambles. Our food was strewn everywhere. Our water jug was fifty yards away. Muddy claw marks were everywhere. . . .

53e Slashes

You will use slashes mainly to indicate alternative forms of words. You can also use slashes to mark quoted lines of poetry when those lines are not set off from your text.

1 Use slashes with alternative words

When used to indicate alternative words, the slash translates as "or" or "and." It is a shorthand often used in technical documents and manuals.

Be certain that the **on/off** switch is in the vertical position.

There is no exemption from the Composition **101/102** sequence.

Combinations such as *he/she* and *him/her* are not entirely acceptable in formal writing. Many good alternatives for these combinations are available. (See 47c.) The term *and/or* appears primarily in legal writing, but it can be used in moderation elsewhere. Different fields or professions may have particular functions for the slash or may use the slash in specific terms.

2 Use slashes when quoting lines of poetry

When you quote lines of poetry *within* your text rather than setting off the material in a block quotation, separate the lines of verse with a slash. Type a space before and after the slash.

> The speaker in Sir Philip Sidney's sonnet addresses the moon by saying, "With how sad steps, O Moon, thou climb'st the skies, / How silently, and with how wan a face."

Exercise 2

A. Find or create a short paragraph that uses as many of the punctuation marks described in this chapter as possible: parentheses, brackets, dashes, ellipses, and slashes. Choose one example of each case, and explain what purpose it serves in the paragraph.

B. Write or type out another version of the paragraph for Exercise 2A, stripped of its special punctuation. Make two copies to exchange with classmates. Ask the members of your group to edit the two copies, which lack parentheses, brackets, dashes, ellipses, and slashes. They should insert these punctuation marks wherever they think the marks are appropriate. Then compare your original and the versions punctuated by your classmates. Decide which marks of punctuation you consider effective and ineffective, and give reasons for your judgments.

CHAPTER 54 Capitalization

Capital letters call attention to themselves and to words containing them. Your readers expect capitalization to signal the start of sentences or to identify specific people, places, and things. Capitalization that follows convention not only makes reading easier but also reflects a general sense that certain people and things deserve the kind of recognition that capital letters can provide. In the passage that follows, notice how hard it is to pay attention to specific details when some capitals have been removed.

> Then, as i cross the state line, i remember a florence, alabama, composer named william christopher handy. After moving to memphis and writing songs about boss crump, beale street, st. james infirmary, and st. louis, he became known as "the father of the blues." Maybe i should turn north.
>
> —Hugh Merrill, *The Blues Route*

The general rules for capitalization are easy to remember.

- Use a capital letter at the beginning of a sentence.
- Capitalize proper nouns, proper adjectives, and most words in titles of works.

Specific conventions are often harder to keep in mind, and sometimes you may need to consult this chapter for answers to your questions: Should I capitalize a sentence after a colon? What about the beginning of a sentence within parentheses? When should I use *president* and *President*? How can I recognize when a noun is "proper" and requires capitalization?

54a Beginning a sentence

Sentences begin with capital letters. This rule applies to regular sentences and sentence fragments used as partial sentences. (See 37c.)

Two national parks, Yellowstone and Grand Teton, are in Wyoming.
Are camping spots in the parks hard to get in the summer?
Make your reservations early!
No camping without a reservation.

1 Capitalize the opening word in a quoted sentence

When you quote someone else's words or sentences, you will ask, "When should I capitalize within the quotation?" The answer generally depends on the relationship between the main (outer) sentence and the material you are quoting within it.

Capitalize the first word in the quotation when it is a complete sentence or when it begins your own sentence.

COMPLETE SENTENCE QUOTED Speaking of *Blind Man with a Pistol*, James Lundquist says, "**T**he novel begins with an opening chapter that, without exaggeration, is one of the strangest in American literature."

If you interrupt a quotation with your own words, do not capitalize after the interruption.

QUOTATION INTERRUPTED "**T**he novel," claims James Lundquist, "**b**egins with an opening chapter that, without exaggeration, is one of the strangest in American literature."

Also drop the capitalization if you integrate the quotation into the structure of your own sentence (see 26h).

INTEGRATED QUOTATION On the other hand, James Lundquist claims that "**t**he novel begins with an opening chapter that, without exaggeration, is one of the strangest in American literature."

If you are quoting only part of someone else's sentence, capitalize the quoted material when you use it to open your sentence but not when you place it in the middle or at the end. (Indicate any changes in capitalization in brackets.)

OPENING QUOTATION "[**O**]ne of the strangest in American literature" is how Lundquist describes the first chapter.

The first word is not capitalized in the source, so the writer indicates the change in brackets.

CONCLUDING QUOTATION James Lundquist overstates his case when he argues that the first chapter remains "**o**ne of the strangest in American literature."

2 Capitalize a freestanding sentence in parentheses

Capitalize the first word of any sentence that stands on its own within parentheses.

FREESTANDING SENTENCE — By this time, the Union forces were split up into nineteen sections. (**G**rant was determined to unite them.)

However, when you place a sentence within parentheses (or dashes) inside another sentence, do not begin the enclosed sentence with a capital.

ONE SENTENCE INSIDE ANOTHER — Saskatchewan's economy depends heavily on farming (**o**ver half of Canada's wheat crop comes from the province), though oil production and mining have also become important in recent decades.

3 Capitalize the first word of a line of poetry

Lines of poetry generally begin with a capital letter, regardless of where the initial word appears in the "sentence."

Long since, we pulled brown oak-leaves to the ground
In a winter of dry trees; we heard the cock
Shout its unplaceable cry, the axe's sound
Delay a moment after the axe's stroke.

—LOUISE BOGAN, "Old Countryside"

For special effect, however, poets sometimes ignore this and other conventions of capitalization.

new **h**ampshire explodes into radio primary,
newspaper headlines & beer—
well-weathered tag-lines from lips of schoolchildren.
we triumph by not being clear.

—T. R. MAYERS, "(snap)shots"

When you are quoting poetry, follow the author's practice.

4 Decide whether to capitalize following a colon

If a complete sentence follows a colon, you can choose to capitalize it or put it in lowercase (see 49b on colon use). Since either choice is correct, you might make your decision on the basis of style or emphasis. But be consistent.

CORRECT — The province of New Brunswick is bilingual both by law and in practice: **O**ne-third of the population is French-speaking and the remainder English-speaking.

ALSO CORRECT — The province of New Brunswick is bilingual both by law and in practice: **o**ne-third of the population is French-speaking and the remainder English-speaking.

In general, do not use a capital letter if the word group following the colon is not a sentence.

> Foremost among the educational issues in New Brunswick is another problem related to language: **b**ilingualism in the schools.

There are special cases in which the word group after a colon takes a capital letter even if it is not a complete sentence. If the word group after a colon states a principle or aphorism, for example, use a capital letter.

> Remember this rule as you go through life: **A**lways look on the bright side.

5 Decide whether to capitalize elements in a series or list

You can treat questions in a series or elements in a list in various ways.

Questions in a series. You can choose whether to use capital letters to highlight the opening of each question in a series.

CORRECT — Should we spend our limited campaign funds on television ads? **O**n billboards? **O**n smaller signs and posters? **O**n flyers?

ALSO CORRECT — Should we spend our limited campaign funds on television ads? **o**n billboards? **o**n smaller signs and posters? **o**n flyers?

Stick to one style throughout an essay.

Run-in lists. If the items in a **run-in list** (a list whose items aren't placed on separate lines) are simple, you may use commas to separate them and a lowercase letter for the first word in each item. If the items themselves in a run-in list contain commas or are very complex and lengthy, you may decide to separate them with semicolons.

> In estimating the project's costs, remember that you need to pay for the following: (1) **l**ab facilities, (2) **u**tilities, and (3) **m**easuring equipment.

> In estimating the project's costs, remember the following: (1) **l**ab facilities must be rented; (2) **l**ight, heat, and other utilities need to be charged to the project's account; (3) **m**easuring equipment should be leased.

If the list following the colon consists of complete sentences, capitalize the first word of each item.

> In estimating the project's costs, remember the following: **F**irst, lab facilities must be rented. **S**econd, light, heat, and other utilities need to be charged to the project's account. **F**inally, measuring equipment should be leased.

Vertical lists. You may choose whether to capitalize the elements in a **vertical list** when they are either words or partial sentences. You must use capitalization with complete sentences, unless they appear in an outline without periods (see 3c on outlining).

CORRECT When you estimate the project's costs, remember the following.

1. **L**ab facilities
2. **U**tilities
3. **M**easuring equipment

ALSO CORRECT When you estimate the project's costs, remember the following.

1. **l**ab facilities
2. **u**tilities
3. **m**easuring equipment

Use the same pattern of capitalization in all the lists in a paper, and make sure the items in each list are parallel in form (see 43d).

54b Proper nouns and adjectives

To capitalize a word is to highlight its importance. Readers pay special attention to words naming specific people, places, and things (proper nouns) and to adjectives created from these nouns (proper adjectives). Capitalizing a title also helps call attention to it.

1 Capitalize proper nouns and adjectives

You should capitalize the names of specific people, places, and things (**proper nouns**) as well as adjectives derived from them (**proper adjectives**).

PROPER NOUNS	PROPER ADJECTIVES
Brazil	Brazilian music
Dickens	Dickensian portrait
Venice	Venetian architecture

An article (*a*, *an*, or *the*) preceding a proper noun or adjective should not be capitalized unless it begins a title (see 54c) or starts a sentence.

All other nouns and adjectives are **common nouns** and **common adjectives.** Do not capitalize them except in special contexts, such as at the beginning of a sentence, in titles of works, or as parts of proper nouns.

COMMON NOUN (LOWERCASE)	PART OF PROPER NOUN (CAPITALIZED)
lake	Lake Jackson
park	Prospect Park
computer company	Mesa Computer Company

Some company and institutional names include both a proper and a common noun. Both parts form a proper name and are capitalized.

proper common	proper common
Sandberg **U**niversity	**R**obinson **C**orporation

People writing documents under the auspices of an institution (for example, a memo to university staff or a corporate report) may decide to capitalize the common noun when used as a shortened name for the institution.

> Sandberg **U**niversity is pleased to announce plans for renovating Smith Hall.
>
> The **U**niversity has contracted with Azar Construction for the project.

If the subject of your paper has a common noun as part of its name, you may wish to follow the same procedure, after first giving the subject's full name, in order to help your readers readily distinguish references to the subject from more generic uses of the word.

> The Democratic **P**arty has always been the dominant **p**arty in this county. However, other political groups have begun to encroach upon the **P**arty's territory.

Sometimes a time period such as a week or season refers to a specific event. In such cases the time period is capitalized because it is part of the name of the event.

PART OF THE EVENT'S NAME
At Bardstown College, **F**all **O**rientation runs from September 3 to 5.

NOT PART OF THE NAME
The **f**all **o**rientation at Bardstown College runs from September 3 to 5.

CAPITALIZATION OF NOUNS AND ADJECTIVES

CAPITALIZED	LOWERCASE
INDIVIDUALS	
President Bush	the president
Michael Jordan	her husband
Georgia O'Keeffe	my teacher's neighbor
RELATIVES	
Aunt Rosa; Cousin Jack	an aunt; my cousin Jack
Mother; Dad	my mother; your dad

CAPITALIZED	LOWERCASE
GROUPS OF PEOPLE AND LANGUAGES	
Caucasian	white
Japanese	
Hopi	
Negro	
African American	black (preferred in general usage)
Russian	
Native American	
TIME PERIODS, HOLIDAYS, AND SEASONS	
Thursday; October	spring; summer; fall; winter
Easter; Ramadan; Yom Kippur; Labor Day	holiday
RELIGIONS AND RELATED SUBJECTS	
Judaism, Jews	
Christianity, Christians	
Islam, Muslims	
Catholic	catholic (meaning "universal")
Protestant	
Hinduism	
Buddhist practices	
Talmud; Bible	talmudic; biblical
God; Jesus Christ	a god, goddess; godly
ORGANIZATIONS, INSTITUTIONS, AND MEMBERS	
Chicago Bulls, the Bulls	the team
Democratic Party, Democrat	democratic (referring to democracy)
Heritage Foundation; Conservative Party; Tory	conservative (referring to a political philosophy)
Girl Scout; Boy Scouts of America	the scout
Metropolitan Opera; Cincinnati Symphony	the opera; the string quartet
Rolling Stones	the band
Florida State Police	the police, the state police
Coast Guard; Virginia Board of Ethics	the sailors; the board
House of Commons; U.S. Senate	a member of parliament; a senator
Air Line Pilots Association	the union, union member
PLACES, THEIR RESIDENTS, AND GEOGRAPHIC REGIONS	
Malaysia, Malaysian	the country; the citizen
Cape Verde Islands, Cape Verdean	the state; the resident

(*continued*)

CAPITALIZATION OF NOUNS AND ADJECTIVES *(continued)*

CAPITALIZED	LOWERCASE
PLACES, THEIR RESIDENTS, AND GEOGRAPHIC REGIONS	
Tibet, Sino-Tibetan	
Berlin, Berliner	the city; the resident
Erie County; Nassau Avenue	the county; the street
South China Sea; Volga River	the sea; the river
Amazon Basin; Mars	the region; the planet
the Southwest, the East; East Coast	southwest, east southeastern, eastern (directions)
BUILDINGS AND MONUMENTS	
Taj Mahal; Peace Bridge	Jim's garden; our backyard
Tower of London; Busch Stadium	the tower; a stadium
Space Needle; Getty Museum	a landmark; a museum
Piazza Navona; Grant's Tomb	the piazza; her tomb
HISTORICAL PERIODS, EVENTS, AND MOVEMENTS	
Thirty Years' War; Dorr's Rebellion	the war; the rebellion
Algerian Revolution	the revolution
Ming Dynasty	a dynasty
Romantic period; Impressionism	the period or style
First Great Awakening; Postmodernism	the movement; a trend
Jazz Age; Renaissance	a cultural epoch
ACADEMIC INSTITUTIONS AND COURSES	
Auburn University; Utica College	a university; the college
English Department	an English department
Department of Chemistry	chemistry department
Sociology 203; English 101	sociology or English course
VEHICLES	
Airbus A300; Pontiac Grand Prix	a passenger plane; my car
J Boat	a sailboat
COMPANY NAMES AND TRADE NAMES	
Samsung; Monsanto Chemical	the company; the chemical company
Intel; Fuji Heavy Industries; Xerox	a manufacturer; an employer
Luvs; New Balance; Kleenex; Toblerone; Patagonia	diapers; shoes; tissues; chocolate bar; outdoor equipment
SCIENTIFIC, TECHNICAL, AND MEDICAL TERMS	
Big Dipper; Earth (planet)	the stars; earth (ground)
Marxism	marxian theory
Heisenberg's uncertainty principle	
Alzheimer's disease; Down syndrome	tuberculosis
organ of Corti	pancreas
Pistacia vera; *Gazella dorcas*	pistachio tree; gazelle

ESL ADVICE: CAPITALIZATION

Rules for beginning words with capital letters can vary considerably from language to language, often differing markedly from those in English. In German, for example, nouns and pronouns are capitalized: *Ich werde Sie ihrer Blumen zuruckgeben* (I will give you your flowers back). In Spanish, pronouns and the names of days and months are not capitalized: *Almuerzo con ella los lunes* (I lunch with her on Mondays).

2 Capitalize the pronoun *I* and the interjection *O*

Whenever **I** try to argue with my parents, they make me feel as if **I'm** still a child.

Trust in him, **O** people, and pour out your heart.

Although *oh* would seem to be capitalized by analogy with *O*, convention requires that *oh* remain in lowercase unless it begins a sentence or is capitalized in material you are quoting.

"**O**h dear, no," said the housekeeper.

—WILKIE COLLINS, *The Woman in White*

54c Titles of works

In titles, you should capitalize the first word, the last word, and all words in between *except* articles (*a*, *an*, and *the*), prepositions under five letters (such as *in*, *of*, and *to*), and conjunctions under five letters (such as *and* or *but*). These rules apply to titles of long works, short works, and parts of works as well as titles for your own papers. If a colon divides the title, capitalize the first word after the colon.

The Mill on the Floss
"Factory of the Future: A Survey"
Reservoir Dogs
"Politics and the English Language"
Fragile Glory: A Portrait of France and the French
"Just like Romeo and Juliet"
"The Civil Rights Movement: What Good Was It?"
"Sumer Is Icumen In"
Developing a Growth Plan for a Small Retail Business [your paper's title; see p. 803]

(For the rules governing the use of italics and quotation marks in titles, see 55a and 51d.)

Exercise 1

A. Add capitalization wherever necessary in the following sentences. Replace unnecessary capitals with lowercase letters. Circle the cases that seem the toughest to figure out.

EXAMPLE

I

Over the next ten years, india will become an increasingly important

N A

trading partner for north america.

1. Located on a subcontinent in the southern part of asia, the republic of india has a territory of about 1.2 million Square Miles.
2. India's population of almost 800 Million falls into two main groups, dravidians and indo-aryans, which in turn are made up of many other cultural groups.
3. Dravidians live mainly in the south, an area that is dominated geographically by the deccan plateau.
4. The religion of the Majority is hinduism, though other religious groups such as sikhs and muslims are important.
5. Recently, religious conflicts have broken out in the provinces of kashmir and uttar pradesh.
6. Indian History is long and complicated, but in Modern Times it has been dominated by the british rule over the Country and by attempts to escape that rule and found a democratic State.
7. British Rule over most of the country began after the sepoy rebellion of 1857–58.
8. It ended after world war II with the independence movement led by mahatma gandhi.
9. The move toward industrialization has been the main goal of indian leaders since Independence, though this movement has at times been complicated by the problem of overpopulation and by conflicts stemming from the hindu social (or caste) system.
10. The dominant political Party since Independence has been the congress Party, with leaders such as jawaharlal nehru, indira gandhi, and rajiv gandhi.

B. In a small group, compare your list of difficult cases from Exercise 1A. What did you do to figure out your answer to each difficult case? Compare your answers.

CHAPTER 55
Italics (Underlining)

Type that slants to the right—***italic type***—gives special emphasis to words and ideas. In handwritten or typed texts, underlining is the equivalent of italic type: The Color Purple = *The Color Purple.*

Convention requires you to use underlining (or italics) to give distinctive treatment to titles of full-length works, foreign words, names of vehicles, and words named as words. (Titles of shorter works or parts of works require quotation marks; see 51d.)

If you write your papers out in longhand, you will underline all such words and phrases. (A typewriter will also provide underlining.) Most computer word-processing programs give you the option of *italics*, though some readers may prefer you to underline.

COMPUTER PRINTOUT Alice Walker's novel *The Color Purple* has been both praised and criticized since it appeared in 1982.

You can occasionally use underlining or italics to add emphasis to your writing or to clarify your meaning.

> Not only was he one of the captains of the Permian team, not only was he number one in his class, but now he was thinking of applying to Harvard.
>
> *Harvard?*
>
> Never in a thousand years could Tony Chavez have imagined it turning out this way. Never in a million.
>
> —H. G. BISSINGER, *Friday Night Lights*

55a Following conventions

Knowing when to use underlining or italics can sometimes be difficult. The lists and discussions that follow can answer most of your questions. For example, should Stephen Crane's novel be written as *Maggie: A Girl of the Streets* or as "Maggie: A Girl of the Streets"? Should the French word "quiche," be written *quiche* or quiche? Should the name of the Star Trek vessel be written as *The Enterprise*, the *Enterprise*, "The Enterprise," or The Enterprise?

1 Underline titles of long or major works

Underline or italicize titles of most long works, such as books, magazines, and films, and of major works such as paintings and sculptures. For parts of works, however, and for short works such as stories, reports, magazine or newspaper articles, and episodes in a television series, use quotation marks rather than underlining. Some titles, such as those of sacred books (like the New Testament, Pentateuch, and Koran), require neither underlining nor quotation marks. (See the following list.)

TREATMENT OF TITLES

UNDERLINE OR ITALICIZE	USE QUOTATION MARKS
BOOKS AND PAMPHLETS	
Generations: The History of America's Future, 1584 to 2069 (nonfiction book)	"Boomers" (book chapter)
Maggie: A Girl of the Streets (novel)	"Preface" (chapter in a novel)
Beetroot (collection of stories)	"The Purloined Letter" (story)
The Wild Flag (collection of essays)	"Once More to the Lake" (essay)
Tracing Your Family's History (pamphlet)	"List Your Relatives" (section of a pamphlet)
POEMS	
Paradise Lost (long poem)	"Richard Cory" (short poem)
	"Whoso list to hunt" (first line of a poem, used as a title)
PLAYS	
Angels in America	
Fences	
MOVIES AND TELEVISION PROGRAMS	
Saving Private Ryan (film)	
Queer as Folk (TV show)	"The Long Suit" (episode in a TV series)
20/20 (TV news show)	"Daycare Dilemmas" (report from a news program)
PAINTINGS AND SCULPTURE	
Nude Descending a Staircase (painting)	
Winged Victory (sculpture)	
MUSICAL WORKS	
Nixon in China (opera)	"Luck Be a Lady" (song in a musical)

UNDERLINE OR ITALICIZE	USE QUOTATION MARKS
Nutcracker Suite (work for orchestra)	"Waltz of the Flowers" (section of a longer work)
Some Kind of Blue (album)	"Big Money" (song on an album)
Camille Saint-Saëns's *Organ Symphony*	
MAGAZINES AND NEWSPAPERS	
Discover (magazine)	"What Can Baby Learn?" (article in a magazine)
Review of Contemporary Fiction (scholarly journal)	"From Krazy Kat to Hoodoo: Aesthetic Discourse in the Fiction of Ishmael Reed" (scholarly article)
the *New York Times* (MLA style) *The New York Times* (alternate style)	"Asbestos Found in Schools" (newspaper article)

NO UNDERLINING, ITALICS, OR QUOTATION MARKS

SACRED BOOKS

Bible, Koran, Talmud, Bhagavad Gita

PUBLIC, LEGAL, OR WELL-KNOWN DOCUMENTS

United States Constitution

Last Will and Testament

TITLE OF YOUR OWN PAPER

The Attitudes of College Students Toward Intramural Sports (paper for a sociology class)

The Role of Verbal Abuse in *The Color Purple* (title of a work being discussed is italicized)

Exception: If your paper has been published and you are citing it, enclose the title in quotation marks.

A reader needs to know whether certain end punctuation (such as a question mark) is part of a title or part of your own sentence in which the title appears. Underline any punctuation *only* when it's part of the title.

INCORRECT What did he think of Jumanji?

CORRECT What did he think of Jumanji?

CORRECT The book What's Up, Doc? provides a history of cartoons.
The comma and question mark are part of the title, so they need to be underlined.

2 Underline names of specific vehicles

Underline or italicize the names of specific ships, airplanes, trains, and spacecraft, but not the names of *types* of vehicles. Note that USS and SS are not underlined. (See also 58a-2.)

SPECIFIC VEHICLES	TYPES OF VEHICLES
Voyager VI	Boeing 767
Orient Express	Sea-Doo
USS *Corpus Christi*	Arctic Cat snowmobile
SS *Norway*	Chevrolet Impala
Memphis Belle	Ducati 750
Mir	Boston Whaler

3 Underline foreign words and phrases

Foreign words and phrases pass through stages of familiarity. When a word or phrase is not used commonly and still seems foreign, highlight it with underlining or italics. Extremely common words and phrases—for example, "quiche," "junta," "taco," and "kvetch"—have lost their foreignness. You need not underline such words. When you can't decide whether to treat a word or phrase as part of the language, look it up in a dictionary.

FOREIGN The code of omertà supported a kind of order in the criminal world.

FOREIGN Many lawyers contribute to their communities by doing pro bono work.

COMMON I served the vegetables grilled on skewers like shish kebab.

Scientific names for the genus and species of plants and animals also require underlining; the common names do not.

SCIENTIFIC NAME The seaweed Chrodus crispus turns up in processed form in ice cream, in nondairy creamer, and even in hamburgers.

COMMON NAME Tests found algae growing in the Swansons' pool.

4 Underline words, letters, and numbers named as words

When you focus attention on a word, letter, or number by discussing it as itself, you should underline it.

DISCUSSED In several Boston accents, r is pronounced ah, so that the words car and park become cah and pahk.

Also underline a word or phrase you are defining.

DEFINED Electricity can also be generated from a piezoelectric crystal, a piece of quartz or similar material that responds to pressure by producing electric current.

Exercise 1

The following sentences contain words that need to be highlighted by underlining (italics) or by quotation marks. Edit each by supplying any necessary underlining or quotation marks. Star the items that are the most challenging to edit.

EXAMPLE

The well-known "Old Farmer's Almanac" contains information about the weather and articles on various topics.

1. I first learned about this famous American almanac from a newspaper article, You Can Look It Up There, that appeared in my local paper, the Record-Advertiser.
2. GQ and Cosmopolitan probably would not print an article like Salt: It's Still Worth Its Salt, which appeared in a recent edition of the almanac.
3. According to this article, the word salary comes from the Latin term for wages paid to some soldiers, salarium argentum, that is, salt money.
4. In an essay on the historic effects of weather, the author points out that freezing temperatures on January 28, 1986, led to the space shuttle Challenger disaster.
5. If you are interested in learning about the ocean, you can find out that high tides occur twice a month at syzygy, the times when the sun and moon are lined up on the same side of the earth or on opposite sides.

55b Emphasis

By underlining or italicizing a word or phrase, you give it special emphasis. Use this strategy on a *very* limited basis, however. Readers become annoyed when you rely too often on underlining to do the work your words should be doing on their own.

EMPHASIZES CONTRAST

A letter of recommendation mixing strong praise with a few reservations seems direct and realistic; a letter filled with faint praise makes the endorsement seem lukewarm.

HIGHLIGHTS IMPORTANT INFORMATION

Whenever you start the generator, make sure there is sufficient oil in the crankcase.

Many kinds of informal writing, such as notes, journal entries, and personal letters, rely on underlining to add a certain "oral" emphasis to the prose. Be careful not to rely on underlining for this purpose when writing formal papers and other documents.

INFORMAL Next time, hand the receipts to me instead of dropping them on my desk.

MORE FORMAL In the future, give the receipts to me personally instead of placing them on my desk.

Exercise 2

A. For each of the following sentences, add underlining as required by convention or needed for appropriate emphasis. Circle words that are underlined but should not be. Star items that are challenging to edit.

EXAMPLE

In 1957, Chevrolet produced the Bel Air, a model now considered a classic.

1. As David Halberstam points out in his book The Fifties, automobiles from the period were so hot they were cool.
2. Cars from that period, with enormous tailfins and lots of chrome, are still eye-catchers today.
3. The musical Grease is set in the same era.
4. Television shows from the period included the Ed Sullivan Show and Lassie.
5. Readers could choose from such now-defunct publications as the Herald Tribune newspaper and Look magazine.

B. In a group, compare your corrections to Exercise 2A. Which were the hardest to make, and why?

CHAPTER 56 Hyphens and Word Division

Hyphens divide words and tie them together as well. At the end of a line, you may need to split a word, completing it on the next line. A hyphen (-) tells readers to treat the divided word as one word, not two. Hyphens also help to divide words that are hard to read without a break, and they link familiar compound words.

56a Dividing words

To make your readers' job easier, use a hyphen to split a word at the end of a line. Also hyphenate words that may be misleading or hard to read without a visual break.

1 Divide words at the end of a line

When you don't have room at the end of a line to complete a word of *two or more syllables*, type it on the next line unless doing so will create a right margin that is jagged and distracting. To create a reasonably even margin, split the word *between syllables*, marking the break with a hyphen.

DISTRACTING The rate of change in home appliance manufacturing has accelerated rapidly over the past decade. Increasingly sophisticated consumers, international competition, and the need for an ozone-safe refrigerant to replace CFCs (chlorofluorocarbons) have provided the impetus.

HYPHENATED The rate of change in home appliance manufacturing has accelerated rapidly over the past decade. Increas-
ingly sophisticated consumers, international compe-
tition, and the need for an ozone-safe refrigerant to replace CFCs (chlorofluorocarbons) have provided the impetus.

If there is no space at the end of a line, a word-processing program will automatically move a word to the next line. This process is called *word wrapping*. You need to be alert for jagged margins created by this process, and hyphenate to make margins more regular.

Type a hyphen as a *single* line (-) with no space on either side. A dash, in contrast, interrupts sentences (see 53c). Type a dash as *two* lines (--) with no space on either side or in between.

INCORRECT HYPHEN	one - fourth of the workforce
CORRECT HYPHEN	one-fourth of the workforce
INCORRECT DASH	surprising ingredients - peanut butter, raisins, and cream
CORRECT DASH	surprising ingredients--peanut butter, raisins, and cream

Divide words only between syllables. Readers have a hard time recognizing words that are split at a place other than a syllable break. For example, the word *adjustable* can be correctly divided in only two places: *ad-just-able.*

CONFUSING	Experts disagree about the wisdom of **adju-** **stable** rates for mortgages.
CLEAR	Experts disagree about the wisdom of **adjust-** **able** rates for mortgages.

Consult a dictionary to determine where to divide a word. If you rely entirely on your own pronunciation, you may divide some words incorrectly. For example, *irrevocable* is divided as *ir-re-vo-ca-ble,* not *ir-rev-oc-able*; *milieu* is *mi-lieu,* not *mil-ieu.* Your pronunciation of a familiar word may also differ from the standard one given in the dictionary and expected by readers.

56a -

Some word-processing programs will hyphenate words at the ends of lines for you. This feature can be timesaving and helpful, but check the results in case the program has split a term incorrectly.

Leave more than one letter at the end of a line and more than two at the beginning.

INCORRECT	Two designers announced they are considering an **a-** **greement** to produce a line of affordable clothes for professional women.
EDITED	Two designers announced they are considering an **agreement** to produce a line of affordable clothes for professional women.
INCORRECT	The concert ended because a stagehand **disconnect-** **ed** the power supply for the main amplifiers.
EDITED	The concert ended because a stagehand **discon-** **nected** the power supply for the main amplifiers.

Newspapers will often begin a line with two letters, but this is to accommodate their narrow margins.

Divide compound words at natural breaks. Generally, divide a compound word at the break between the words making it up. If a compound already includes a hyphen, divide it at that point.

DISTRACTING If the sports car is the classic European car, the **Volkswa-gen** is the classic California car.

EDITED If the sports car is the classic European car, the **Volks-wagen** is the classic California car.

DISTRACTING In his new movie, the actor plays a bumbling, **acci-dent-prone** police detective.

EDITED In his new movie, the actor plays a bumbling, **accident-prone** police detective.

Don't divide one-syllable words. Relatively long words such as *touched*, *drought*, and *through* have no stopping points in pronunciation and should be left intact. If the undivided word doesn't fit on a line, move it to the next line.

Avoid confusing divisions. When some words are correctly divided, they form other words with meanings that may be distracting.

DISTRACTING The school board is proposing a solution for **sin-gle** parents unable to afford child care.

CLEAR The school board is proposing a solution for **single** parents unable to afford child care.

Don't split abbreviations, numerals, or contractions. Abbreviations and acronyms (NATO, DVD, NCAA), numerals (528; 100,000), and contractions (didn't, should've) can be sounded out with syllables, but splitting them will distract your readers.

DISTRACTING Foreign policy experts disagree about funding the **NA-TO** alliance at present levels.

CLEAR Foreign policy experts disagree about funding the **NATO** alliance at present levels.

Exercise 1

A. Look at each hyphen in the following sentences and decide whether to retain it, to change the division within the word, or to eliminate it in favor of placing the entire word on the next line. Use your dictionary if you need to, and keep track of the toughest cases.

EXAMPLE

Although receiving a present can be very pleasant, gift-~~giv-~~
giving
~~ing~~ can be equally rewarding.

1. Looking for a job that would be challenging, Jen thought long and hard about taking the position at Hammond's Gift Shop.
2. By the next Saturday, however, she was unpacking a truck-
load of the exquisite vases and figurines that the gift shop sells.
3. Hank wanted only one thing for his birthday: an ornamental Chinese vase that was way beyond Rachel's budget.
4. When he came home one afternoon and saw the vase on the man-
tle, Hank went right out to get flowers as a way of saying "thank you."
5. The bouquet was lovely, redolent of roses, tulips, and baby's-
breath.

B. In a small group, compare your edited sentences from Exercise 1A. Which were the most difficult, and why?

---

2 Divide words to prevent misreading

You can use a hyphen to help readers distinguish between words that are spelled the same but have very different meanings.

In the spirit of **reform** politics, the party sought to **re-form** a defunct citizens' action committee.

For **recreation,** the Prichards staged a hilarious **re-creation** of the argument between Joe and Arnold.

You should also hyphenate words that are difficult to read because of repeated letters or odd combinations of letters.

post-traumatic (*not* posttraumatic)

co-owner (*not* coowner)

56b Joining words

Instead of *dividing* whole words, hyphens are often used to *tie together* the elements of compound words and phrases. The conventions for linking compounds, however, tend to be mixed; for example, should the mechanical heart regulator be written as *pacemaker*, *pace maker*, or *pace-maker*?

1 Check hyphens in compound words

A compound word is made from two or more words. Some compounds are hyphenated (*double-decker*, *time-lapse*), some treated as one word (*backfire*, *timekeeper*), and some treated as separate words (*mail carrier*, *time bomb*). A dictionary will tell you how to treat a particular compound. Make sure the dictionary is up to date, however, because usage changes.

2 Hyphenate familiar compounds correctly

Some familiar compounds generally require hyphens.

Numbers. Hyphenate all numbers between twenty-one and ninety-nine when they are spelled out.

forty-one   eighty-six   twenty-five

This rule holds even if the number is part of a larger number.

fifty-eight thousand   twenty-three million

Use a hyphen to show inclusive numbers.

pages 163-78   volumes 9-14

Fractions. Hyphenate fractions when you spell them out.

five-eighths of the liquid in the container

Prefixes and suffixes. Hyphenate a prefix attached to a capitalized word or a number.

Cro-Magnon   non-Euclidean   post-Victorian   pre-1989

Hyphenate a capital letter and a word that together form a compound.

A-frame   I-beam   T-shirt

Some specialized terms, such as those used in music, do not require a hyphen.

A minor   G sharp   C clef

The prefixes *ex-*, *self-*, and *all-* and the suffixes *-elect* and *-odd* should generally be hyphenated in compounds.

all-encompassing   self-centered   president-elect
ex-partner   self-denial   twenty-odd

3 Hyphenate compound modifiers correctly

When you ask two or more words to work as a single modifier and you place them *before* a noun, hyphenate them.

BEFORE NOUN The **second-largest** supplier of crude oil to the United States is Nigeria.

BEFORE NOUN Ayn Rand's works are among the most popular **twentieth-century** novels.

When the modifiers come *after* a noun, you generally do not need to hyphenate them.

AFTER NOUN Many of the drugs used to treat cancer are **nausea inducing.**

Remember that modifying compounds can mean something quite different from the sum of their independent meanings. Hyphens help readers to know which meaning to assign the compound.

The director needed three **extra wild** monkeys for the scene.

The director needed three **extra-wild** monkeys for the scene.

Do not hyphenate compound modifiers containing *-ly* adverbs or comparative and superlative forms.

The new products were developed by the company's **highly regarded** research team.

Nigeria is the **most populous** country in Africa.

(Compound modifiers differ from coordinate adjectives, which are joined with a comma. See 48f.)

4 Use hyphens to create new compounds

To add vividness and emphasis to your writing, you can occasionally create (or "coin") a new compound word or phrase. Join the elements in such a compound with hyphens to indicate its original, temporary nature.

She entered the program with a **prove-it-to-me** attitude.

Exercise 2

A. Insert hyphens in the following sentences wherever appropriate. Consult a dictionary if necessary.

EXAMPLE

The company hired a well-regarded accounting firm as part of its financial reorganization.

1. Alejo enjoys painstakingly exact work, such as building scale model ships.
2. While working, he likes to listen to Francis Poulenc's jazz influenced classical music.
3. One fourth of all his model ships are sold at auction.
4. Tony, his assistant, keeps track of the profits in a pre and post auction sale log.
5. Although his creations are awesome, Alejo harbors many insecurities that are mostly selfinflicted.

B. In a small group, compare your edited versions of the sentences in Exercise 2A. Which were the most difficult decisions, and why? Did your dictionaries give all members of the group the same advice?

CHAPTER 57 Numbers

You can convey numbers in several ways in your writing—as numerals (37; 18.6), as words (eighty-one; two million), or as a combination of numerals and letters (7th, 2nd). Understanding the appropriate ways to present numbers is important because unconventional or inconsistent usage can mislead your readers. This chapter shows you how to present numbers appropriately in general academic writing. For advice about the use of numbers in business, technical, and professional writing, see the reference guides listed in Chapters 28–31.

57a Spelling out or using numerals

Whenever you use numbers in your writing, you need to decide whether to spell them out (twenty-five) or use numerals (25). The rules that follow tell you how to use numbers in general writing, including much academic writing. Conventions for the use of numbers may vary according to academic discipline and profession, however, so check with your instructor or with one of the style sheets describing conventions for specific fields (see Chapters 28–31).

1 Spell out numbers of one or two words

Spell out a number if you can write it in one or two words.

CORRECT We are ordering **twenty-seven** personal computers.

CORRECT Folktales have been popular in children's storybooks for the past **two hundred** years.

Treat hyphenated numbers (see 56b-2) as a single word.

CORRECT Last year, our farm produced more than **seventy-eight thousand** eggs.

2 Spell out numbers that begin a sentence

Readers expect every sentence to begin with a capital letter. To avoid unsettling your readers, spell out any number that opens a sentence, even if the number contains more than two words. If the number is long enough to be distracting, rewrite so that it appears elsewhere in the sentence.

INAPPROPRIATE **428** of the houses in Talcottville are built on leased land.

DISTRACTING **Four hundred twenty-eight** of the houses in Talcottville are built on leased land.

EASY TO READ **In Talcottville, 428** houses are built on leased land.

3 Express related numbers in a consistent form

When the numbers in a sentence or passage refer to the same category, treat them consistently by sticking to either words or numerals. If one of the numbers would require numerical form on its own, expressing the rest in numerals will help you keep sentences direct and concise.

INCONSISTENT Café Luna opened with a menu of **twenty-six** items, which soon expanded to **eighty-five** and then **104** items as word spread about the good food.

CONSISTENT Café Luna opened with a menu of **26** items, which soon expanded to **85** and then **104** items as word spread about the good food.

57b Special conventions

In using numbers as part of dates, measurements, addresses, and the like, you need to follow some special conventions.

1 Use numerals when appropriate

ADDRESSES AND ROUTES

1005 Avenue of the Americas Interstate 6 Route 102
2450 Ridge Road, Apartment B3, Alhambra, CA 91801

DATES

September 7, 1989	2002	1880–1910
class of '01 (informal)	the '80s (informal)	1930s
486 B.C. (or B.C.E.)	A.D. 980 (or 980 C.E.)	
from 1955 to 1957	between 1872 and 1876	

PARTS OF A WRITTEN WORK

Chapter 12 page 278
Macbeth 2.4.25–28 (or act II, scene iv, lines 25–28)
Genesis 1:1–6 (reference to the Bible)

MEASUREMENTS USING SYMBOLS OR ABBREVIATIONS

128 MB	65 mph	80 kph
6'4"	47 psi	21 ml

PERCENTAGES, DECIMALS, AND FRACTIONS

7 5/8 27.3 67 percent (or 67%)

TIME OF DAY

10:52	2 p.m.	6:17 a.m.
12 p.m. (noon)	12 a.m. (midnight)	

EXCEPTION

seven o'clock, not 7 o'clock

MONEY (SPECIFIC AMOUNTS)

$7,883 (or $7883) $4.29 $7.2 million (or $7,200,000)

SURVEYS, RATIOS, STATISTICS, AND SCORES

7 out of 10 3 to 1 a mean of 23
a standard deviation of 2.5
the Bills defeated the Packers 21 to 17

CLUSTERED NUMBERS

paragraphs 2, 4, 9, and 13–15 (or 13 through 15)
units 23, 145, and 210

57b num

2 Spell out numbers when appropriate

DATES AND TIMES

the sixties October seventh the nineteenth century
four o'clock (or four in the morning)
times rounded to the quarter hour: half past eight, a quarter after one

ROUNDED NUMBERS OR ROUNDED AMOUNTS OF MONEY

about three hundred thousand citizens
close to eleven thousand dollars
sixty cents (and other small dollar or cent amounts)

RANGES OF NUMBERS

LESS THAN 100 Supply the full second number.
9–13 27–34 58–79 94–95

OVER 100 Simply supply the last two figures of the second number unless more are needed to prevent confusion. Do not use a comma in page numbers.
134–45 95–102 (not 95–02) 370–420
1534–620 (not 1534–20) 1007–09

YEARS	Supply both years in a range except when they belong to the same century. 1890–1920 1770–86 476–823 42–38 B.C.
LARGE NUMBERS	For especially large numbers, combine numerals and words. 75 million years 2.3 million new automobiles

57c Too many numbers

Using too many numbers in a sentence or passage can confuse readers. If numbers come next to each other, first check for any needed hyphens (see 56b).

CONFUSING For the company picnic we can buy either **forty six packs** of soda pop or **twenty two liter** bottles.

HYPHENS ADDED For the company picnic we can buy either **forty six-packs** of soda pop or **twenty two-liter** bottles.

When a passage contains so many numbers that readers might have trouble keeping track of the relationships, consider organizing the numbers in a table or chart.

DETAILED DESCRIPTION

The origins of Canada's population include the British Isles (40%), France (27%), other European regions (20%), and Indian (indigenous) or Eskimo (1.5%).

57c num

CHARTED NUMBERS

Canadian Population

ORIGIN	PERCENTAGE
British Isles	40.0
France	27.0
Other European	20.0
Indian (indigenous) or Eskimo	1.5

This alternative is appropriate only when the numbers identify comparable categories. In other instances, you can avoid confusing readers by rewriting in order to simplify or to separate numbers so they are easier to understand.

Exercise 1

A. In the following sentences, correct any errors in the use of numbers. Circle any especially difficult items. You may need to rewrite some sentences.

EXAMPLE

When the list of cities for the Rock and Roll Hall of Fame was narrowed down to ~~1~~ one, the choice was Cleveland.

1. Of the groups and individuals elected to the Rock and Roll Hall of Fame from 1986 to 1990, 5 were female and 68 were male.
2. The Hall of Fame is increasing its membership goals from nineteen thousand to twenty-one thousand five hundred.
3. 411 of the 2000 questionnaires about favorite rockers were returned by the deadline.
4. This year the Hall of Fame purchased twenty-six articles of clothing, 127 signed memorabilia, and 232 unused concert tickets for the museum.
5. Although subscribers were told the museum would open by 10:30 in the morning on the twelfth, the personnel weren't ready for the large crowd until about 2 o'clock.

B. In a small group, compare your edited versions of the sentences in Exercise 1A. Which cases gave you the most trouble? How did you resolve them?

CHAPTER 58 Abbreviations

When they are understood and agreed upon by both writer and reader, abbreviations make a sentence quicker to write and easier to read.

SPELLED OUT In her course Reporting Economic Issues, new faculty member **Doctor** Marian Hwang will be drawing heavily on her prior employment at both the **Internal Revenue Service** and **the National Broadcasting Company.**

ABBREVIATED In her course Reporting Economic Issues, new faculty member **Dr.** Marian Hwang will be drawing heavily on her prior employment at both the **IRS** and **NBC.**

Improper or badly placed abbreviations, however, can make a sentence *harder* to read and understand.

CONFUSING The legal theory known as Law **&** Economics has a strong advocate in **Jg. Rich.** Posner. He is a former **U of C** law **prof.** who now sits on the Seventh **U.S. Cir. Ct. of App.** in Chicago.

READER'S REACTION: Am I supposed to know all these abbreviations? What is "Cir. Ct. of App."? Is "U of C" the University of California? Cincinnati? Chicago?

CLEAR The legal theory known as Law **and** Economics has a strong advocate in **Judge** Richard Posner. He is a former **University of Chicago** law **professor** who now sits on the Seventh U.S. **Circuit Court of Appeals** in Chicago.

Abbreviations should aid your readers, not distract them.

58a Familiar abbreviations

Many abbreviations are so widely used that readers have no trouble recognizing them. These abbreviations are acceptable in all kinds of writing as long as you present them in standard form.

1 Abbreviate titles with proper names

When people's titles come right before or after their names, you should use standard abbreviations such as *Dr.*, *Rev.*, *Ms.*, and *Prof.*

BEFORE NAME **Dr.** Antoinette Plocek; **Mr.** William Choi; **Ms.** Rutkowski; **Mrs.** Stephanie Chenier; **Rev.** Richard Valantasis; **Hon.** Patricia Hacaj; **St.** Rose of Lima.

AFTER NAME Christine Carruthers, **M.D.;** Cathy Harrington, **D.V.M.;** Angelo Iacono, **Jr.;** James Guptil, **Sr.**; Ralph Romero, **S.J.;** Jane Berger, **M.A.;** Rosemary Anzaldua, **C.P.A.**

If the person's title is preceded by *the*, the title should be spelled out.

The **Reverend** Robert Marsh

When you give a person's entire name, you may abbreviate the title, but if you use it *as part of your reference to the person*, spell out the entire title.

INCORRECT The list included **Prof.** Levesque, **Brig. Gen.** Washington, and **Rep.** Schroeder.

ACCEPTABLE The list included **Professor** Levesque, **Brigadier General** Washington, and **Representative** Schroeder.

58a abbrev

ALTERNATIVE The list included **Prof. Roland** Levesque, **Brig. Gen. William** Washington, and **Rep. Patricia** Schroeder.

EXCEPTIONS **Rev.** Mills and **Dr.** Smith were not invited.

Spell out a title when it does not come next to a proper name.

INCORRECT You should consult the **Dr.** about that knee.

EDITED You should consult the **doctor** about that knee.

EDITED You should consult **Dr. Boyajian** about that knee.

Use only one form of a person's title at a time.

INCORRECT **Dr.** Vonetta McGee, **D.D.S.**

CORRECT **Dr.** Vonetta McGee

CORRECT Vonetta McGee, **D.D.S.**

Academic titles such as *M.A.*, *Ph.D.*, *B.S.*, *Ed.D.*, and *M.D.* can be used on their own in abbreviated form.

ACCEPTABLE The university offers an **Ed.D.** specifically designed for school-teachers who want to become administrators.

2 Abbreviate references to people and organizations

Your readers may be more familiar with some abbreviations (3M, IBM, NAFTA) than with the names for which they stand (Minnesota Mining and Manufacturing, International Business Machines, North American Free Trade Agreement). Such abbreviations are almost always acceptable, as are those that simplify complicated names (AFL-CIO for American Federation of Labor and Congress of Industrial Organizations).

In some abbreviations the letters are pronounced singly (YMCA, USDA). In others, called **acronyms,** the letters form a pronounceable word (AIDS, SALT). Abbreviations and acronyms in which each letter stands for a word are usually written in capitals without periods.

ORGANIZATIONS NAACP, AMA, NBA, FDA, NCAA, UNESCO, IBEW

CORPORATIONS USX, PBS, GM, CNN, AT&T, PBS, BBC

COUNTRIES USA (*or* U.S.A.), UK (*or* U.K.)

PEOPLE JFK, LBJ, FDR, MLK

THINGS OR EVENTS FM, AM, TB, MRI, AWOL, DWI, TGIF

If your reader won't recognize an unfamiliar abbreviation, you can still use it in your document as long as you give the full word or phrase once and show the abbreviation in parentheses. From then on, you can use the abbreviation without confusion.

EXPLAINED The **American Library Association (ALA)** has taken stands on access to information. The **ALA** opposes book censorship and favors privacy for records of borrowing.

This technique is especially useful in academic or technical writing because it enables you to shorten complicated and often-repeated terms.

3 Abbreviate dates and numbers correctly

Abbreviations of dates and numbers may be used only when they *specify* a number or amount; they are not a substitute for the general term.

ABBREVIATION	MEANING
A.D. or AD	*anno Domini*, meaning "in the year of Our Lord"
B.C. or BC	*b*efore *C*hrist
B.C.E. or BCE	*b*efore *c*ommon *e*ra, used in place of *B.C.*
C.E. or CE	*C*ommon *E*ra, used in place of *A.D.*
a.m.	*a*nte *m*eridiem, meaning "morning"; some writers use *A.M.* or small capitals
p.m.	*p*ost *m*eridiem, meaning "after noon"; some writers use *P.M.* or small capitals
no.	number
$	dollars

INCORRECT Because of the lack of capable leadership, the bill providing **$** for inspection of meat-processing plants was not passed until late in the **p.m.,** just before the legislature adjourned.

EDITED Because of the lack of capable leadership, the bill providing **money** for inspection of meat-processing plants was not passed until late in the **evening,** just before the legislature adjourned.

You may use either *a.m.* and *p.m.* or *A.M.* and *P.M.* in hand- or typewritten papers. Book and magazine printers generally set these abbreviations in small capitals (A.M., P.M.). Your word processor may allow you to do this.

In a hurried, informal note, you can use abbreviations to avoid spelling out words as long as your reader understands your shortcuts. In formal writing, however, use only familiar, acceptable abbreviations.

INFORMAL If I'm not in the office during the **a.m.,** leave your **ID no.** and have the **$** delivered to **Dr. B.** at the Oak **Blvd.** office.

FORMAL If I'm not in the office during the **morning,** leave your **identification number** and have the **money** delivered to **Dr. Baruti** at the Oak **Boulevard** office.

58b Using abbreviations sparingly

You can shorten many words and turn most names into initials, but the resulting sentences are likely to be hard to read and irritating. Their only real use is in shorthand notes to yourself or as a quick drafting technique (see 7b).

UNREADABLE The descr. in the opening ch. is ~ to that in B. House except for the hum. tone and the emph. on a single char.'s pt. of view.

In most formal writing, your readers will expect words in full form except for certain familiar abbreviations (discussed in 58a). In special situations, such as research papers and scientific or technical writing, you can draw on a wider range of appropriate abbreviations to save space, particularly in documenting sources.

1 Avoid inappropriate abbreviations

The following lists should help alert you to inappropriate abbreviations.

DAYS, MONTHS, AND HOLIDAYS

AVOID	Thurs., Thur., Th.	Oct.	Xmas
USE	Thursday	October	Christmas

PLACES

AVOID	Wasatch Mts.	Lk. Erie	Phil.	Ont.	Ave.
USE	Wasatch Mountains	Lake Erie	Philadelphia	Ontario	Avenue

EXCEPTION 988 Dunkerhook Road, Paramus, **NJ** 07659
Use accepted postal abbreviations in all addresses with zip codes.

If an abbreviation is officially part of a company name, you may use it (for example, Sugarn *& Son Mfg.* for Sugarn *and Son Manufacturing*). Otherwise, spell out the entire name.

COMPANY NAMES

QUESTIONABLE The switches were installed by **LaForce Bros. Electrical Conts.**

EDITED The switches were installed by **LaForce Brothers Electrical Contractors.**

Some contexts require you to use abbreviations in a particular way. The Modern Language Association (MLA) reference style, for example, requires abbreviations of publishing companies; thus, Holt, Rinehart and Winston, Incorporated, becomes just Holt (see 28d). Otherwise, spell out the entire name.

PEOPLE'S NAMES

AVOID Wm. and Kath. Newholtz will attend.

EDITED William and Katherine Newholtz will attend.

DISCIPLINES AND PROFESSIONS

INCORRECT	econ.	bio.	poli. sci.	phys. ed.	OT
EDITED	economics	biology	political science	physical education	occupational therapy

Abbreviations may be acceptable in particular contexts; for example, reports in medicine or education routinely refer to PT (physical therapy) and OT (occupational therapy).

PARTS OF WRITTEN WORKS

IN DOCUMENTATION	ch.	p.	pp.	fig.
IN WRITTEN TEXT	chapter	page	pages	figure

Check style guide for academic field or profession (see Chapters 28–31).

Use symbols such as @, #, =, ~, and + only in tables or graphs, not in the text of a paper. In general, spell out units of measurement such as *quart* and *mile* when you use them in sentences. You may, however, abbreviate phrases such as *rpm* and *mph*, with or without periods. You may also use @ when including an email address in text.

Write to her at jmjones@adcorp.com

SYMBOLS AND UNITS OF MEASUREMENT

AVOID	pt.	qt.	in.	mi.	kg.
USE	pint	quart	inch	mile	kilogram

CORRECT Above 5600 **rpm,** viscosity breaks down.

CORRECT Above 5600 **r.p.m.,** viscosity breaks down.

2 Limit Latin abbreviations

Limit your use of Latin abbreviations such as *et al.* and *e.g.* to documenting sources and making parenthetical comments.

c.f.	compare (*confer*)	i.e.	that is (*id est*)
e.g.	for example (*exempli gratia*)	N.B.	note well (*nota bene*)
et al.	and others (*et alii*)	viz.	namely (*videlicet*)
etc.	and so forth (*et cetera*)		

INCORRECT	Many products, **e.g.,** laptops, have flat-screen displays.
APPROPRIATE IN PARENTHESES	Many products (**e.g.,** laptops) have flat-screen displays.
PREFERABLE	Many products, **such as** laptop computers, have flat-screen displays.

The abbreviation *et al.* is very often used incorrectly. Meaning "and others," *et al.* comes from the longer Latin phrase *et alii.* No period appears at the end of the word *et*, but a period *always* appears at the end of *al.* because it is an abbreviation. Making the phrase possessive can be awkward; avoid such constructions as "Johnson et al.'s new book." Instead, use "a new book by Johnson et al."

Exercise 1

A. Revise the following sentences, adding or correcting abbreviations when appropriate and spelling out or rewriting any inappropriate abbreviations. Assume that these sentences are all written in a fairly formal academic context.

EXAMPLE

New York, Los Angeles,
People think of ~~NY, LA,~~ and Montreal as international cities, but many small- to-medium-sized towns are just as cosmopolitan.

1. At a drugstore in a small Montana town, I talked with a clerk who told me about the Wine Appreciation Guild, Ltd. (155 Conn. St., San Francisco, CA 94107), which publishes books on food, wine, etc., e.g., *Wine Technology and Operations* by Yair Margalit, PhD.
2. According to a study by Ernest D. Abrams Consulting, smaller towns like Sioux City, IA, and Vero Bch., Fla., are even more likely to be the homes of inventors and innovators.
3. In one town in upstate NY, an engineer, Chas. D'Angelis, has created a device that measures rpms by counting the # of times a gear with a single tooth interrupts a laser beam.
4. While I was driving through the rural Midwest, I visited Rich. Forer, D.O., who examined my sore back, prescribed a new exercise rout. he had developed, and gave me an Rx for a mild painkiller.
5. In a city of twenty thou. people in eastern Tenn. I came across a health coop. that is pioneering a new phys. therapy program.

B. Meet in a small group and compare your editing of the sentences in Exercise 1A. Which ones seemed the hardest? Why?

CHAPTER 59 Spelling

Consider the fact that the sound represented by the word *see* can be spelled in at least a dozen different ways, as illustrated in the words *see*, *se*nile, *sea*, *sc*enic, *cei*ling, *ce*dar, jui*cy*, glo*ssy*, se*xy*, *cea*se, *sei*ze, and si*tu*. Or consider the six different pronunciations of the letters *ough* in the words *cough, tough, bough, through, though,* and *thoroughfare.* English spelling is often difficult, and unless you have been gifted with a marvelous visual memory for the way words are spelled, the best you can do is to develop some practical strategies.

59a Spelling as you write

Spelling errors are most likely to occur as you draft. You can deal with them immediately, during drafting, or later, as you edit and proofread. Worrying about spelling can draw your attention away from the most important parts of drafting and revising—exploring ideas and expressing them in effective ways. Stopping to check every word you *might* have misspelled is a sure way to disrupt your train of thought.

Giving special attention to spelling is therefore something often best reserved for proofreading. Nonetheless, you can take positive steps to deal with spelling errors as you write.

1 Recognize possible errors

To recognize possible spelling errors as you draft, consider the following sources of incorrect spelling.

Inattention. You know the correct spelling of a word, but you don't use it. You might make a keyboard mistake. You might focus so hard on what you want to say or how to say it that you overlook a misspelling. Usually, you can recognize errors of this sort quickly when you review what you have written.

Guessing. You don't know the correct spelling of a word, so you guess. You know, for example, that the words *irreconcilable, reasonable, honorable, justifiable,* and *probable* all end with *-able,* so you reason that the word you don't know, *irresistible,* must do the same—and you get it wrong.

"Sounding out." You don't know the correct spelling of a word, so you "sound it out." This strategy can often lead you astray because of the sound/spelling discrepancies in English. And if you mispronounce a word, your spelling will probably be wrong. Many a motel billboard has mistakenly offered "congradulations" to a graduating class. Sounding out a word can be helpful during the drafting process, when you need to get the word down on the page and can't, for the moment, look it up. Nonetheless, you can recognize right away that the spelling *might* be wrong.

2 Note possible misspellings as you draft

Instead of interrupting your thoughts to check every possible spelling error while you draft, try the following strategy.

Circle possible misspellings as you write. As you draft, regularly glance over a sentence or two in order to review what you have said. When you do this, circle any obvious spelling errors that have slipped into your work as well as any words you think *might* be spelled wrong. You may want to correct some errors right away, but don't allow correcting to distract you from the more important practice of drafting and developing your ideas. Come back to the circled words later, after you have completed drafting, and check them for misspellings.

59b Recognizing and correcting spelling errors

As you edit and proofread, use one or more of the following methods to recognize and correct misspellings.

1 Pause to think

Remind yourself to pay attention to spelling. If you suspect for whatever reason that a word might be misspelled, pause to check the spelling. Think about the sequence of letters, concentrating especially on sequences that are likely to be misspelled. Correct any words whose spelling you know; look up any unfamiliar spellings (see 59b-2). Develop some way to remember the correct spelling for future use. For example, if you often misspell the plural of *quiz*, try to remember that *quizzes* has two *z*'s—perhaps by associating quizzes with boredom (*zzzzzzz*).

2 Look it up

A dictionary will give you the correct spelling of a word, and it may even offer spelling advice. *Merriam-Webster's Collegiate Dictionary* (11th ed.), the *New World Dictionary of the American Language*, the *American Heritage Dictionary of the English Language*, or any other standard dictionary is a good place to start. If you have a general idea of how a word is spelled, especially in•fer \in-ˈfər\ *vb* **in•ferred; in•fer•ring** [MF or L; MF *inferer,* fr. L *inferre,* lit., to carry or bring into, fr. *in-* + *ferre* to carry — more at BEAR] *vt* (1528) **1** : to derive as a conclusion from facts or premises ⟨we see smoke and ~ fire —L. A. White⟩ — compare IMPLY **2** : GUESS, SURMISE ⟨your letter . . . allows me to ~ that you are as well as ever —O. W. Holmes †1935⟩ **3 a** : to involve as a normal outcome of thought **b** : to point out: INDICATE ⟨this doth ~ the zeal I had to see him —Shak.⟩ ⟨another survey . . . ~*s* that two-thirds of all present computer installations are not paying for themselves —H. R. Chellman⟩ **4** : SUGGEST, HINT ⟨are you *inferring* I'm incompetent?⟩ ~ *vi:* to draw inferences ⟨men . . . have observed, *inferred,* and reasoned . . . to all kinds of results —John Dewey⟩ — **in•fer•able** *also* **in•fer•ri•ble** \in-ˈfər-ə-bəl\ *adj*— **in•fer•rer** \-ˈfər-ər\ *n*

syn INFER, DEDUCE, CONCLUDE, JUDGE, GATHER mean to arrive at a mental conclusion. INFER implies arriving at a conclusion by reasoning from evidence; if the evidence is slight, the term comes close to *surmise* ⟨from that remark, I *inferred* that they knew each other⟩. DEDUCE often adds to INFER the special implication of drawing a particular inference from a generalization ⟨denied we could *deduce* anything important from human mortality⟩. CONCLUDE implies arriving at a necessary inference at the end of a chain of reasoning ⟨*concluded* that only the accused could be guilty⟩. JUDGE stresses a weighing of the evidence on which a conclusion is based ⟨*judge* people by their actions⟩. GATHER suggests an intuitive forming of a conclusion from implications ⟨*gathered* their desire to be alone without a word⟩.

usage Sir Thomas More is the first writer known to have used both *infer* and *imply* in their approved senses (1528). He is also the first to have used *infer* in a sense close in meaning to *imply* (1533). Both of these uses of *infer* coexisted without comment until some time around the end of World War I. Since then, senses 3 and 4 of *infer* have been frequently condemned as an undesirable blurring of a useful distinction. The actual blurring has been done by the commentators. Sense 3, descended from More's use of 1533, does not occur with a personal subject. When objections arose, they were to a use with a personal subject (now sense 4). Since dictionaries did not recognize this use specifically, the objectors assumed that sense 3 was the one they found illogical, even though it had been in respectable use for four centuries. The actual usage condemned was a spoken one never used in logical discourse. At present sense 4 is found in print chiefly in letters to the editor and other informal prose, not in serious intellectual writing. The controversy over sense 4 has apparently reduced the frequency of use of sense 3.

in•fer•ence \ˈin-f(ə-)rən(t)s, -fərn(t)s\ *n* (1594) **1** : the act or process of inferring: as **a** : the act of passing from one proposition, statement, or judgment considered as true to another whose truth is believed to follow from that of the former **b** : the act of passing from statistical sample data to generalizations (as of the value of population parameters) usu. with calculated degrees of certainty **2** : something that is inferred; *esp*: a proposition arrived at by inference **3** : the premises and conclusion of a process of inferring

in•fer•en•tial \ˌin-fə-ˈren(t)-shəl\ *adj* [ML *inferentialis*, fr. L *inferent-, inferens,* prp. of *inferre*] (1657) **1** : relating to, involving, or resembling inference **2** : deduced or deducible by inference

in•fer•en•tial•ly \-ˈren(t)-sh(ə-)lē\ *adv* (1691) : by way of inference : through inference

FIGURE 59.1 Detail from *Merriam-Webster's Collegiate Dictionary,* 11th ed. Springfield, MA: Merriam-Webster, 2003.

how it begins, you can usually locate it in a dictionary with a little looking around. If you know how a word sounds but are not sure about the spelling, you can use the lists of correspondences between sound and spelling that some dictionaries offer. If you still can't find your word, you may wish to use a specialized dictionary or handheld electronic speller designed for people who have considerable trouble with spelling. These dictionaries list words both under the correct spelling (*phantom,* for example) and under likely misspellings (*fantom*). Electronic spellers work like computer spell checkers.

As shown in the samples from *Merriam-Webster's Collegiate Dictionary* (11th ed.), a dictionary entry will tell you a word's correct spelling and also the spelling of its various forms (see Figure 59.1). The entry will indicate preferred spellings and alternative forms, and it will contain listings for related words. It will also provide information about the word's roots and history, and this information may help you remember the spelling.

Exercise 1

A. Assume that you've circled the following words in italics in one of your papers. You're done with your draft, and now you want to double-check your spellings. Look up each word, make any necessary corrections, and then write out one way to remember each correct spelling. Do this whether or not you already know how to spell the word.

EXAMPLE

school *principle* pal

The school principal is not always every kid's "pal."

coal *minor*	*precede* to the gate	*stationery* car
vacume the rug	she was *lieing*	*likelyhood*

B. In a group, share your devices for remembering the spellings in Exercise 1A. Write out those the group thinks are best, and share them with the rest of the class.

3 Be alert for common patterns of misspelling

Many words contain groups of letters that can trip up even the best spellers. Other words have plural or compound forms that may be confusing, and others add suffixes and prefixes that need special attention.

Plurals. For most words, you can form a plural simply by adding *-s* (*novel, novels*; *experiment, experiments*; *contract, contracts*). Watch out for words that end in *-o* preceded by a consonant; they often add *-es* for the plural.

ADD *-ES*	potato, potatoes	tomato, tomatoes
	hero, heroes	zero, zeroes
ADD *-S*	cello, cellos	memo, memos

When a vowel comes before the *-o*, add *-s*.

ADD *-S*	stereo, stereos	video, videos

For words ending in a consonant plus *-y*, change *y* to *i* and add *-es*.

etiology, etiologies gallery, galleries notary, notaries

Exception: Add *-s* for proper nouns *(Kennedy, Kennedys; Tanury, Tanurys)*.

For words ending in a vowel plus *y*, however, keep the *y* and add *-s*.

day, days   journey, journeys   pulley, pulleys

For words ending in *-f* or *-fe*, you often change *f* to *v* and add *-s* or *-es*.

hoof, hooves   knife, knives   life, lives   self, selves

Remember, however, that some words simply add *-s*.

belief, beliefs   roof, roofs   turf, turfs

Words ending with a hiss (*-ch*, *-s*, *-ss*, *-sh*, *-x*, or *-z*) generally add *-es*.

bench, benches	bus, buses	bush, bushes
buzz, buzzes	fox, foxes	kiss, kisses

A number of one-syllable words ending in *-s* or *-z* double the final consonant: *quiz, quizzes.*

Though most plurals follow these simple rules, some do not, and you need to be alert for their irregular forms. Words with foreign roots often follow the patterns of the original language, as is the case with the following words drawn from Latin and Greek.

alumna, alumnae (female)	criterion, criteria
alumnus, alumni (male)	datum, data
bacterium, bacteria	vertebra, vertebrae

Some familiar words form irregular plurals: *foot, feet; woman, women; mouse, mice; man, men.* (If you suspect that a word has an irregular plural, be sure to check a dictionary for its form.)

For compound words, use the plural form of the last word except in those few cases where the first word is clearly the most important.

basketball, basketballs	pegboard, pegboards
meadowland, meadowlands	snowflake, snowflakes

Exception: sister-in-law, sisters-in-law.

Word beginnings and endings. **Prefixes** do not change the spelling of the root word that follows.

precut   dissatisfied   misspell   unendurable

The prefixes *in-* and *im-* have the same meaning, but you should use *im-* before the letters *b*, *m*, and *p*.

USE *IN-*	incorrect	inadequate	incumbent
USE *IM-*	immobile	impatient	imbalance

Suffixes may change the spelling of the root word that comes before, and they may pose spelling problems in themselves.

Retain the silent *-e* at the end of a word when you add a suffix beginning with a consonant.

KEEP *-E* fate, fateful gentle, gentleness

Exceptions: words like *judgment, argument, truly,* and *ninth.*

Drop the silent *-e* when you add a suffix beginning with a vowel.

DROP *-E*	imagine, imaginary	generate, generation
	decrease, decreasing	define, definable

Exceptions: words like *noticeable* and *changeable.*

Four familiar words end in *-ery*: *stationery* (paper), *cemetery, monastery, millinery.* Most others end in *-ary*: *stationary* (fixed in place), *secretary, primary, military,* and *culinary.*

Most words with a final "seed" sound end in *-cede*: *precede, recede,* and *intercede,* for example. Only three are spelled *-ceed*: *proceed, succeed,* and *exceed.* One is spelled *-sede: supersede.*

The endings *-able* and *-ible* are easy to confuse because they sound alike. Add *-able* to words that can stand on their own and *-ible* to word roots that cannot stand on their own.

59b spell

USE *-ABLE* charitable, habitable, advisable, mendable

Drop the e for word roots ending in one *e* (*comparable, detestable*), but keep it for words ending in double *e* (*agreeable*).

USE *-IBLE* credible, irreducible, frangible

Words containing *ie* and *ei*. Here is an old rhyme that tells you when to use *ie* and *ei*.

> *I* before *e*
> Except after *c*,
> Or when sounding like *a*
> As in n*ei*ghbor and w*ei*gh.

Most words follow the rule.

USE *IE* believe, thief, grief, friend, chief, field, niece

USE *EI* receive, deceit, perceive, ceiling, conceited

Exceptions: weird, seize, foreign, ancient, height, either, neither, their, leisure, forfeit.

4 Watch for commonly misspelled words

Words that sound like each other but are spelled differently (*accept/except*, *assent/ascent*) are known as **homophones.** Writers often confuse them, creating errors in both spelling and meaning.

INCORRECT The city will not **except** any late bids for the project.

EDITED The city will not **accept** any late bids for the project.

The list of homophones and other often-confused words on pages 862–864 will help you recognize errors in spelling or meaning as you proofread.

5 Try alternatives to the dictionary

Sometimes when you want to use a particular word, you can't find the correct spelling in a dictionary, no matter how hard you look. Try these alternatives.

- List as many possible spellings as you can, even if they seem odd. Look them all up. Often you will be able to locate the word with a little more searching.
- Try a thesaurus (see 46e) if you know a suitable synonym; the word may be listed there in its correct spelling.
- Ask friends or classmates if they know the spelling, especially for technical terms; then look up the word in the dictionary to be sure you got good information.
- Check the indexes of books that deal with the topic the word relates to.
- Check your textbook, class notes, or handouts to see whether the word appears there.

COMMONLY MISSPELLED OR CONFUSED WORD PAIRS

WORD	MEANING	WORD	MEANING
accept	receive	allusion	indirect reference
except	other than	illusion	faulty belief or perception
affect	to influence; an emotional response	ascent	upward movement
		assent	agreement
effect	result	assure	state positively
all ready	prepared	ensure	make certain
already	by this time	insure	indemnify

WORD	MEANING	WORD	MEANING
bare	naked	gorilla	an ape
bear	carry; an animal	guerrilla	kind of soldier or warfare
board	get on; flat piece of wood	hear	perceive sound
bored	not interested	here	in this place
brake	stop	heard	past tense of *hear*
break	shatter, destroy; a gap; a pause	herd	group of animals
capital	seat of government; monetary resources	hole	opening
capitol	building that houses government	whole	complete
cite	quote an authority	its	possessive form of *it*
sight	ability to see; a view	it's	contraction for *it is*
site	a place	later	following in time
complement	to complete or supplement	latter	last in a series
compliment	to praise	lessen	make less
desert	abandon; sandy wasteland	lesson	something learned
dessert	sweet course at conclusion of meal	loose	not tight
discreet	tactful, reserved	lose	misplace
discrete	separate or distinct	meat	flesh
elicit	draw out, evoke	meet	encounter
illicit	illegal	no	negative
eminent	well known, respected	know	understand or be aware of
immanent	inherent	passed	past tense of *pass*
imminent	about to happen	past	after; events occurring at a prior time
fair	lovely; light-colored; just	patience	calm endurance
fare	fee for transportation	patients	people getting medical treatment
foreword	prefatory comment in book	peace	calm or absence of war
forward	advance, ahead	piece	part of something
forth	forward	plain	clear, unadorned
fourth	after *third*	plane	woodworking tool; airplane

(continued)

59b spell

COMMONLY MISSPELLED OR CONFUSED WORD PAIRS *(continued)*

WORD	MEANING	WORD	MEANING
persecute	harass	stationary	fixed in place or still
prosecute	take legal action against	stationery	paper for writing
personal	relating to oneself	straight	unbending
personnel	employees	strait	water passageway
precede	come before	than	compared with
proceed	go ahead, continue	then	at that time; next
principal	most important; head of a school; invested money	their	possessive form of *they*
		there	in that place
principle	basic truth, rule of behavior	they're	contracton for *they* are
rain	precipitation	to	toward
reign	to rule; period of ruling	too	in addition, also
		two	number after *one*
rein	strap for guiding an animal	waist	middle of body
		waste	leftover or discarded material
raise	lift up or build up		
raze	tear down		
right	correct	which	one of a group
rite	ritual	witch	person with magical powers
write	compose; put words into a text	who's	contraction for *who is*
road	street		
rode	past tense of *ride*	whose	possessive of *who*
scene	section of a play: setting of an action	your	possessive of *you*
		you're	contraction for *you are*
seen	visible		

6 Get help

All writers make some spelling errors that they simply can't fix because they don't know the word is misspelled. If at all possible, ask members of a revision group to identify any spelling errors you haven't caught. But first clean up all the errors you already know, even if you simply circle the words to identify them as misspelled. If someone else finds any more misspellings in your paper, you have the chance not just to fix them before sending the paper on to its reader but also to learn the correct spellings along the way.

59c Long-term strategies

Improving your spelling in general is like improving anything that develops slowly: you need to practice.

1 Use memory devices and pronunciation aids

The use of **mnemonics** (memory aids) can greatly improve your spelling by reminding you of odd spelling conventions that don't correspond with pronunciation. In *Beyond the "SP" Label*, Patricia McAlexander, Ann Dobie, and Noel Gregg offer a number of memory aids, including the following.

> *All right* is spelled like *all wrong*.
>
> *A lot* is like *a little*.
>
> *Emigrant, immigrant*: An *e*migrant leaves; an *i*mmigrant comes *i*n.
>
> *Separate*: *separate* rates two *a*'s; there's a rat in *separate*.

Use these as models to create memory aids of your own.

Some words get misspelled because they are often pronounced incorrectly. You need to develop an ear for pronunciations equivalent to spelling. Instead of hearing *new-cue-lar*, a common pronunciation of *nuclear*, hear the word in its carefully pronounced spelling form: *new-clee-ar*.

2 Read more and attend to spellings

Nothing boosts literacy (spelling included) so powerfully as reading. The more you read, the more likely you are to see words spelled correctly. When reading, keep a list of words you might use (and might otherwise misspell) someday. Focus consciously on words with difficult spellings.

3 Build your own speller

The most useful spelling aid should look like someone's personal telephone book: filled with names and numbers generally meaningless to other people. If you keep track of words you commonly misspell, perhaps in a little notebook or file, you'll find yourself looking up possible candidates for misspellings much more quickly.

Exercise 2

A. Without using a dictionary, circle the words that are misspelled in this list.

supercede	conceed	procede
idiosyncracy	concensus	accomodate
dexterous	impressario	irresistable
rhythym	opthalmologist	diptheria
anamoly	afficianado	caesarian
grafitti	judgement	liason

B. Working with a partner or in a small group, compare your answers to Exercise 2A, and *then* resolve any debates with a dictionary.

59d Spelling and the computer

You're no doubt aware of the virtues of the spell checker, a program that searches your document for misspellings and asks you whether they're correct. But spell checkers need to be used with care.

1 Understand how spell checkers work

Most spell checkers on personal computers work in conjunction with a dictionary that must be present in the computer's memory. When you ask the computer to screen your document for spelling errors, it compares each word in your text with the words in the dictionary. If the word matches a word in the dictionary, the computer moves on to the next word.

When the computer encounters a word that does *not* match any word in its dictionary, it asks you whether the word is misspelled. A typical program also allows you to add words to its dictionary. In this way, you can personalize the dictionary so that an unusual word or technical term won't be flagged every time the computer finds it in your paper.

2 Use a spell checker cautiously

Using a spell checker, especially on longer documents, is likely to reveal at least one or two errors. But whatever you do, don't rely *entirely* on a spell checker to fix your writing.

A spell checker can't reveal words that are properly spelled but used incorrectly. The computer may flag a word as misspelled and then, on command, offer you other correct spelling options. If you're not careful, you can mistakenly choose the wrong word to be inserted in place of the misspelled one.

Glossary of Usage and Terms

Three kinds of entries are found in this glossary: grammatical terms (such as *irregular verb*), rhetorical terms (such as *freewriting*), and words that writers frequently find confusing or difficult (such as *farther* and *further*). The latter entries, which deal with matters of usage, are indicated by an arrow (→).

→**a, an** When the word that follows the article *a* or *an* begins with a vowel, use *an*: *an apple, an outrageous film*. Use *a* before consonants: *a banana, a shocking film*. (*See 32a.*)

abridged dictionary Any type of abbreviated dictionary that does not aim to be exhaustive in its treatment of English vocabulary. (*See 46e.*)

absolute phrase A phrase consisting of a noun, a pronoun, or a word group acting as a noun followed by a present or past participle and any modifiers; it is used to modify a noun or an entire clause. (*See 32c-2, 40d.*)

> **Their lungs burning from the acrid smoke,** the firefighters pressed ahead into the burning building.

abstract A concise summary of a paper, sometimes used as an overview or preface at the beginning of the paper itself. (*See 18i.*)

academic community The interacting population of individuals involved in scholarly pursuits, from teachers to researchers to students, both within one institution and outside in the broader arena available through publication and the Internet. (*See 1a.*)

academic thesis Statement of conclusion and plan to support it in a paper or report directed to an academic audience. (*See 3d.*)

→**accept, except** Use *accept* to mean "to take or receive." Use *except* to mean "excluding."

> She **accepted** the invitation.
> Everyone finished the race **except** Larry.

acronym An abbreviation whose letters begin some or all of the words in the full version: *NASA* (National Aeronautics and Space Administration), *AIDS* (acquired immune deficiency syndrome). (*See 58a-2.*)

action statement In a writing assignment, the directions that specify the processes the writer should go through in completing the assignment.

action verb A verb that indicates an action or activity: *swim, analyze, dig, turn, negotiate*. (*See 32a-3; compare* **linking verb.**)

active voice The form of a verb in a sentence in which the doer (or agent) takes the position of the main subject, before the main verb. (*See 7c-3, 32a-3, 33e, 41c; compare* **passive voice.**)

ad hominem A **fallacy** in which an argument is based on personal attack rather than rational support and evidence. (*See 11i.*)

ad populum A **fallacy** in which an argument appeals to an audience's biases instead of using rational support. (*See 11i.*)

adaptation The principle of adjusting writing style, organization, and language to the expectations of readers in particular settings.

adjective A word that modifies a noun, pronoun, or word group acting as a noun by answering such questions as "How many?" "What kind?" and "Which one?" (*See 32a-4, 36a, 36b.*)

adjective clause (*See* **relative clause.**)

adjective phrase A phrase that modifies a noun. (*See 32c.*)

adverb A word that modifies a verb, an adjective, an adverb, or an entire sentence by answering such questions as "When?" "Where?" "Why?" "How often?" "Which direction?" "What conditions?" and "What degree?" (*See 32a-5, 36a, 36b.*)

adverb clause A clause that acts as an adverb. (*See 32c.*)

→**adverse, averse** Someone opposed to something is *averse* to it; if conditions stand in opposition to achieving a goal, they are *adverse.*

> Bill wasn't **averse** to going on the ski trip unless the warm temperature would be **adverse** to good skiing conditions.

→**advice, advise** *Advice* is a noun meaning "counsel" or "recommendations." *Advise* is a verb meaning "to give counsel or recommendations."

> Professor Raul wanted to **advise** his students, but they believed they needed no **advice.**

advocacy Web site A Web site explaining or defending an organization's actions and beliefs, and often arguing for specific policies. (*See 24c-4.*)

→**affect, effect** *Affect* is a verb meaning "to influence." *Effect* is a noun meaning "a result." More rarely, *effect* is a verb meaning "to cause something to happen."

> It is thought that CFCs **affect** the ozone layer. The **effect** on global warming is uncertain. Lawmakers need to **effect** changes in public attitudes toward our environment.

agenda A plan of action for a business meeting.

→**aggravate, irritate** *Aggravate* means "to worsen"; *irritate* means "to bother or pester."

> He was **irritated** that the hotel had no humidifiers because the dry air **aggravated** his skin condition.

agreement The correct matching, in **person, number,** and **gender,** of subjects and verbs or pronouns and their antecedents. (*See Chapter 35.*)

SUBJECT-VERB AGREEMENT	*The dog and the boy* **are running** in the field. *The dog* **is running** in the field.
PRONOUN-ANTECEDENT AGREEMENT	*A memo* should address the needs of **its** audience. *Memos* should address the needs of **their** audience.

→**ain't** Although widely used colloquially, *ain't* is inappropriate in formal writing. Use *am not, is not,* or *are not;* the contracted forms *aren't* and *isn't* are more acceptable than *ain't* but may still be too informal in some contexts.

all-purpose modifier A modifier that adds little or no meaning to a sentence and often can be cut: *very, totally, major, central.* (*See 45a-1.*)

all-purpose word A filler word that carries little or no meaning and often can be cut: *factor, aspect, field, thing, kind.* (*See 45a-1.*)

→**all ready, already** *All ready* means "prepared for"; *already* means "by that time."

Sam was **all ready** for the kickoff, but when he had climbed to his bleacher seat, the game had **already** started.

→**all right** This expression is always spelled as two words, not as *alright*.

→**all together, altogether** Use *all together* to mean "everyone"; use *altogether* to mean "completely."

We were **all together** on our decision to climb the cliff, but it was **altogether** too hard for us to leave Jennie behind.

→**allude, elude** Use *allude* to mean "hint at" or "refer to indirectly"; use *elude* to mean "escape."

Francis **alluded** to the time the refrigerator broke when he was on vacation; the rotten smell had **eluded** the house sitter, who never thought to open the refrigerator.

→**allusion, illusion** An *allusion* is a reference to something; an *illusion* is a vision or false belief.

Peter found an interesting **allusion** to UFOs in a government document. It turned out that the UFOs were just an **illusion.**

→**a lot** This expression is always spelled as two words, not as *alot*. Even when spelled correctly, *a lot* may be too informal for some academic writing. Use *many*, *much*, or some other modifier instead.

→**a.m., p.m.** These abbreviations may be capital or lowercase letters. (*See 58a-3.*)

ambiguous reference A sentence in which a reader cannot identify a pronoun with its antecedent. (*See 39a-1.*)

→**among, between** Use *between* to describe something involving two people, things, or ideas; use *among* to refer to three or more people, things, or ideas.

A fight broke out **between** the umpire and the catcher; then there was a discussion **among** the catcher, the umpire, and the team managers.

→**amount, number** Use *amount* to refer to a quantity of something that can't be divided into separate units. Use *number* when you want to refer to countable objects.

A large **number** of spices may be used in Thai dishes. This recipe calls for a small **amount** of coconut milk.

→**an, a** (*See* **a, an.**)

analogy A comparison between two things, often on the basis of shared characteristics. (*See 11i, see also* **false analogy.**)

analysis Writing that analyzes or "takes apart" a topic, often looking at how the parts relate to one another. (*See 17d–f.*)

analytical synthesis Bringing together summaries of several sources and pointing out their relationships in order to provide background information. (*See 26g.*)

analyze To divide or break something up into its constituent parts to examine their relationships. (*See 3a-2.*)

→**and etc.** (*See* **etc.**)

→**and/or** Although widely used, *and/or* is usually imprecise and may distract your reader. Choose one of the words, or revise your sentence.

IMPRECISE	The police **and/or** the fire department will usually arrive first when someone calls 911.
EDITED	The police **or** the fire department will usually arrive first when someone calls 911.

anecdote A brief story or account of a personal experience, often used in an introductory paragraph to spark a reader's interest. (*See 6f-1.*)

annotated bibliography A bibliography that includes annotations (short descriptions of each entry, sometimes with accompanying evaluative comments). (*See 16e.*)

annotations Notes written about (or sometimes directly on) a draft or a published text. Annotations can include **interpretations,** questions, **counterarguments,** restatements, or **evaluations.** (*See 9a.*)

→**ante-, anti-** Use *ante-* as a prefix to mean "before" or "predating"; use *anti-* to mean "against" or "opposed."

> Some people experience strong **antiracist** feelings when touring the slave quarters of **antebellum** Southern plantations that survived the Civil War.

antecedent The noun or pronoun to which another word (usually a **pronoun**) refers. (*See 32a-2, 35c, Chapter 39.*)

> antecedent pronoun
> **Jean** presented **her** proposal to the committee.

antithesis The use of parallelism to emphasize contrast within sentences. (*See 7d-4, 43a–b.*)

antonym A word opposite in meaning to another word: *hot* and *cold.* (*See 46e; see also* **thesaurus.**)

→**anyone, any one** *Anyone* as one word is an indefinite pronoun. Occasionally you may want to use *any* to modify *one,* in the sense of "any individual thing or person." (The same distinction applies to **everyone, every one;** *somebody, some body;* and *someone, some one.*)

> **Anyone** can learn to parachute without fear. But the instructors are told not to spend too much time with **any one** person.

→**anyplace** Avoid using this term in formal writing; instead, use *anywhere* or revise your sentence.

→**anyways, anywheres** Avoid these incorrect versions of *anyway* and *anywhere.*

APA documentation style The style of documentation suggested by the American Psychological Association and described in its manual. (*See Chapter 29.*)

application letter A brief letter inquiring about a job, usually accompanied by a **résumé.** (*See 20f.*)

appositive A noun or pronoun that renames or stands for a preceding noun (*See 48c-3.*)

appositive phrase A phrase consisting of an appositive (usually a noun) along with its modifiers, used to rename a noun in order to add information to a sentence. (*See 32c-3.*)

> Ken Choi and Stephanie Almagno, **my classmates,** won an award for their innovative packaging design.

→**apt, likely, liable** Use *apt* to mean "a tendency to." Use *likely* to mean "probable." Use *liable* only to imply risk, or, in a legal context, obligation or responsibility.

Claude was **apt** to ski the most treacherous slopes when he was young, but he will **likely** keep to the moderate slopes now because he is **liable** to hurt himself again if he skis the expert slopes. The ski resort was **liable** for Claude's injuries because it did not mark the location of the cliff.

archaic word A word that is no longer in general use or is in the process of dropping from the language, such as *save* in the sense of "except." (*See 46c-4.*)

archival Web site A Web site that serves as a repository for stored (archived) information, such as collections of documents, images, data, and the like. (*See 24c-7.*)

argue To prove a point or persuade a reader to accept or entertain a particular position. (*See 3d; see also* **argument; argumentative writing.**)

argument Not a disagreement, but the reasons, evidence, and explanations used in an attempt to resolve a disagreement by encouraging readers (listeners) to agree with the writer (speaker). (*See Chapters 8–12.*)

argumentative thesis Statement of opinion or proposition in the presentation of an argument. (*See 3d.*)

argumentative writing Writing that presents and defends a position or point of view. (*See Chapters 8–12.*)

article One of three words that precede a noun: *a*, *an*, or *the*. An **indefinite article** (*a* or *an*) precedes a general noun (one that does not refer to a specific thing). The **definite article** *the* precedes a specific noun. (*See 32a.*)

→**as, like** Used as a preposition, *as* indicates a precise comparison. *Like* indicates a resemblance or similarity.

Remembered **as** a man of habit, Kant would take his walk at exactly the same time each day. He was **like** many other philosophers: brooding, thoughtful, and at times intense.

→**as to** *As to* is considered informal in many academic contexts and should be avoided.

INFORMAL	The media had many speculations **as to** the skater's involvement in the attack against her rival.
EDITED	The media had many speculations **about** the skater's involvement in the attack against her rival.

→**assure, ensure, insure** Use *assure* to imply a promise; use *ensure* to imply a certain outcome. Use *insure* only when you imply something legal or financial.

The surgeon **assured** the world-renowned pianist that his fingers would heal in time for the performance. To **ensure** that, the pianist could not practice for three weeks. In case of an even worse accident, the pianist had **insured** his hands with Lloyd's of London.

→**at** In any writing, avoid using *at* in direct and indirect questions.

COLLOQUIAL	Jones wondered where his attorney was **at.**
EDITED	Jones wondered where his attorney **was.**

atlas A book containing maps and related information.

audience The implied or intended readers for a particular piece of writing. (*See Chapter 3, 21i.*)

audience inventory A checklist or set of questions adapted to a specific audience that helps to tailor your research and writing. (*See 21i.*)

audiovisual collection A library collection of videotapes, films, audio recordings, and similar resources.

auxiliary verb (*See* **helping verb.**)

→**awful, awfully** Use *awful* as an adjective modifying a noun; use *awfully* as an adverb in verbal structures.

> Sanders played **awfully** at the U.S. Open Golf Tournament. On the sixth hole, an **awful** shot landed his ball in the pond.

→**awhile, a while** *Awhile* (one word) functions as an adverb; it is not preceded by a preposition. *A while* functions as a noun (*while*) preceded by an article (*a*) and is often used in prepositional phrases.

> The shelter suggested that the homeless family stay **awhile.** It turned out that the children had not eaten for **a while.**

background information Information that helps readers understand the scope and substance of an issue, subject, or problem by providing knowledge of its history, context, or consequences.

→**bad, badly** Use *bad* as an adjective that modifies nouns or with a linking verb expressing feelings. Use *badly* as an adverb.

> The summit was scheduled at a **bad** time of year for some delegates. The British prime minister felt **bad** that some countries weren't represented. Several heads of state spoke **badly** of East–West relations.

balanced sentence A sentence built around pairs of parallel phrases and clauses, used to create emphasis. (*See 43b.*)

bandwagon argument A **fallacy** in argumentative writing in which the writer tries to convince the reader that everyone else feels a particular way about a topic and that the reader ought to as well. (*See 11i.*)

base form The present tense form of a verb. (*See* **tense;** *see 33a.*)

→**because, since** In general, avoid using *since* in place of *because*, which is more formal and precise. Use *since* to indicate time, not causality.

INFORMAL	**Since** the meeting was canceled, Sam gave his nonrefundable plane tickets to a friend.
EDITED	**Because** the meeting was canceled, Sam gave his nonrefundable plane tickets to a friend.
CORRECT	**Since** then, Sam has avoided buying nonrefundable tickets for meetings.

begging the question In argument, a **fallacy** in which assumptions are presented as facts, sometimes using words like *obviously* or *clearly*. (Also known as *overgeneralization* or *hasty generalization*.) (*See 11i.*)

→**being as, being that** Avoid using *being as* or *being that* in academic and other formal writing when you mean *because*.

→**beside, besides** Use *beside* as a preposition to mean "next to." Use *besides* as an adverb meaning "also" or an adjective meaning "except."

Betsy placed the documents **beside** Mr. Klein. **Besides** being the best lawyer at the firm, Klein was also the most cautious.

→**better, had better** Avoid using *better* or *had better* in place of *ought to* or *should* in formal writing.

COLLOQUIAL	Fast-food chains **better** realize that Americans are more health-conscious today.
EDITED	Fast-food chains **ought** to realize that Americans are more health-conscious today.

→**between, among** (*See* **among, between.**)

bibliographic sources Lists of resources you can consult in your research. **Bibliographies,** indexes, electronic databases, and catalogs all provide information about possible sources.

bibliographies Lists of library or other resources available in specific subject areas. (*See 22b.*)

bibliography A list of the sources used by the writer of a research paper, an article, or a book, prepared so that a reader can easily find the same materials. (*See, for instance, the formats in Chapters 28–31; see also* **annotated bibliography.**)

biographical sources Source materials that supply information about the lives and times of important people.

block format A format for short letters in which all the paragraphs are flush at the left margin. (*See 20c; compare* **modified block format.**)

block quotation A quotation of sufficient length to justify separating it from the body of a text in an indented block of prose. (*See 26h-1.*)

blog Short for "Web log," a kind of interactive journal that invites readers to respond to the blog owner or writer's ideas. (*See 14d-2, 24c-2.*)

body The main section of a paper or written document. It is preceded by an **introduction** and followed by a **conclusion.** (*See 4a-2.*)

Boolean logic An electronic search strategy whereby you use *and*, *or*, and *not* to link terms in a subject you are searching for; usage selected will expand or limit your search. (*See 24b.*)

boundary statement A sentence at the start of a paragraph that acts as a bridge from the paragraph before. (*See 6d-2.*)

brainstorming A technique for generating material for possible use in a written document. Brainstorming involves concentrating on a topic, thinking associatively, and finding connections among different ideas.

→**bring, take** *Bring* implies a movement from somewhere else to close at hand; *take* implies a movement in the opposite direction.

Please **bring** me a coffee refill, and **take** away these leftover muffins.

broad pronoun reference Using a pronoun to refer to an entire idea rather than a specific **antecedent.** (*See 39a.*)

→**broke** *Broke* is the past tense of *break;* avoid using it as the past participle.

INCORRECT	The computer was **broke.**
EDITED	The computer was **broken.**

browser A computer software program, such as *Netscape Navigator* or Microsoft *Internet Explorer*, allowing you access to Web sites. (*See Chapter 24.*)

→**burst, bursted** *Burst* implies an outward explosion. Do not use the form *bursted* for the past tense.

CORRECT The gang of boys **burst** the balloon.

→**bust, busted** Avoid the use of *bust* or *busted* to mean "broke."

COLLOQUIAL The senator's limousine **bust** down on the trip to Washington.

EDITED The senator's limousine **broke** down on the trip to Washington.

→**but however, but yet** These are **redundant pairs;** choose one word of each pair, not both.

INCORRECT The medfly was a nuisance, **but yet** the state of California was finally able to control it.

EDITED The medfly was a nuisance, **but** the state of California was finally able to control it.

→**calculate, figure, reckon** These three terms are sometimes used informally to mean "imagine" or "think." When in doubt, avoid them.

INFORMAL John **figured** he had never seen such a large pike.

EDITED John **thought** he had never seen such a large pike.

→**can, may** *Can* implies ability; *may* implies permission or uncertainty.

Bart **can** drive now, but his parents **may** not lend him their new car.

→**can't hardly, can't scarcely** Use these pairs positively, not negatively: *can hardly* and *can scarcely*, or simply *can't.*

→**capital, capitol** *Capital* refers to a government center or to money; *capitol* refers to a government building.

Madison is the **capital** of Wisconsin.

card catalog A file of printed cards listing a library's books and other holdings. An individual work usually has several cards that list it by author, title, and subject area(s). (*See* **online catalog.**)

case The grammatical role that a pronoun or noun plays in a sentence (as subject, object, direct object, and the like). *Subjective case* refers to the role played as the subject of a sentence. *Objective case* refers to the role played as the object of a sentence. *Possessive case* refers to the role played in a sentence to indicate possession or ownership. (*See 34a.*)

glos

cause-effect paragraph A paragraph explaining why something has occurred and exploring consequences. (*See 6e.*)

CBE/CSE documentation style The style of documentation suggested by the Council of Science Editors and described in its guide. (*See Chapter 31.*)

→**censor, censure** *Censor* means the act of shielding something from the public eye, such as a book or movie. *Censure* implies a punishment or critical labeling.

The school board **censored** *Catcher in the Rye*, but a group of parents **censured** the school by naming it on a list of "anti-intellectual" schools in the area.

→**center around** Something can't center *around* something else. *Use center on* or *focus on* instead, or reword as *revolve around.*

chain of reasoning In writing, the path a writer takes and asks others to follow. (*See 8c.*)

→**chairman, chairperson, chair** The use of *chairman* is now considered sexist. *Chairperson* is an awkward but acceptable substitute. *Chair* is now a common nonsexist alternative.

SEXIST	Gayle is now **chairman** of the provost's academic standards council.
EDITED	Gayle is now **chair** of the provost's academic standards council.

character Any person, usually fictional, in a work of literature. (*See 17b-2.*)

chat rooms Informal real-time communities hosted by private Internet services or available via the Internet Relay Chat (IRC) network. (*See 14d-3.*)

→**choose, chose** Incorrect use of these terms often has its source in a simple spelling error. Use *choose* for the present tense form of the verb; use *chose* for the past tense form.

chronological order A pattern for structuring writing in which elements of an event are presented in the order in which they happened. (*See also* **sequential order.**)

circular reasoning In argumentative writing, a fallacy in which an assertion is supported with the assertion itself. (Also known as *tautology.*) (*See 11g.*)

→**cite, site** *Cite* means to acknowledge someone else's work; *site* means a place or location.

> Phil decided to **cite** Chomsky's theory of syntax as evidence for his thesis.
> We chose the perfect **site** to pitch our tent.

claim (*See* **data-warrant-claim reasoning.**)

clarifying sentence (*See* **limiting sentence.**)

classification The organization of information into groups, categories, or parts.

classification paragraph A paragraph in which several subjects are sorted into groups based on their similarities or relationships. (*See 6e.*)

cliché An overused or trite word or expression: *right off the bat, out of the blue, needle in a haystack.* (*See 45b-1.*)

→**climactic, climatic** *Climactic* refers to the culmination of something; *climatic* refers to the weather conditions.

climactic sentence order A sentence structured to build to a climax, often through the use of elements in a series. (*See 7c-2.*)

> What every truly modern home has, she said, is a dishwasher, a gas grill, a Jacuzzi, and a divorce.

clustering A planning strategy in which groups of ideas are related graphically to a kernel topic. (*See 2c-1.*)

CMS documentation style The style of documentation described in *The Chicago Manual of Style.* (*See Chapter 30.*)

coherence Writing in which each sentence or paragraph follows clearly from the one before and leads clearly to the next in a recognizable, easy-to-understand arrangement. (*See 6c, 6d.*)

collaborative revision The process of working with one or more people in order to revise writing drafts. (*See 5c.*)

collective noun A kind of noun that refers to a unit composed of more than one individual or thing: *group, board of directors, family.* Such nouns generally take a singular form even though they refer to more than one thing. (*See 32a, 35b-2, 35c-3; see also* **noun; count noun; mass noun.**)

comma splice Two or more sentences (independent or main clauses) incorrectly joined with a comma. (*See Chapter 38, 48a; compare* **fused sentence.**)

COMMA SPLICE	The human eye is not like that of the cat, it has many more color-sensitive cells.
EDITED	The human eye is not like that of the cat; it has many more color-sensitive cells.

common adjective Any adjective that is not a **proper adjective.** (*See 54b-2.*)

common knowledge Information that most readers of a document, such as a research paper or report, will know, making it unnecessary to cite a source for it. (*See 26i.*)

common noun Any noun that is not a **proper noun.** (*See 32a-1, 54b-2.*)

comparative form One of three forms taken by an adjective or adverb to indicate that the noun or verb modified is being compared to something else. The comparative form adds *-er* or *more* to the adjective or adverb. (*See 36c; compare* **positive form** and **superlative form.**)

ADJECTIVE	This oven is **cleaner** than mine. She is the **more imaginative** designer of the two.
ADVERB	Sometimes you can travel **faster** in Manhattan by foot than by car. Peggy designs **more imaginatively** than Horace.

→**compare to, compare with** Use *compare to* when you want to imply similarities between two things—the phrase is close in meaning to *liken to*. Use *compare with* when you want to imply both similarities and differences.

CORRECT	To help the child understand his virus, the doctor **compared** it **to** a tiny army in his body.
CORRECT	**Compared with** his last illness, this one was mild.

comparing and contrasting A technique for organizing an entire paper or for developing individual paragraphs or sentences. Opinions, characteristics, or objects are compared for similarities and differences, which often are presented in alternating form. (*See 43b-3e on* **parallelism;** *see also* **point-by-point organization** and **subject-by-subject organization.**)

complement A word (noun, pronoun, or adjective) or phrase tied by a linking verb to a subject. (*See 32b-2, 34b-3, 36b-2.*) *A subject complement* "completes" the linking verb by describing the subject or renaming it. An *object complement* renames or describes the *direct object*.

→**complement, compliment** *Complement* means "an accompaniment"; *compliment* means "words of praise."

The diplomats **complimented** the ambassador on her choice of opera.
The theater's grand ceiling **complemented** the theme of the opera perfectly.

complete predicate (*See* **predicate.**)

complete sentence A sentence that contains both a subject and a complete predicate and is therefore grammatical. (*See Chapter 37; compare* **sentence fragment.**)

glos

complete subject (*See* **subject.**)

complex sentence A sentence with one **main clause** and one or more **subordinate clauses**. (*See 32d, 44b-1; compare* **compound sentence; compound-complex sentence; simple sentence.**)

compound antecedent A group of words to which a pronoun or noun refers. (*See 39a; see also* **antecedent.**)

compound-complex sentence A sentence with two or more **main clauses** and one or more **subordinate clauses.** (*See 32d; compare* **compound sentence; complex sentence; simple sentence.**)

compound predicate A predicate that contains two or more complete verbs, usually connected with *and.*

The car **struck and injured** the bystander.

compound sentence A sentence with two or more **main clauses** and no **subordinate clauses.** (*See 32d; compare* **complex sentence; compound-complex sentence; simple sentence.**)

compound subject Two or more subjects joined with *and* or *both . . . and.* (*See 34b, 35b.*)

Jim and the rest of the Boy Scouts were responsible for the rescue.

conclusion The ending section of a paper, preceded by the **introduction** and **body** (*see 4a-2*), also the necessary consequence of a line of reasoning, especially in **deductive argument.** (*See 11e.*)

conditional statement A sentence that expresses something improbable or hypothetical, often beginning with *if.* Conditional statements use the *subjunctive* form of the verb. (*See 33g.*)

conjunction A word that joins two elements in a sentence. (*See 32a-7, 35b, 43b-3, 48a.*) *Coordinating conjunctions* (*and, but, or, nor, for, yet,* and *so*) link grammatically equal elements such as parts of compound subjects, verbs, objects, and modifiers.

We analyzed **and** discussed the theory in class.
Fresh orange juice **or** grapefruit juice contains citric acid.

Subordinating conjunctions (*because, although, while, if,* or *since*) create a **subordinate** (or *modifying*) **clause.**

Because they were tired, they did not notice that the pot was boiling over.

conjunctive adverb An adverb such as *however, moreover, thus,* or *therefore* that joins sentences or elements within sentences and indicates a logical relationship between them. (*See 32a-5, 48b-3, 49a-2.*)

connotation The associative or affective "shades of meaning" conveyed by a word, as opposed to its literal meaning. If someone is said to have *retreated* from a gathering, the word connotes that the person was feeling attacked or bewildered. (*See 46c-2.*)

→**consensus of opinion** Avoid this redundancy by using *consensus.*

content The specific ideas or information presented in a piece of writing. (*See 8c.*)

→**continual, continuous** *Continual* implies that something is recurring; *continuous* implies that something is constant and unceasing.

The **continual** noise of landing jets didn't bother the homeowners as much as the foul odor that drifted **continuously** from the landfill near the airport.

contraction A form in which two words are brought together, usually by eliminating one or more letters and adding an apostrophe to mark the omission(s): *it's, they're, can't.* (*See 50b-1.*)

controlling idea (*See* **thesis statement.**)

conversational speaking (*See* **extemporaneous speaking.**)

coordinate adjectives A pair of adjectives, each modifying a noun on its own and therefore separated by a comma. In *noncoordinate adjectives,* which are not separated by commas, the first adjective modifies the second, which modifies the noun. (*See 48f.*)

COORDINATE	These drawings present a **quick, simple** solution to the drainage problem.
NONCOORDINATE	We can use **flexible plastic** pipe to carry water away from the building.

coordinating conjunction (*See* **conjunction.**)

coordination A sentence structure that links and equally weights main clauses using *coordinating conjunctions.* (*See 48a; compare* **subordination.**)

correlative conjunctions Pairs of conjunctions (*not only . . . but also; either . . . or; neither . . . nor; both . . . and; whether . . . or*) that join sentence elements that are grammatically equal. (*See 32a-8, 43b-3* on **parallelism.**)

→**could of, would of** These incorrect pairs are common because they are often pronounced as if they are spelled this way. Use the correct verb forms *could have* and *would have.*

INCORRECT	I **could of** majored in psychology.
EDITED	I **could have** majored in psychology.

count noun A type of noun that refers to individual ("countable") items: *chair, bean, cup.* Most count nouns can be made plural by the addition of an *-s.* (*See 32a-1; see also* **noun; collective noun; mass noun.**)

counterargument A claim or opinion opposed to the one being supported in an argumentative paper. (*See 11b–c.*)

→**couple, couple of** These terms are used colloquially; in formal writing, use *a few* or *two* instead.

COLLOQUIAL	Watson took a **couple of** days to examine the data.
EDITED	Watson took **a few** days to examine the data.
EDITED	Watson took **two or three** days to examine the data.

criteria *Criteria* is the plural form of *criterion.* Make sure your verbs agree in number with this noun.

SINGULAR	One **criterion** for winning the bonus was selling ten cars in two weeks.
PLURAL	The **criteria** were too strict to follow.

critical notes Research notes that include comments, interpretations, or evaluations of a source.

critical reading Evaluating information and ideas presented by using your own knowledge and insight, identifying unanswered questions, and interpreting sources. (*See Chapter 9, 21h.*)

critical synthesis Brings together perspectives, opinions, interpretations, and evidence from a variety of sources and explores their potential connections. (*See 21h-2.*)

critique A paper that summarizes and presents a critical reaction to a specific work, such as a speech or book. (*See 16i.*)

cumulative sentence A sentence that begins with the main clause and then adds details and statements in the form of modifying phrases, clauses, and words. (*See 7c.*)

→**curriculum** *Curriculum* is the singular form of this noun. For the plural, use either *curricula* or *curriculums*, but be consistent.

dangling modifier A sentence that contains no **headword** or **phrase** to which a modifier can be correctly linked. (*See Chapter 40; compare* **disruptive modifier** and **misplaced modifier.**)

DANGLING	Staring from his study, **Paul's stomach** tied itself into knots.
EDITED	Staring from his study, **Paul** felt his stomach tying itself into knots.

→**data** Although now widely used for both the singular and plural, *data* technically is a plural noun; *datum* refers to a single piece of data. If in doubt, use the more formal distinction between the two, and make sure your verbs agree in number.

SINGULAR	This one **datum** is astonishing.
PLURAL	These **data** are not very revealing.

data-warrant-claim reasoning A reasoning or argumentative strategy in which data (indisputable facts) lead to a claim (or conclusion) through a mental process involving probable facts and assertions (warrants). Also called Toulmin reasoning. (*See 11g.*)

database A computerized (CD-ROM or online) collection of resources available to researchers. Databases contain a wide variety of materials such as articles, graphics, bibliographies, and statistics and usually focus on a particular area of study or a particular topic. (*See 22b, Chapter 23.*)

declarative sentence A type of sentence that makes a statement. (*See 32d; compare* **exclamatory sentence; imperative sentence; interrogative sentence.**)

The motor is making a rattling noise.

decorum Proper conduct and behavior; in writing, style and tone that fit the expectations of a particular social context. (*See 47a.*)

deductive argument An argument that begins with an explicitly stated premise and goes on to support that premise, using **syllogism** as the basic logical format. (*See 11e; compare* **inductive argument.**)

definite article (*See* **article.**)

definition paragraph A paragraph designed to adequately introduce a term or concept to your readers. (*See 6e.*)

demonstrative adjective (*See* **demonstrative pronoun.**)

demonstrative pronoun A pronoun (*this, that, these,* or *those*) that points out or highlights an antecedent. (*See 34a-2, 35c-3.*)

dependent clause (*See* **subordinate clause.**)

description A kind of writing and a means of developing paragraphs that uses specific details to evoke images of places, objects, characters, or feelings. (*See also* **objective description** and **subjective description.**)

desk dictionary A midsized dictionary suitable for most professional and academic contexts. (*See 46e.*)

detailing list A prewriting and revision strategy for creating more detailed prose. (*See 2a-3.*)

dialogue journal A kind of collaborative **working journal** in which partners swap journal entries and respond to each other's ideas.

diction The choice of words and phrases in a piece of writing. (*See Chapter 45.*)

→**different from, different than** The subtle difference between these two phrases is marked by what follows them: use *different from* when an object follows, and use *different than* when an entire clause follows.

> Jack's quiche recipe is **different from** Marlene's, but his cooking method is **different** now **than** when he was an apprentice.

direct object (*See* **object.**)

direct quotation A quotation that presents a speaker's or writer's ideas and feelings in the same words the speaker used, set off by quotation marks. (*See 41d.*)

directions One type of process explanation in which the writer gives a step-by-step guide for assembling or creating something or for following a procedure.

→**discreet, discrete** *Discreet* means "reserved or cautious"; *discrete* means "distinctive, different, or explicit."

> Emmons was as **discreet** as an anthropologist could be, but he violated some of the **discrete** codes of research when he lived among the tribe.

discriminatory language Language that implies or reinforces racist or discriminatory views toward other cultures or groups. (*See 47d.*)

discussion group A type of electronic bulletin board with a specialized membership in a specific academic, work, or public community. (*See 24c-10.*)

→**disinterested, uninterested** *Uninterested* implies boredom or lack of interest; *disinterested* implies impartiality or objectivity.

> It wasn't that Reagan was **uninterested** in environmental issues; he was simply a **disinterested** party when it came to special-interest groups.

disruptive modifier A sentence in which two closely connected elements such as a noun and a verb are inappropriately disrupted by a modifier. (*See 40c; compare* **dangling modifier** and **misplaced modifier.**)

DISRUPTIVE — The engineer, **even though he could have lost his life if he had become trapped in the burning plant,** was able to shut off the gas valve and prevent millions of dollars in damage.

EDITED	**Even though he could have lost his life if he had become trapped in the burning plant,** the engineer was able to shut off the gas valve and prevent millions of dollars in damage.

division paragraph A paragraph in which a subject is split into its constituent parts so that the relationship between these parts can be highlighted or explained. (*See 6e-2.*)

documentation The process of citing the source or reference for an idea, sentence, passage, or text in a research paper. (*See Chapters 28–31.*)

domain name The name a company, organization, or other entity uses to identify itself on the Internet (such as naacp.org). (*See 14c-2.*)

→**done** Avoid using *done* as a simple past tense; it is a *past participle.* (*See 33d.*)

INCORRECT	The skater **done** the best she could at the Olympics.
EDITED	The skater **did** the best she could at the Olympics.

→**don't, doesn't** These and other contractions may strike some academic readers as too informal. Check with your reader, or err on the side of formality (*do not, does not*) when in doubt.

double negative Avoid the incorrect use of two negative forms. (*See 36d.*)

INCORRECT	The state **hasn't** done **nothing** about it.
EDITED	The state **has** done **nothing** about it.
EDITED	The state **hasn't** done **anything** about it.

drafting The process of creating a preliminary but readable version of an essay or other text. (*See Chapter 4.*)

draft thesis statement (*See* **tentative thesis statement.**)

→**due to** When meaning "because," use *due to* only after some form of the verb *be.* Avoid *due to the fact that,* which is wordy.

INCORRECT	The mayor collapsed **due to** campaign fatigue.
EDITED	The mayor's collapse was **due to** campaign fatigue.
EDITED	The mayor collapsed **because** of campaign fatigue.

editing The process of fine tuning a rough draft for problems in grammar, wording, style, sentence rhythm or length, and other details. (*See Chapter 5; compare* **proofreading** and **revision.**)

→**effect, affect** (*See* **affect, effect.**)

→**e.g.** From a Latin term meaning "for example," this abbreviation is common in much writing but should be avoided when possible.

AWKWARD	Her positions on major issues, **e.g.,** gun control, abortion, and the death penalty, are very liberal.
EDITED	Her positions on major issues **such as** gun control, abortion, and the death penalty are very liberal.

either/or strategy In argumentative writing, a **fallacy** in which an issue is oversimplified, usually into two sides or positions. (*See 11i.*)

e-journals Scholarly journals published (or distributed) through electronic computer networks.

electronic community Writers and readers who participate in one of the many clusters of related sites that form and re-form on the Internet and World Wide Web. (*See Chapter 1.*)

electronic indexes Computerized (CD-ROM or online) indexes to articles in magazines, newspapers, or scholarly journals. Indexes enable researchers to identify possible sources. (*See Chapter 24b; see also* **printed indexes.**)

electronic mailing list The most common type of subscriber-based mailing list. (*See 20c.*)

electronic research Research conducted using electronic media or technology, such as CD-ROM databases, online resources, or electronic card catalogs. (*See Chapter 24; see also* **research.**)

ellipsis A series of three evenly spaced periods telling a reader that something has been left out of a quotation. (*See 53d.*)

> As Fielding describes it, Squire Allworthy's house had "an Air of Grandeur in it, that struck you with awe . . . and it was as commodious within, as venerable without."

elliptical construction The omission of an otherwise repeated element in a sentence; appropriate omissions are not misleading or confusing. (*See 42b-2.*)

LEFT IN	Some car owners invest lots of time caring for their cars; others **invest little time caring for their cars.**
OMITTED BUT CLEAR	Some car owners invest lots of time caring for their cars; **others invest little.**

email Mail exchanged through electronic computer networks. (*See 20e.*)

embedded quotation A quotation used within a sentence you have written, as contrasted to a **block quotation.**

→**emigrate from, immigrate to** Foreigners *emigrate from* one country and *immigrate to* another. *Migrate* implies moving around (as in *migrant workers*) or settling temporarily.

emoticons Faces drawn with keyboard characters. (*See 14c-3.*)

emotional strategy In argumentative writing, a focus on the values, attitudes, systems of beliefs, and emotions that guide people's lives and are central to most decision-making processes. (*See 11f.*)

empty phrase A phrase that adds little or no meaning to a sentence and can be cut or reduced: *at this point in time, due to the fact that, each and every.* (*See 45a-1.*)

e-newsletters Scholarly or professional newsletters containing current information and announcements, published (or distributed) through electronic computer networks.

→**ensure, assure, insure** (*See* **assure, ensure, insure.**)

→**enthused** Avoid *enthused* to mean *enthusiastic* in formal writing.

equivocation (*See* **misleading language/misleading evidence.**)

→**especially, specially** *Especially* implies "in particular"; *specially* means "for a specific purpose."

> It was **especially** important that Nakita follow the workouts **specially** designed by her coach.

essay exam A test written out in essay form, either during a timed, in-class session or at home between class sessions. (*See 16f.*)

→**etc.** Avoid this abbreviation in formal writing by supplying a complete list of items or by using a phrase like *and so forth*.

INFORMAL	The Washington march was a disaster: it was cold and rainy, the protesters had no food, **etc.**
EDITED	The Washington march was a disaster: the protesters were cold, wet, and hungry.

ethnographic research Research that interprets the practices, behaviors, language, and attitudes of particular groups that are tied together by their interests or ways of understanding and acting in the world. (*See 25f.*)

ethnography The written report of ethnographic research. (*See 25f.*)

etymological dictionary (*See* **etymology.**)

etymology The history of a word, including its source(s) and the changes it has undergone. (*See 46e.*)

evaluation The process of deciding the relative worth of a source, phenomenon, or opinion, including the credibility or authority of a researched source. (*See 21h, 24d.*)

evaluative summary (*See* **summary.**)

→**eventually, ultimately** Use *eventually* to imply that an outcome follows a series of events or a lapse of events. Use *ultimately* to imply that a final or culminating act ends a series of events.

> **Eventually,** the rescue team managed to pull the last of the survivors from the wreck, and **ultimately** there were no casualties.

→**everyday, every day** *Everyday* is an adjective that modifies a noun. *Every day* is an adjective followed by a noun.

> **Every day** in the Peace Corps, Monique faced the **everyday** task of boiling her drinking water.

→**everyone, every one** *Everyone* is a pronoun; *every one* is an adjective followed by a noun. (*See also* **anyone, any one.**)

> **Everyone** was tantalized by **every one** of the items on the dessert menu.

evidence Information that gives readers reasons for accepting the accuracy, value, or importance of conclusions. (*See 8b-2.*)

→**exam** In formal writing, some readers may be bothered by this abbreviation of the word *examination*.

→**except, accept** (*See* **accept, except.**)

exclamatory sentence A type of sentence that expresses something emphatically. (*See 7d-2, 32d-2; compare* **declarative sentence; imperative sentence; interrogative sentence.**)

> The car is on fire!

explanation A kind of writing that provides details on how a mechanism or procedure works.

expletive construction In indirect sentences, the use of opening expletives such as *there is, there are,* or *it is* to delay the actual subject until further into the sentence. (*See 7b, 45a-2.*)

This is the case in which the man bit the dog.

explication A line-by-line analysis of a text. (*See 34d.*)

→**explicit, implicit** *Explicit* means that something is outwardly or openly stated; *implicit* means that it is implied or suggested.

The conductors **explicitly** assured the passengers that they were traveling to a comfortable new life, but **implicit** in their voices was the Nazi menace that the Jews had come to recognize.

exploratory sources (*See* **preliminary sources.**)

extemporaneous speaking A style of oral presentation in which the speaker does not read a written text out loud but presents ideas from memory, using cues and notes.

extend In writing assignments, to take an idea or concept and apply it more extensively. (*See 3a-2.*)

fallacy Any flaw in reasoning, particularly in the context of persuasive or argumentative writing. (*See 11i.*)

false analogy A **fallacy** in which two things that are presented as comparable are actually not. (*See 11i.*)

→**farther, further** *Farther* implies a measurable distance; *further* implies something that cannot be measured.

The **farther** they trekked into the wilderness, the **further** their relationship deteriorated.

faulty cause-effect relationship A **fallacy** in which one event is assumed or implied to have caused another event. (*See 11i.*)

faulty parallelism (*See* **parallelism.**)

faulty predication A sentence in which the second part comments on or names a topic different from the one announced in the first part. (*See 42a-1; see* **shift.**)

FAULTY	The **presence** of ozone in smog is **the chemical** that causes eye irritation.
EDITED	The **ozone** in smog is the **chemical** that causes eye irritation.

→**female, male** Use these terms only when you want to call attention to gender specifically, as in a research report. Otherwise, use the simpler *man* and *woman* or *boy* and *girl*, unless such usage is sexist. (*See Chapter 47.*)

→**fewer, less** Use *fewer* for things that can be counted, and use *less* for quantities that cannot be divided.

Bush had **fewer** supporters for the bill than before, but there was much **less** media coverage this time.

field research (*See* **research.**)

field resources Original documents, interviews, surveys, questionnaires, and personal observations gathered during the process of **research.**

figure, calculate, reckon (*See* **calculate, figure, reckon.**)

→**finalize** Some readers object to adjectives and nouns that are turned into verbs ending in *-ize* (*finalize, prioritize, objectivize*). When in doubt, use *make final* or some other construction.

→**firstly** Use *first, second, third*, and so forth when enumerating points in writing.

INAPPROPRIATE **Firstly,** I will compare Sartre's and Camus's versions of existentialism.

EDITED **First,** I will compare Sartre's and Camus's versions of existentialism.

first person (*See* **person.**)

five-paragraph theme A kind of academic paper that has a simple, clearly defined structure including an **introduction,** a **body** of three paragraphs each starting with a **topic sentence,** and a **conclusion.**

focus-imagine-choose strategy A strategy for choosing the correct case of pronouns: focus on the pronoun, imagine each possible choice, and choose the correct form. (*See 34b-1.*)

focused freewriting Writing quickly, without stopping, about a particular idea or topic. (*See 2c; see also* **freewriting.**)

focused paragraph (*See* **paragraph.**)

format A general plan for the organization, such as length, level of formality, and the actual appearance of a document. (*See Chapter 13.*)

→**former, latter** *Former* means "the one before" and *latter* means "the one after." They can be used only when referring to two things.

fragment (*See* **sentence fragment.**)

freewriting A technique involving writing as quickly as possible without concern for style or grammar. Freewriting is often used to avoid writer's block, to "warm up" for more formal writing, or to generate ideas for a paper. (*See 2a; see also* **focused freewriting.**)

→**freshman, freshmen** Many readers consider these terms sexist and archaic. Unless you are citing an established term or group (such as the Freshman Colloquium at Midwest University), use *first-year student* instead.

full-text database A database that provides access to complete texts, such as articles or papers, instead of just abstracts or summaries. (*See 23b.*)

further, farther (*See* **farther, further.**)

fused sentence Two or more complete sentences incorrectly joined without any punctuation. (*See Chapter 38; compare* **comma splice.**)

FUSED Frank Lloyd Wright's Robie House is a good example of his architectural principles it embodies the idea of "space, not mass."

EDITED Frank Lloyd Wright's Robie House is a good example of his architectural principles; it embodies the idea of "space, not mass."

future perfect tense (*See* **perfect tense.**)

future progressive tense (*See* **progressive tense.**)

future tense (*See* **tense.**)

gazetteer A dictionary of geographical places and cities.

gender Labeling of nouns and pronouns according to whether they are masculine, feminine, or neuter. Pronouns must agree in gender with the nouns to which they refer. *(See 32a-2, 49a.)*

> **Harry** put on **his** shirt.

general academic writing Writing typically found in introductory courses across the college curriculum, including term papers, essay exams, short reports, abstracts, summaries, and argumentative analyses.

general-interest magazines Magazines that appear monthly or weekly, with each issue paginated separately. *(See 22d.)*

general pattern of development A type of paragraph development such as **narration, comparison,** or **cause-effect,** used to shape a paragraph's content and arrangement. *(See 6e-2.)*

general reference A reference to the main ideas in a source or to information presented throughout the work, not in a single place. *(See 28a; compare* **informational reference** and **specific reference.**)

general sources Books, indexes, databases, and nonspecialized periodicals used for background and to point the way to **specialized sources.** *(See 21j.)*

general thesis Perspective on a topic explained to a general audience. *(See 10c.)*

general-to-specific pattern *(See* **logical order.**)

generalizations Conclusions reached on the basis of facts (*see Chapter 8*) and summing up their meaning or qualities, or broad conclusions about what your research has to say about your topic. *(See 21g.)*

genre The form, or category of discourse, to which a work conforms (e.g., poem, play, novel, novella, film). *(See 34a-2.)*

gerund An *-ing* form of a verb that acts as a noun. *(See 32a-3, 32c-4, 34b-6; see also* **verbal phrase.**)

> **Running** can be enjoyable.

→**get** Avoid imprecise or frequent use of *get* in formal writing; use more specific verbs instead.

INFORMAL	Martin Luther King, Jr., had a premonition that he would **get** shot; his sermons and speeches before his death **got** nostalgic at times.
EDITED	Martin Luther King, Jr., had a premonition that he would **be** shot; his sermons and speeches before his death **waxed** nostalgic at times.

→**goes, says** In very informal contexts, some speakers use *go* and *goes* colloquially to mean *say* and *says*. This usage is considered inappropriate in all writing.

INAPPROPRIATE	Hjalmar **goes** to Gregers, "I thought it best to make a clean break."
EDITED	Hjalmar **says** to Gregers, "I thought it best to make a clean break."

→**gone, went** Do not use *went* (the past tense of *go*) in place of the past participle form *gone*.

INCORRECT	The players **should have went** to their captain.
EDITED	The players **should have gone** to their captain.

→**good and** This is a colloquial term when used to mean "very" (*good and* tired; *good and* hot). Avoid it in formal writing.

→**good, well** *Good* is an adjective meaning "favorable" (a *good* trip). *Well* is an adverb meaning "done favorably." Avoid colloquial uses of *good* for *well.*

COLLOQUIAL	The vikings played real **good** in the playoffs.
CORRECT	A **good** shot in the game of golf is not a hard-hit shot but a shot that is placed **well.**

→**got to** Avoid the colloquial use of *got* or *got to* in place of *must* or *have to.*

COLLOQUIAL	I **got to** improve my ratings in the opinion polls.
EDITED	I **must** improve my ratings in the opinion polls.

government documents Archives of congressional reports and papers issued by federal agencies as well as state and local governments. (*See 22d.*)

→**great** In formal writing, avoid using *great* as an adjective meaning "wonderful." Use *great* in the sense of "large" or "monumental."

INFORMAL	Our trip to Stone Mountain was **great.**
APPROPRIATE	As you approach Stone Mountain, **a great** carving appears on the rock face.

guessing Unsure of the correct spelling of a word and deciding it on the basis of reason or similar sounding words. (*See 59a-1.*)

guiding question In research, a specific question that helps to determine the kinds of sources to consult, the process of locating sources, and the possibilities for organizing the paper. (*See 21e.*)

→**hanged, hung** Although the distinction between these terms is disappearing, some readers may expect you to use *hanged* exclusively to mean execution by hanging and *hung* to refer to anything else.

The convict was **hanged** at dawn.
The farmer **hung** the dead pheasant upside down for a day before cooking it.

hasty generalization (*See* **begging the question.**)

→**have, got** (*See* **got to.**)

→**have, of** (*See* **could of, would of.**)

→**he, she, he or she, his/her** When you use gender-specific pronouns, be careful not to privilege the male versions. Look for ways to avoid awkward alternations of *he* and *she* or *his* and *her* by revising structures that require them. (*See 47a-3.*)

headword The word a modifier refers to. (*See introduction to Chapter 39.*)

helping verb The different forms of *be, do,* and *have* that link to main verbs and create complex verb forms. Helping verbs are sometimes called **auxiliary verbs** or **modal auxiliaries**. (*See 32a-3, 33b.*)

helping verb / main verb

The tourist agency is planning to make a video of the local attractions.

glos

homophones Words that sound like each other but are spelled differently (*accept/except*; *assent/ascent*; *principal/principle*; *stationary/stationery*). (*See 59b-4.*)

→**hopefully** Although the word is widely used to modify entire clauses (as in "Hopefully, her condition will improve"), some readers may object. When in doubt, use *hopefully* only to mean "feeling hopeful."

> Bystanders watched **hopefully** as the workers dug their way to the trapped spelunkers.

→**however, yet, but** (*See* **but however, but yet.**)

→**hung, hanged** (*See* **hanged, hung.**)

hypercorrection The phenomenon in which speakers using nonmainstream dialect unwittingly create a new error in trying to "repair" their speech. (*See 47b-4.*)

hyphenated noun A single noun that consists of two or more words linked by hyphens: *father-in-law*. (*See 56b.*)

hypothesis A tentative assertion to be explored in an argument. (*See 11e.*)

idiom A common expression that typically means something different from its literal interpretation (e.g., *kick the bucket*). (*See 46c-5.*)

→**if, whether** Use *if* before a specific outcome (either stated or implied); use *whether* when you are considering alternatives.

> **If** holographic technology can be perfected, we may soon be watching three-dimensional television. But **whether** any of us will be able to afford it is another question.

illogical comparison (*See* **incomplete sentence.**)

→**illusion, allusion** (*See* **allusion, illusion.**)

→**immigrate to, emigrate from** (*See* **emigrate from, immigrate to.**)

imperative mood (*See* **mood.**)

imperative sentence A type of sentence that makes a request or command. (*See 7d-2, 32d; compare* **declarative sentence; exclamatory sentence; interrogative sentence.**)

> Do your chores immediately.

→**implicit, explicit** (*See* **explicit, implicit.**)

inattention Knowing the correct spelling of a word but failing to use it. (*See 59a-1.*)

incomplete comparison (*See* **incomplete sentence.**)

incomplete sentence A sentence that fails to complete an expected logical or grammatical pattern. An *incomplete comparison* leaves out the element to which something is being compared. An *illogical comparison* is worded so that it seems to be comparing things that cannot be reasonably compared. (*See 42b.*)

INCOMPLETE COMPARISON	The sound quality of the new digital audiotapes is much better.
EDITED	The sound quality of the new digital audiotapes is much better **than that of the old analog tapes.**

indefinite article (*See* **article.**)

indefinite pronoun A pronoun that refers to people, things, or ideas in general rather than to specific antecedents. Indefinite pronouns include *all*, *another*, *any*, *anybody*, *anyone*, *anything*, *both*, *each*, *every*, and *everyone*. (*See 32a-2, 34a-2.*)

glos

independent clause (*See* **main clause.**)
indicative mood (*See* **mood.**)
indirect object (*See* **object.**)
indirect question A sentence whose main clause is a statement and whose embedded clause asks a question. Such sentences usually behave as statements, not as questions. (*See 52b-1.*)

> Phil wondered whether it would be too much work to take on an additional course.

indirect quotation A quotation in which a writer reports the substance of someone's words but not the exact words the person used. Quotation marks are not needed. (*See 41b-2, 41d.*)
inductive argument An argument that does not explicitly state a premise but leads the reader through an accumulating body of evidence to a conclusion. (*See 11e; compare* **deductive argument.**)
inferences Conclusions reached on the basis of facts. (*See 47b-2.*)
infinitive The "root," tenseless form of a verb. In English, infinitives are preceded by *to*: *to live, to perform, to abolish.* (*See 32c-4; see also* **split infinitive** and **verbal phrase.**)
infinitive phrase A phrase that uses the *to* form of a verbal. It can be used as an adjective, an adverb, or a noun. (*See 32c-4.*)
inform In a writing assignment, to tell the reader about some facts, views, or phenomena.
informants In field research, people interviewed or surveyed. (*See 25c.*)
informational notes Research notes that record facts, details, concepts, interpretations, and quotations from sources.
informational reference A reference that provides background information or material potentially useful for readers but too cumbersome to include in the text itself. (*Compare* **general reference** and **specific reference.**)
informational Web site A Web site that provides tables of data, historical information, reports of research, **FAQs,** and references. (*See 24c-5.*)
informative thesis A thesis used when writing to present and explain information. (*See 3d.*)
informative writing Writing whose content and strategies are shaped by the purpose of conveying, explaining, or analyzing information. (*See Chapter 16.*)
→**in regard to** Although it may sound sophisticated, *in regard to* is wordy and unnecessary. Use *about* instead.

WORDY	The cruise company was adamant **in regard to** its docking rights at Christiansted.
EDITED	The cruise company was adamant **about** its docking rights at Christiansted.

→**inside of, outside of** When you use *inside* or *outside* to mark locations, do not pair them with *of.*

INAPPROPRIATE	**Inside of** the hut was a large stock of rootwater.
EDITED	**Inside** the hut was a large stock of rootwater.

→**insure, assure, ensure** (*See* **assure, ensure, insure.**)

glos

intensifying phrase A phrase that is meant to make a sentence more forceful but carries little or no additional meaning; *for all intents and purposes, in my opinion, all things considered.* (*See 45a-1.*)
intensive drafting Creating a preliminary version of an essay in collaboration with a close friend or colleague. (*See 4c.*)
intensive pronoun A **reflexive pronoun** used to give emphasis to, or intensify, a sentence. (*See 32a-2, 34b-7.*)

He was able to move the heavy refrigerator **himself.**
She **herself** was responsible for the mismanagement of the firm.

intentional fragment (*See* **partial sentence.**)
interjection An emphatic word or phrase used to convey a strong reaction or emotion, such as surprise (*Hey!*) or disappointment (*Oh no!*). (*See 32a-8.*)
interlibrary loans Systems that allow for the exchange of books, articles, and other resources between libraries to serve users of a library that does not have an item in its own holdings.
Internet A network that links computers of all kinds through email, discussion groups, resource sites, and the World Wide Web. (*See Chapter 24.*)
interpolation The introduction of your own words, marked with brackets, into a verbatim quotation from someone else. (*See 53b-1.*)

Kent said, "Captain Sims **[the boat's owner]** has chosen a special place within two hours of Key West."

interpretation The process of reading into or adding your own understandings to a source, concept, or phenomenon. (*See 9b.*)
interpretive reading A kind of **critical reading** to determine the meaning, perspective, and purposes, both explicit and implicit, of a text. (*See Chapter 9.*)
interrogative pronoun The pronouns *who* and *which* when they are used to introduce questions. (*See 32a-2.*)
interrogative sentence A type of sentence that poses a question. (*See 32d-2; compare* **declarative sentence; exclamatory sentence; imperative sentence.**)
interrupters Parenthetical remarks such as *in fact* or *more importantly.* (*See 45a.*)
interviews Conversations, verbal or written, with a person in order to gather information or ideas. (*See 25d.*)
in-text citation In research writing, a citation that is placed within the text of the paper rather than at the end in a works cited page or bibliography. (*See 26f.*)
intransitive verb A verb that is not followed by an **object** or **complement.** (*See 32b-2; compare* **transitive verb.**)

verb no object
The president **dreamed.**

introduction The first part of a paper or other document, often leading up to or containing a **thesis.** (*See 4a-2.*)
invention A term from classical rhetoric referring to the process of generating and exploring ideas before writing a draft. (*See Chapter 2; see also* **brainstorming; planning; prewriting strategies.**)
inverted sentence order A sentence in which the normal subject-verb-object/complement word order is shifted by placing a subsidiary element at the beginning of the sentence in order to call attention to it. (*See 7d-3.*)

glos

NORMAL	**The director's voice thundered** from the darkness near the rear of the auditorium with criticisms of our acting.
INVERTED	**From the darkness near the rear of the auditorium thundered the director's voice** with criticisms of our acting.

IRB approval The process of obtaining approval to conduct research on human subjects by an "Institutional Review Board." (*See 25e.*)

→**irregardless** Avoid this erroneous form of the word *regardless*, commonly used because *regardless* and *irrespective* are often used synonymously.

→**irregular verb** A verb that does not follow the usual pattern for distinguishing forms for the present, past, and past participle. (*See 33a-3.*)

	PRESENT	PAST	PAST PARTICIPLE
REGULAR VERB	bake	baked	baked
IRREGULAR VERB	swim	swam	swum

→**irritate, aggravate** (*See* **aggravate, irritate.**)

issue A subject about which there are two (or more) clearly differing opinions. (*See 10a.*)

italic type Type that *slants to the right* and is the equivalent of underlining for emphasis or for some titles. (*See Chapter 55.*)

→**its, it's** Use *its* as a possessive pronoun and *it's* as a contraction of *it* and *is*. (Some readers may also object to *it's* for *it is* in formal writing.) (*See 50b.*)

The porcupine raised **its** quills threateningly. **It's** a shame that dogs must learn about porcupines the hard way.

→**-ize, -wise** Some readers object to the process of turning nouns or adjectives into verbs by adding *-ize* at the end (*finalize, itemize, computerize*). When in doubt, opt for different verbs. Also avoid adding the suffix *-wise* to words, as in "Weather*wise*, it will be a chilly night all over the region."

journalist's questions A set of questions (*who? what? when? where? why? how?*) used during the planning or prewriting process to generate or explore ideas or existing material.

keywording Using keywords to follow leads during the research process. (*See 21d-4.*)

keywords Most **database** resources and other electronic sources of information such as **online catalogs** and **electronic indexes** allow researchers to retrieve information and listings by typing in important (key) words identifying the subject or important ideas or details related to the subject.

→**kind, sort, type** These words are singular nouns; precede them with *this*, not *these*. In general, use more precise words.

→**kind of, sort of** Considered by most readers to be informal, these phrases should be avoided in academic and professional writing.

lab report A paper that summarizes the methods and results of a laboratory experiment. (*See 18h.*)

→**latter, former** (*See* **former, latter.**)

→**lay, lie** *Lay* is a transitive verb requiring a direct object (but not the self). *Lie,* when used to mean "place in a resting position," refers to the self but takes the form *lay* in the past tense. (*See 33d.*)

INCORRECT	I was going to **lay** down for a while.
EDITED	I was going to **lie** down for a while.

→**less, fewer** (*See* **fewer, less.**)
→**liable** (*See* **apt, likely, liable.**)
library research (*See* **research.**)
→**lie, lay** (*See* **lay, lie.**)
→**like, as** (*See* **as, like.**)
→**likely, apt, liable** (*See* **apt, likely, liable.**)
limiting modifier A **modifier** such as *only, almost, hardly, just, scarcely, merely, simply, exactly,* or *even* that limits or qualifies a word, usually the one that follows it. (*See 40a-2.*)
limiting sentence A sentence that limits, or narrows, the focus of a **topic sentence.** (*See 6b-2.*)
linking verb Verbs that express a state of being or an occurrence: *is, seems, becomes, grows.* Also known as **state-of-being verbs.** (*See 32a-3, 32b-2.*)
listing A technique for exploring ideas by making a detailing list, usually in preparation for writing a formal paper. (*See 2a-2.*)
listserv (*See* **electronic mailing list.**)
→**literally** Avoid using *literally* in a figurative statement (one that is not true to fact). Even when used correctly, *literally* is redundant because the statement will be taken as fact anyway.

INCORRECT	The visiting scholars **literally** died when they saw their accommodations.
REDUNDANT	The visiting scholars **literally gasped** when they saw their accommodations.
EDITED	The visiting scholars gasped when they saw their accommodations.

literature review A paper or part of a paper that provides a **synthesis** of existing literature or research on a specific topic. (*See 17d.*)
logical order A pattern for paragraph development in which details and generalizations are arranged according to a *question-answer pattern,* a *problem-solution pattern,* a *general-to-specific pattern,* or a *specific-to-general pattern,* suggesting an internal logic to the flow of sentences and ideas.
logical strategies The arrangement of ideas and evidence in ways that correspond with patterns of thought that most people accept as reasonable and convincing. (*See 11e.*)
looping A technique involving successively **freewriting,** reviewing the material produced from freewriting in order to find new ideas or concepts, and then freewriting on those ideas or concepts.
→**loose, lose** Commonly misspelled, these words are pronounced differently. *Loose* (rhyming with *moose*) is an adjective meaning "not tight." *Lose* (rhyming with *snooze*) is a present tense verb meaning "to misplace."

I was afraid that I would **lose** my ring because it was very **loose.**

→**lots, lots of, a lot of** (*See* **a lot.**)

glos

main clause A word group that contains a subject and a verb and can act as a complete sentence. Also called an *independent clause.* (*See 32c*; *compare* **phrase.**)

main conclusion The end point of a chain of reasoning. (*See 8b-1.*)

main verb The central verb (word showing action or state of being) in a sentence; it can stand alone or be accompanied by one or more **helping verbs.** (*See 32a-3.*)

major premise (*See* **premise.**)

major revision (*See* **revision.**)

→**man, mankind** For many readers, these terms represent sexist usage when they refer to all humans. Use *people, humans, humanity,* or some other substitute. (*See 47d.*)

mass noun A kind of noun that refers to material that cannot be "counted," or divided into separate units to form a usual plural. (*See 32a-1*; *see also* **noun; collective noun; count noun.**)

COUNT NOUNS	Chair + *s*, cake + *s*, shadow + *s*, pea + *s*
NONCOUNT NOUNS	Flour, rice, sugar, steel, sunlight, earth, water

→**may, can** (*See* **can, may**.)

→**maybe, may be** *Maybe* means *possibly; may be* is part of a verb structure.

The President **may be** addressing the nation tonight, so **maybe** we should turn on the news.

→**media, medium** Technically, *media* is a plural noun requiring a verb that agrees in number. Many people now use *media* as a singular noun when referring to the press.

The **media** *is* not covering the story accurately.

Medium generally refers to a conduit or method of transmission.

The telephone was not a good **medium** for reviewing all the budget figures.

meeting minutes A report of the items discussed during a business meeting. (*See 20b.*)

memo A short, usually internal, note between or among people working in a business. (*See 20d.*)

metasearch site A site that allows you to conduct a search using several search engines simultaneously. (*See 24b.*)

→**might of, may of** (*See* **could of, would of.**)

→**mighty** Avoid this adjective in formal writing.

INFORMAL	It was a **mighty** proud moment for NASA.
EDITED	It was a **very** proud moment for NASA.

minor premise (*See* **premise.**)

minor revision (*See* **revision.**)

minutes (*See* **meeting minutes.**)

misleading language/misleading evidence A **fallacy** in which a writer deceives a reader through the use of language or information. Using misleading language, the writer shifts the meaning of a term from one sense to another but still gives the erroneous impression of supporting the argument. Using misleading evidence, the writer uses faulty statistics, survey results, and other material slanted in favor of only one side of an argument. (*See 11i.*)

misplaced modifier A modifier incorrectly placed relative to its intended **headword,** giving the impression that it modifies something else. (*See Chapter 40; compare* **dangling modifier** and **disruptive modifier.**)

MISPLACED In *Walden*, Thoreau describes how he **simply** lived, conserving his resources.

EDITED In *Walden*, Thoreau describes how he lived **simply,** conserving his resources.

mixed sentence A sentence with mismatched topics or with a shifted grammatical structure. (*See 42a; see* **faulty predication.**)

MLA documentation style The style of **documentation** suggested by the Modern Language Association and described in its guide. (*See Chapter 28.*)

mnemonic An aid to memorization, for example, of correct spellings. (*See 59c-1.*)

modal auxiliary verbs (*See* **helping verbs.**)

moderator The person who decides which messages will be posted on an electronic mailing list. (*See 14d.*)

modified block format A format for longer letters in which the return address and the closing and signature are indented but paragraphs are not. (*See 20c; compare* **block format.**)

modifier A word or word group, functioning as an adjective or adverb, that qualifies or adds to a noun or verb. (*See Chapter 40.*)

mood The verb form that indicates the speaker's attitude in a sentence. *Indicative mood* characterizes statements intended as truthful or factual. *Imperative mood* characterizes statements that function as commands. *Subjunctive mood* characterizes statements expressing uncertainty. Many **conditional sentences** require the subjunctive mood. (*See 33g.*)

INDICATIVE MOOD It will rain today.

IMPERATIVE Beware of lightning!

SUBJUNCTIVE MOOD Were it to rain, we would not play golf.

→**Ms.** To avoid the sexist labeling of women as "married" or "unmarried" (a condition not marked in men's titles), use *Ms.* unless you have reason to use *Miss* or *Mrs.* (for example, when giving the name of a character such as *Mrs. Dalloway*). Use professional titles when appropriate (*Dr., Professor, Senator, Mayor*). (*See Chapter 47d.*)

multiple-word noun A noun consisting of two or more words that are treated as a single unit when marking plurality or possession. (*See 50a-3.*)

The **union leaders'** negotiations fell through.

→**must of, must have** (*See* **could of, would of.**)

glos

narrative A type of writing, or **genre,** in which the writer usually traces events in the past, present, or imagined future. Narratives tell stories about people, places, or events, often from the writer's own experience.

narrowing The process of taking a more specific perspective on a chosen topic. (*See 3c-4.*)

neologism A word that has entered into general use very recently, sometimes not yet having been put into any dictionaries. (*See 46b-4.*)

netiquette Commonsense guidelines that apply across nearly all Internet communities. (*See 14a-3.*)

nominalization A sentence in which a verb or adjective is (sometimes inappropriately) turned into a noun: *completion* (noun) from *complete* (verb), *happiness* (noun) from *happy* (adjective). (*See 7a-2, 45a-2.*)

noncoordinate adjectives (*See* **coordinate adjectives.**)

noncount noun (*See* **mass noun.**)

nonrestrictive clause (*See* **restrictive modifier.**)

nonrestrictive modifier (*See* **restrictive modifier.**)

→**nor, or** Use *nor* in negative constructions and *or* in positive ones.

NEGATIVE	Neither rain **nor** snow will slow the team.
POSITIVE	Either rain **or** snow may delay the game.

→**nothing like, nowhere near** These phrases are considered informal when used to compare two things (as in "Gibbon's position is **nowhere near** as justified as Carlyle's"). Avoid them in formal writing.

noun A word that names a person, place, or thing and is often preceded by an **article** (*a*, *an*, or *the*). (*See 32a-1; see also* **collective noun; count noun; mass noun.**)

noun clause A clause that functions as a noun. (*See 32d.*)

noun string A string of nouns used as modifiers (usually adjectives) of a main noun. Such strings are grammatically correct but may seem overly abstract or technical. (*See 7a-4.*)

The **area computer network downlink access program** failed.

→**nowheres** Use *nowhere* instead.

number A grammatical concept referring to whether a noun or pronoun is singular or plural. Pronouns must agree in number with the nouns they modify, and subjects and verbs must also agree in number. (*See 32a-2, 33b, 34a, 35a, 35b.*)

→**number, amount** (*See* **amount, number.**)

object A noun, pronoun, or group of words functioning as a noun to which the action of a verb applies. *Direct objects* receive the action of **transitive verbs;** *indirect objects* are affected indirectly by the action of a transitive verb. (*See 32b-2; see also* **complement.**)

object complement (*See* **complement.**)

object of a preposition The noun or pronoun that follows a preposition. (*See 32c-1.*)

object pronoun A pronoun that is the **object** of a verb. (*See 32c-1.*)

objective case (*See* **case.**)

objective description Description that emphasizes physical details and avoids attention to their emotional impact. (*Compare* **subjective description.**)

objective summary (*See* **summary.**)

observation A kind of ethnographic research involving firsthand research (*onsite visiting and note taking*) of people, events, or settings. (*See 25f.*)

→**of, have** (*See* **could of, would of.**)

→**off of** Use simply *off* instead.

→**OK** When you write formally, use *OK* only in dialogue. If you mean "good" or "acceptable," use one of these terms.

→**on account of** Avoid this expression in formal writing. Use *because* instead.

online catalog A computerized listing of books, magazines, and other holdings in a library. A researcher can retrieve individual listings by author, title, or subject area. Many online catalogs list resources in more than one library and can be accessed through computer networks as well as by terminals in a library. (*See 22c; see also* **card catalog.**)

online community A community of people defined or organized by a means of online communication such as a listserv or an Internet forum. (*See introduction to Chapter 14.*)

online database File of information available through the Internet or Web, or, occasionally, on CD-ROM. (*See Chapter 23.*)

online (electronic) periodicals Periodicals available through the Internet, with past issues or selected articles sometimes available in electronic archives. (*See 24c-8.*)

outline A list, usually hierarchical, showing the main contents of a paper. (*See 3c-3.*) A *working outline* shows the general sequence of information in a paper and the relationships among the segments of information. (*See 2d-3.*)

→**outside of, inside of** (*See* **inside of, outside of.**)

overblown language **Diction** that is too formal or technical for the writer's purpose and audience, often used out of a misguided attempt to impress the reader. (*See 45b-2.*)

overgeneralization (*See* **begging the question.**)

paragraph A unit of prose marked by an indent at the left margin and consisting of a topic and its **development.** A *focused paragraph* is one in which the topic, main idea, or perspective is evident and is maintained throughout the paragraph. A *unified paragraph* contains sentences that are clearly and directly related to the main idea. (*See Chapter 6.*)

paragraph development The examples, facts, concrete details, explanatory statements, or supporting arguments that make a paragraph informative and give it a sense of structure. (*See Chapter 6.*)

parallel drafting Preparing a preliminary version of a document by having each member of a group responsible for a specific section. (*See 4c.*)

parallelism The expression of similar or related ideas in similar grammatical form. *Faulty parallelism* occurs when elements in parallel are given incorrect or unequal grammatical form. (*See Chapter 43.*) In paragraphs, parallelism refers to a technique in which grammatical structures are repeated in order to highlight similar or related ideas. (*See 6d.*)

paraphrase A rewriting of an original sentence or passage in your own words, preserving the essence and level of detail of the original. (*See 21g, 51a-2.*)

partial sentence An effective sentence fragment used for emphasis. (*See 37c.*)

participle The form a verb takes when it is linked to a helping verb. Verbs can take two participial forms, the *present participle* and the *past participle.* (*See 32b-4, 33b.*)

particle (*See* **phrasal verb.**)

passive voice The form of a verb in a sentence in which the doer (or agent) takes the position of the direct object. (*See 7c-3, 33e, 41c, 45a-2; compare* **active voice.**)

subject verb
The ball was caught by the outfielder.

past participle (*See* **participle.**)
past perfect tense (*See* **perfect tense.**)
past progressive tense (*See* **progressive tense.**)
past tense (*See* **tense.**)
peer group A group of fellow writers, usually in a classroom, who participate in collaborative writing activities. (*See 3g-2.*)

→**per** Use *per* only to mean "by the," as in *per hour* or *per day*. Avoid using it to mean "according to," as in "per your instructions."

→**percent, percentage** Use *percent* only with numerical data. Use *percentage* to imply a statistical part of something.

INCORRECT	**A percentage** of my commute is through Tomkins State Park.
CORRECT	Ten **percent** of the sample returned the questionnaire.
CORRECT	A large **percentage** of the revenue from the parking meters was stolen.

perfect tense A tense used to indicate that something happens before something else happens. Three perfect tenses can be marked in verb phrases: present perfect, past perfect, and future perfect. (*See 33c.*)

PRESENT PERFECT	**I have reported** the fire already.
PAST PERFECT	The fires **had burned** for an hour before the brigade arrived.
FUTURE PERFECT	Nancy **will have finished** by the time the dentist is ready.

periodic sentence A sentence structured so that subsidiary phrases, clauses, or other elements are piled up at the beginning, delaying the sentence's main clause. (*See 7c-2.*)

Because she knows that inspired designs often spring from hard work, because she loves perfection yet fears failure, and because she believes that risk-taking ought to be accompanied by attention to detail, Janelle is working up to eighteen hours a day on the clothing for her fall collection.

periodical A recurring publication that contains articles by different authors. Periodicals include magazines, scholarly journals, and newspapers. (*See 22d.*)
person The form that a noun or a pronoun takes to identify the subject of a sentence. *First person* is someone speaking (*I, we*); *second person* is someone spoken to (*you*); *third person* is someone being spoken about (*he, she, it, they*). Verbs must agree in person with their subjects. (*See 32a-3, 35b, 41a.*)
persona The way a writer chooses to characterize himself or herself through the choice of words and phrases, voice, and other devices. (*See 14a-2.*)
personal home page A category of Web page in which an individual author creates a personal space online. (*See 14d.*)

personal pronoun A pronoun that designates persons or things. (*See 34a-2.*)

SINGULAR	I, me, you, he, him, she, her, it
PLURAL	we, us, you, they, them

phrasal verb A verb plus a closely associated word (**particle**) that looks like a preposition (*run down, burn up, call up, clear out*). Unlike prepositions, particles can be moved from a position after the verb to a position after a direct object. (*See 32a-3.*)

BEFORE OBJECT	Mr. Sims **burned up** all the wood.
AFTER OBJECT	Mr. Sims **burned** all the wood **up.**

phrase A word group lacking one or more elements (such as a subject or predicate) that would make it a complete sentence. (*See 32c; compare* **main clause.**)

plagiarism The unethical practice of claiming that another writer's words or text are your own, or citing another person's words or text without credit, thereby giving the illusion that that person's words are your own. (*See 14b, Chapter 26.*)

planning A set of writing strategies through which the writer generates material and makes decisions about the content, organization, and style of a piece of formal writing. (*See Chapter 2; see also* **brainstorming; prewriting; invention.**)

plot The chain of events in a work of fiction. (*See 34a-2.*)

→**plus** Avoid using *plus* as a conjunction joining two independent clauses.

INFORMAL	The school saved money through its "lights off" campaign, **plus** it generated income by recycling aluminum cans.
EDITED	The school saved money through its "lights off" campaign and also generated income by recycling aluminum cans.

Use *plus* only to mean "in addition to."

ACCEPTABLE	The wearisome reelection campaign, **plus** the pressures from the media, exhausted the senator.

→**p.m., a.m.** (*See* **a.m., p.m.**)

pocket dictionary An abbreviated or abridged dictionary useful for quick checks on spelling or definitions. (*See 46e.*)

point-by-point organization A strategy for arranging paragraphs that make use of **comparing and contrasting.** Comparable features of two different or opposed subjects are described one by one. (*See 6c-2; compare* **subject-by-subject organization.**)

point of view The perspective from which something (particularly a work of fiction) is told. (*See 34a-2; see also* **person** and **persona.**)

policy In argumentative writing, a position that a particular course of action is one that should be undertaken or avoided. (*See 10c.*)

poll In fieldwork, research gathered by questioning a representative sample of people to obtain information or opinion. (*See 25c.*)

position paper A short, often documented paper that defines an issue, considers an audience, and draws on evidence and logical strategies to make its point.

positive form One of three forms taken by an adjective or adverb to indicate whether the noun or verb modified is being compared to something else. The positive form is used when no comparison is indicated. (*See 36c*; *compare* **comparative form** and **superlative form.**)

ADJECTIVE	This is a **clean** oven. She is an **imaginative** designer.
ADVERB	You can travel **fast** in Manhattan by foot. Peggy designs **imaginatively.**

possessive case (*See* **case.**)

possessive noun A noun that expresses ownership. Possession is usually marked with an apostrophe to distinguish the form from a plural. (*See 50a.*)

The bird's call is becoming fainter.

possessive pronoun A pronoun that shows ownership. (*See 32a-2.*)

SINGULAR	my, mine, your, yours, her, hers, his, its
PLURAL	our, ours, your, yours, their, theirs

post hoc **fallacy** (*See* **faulty cause-effect relationship.**)

PowerPoint Commercial software that produces slides and other visuals that can be projected from a computer onto a screen in oral presentations.

→**precede, proceed** *Precede* means "come before"; *proceed* means "go ahead."

The Mickey Mouse float **preceded** the mayor's car. The parade **proceeded** down Fifth Avenue.

predicate In a sentence, the word or words indicating an action, a relationship, consequences, or conditions. A predicate typically takes the form of a **verb phrase** preceded by the subject of the sentence. A *simple predicate* consists only of a verb or verb phrase; a *complete predicate* consists of a verb or verb phrase plus any modifiers and other words that receive action or complete the verb. (*See 32b-2.*)

prefix An affix, such as *un-* in *unforgiving*, placed before a word. (*See 59b-3.*)

preliminary sources Reference works (such as encyclopedias) or electronic sites (such as mail lists or bulletin boards) that you can consult early in a research project for background information or for issues and questions of current interest. Preliminary (or *exploratory*) sources help you explore broad topics and identify areas for further, more intensive research. (*See 21d-4.*)

premise A claim or assertion that serves as the foundation of an argument. **Syllogistic reasoning** includes both *major* and *minor premises*—assertions or claims on which conclusions can be based. (*See 11e.*)

preposition A word that indicates a location, direction, or time (for example, *to, from, with, under, in, over*). (*See 32a-6*; *see also* **object of a preposition.**)

prepositional phrase A phrase, created from a preposition plus a noun phrase, that can add information to a sentence or make it more precise or detailed. (*See 32a-6.*)

A faint smell **of grilled onions** came **through the window.**

prereading strategies A set of reading strategies in which the reader previews, skims, and samples a reading before working through it more formally. (*See 9a-1.*)

present participle (*See* **participle.**)

present perfect tense (*See* **perfect tense.**)

present progressive tense (*See* **progressive tense.**)

present tense (*See* **tense.**)

→**pretty** Avoid using *pretty* (as in *pretty good, pretty hungry, pretty sad*) to mean "somewhat" or "rather." Use *pretty* in the sense of "attractive."

prewriting strategies A set of writing strategies used to explore ideas and information in order to generate material for a formal paper. (*See Chapter 2; see also* **brainstorming; invention; planning.**)

primary sources (*See* **research.**)

→**principal, principle** Principal is a noun meaning "an authority" or "head of a school" or an adjective meaning "leading" ("a *principal* objection to the testimony"). *Principle* is a noun meaning "belief or conviction."

printed indexes Books listing articles that appear in magazines, newspapers, or scholarly journals. Indexes help researchers locate useful sources. (*See 22d; see also* **electronic indexes.**)

problem-solution grid A planning strategy through which a variety of hypothetical solutions are generated to solve a specific problem. (*See 2d-2.*)

problem-solution sequence A piece of writing in which a problem is presented followed by a proposal for one or more solutions, perhaps with their advantages and disadvantages. (*See 2d-2.*)

→**proceed, precede** (*See* **precede, proceed.**)

process Any kind of operation, mental or physical, including the specific steps and materials or mechanism involved in the operation. (*See 6c-2.*)

progressive tense A tense used to show an ongoing action in progress at some point in time. Verb forms can show three types of progressive tense: *present progressive, past progressive,* and *future progressive.* (*See 33c.*)

PRESENT PROGRESSIVE	The carousel **is turning** too quickly.
PAST PROGRESSIVE	The horses **were bobbing** up and down.
FUTURE PROGRESSIVE	The children **will be laughing.**

glos

pronoun A word that takes the place of a noun, such as *them, his, she,* and *it.* Pronouns are often used to avoid repeating the nouns used in the sentence. (*See 32a-2, 35c.*)

Jim changed **his shirt** after spilling gravy on **it**.

pronoun-antecedent agreement (*See* **agreement.**)

pronoun reference The connection between a pronoun (*its, him, them,* etc.) and its antecedent, or the noun or person to which it refers. (*See Chapter 39.*)

proofreading The process of reading a draft in order to identify and correct distracting and usually minor errors in spelling, punctuation, incorrect hyphenation, and word division. (*See 5h; compare* **editing.**)

proper adjective An adjective derived from a proper noun, used to modify a noun: *Brazilian music, Dickensian portrait.* (*See 54b-1.*)

proper noun A noun that refers to specific people, places, titles, or things and is capitalized: *Miss America, New Orleans, Xerox Corporation.* (*See 32a-1, 54b-1.*)

proposition A **thesis statement** offering an opinion or conclusion that the writer wishes readers to accept or agree with. A proposition is supported or made convincing by an **argument.**

public community People linked by their interest in or participation in activities or organizations addressing the welfare or concerns of either the residents of a particular area or a clearly recognizable social group. A general, diverse population, rather than a specific one, such as a **work community.** (*See 1a.*)

purpose The writer's rhetorical goals or aim for a piece of writing. (*See Chapter 3, 10a, 46b-2.*)

purpose structure A series of statements briefly describing the function of each paragraph or section of a paper. (*See 3b.*)

quantifier A word like *each*, *one*, or *many* that indicates the quantity of a subject. (*See 35b.*)

question-answer pattern (*See* **logical order.**)

questionnaire A printed set of questions used in a **survey** or often mailed to a large number of people, to extract information, possibly in-depth. (*See 25c.*)

→**quote, quotation** Formally, *quote* is a verb and *quotation* is a noun. *Quote* is sometimes used as a short version of the noun *quotation*, but this may bother some readers. Use *quotation* instead.

→**raise, rise** Raise is a transitive verb meaning "to lift up." *Rise* is an intransitive verb (it takes no object) meaning "to get up or move up."

He **raised** his head from the newspaper and watched the fog **rise** from the lake.

→**rarely ever** Use *rarely* alone, not paired with *ever*.

REDUNDANT He **rarely ever** spoke about the gulag.

EDITED He **rarely** spoke about the gulag.

reader The intended or imagined **audience** for a piece of writing. (*See Chapter 3.*)

reading plan A prereading strategy in which the reader decides which goals, generalizations, and kinds of information to pay attention to in a reading. (*See 9a-1.*)

→**real, really** Use *real* as an adjective modifying a noun; use *really* as an adverb.

Emmons drove **really** well in the race because for once she was in a **real** stock car.

real time Electronic discussions that take place without delay. (*See 14d-3.*)

→**reason is because, reason is that** Avoid these phrases in formal writing; they are wordy and awkward.

reciprocal pronoun A pronoun (*one another, each other*) that enables a writer to refer to individual parts of a plural antecedent. (*See 32a-2.*)

The two kinds of birds compete for territory by destroying **each other's** nests.

→**reckon, calculate, figure** (see **calculate, figure, reckon.**)

red herring A **fallacy** in which some fact or information distracts a reader from the real argument. (*See 11i.*)

redrafting Part of the revision process that involves writing unworkable material over again. (*See* **revision.**)

redundancy The use of unnecessary or repeated words and phrases that can be reduced through **editing.** (*See Chapters 5, 45.*) *Redundant pairs* are two words used when only one is needed: *aid and abet, one and only, part and parcel, kith and kin. Redundant phrases* say the same thing twice: *each individual, fresh news, free gifts.* (*See 45a.*)

redundant pair (*See* **redundancy.**)

redundant phrase (*See* **redundancy.**)

reference chain A chain of pronouns whose antecedent is stated in the opening sentence of a passage. Reference chains can help to guide readers through a passage and remind them of the controlling topic. (*See 39a-4.*)

reference list List of sources found at the end of a document. (*See Chapter 29.*)

reflexive pronoun A pronoun that enables a subject or doer of an action also to be the receiver of the action. (*See 32a-2.*)

> **He** paid **himself** for the work.

→**regarding, in regard, with regard to** (*See* **in regard to.**)

→**regardless, irregardless** (*See* **irregardless.**)

register In communication, the form language takes in a particular context, showing variations in pronunciation, grammar, or word choice. (*See 47b.*)

relative clause An adjective-like clause that modifies a noun or pronoun and begins with a **relative pronoun.** (*See 32a-2, 16c, 34c-1.*)

> I reminisced about all the shellfish **that I had bought in Seattle.**

relative pronoun A pronoun (*who, whom, whose, which,* or *that*) introducing a subordinate clause that modifies or adds information to a main clause. (*See 32a-2, 32d, 34c-1, 44c.*)

remote reference Placing a **pronoun** at a distance from its **antecedent.** (*See 39a-2.*)

rereading The process of going back over a reading in order to review, summarize, or understand it. (*See 9a-2.*)

research The process of investigating a topic, either through *primary sources* such as interviews or observations or through *secondary sources* such as other writers' books and articles on the same topic. *Library research* is conducted primarily using the print and electronic materials in libraries; *field research* is conducted in settings where the subject of the research can be found in primary form. (*See Chapter 21.*)

research conversation An exchange among writers, readers, and speakers investigating certain aspects of a subject. (*See introduction to Chapter 21.*)

research file A detailed set of records for a research project. (*See 21a.*)

research-oriented Web site A broadly informational Web site that is focused on a specific research question or set of questions. (*See 24c-6.*)

research plan An anticipated sequence of activities that guides the work of a research paper. (*See 21f.*)

research question A specific question that drives a research project, giving it focus and purpose. (*See 21a-1.*)

→**respectfully, respectively** *Respectfully* means "with respect"; *respectively* implies a certain order for events or things.

> The senior class **respectfully** submitted the planning document. The administration considered items 3, 6, and 10, **respectively.**

restrictive clause (*See* **restrictive modifier.**)

restrictive modifier A midsentence clause that presents information essential to the meaning of a passage. In contrast, a *nonrestrictive modifier* adds information that is useful or interesting but not essential to the sentence's meaning. (*See 44c, 48c.*)

RESTRICTIVE MODIFIER	The charts **drawn by hand** were hard to read.
NONRESTRICTIVE MODIFIER	The charts, **drawn by hand,** were hard to read.

résumé A synthesis (in one or two pages) of one's education and employment history, usually prepared for the purpose of applying for a job. (*See 20f.*)

resumptive modifier A modifying clause or phrase used to extend a sentence that appears to have ended, adding new information or twists of thought. (*See 7d-4.*)

> People who are careful about what they eat may lead healthier lives, **healthier, though not necessarily longer.**

review A critical appraisal of an event, object, or phenomenon, such as an art show, a concert, or a book. Most reviews are both descriptive and evaluative. (*See 16j.*)

revision The process of improving rough or preliminary versions of a document by making large-scale changes, additions, or deletions in the material. *Major revision* involves redrafting, reorganizing, adding, or deleting significant material; *minor revision* involves changes within paragraphs, often at the sentence level. (*See Chapter 5; see also* **editing** and **proofreading.**)

rhetorical purpose (*See* **purpose.**)

rhetorical question A question asked not in expectation of an answer but for the purpose of providing the answer. (*See 7d-2.*)

rhyming dictionary A dictionary that gives rhymes for words. (*See 46e.*)

→**rise, raise** (*See* **raise, rise.**)

Rogerian argument A strategy for argument that calls for acknowledging the reasonableness of the opposing point(s) of view rather than strong opposition to alternative perspectives. (*See 11h.*)

rough draft A preliminary version of a paper which will later undergo **revision.** (*See Chapter 4.*)

rough thesis A statement of the major ideas to be covered in a paper, used to guide further planning and drafting. A rough thesis often appears in a draft but is usually revised by the final version. (*See 3c-2.*)

run-in list A list whose items aren't placed on separate lines. Such lists can present items in full or partial sentences. (*See 54a-5; compare* **vertical list.**)

run-on sentence (*See* **fused sentence.**)

→**says, goes** (*See* **goes, says.**)

scholarly journals Journals that appear approximately four times a year, with the page numbering running continuously throughout the separate issues making up an annual volume. (*See 22d.*)

screen name A self-identifier the email user chooses. (*See 14c-2.*)

search engines Software dedicated to indexing and sorting Web pages for user convenience. (*See 14d, 24b.*)

search strategy A strategy for research papers in which you identify the type of research you are conducting, the sources you might consult, and the tasks you need to perform. (*See 21j.*)

second person (*See* **person.**)

secondary sources (*See* **research.**)

semidrafting While creating a **rough draft,** the process of writing out full sentences interspersed with *etc.* or other words indicating that something needs to be added later. (*See 4b-3.*)

sentence A group of words containing a complete subject and predicate. (*See also* **compound sentence; compound-complex sentence; declarative sentence; exclamatory sentence; imperative sentence; interrogative sentence; simple sentence.**)

sentence adverb An adverb used to modify an entire sentence. (*See 32a-5.*)

sentence cluster A group of sentences that develop related ideas or information, often arranged using **parallelism.** (*See 43c-1.*)

sentence fragment A part of a sentence incorrectly treated as a complete sentence with a capital letter at the beginning and a period at the end. (*See Chapter 37.*)

FRAGMENT	They were able to get the pump started again. **By replacing the gas filter.**
EDITED	They were able to get the pump started again by replacing the gas filter.
EDITED	By replacing the gas filter, they were able to get the pump started again.

sequential order A way to organize information in a pattern within a particular perspective or focus, such as spatially or chronologically. (*See 6e-2.*)

→**set, sit** *Set* means "to place"; *sit* means "to place oneself."

The research assistant **set** the sample near the centrifuge and then **sat** down on the stool.

glos

setting The physical and temporal context of a work of fiction. (*See 17b-2.*)

sexist language Language that implies or reinforces unfair, misleading, or discriminatory stereotypes on the basis of gender. (*See Chapter 47.*)

shift An incorrect or inappropriate switch in **person, number, mood, tense,** or **topic.** (*See Chapter 41, 42a-4.*)

→**should of** (*See* **could of, would of.**)

show In a writing assignment, to demonstrate or provide evidence for something.

signal paragraph A type of transition paragraph used to alert readers to a major change in direction or the start of a new section of the discussion.

simple predicate (*See* **predicate.**)

simple sentence A sentence with one main (independent) clause and no subordinate (dependent) clauses. (*See 32d-1; compare* **complex sentence; compound sentence; compound-complex sentence.**)

simple subject (*See* **subject.**)

→**since, because** (*See* **because, since.**)

→**sit, set** (*See* **set, sit.**)

site, cite (*See* **cite, site.**)

slang New words not yet, possibly never to be, shared by the general population, but used by a limited social group. (*See 47b.*)

slanted statistics (*See* **misleading language/misleading evidence.**)

→**so** Some readers object to the use of *so* in place of *very*.

INFORMAL	The filmmaker is **so** thoughtful about giving his films distinct themes.
EDITED	The filmmaker is **very** thoughtful about giving his films distinct themes.

social context The social, cultural, generational, or economic circumstances of a writer; of an intended **audience;** or of a piece of writing. (*See 3f.*)

→**somebody, some body** (*See* **anybody, any body.**)

→**someone, some one** (*See* **anybody, any body.**)

→**sometime, some time, sometimes** *Sometime* refers to an indistinct time in the future; *sometimes* means "every once in a while." *Some time* is an adjective (*some*) modifying a noun (*time*).

The probe will reach the nebula **sometime** in the next decade. **Sometimes** such probes fail to send back any data. It takes **some time** before images will come back to us from Neptune.

→**sort, kind** (*See* **kind, sort, type.**)

"sounding out" Trying to determine the correct spelling of a word by its sound. (*See 59a-1.*)

spatial order In paragraph development, a pattern for arranging descriptive sentences based on the spatial or visual arrangement of a scene, work of art, person, mechanism, or phenomenon (left to right, top to bottom, and so on).

specialized dictionary A dictionary that lists terms from a particular field or about a specific topic.

specialized sources Focused, often complex or technical resources for research that provide detailed information on narrow topics and often include the latest scholarly findings. Sources of this kind include research reports, scholarly articles, specialized electronic databases, and interviews with experts (*See 22d.*)

→**specially, especially** (*See* **especially, specially.**)

specific pattern of development A preferred way of developing paragraphs reflecting reader and writer coming from a specific community; compare with **general pattern of development.** (*See 6e-2.*)

specific pronoun reference Using pronouns to clearly specify the relationships between statements. (*See 39b.*)

specific reference A reference that documents the exact location of a word, idea, or fact in a source (for example, on a specific page or in a chart or drawing). (*See 26g; compare* **general reference** and **informational reference.**)

specific-to-general pattern (*See* **logical order.**)

speculative writing Writing that explores and considers a topic without taking a position on it.

spelling dictionary A dictionary that gives the spellings of words but not their definitions or etymologies. (*See 46e.*)

split infinitive An **infinitive** in which a word separates *to* from the verb. Some readers object to split infinitives. (*See 40c-3.*)

SPLIT INFINITIVE The office designer tried **to** respectively **address** each of the workers' concerns.

EDITED The office designer tried **to address** each of the workers' concerns respectively.

sponsored Web site A Web site prepared and maintained by an organization (public, private, corporate, etc.). (*See 24c-3.*)

squinting modifier A modifier that incorrectly appears to modify both the word or phrase that comes before it and the one that comes after it. (*See 40a-3.*)

SQUINTING Those who smoke **seldom** seem concerned about the potential health hazards.

EDITED Those who **seldom** smoke seem concerned about the potential health hazards.

state-of-being verb (*See* **linking verb.**)

→**stationary, stationery** *Stationary* means "standing still"; *stationery* refers to writing paper.

structure The arrangement of ideas, sections, or paragraphs in a paper or other text. (*See 3g-1; see also* **outline** and **purpose structure.**)

structured observation Carefully planned and focused observation of events, people, or situations intended to produce research data from which conclusions can be drawn. (*See Chapter 25.*)

style The distinctive choice of words (**diction**), sentence structures, and **persona** in a piece of writing. (*See 3g-1.*)

subject In a sentence, the doer or the thing talked about—typically the first noun phrase followed by a verb phrase. A *simple subject* consists of one or more nouns (or pronouns) naming the doer or the topic. A *complete subject* consists of the simple subject plus all its modifying words or phrases. (*See 32b-1.*)

subject-by-subject organization A strategy for arranging paragraphs that make use of **comparing and contrasting.** The writer considers one subject in its entirety and then the other, instead of presenting one point for both and then the next point. (*See 6e; compare* **point-by-point organization.**)

subject complement (*See* **complement.**)

subject pronoun A pronoun that is the subject of a clause. (*See 32d.*)

subjective case (*See* **case.**)

subjective description Description that emphasizes the emotional impact of events or phenomena. (*See 6e; compare* **objective description.**)

subject-verb agreement The verb agrees with the subject in grammatical form. (*See 35a, 35b.*)

subjunctive mood (*See* **mood.**)

subordinate clause A word group that contains both a subject and a predicate but cannot stand on its own as a sentence because it begins with a subordinating word such as *because, since, although, which,* or *that*. Also called a *dependent clause*. (*See 32c-5, 32d, 44c.*)

subordinating conjunction (*See* **conjunction.**)

subordination A sentence structure in which one clause modifies another, helping readers perceive the links between ideas and understand the relative importance of information. The **main clause** is accompanied by a **subordinate clause** that modifies, qualifies, or comments on the ideas or the information in the main clause. (*See 44c; compare* **coordination.**)

→**such** Some academic readers will expect you to avoid using *such* without *that*.

INFORMAL	Anne Frank had **such** a difficult time living the life of a normal young girl.
EDITED	Anne Frank had **such** a difficult time growing up **that** her diary writing became her only solace.

suffix An affix added to the end of a word in order to form a derived word (*bold + ness*) or to provide a grammatical inflection (*talk + ing*). (*See 59b.*)

summarize (*See* **summary.**)

summary A précis in your own words of an original passage, preserving the essence of the original but boiling it down to its essential points. An *objective summary* focuses on the content of the original passage, without any authorial judgment or commentary. An *evaluative summary* contains the author's opinions and comments on the passage. (*See 21g, 26h, 51a-2.*)

summary paragraph A transitional or concluding paragraph used to mark the end of a discussion or to help readers remember main points.

summative modifier A modifying phrase or clause that summarizes the preceding part of a sentence and then takes the sentence on a new course. (*See 7d-4.*)

To protect your vegetables against harmful insects, you can use soap sprays, scatter insect-repelling plants among the beds, or introduce "friendly" insects like ladybugs and praying mantises—**three techniques** that will not leave a harmful chemical residue on the food you grow.

superlative form One of the three forms taken by adjectives and adverbs to indicate whether the noun or verb modified is being compared to something else. The superlative form adds *-est* or *-most* to the adjective or adverb and indicates a comparison of three or more objects or actions. (*See 35c; compare* **comparative form** and **positive form.**)

ADJECTIVE	This is the **cleanest** oven I've seen. She is the **most imaginative** designer of the three.
ADVERB	You can travel **fastest** in Manhattan if you ride a bicycle. Peggy designs **most imaginatively** of the three.

supporting conclusions The links in the chain of reasoning. (*See 8b-1.*)

supporting evidence Material that supports a central claim or **thesis,** including examples from personal experience, examples from other people's experience, quotations and ideas from recognized authorities, technical information and statistics, data from surveys and interviews, background and historical information, and comparisons to similar situations and problems. (*See 11a, 11b.*)

supporting idea Material that supports an assertion or **thesis.** (*See 3c; see also* **supporting evidence.**)

→**suppose to, supposed to** The correct form of this phrase is *supposed to;* the *-d* is sometimes mistakenly left off because it is not always heard in pronunciation.

→**sure, surely** In formal writing, use *sure* to mean "certain." *Surely* is an adverb; don't use *sure* in its place.

He is **sure** to pass the exam.
He has **surely** studied hard for the exam.

→**sure and, try and** *And* is sometimes used in place of *to* with *sure* and *try.* Write *sure to* and *try to* instead.

INCORRECT	We will be *sure and* bring our rackets.
CORRECT	Bob will *try to* win the match.

survey A research tool to obtain data for analysis, usually more complex than a **poll.** (*See 25c.*)

syllabification The correct division of words into their syllables. (*See 46e.*)

syllogism (*See* **syllogistic reasoning.**)

syllogistic reasoning A kind of logical reasoning that includes a *major premise*, a *minor premise*, and a conclusion. (*See 8b; see* **premise.**)

MAJOR PREMISE	All landowners in Clarksville must pay taxes.
MINOR PREMISE	Fred Hammil owns land in Clarksville.
CONCLUSION	Therefore, Fred Hammil must pay taxes.

synonym A word that is identical or nearly identical in meaning to another word: *ill* and *sick, large* and *big.* (*See 46c-2, 46e; see* **thesaurus.**)

synthesis The combining or distilling of separate elements into a single, unified entity. Synthesizing source material for a research paper involves combining concepts and details from a variety of sources to form a unified discussion of a topic. (*See 26h.*)

glos

→**take, bring** (*See* **bring, take.**)

talking points Notes taken in advance of an oral presentation in which the presenter outlines major points and provides speaking cues and reminders for him- or herself.

tautology (*See* **circular reasoning.**)

team drafting A method of preparing a preliminary version of a document in which one member of a group begins, then turns it over to a second, and so on; drafts are recirculated before revision. (*See 4c.*)

tense The form a verb takes to indicate time—whether the verb's action occurred in the past (*past tense*) or the present (*present tense*). The present tense form is also called the **base form** of the verb. *Future tense* is marked with the use of **helping verbs.** (*See 32a, 33a, 33b, 41b.*)

PAST	Her grandmother **made** possum stew.
PRESENT	Her friends **stop** to pick up "road kill."
FUTURE	Her children **will find** these old customs offensive.

tense sequence The pattern of tenses in a piece of writing. Incorrect tense shifts can confuse or annoy a reader. (*See 33f.*)

tentative thesis statement A preliminary statement of your key ideas and purposes used to help focus planning for the drafting of a paper. (*See 21f.*)

text analysis A paper that provides a close, analytical reading of a particular text, often a work of literature. The analysis can focus on elements of the text such as technique or meaning. (*See 17c.*)

→**than, then** *Than* is a word used to compare something; *then* implies a sequence of events or a causal relationship.

Gregorian chants are more lugubrious **than** other vocal music from that period. As a result, we were lulled by the Gregorian chants, but **then** the organ recital started.

→**that, which** Although the distinction between *that* and *which* is weakening in many contexts, formal academic writing often requires you to know the difference. Use *that* in a clause that is essential to the meaning of a sentence (**restrictive modifier**); use *which* with a clause that does not provide essential information (*nonrestrictive modifier*).

THAT	He has the report **that** will vindicate Clareson.
WHICH	He has a penchant for emotionalism, **which** may help him win the jury's favor.

→**theirself, theirselves, themself** All these forms are incorrect; use *themselves* to refer to more than one person, *himself* or *herself* to refer to one person.

→**them** Avoid using *them* as a subject or to modify a subject, as in "*Them* are delicious" or "*Them* apples are very crisp."

theme In literary works, an idea, perspective, or cluster of feelings and insights conveyed to a reader through various fictional devices. (*See 17b.*)

→**then, than** (See **than, then.**)

→**there, their, they're** These forms are often confused in spelling because they all sound alike. *There* indicates location; *their* is a possessive pronoun; *they're* is a contraction of *they* and *are*.

THERE	Look over **there.**
THEIR	**Their** car ran out of gas.
THEY'RE	**They're** not eager to hike to the nearest gas station.

thesaurus A dictionary of **synonyms** and **antonyms**—words similar or opposite in meaning to each other. (*See 46d-2, 46e.*)

thesis or thesis statement A sentence, often at the conclusion of an essay's first paragraph, that establishes the point, main argument, or direction of a paper, giving the reader a sense of purpose and an understanding of the essay's contents. (*See 3c, 10c, 21f.*)

third person (*See* **person.**)

→**thusly** Avoid this term; use *thus* or *therefore* instead.

→**till, until, 'til** Some readers will find *'til* and *till* too informal; use *until.*

time sequence A planning strategy, particularly for papers involving chronological or temporal structures, in which events are labeled along a timeline. (*See 2c-3.*)

→**to, as** (*See* **as, to.**)

→**to, too, two** Because these words sound the same, they may be confused. *To* is a preposition indicating location. *Too* means "also." *Two* is a number.

> The Birdsalls went **to** their lake cabin. They invited the Corbetts **too.** That made **two** trips so far this season.

topic The focus or subject of a piece of writing. (*See 3c-1, 21d-1.*)

topic sentence A sentence, usually located at the beginning of a paragraph, that announces its main idea or perspective. (*See 6b.*)

topic shift (*See* **faulty predication, shift.**)

→**toward, towards** Prefer *toward* in formal writing. (You may see *towards* used in England and Canada.)

trace In a writing assignment, mapping out a history or chronology or identifying the origins of something. (*See 3a-2.*)

transition (*See* **transitional expression.**)

transitional expression Words or phrases (*in addition to, on the other hand, therefore, without a doubt*) that link one idea, sentence, or paragraph to the next, helping readers to see relationships among ideas by connecting them logically. (*See 6d-2, 48b-3, 49a-2.*)

transitive verb A verb followed by an **object** or **complement.** (*See 32b-2; compare* **intransitive verb.**)

> transitive verb — object
> The President **called** the British Prime Minister.

tree diagram A planning strategy in which a central idea (or trunk) generates many subsidiary or associative ideas (branches), which can branch off into even more subsidiary twigs. (*See 2b-2; compare* **clustering.**)

→**try and, try to, sure and** (*See* **sure and, try and.**)

→**ultimately, eventually** (*See* **eventually, ultimately.**)

unabridged dictionary A full-size reference dictionary, generally available in a library, that has not been abbreviated to save space. (*See 46e.*)

uncountable noun (*See* **noncount noun.**)

unified paragraph (*See* **paragraph.**)

→**uninterested, disinterested** (*See* **disinterested, uninterested.**)

→**unique** Use *unique* alone; don't write *most unique* or *more unique* since the word indicates an absolute condition.

→**until, till** (*See* **till, until, 'til.**)

URL Standing for Universal Resource Locator, a standardized notation specifying the address or location of files on the Internet. (*See 24b.*)

→**use to, used to** Like *supposed to,* this phrase may be mistakenly written as *use to* because the *-d* is not always clearly pronounced. Write *used to.*

usenet newsgroups Electronic bulletin boards tending to attract diverse membership from many geographic regions and professions. (*See 24c-10.*)

vague generalization A sentence or passage that offers so little specific information that it is not meaningful. (*See 45b-1.*)

vague pronoun reference Using pronouns that refer to antecedents that are implied rather than stated, or pronouns that are not connected explicitly to a specific antecedent. (*See 39b.*)

value judgment An argument that an activity, belief, or arrangement is desirable or undesirable. (See *10c.*)

verb The word in a sentence that indicates the action that has occurred, is occurring, or will occur. (*See 32a-3.*)

verb phrase A phrase that consists of a main verb plus a helping verb. (*See 32a-3, 33b.*)

verbal phrase A verbal plus its modifiers, object, or complements. (*See 32c-4.*)

verbals Verbs or parts of verb phrases that are used to function as nouns, adjectives, or adverbs. The three kinds of verbals are **infinitives, participles,** and **gerunds.** (*See 32a-3, 32c-4.*)

vertical file A library file of clippings, pamphlets, and other useful materials.

vertical list A list whose items are placed on separate lines. (*See 54a-5; compare* **run-in list.**)

visuals Drawings, photos, graphs, and other visual representations. (*See Chapters 12 and 13, 25c-3.*)

voice (*See* **active voice, passive voice.**)

→**wait for, wait on** Use *wait on* only to refer to a clerk's or server's job; use *wait for* to mean "to await someone's arrival."

Julie **waited on** the customers while she **waited for** Melissa to arrive.

warrant (*See* **data-warrant-claim reasoning.**)

Web sites Provide text and graphics with numerous links to related sites. (*See 22b.*)

→**well, good** (*See* **good, well.**)

→**went, gone** (*See* **gone, went.**)

→**were, we're** *Were* is the past plural form of the verb *was*; *we're* is a contraction of *we* and *are.*

We're going to the ruins where the fiercest battles **were.**

→**where . . . at** (*See* **at.**)

→**whether, if** (*See* **if, whether.**)

→**which, that** (*See* **that, which.**)

white space In document design, the amount or use of blank (white) space around text or visuals. (*See 13c-2.*)

→**who, whom** Although the distinction between these words is slowly disappearing from the language, many readers will expect you to use *whom* in the objective case. When in doubt, err on the side of formality. (Sometimes editing can eliminate the need to choose.) (*See 34c.*)

QUESTIONABLE	The person **who** we chose to be the next board president was Harland Clasgow.
EDITED	The person **whom** we chose to be the next board president was Harland Clasgow.
EDITED	We chose Harland Clasgow to be the next board president.

→**who's, whose** *Who's* is the contracted form of *who* and *is*. *Whose* indicates possession.

The man **who's** going to Frankfurt tried to find the man **whose** bag he mistakenly took at the airport.

→**wise, -ize** (*See* **-ize, -wise.**)

wordiness Use of too many words. (*See Chapter 22.*)

work communities Groups of people or audiences that are involved in specific business or work environments, as well as governmental agencies. (*See 1a.*)

working bibliography An in-progress bibliography or list of references kept during the **research** process.

working journal A place to explore ideas, develop insights, experiment with prose, write rough drafts, and reflect on reading. (*See 2b.*)

working outline (*See* **outline.**)

working thesis (*See* **rough thesis.**)

works cited List of the works to which the writer makes reference in the body of a research paper, either through in-text (parenthetical) citations or through footnotes or endnotes. (*See 28d.*)

→**would of, could of** (*See* **could of, would of.**)

writer's commentary A writer's direct address of the reader or reference to himself or herself in prose that is not intended to convey personal feelings. (*See 45b-3.*)

writing and reading community People with similar goals, preferences, and uses for both verbal and visual texts. (*See 1a.*)

→**yet, however, but** (*See* **but however, but yet.**)

→**your, you're** *Your* is a possessive pronoun; *you're* is a contraction of *you* and *are*.

If **you're** going to take physics, you'd better know **your** math.

Credits

4Control Media Website. Copyright 1995–2001, 4Control Media, Inc., Jersey City, NJ. Reprinted by permission.
Abbey, Edward. *Down the River.* (New York: Dutton, 1982).
Abbey, Edward. *The Journey Home.* (New York: Plume, 1991).
American Psychological Association (APA) Home Page (www.apa.org). Copyright © 2006 by the American Psychological Association. Reproduced with permission.
Animal Rights Project Website. Copyright © 1996–2004. Reprinted by permission of Gary L. Francione and Anna E. Charlton.
Anson, Chris M., Schwegler, Robert A., and Muth, Marcia, F. Chapter 18 from *The Longman Writer's Companion*, 3/e. Copyright © 2005 by Pearson Education, Inc. Reprinted by permission.
Arreola, Daniel D. "Forget the Alamo: The Border as Place in John Sayles' Lone Star." *Journal of Cultural Geography*, Fall/Winter 2005. By permission of JCG Press, Oklahoma State University.
Atlanta Journal and Constitution, Staff Writer. "Restrict Right to Sue or We'll Pay in the End." Copyright © 2001 by Atlanta Jour-Constitution. Reproduced with permission of Atlanta Journal-Constitution in the format Textbook and Other Book via Copyright Clearance Center.
Baldwin, Hanson W. " R.M.S. Titanic." *Harper's Magazine*, 1933.
Bickner, Robert, and Peyasantiwong, Patcharin. "Cultural Variation in Reflective Writing"; and Kachru, Yamuna. "Writers in Hini and English" from *Writing Across Languages and Cultures*, Alan C. Purves, Ed. (Newbury Park: Sage, 1988), pp. 160–174, 109–137.
Bissinger, H. G. *Friday Night Lights.* (Reading, MA: Addison-Wesley, 1990).
Bogan, Louise. Excerpt from "Old Countryside" from *The Blue Estuaries: Poems 1923–1968.* Copyright © 1968 by Louise Bogan. Copyright renewed © 1996 by Ruth Limmer. Reprinted by permission of Farrar, Straus and Giroux, LLC.
Braun, Cary. "Whenever we went to my grandfather's house . . ." Reprinted by permission of the author.
Brilliant, Sara. "Breakfast cereals can differ . . ." Reprinted by permission of the author.
Bronowski, Jacob. *The Ascent of Man.* (Boston: Little, Brown, 1973).
Brown, Marcia. *Stone Soup*. Reprinted with permission of Atheneum Books for Young Readers, an imprint of Simon & Schuster Children's Publishing Division. Copyright © 1947 Marcia Brown; copyright renewed © 1975 Marcia Brown.
Jimmy Buffett, *Where Is Joe Merchant* (New York: Harcourt, Brace, Jovanovich, 1992).
Carroll, Cathryn. *Laurent Clerc: The Story of His Early Years.* (Washington, DC: Gallaudet University Press, 1991).
Collins, Wilkie. *The Woman in White.* (New York: Dutton, 1969).
Colorado Division of Wildlife. "Tips." *The Denver Post*, July 30, 1998, p. 15. Reprinted by permission of the Colorado Division of Wildlife. For more information, go to http://wildlife.state.co.us/WildlifeSpecies/CoexistingWithWildlife/Mammals/CoyoteCountry.htm and http://wildlife.state.co.us/WildlifeSpecies/CoexistingWithWildlife/.
Conrad, Joseph. *Heart of Darkness*, 1899.
Coontz, Stephanie. "The Way We Weren't." *National Forum: Phi Beta Kappa Phi Journal*, Vol. 75, No. 3 (Summer 1995). Copyright © by Stephanie Coontz. Reprinted by permission of the publisher.
Curtin, Sharon R. *Nobody Ever Died of Old Age.* (Boston, MA: Little, Brown, 1972).
Health Reference Center—Academic Database. Sample of Abstracts. From the online catalog of the Providence Public Library, Health & Wellness Resource Center. Reprinted by permission of the Providence Public Library, Providence, RI. Screen shot powered by InfoTrac from the online database Health Reference Center—Academic. Copyright © 2007. Reprinted by permission of Thomson Gale, a division of Thomson Learning: www.thomsonrights.com. Fax 800-730-2215.
Davis, Mike. "House of Cards." *Sierra* © 1995.
Dawes, Robyn M. From "Why Believe That for Which There Is No Good Evidence?" (Fall 1992). The False Memory Syndrome Web Site, www.fmsfonline.org.
DeGregorio, Jessica. Paper in Process (Planning, Drafting, Revisiing). Reprinted by permission of the author.

Didion, Joan. *After Henry.* (New York: Simon & Schuster, 1992).
Drummond, A. H., Jr. *The Complete Guide to Sailing.* (New York: Simon & Schuster, 1986).
Edmondson, Brad. "Making Yourself at Home."
Elkind, David. "The Family in the Postmodern World." *National Forum: Phi Beta Kappa Phi Journal*, Vol. 75, No. 3 (Summer 1995). Copyright © by David Elkind. Reprinted by permission of the publisher.
Exxon Valdez Oil Spill Trustee Council Website, excerpts. www.oilspill.state.ak.us/resoration/index.html. Used by permission.
Fast-Track Recalls. *Consumer Product Safety Review*, Fall, 1998 issue, Vol. 3, No. 1.
"Fire Safety Tips for a Safe Holiday Season" from www.sema.state.mo.us/firexmas.html.
Fussell, Paul. *Uniforms: Why We Are What We Wear.* (New York: Houghton Mifflin-Marnier Books, 2003).
Gallagher, Tess. "Under Stars." Copyright © 1987 by Tess Gallagher. Reprinted from *Amplitude: New and Selected Poems* with permission of Graywolf Press, Saint Paul, Minnesota.
Garrett, Laurie. *The Coming Plague.* (New York: Penguin, 1994), p. 199.
Geertz, Clifford. *The Interpretation of Cultures.* (New York: Basic Books, 1973).
Giannetti, Louis D. *Understanding Movies*, 6th Ed. (Englewood Cliffs, NJ: Prentice Hall, 1993).
Giovanni, Nikki. From "Pioneers: A View of Home." *Sacred Cows—and Other Edibles.* (New York: Morrow, 1988).
GlobalReach. Pie graph "Online Language Populations" found at www.glreach.com. Reprinted by permission of Neutralize, United Kingdom.
Goddio, Frank. "San Diego: An Account of Adventure, Deceit, and Intrigue." *National Geographic*, 1994.
Goleman, Daniel. "Too Little, Too Late." *American Health*, © 1992.
Gonzalez, Anson. "The Little Rosebud Girl." Copyright © 1972 by Anson Gonzalez. Reprinted by permission.
Goodman, Ellen. Excerpt from "Religion in Textbooks." *The Boston Globe*, 1994. Copyright © 1994, The Washington Post Writers Group. Reprinted with permission.
Google™ Logo and Search Code Copyright © 2007 Google. The Google search code and Google Logo used on the main page of this site are provided by and used with permission of http://www.google.com.
Gore, Al. *Earth in Balance.* (Boston, MA: Houghton Mifflin, 1992).
Gore, Rick. "Dinosaurs." *National Geographic*, January 1993.
Gormen, Christine. Excerpt from "Sizing Up the Sexes," *Time*, January 20, 1992.
Green, Beverly. "African American Families: A Legacy of Vulnerability and Resilience." *National Forum: Phi Beta Kappa Phi Journal*, Vol. 75, No. 3 (Summer 1995). Copyright © by Beverly Green. Reprinted by permission of the publisher.
Green, Kenneth C. "Web Site Services, 2005." from *Campus Computing 2005: The 16th National Survey of Computing and Information Technology in American Education.* www.campuscomputing.net. Reprinted by permission of The Campus Computing Project.
Hall, Donald. Excerpt from "The Black-Faced Sheep" from *Old and New Poems.* Copyright © 1990 by Donald Hall. Reprinted by permission of Houghton Mifflin Company. All rights reserved.
Harris Interactive Website. (www.harrisinteractive.com). Reprinted with permission.
Hawthorne, Nathaniel. "Young Goodman Brown," 1846, and "The Birthmark," 1843.
Hemingway, Ernest. *The Old Man and The Sea.* (New York: Scribner, 1952).
Hermann, Andrea. "When you hear the word crystal . . ." Reprinted by permission of the author.
Hurston, Zora Neale. *Their Eyes Were Watching God.* (New York: Harper & Row, 1937).
Images Journal Website. Copyright © Images Journal Website.
"Is Anyone Out There?" *Discover*, November 1992.
Jastrow, Robert. *Journey to the Stars.* (New York: Bantam Books, 1989).
Jastrow, Robert. *The Enchanted Loom.* (New York: Simon & Schuster, 1981).
Joseph, Lawrence E. "The Scoop on Ice Cream." *Discover*, August 1992.
Kingston, Maxine Hong. *The Woman Warrior.* (New York: Alfred A. Knopf, 1976).
Kitwana, Bakari. *Hip Hop Generation: Young Blacks and the Crisis in African-American Culture.* (New York: Perseus Book Group, 2002).
Kowinski, William Severini. *The Malling of America.* (New York: Morrow, 1985).
Levine, Robert. *A Geography of Time.* Copyright © 1997 by Robert Levine. Reprinted by permission of Basic Books, a member of Perseus Books Group.
Lundquist, James. *Chester Himes.* (New York: Random House, 1988).
Lynn, Steve. *Texts and Contexts: Writing About Literature with Critical Theory.* (New York, HarperCollins, 1994).

Macklin, Ruth. *Mortal Choices*. (Boston: Houghton Mifflin, 1987).
Mayers, T.R. From "(snap) shots." Reprinted by permission of the author.
McCord, Holly, and McVeigh, Gloria. Excerpt from "Zero in on Hidden Fats" from *Prevention*, February, 2003. Reprinted by permission of *Prevention* Magazine. Copyright 2003, Rodale Inc. All rights reserved. For more articles visit Prevention.com. For subscription information call 1-800-813-8070.
Mead, Margaret. *Male and Female*. (New York: Morrow, 1949).
Mellix, Barbara. "From Outside In." *The Georgia Review*, Vol. 47 (Summer 1987).
Merriam-Webster, Incorporated. By permission, from *Merriam-Webster's Collegiate® Dictionary, Eleventh Edition* © 2005 by Merriam-Webster, Inc. (www.Merriam-Webster.com).
Merrill, Hugh. *The Blues Route*. (New York: Morrow, 1990).
Morris, Desmond. *Body Watching*. (New York: Crown, 1985).
MountainLion Foundation Website (www.mountainlion.org) Reprinted by permission.
Mungo, Paul, and Clough, Bryan. "The Bulgarian Connection." *Discover*, February 1993.
Murrow, Edward R. *In Search of Light*. (New York: Alfred A. Knopf, 1967).
Neal, Bill. "How to Cure a Pig." *Esquire* © 1991.
Noda, Kesaya. "Growing Up Asian in America," as it appeared in *Making Waves* edited by Asian Women United. (Boston: Beacon Press, 1989).
Open Society Institute. *Gun Control in the United States: A Comparative Survey of State Firearm Laws*, April 2000.
Orlean, Susan. *Saturday Night*. (New York: Random House, 1990).
Ortiz, Alfonso. "Some Concerns Central to the Writing of Indian History." *The Indian Historian* 10, 1977.
Patton, Phil. "How a Ridiculous Idea Mutated into a Marketing Star." *Smithsonian*, 1992.
Phillips Park Zoolennium Fall Festival 2004! Website. Reprinted by permission of City of Aurora, IL Parks Department, www.aurora-il.org/parks.
Plimpton, George. "Bonding with the Grateful Dead." *Esquire*.
Popenoe, David. "The American Family Crisis." *National Forum: Phi Beta Kappa Phi Journal*, Vol. 75, No. 3 (Summer 1995). Copyright © David Popenoe. Reprinted by permission of the publisher.
Postman, Neil. *Amusing Ourselves to Death*. (New York: Penguin, 1985).
Preeth, Samuel J. "Incident at Lake Nyos." *The Sciences* © 1992.
Riddle, Karyn, et al. "Judging the Degree of Violence in Media Portrayals." *Journal of Broadcasting & Electronic Media* 50(2), 2006, p. 270. Copyright 2006. Reproduced by permission of Taylor & Francis Group, LLC, http://www.taylorandfrancis.com.
Rodeghier, Mark. From "The Center for UFO Studies Response to the Air Force's 1997 Report 'The Roswell Report: Case Closed.'" www.cufos.org/airforce.htm.
Rodriguez, Richard. *Hunger of Memory*. (Boston: David R. Godine, 1983).
Russell, Peter. *The Brain Book*. Copyright © 1979 by Peter Russell. Used by permission of Dutton Signet, a division of Penguin Group (USA) Inc.
Sankey, Jay. *Zen and the Art of Stand-Up Comedy*. Copyright © 1998 by Jay Sankey.
From "Save the Children" web site, www.savethechildren.org. Text and photo reprinted by permission of Save the Children U.S. Headquarters.
Screen shot of search results for keywords *Afro-Cuban music* from HELIN Library Catalog. Used by permission of the HELIN Consortium.
Screen shot of detailed information for one entry under *Afro-Cuban music* from HELIN Library Catalog. Used by permission of the HELIN Consortium.
Screen shot of search results in HTML and PDF formats from Blackwell Synergy online database for article "A Queen for Whose Time? Elizabeth I as Icon for the Twentieth Century" by David Grant, *Journal of Popular Culture*, 39 (2006). By permission of Blackwell Publishing.
Screen shot, CBS News web site from 11/20/06. *www.CBSNews.com*. Copyright © 2006 CBS Interactive, Inc. Reprinted by permission of the CBS News Archives.
Screen shot of search results in HTML and PDF formats from EBSCOhost Academic Search Premier online database for article "Treatment Approaches for Sleep Difficulties among College Students" by Walter C. Buboltz et al. from *Counselling Psychology Quarterly*, September 2002, Vol. 15, No. 2. Reprinted by permission of the publisher, Taylor & Francis Ltd, *http://informaworld.com* and EBSCO Publishing.
Screen shot for search terms "hydrogenated oils and food" from EBSCOhost *Academic Search Premier* online database. Reprinted by permission of EBSCO Publishing.
Screenshot from Inanimate.com, http://Inanimate.com/portfolio.html. Original Web design by Jared Cole, jaredcole.com. Reprinted by permission.

Screen shot from the JASA web site. Reprinted by permission of The Jane Austen Society of Australia Inc., 45 Sylvan Avenue, Linfield Avenue, Linfield NSW 2070, Australia, *info@jasa.net.au.*

Screen shot "Lactose Intolerance" from National Digestive Diseases Information Clearinghouse, National Institutes of Health. www.niddk.gov.

Screen shot "Mmm . . . milk—Got Milk?" from Southeast United Dairy Industry Association Web Site (SUDIA). www.southeastdairy.org. Reprinted by permission of SUDIA.

Screen shot from NOTMILK web site featuring excerpt from "Milk and the Cancer Connection" by Hans R. Larsen. www.notmilk.com. Reprinted by permission.

Screen shot from *Student Affairs On-Line*, Summer 2006, Vol. 7, No. 2 with excerpt from article "Student Affairs and Podcasting: The New Frontier?" by Stuart Brown. http://studentaffairs.com/ © 2007 StudentAffairs.com. All rights reserved. Used by permission of StudentAffairs.com LLC.

Screen shot from *T.H.E. Journal*, March 2007 with excerpt from article "What Students Want : : Leave Me Alone . . . I'm Socializing" by Neal Starkman. Copyright © 2007. http://www.thejournal.com/articles/20336. Reprinted by permission of PARS International on behalf of *T.H.E. Journal.* Photo: Masterfile.

Screen shot for search result "Treatment Approaches for Sleep Difficulties in College Students" from EBSCOhost *Academic Search Premier* online database. Reprinted by permission of EBSCO Publishing.

Screen shot from University of Florida website, SFA Survey (www.ufsa.edu). Reprinted by permission of University of Florida.

Screen shot for search results "Zero in on Hidden Fats" from EBSCOhost *Academic Search Premier* online database. Reprinted by permission of EBSCO Publishing.

Schor, Juliet B. *The Overworked American.* (New York: Harper Collins, 1998).

Stacey, Judith. "The Family Values Fable." *National Forum: Phi Beta Kappa Phi Journal*, Vol. 75, No. 3 (Summer 1995). Copyright © Judith Stacey. Reprinted by permission of the publisher.

Stern, Jane, and Stern, Michael. *Roadfood.* (New York: HarperCollins, © 1992).

Tannen, Deborah. *You Just Don't Understand: Women and Men in Conversation.* (New York: Morrow, 1990).

Thomas, Lewis. "Clever Animals" from *Late Night Thoughts on Listening to Mahler's Ninth Symphony.* (New York: Penguin, 1982). Used by permission of Viking Penguin, a division of Penguin Group (USA), Inc.

The Treasures of Tutenkhamun. (New York: Metropolitan Museum of Art, 1976).

The U.S. Global Change Research Information Office. Fig. 1. From "Population Reference Bureau Estimates and UN (Medium Series) Long Range Projections of 1992" as appeared in "Global and US National Population Trends," *Consequences*, Vol. 1, No. 2 (1995). *www.grico.org.*

"U.S. Public School Student Membership, 1990–2000." National Center for Education Statistics, Common Core Data (CCD). http://nces.ed.gov.

Wagner, Richard H. *Environment and Man.* (New York: Norton, 1978).

"What research has been done on St. John's Wort?" from www.athleticnutrition.com/Stjohns.html.

Wideman, John Edgar. *Philadelphia Fire.* (New York: Henry Holt, 1990).

Wilson, William Julius. *When Work Disappears: The World of the New Urban Poor.* (New York: Knopf, 1996).

Wisniewski, Richard, and Kleine, Paul. "Teacher Moonlighting: An Unstudied Phenomenon" from ERIC © 1983.

Zimmer, Carl. "The Body Electric." *Discover*, February, 1993.

Student Acknowledgments: David Aharonian, Summer Arrigo-Nelson, Heloise Benet, Amy Braegelman, Nicholas Branahan, Carey Braun, Sara Brilliant, Justine Buhl, Zachary Carter, Paul Copass, Kimlee Cunningham, Jessica DiGregorio, Jason Fester, Jennifer Figliozzi, Daisy Garcia, Lily Germaine, Chantele Giles, Jen Halliday, Andrea Hermann, Jenny Latimer, Fredza Leger, Reid Nelson, James Newlands, Jennifer O'Berry, Michael Perry, Ian Preston, Paul Pusateri, Andrew Quadros, Sam Roles, Sharon Salamone, Amy Singh, Pete Sodeberg, Metili Sovan, Ted Wolfe.

Index

index

dex

dex

dex

dex

GUIDE TO ESL ADVICE

If your first language is not English, look for special advice integrated throughout the handbook. Each ESL Advice section is labeled and highlighted so it's easy to spot. *The Longman Handbook* offers special help on these topics.

ESL ESL exercises can be found on MyCompLab.

Revision and Editing Symbols

abbrev	incorrect abbreviation, **58**
agr	error in subject-verb or pronoun-antecedent agreement, **35**
apos	lack of (or incorrect) possessive apostrophe, **50**
art	article used incorrectly, **32**
awk	awkward construction, **7a–b**
cap	capital letter needed, **54**
case	incorrect pronoun case, **34**
clear	clearer sentence needed, **7a**
coh	paragraph or essay coherence needed, **6c–d**
cs	comma splice, **38**
coord	faulty coordination, **44a–b**
dev	paragraph or essay development needed, **6e**
discrm	sexist or discriminatory language, **47c–d**
dm	dangling modifier, **40b**
dneg	double negative, **36d**
emph	emphasis needed, **7c**
foc	paragraph or essay focus needed, **6a–b**
frag	sentence fragment, **37**
fs	fused sentence, **38**
hyph	hyphen (-) needed, **56**
inc	incomplete sentence, **42b**
ital	italics (underlining), **55**
lc	lowercase letter needed, **54**
link	paragraph linkage needed, **6d**
log	faulty reasoning, **8c–d**
mixed	grammatically mixed sentence, **42a**
mm	misplaced modifier, **40a**
modif	incorrect adjective or adverb, **36a–b**
num	incorrect numbering style, **57**
//	parallel elements needed, **43**
¶	new paragraph, **6**
no ¶	no new paragraph, **6**
p	error in punctuation, **48–53**
punc	error in punctuation, **48–53**
^,	comma, **48a–j**
no ^,	no comma, **48j**
;	semicolon, **49a**
:	colon, **49b**
’	apostrophe, **50**
“ ”	quotation marks, **51**
.	period, **52a**
?	question mark, **52b**
!	exclamation point, **52c**
( ) [ ] —	parentheses, brackets, dashes, **53a–c**
. . . /	ellipses, slashes, **53d–e**
prep	preposition error, **32a**
pr ref	pronoun reference error, **39**
ref	pronoun reference error, **39**
rep	repetitious, **45**
sent	sentence revision needed, **7**
shift	shift, **41**
sp	word spelled incorrectly, **59**
spell	word spelled incorrectly, **59**
sub	faulty subordination, **44c–d**
t	wrong verb tense, **33a–c**
tense	wrong verb tense, **33a–c**
trans	transition needed, **6c–d**
und	underlining (italics), **55**
us	error in usage, **Glossary**
var	sentence variety needed, **7d**
verb	incorrect verb form, **33**
wc	faulty word choice, **46b**
wordy	too many words, **45**
ww	wrong word, **46a–d**
^	insert
[delete mark]	delete
⁀	close up space
[transpose mark]	transpose letters or words
#	add a space
X	obvious error